# GEORGE BERNARD SHAW

## SELECTED PLAYS

# GEORGE BERNARD SHAW

## SELECTED PLAYS

Mrs. Warren's Profession

Caesar and Cleopatra

Man and Superman

Major Barbara

Pygmalion

Heartbreak House

GRAMERCY BOOKS
New York • Avenel

This 1996 edition is published by Gramercy Books,
a division of Random House Value Publishing, Inc.,
40 Engelhard Avenue,
Avenel, New Jersey 07001.

Random House
New York • Toronto • London • Sydney • Auckland

Printed and bound in the United States

**Library of Congress Cataloging-in-Publication Data**

A catalog record for this book is available from the Library of Congress.

George Bernard Shaw: Selected Works

ISBN: 0-517-12428-9

8 7 6 5 4 3 2 1

# Contents

# INTRODUCTION

George Bernard Shaw was born in Dublin, Ireland, on July 26, 1856. He was the third child of George Carr Shaw and Lucinda Elizabeth Shaw. His mother was a talented singer and financially supported the family by giving voice lessons. His father was an alcoholic and an unsuccessful businessman. Shaw left school at the age of thirteen out of boredom and, in 1871, became a clerk at the C. Uniack Townshend and Company real-estate office. Although he hated the job, he remained there for four and a half years. In 1876, Shaw moved to London, where his sister Lucy and his mother—who had left her husband behind—had relocated three years earlier, in part to help Lucy's singing career. For a brief period of time in 1879 he worked for the Edison Company, which made and installed telephones. However, Shaw soon quit and attempted to become a novelist. He wrote five unsuccessful novels and began a sixth before giving up in 1883. During this time he spent much of his time at the reading room of the British Museum, where he read voraciously on a variety of subjects, including economics and art. There he read *Das Kapital* by Karl Marx, which influenced his conversion to socialism. In 1884, he joined a group of radicals and helped found the Fabian Society, a Socialist organization that later included the writer H. G. Wells. Shaw began writing essays and, although rather shy at the time, made public speeches on the society's behalf.

In 1885, Shaw began a career in journalism, writing art criticism for *The World*, a job he obtained with the help of William Archer, the drama critic for the paper, whom he had met at the British Museum. Three years later he was writing music reviews under the pseudonym "Corno di Bassetto," and in 1894 he became the drama critic for the *Saturday Review*, a position he held for three years. By then, however, he had already begun his career as a dramatist. He finished writing his first play, *Widowers' Houses*, in 1892. Although it caused controversy with its depiction of slum landlords, it was a commercial failure. However, delighted at the uproar he had caused, Shaw continued to write undeterred. He was greatly influenced by the Norwegian playwright Henrik Ibsen whose plays emphasized the provocative social issues of the day. Following in Ibsen's footsteps, Shaw wrote *Mrs. Warren's Profession* in 1893. The play focused on prostitution and was banned in London by the Lord Chamberlain.

A steady stream of plays followed in a career than spanned almost sixty years, most notably *Caesar and Cleopatra* (1901), *Man and Superman* (1904), *Major Barbara* (1907), *Pygmalion* (1912), and *Heartbreak House* (1917). In 1925, Shaw was awarded the Nobel Prize for Literature, which he at first refused, but finally accepted after he found out that he could donate the money that accompanied the prize to a fund popularizing Scandinavian literature. Shaw died at the age of ninety-four on November 2, 1950, after succumbing to injuries sustained from falling off a ladder while pruning an apple tree.

All of Shaw's plays reflect his zeal for political, social, and economic reform. His goal was to shock audiences out of their complacency and their hypocrisy. Unlike Oscar Wilde's wit, which was an end unto itself, Shaw's comedy and humor were used to entertain the audience and to overturn people's preconceived, middlebrow expectations. He wrote, "I must warn my readers that my attacks are directed against themselves not against my stage figures." At the core of his beliefs was what he called the Life Force, a sort of immanent Holy Spirit. Shaw was convinced that the human race, guided by the Life Force, was moving toward a self-willed evolution that would improve and perfect humankind and the world. With an end to educating his audience toward greater awareness, his plays preached, among other things, socialism, the abolition of prisons, women's equality, and the stupidity of war. Shaw brought serious themes and issues back to English drama, and the six plays collected in this volume show that he remains one of the great playwrights of the twentieth century.

*Mrs. Warren's Profession* was Shaw's third play. Although it was banned for a long time because of its topic, prostitution, the play is not an exposé upon the more prurient aspects of the subject. Shaw states that Mrs. Warren is "an organism of prostitution—a woman who owns and manages brothels in every big city in Europe and is proud of it." With the profits from her enterprise, Mrs. Warren is able to support a high standard of living, including sending her daughter Vivie to school at Cambridge. He further goes on to describe Mrs. Warren as "rather spoiled and domineering, and decidedly vulgar, but on the whole a genial and fairly presentable old blackguard of a woman." In the course of the play, Vivie, who is unsuspecting of her mother's illegal activities, finally finds out. But Shaw, ever trying to subvert audience expectation, has Vivie, who he created as a paragon of the New Woman—level-headed, educated, and independent—reject her mother not because she managed brothels but because, "You are a conventional woman at heart." Shaw does not scorn or romanticize prostitution, his intent is to uncover the economic basis of the occupation—the laws of supply and demand keeping prostitution going. Under society's moral indignation is its overt complicity—women would not need to sell themselves if they could be independent of men and have an opportunity to earn a living in legitimate enterprises.

When Shaw wrote *Caesar and Cleopatra* in 1901, he claimed that his Caesar was "an improvement on Shakespear's." What he meant was that, in creating his Caesar, he was able to draw upon the more accurate historical scholarship of the nineteenth century that was unavailable to Shakespeare. Shaw's Caesar is more human than Shakespeare's "great Caesar." He is a master statesman and philosopher with "abundant evidence of his light-heartedness and adventurousness." As one critic pointed out he is "an idealized picture of Shaw in a toga." Shaw's Cleopatra, rather than Shakespeare's "serpent of old Nile . . . wrinkled deep in time," is a coquettish girl of sixteen with more charm than intelligence. The focus of the play is the middle-aged Caesar's attempts to teach Cleopatra—who he declares is "as yet but a child that is whipped by her nurse"—how to develop into a ruler of a nation. The play, one of Shaw's finest achievements, is highlighted by his masterfully drawn characters. It was made into a movie in 1945 with Claude Rains as Caesar and Vivien Leigh as Cleopatra.

*Man and Superman,* finished in 1903, was written in response to a suggestion from a friend that Shaw write a play based on the legend of Don Juan. But Shaw's Don Juan, Jack Tanner, is not a man who fits the lothario image of the legend. Tanner is the center of a play that most fully illustrates Shaw's conception of his philosophy of the Life Force. The plot of the play is concerned with the love affair between Tanner, a witty and intellectual member of the English idle-rich, and his ward, Ann Whitefield, who has set her sights upon him. Both characters are in the power of the Life Force that Shaw believed to be the true basis of sexual attraction. At the heart of the play is the famous "Don Juan in Hell" dream sequence from Act III which is often produced by itself. Tanner, after being captured by a group of bandits led by an Englishman called Mendoza, has a dream in which he, as Don Juan, is in Hell where he encounters, among others, the Devil (Mendoza). There they discuss and debate on many subjects: the nature of Heaven and Hell, socialism, war, love, politics, evolution, marriage, and the Life Force. *Man and Superman,* although one of Shaw's longest plays, is one of his most popular and one of his most ambitious. As he wrote when referring to Act III: it "is a careful attempt to write a new Book of Genesis . . ."

Shaw referred to *Major Barbara: A Discussion in Three Acts,* from 1907, as "all religion and morals and Fabian debates." The major preoccupations of the play are poverty, money, capitalism, socialism, and the Salvation Army. In this play Shaw is preaching a lesson that is the opposite of Christian teachings, and can be summed up by the novelist Samuel Butler's heretical rephrasing of St. Paul: "The lack of money is the root of all evil." At the center of the play is Andrew Undershaft, a millionaire arms manufacturer. The action of the play turns around his efforts to convince his daughter, Barbara, who works for the Salvation Army, that he is actually helping mankind more than she is. Shaw's ultimate paradox is that while Undershaft is selling death and destruction—a profession that seems on the surface morally questionable—he has created a Utopian society for his workers. Undershaft believes that "the vilest sin of man and society" is poverty and Barbara soon comes to realize charitable organizations like the Salvation Army, while aiding the poor temporarily, are not doing anything to fundamentally change or "save" the people they claim they are helping. The play explores the timeless question of how to cure poverty through Shaw's unique perspective. Winston Churchill, on seeing *Major Barbara* again after twenty years, said of it: "there was not a character requiring to be redrawn, not a sentence nor a suggestion that was out of date. . . . [it is] the very acme of modernity."

*Pygmalion: A Romance in Five Acts*, written in 1912, is probably Shaw's most famous and entertaining play. It was immortalized in 1956 when it was turned into the extremely popular musical *My Fair Lady* by Lerner and Loewe. Shaw based the play on the Greek myth about the sculptor, Pygmalion, who creates a statue, Galatea, that he falls in love with. In his play Pygmalion is Professor Higgins, a speech teacher, who teaches Eliza Doolittle, a Cockney flowergirl, how to speak properly and pass for a lady of the English aristocracy. The original comedy is a penetrating and amusing investigation into the correlation between accent and social class in England.

Shaw considered *Heartbreak House: A Fantasia in the Russian Manner on English Themes* to be his "greatest play." A dreamlike and symbolic play, it remains one of his most important and interesting works. It was written mostly in 1913 but Shaw held it back until after the end of World War I. He considered the play too powerful for the English public during wartime, as he wrote: "War cannot bear the terrible castigation of comedy, the ruthless light of laughter that glares on the stage." The influence of Anton Chekov, the great Russian playwright, is apparent in its title as well as the setting and social milieu of the play that are reminiscent of such plays as *The Cherry Orchard*. Set in Heartbreak House, a country estate in Sussex owned by Captain Shotover, Shaw assembles representatives of "cultured, leisured Europe before the war." He portrays an aristocracy interested only in amusement rather than in any meaningful activities such as politics. The violent ending of the play reflects Shaw's pessimistic outlook and political disillusionment just before the outbreak of the catastrophic First World War. Shaw has Shotover assess the situation at the end of the play with the foreboding, "The judgment has come." After two world wars, a cold war, and the ongoing insanity of mankind's propensity for inhumane violence, Shaw may be right.

# Mrs. Warren's
# Profession

# Act I

*Summer afternoon in a cottage garden on the eastern slope of a hill a little south of Haslemere in Surrey. Looking up the hill, the cottage is seen in the left hand corner of the garden, with its thatched roof and porch, and a large latticed window to the left of the porch. Farther back a little wing is built out, making an angle with the right side wall. From the end of this wing a paling curves across and forward, completely shutting in the garden, except for a gate on the right. The common rises uphill beyond the paling to the sky line. Some folded canvas garden chairs are leaning against the side bench in the porch. A lady's bicycle is propped against the wall, under the window. A little to the right of the porch, a hammock is slung from two posts. A big canvas umbrella, stuck in the ground, keeps the sun off the hammock, in which a young lady lies reading and making notes, her head towards the cottage and her feet towards the gate. In front of the hammock, and within reach of her hand, is a common kitchen chair, with a pile of serious-looking books and a supply of writing paper upon it.*

    *A gentleman walking on the common comes into sight from behind the cottage. He is hardly past middle age, with something of the artist about him, unconventionally but carefully dressed, and clean-shaven except for a moustache, with an eager, susceptible face and very amiable and considerate manners. He has silky black hair, with waves of grey and white in it. His eyebrows are white, his moustache black. He seems not certain of his way. He looks over the paling; takes stock of the place; and sees the young lady.*

THE GENTLEMAN (*taking off his hat*):
    I beg your pardon. Can you direct me to Hindhead View—
    Mrs. Alison's?

THE YOUNG LADY (*glancing up from her book*):
    This is Mrs. Alison's. (*She resumes her work.*)

THE GENTLEMAN:
    Indeed! Perhaps—may I ask are you Miss Vivie Warren?

THE YOUNG LADY (*sharply, as she turns on her elbow to get a good look at
    him*):
    Yes.

THE GENTLEMAN (*daunted and conciliatory*):

> I'm afraid I appear intrusive. My name is Praed. (*Vivie at once throws her books upon the chair, and gets out of the hammock.*) Oh, pray don't let me disturb you.

VIVIE (*striding to the gate and opening it for him*):

> Come in, Mr. Praed. (*He comes in.*) Glad to see you. (*She proffers her hand and takes his with a resolute and hearty grip. She is an attractive specimen of the sensible, able, highly-educated young middle-class English-woman. Age 22. Prompt, strong, confident, self-possessed. Plain, business-like dress, but not dowdy. She wears a chatelaine at her belt, with a fountain pen and a paper knife among its pendants.*)

PRAED:

> Very kind of you indeed, Miss Warren. (*She shuts the gate with a vigorous slam: he passes in to the middle of the garden, exercising his fingers, which are slightly numbed by her greeting.*) Has your mother arrived?

VIVIE (*quickly, evidently scenting aggression*):

> Is she coming?

PRAED (*surprised*):

> Didn't you expect us?

VIVIE:

> No.

PRAED:

> Now, goodness me, I hope I've not mistaken the day. That would be just like me, you know. Your mother arranged that she was to come down from London and that I was to come over from Horsham to be introduced to you.

VIVIE (*not at all pleased*):

> Did she? H'm! My mother has rather a trick of taking me by surprise—to see how I behave myself when she's away, I suppose. I fancy I shall take my mother very much by surprise one of these days, if she makes arrangements that concern me without consulting me beforehand. She hasn't come.

PRAED (*embarrassed*):

> I'm really very sorry.

VIVIE (*throwing off her displeasure*):

> It's not your fault, Mr. Praed, is it? And I'm very glad you've come, believe me. You are the only one of my mother's friends I have asked her to bring to see me.

PRAED (*relieved and delighted*):

> Oh, now this is really very good of you, Miss Warren!

VIVIE:

> Will you come indoors; or would you rather sit out here whilst we talk?

PRAED:

It will be nicer out here, don't you think?

VIVIE:

Then I'll go and get you a chair. (*She goes to the porch for a garden chair.*)

PRAED (*following her*):

Oh, pray, pray! Allow me. (*He lays hands on the chair.*)

VIVIE (*letting him take it*):

Take care of your fingers: they're rather dodgy things, those chairs. (*She goes across to the chair with the books on it; pitches them into the hammock; and brings the chair forward with one swing.*)

PRAED (*who has just unfolded his chair*):

Oh, now do let me take that hard chair! I like hard chairs.

VIVIE:

So do I. (*She sits down.*) Sit down, Mr. Praed. (*This invitation is given with genial peremptoriness, his anxiety to please her clearly striking her as a sign of weakness of character on his part.*)

PRAED:

By the way, though, hadn't we better go to the station to meet your mother?

VIVIE (*coolly*):

Why? She knows the way. (Praed *hesitates, and then sits down in the garden chair, rather disconcerted.*) Do you know, you are just like what I expected. I hope you are disposed to be friends with me?

PRAED (*again beaming*):

Thank you, my dear Miss Warren; thank you. Dear me! I'm so glad your mother hasn't spoilt you!

VIVIE:

How?

PRAED:

Well, in making you too conventional. You know, my dear Miss Warren, I am a born anarchist. I hate authority. It spoils the relations between parent and child—even between mother and daughter. Now I was always afraid that your mother would strain her authority to make you very conventional. It's such a relief to find that she hasn't.

VIVIE:

Oh! have I been behaving unconventionally?

PRAED:

Oh, no: oh, dear no. At least not conventionally unconventionally, you understand. (*She nods. He goes on, with a cordial outburst.*) But it was so charming of you to say that you were disposed to be friends with me! You modern young ladies are splendid—perfectly splendid!

VIVIE (*dubiously*):

Eh? (*watching him with dawning disappointment as to the quality of his brains and character.*)

PRAED:

When I was your age, young men and women were afraid of each other: there was no good fellowship—nothing real—only gallantry copied out of novels, and as vulgar and affected as it could be. Maidenly reserve!—gentlemanly chivalry!—always saying no when you meant yes!—simple purgatory for shy and sincere souls!

VIVIE:

Yes, I imagine there must have been a frightful waste of time—especially women's time.

PRAED:

Oh, waste of life, waste of everything. But things are improving. Do you know, I have been in a positive state of excitement about meeting you ever since your magnificent achievements at Cambridge—a thing unheard of in my day. It was perfectly splendid, your tieing with the third wrangler. Just the right place, you know. The first wrangler is always a dreamy, morbid fellow, in whom the thing is pushed to the length of a disease.

VIVIE:

It doesn't pay. I wouldn't do it again for the same money.

PRAED (*aghast*):

The same money!

VIVIE:

I did it for £50. Perhaps you don't know how it was. Mrs. Latham, my tutor at Newnham, told my mother that I could distinguish myself in the mathematical tripos if I went for it in earnest. The papers were full just then of Phillipa Summers beating the senior wrangler—you remember about it; and nothing would please my mother but that I should do the same thing. I said flatly that it was not worth my while to face the grind since I was not going in for teaching; but I offered to try for fourth wrangler or thereabouts for £50. She closed with me at that, after a little grumbling; and I was better than my bargain. But I wouldn't do it again for that. £200 would have been nearer the mark.

PRAED (*much damped*):

Lord bless me! That's a very practical way of looking at it.

VIVIE:

Did you expect to find me an unpractical person?

PRAED:

No, no. But surely it's practical to consider not only the work these honors cost, but also the culture they bring.

VIVIE:

Culture! My dear Mr. Praed: do you know what the mathematical tripos means? It means grind, grind, grind, for six to eight hours a day at mathematics, and nothing but mathematics. I'm supposed to know something about science; but I know nothing except the mathematics it involves. I can make calculations for engineers, electricians, insurance companies, and so on; but I know next to nothing about engineering or electricity or insurance. I don't even know arithmetic well. Outside mathematics, lawn-tennis, eating, sleeping, cycling, and walking, I'm a more ignorant barbarian than any woman could possibly be who hadn't gone in for the tripos.

PRAED (*revolted*):

What a monstrous, wicked, rascally system! I knew it! I felt at once that it meant destroying all that makes womanhood beautiful.

VIVIE:

I don't object to it on that score in the least. I shall turn it to very good account, I assure you.

PRAED:

Pooh! In what way?

VIVIE:

I shall set up in chambers in the city and work at actuarial calculations and conveyancing. Under cover of that I shall do some law, with one eye on the Stock Exchange all the time. I've come down here by myself to read law—not for a holiday, as my mother imagines. I hate holidays.

PRAED:

You make my blood run cold. Are you to have no romance, no beauty in your life?

VIVIE:

I don't care for either, I assure you.

PRAED:

You can't mean that.

VIVIE:

Oh yes I do. I like working and getting paid for it. When I'm tired of working, I like a comfortable chair, a cigar, a little whisky, and a novel with a good detective story in it.

PRAED (*in a frenzy of repudiation*):

I don't believe it. I am an artist; and I can't believe it: I refuse to believe it. (*Enthusiastically.*) Ah, my dear Miss Warren, you haven't discovered yet, I see, what a wonderful world art can open up to you.

VIVIE:

Yes, I have. Last May I spent six weeks in London with Honoria Fraser. Mamma thought we were doing a round of sightseeing together; but I was really at Honoria's chambers in Chancery Lane every day, working away at actuarial calculations for her, and helping her as well as a greenhorn could. In the evenings we smoked and talked, and never dreamt of going out except for exercise. And I never enjoyed myself more in my life. I cleared all my expenses and got initiated into the business without a fee into the bargain.

PRAED:

But bless my heart and soul, Miss Warren, do you call that trying art?

VIVIE:

Wait a bit. That wasn't the beginning. I went up to town on an invitation from some artistic people in Fitzjohn's Avenue; one of the girls was a Newnham chum. They took me to the National Gallery, to the Opera, and to a concert where the band played all the evening—Beethoven and Wagner and so on. I wouldn't go through that experience again for anything you could offer me. I held out for civility's sake until the third day; and then I said, plump out, that I couldn't stand any more of it, and went off to Chancery Lane. Now you know the sort of perfectly splendid modern young lady I am. How do you think I shall get on with my mother?

PRAED (*startled*):

Well, I hope—er——

VIVIE:

It's not so much what you hope as what you believe, that I want to know.

PRAED:

Well, frankly, I am afraid your mother will be a little disappointed. Not from any shortcoming on your part—I don't mean that. But you are so different from her ideal.

VIVIE:

What is her ideal like?

PRAED:

Well, you must have observed, Miss Warren, that people who are dissatisfied with their own bringing up generally think that the world would be all right if everybody were to be brought up quite differently. Now your mother's life has been—er—I suppose you know——

VIVIE:

I know nothing. (*Praed is appalled. His consternation grows as she continues.*) That's exactly my difficulty. You forget, Mr. Praed, that I hardly know my mother. Since I was a child I have lived in England, at school or college, or with people paid to take charge of me. I have been boarded out all my life; and my mother has lived in Brussels or Vienna and never let me go to her. I only see her when she visits England for a few days. I don't complain: it's been very pleasant; for people have been very good to me; and there has always been plenty of money to make things smooth. But don't imagine I know anything about my mother. I know far less than you do.

PRAED (*very ill at ease*):

In that case— (*He stops, quite at a loss. Then, with a forced attempt at gaiety.*) But what nonsense we are talking! Of course you and your mother will get on capitally. (*He rises, and looks abroad at the view.*) What a charming little place you have here!

VIVIE (*unmoved*):

If you think you are doing anything but confirming my worst suspicions by changing the subject like that, you must take me for a much greater fool than I hope I am.

PRAED:

Your worst suspicions! Oh, pray don't say that. Now don't.

VIVIE:

Why won't my mother's life bear being talked about?

PRAED:

Pray think, Miss Vivie. It is natural that I should have a certain delicacy in talking to my old friend's daughter about her behind her back. You will have plenty of opportunity of talking to her about it when she comes. (*Anxiously.*) I wonder what is keeping her.

VIVIE:

No: she won't talk about it either. (*Rising.*) However, I won't press you. Only mind this, Mr. Praed. I strongly suspect there will be a battle royal when my mother hears of my Chancery Lane project.

PRAED (*ruefully*):

I'm afraid there will.

VIVIE:

I shall win the battle, because I want nothing but my fare to London to start there to-morrow earning my own living by devilling for Honoria. Besides, I have no mysteries to keep up; and it seems she has. I shall use that advantage over her if necessary.

PRAED (*greatly shocked*):

Oh, no. No, pray. You'd not do such a thing.

VIVIE:

Then tell me why not.

PRAED:

I really cannot. I appeal to your good feeling. (*She smiles at his sentimentality.*) Besides, you may be too bold. Your mother is not to be trifled with when she's angry.

VIVIE:

You can't frighten me, Mr. Praed. In that month at Chancery Lane I had opportunities of taking the measure of one or two women, very like my mother, who came to consult Honoria. You may back me to win. But if I hit harder in my ignorance than I need, remember that it is you who refuse to enlighten me. Now let us drop the subject. (*She takes her chair and replaces it near the hammock with the same vigorous swing as before.*)

PRAED (*taking a desperate resolution*):

One word, Miss Warren. I had better tell you. It's very difficult; but——

Mrs. Warren *and* Sir George Crofts *arrive at the gate.* Mrs. Warren *is a woman between 40 and 50, good-looking, showily dressed in a brilliant hat and a gay blouse fitting tightly over her bust and flanked by fashionable sleeves. Rather spoiled and domineering, but, on the whole, a genial and fairly presentable old blackguard of a woman.*

Crofts *is a tall, powerfully-built man of about 50, fashionably dressed in the style of a young man. Nasal voice, reedier than might be expected from his strong frame. Clean-shaven, bull-dog jaws, large flat ears, and thick neck, gentlemanly combination of the most brutal types of city man, sporting man, and man about town.*

VIVIE:

Here they are. (*Coming to them as they enter the garden.*) How do, mater. Mr. Praed's been here this half hour, waiting for you.

MRS. WARREN:

Well, if you've been waiting, Praddy, it's your own fault: I thought you'd have had the gumption to know I was coming by the 3:10 train. Vivie, put your hat on, dear: you'll get sunburnt. Oh, forgot to introduce you. Sir George Crofts, my little Vivie.

Crofts *advances to* Vivie *with his most courtly manner. She nods, but makes no motion to shake hands.*

CROFTS:

> May I shake hands with a young lady whom I have known by reputation very long as the daughter of one of my oldest friends?

VIVIE (*who has been looking him up and down sharply*):

> If you like. (*She take his tenderly proffered hand and gives it a squeeze that makes him open his eyes; then turns away and says to her mother*) Will you come in, or shall I get a couple more chairs? (*She goes into the porch for the chairs.*)

MRS. WARREN:

> Well, George, what do you think of her?

CROFTS (*ruefully*):

> She has a powerful fist. Did you shake hands with her, Praed?

PRAED:

> Yes: it will pass off presently.

CROFTS:

> I hope so. (Vivie *reappears with two more chairs. He hurries to her assistance.*) Allow me.

MRS. WARREN (*patronizingly*):

> Let Sir George help you with the chairs, dear.

VIVIE (*almost pitching two into his arms*):

> Here you are. (*She dusts her hands and turns to* Mrs. Warren.) You'd like some tea, wouldn't you?

MRS. WARREN (*sitting in* Praed's *chair and fanning herself*):

> I'm dying for a drop to drink.

VIVIE:

> I'll see about it. (*She goes into the cottage.* Sir George *has by this time managed to unfold a chair and plant it beside* Mrs. Warren, *on her left. He throws the other on the grass and sits down, looking dejected and rather foolish, with the handle of his stick in his mouth.* Praed, *still very uneasy, fidgets about the garden on their right.*)

MRS. WARREN (*to* Praed, *looking at* Crofts):

> Just look at him, Praddy: he looks cheerful, don't he? He's been worrying my life out these three years to have that little girl of mine shewn to him; and now that I've done it, he's quite out of countenance. (*Briskly.*) Come! sit up, George; and take your stick out of your mouth. (Crofts *sulkily obeys.*)

PRAED:

> I think, you know—if you don't mind my saying so—that we had better get out of the habit of thinking of her as a little girl.

You see she has really distinguished herself; and I'm not sure, from what I have seen of her, that she is not older than any of us.

MRS. WARREN (*greatly amused*):

Only listen to him, George! Older than any of us! Well, she has been stuffing you nicely with her importance.

PRAED:

But young people are particularly sensitive about being treated in that way.

MRS. WARREN:

Yes; and young people have to get all that nonsense taken out of them, and a good deal more besides. Don't you interfere, Praddy. I know how to treat my own child as well as you do. (Praed, *with a grave shake of his head, walks up the garden with his hands behind his back.* Mrs. Warren *pretends to laugh, but looks after him with perceptible concern. Then she whispers to* Crofts.) What's the matter with him? What does he take it like that for?

CROFTS (*morosely*):

You're afraid of Praed.

MRS. WARREN:

What! Me! Afraid of dear old Praddy! Why, a fly wouldn't be afraid of him.

CROFTS:

You're afraid of him.

MRS. WARREN (*angry*):

I'll trouble you to mind your own business, and not try any of your sulks on me. I'm not afraid of you, anyhow. If you can't make yourself agreeable, you'd better go home. (*She gets up, and, turning her back on him, finds herself face to face with* Praed.) Come, Praddy, I know it was only your tender-heartedness. You're afraid I'll bully her.

PRAED:

My dear Kitty: you think I'm offended. Don't imagine that: pray don't. But you know I often notice things that escape you; and though you never take my advice, you sometimes admit afterwards that you ought to have taken it.

MRS. WARREN:

Well, what do you notice now?

PRAED:

Only that Vivie is a grown woman. Pray, Kitty, treat her with every respect.

MRS. WARREN (*with genuine amazement*):

Respect! Treat my own daughter with respect! What next, pray!

VIVIE (*appearing at the cottage door and calling to* Mrs. Warren):

> Mother: will you come up to my room and take your bonnet off before tea?

MRS. WARREN:

> Yes, dearie. (*She laughs indulgently at* Praed *and pats him on the cheek as she passes him on her way to the porch. She follows* Vivie *into the cottage.*)

CROFTS (*furtively*):

> I say, Praed.

PRAED:

> Yes.

CROFTS:

> I want to ask you a rather particular question.

PRAED:

> Certainly. (*He takes* Mrs. Warren's *chair and sits close to Crofts.*)

CROFTS:

> That's right: they might hear us from the window. Look here: did Kitty ever tell you who that girl's father is?

PRAED:

> Never.

CROFTS:

> Have you any suspicion of who it might be?

PRAED:

> None.

CROFTS (*not believing him*):

> I know, of course, that you perhaps might feel bound not to tell if she had said anything to you. But it's very awkward to be uncertain about it now that we shall be meeting the girl every day. We don't exactly know how we ought to feel towards her.

PRAED:

> What difference can that make? We take her on her own merits. What does it matter who her father was?

CROFTS (*suspiciously*):

> Then you know who he was?

PRAED (*with a touch of temper*):

> I said no just now. Did you not hear me?

CROFTS:

> Look here, Praed. I ask you as a particular favor. If you do know (*movement of protest from* Praed)—I only say, if you know, you might at least set my mind at rest about her. The fact is I feel attracted towards her. Oh, don't be alarmed: it's quite an innocent feeling. That's what puzzles me about it. Why, for all I know, *I* might be her father.

PRAED:

> You! Impossible! Oh, no, nonsense!

CROFTS (*catching him up cunningly*):

> You know for certain that I'm not?

PRAED:

> I know nothing about it, I tell you, any more than you. But really, Crofts—oh, no, it's out of the question. There's not the least resemblance.

CROFTS:

> As to that, there's no resemblance between her and her mother that I can see. I suppose she's not your daughter, is she?

PRAED (*He meets the question with an indignant stare; then recovers himself with an effort and answers gently and gravely*):

> Now listen to me, my dear Crofts. I have nothing to do with that side of Mrs. Warren's life, and never had. She has never spoken to me about it; and of course I have never spoken to her about it. Your delicacy will tell you that a handsome woman needs some friends who are not—well, not on that footing with her. The effect of her own beauty would become a torment to her if she could not escape from it occasionally. You are probably on much more confidential terms with Kitty than I am. Surely you can ask her the question yourself.

CROFTS (*rising impatiently*):

> I have asked her often enough. But she's so determined to keep the child all to herself that she would deny that it ever had a father if she could. No: there's nothing to be got out of her—nothing that one can believe, anyhow. I'm thoroughly uncomfortable about it, Praed.

PRAED (*rising also*):

> Well, as you are, at all events, old enough to be her father, I don't mind agreeing that we both regard Miss Vivie in a parental way, as a young girl whom we are bound to protect and help. All the more, as the real father, whoever he was, was probably a blackguard. What do you say?

CROFTS (*aggressively*):

> I'm no older than you, if you come to that.

PRAED:

> Yes, you are, my dear fellow: you were born old. I was born a boy: I've never been able to feel the assurance of a grown-up man in my life.

MRS. WARREN (*calling from within the cottage*):

> Prad-dee! George! Tea-ea-ea-ea!

CROFTS (*hastily*):

> She's calling us. (*He hurries in.* Praed *shakes his head bodingly, and is following slowly when he is hailed by a young gentleman who has just appeared on the common, and is making for the gate. He is a pleasant, pretty, smartly dressed, and entirely good-for-nothing young fellow, not long turned 20, with a charming voice and agreeably disrespectful manner. He carries a very light sporting magazine rifle.*)

THE YOUNG GENTLEMAN:

> Hallo! Praed!

PRAED:

> Why, Frank Gardner! (Frank *comes in and shakes hands cordially.*) What on earth are you doing here?

FRANK:

> Staying with my father.

PRAED:

> The Roman father?

FRANK:

> He's rector here. I'm living with my people this autumn for the sake of economy. Things came to a crisis in July: the Roman father had to pay my debts. He's stony broke in consequence; and so am I. What are you up to in these parts? Do you know the people here?

PRAED:

> Yes: I'm spending the day with a Miss Warren.

FRANK (*enthusiastically*):

> What! Do you know Vivie? Isn't she a jolly girl! I'm teaching her to shoot—you see (*shewing the rifle.*)! I'm so glad she knows you: you're just the sort of fellow she ought to know. (*He smiles, and raises the charming voice almost to a singing tone as he exclaims*) It's ever so jolly to find you here, Praed. Ain't it, now?

PRAED:

> I'm an old friend of her mother's. Mrs. Warren brought me over to make her daughter's acquaintance.

FRANK:

> The mother! Is she here?

PRAED:

> Yes—inside at tea.

MRS. WARREN (*calling from within*):

> Prad-dee-ee-ee-eee! The tea-cake'll be cold.

PRAED (*calling*):

> Yes, Mrs. Warren. In a moment. I've just met a friend here.

MRS. WARREN:

A what?

PRAED (*louder*):

A friend.

MRS. WARREN:

Bring him up.

PRAED:

All right. (*To* Frank.) Will you accept the invitation?

FRANK (*incredulous, but immensely amused*):

Is that Vivie's mother?

PRAED:

Yes.

FRANK:

By Jove! What a lark! Do you think she'll like me?

PRAED:

I've no doubt you'll make yourself popular, as usual. Come in and try (*moving towards the house*).

FRANK:

Stop a bit. (*Seriously.*) I want to take you into my confidence.

PRAED:

Pray don't. It's only some fresh folly, like the barmaid at Redhill.

FRANK:

It's ever so much more serious than that. You say you've only just met Vivie for the first time?

PRAED:

Yes.

FRANK (*rhapsodically*):

Then you can have no idea what a girl she is. Such character! Such sense! And her cleverness! Oh, my eye, Praed, but I can tell you she is clever! And the most loving little heart that——

CROFTS (*putting his head out of the window*):

I say, Praed: what are you about? Do come along. (*He disappears.*)

FRANK:

Hallo! Sort of chap that would take a prize at a dog show, ain't he? Who's he?

PRAED:

Sir George Crofts, an old friend of Mrs. Warren's. I think we had better come in.

*On their way to the porch they are interrupted by a call from the gate. Turning, they see an elderly clergyman looking over it.*

THE CLERGYMAN (*calling*):

Frank!

FRANK:

> Hallo! (*To* Praed.) The Roman father. (*To* the clergyman.) Yes, gov'nor: all right: presently. (*To* Praed.) Look here, Praed: you'd better go in to tea. I'll join you directly.

PRAED:

> Very good. (*He raises his hat to* the clergyman, *who acknowledges the salute distantly.* Praed *goes into the cottage.* The clergyman *remains stiffly outside the gate, with his hands on the top of it. The* Rev. Samuel Gardner, *a beneficed clergyman of the Established Church, is over 50. He is a pretentious, booming, noisy person, hopelessly asserting himself as a father and a clergyman without being able to command respect in either capacity.*)

REV. S.:

> Well, sir. Who are your friends here, if I may ask?

FRANK:

> Oh, it's all right, gov'nor! Come in.

REV. S.:

> No, sir; not until I know whose garden I am entering.

FRANK:

> It's all right. It's Miss Warren's.

REV. S.:

> I have not seen her at church since she came.

FRANK:

> Of course not: she's a third wrangler—ever so intellectual!—took a higher degree than you did; so why should she go to hear you preach?

REV. S.:

> Don't be disrespectful, sir.

FRANK:

> Oh, it don't matter: nobody hears us. Come in. (*He opens the gate, unceremoniously pulling his father with it into the garden.*) I want to introduce you to her. She and I get on rattling well together: she's charming. Do you remember the advice you gave me last July, gov'nor?

REV. S. (*severely*):

> Yes. I advised you to conquer your idleness and flippancy, and to work your way into an honorable profession and live on it and not upon me.

FRANK:

> No: that's what you thought of afterwards. What you actually said was that since I had neither brains nor money, I'd better turn my good looks to account by marrying somebody with both. Well, look here. Miss Warren has brains: you can't deny that.

REV. S.:

Brains are not everything.

FRANK:

No, of course not: there's the money——

REV. S. (*interrupting him austerely*):

I was not thinking of money, sir. I was speaking of higher things—social position, for instance.

FRANK:

I don't care a rap about that.

REV. S.:

But I do, sir.

FRANK:

Well, nobody wants you to marry her. Anyhow, she has what amounts to a high Cambridge degree; and she seems to have as much money as she wants.

REV. S. (*sinking into a feeble vein of humor*):

I greatly doubt whether she has as much money as you will want.

FRANK:

Oh, come: I haven't been so very extravagant. I live ever so quietly; I don't drink; I don't bet much; and I never go regularly on the razzle-dazzle as you did when you were my age.

REV. S. (*booming hollowly*):

Silence, sir.

FRANK:

Well, you told me yourself, when I was making ever such an ass of myself about the barmaid at Redhill, that you once offered a woman £50 for the letters you wrote to her when——

REV. S. (*terrified*):

Sh-sh-sh, Frank, for Heaven's sake! (*He looks round apprehensively. Seeing no one within earshot he plucks up courage to boom again, but more subduedly.*) You are taking an ungentlemanly advantage of what I confided to you for your own good, to save you from an error you would have repented all your life long. Take warning by your father's follies, sir; and don't make them an excuse for your own.

FRANK:

Did you ever hear the story of the Duke of Wellington and his letters?

REV. S.:

No, sir; and I don't want to hear it.

FRANK:

The old Iron Duke didn't throw away £50—not he. He just

wrote: "My dear Jenny: Publish and be damned! Yours affectionately, Wellington." That's what you should have done.

REV. S. (*piteously*):

Frank, my boy: when I wrote those letters I put myself into that woman's power. When I told you about her I put myself, to some extent, I am sorry to say, in your power. She refused my money with these words, which I shall never forget: "Knowledge is power," she said; "and I never sell power." That's more than twenty years ago; and she has never made use of her power or caused me a moment's uneasiness. You are behaving worse to me than she did, Frank.

FRANK:

Oh, yes, I dare say! Did you ever preach at her the way you preach at me every day?

REV. S. (*wounded almost to tears*):

I leave you, sir. You are incorrigible. (*He turns towards the gate.*)

FRANK (*utterly unmoved*):

Tell them I shan't be home to tea, will you, gov'nor, like a good fellow? (*He goes towards the cottage door and is met by* Vivie *coming out, followed by* Praed, Crofts, *and* Mrs. Warren.)

VIVIE (*to* Frank):

Is that your father, Frank? I do so want to meet him.

FRANK:

Certainly. (*Calling after his father.*) Gov'nor. (*The* Rev. S. *turns at the gate, fumbling nervously at his hat.* Praed *comes down the garden on the opposite side, beaming in anticipation of civilities.* Crofts *prowls about near the hammock, poking it with his stick to make it swing.* Mrs. Warren *halts on the threshold, staring hard at the clergyman.*) Let me introduce—my father: Miss Warren.

VIVIE (*going to* the clergyman *and shaking his hand*):

Very glad to see you here, Mr. Gardner. Let me introduce everybody. Mr. Gardner—Mr. Frank Gardner—Mr. Praed—Sir George Crofts, and—(*As the men are raising their hats to one another,* Vivie *is interrupted by an exclamation from her mother, who swoops down on the* Reverend Samuel).

MRS. WARREN:

Why, it's Sam Gardner, gone into the church! Don't you know us, Sam? This is George Crofts, as large as life and twice as natural. Don't you remember me?

REV. S. (*very red*):

I really—er——

MRS. WARREN:

Of course you do. Why, I have a whole album of your letters still: I came across them only the other day.

REV. S. (*miserably confused*):

Miss Vavasour, I believe.

MRS. WARREN (*correcting him quickly in a loud whisper*):

Tch! Nonsense—Mrs. Warren: don't you see my daughter there?

# Act II

*Inside the cottage after nightfall. Looking eastward from within instead of westward from without, the latticed window, with its curtains drawn, is now seen in the middle of the front wall of the cottage, with the porch door to the left of it. In the left-hand side wall is the door leading to the wing. Farther back against the same wall is a dresser with a candle and matches on it, and Frank's rifle standing beside them, with the barrel resting in the plate-rack. In the centre a table stands with a lighted lamp on it. Vivie's books and writing materials are on a table to the right of the window, against the wall. The fireplace is on the right, with a settle: there is no fire. Two of the chairs are set right and left of the table.*

*The cottage door opens, shewing a fine starlit night without; and Mrs. Warren, her shoulders wrapped in a shawl borrowed from Vivie, enters, followed by Frank. She has had enough of walking, and gives a gasp of relief as she unpins her hat; takes it off; sticks the pin through the crown; and puts it on the table.*

MRS. WARREN:

O Lord! I don't know which is the worst of the country, the walking or the sitting at home with nothing to do: I could do a whisky and soda now very well, if only they had such a thing in the place.

FRANK (*helping her to take off her shawl, and giving her shoulders the most delicate possible little caress with his fingers as he does so*):

Perhaps Vivie's got some.

MRS. WARREN (*glancing back at him for an instant from the corner of her eye as she detects the pressure*):

Nonsense! What would a young girl like her be doing with such things! Never mind: it don't matter. (*She throws herself wearily into a chair at the table.*) I wonder how she passes her time here! I'd a good deal rather be in Vienna.

FRANK:

Let me take you there. (*He folds the shawl neatly; hangs it on the back of the other chair; and sits down opposite Mrs. Warren.*)

MRS. WARREN:

Get out! I'm beginning to think you're a chip off the old block.

FRANK:

Like the gov'nor, eh?

MRS. WARREN:

Never you mind. What do you know about such things? You're only a boy.

FRANK:

Do come to Vienna with me? It'd be ever such larks.

MRS. WARREN:

No, thank you. Vienna is no place for you—at least not until you're a little older. (*She nods at him to emphasize this piece of advice. He makes a mock-piteous face, belied by his laughing eyes. She looks at him; then rises and goes to him.*) Now, look here, little boy (*taking his face in her hands and turning it up to her*): I know you through and through by your likeness to your father, better than you know yourself. Don't you go taking any silly ideas into your head about me. Do you hear?

FRANK (*gallantly wooing her with his voice*):

Can't help it, my dear Mrs. Warren: it runs in the family. (*She pretends to box his ears; then looks at the pretty, laughing, upturned face for a moment, tempted. At last she kisses him and immediately turns away, out of patience with herself.*)

MRS. WARREN:

There! I shouldn't have done that. I am wicked. Never you mind, my dear: it's only a motherly kiss. Go and make love to Vivie.

FRANK:

So I have.

MRS. WARREN (*turning on him with a sharp note of alarm in her voice*):

What!

FRANK:

Vivie and I are ever such chums.

MRS. WARREN:

What do you mean? Now, see here: I won't have any young scamp tampering with my little girl. Do you hear? I won't have it.

FRANK (*quite unabashed*):

My dear Mrs. Warren: don't you be alarmed. My intentions are honorable—ever so honorable; and your little girl is jolly well able to take care of herself. She don't need looking after half so much as her mother. She ain't so handsome, you know.

MRS. WARREN (*taken aback by his assurance*):

Well, you have got a nice, healthy two inches thick of cheek all over you. I don't know where you got it—not from your father, anyhow. (*Voices and footsteps in the porch.*) Sh! I hear the others coming in. (*She sits down hastily.*) Remember: you've got your warning. (*The* Rev. Samuel *comes in, followed by* Crofts.) Well, what became of you two? And where's Praddy and Vivie?

CROFTS (*putting his hat on the settle and his stick in the chimney corner*): They went up the hill. We went to the village. I wanted a drink. (*He sits down on the settle, putting his legs up along the seat.*)

MRS. WARREN:

Well, she oughtn't to go off like that without telling me. (*To* Frank.) Get your father a chair, Frank: where are your manners? (Frank *springs up and gracefully offers his father his chair; then takes another from the wall and sits down at the table, in the middle, with his father on his right and* Mrs. Warren *on his left.*) George: where are you going to stay to-night? You can't stay here. And what's Praddy going to do?

CROFTS:

Gardner'll put me up.

MRS. WARREN:

Oh, no doubt you've taken care of yourself! But what about Praddy?

CROFTS:

Don't know. I suppose he can sleep at the inn.

MRS. WARREN:

Haven't you room for him, Sam?

REV. S.:

Well, er—you see, as rector here, I am not free to do as I like exactly. Er—what is Mr. Praed's social position?

MRS. WARREN:

Oh, he's all right: he's an architect. What an old-stick-in-the-mud you are, Sam!

FRANK:

Yes, it's all right, gov'nor. He built that place down in Monmouthshire for the Duke of Beaufort—Tintern Abbey they call it. You must have heard of it. (*He winks with lightning smartness at* Mrs. Warren, *and regards his father blandly.*)

REV. S.:

Oh, in that case, of course we shall only be too happy. I suppose he knows the Duke of Beaufort personally.

FRANK:

Oh, ever so intimately! We can stick him in Georgina's old room.

MRS. WARREN:

Well, that's settled. Now, if those two would only come in and let us have supper. They've no right to stay out after dark like this.

CROFTS (*aggressively*):
> What harm are they doing you?

MRS. WARREN:
> Well, harm or not, I don't like it.

FRANK:
> Better not wait for them, Mrs. Warren. Praed will stay out as long as possible. He has never known before what it is to stray over the heath on a summer night with my Vivie.

CROFTS (*sitting up in some consternation*):
> I say, you know. Come!

REV. S. (*startled out of his professional manner into real force and sincerity*):
> Frank, once for all, it's out of the question. Mrs. Warren will tell you that it's not to be thought of.

CROFTS:
> Of course not.

FRANK (*with enchanting placidity*):
> Is that so, Mrs. Warren?

MRS. WARREN (*reflectively*):
> Well, Sam, I don't know. If the girl wants to get married, no good can come of keeping her unmarried.

REV. S. (*astounded*):
> But married to him!—your daughter to my son! Only think: it's impossible.

CROFTS:
> Of course it's impossible. Don't be a fool, Kitty.

MRS. WARREN (*nettled*):
> Why not? Isn't my daughter good enough for your son?

REV. S.:
> But surely, my dear Mrs. Warren, you know the reason—

MRS. WARREN (*defiantly*):
> I know no reasons. If you know any, you can tell them to the lad, or to the girl, or to your congregation, if you like.

REV. S. (*helplessly*):
> You know very well that I couldn't tell anyone the reasons. But my boy will believe me when I tell him there are reasons.

FRANK:
> Quite right, Dad: he will. But has your boy's conduct ever been influenced by your reasons?

CROFTS:
> You can't marry her; and that's all about it. (*He gets up and stands on the hearth, with his back to the fireplace, frowning determinedly.*)

MRS. WARREN (*turning on him sharply*):
> What have you got to do with it, pray?

FRANK (*with his prettiest lyrical cadence*):

Precisely what I was going to ask, myself, in my own graceful fashion.

CROFTS (*to Mrs. Warren*):

I suppose you don't want to marry the girl to a man younger than herself and without either a profession or twopence to keep her on. Ask Sam, if you don't believe me. (*To the* Rev. S.) How much more money are you going to give him?

REV. S.:

Not another penny. He has had his patrimony; and he spent the last of it in July. (*Mrs. Warren's face falls.*)

CROFTS (*watching her*):

There! I told you. (*He resumes his place on the settle and puts up his legs on the seat again, as if the matter were finally disposed of.*)

FRANK (*plaintively*):

This is ever so mercenary. Do you suppose Miss Warren's going to marry for money? If we love one another—

MRS. WARREN:

Thank you. Your love's a pretty cheap commodity, my lad. If you have no means of keeping a wife, that settles it: you can't have Vivie.

FRANK (*much amused*):

What do you say, gov'nor, eh?

REV. S.:

I agree with Mrs. Warren.

FRANK:

And good old Crofts has already expressed his opinion.

CROFTS (*turning angrily on his elbow*):

Look here: I want none of your cheek.

FRANK (*pointedly*):

I'm ever so sorry to surprise you, Crofts; but you allowed yourself the liberty of speaking to me like a father a moment ago. One father is enough, thank you.

CROFTS (*contemptuously*):

Yah! (*He turns away again.*)

FRANK (*rising*):

Mrs. Warren: I cannot give my Vivie up even for your sake.

MRS. WARREN (*muttering*):

Young scamp!

FRANK (*continuing*):

And as you no doubt intend to hold out other prospects to her, I shall lose no time in placing my case before her. (*They stare at him; and he begins to declaim gracefully*)

He either fears his fate too much,
    Or his deserts are small,
That dares not put it to the touch
    To gain or lose it all.

*The cottage door opens whilst he is reciting; and* Vivie *and* Praed *come in.
He breaks off.* Praed *puts his hat on the dresser. There is an immediate
improvement in the company's behaviour.* Crofts *takes down his legs from
the settle and pulls himself together as* Praed *joins him at the fireplace.*
Mrs. Warren *loses her ease of manner, and takes refuge in querulousness.*

MRS. WARREN:
Wherever have you been, Vivie?

VIVIE (*taking off her hat and throwing it carelessly on the table*):
On the hill.

MRS. WARREN:
Well, you shouldn't go off like that without letting me know.
How could I tell what had become of you—and night coming
on, too!

VIVIE (*going to the door of the inner room and opening it, ignoring her
mother*):
Now, about supper? We shall be rather crowded in here, I'm
afraid.

MRS. WARREN:
Did you hear what I said, Vivie?

VIVIE (*quietly*):
Yes, mother. (*Reverting to the supper difficulty.*) How many are
we? (*Counting.*) One, two, three, four, five, six. Well, two will
have to wait until the rest are done: Mrs. Alison has only plates
and knives for four.

PRAED:
Oh, it doesn't matter about me. I——

VIVIE:
You have had a long walk and are hungry, Mr. Praed: you shall
have your supper at once. I can wait myself. I want one person
to wait with me. Frank: are you hungry?

FRANK:
Not the least in the world—completely off my peck, in fact.

MRS. WARREN (*to* Crofts):
Neither are you, George. You can wait.

CROFTS:
Oh, hang it, I've eaten nothing since teatime. Can't Sam do it?

FRANK:
Would you starve my poor father?

REV. S. (*testily*):

Allow me to speak for myself, sir. I am perfectly willing to wait.

VIVIE (*decisively*):

There's no need. Only two are wanted. (*She opens the door of the inner room.*) Will you take my mother in, Mr. Gardner. (*The Rev. S. takes Mrs. Warren; and they pass into the next room. Praed and Crofts follow. All except Praed clearly disapprove of the arrangement, but do not know how to resist it. Vivie stands at the door looking in at them.*) Can you squeeze past to that corner, Mr. Praed: it's rather a tight fit. Take care of your coat against the white-wash—that's right. Now, are you all comfortable?

PRAED (*within*):

Quite, thank you.

MRS. WARREN (*within*):

Leave the door open, dearie. (*Frank looks at Vivie; then steals to the cottage door and softly sets it wide open.*) Oh, Lor', what a draught! You'd better shut it, dear. (*Vivie shuts it promptly. Frank noiselessly shuts the cottage door.*)

FRANK (*exulting*):

Aha! Got rid of 'em. Well, Vivvums: what do you think of my governor!

VIVIE (*preoccupied and serious*):

I've hardly spoken to him. He doesn't strike me as being a particularly able person.

FRANK:

Well, you know, the old man is not altogether such a fool as he looks. You see, he's rector here; and in trying to live up to it he makes a much bigger ass of himself than he really is. No, the gov'nor ain't so bad, poor old chap; and I don't dislike him as much as you might expect. He means well. How do you think you'll get on with him?

VIVIE (*rather grimly*):

I don't think my future life will be much concerned with him, or with any of that old circle of my mother's, except perhaps Praed. What do you think of my mother?

FRANK:

Really and truly?

VIVIE:

Yes, really and truly.

FRANK:

Well, she's ever so jolly. But she's rather a caution, isn't she? And Crofts! Oh, my eye, Crofts!

VIVIE:

What a lot, Frank!

FRANK:

What a crew!

VIVIE (*with intense contempt for them*):

If I thought that *I* was like that—that I was going to be a waster, shifting along from one meal to another with no purpose, and no character, and no grit in me, I'd open an artery and bleed to death without one moment's hesitation.

FRANK:

Oh, no, you wouldn't. Why should they take any grind when they can afford not to? I wish I had their luck. No: what I object to is their form. It isn't the thing: it's slovenly, ever so slovenly.

VIVIE:

Do you think your form will be any better when you're as old as Crofts, if you don't work?

FRANK:

Of course I do—ever so much better. Vivvums mustn't lecture: her little boy's incorrigible. (*He attempts to take her face caressingly in his hands.*)

VIVIE (*striking his hands down sharply*):

Off with you: Vivvums is not in a humor for petting her little boy this evening.

FRANK:

How unkind!

VIVIE (*stamping at him*):

Be serious. I'm serious.

FRANK:

Good. Let us talk learnedly. Miss Warren: do you know that all the most advanced thinkers are agreed that half the diseases of modern civilization are due to starvation of the affections in the young. Now, *I*——

VIVIE (*cutting him short*):

You are getting tiresome. (*She opens the inner door.*) Have you room for Frank there? He's complaining of starvation.

MRS. WARREN (*within*):

Of course there is (*clatter of knives and glasses as she moves the things on the table*). Here: there's room now beside me. Come along, Mr. Frank.

FRANK (*aside to Vivie, as he goes*):

Her little boy will be ever so even with his Vivvums for this. (*He goes into the other room.*)

MRS. WARREN (*within*):

Here, Vivie: come on, you too, child. You must be famished. (*She enters, followed by Crofts, who holds the door open for Vivie with marked deference. She goes out without looking at him; and he shuts the door after her.*) Why, George, you can't be done: you've eaten nothing.

CROFTS:

Oh, all I wanted was a drink. (*He thrusts his hands in his pockets and begins prowling about the room, restless and sulky.*)

MRS. WARREN:

Well, I like enough to eat. But a little of that cold beef and cheese and lettuce goes a long way. (*With a sigh of only half repletion she sits down lazily at the table.*)

CROFTS:

What do you go encouraging that young pup for?

MRS. WARREN (*on the alert at once*):

Now see here, George: what are you up to about that girl? I've been watching your way of looking at her. Remember: I know you and what your looks mean.

CROFTS:

There's no harm in looking at her, is there?

MRS. WARREN:

I'd put you out and pack you back to London pretty soon if I saw any of your nonsense. My girl's little finger is more to me than your whole body and soul. (Crofts *receives this with a sneering grin.* Mrs. Warren, *flushing a little at her failure to impose on him in the character of a theatrically devoted mother, adds in a lower key.*) Make your mind easy, the young pup has no more chance than you have.

CROFTS:

Mayn't a man take an interest in a girl?

MRS. WARREN:

Not a man like you.

CROFTS:

How old is she?

MRS. WARREN:

Never you mind how old she is.

CROFTS:

Why do you make such a secret of it?

MRS. WARREN:

Because I choose.

CROFTS:

Well, I'm not fifty yet; and my property is as good as ever it was——

MRS. WARREN (*interrupting him*):

Yes; because you're as stingy as you're vicious.

CROFTS (*continuing*):

And a baronet isn't to be picked up every day. No other man in my position would put up with you for a mother-in-law. Why shouldn't she marry me?

MRS. WARREN:

You!

CROFTS:

We three could live together quite comfortably. I'd die before her and leave her a bouncing widow with plenty of money. Why not? It's been growing in my mind all the time I've been walking with that fool inside there.

MRS. WARREN (*revolted*):

Yes; it's the sort of thing that would grow in your mind. (*He halts in his prowling; and the two look at one another, she stead-fastly, with a sort of awe behind her contemptuous disgust: he stealthily, with a carnal gleam in his eye and a loose grin, tempting her.*)

CROFTS (*suddenly becoming anxious and urgent as he sees no sign of sympathy in her*):

Look here, Kitty: you're a sensible woman: you needn't put on any moral airs. I'll ask no more questions; and you need answer none. I'll settle the whole property on her; and if you want a cheque for yourself on the wedding day, you can name any figure you like—in reason.

MRS. WARREN:

Faugh! So it's come to that with you, George, like all the other worn out old creatures.

CROFTS (*savagely*):

Damn you! (*She rises and turns fiercely on him; but the door of the inner room is opened just then; and the voices of the others are heard returning.* Crofts, *unable to recover his presence of mind, hurries out of the cottage.* The clergyman *comes back.*)

REV. S. (*looking round*):

Where is Sir George?

MRS. WARREN:

Gone out to have a pipe. (*She goes to the fireplace, turning her back on him to compose herself. The clergyman goes to the table for his hat. Meanwhile* Vivie *comes in, followed by* Frank, *who collapses into the nearest chair with an air of extreme exhaustion.* Mrs. Warren *looks round at* Vivie *and says, with her affectation of maternal patronage even more forced than usual.*) Well, dearie: have you had a good supper?

VIVIE:

You know what Mrs. Alison's suppers are. (*She turns to* Frank *and pets him.*) Poor Frank! was all the beef gone? did it get nothing but bread and cheese and ginger beer? (*Seriously, as if she had done quite enough trifling for one evening.*) Her butter is really awful. I must get some down from the stores.

FRANK:

Do, in Heaven's name!

Vivie *goes to the writing-table and makes a memorandum to order the butter.* Praed *comes in from the inner room, putting up his handkerchief, which he has been using as a napkin.*

REV. S.:

Frank, my boy: it is time for us to be thinking of home. Your mother does not know yet that we have visitors.

PRAED:

I'm afraid we're giving trouble.

FRANK:

Not the least in the world, Praed: my mother will be delighted to see you. She's a genuinely intellectual, artistic woman; and she sees nobody here from one year's end to another except the gov'nor; so you can imagine how jolly dull it pans out for her. (*To the* Rev. S.) You're not intellectual or artistic, are you, pater? So take Praed home at once; and I'll stay here and entertain Mrs. Warren. You'll pick up Crofts in the garden. He'll be excellent company for the bull-pup.

PRAED (*taking his hat from the dresser, and coming close to* Frank):

Come with us, Frank. Mrs. Warren has not seen Miss Vivie for a long time; and we have prevented them from having a moment together yet.

FRANK (*quite softened, and looking at* Praed *with romantic admiration*):

Of course: I forgot. Ever so thanks for reminding me. Perfect gentleman, Praddy. Always were—my ideal through life. (*He rises to go, but pauses a moment between the two older men, and puts his hand on* Praed's *shoulder.*) Ah, if you had only been my father instead of this unworthy old man! (*He puts his other hand on his father's shoulder.*)

REV. S. (*blustering*):

Silence, sir, silence: you are profane.

MRS. WARREN (*laughing heartily*):

You should keep him in better order, Sam. Good-night. Here: take George his hat and stick with my compliments.

REV. S. (*taking them*):

Good-night. (*They shake hands. As he passes* Vivie *he shakes hands with her also and bids her good-night. Then, in booming command, to* Frank.) Come along, sir, at once. (*He goes out. Meanwhile* Frank *has taken his cap from the dresser and his rifle from the rack.*

(*Praed shakes hands with* Mrs. Warren *and* Vivie *and goes out,*
Mrs. Warren *accompanying him idly to the door, and looking out
after him as he goes across the garden.* Frank *silently begs a kiss from*
Vivie; *but she, dismissing him with a stern glance, takes a couple of
books and some paper from the writing-table, and sits down with
them at the middle table, so as to have the benefit of the lamp.*)

FRANK (*at the door, taking* Mrs. Warren's *hand*):

Good-night, dear Mrs. Warren. (*He squeezes her hand. She
snatches it away, her lips tightening, and looks more than half disposed to box his ears. He laughs mischievously and runs off, clapping-
to the door behind him.*)

MRS. WARREN (*coming back to her place at the table, opposite* Vivie,
*resigning herself to an evening of boredom now that the men
are gone*):

Did you ever in your life hear anyone rattle on so? Isn't he
a tease? (*She sits down.*) Now that I think of it, dearie, don't
you go encouraging him. I'm sure he's a regular good-for-
nothing.

VIVIE:

Yes: I'm afraid poor Frank is a thorough good-for-nothing. I
shall have to get rid of him; but I shall feel sorry for him,
though he's not worth it, poor lad. That man Crofts does not
seem to me to be good for much either, is he?

MRS. WARREN (*galled by* Vivie's *cool tone*):

What do you know of men, child, to talk that way about them?
You'll have to make up your mind to see a good deal of Sir
George Crofts, as he's a friend of mine.

VIVIE (*quite unmoved*):

Why? Do you expect that we shall be much together—you and
I, I mean?

MRS. WARREN (*staring at her*):

Of course—until you're married. You're not going back to college again.

VIVIE:

Do you think my way of life would suit you? I doubt it.

MRS. WARREN:

Your way of life! What do you mean?

VIVIE (*cutting a page of her book with the paper knife on her chatelaine*):

Has it really never occurred to you, mother, that I have a way
of life like other people?

MRS. WARREN:

What nonsense is this you're trying to talk? Do you want to
shew your independence, now that you're a great little person
at school? Don't be a fool, child.

VIVIE (*indulgently*):

That's all you have to say on the subject, is it, mother?

MRS. WARREN (*puzzled, then angry*):

Don't you keep on asking me questions like that. (*Violently.*) Hold your tongue. (Vivie *works on, losing no time, and saying nothing.*) You and your way of life, indeed! What next? (*She looks at* Vivie *again. No reply.*) Your way of life will be what I please, so it will. (*Another pause.*) I've been noticing these airs in you ever since you got that tripos or whatever you call it. If you think I'm going to put up with them you're mistaken; and the sooner you find it out, the better. (*Muttering.*) All I have to say on the subject, indeed! (*Again raising her voice angrily.*) Do you know who you're speaking to, Miss?

VIVIE (*looking across at her without raising her head from her book*):

No. Who are you? What are you?

MRS. WARREN (*rising breathless*):

You young imp!

VIVIE:

Everybody knows my reputation, my social standing, and the profession I intend to pursue. I know nothing about you. What is that way of life which you invite me to share with you and Sir George Crofts, pray?

MRS. WARREN:

Take care. I shall do something I'll be sorry for after, and you, too.

VIVIE (*putting aside her books with cool decision*):

Well, let us drop the subject until you are better able to face it. (*Looking critically at her mother.*) You want some good walks and a little lawn tennis to set you up. You are shockingly out of condition: you were not able to manage twenty yards uphill to-day without stopping to pant; and your wrists are mere rolls of fat. Look at mine. (*She holds out her wrists.*)

MRS. WARREN (*after looking at her helplessly, begins to whimper*):

Vivie——

VIVIE (*springing up sharply*):

Now pray don't begin to cry. Anything but that. I really cannot stand whimpering. I will go out of the room if you do.

MRS. WARREN (*piteously*):

Oh, my darling, how can you be so hard on me? Have I no rights over you as your mother?

VIVIE:

Are you my mother?

MRS. WARREN (*appalled*):

Am I your mother! Oh, Vivie!

VIVIE:

Then where are our relatives—my father—our family friends? You claim the rights of a mother: the right to call me fool and child; to speak to me as no woman in authority over me at college dare speak to me; to dictate my way of life; and to force on me the acquaintance of a brute whom anyone can see to be the most vicious sort of London man about town. Before I give myself the trouble to resist such claims, I may as well find out whether they have any real existence.

MRS. WARREN (*distracted, throwing herself on her knees*):

Oh, no, no. Stop, stop. I am your mother: I swear it. Oh, you can't mean to turn on me—my own child: it's not natural. You believe me, don't you? Say you believe me.

VIVIE:

Who was my father?

MRS. WARREN:

You don't know what you're asking. I can't tell you.

VIVIE (*determinedly*):

Oh, yes, you can, if you like. I have a right to know; and you know very well that I have that right. You can refuse to tell me, if you please; but if you do, you will see the last of me tomorrow morning.

MRS. WARREN:

Oh, it's too horrible to hear you talk like that. You wouldn't— you couldn't leave me.

VIVIE (*ruthlessly*):

Yes, without a moment's hesitation, if you trifle with me about this. (*Shivering with disgust.*) How can I feel sure that I may not have the contaminated blood of that brutal waster in my veins?

MRS. WARREN:

No, no. On my oath it's not he, nor any of the rest that you have ever met. I'm certain of that, at least. (Vivie's *eyes fasten sternly on her mother as the significance of this flashes on her.*)

VIVIE (*slowly*):

You are certain of that, at least. Ah! You mean that that is all you are certain of. (*Thoughtfully.*) I see. (Mrs. Warren *buries her face in her hands.*) Don't do that, mother: you know you don't feel it a bit. (Mrs. Warren *takes down her hands and looks up deplorably at* Vivie, *who takes out her watch and says*) Well, that is enough for to-night. At what hour would you like breakfast? Is half-past eight too early for you?

MRS. WARREN (*wildly*):

My God, what sort of woman are you?

VIVIE (*coolly*):

> The sort the world is mostly made of, I should hope. Otherwise I don't understand how it gets its business done. Come (*taking her mother by the wrist, and pulling her up pretty resolutely*): pull yourself together. That's right.

MRS. WARREN (*querulously*):

> You're very rough with me, Vivie.

VIVIE:

> Nonsense. What about bed? It's past ten.

MRS. WARREN (*passionately*):

> What's the use of my going to bed? Do you think I could sleep?

VIVIE:

> Why not? I shall.

MRS. WARREN:

> You! you've no heart. (*She suddenly breaks out vehemently in her natural tongue—the dialect of a woman of the people—with all her affectations of maternal authority and conventional manners gone, and an overwhelming inspiration of true conviction and scorn in her.*) Oh, I won't bear it: I won't put up with the injustice of it. What right have you to set yourself up above me like this? You boast of what you are to me—to me, who gave you the chance of being what you are. What chance had I? Shame on you for a bad daughter and a stuck-up prude!

VIVIE (*cool and determined, but no longer confident; for her replies, which have sounded convincingly sensible and strong to her so far, now begin to ring rather woodenly and even priggishly against the new tone of her mother*):

> Don't think for a moment I set myself above you in any way. You attacked me with the conventional authority of a mother: I defended myself with the conventional superiority of a respectable woman. Frankly, I am not going to stand any of your nonsense; and when you drop it I shall not expect you to stand any of mine. I shall always respect your right to your own opinions and your own way of life.

MRS. WARREN:

> My own opinions and my own way of life! Listen to her talking! Do you think I was brought up like you—able to pick and choose my own way of life? Do you think I did what I did because I liked it, or thought it right, or wouldn't rather have gone to college and been a lady if I'd had the chance?

VIVIE:

> Everybody has some choice, mother. The poorest girl alive may not be able to choose between being Queen of England or

Principal of Newnham; but she can choose between ragpicking and flowerselling, according to her taste. People are always blaming their circumstances for what they are. I don't believe in circumstances. The people who get on in this world are the people who get up and look for the circumstances they want, and, if they can't find them, make them.

MRS. WARREN:

Oh, it's easy to talk, very easy, isn't it? Here!—would you like to know what my circumstances were?

VIVIE:

Yes: you had better tell me. Won't you sit down?

MRS. WARREN:

Oh, I'll sit down: don't you be afraid. (*She plants her chair farther forward with brazen energy, and sits down.* Vivie *is impressed in spite of herself.*) D'you know what your gran'mother was?

VIVIE:

No.

MRS. WARREN:

No, you don't. I do. She called herself a widow and had a fried-fish shop down by the Mint, and kept herself and four daughters out of it. Two of us were sisters: that was me and Liz; and we were both good-looking and well made. I suppose our father was a well-fed man: mother pretended he was a gentleman; but I don't know. The other two were only half sisters—undersized, ugly, starved looking, hard-working, honest poor creatures: Liz and I would have half-murdered them if mother hadn't half-murdered us to keep our hands off them. They were the respectable ones. Well, what did they get by their respectability? I'll tell you. One of them worked in a whitelead factory twelve hours a day for nine shillings a week until she died of lead poisoning. She only expected to get her hands a little paralyzed; but she died. The other was always held up to us as a model because she married a Government labourer in the Deptford victualling yard, and kept his room and the three children neat and tidy on eighteen shillings a week—until he took to drink. That was worth being respectable for, wasn't it?

VIVIE (*now thoughtfully attentive*):

Did you and your sister think so?

MRS. WARREN:

Liz didn't, I can tell you: she had more spirit. We both went to a church school—that was part of the ladylike airs we gave ourselves to be superior to the children that knew nothing and went nowhere—and we stayed there until Liz went out one night and never came back. I know the schoolmistress thought

I'd soon follow her example; for the clergyman was always warning me that Lizzie'd end by jumping off Waterloo Bridge. Poor fool: that was all he knew about it! But I was more afraid of the whitelead factory than I was of the river; and so would you have been in my place. That clergyman got me a situation as scullery maid in a temperance restaurant where they sent out for anything you liked. Then I was waitress; and then I went to the bar at Waterloo station—fourteen hours a day serving drinks and washing glasses for four shillings a week and my board. That was considered a great promotion for me. Well, one cold, wretched night, when I was so tired I could hardly keep myself awake, who should come up for a half of Scotch but Lizzie, in a long fur cloak, elegant and comfortable, with a lot of sovereigns in her purse.

VIVIE (*grimly*):

My aunt Lizzie!

MRS. WARREN:

Yes: and a very good aunt to have, too. She's living down at Winchester now, close to the cathedral, one of the most respectable ladies there—chaperones girls at the county ball, if you please. No river for Liz, thank you! You remind me of Liz a little: she was a first-rate business woman—saved money from the beginning—never let herself look too like what she was—never lost her head or threw away a chance. When she saw I'd grown up good-looking she said to me across the bar: "What are you doing there, you little fool? wearing out your health and your appearance for other people's profit!" Liz was saving money then to take a house for herself in Brussels: and she thought we two could save faster than one. So she lent me some money and gave me a start; and I saved steadily and first paid her back, and then went into business with her as her partner. Why shouldn't I have done it? The house in Brussels was real high class—a much better place for a woman to be in than the factory where Anne Jane got poisoned. None of our girls were ever treated as I was treated in the scullery of that temperance place, or at the Waterloo bar, or at home. Would you have had me stay in them and become a worn out old drudge before I was forty?

VIVIE (*intensely interested by this time*):

No; but why did you choose that business? Saving money and good management will succeed in any business.

MRS. WARREN:

Yes, saving money. But where can a woman get the money to save in any other business? Could you save out of four shillings a week and keep yourself dressed as well? Not you. Of course, if you're a plain woman and can't earn anything more; or if you have a turn for music, or the stage, or newspaper-writing: that's different. But neither Liz nor I had any turn for such things: all we had was our appearance and our turn for pleasing men. Do you think we were such fools as to let other people trade in our good looks by employing us as shopgirls, or barmaids, or waitresses, when we could trade in them ourselves and get all the profits instead of starvation wages? Not likely.

VIVIE:

You were certainly quite justified—from the business point of view.

MRS. WARREN:

Yes; or any other point of view. What is any respectable girl brought up to do but to catch some rich man's fancy and get the benefit of his money by marrying him?—as if a marriage ceremony could make any difference in the right or wrong of the thing! Oh, the hypocrisy of the world makes me sick! Liz and I had to work and save and calculate just like other people; elseways we should be as poor as any good-for-nothing, drunken waster of a woman that thinks her luck will last for ever. (*With great energy.*) I despise such people: they've no character; and if there's a thing I hate in a woman, it's want of character.

VIVIE:

Come, now, mother: frankly! Isn't it part of what you call character in a woman that she should greatly dislike such a way of making money?

MRS. WARREN:

Why, of course. Everybody dislikes having to work and make money; but they have to do it all the same. I'm sure I've often pitied a poor girl, tired out and in low spirits, having to try to please some man that she doesn't care two straws for—some half-drunken fool that thinks he's making himself agreeable when he's teasing and worrying and disgusting a woman so that hardly any money could pay her for putting up with it. But she has to bear with disagreeables and take the rough with the smooth, just like a nurse in a hospital or anyone else. It's not work that any woman would do for pleasure, goodness knows; though to hear the pious people talk you would suppose it was a-bed of roses.

VIVIE:

Still you consider it worth while. It pays.

MRS. WARREN:

> Of course it's worth while to a poor girl, if she can resist temptation and is good-looking and well conducted and sensible. It's far better than any other employment open to her. I always thought that oughtn't to be. It can't be right, Vivie, that there shouldn't be better opportunities for women. I stick to that: it's wrong. But it's so, right or wrong; and a girl must make the best of it. But, of course, it's not worth while for a lady. If you took to it you'd be a fool; but I should have been a fool if I'd taken to anything else.

VIVIE (*more and more deeply moved*):

> Mother: suppose we were both as poor as you were in those wretched old days, are you quite sure that you wouldn't advise me to try the Waterloo bar, or marry a labourer, or even go into the factory?

MRS. WARREN (*indignantly*):

> Of course not. What sort of mother do you take me for! How could you keep your self-respect in such starvation and slavery? And what's a woman worth? what's life worth? without self-respect! Why am I independent and able to give my daughter a first-rate education, when other women that had just as good opportunities are in the gutter? Because I always knew how to respect myself and control myself. Why is Liz looked up to in a cathedral town? The same reason. Where would we be now if we'd minded the clergyman's foolishness? Scrubbing floors for one and sixpence a day and nothing to look forward to but the workhouse infirmary. Don't you be led astray by people who don't know the world, my girl. The only way for a woman to provide for herself decently is for her to be good to some man that can afford to be good to her. If she's in his own station of life, let her make him marry her; but if she's far beneath him she can't expect it—why should she? It wouldn't be for her own happiness. Ask any lady in London society that has daughters; and she'll tell you the same, except that I tell you straight and she'll tell you crooked. That's all the difference.

VIVIE (*fascinated, gazing at her*):

> My dear mother: you are a wonderful woman—you are stronger than all England. And are you really and truly not one wee bit doubtful—or—or—ashamed?

MRS. WARREN:

> Well, of course, dearie, it's only good manners to be ashamed of it; it's expected from a woman. Women have to pretend to feel a great deal that they don't feel. Liz used to be angry with me for plumping out the truth about it. She used to say that

when every woman could learn enough from what was going on in the world before her eyes, there was no need to talk about it to her. But then Liz was such a perfect lady! She had the true instinct of it; while I was always a bit of a vulgarian. I used to be so pleased when you sent me your photographs to see that you were growing up like Liz: you've just her ladylike, determined way. But I can't stand saying one thing when everyone knows I mean another. What's the use in such hypocrisy? If people arrange the world that way for women, there's no good pretending that it's arranged the other way. I never was a bit ashamed really. I consider that I had a right to be proud that we managed everything so respectably, and never had a word against us, and that the girls were so well taken care of. Some of them did very well: one of them married an ambassador. But of course now I daren't talk about such things: whatever would they think of us! (*She yawns.*) Oh, dear! I do believe I'm getting sleepy after all. (*She stretches herself lazily, thoroughly relieved by her explosion, and placidly ready for her night's rest.*)

VIVIE:

I believe it is I who will not be able to sleep now. (*She goes to the dresser and lights the candle. Then she extinguishes the lamp, darkening the room a good deal.*) Better let in some fresh air before locking up. (*She opens the cottage door, and finds that it is broad moonlight.*) What a beautiful night! Look! (*She draws aside the curtains of the window. The landscape is seen bathed in the radiance of the harvest moon rising over Blackdown.*)

MRS. WARREN (*with a perfunctory glance at the scene*):

Yes, dear: but take care you don't catch your death of cold from the night air.

VIVIE (*contemptuously*):

Nonsense.

MRS. WARREN (*querulously*):

Oh, yes: everything I say is nonsense, according to you.

VIVIE (*turning to her quickly*):

No: really that is not so, mother. You have got completely the better of me to-night, though I intended it to be the other way. Let us be good friends now.

MRS. WARREN (*shaking her head a little ruefully*):

So it has been the other way. But I suppose I must give in to it. I always got the worst of it from Liz; and now I suppose it'll be the same with you.

VIVIE:

Well, never mind. Come; good-night, dear old mother. (*She takes her mother in her arms.*)

MRS. WARREN (*fondly*):

> I brought you up well, didn't I, dearie?

VIVIE:

> You did.

MRS. WARREN:

> And you'll be good to your poor old mother for it, won't you?

VIVIE:

> I will, dear. (*Kissing her.*) Good-night.

MRS. WARREN (*with unction*):

> Blessings on my own dearie darling—a mother's blessing! (*She embraces her daughter protectingly, instinctively looking upward as if to call down a blessing.*)

# Act III

*In the rectory garden next morning, with the sun shining and the birds in full song. The garden wall has a five-barred wooden gate, wide enough to admit a carriage, in the middle. Beside the gate hangs a bell on a coiled spring, communicating with a pull outside. The carriage drive comes down the middle of the garden and then swerves to its left, where it ends in a little gravelled circus opposite the rectory porch. Beyond the gate is seen the dusty high road, parallel with the wall, bounded on the farther side by a strip of turf and an unfenced pine wood. On the lawn, between the house and the drive, is a clipped yew tree, with a garden bench in its shade. On the opposite side the garden is shut in by a box hedge; and there is a sundial on the turf, with an iron chair near it. A little path leads off through the box hedge, behind the sundial.*

*Frank, seated on the chair near the sundial, on which he has placed the morning papers, is reading the* Standard. *His father comes from the house, red-eyed and shivery, and meets Frank's eye with misgiving.*

FRANK (*looking at his watch*):

> Half-past eleven. Nice hour for a rector to come down to breakfast!

REV. S.:

> Don't mock, Frank: don't mock. I'm a little—er—(*Shivering.*)——

FRANK:

> Off colour?

REV. S. (*repudiating the expression*):

> No, sir: unwell this morning. Where's your mother?

FRANK:

> Don't be alarmed: she's not here. Gone to town by the 11:13

with Bessie. She left several messages for you. Do you feel
equal to receiving them now, or shall I wait till you've
breakfasted?

REV. S.:

I have breakfasted, sir. I am surprised at your mother going to
town when we have people staying with us. They'll think it
very strange.

FRANK:

Possibly she has considered that. At all events, if Crofts is going
to stay here, and you are going to sit up every night with him
until four, recalling the incidents of your fiery youth, it is
clearly my mother's duty, as a prudent housekeeper, to go up to
the stores and order a barrel of whisky and a few hundred
siphons.

REV. S.:

I did not observe that Sir George drank excessively.

FRANK:

You were not in a condition to, gov'nor.

REV. S.:

Do you mean to say that I——

FRANK (*calmly*):

I never saw a beneficed clergyman less sober. The anecdotes
you told about your past career were so awful that I really
don't think Praed would have passed the night under your
roof if it hadn't been for the way my mother and he took to
one another.

REV. S.:

Nonsense, sir. I am Sir George Crofts' host. I must talk to him
about something; and he has only one subject. Where is Mr.
Praed now?

FRANK:

He is driving my mother and Bessie to the station.

REV. S.:

Is Crofts up yet?

FRANK:

Oh, long ago. He hasn't turned a hair: he's in much better
practice than you—has kept it up ever since, probably. He's
taken himself off somewhere to smoke. (Frank *resumes his paper.
The* Rev. S. *turns disconsolately towards the gate; then comes back
irresolutely.*)

REV. S.:

Er—Frank.

FRANK:

Yes.

REV. S.:

> Do you think the Warrens will expect to be asked here after yesterday afternoon?

FRANK:

> They've been asked already. Crofts informed us at breakfast that you told him to bring Mrs. Warren and Vivie over here today, and to invite them to make this house their home. It was after that communication that my mother found she must go to town by the 11:13 train.

REV. S. (*with despairing vehemence*):

> I never gave any such invitation. I never thought of such a thing.

FRANK (*compassionately*):

> How do you know, gov'nor, what you said and thought last night? Hallo! here's Praed back again.

PRAED (*coming in through the gate*):

> Good morning.

REV. S.:

> Good morning. I must apologize for not having met you at breakfast. I have a touch of—of——

FRANK:

> Clergyman's sore throat, Praed. Fortunately not chronic.

PRAED (*changing the subject*):

> Well, I must say your house is in a charming spot here. Really most charming.

REV. S.:

> Yes: it is indeed. Frank will take you for a walk, Mr. Praed, if you like. I'll ask you to excuse me: I must take the opportunity to write my sermon while Mrs. Gardner is away and you are all amusing yourselves. You won't mind, will you?

PRAED:

> Certainly not. Don't stand on the slightest ceremony with me.

REV. S.:

> Thank you. I'll—er—er—(*He stammers his way to the porch and vanishes into the house*).

PRAED (*sitting down on the turf near* Frank, *and hugging his ankles*):

> Curious thing it must be writing a sermon every week.

FRANK:

> Ever so curious, if he did it. He buys 'em. He's gone for some soda water.

PRAED:

> My dear boy: I wish you would be more respectful to your father. You know you can be so nice when you like.

FRANK:

My dear Praddy: you forget that I have to live with the governor. When two people live together—it don't matter whether they're father and son, husband and wife, brother and sister— they can't keep up the polite humbug which comes so easy for ten minutes on an afternoon call. Now the governor, who unites to many admirable domestic qualities the irresoluteness of a sheep and the pompousness and aggressiveness of a jack-ass——

PRAED:

No, pray, pray, my dear Frank, remember! He is your father.

FRANK:

I give him due credit for that. But just imagine his telling Crofts to bring the Warrens over here! He must have been ever so drunk. You know, my dear Praddy, my mother wouldn't stand Mrs. Warren for a moment. Vivie mustn't come here until she's gone back to town.

PRAED:

But your mother doesn't know anything about Mrs. Warren, does she?

FRANK:

I don't know. Her journey to town looks as if she did. Not that my mother would mind in the ordinary way: she has stuck like a brick to lots of women who had got into trouble. But they were all nice women. That's what makes the real difference. Mrs. Warren, no doubt, has her merits; but she's ever so rowdy; and my mother simply wouldn't put up with her. So—hallo! (*This exclamation is provoked by the reappearance of* the clergyman, *who comes out of the house in haste and dismay.*)

REV. S.:

Frank: Mrs. Warren and her daughter are coming across the heath with Crofts: I saw them from the study windows. What am I to say about your mother?

FRANK (*jumping up energetically*):

Stick on your hat and go out and say how delighted you are to see them; and that Frank's in the garden; and that mother and Bessie have been called to the bedside of a sick relative, and were ever so sorry they couldn't stop; and that you hope Mrs. Warren slept well; and—and—say any blessed thing except the truth, and leave the rest to Providence.

REV. S.:

But how are we to get rid of them afterwards?

FRANK:

There's no time to think of that now. Here! (*He bounds into the porch and returns immediately with a clerical felt hat, which he claps on his father's head.*) Now: off with you. Praed and I'll wait here, to give the thing an unpremeditated air. (*The clergyman, dazed, but obedient, hurries off through the gate. Praed gets up from the turf, and dusts himself.*)

FRANK:

We must get that old lady back to town somehow, Praed. Come! honestly, dear Praddy, do you like seeing them together—Vivie and the old lady?

PRAED:

Oh, why not?

FRANK (*his teeth on edge*):

Don't it make your flesh creep ever so little?—that wicked old devil, up to every villainy under the sun, I'll swear, and Vivie—ugh!

PRAED:

Hush, pray. They're coming. (*The clergyman and* Crofts *are seen coming along the road, followed by* Mrs. Warren *and* Vivie *walking affectionately together.*)

FRANK:

Look: she actually has her arm round the old woman's waist. It's her right arm: she began it. She's gone sentimental, by God. Ugh! ugh! Now do you feel the creeps? (*The clergyman opens the gate; and* Mrs. Warren *and* Vivie *pass him and stand in the middle of the garden looking at the house.* Frank, *in an ecstasy of dissimulation, turns gaily to* Mrs. Warren, *exclaiming*) Ever so delighted to see you, Mrs. Warren. This quiet old rectory garden becomes you perfectly.

MRS. WARREN:

Well, I never! Did you hear that, George? He says I look well in a quiet old rectory garden.

REV. S.: (*still holding the gate for* Crofts, *who loafs through it, heavily bored*):

You look well everywhere, Mrs. Warren.

FRANK:

Bravo, gov'nor! Now look here: let's have an awful jolly time of it before lunch. First let's see the church. Everyone has to do that. It's a regular old thirteenth century church, you know: the gov'nor's ever so fond of it, because he got up a restoration fund and had it completely rebuilt six years ago. Praed will be able to show its points.

REV. S. (*mooning hospitably at them*):

I shall be pleased, I'm sure, if Sir George and Mrs. Warren really care about it.

MRS. WARREN:

Oh, come along and get it over. It'll do George good: I'll lay he doesn't trouble church much.

CROFTS (*turning back towards the gate*):

I've no objection.

REV. S.:

Not that way. We go through the fields, if you don't mind. Round here. (*He leads the way by the little path through the box hedge.*)

CROFTS:

Oh, all right. (*He goes with the parson. Praed follows with Mrs. Warren. Vivie does not stir, but watches them until they have gone, with all the lines of purpose in her face marking it strongly.*)

FRANK:

Ain't you coming.

VIVIE:

No. I want to give you a warning, Frank. You were making fun of my mother just now when you said that about the rectory garden. That is barred in future. Please treat my mother with as much respect as you treat your own.

FRANK:

My dear Viv: she wouldn't appreciate it. She's not like my mother: the same treatment wouldn't do for both cases. But what on earth has happened to you? Last night we were perfectly agreed as to your mother and her set. This morning I find you attitudinizing sentimentally with your arm round your parent's waist.

VIVIE (*flushing*):

Attitudinizing!

FRANK:

That was how it struck me. First time I ever saw you do a second-rate thing.

VIVIE (*controlling herself*):

Yes, Frank: there has been a change; but I don't think it a change for the worse. Yesterday I was a little prig.

FRANK:

And to-day?

VIVIE (*wincing; then looking at him steadily*):

To-day I know my mother better than you do.

FRANK:

Heaven forbid!

VIVIE:

What do you mean?

FRANK:

Viv; there's a freemasonry among thoroughly immoral people that you know nothing of. You've too much character. That's the bond between your mother and me: that's why I know her better than you'll ever know her.

VIVIE:

You are wrong: you know nothing about her. If you knew the circumstances against which my mother had to struggle——

FRANK (*adroitly finishing the sentence for her*):

I should know why she is what she is, shouldn't I? What difference would that make? Circumstances or no circumstances, Viv, you won't be able to stand your mother.

VIVIE (*very angry*):

Why not?

FRANK:

Because she's an old wretch, Viv. If you ever put your arm round her waist in my presence again, I'll shoot myself there and then as a protest against an exhibition which revolts me.

VIVIE:

Must I choose between dropping your acquaintance and dropping my mother's?

FRANK (*gracefully*):

That would put the old lady at ever such a disadvantage. No, Viv: your infatuated little boy will have to stick to you in any case. But he's all the more anxious that you shouldn't make mistakes. It's no use, Viv: your mother's impossible. She may be a good sort; but she's a bad lot, a very bad lot.

VIVIE (*hotly*):

Frank—! (*He stands his ground. She turns away and sits down on the bench under the yew tree, struggling to recover her self-command. Then she says*) Is she to be deserted by all the world because she's what you call a bad lot? Has she no right to live?

FRANK:

No fear of that, Viv: she won't ever be deserted. (*He sits on the bench beside her.*)

VIVIE:

But I am to desert her, I suppose.

FRANK (*babyishly, lulling her and making love to her with his voice*):

Mustn't go live with her. Little family group of mother and daughter wouldn't be a success. Spoil our little group.

VIVIE (*falling under the spell*):

What little group?

FRANK:

> The babes in the wood: Vivie and little Frank. (*He slips his arm round her waist and nestles against her like a weary child.*) Let's go and get covered up with leaves.

VIVIE (*rhythmically, rocking him like a nurse*):

> Fast asleep, hand in hand, under the trees.

FRANK:

> The wise little girl with her silly little boy.

VIVIE:

> The dear little boy with his dowdy little girl.

FRANK:

> Ever so peaceful, and relieved from the imbecility of the little boy's father and the questionableness of the little girl's——

VIVIE (*smothering the word against her breast*):

> Sh-sh-sh-sh! little girl wants to forget all about her mother. (*They are silent for some moments, rocking one another. Then* Vivie *wakes up with a shock, exclaiming*) What a pair of fools we are! Come: sit up. Gracious! your hair. (*She smooths it.*) I wonder do all grown up people play in that childish way when nobody is looking. I never did it when I was a child.

FRANK:

> Neither did I. You are my first playmate. (*He catches her hand to kiss it, but checks himself to look round first. Very unexpectedly he sees* Crofts *emerging from the box hedge.*) Oh, damn!

VIVIE:

> Why damn, dear?

FRANK (*whispering*):

> Sh! Here's this brute Crofts. (*He sits farther away from her with an unconcerned air.*)

VIVIE:

> Don't be rude to him, Frank. I particularly wish to be polite to him. It will please my mother. (Frank *makes a wry face.*)

CROFTS:

> Could I have a few words with you, Miss Vivie?

VIVIE:

> Certainly.

CROFTS (*to* Frank):

> You'll excuse me, Gardner. They're waiting for you in the church, if you don't mind.

FRANK (*rising*):

> Anything to oblige you, Crofts—except church. If you want anything, Vivie, ring the gate bell, and a domestic will appear. (*He goes into the house with unruffled suavity.*)

CROFTS (*watching him with a crafty air as he disappears, and speaking to* Vivie *with an assumption of being on privileged terms with her*):
Pleasant young fellow that, Miss Vivie. Pity he has no money, isn't it?

VIVIE:
Do you think so?

CROFTS:
Well, what's he to do? No profession, no property. What's he good for?

VIVIE:
I realize his disadvantages, Sir George.

CROFTS (*a little taken back at being so precisely interpreted*):
Oh, it's not that. But while we're in this world we're in it; and money's money. (Vivie *does not answer.*) Nice day, isn't it?

VIVIE (*with scarcely veiled contempt for this effort at conversation*):
Very.

CROFTS (*with brutal good humor, as if he liked her pluck*):
Well, that's not what I came to say. (*Affecting frankness.*) Now listen, Miss Vivie. I'm quite aware that I'm not a young lady's man.

VIVIE:
Indeed, Sir George?

CROFTS:
No; and to tell you the honest truth, I don't want to be either. But when I say a thing I mean it; when I feel sentiment I feel it in earnest; and what I value I pay hard money for. That's the sort of man I am.

VIVIE:
It does you great credit, I'm sure.

CROFTS:
Oh, I don't mean to praise myself. I have my faults, Heaven knows: no man is more sensible of that than I am. I know I'm not perfect: that's one of the advantages of being a middle-aged man; for I'm not a young man, and I know it. But my code is a simple one, and, I think, a good one. Honor between man and man; fidelity between man and woman; and no cant about this religion, or that religion, but an honest belief that things are making for good on the whole.

VIVIE (*with biting irony*):
"A power, not ourselves, that makes for righteousness," eh?

CROFTS (*taking her seriously*):
Oh, certainly, not ourselves, of course. You understand what I mean. (*He sits down beside her, as one who has found a kindred spirit.*) Well, now as to practical matters. You may have an idea

that I've flung my money about; but I haven't: I'm richer to-day than when I first came into the property. I've used my knowledge of the world to invest my money in ways that other men have overlooked; and whatever else I may be, I'm a safe man from the money point of view.

VIVIE:

It's very kind of you to tell me all this.

CROFTS:

Oh, well, come, Miss Vivie: you needn't pretend you don't see what I'm driving at. I want to settle down with a Lady Crofts. I suppose you think me very blunt, eh?

VIVIE:

Not at all: I am much obliged to you for being so definite and business-like. I quite appreciate the offer: the money, the position, Lady Crofts, and so on. But I think I will say no, if you don't mind. I'd rather not. (*She rises, and strolls across to the sundial to get out of his immediate neighborhood.*)

CROFTS (*not at all discouraged, and taking advantage of the additional room left him on the seat to spread himself comfortably, as if a few preliminary refusals were part of the inevitable routine of courtship*):

I'm in no hurry. It was only just to let you know in case young Gardner should try to trap you. Leave the question open.

VIVIE (*sharply*):

My no is final. I won't go back from it. (*She looks authoritatively at him. He grins; leans forward with his elbows on his knees to prod with his stick at some unfortunate insect in the grass; and looks cunningly at her. She turns away impatiently.*)

CROFTS:

I'm a good deal older than you—twenty-five years—quarter of a century. I shan't live for ever; and I'll take care that you shall be well off when I'm gone.

VIVIE:

I am proof against even that inducement, Sir George. Don't you think you'd better take your answer? There is not the slightest chance of my altering it.

CROFTS (*rising, after a final slash at a daisy, and beginning to walk to and fro*):

Well, no matter. I could tell you some things that would change your mind fast enough; but I won't, because I'd rather win you by honest affection. I was a good friend to your mother: ask her whether I wasn't. She'd never have made the money that paid for your education if it hadn't been for my advice and help, not to mention the money I advanced her.

There are not many men would have stood by her as I have. I put not less than £40,000 into it, from first to last.

VIVIE (*staring at him*):

Do you mean to say you were my mother's business partner?

CROFTS:

Yes. Now just think of all the trouble and the explanations it would save if we were to keep the whole thing in the family, so to speak. Ask your mother whether she'd like to have to explain all her affairs to a perfect stranger.

VIVIE:

I see no difficulty, since I understand that the business is wound up, and the money invested.

CROFTS (*stopping short, amazed*):

Wound up! Wind up a business that's paying 35 per cent in the worst years! Not likely. Who told you that?

VIVIE (*her color quite gone*):

Do you mean that it is still—? (*She stops abruptly, and puts her hand on the sundial to support herself. Then she gets quickly to the iron chair and sits down.*) What business are you talking about?

CROFTS:

Well, the fact is, it's not what would be considered exactly a high-class business in my set—the county set, you know—our set it will be if you think better of my offer. Not that there's any mystery about it: don't think that. Of course you know by your mother's being in it that it's perfectly straight and honest. I've known her for many years; and I can say of her that she'd cut off her hands sooner than touch anything that was not what it ought to be. I'll tell you all about it if you like. I don't know whether you've found in travelling how hard it is to find a really comfortable private hotel.

VIVIE (*sickened, averting her face*):

Yes: go on.

CROFTS:

Well, that's all it is. Your mother has a genius for managing such things. We've got two in Brussels, one in Berlin, one in Vienna, and two in Budapest. Of course there are others besides ourselves in it; but we hold most of the capital; and your mother's indispensable as managing director. You've noticed, I daresay, that she travels a good deal. But you see you can't mention such things in society. Once let out the word hotel and everybody says you keep a public-house. You wouldn't like people to say that of your mother, would you? That's why we're so reserved about it. By the bye, you'll keep it to yourself, won't you? Since it's been a secret so long, it had better remain so.

VIVIE:

And this is the business you invite me to join you in?

CROFTS:

Oh, no. My wife shan't be troubled with business. You'll not be in it more than you've always been.

VIVIE:

*I* always been! What do you mean?

CROFTS:

Only that you've always lived on it. It paid for your education and the dress you have on your back. Don't turn up your nose at business, Miss Vivie: where would your Newnhams and Girtons be without it?

VIVIE (*rising, almost beside herself*):

Take care. I know what this business is.

CROFTS (*starting, with a suppressed oath*):

Who told you?

VIVIE:

Your partner—my mother.

CROFTS (*black with rage*):

The old—(Vivie *looks quickly at him. He swallows the epithet and stands swearing and raging foully to himself. But he knows that his cue is to be sympathetic. He takes refuge in generous indignation.*) She ought to have had more consideration for you. I'd never have told you.

VIVIE:

I think you would probably have told me when we were married: it would have been a convenient weapon to break me in with.

CROFTS (*quite sincerely*):

I never intended that. On my word as a gentleman I didn't.

Vivie *wonders at him. Her sense of the irony of his protest cools and braces her. She replies with contemptuous self-possession.*

VIVIE:

It does not matter. I suppose you understand that when we leave here to-day our acquaintance ceases.

CROFTS:

Why? Is it for helping your mother?

VIVIE:

My mother was a very poor woman who had no reasonable choice but to do as she did. You were a rich gentleman; and you did the same for the sake of 35 per cent. You are a pretty common sort of scoundrel, I think. That is my opinion of you.

CROFTS (*after a stare—not at all displeased, and much more at his ease on these frank terms than on their former ceremonious ones*):

Ha, ha, ha, ha! Go it, little missie, go it: it doesn't hurt me and it amuses you. Why the devil shouldn't I invest my money that way? I take the interest on my capital like other people: I hope you don't think I dirty my own hands with the work. Come: you wouldn't refuse the acquaintance of my mother's cousin, the Duke of Belgravia, because some of the rents he gets are earned in queer ways. You wouldn't cut the Archbishop of Canterbury, I suppose, because the Ecclesiastical Commissioners have a few publicans and sinners among their tenants? Do you remember your Crofts scholarship at Newnham? Well, that was founded by my brother the M.P. He gets his 22 per cent out of a factory with 600 girls in it, and not one of them getting wages enough to live on. How d'ye suppose most of them manage? Ask your mother. And do you expect me to turn my back on 35 per cent when all the rest are pocketing what they can, like sensible men? No such fool! If you're going to pick and choose your acquaintances on moral principles, you'd better clear out of this country, unless you want to cut yourself out of all decent society.

VIVIE (*conscience stricken*):

You might go on to point out that I myself never asked where the money I spent came from. I believe I am just as bad as you.

CROFTS (*greatly reassured*):

Of course you are; and a very good thing, too! What harm does it do after all? (*Rallying her jocularly.*) So you don't think me such a scoundrel now you come to think it over. Eh?

VIVIE:

I have shared profits with you; and I admitted you just now to the familiarity of knowing what I think of you.

CROFTS (*with serious friendliness*):

To be sure you did. You won't find me a bad sort: I don't go in for being superfine intellectually; but I've plenty of honest human feeling; and the old Crofts breed comes out in a sort of instinctive hatred of anything low, in which I'm sure you'll sympathize with me. Believe me, Miss Vivie, the world isn't such a bad place as the croakers make out. So long as you don't fly openly in the face of society, society doesn't ask any inconvenient questions; and it makes precious short work of the cads who do. There are no secrets better kept than the secrets that everybody guesses. In the society I can introduce you to, no lady or gentleman would so far forget themselves as to discuss

my business affairs or your mother's. No man can offer you a
safer position.

VIVIE (*studying him curiously*):

I suppose you really think you're getting on famously with me.

CROFTS:

Well, I hope I may flatter myself that you think better of me
than you did at first.

VIVIE (*quietly*):

I hardly find you worth thinking about at all now. (*She rises and
turns towards the gate, pausing on her way to contemplate him and
say almost gently, but with intense conviction.*) When I think of
the society that tolerates you, and the laws that protect you—
when I think of how helpless nine out of ten young girls would
be in the hands of you and my mother—the unmentionable
woman and her capitalist bully——

CROFTS (*livid*):

Damn you!

VIVIE:

You need not. I feel among the damned already.

*She raises the latch of the gate to open it and go out. He follows her and
puts his hand heavily on the top bar to prevent its opening.*

CROFTS (*panting with fury*):

Do you think I'll put up with this from you, you young devil,
you?

VIVIE (*unmoved*):

Be quiet. Some one will answer the bell. (*Without flinching a
step she strikes the bell with the back of her hand. It clangs harshly;
and he starts back involuntarily. Almost immediately* Frank *appears
at the porch with his rifle.*)

FRANK (*with cheerful politeness*):

Will you have the rifle, Viv; or shall I operate?

VIVIE:

Frank: have you been listening?

FRANK:

Only for the bell, I assure you; so that you shouldn't have to
wait. I think I showed great insight into your character, Crofts.

CROFTS:

For two pins I'd take that gun from you and break it across
your head.

FRANK (*stalking him cautiously*):

Pray don't. I'm ever so careless in handling firearms. Sure to be a fatal accident, with a reprimand from the coroner's jury for my negligence.

VIVIE:

Put the rifle away, Frank: it's quite unnecessary.

FRANK:

Quite right, Viv. Much more sportsmanlike to catch him in a trap. (Crofts, *understanding the insult, makes a threatening movement.*) Crofts: there are fifteen cartridges in the magazine here; and I am a dead shot at the present distance at an object of your size.

CROFTS:

Oh, you needn't be afraid. I'm not going to touch you.

FRANK:

Ever so magnanimous of you under the circumstances! Thank you.

CROFTS:

I'll just tell you this before I go. It may interest you, since you're so fond of one another. Allow me, Mister Frank, to introduce you to your half-sister, the eldest daughter of the Reverend Samuel Gardner. Miss Vivie: your half-brother. Good morning. (*He goes out through the gate and along the road.*)

FRANK (*after a pause of stupefaction, raising the rifle*):

You'll testify before the coroner that it's an accident, Viv. (*He takes aim at the retreating figure of* Crofts. Vivie *seizes the muzzle and pulls it round against her breast.*)

VIVIE:

Fire now. You may.

FRANK (*dropping his end of the rifle hastily*):

Stop! take care. (*She lets it go. It falls on the turf.*) Oh, you've given your little boy such a turn. Suppose it had gone off— ugh! (*He sinks on the garden seat, overcome.*)

VIVIE:

Suppose it had: do you think it would not have been a relief to have some sharp physical pain tearing through me?

FRANK (*coaxingly*):

Take it ever so easy, dear Viv. Remember: even if the rifle scared that fellow into telling the truth for the first time in his life, that only makes us the babes in the wood in earnest. (*He holds out his arms to her.*) Come and be covered up with leaves again.

VIVIE (*with a cry of disgust*):

Ah, not that, not that. You make all my flesh creep.

FRANK:

Why, what's the matter?

VIVIE:

Good-bye. (*She makes for the gate.*)

FRANK (*jumping up*):

Hallo! Stop! Viv! Viv! (*She turns in the gateway.*) Where are you going to? Where shall we find you?

VIVIE:

At Honoria Fraser's chambers, 67 Chancery Lane, for the rest of my life. (*She goes off quickly in the opposite direction to that taken by* Crofts.)

FRANK:

But I say—wait—dash it! (*He runs after her.*)

# Act IV

*Honoria Fraser's chambers in Chancery Lane. An office at the top of New Stone Buildings, with a plate-glass window, distempered walls, electric light, and a patent stove. Saturday afternoon. The chimneys of Lincoln's Inn and the western sky beyond are seen through the window. There is a double writing table in the middle of the room, with a cigar box, ash pans, and a portable electric reading lamp almost snowed up in heaps of papers and books. This table has knee holes and chairs right and left and is very untidy. The clerk's desk, closed and tidy, with its high stool, is against the wall, near a door communicating with the inner rooms. In the opposite wall is the door leading to the public corridor. Its upper panel is of opaque glass, lettered in black on the outside, "Fraser and Warren." A baize screen hides the corner between this door and the window.*

Frank, *in a fashionable light-colored coaching suit, with his stick, gloves, and white hat in his hands, is pacing up and down the office. Somebody tries the door with a key.*

FRANK (*calling*):

Come in. It's not locked.

Vivie *comes in, in her hat and jacket. She stops and stares at him.*

VIVIE (*sternly*):

What are you doing here?

FRANK:

Waiting to see you. I've been here for hours. Is this the way you attend to your business? (*He puts his hat and stick on the table, and perches himself with a vault on the clerk's stool, looking at her with every appearance of being in a specially restless, teasing, flippant mood.*)

VIVIE:

> I've been away exactly twenty minutes for a cup of tea. (*She takes off her hat and jacket and hangs them up behind the screen.*) How did you get in?

FRANK:

> The staff had not left when I arrived. He's gone to play football on Primrose Hill. Why don't you employ a woman, and give your sex a chance?

VIVIE:

> What have you come for?

FRANK (*springing off the stool and coming close to her*):

> Viv: let's go and enjoy the Saturday half-holiday somewhere, like the staff. What do you say to Richmond, and then a music hall, and a jolly supper?

VIVIE:

> Can't afford it. I shall put in another six hours' work before I go to bed.

FRANK:

> Can't afford it, can't we? Aha! Look here. (*He takes out a handful of sovereigns and makes them chink.*) Gold, Viv, gold!

VIVIE:

> Where did you get it?

FRANK:

> Gambling, Viv, gambling. Poker.

VIVIE:

> Pah! It's meaner than stealing it. No: I'm not coming. (*She sits down to work at the table, with her back to the glass door, and begins turning over the papers.*)

FRANK (*remonstrating piteously*):

> But, my dear Viv, I want to talk to you ever so seriously.

VIVIE:

> Very well: sit down in Honoria's chair and talk here. I like ten minutes' chat after tea. (*He murmurs.*) No use groaning: I'm inexorable. (*He takes the opposite seat disconsolately.*) Pass that cigar box, will you?

FRANK (*pushing the cigar box across*):

> Nasty womanly habit. Nice men don't do it any longer.

VIVIE:

> Yes: they object to the smell in the office; and we've had to take to cigarets. See! (*She opens the box and takes out a cigaret, which she lights. She offers him one; but he shakes his head with a wry face. She settles herself comfortably in her chair, smoking.*) Go ahead.

FRANK:

Well, I want to know what you've done—what arrangements you've made.

VIVIE:

Everything was settled twenty minutes after I arrived here. Honoria has found the business too much for her this year; and she was on the point of sending for me and proposing a partnership when I walked in and told her I hadn't a farthing in the world. So I installed myself and packed her off for a fortnight's holiday. What happened at Haslemere when I left?

FRANK:

Nothing at all. I said you'd gone to town on particular business.

VIVIE:

Well?

FRANK:

Well, either they were too flabbergasted to say anything, or else Crofts had prepared your mother. Anyhow, she didn't say anything; and Crofts didn't say anything; and Praddy only stared. After tea they got up and went; and I've not seen them since.

VIVIE (*nodding placidly with one eye on a wreath of smoke*):

That's all right.

FRANK (*looking round disparagingly*):

Do you intend to stick in this confounded place?

VIVIE (*blowing the wreath decisively away and sitting straight up*):

Yes. These two days have given me back all my strength and self-possession. I will never take a holiday again as long as I live.

FRANK (*with a very wry face*):

Mps! You look quite happy—and as hard as nails.

VIVIE (*grimly*):

Well for me that I am!

FRANK (*rising*):

Look here, Viv: we must have an explanation. We parted the other day under a complete misunderstanding.

VIVIE (*putting away the cigaret*):

Well: clear it up.

FRANK:

You remember what Crofts said?

VIVIE:

Yes.

FRANK:

That revelation was supposed to bring about a complete

change in the nature of our feeling for one another. It placed us on the footing of brother and sister.

VIVIE:

Yes.

FRANK:

Have you ever had a brother?

VIVIE:

No.

FRANK:

Then you don't know what being brother and sister feels like? Now I have lots of sisters: Jessie and Georgina and the rest. The fraternal feeling is quite familiar to me; and I assure you my feeling for you is not the least in the world like it. The girls will go their way; I will go mine; and we shan't care if we never see one another again. That's brother and sister. But as to you, I can't be easy if I have to pass a week without seeing you. That's not brother and sister. It's exactly what I felt an hour before Crofts made his revelation. In short, dear Viv, it's love's young dream.

VIVIE (*bitingly*):

The same feeling, Frank, that brought your father to my mother's feet. Is that it?

FRANK (*revolted*):

I very strongly object, Viv, to have my feelings compared to any which the Reverend Samuel is capable of harboring; and I object still more to a comparison of you to your mother. Besides, I don't believe the story. I have taxed my father with it, and obtained from him what I consider tantamount to a denial.

VIVIE:

What did he say?

FRANK:

He said he was sure there must be some mistake.

VIVIE:

Do you believe him?

FRANK:

I am prepared to take his word against Crofts'.

VIVIE:

Does it make any difference? I mean in your imagination or conscience; for of course it makes no real difference.

FRANK (*shaking his head*):

None whatever to me.

VIVIE:

Nor to me.

FRANK (*staring*):

But this is ever so surprising! I thought our whole relations were altered in your imagination and conscience, as you put it, the moment those words were out of that brute's muzzle.

VIVIE:

No: it was not that. I didn't believe him. I only wish I could.

FRANK:

Eh?

VIVIE:

I think brother and sister would be a very suitable relation for us.

FRANK:

You really mean that?

VIVIE:

Yes. It's the only relation I care for, even if we could afford any other. I mean that.

FRANK (*raising his eyebrows like one on whom a new light has dawned, and speaking with quite an effusion of chivalrous sentiment*):

My dear Viv: why didn't you say so before? I am ever so sorry for persecuting you. I understand, of course.

VIVIE (*puzzled*):

Understand what?

FRANK:

Oh, I'm not a fool in the ordinary sense—only in the Scriptural sense of doing all the things the wise man declared to be folly, after trying them himself on the most extensive scale. I see I am no longer Vivvums' little boy. Don't be alarmed: I shall never call you Vivvums again—at least unless you get tired of your new little boy, whoever he may be.

VIVIE:

My new little boy!

FRANK (*with conviction*):

Must be a new little boy. Always happens that way. No other way, in fact.

VIVIE:

None that you know of, fortunately for you. (*Someone knocks at the door.*)

FRANK:

My curse upon yon caller, whoe'er he be!

VIVIE:

It's Praed. He's going to Italy and wants to say good-bye. I asked him to call this afternoon. Go and let him in.

FRANK:

We can continue our conversation after his departure for Italy.

I'll stay him out. (*He goes to the door and opens it.*) How are you, Praddy? Delighted to see you. Come in. (Praed, *dressed for travelling, comes in, in high spirits, excited by the beginning of his journey.*)

PRAED:

How do you do, Miss Warren. (*She presses his hand cordially, though a certain sentimentality in his high spirits jars on her.*) I start in an hour from Holborn Viaduct. I wish I could persuade you to try Italy.

VIVIE:

What for?

PRAED:

Why, to saturate yourself with beauty and romance, of course. (Vivie, *with a shudder, turns her chair to the table, as if the work waiting for her there were a consolation and support to her.* Praed *sits opposite to her.* Frank *places a chair just behind* Vivie, *and drops lazily and carelessly into it, talking at her over his shoulder.*)

FRANK:

No use, Praddy. Viv is a little Philistine. She is indifferent to my romance, and insensible to my beauty.

VIVIE:

Mr. Praed: once for all, there is no beauty and no romance in life for me. Life is what it is; and I am prepared to take it as it is.

PRAED (*enthusiastically*):

You will not say that if you come to Verona and on to Venice. You will cry with delight at living in such a beautiful world.

FRANK:

This is most eloquent, Praddy. Keep it up.

PRAED:

Oh, I assure you *I* have cried—I shall cry again, I hope—at fifty! At your age, Miss Warren, you would not need to go so far as Verona. Your spirits would absolutely fly up at the mere sight of Ostend. You would be charmed with the gaiety, the vivacity, the happy air of Brussels. (Vivie *recoils.*) What's the matter?

FRANK:

Hallo, Viv!

VIVIE (*to* Praed *with deep reproach*):

Can you find no better example of your beauty and romance than Brussels to talk to me about?

PRAED (*puzzled*):

Of course it's very different from Verona. I don't suggest for a moment that——

VIVIE (*bitterly*):

Probably the beauty and romance come to much the same in both places.

PRAED (*completely sobered and much concerned*):

My dear Miss Warren: I—(*looking enquiringly at* Frank). Is anything the matter?

FRANK:

She thinks your enthusiasm frivolous, Praddy. She's had ever such a serious call.

VIVIE (*sharply*):

Hold your tongue, Frank. Don't be silly.

FRANK (*calmly*):

Do you call this good manners, Praed?

PRAED (*anxious and considerate*):

Shall I take him away, Miss Warren? I feel sure we have disturbed you at your work. (*He is about to rise.*)

VIVIE:

Sit down: I'm not ready to go back to work yet. You both think I have an attack of nerves. Not a bit of it. But there are two subjects I want dropped, if you don't mind. One of them (*to* Frank) is love's young dream in any shape or form: the other (*to* Praed) is the romance and beauty of life, especially as exemplified by the gaiety of Brussels. You are welcome to any illusions you may have left on these subjects: I have none. If we three are to remain friends, I must be treated as a woman of business, permanently single (*to* Frank) and permanently unromantic (*to* Praed).

FRANK:

I also shall remain permanently single until you change your mind. Praddy: change the subject. Be eloquent about something else.

PRAED (*diffidently*):

I am afraid there's nothing else in the world that I can talk about. The Gospel of Art is the only one I can preach. I know Miss Warren is a great devotee of the Gospel of Getting On; but we can't discuss that without hurting your feelings, Frank, since you are determined not to get on.

FRANK:

Oh, don't mind my feelings. Give me some improving advice by all means; it does me ever so much good. Have another try to make a successful man of me, Viv. Come: let's have it all: energy, thrift, foresight, self-respect, character. Don't you hate people who have no character, Viv?

VIVIE (*wincing*):

Oh, stop: stop: let us have no more of that horrible cant. Mr.

Praed: if there are really only those two gospels in the world, we had better all kill ourselves; for the same taint is in both, through and through.

FRANK (*looking critically at her*):

There is a touch of poetry about you to-day, Viv, which has hitherto been lacking.

PRAED (*remonstrating*):

My dear Frank: aren't you a little unsympathetic?

VIVIE (*merciless to herself*):

No: it's good for me. It keeps me from being sentimental.

FRANK (*bantering her*):

Checks your strong natural propensity that way, don't it?

VIVIE (*almost hysterically*):

Oh, yes: go on: don't spare me. I was sentimental for one moment in my life—beautifully sentimental—by moonlight; and now——

FRANK (*quickly*):

I say, Viv: take care. Don't give yourself away.

VIVIE:

Oh, do you think Mr. Praed does not know all about my mother? (*Turning on* Praed.) You had better have told me that morning, Mr. Praed. You are very old-fashioned in your delicacies, after all.

PRAED:

Surely it is you who are a little old-fashioned in your prejudices, Miss Warren. I feel bound to tell you, speaking as an artist, and believing that the most intimate human relationships are far beyond and above the scope of the law, that though I know that your mother is an unmarried woman, I do not respect her the less on that account. I respect her more.

FRANK (*airily*):

Hear, hear!

VIVIE (*staring at him*):

Is that all you know?

PRAED:

Certainly that is all.

VIVIE:

Then you neither of you know anything. Your guesses are innocence itself compared to the truth.

PRAED (*startled and indignant, preserving his politeness with an effort*):

I hope not. (*More emphatically.*) I hope not, Miss Warren. (*Frank's face shows that he does not share* Praed's *incredulity. Vivie utters an exclamation of impatience.* Praed's *chivalry droops before their conviction. He adds, slowly*) If there is anything worse—that is, anything else—are you sure you are right to tell us, Miss Warren?

VIVIE:

I am sure that if I had the courage I should spend the rest of my life in telling it to everybody—in stamping and branding it into them until they felt their share in its shame and horror as I feel mine. There is nothing I despise more than the wicked convention that protects these things by forbidding a woman to mention them. And yet I can't tell you. The two infamous words that describe what my mother is are ringing in my ears and struggling on my tongue; but I can't utter them: my instinct is too strong for me. (*She buries her face in her hands. The two men, astonished, stare at one another and then at her. She raises her head again desperately and takes a sheet of paper and a pen.*) Here: let me draft you a prospectus.

FRANK:

Oh, she's mad. Do you hear, Viv, mad. Come: pull yourself together.

VIVIE:

You shall see. (*She writes.*) "Paid up capital: not less than £40,000 standing in the name of Sir George Crofts, Baronet, the chief shareholder." What comes next?—I forget. Oh, yes: "Premises at Brussels, Berlin, Vienna and Budapest. Managing director: Mrs. Warren;" and now don't let us forget her qualifications: the two words. There! (*She pushes the paper to them.*) Oh, no: don't read it: don't! (*She snatches it back and tears it to pieces; then seizes her head in her hands and hides her face on the table. Frank, who has watched the writing carefully over her shoulder, and opened his eyes very widely at it, takes a card from his pocket; scribbles a couple of words, and silently hands it to Praed, who looks at it with amazement. Frank then remorsefully stoops over Vivie.*)

FRANK (*whispering tenderly*):

Viv, dear: that's all right. I read what you wrote: so did Praddy. We understand. And we remain, as this leaves us at present, yours ever so devotedly. (*Vivie slowly raises her head.*)

PRAED:

We do, indeed, Miss Warren. I declare you are the most splendidly courageous woman I ever met. (*This sentimental compliment braces Vivie. She throws it away from her with an impatient shake, and forces herself to stand up, though not without some support from the table.*)

FRANK:

Don't stir, Viv, if you don't want to. Take it easy.

VIVIE:

> Thank you. You can always depend on me for two things, not to cry and not to faint. (*She moves a few steps towards the door of the inner rooms, and stops close to* Praed *to say*) I shall need much more courage than that when I tell my mother that we have come to the parting of the ways. Now I must go into the next room for a moment to make myself neat again, if you don't mind.

PRAED:

> Shall we go away?

VIVIE:

> No: I'll be back presently. Only for a moment. (*She goes into the other room,* Praed *opening the door for her.*)

PRAED:

> What an amazing revelation! I'm extremely disappointed in Crofts: I am indeed.

FRANK:

> I'm not in the least. I feel he's perfectly accounted for at last. But what a facer for me, Praddy! I can't marry her now.

PRAED (*sternly*):

> Frank! (*The two look at one another,* Frank *unruffled,* Praed *deeply indignant.*) Let me tell you, Gardner, that if you desert her now you will behave very despicably.

FRANK:

> Good old Praddy! Ever chivalrous! But you mistake: it's not the moral aspect of the case: it's the money aspect. I really can't bring myself to touch the old woman's money now?

PRAED:

> And was that what you were going to marry on?

FRANK:

> What else? *I* haven't any money, nor the smallest turn for making it. If I married Viv now she would have to support me; and I should cost her more than I am worth.

PRAED:

> But surely a clever, bright fellow like you can make something by your own brains.

FRANK:

> Oh, yes, a little. (*He takes out his money again.*) I made all that yesterday—in an hour and a half. But I made it in a highly speculative business. No, dear Praddy: even if Jessie and Georgina marry millionaires and the governor dies after cutting them off with a shilling, I shall have only four hundred a year. And he won't die until he's three score and ten: he hasn't originality enough. I shall be on short allowance for the next

twenty years. No short allowance for Viv, if I can help it. I withdraw gracefully and leave the field to the gilded youth of England. So that's settled. I shan't worry her about it: I'll just send her a little note after we're gone. She'll understand.

PRAED (*grasping his hand*):
Good fellow, Frank! I heartily beg your pardon. But must you never see her again?

FRANK:
Never see her again! Hang it all, be reasonable. I shall come along as often as possible, and be her brother. I cannot understand the absurd consequences you romantic people expect from the most ordinary transactions. (*A knock at the door.*) I wonder who this is. Would you mind opening the door? If it's a client it will look more respectable than if I appeared.

PRAED:
Certainly. (*He goes to the door and opens it.* Frank *sits down in* Vivie's *chair to scribble a note.*) My dear Kitty: come in, come in.

Mrs. Warren *comes in, looking apprehensively round for* Vivie. *She has done her best to make herself matronly and dignified. The brilliant hat is replaced by a sober bonnet, and the gay blouse covered by a costly black silk mantle. She is pitiably anxious and ill at ease—evidently panic-stricken.*

MRS. WARREN (*to* Frank):
What! You're here, are you?

FRANK (*turning in his chair from his writing, but not rising.*):
Here, and charmed to see you. You come like a breath of spring.

MRS. WARREN:
Oh, get out with your nonsense. (*In a low voice.*) Where's Vivie?

Frank *points expressively to the door of the inner room, but says nothing.*

MRS. WARREN (*sitting down suddenly and almost beginning to cry*):
Praddy: won't she see me, don't you think?

PRAED:
My dear Kitty: don't distress yourself. Why should she not?

MRS. WARREN:
Oh, you never can see why not: you're too amiable. Mr. Frank: did she say anything to you?

FRANK (*folding his note*):
She must see you, if (*very expressively*) you wait until she comes in.

MRS. WARREN (*frightened*):

Why shouldn't I wait?

Frank *looks quizzically at her; puts his note carefully on the ink-bottle, so that Vivie cannot fail to find it when next she dips her pen; then rises and devotes his attention entirely to her.*

FRANK:

My dear Mrs. Warren: suppose you were a sparrow—ever so tiny and pretty a sparrow hopping in the roadway—and you saw a steam roller coming in your direction, would you wait for it?

MRS. WARREN:

Oh, don't bother me with your sparrows. What did she run away from Haslemere like that for?

FRANK:

I'm afraid she'll tell you if you wait until she comes back.

MRS. WARREN:

Do you want me to go away?

FRANK:

No. I always want you to stay. But I advise you to go away.

MRS. WARREN:

What! And never see her again!

FRANK:

Precisely.

MRS. WARREN (*crying again*):

Praddy: don't let him be cruel to me. (*She hastily checks her tears and wipes her eyes.*) She'll be so angry if she sees I've been crying.

FRANK (*with a touch of real compassion in his airy tenderness*):

You know that Praddy is the soul of kindness, Mrs. Warren. Praddy: what do you say? Go or stay?

PRAED (*to* Mrs. Warren):

I really should be very sorry to cause you unnecessary pain; but I think perhaps you had better not wait. The fact is—(Vivie *is heard at the inner door.*)

FRANK:

Sh! Too late. She's coming.

MRS. WARREN:

Don't tell her I was crying. (Vivie *comes in. She stops gravely on seeing* Mrs. Warren, *who greets her with hysterical cheerfulness.*) Well, dearie. So here you are at last.

VIVIE:

I am glad you have come: I want to speak to you. You said you were going, Frank, I think.

FRANK:

> Yes. Will you come with me, Mrs. Warren? What do you say to a trip to Richmond, and the theatre in the evening? There is safety in Richmond. No steam roller there.

VIVIE:

> Nonsense, Frank. My mother will stay here.

MRS. WARREN (*scared*):

> I don't know: perhaps I'd better go. We're disturbing you at your work.

VIVIE (*with quiet decision*):

> Mr. Praed: please take Frank away. Sit down, mother. (Mrs. Warren *obeys helplessly.*)

PRAED:

> Come, Frank. Good-bye, Miss Vivie.

VIVIE (*shaking hands*):

> Good-bye. A pleasant trip.

PRAED:

> Thank you: thank you. I hope so.

FRANK (*to* Mrs. Warren):

> Good-bye: you'd ever so much better have taken my advice. (*He shakes hands with her. Then airily to* Vivie.) Bye-bye, Viv.

VIVIE:

> Good-bye. (*He goes out gaily without shaking hands with her.* Praed *follows.* Vivie, *composed and extremely grave, sits down in Honoria's chair, and waits for her mother to speak.* Mrs. Warren, *dreading a pause, loses no time in beginning.*)

MRS. WARREN:

> Well, Vivie, what did you go away like that for without saying a word to me? How could you do such a thing! And what have you done to poor George? I wanted him to come with me; but he shuffled out of it. I could see that he was quite afraid of you. Only fancy: he wanted me not to come. As if (*trembling*) I should be afraid of you, dearie. (Vivie's *gravity deepens.*) But of course I told him it was all settled and comfortable between us, and that we were on the best of terms. (*She breaks down.*) Vivie: what's the meaning of this? (*She produces a paper from an envelope; comes to the table; and hands it across.*) I got it from the bank this morning.

VIVIE:

> It is my month's allowance. They sent it to me as usual the other day. I simply sent it back to be placed to your credit, and asked them to send you the lodgment receipt. In future I shall support myself.

MRS. WARREN (*not daring to understand*):

> Wasn't it enough? Why didn't you tell me? (*With a cunning*

*gleam in her eye.*) I'll double it: I was intending to double it. Only let me know how much you want.

VIVIE:

You know very well that that has nothing to do with it. From this time I go my own way in my own business and among my own friends. And you will go yours. (*She rises.*) Good-bye.

MRS. WARREN (*appalled*):

Good-bye?

VIVIE:

Yes: good-bye. Come: don't let us make a useless scene: you understand perfectly well. Sir George Crofts has told me the whole business.

MRS. WARREN (*angrily*):

Silly old—(*She swallows an epithet, and turns white at the narrowness of her escape from uttering it.*) He ought to have his tongue cut out. But I explained it all to you; and you said you didn't mind.

VIVIE (*steadfastly*):

Excuse me: I do mind. You explained how it came about. That does not alter it.

Mrs. Warren, *silenced for a moment, looks forlornly at* Vivie, *who waits like a statue, secretly hoping that the combat is over. But the cunning expression comes back into* Mrs. Warren's *face; and she bends across the table, sly and urgent, half whispering.*

MRS. WARREN:

Vivie: do you know how rich I am?

VIVIE:

I have no doubt you are very rich.

MRS. WARREN:

But you don't know all that that means: you're too young. It means a new dress every day; it means theatres and balls every night; it means having the pick of all the gentlemen in Europe at your feet; it means a lovely house and plenty of servants; it means the choicest of eating and drinking; it means everything you like, everything you want, everything you can think of. And what are you here? A mere drudge, toiling and moiling early and late for your bare living and two cheap dresses a year. Think over it. (*Soothingly.*) You're shocked, I know. I can enter into your feelings; and I think they do you credit; but trust me, nobody will blame you: you may take my word for that. I know what young girls are; and I know you'll think better of it when you've turned it over in your mind.

VIVIE:

So that's how it's done, is it? You must have said all that to many a woman, mother, to have it so pat.

MRS. WARREN (*passionately*):

What harm am I asking you to do? (Vivie *turns away contemptuously*. Mrs. Warren *follows her desperately*.) Vivie: listen to me: you don't understand: you've been taught wrong on purpose: you don't know what the world is really like.

VIVIE (*arrested*):

Taught wrong on purpose! What do you mean?

MRS. WARREN:

I mean that you're throwing away all your chances for nothing. You think that people are what they pretend to be—that the way you were taught at school and college to think right and proper is the way things really are. But it's not: it's all only a pretence, to keep the cowardly, slavish, common run of people quiet. Do you want to find that out, like other women, at forty, when you've thrown yourself away and lost your chances; or won't you take it in good time now from your own mother, that loves you and swears to you that it's truth—gospel truth? (*Urgently.*) Vivie: the big people, the clever people, the managing people, all know it. They do as I do, and think what I think. I know plenty of them. I know them to speak to, to introduce you to, to make friends of for you. I don't mean anything wrong: that's what you don't understand: your head is full of ignorant ideas about me. What do the people that taught you know about life or about people like me? When did they ever meet me, or speak to me, or let anyone tell them about me?—the fools! Would they ever have done anything for you if I hadn't paid them? Haven't I told you that I want you to be respectable? Haven't I brought you up to be respectable? And how can you keep it up without my money and my influence and Lizzie's friends? Can't you see that you're cutting your own throat as well as breaking my heart in turning your back on me?

VIVIE:

I recognise the Crofts philosophy of life, mother. I heard it all from him that day at the Gardners'.

MRS. WARREN:

You think I want to force that played-out old sot on you! I don't, Vivie: on my oath I don't.

VIVIE:

It would not matter if you did: you would not succeed. (Mrs. Warren *winces, deeply hurt by the implied indifference towards her affectionate intention.* Vivie, *neither understanding this nor concerning herself about it, goes on calmly*) Mother: you don't at all know the sort of person I am. I don't object to Crofts more than to any other coarsely built man of his class. To tell you the truth, I rather admire him for being strong-minded enough to enjoy himself in his own way and make plenty of money instead of living the usual shooting, hunting, dining-out, tailoring, loafing life of his set merely because all the rest do it. And I'm perfectly aware that if I'd been in the same circumstances as my aunt Liz, I'd have done exactly what she did. I don't think I'm more prejudiced or straitlaced than you: I think I'm less. I'm certain I'm less sentimental. I know very well that fashionable morality is all a pretence: and that if I took your money and devoted the rest of my life to spending it fashionably, I might be as worthless and vicious as the silliest woman could possibly want to be without having a word said to me about it. But I don't want to be worthless. I shouldn't enjoy trotting about the park to advertise my dressmaker and carriage builder, or being bored at the opera to show off a shop windowful of diamonds.

MRS. WARREN (*bewildered*):

But——

VIVIE:

Wait a moment: I've not done. Tell me why you continue your business now that you are independent of it. Your sister, you told me, has left all that behind her. Why don't you do the same?

MRS. WARREN:

Oh, it's all very easy for Liz: she likes good society, and has the air of being a lady. Imagine me in a cathedral town! Why, the very rooks in the trees would find me out even if I could stand the dulness of it. I must have work and excitement, or I should go melancholy mad. And what else is there for me to do? The life suits me: I'm fit for it and not for anything else. If I didn't do it somebody else would; so I don't do any real harm by it. And then it brings in money; and I like making money. No: it's no use: I can't give it up—not for anybody. But what need you know about it? I'll never mention it. I'll keep Crofts away. I'll not trouble you much: you see I have to be constantly running about from one place to another. You'll be quit of me altogether when I die.

VIVIE:

No: I am my mother's daughter. I am like you: I must have work, and must make more money than I spend. But my work is not your work, and my way not your way. We must part. It will not make much difference to us: instead of meeting one another for perhaps a few months in twenty years, we shall never meet: that's all.

MRS. WARREN (*her voice stifled in tears*):

Vivie: I meant to have been more with you: I did indeed.

VIVIE:

It's no use, mother: I am not to be changed by a few cheap tears and entreaties any more than you are, I dare say.

MRS. WARREN (*wildly*):

Oh, you call a mother's tears cheap.

VIVIE:

They cost you nothing; and you ask me to give you the peace and quietness of my whole life in exchange for them. What use would my company be to you if you could get it? What have we two in common that could make either of us happy together?

MRS. WARREN (*lapsing recklessly into her dialect*):

We're mother and daughter. I want my daughter. I've a right to you. Who is to care for me when I'm old? Plenty of girls have taken to me like daughters and cried at leaving me; but I let them all go because I had you to look forward to. I kept myself lonely for you. You've no right to turn on me now and refuse to do your duty as a daughter.

VIVIE (*jarred and antagonized by the echo of the slums in her mother's voice*):

My duty as a daughter! I thought we should come to that presently. Now once for all, mother, you want a daughter and Frank wants a wife. I don't want a mother; and I don't want a husband. I have spared neither Frank nor myself in sending him about his business. Do you think I will spare you?

MRS. WARREN (*violently*):

Oh, I know the sort you are—no mercy for yourself or anyone else. *I* know. My experience has done that for me anyhow: I can tell the pious, canting, hard, selfish woman when I meet her. Well, keep yourself to yourself: *I* don't want you. But listen to this. Do you know what I would do with you if you were a baby again—aye, as sure as there's a Heaven above us?

VIVIE:

Strangle me, perhaps.

MRS. WARREN:

No: I'd bring you up to be a real daughter to me, and not what you are now, with your pride and your prejudices and the college education you stole from me—yes, stole: deny it if you can: what was it but stealing? I'd bring you up in my own house, so I would.

VIVIE (*quietly*):

In one of your own houses.

MRS. WARREN (*screaming*):

Listen to her! listen to how she spits on her mother's grey hairs! Oh! may you live to have your own daughter tear and trample on you as you have trampled on me. And you will: you will. No woman ever had luck with a mother's curse on her.

VIVIE:

I wish you wouldn't rant, mother. It only hardens me. Come: I suppose I am the only young woman you ever had in your power that you did good to. Don't spoil it all now.

MRS. WARREN:

Yes. Heaven forgive me, it's true; and you are the only one that ever turned on me. Oh, the injustice of it, the injustice, the injustice! I always wanted to be a good woman. I tried honest work; and I was slave-driven until I cursed the day I ever heard of honest work. I was a good mother; and because I made my daughter a good woman she turns me out as if I was a leper. Oh, if I only had my life to live over again! I'd talk to that lying clergyman in the school. From this time forth, so help me Heaven in my last hour, I'll do wrong and nothing but wrong. And I'll prosper on it.

VIVIE:

Yes: it's better to choose your line and go through with it. If I had been you, mother, I might have done as you did; but I should not have lived one life and believed in another. You are a conventional woman at heart. That is why I am bidding you good-bye now. I am right, am I not?

MRS. WARREN (*taken aback*):

Right to throw away all my money!

VIVIE:

No: right to get rid of you? I should be a fool not to? Isn't that so?

MRS. WARREN (*sulkily*):

Oh, well, yes, if you come to that, I suppose you are. But Lord help the world if everybody took to doing the right thing! And now I'd better go than stay where I'm not wanted. (*She turns to the door.*)

VIVIE (*kindly*):

Won't you shake hands?

MRS. WARREN (*after looking at her fiercely for a moment with a savage impulse to strike her*):

No, thank you. Good-bye.

VIVIE (*matter-of-factly*):

Good-bye. (*Mrs. Warren goes out, slamming the door behind her. The strain on Vivie's face relaxes; her grave expression breaks up into one of joyous content; her breath goes out in a half sob, half laugh of intense relief. She goes buoyantly to her place at the writing-table; pushes the electric lamp out of the way; pulls over a great sheaf of papers; and is in the act of dipping her pen in the ink when she finds Frank's note. She opens it unconcernedly and reads it quickly, giving a little laugh at some quaint turn of expression in it.*) And good-bye, Frank. (*She tears the note up and tosses the pieces into the wastepaper basket without a second thought. Then she goes at her work with a plunge, and soon becomes absorbed in her figures.*)

# Caesar and Cleopatra

# Better than Shakespeare*

As to the other plays in this volume, the application of my title is less obvious, since neither Julius Caesar, Cleopatra nor Lady Cecily Waynflete have any external political connection with Puritanism. The very name of Cleopatra suggests at once a tragedy of Circe, with the horrible difference that whereas the ancient myth rightly represents Circe as turning heroes into hogs, the modern romantic convention would represent her as turning hogs into heroes. Shakespeare's *Antony and Cleopatra* must needs be as intolerable to the true Puritan as it is vaguely distressing to the ordinary healthy citizen, because, after giving a faithful picture of the soldier broken down by debauchery, and the typical wanton in whose arms such men perish, Shakespeare finally strains all his huge command of rhetoric and stage pathos to give a theatrical sublimity to the wretched end of the business, and to persuade foolish spectators that the world was well lost by the twain. Such falsehood is not to be borne except by the real Cleopatras and Antonys (they are to be found in every public house) who would no doubt be glad enough to be transfigured by some poet as immortal lovers. Woe to the poet who stoops to such folly! The lot of the man who sees life truly and thinks about it romantically is Despair. How well we know the cries of that despair! Vanity of vanities, all is vanity! moans the Preacher, when life has at last taught him that Nature will not dance to his moralist-made tunes. Thackeray, scores of centuries later, is still baying the moon in the same terms. Out, out, brief candle! cries Shakespeare, in his tragedy of the modern literary man as murderer and witch consulter. Surely the time is past for patience with writers who, having to choose between giving up life in despair and discarding the trumpery moral kitchen scales in which they try to weigh the universe, superstitiously stick to the scales, and spend the rest of the lives they pretend to despise in breaking men's spirits. But even in pessimism there is a choice between intellectual honesty and dishonesty. Hogarth drew the rake and the harlot without glorifying their end. Swift, accepting our system of morals and religion, deliv-

*From *Three Plays for Puritans*, published in 1900. Collection included *The Devil's Disciple* and *Captain Brassbound's Conversion* in addition to *Caesar and Cleopatra*.

ered the inevitable verdict of that system on us through the mouth of the king of Brobdingnag, and described man as the Yahoo, shocking his superior the horse by his every action. Strindberg, the only living genuine Shakespearean dramatist, shows that the female Yahoo, measured by romantic standards, is viler than her male dupe and slave. I respect these resolute tragi-comedians: they are logical and faithful: they force you to face the fact that you must either accept their conclusions as valid (in which case it is cowardly to continue living) or admit that your way of judging conduct is absurd. But when your Shakespeares and Thackerays huddle up the matter at the end by killing somebody and covering your eyes with the undertaker's handkerchief, duly onioned with some pathetic phrase, as The flight of angels sing thee to they rest, or Adsum, or the like, I have no respect for them at all: such maudlin tricks may impose on tea-drunkards, not on me.

Besides, I have a technical objection to making sexual infatuation a tragic theme. Experience proves that it is only effective in the comic spirit. We can bear to see Mrs. Quickly pawning her plate for love of Falstaff, but not Antony running away from the battle of Actium for love of Cleopatra. Let realism have its demonstration, comedy its criticism, or even bawdry its horselaugh at the expense of sexual infatuation, if it must; but to ask us to subject our souls to its ruinous glamor, to worship it, deify it, and imply that it alone makes our life worth living, is nothing but folly gone mad erotically—a thing compared to which Falstaff's unbeglamored drinking and drabbing is respectable and rightminded. Whoever, then, expects to find Cleopatra a Circe and Caesar a hog in these pages, had better lay down my book and be spared a disappointment.

In Caesar, I have used another character with which Shakespeare has been beforehand. But Shakespeare, who knew human weakness so well, never knew human strength of the Caesarian type. His Caesar is an admitted failure; his Lear is a masterpiece. The tragedy of disillusion and doubt, of the agonized struggle for a foothold on the quicksand made by an acute observation striving to verify its vain attribution of morality and respectability to Nature, of the faithless will and the keen eyes that the faithless will is too weak to blind; all this will give you a Hamlet or a Macbeth, and win you great applause from literary gentlemen; but it will not give you a Julius Caesar. Caesar was not in Shakespeare, nor in the epoch, now fast waning, which he inaugurated. It cost Shakespeare no pang to write Caesar down for the merely technical purpose of writing Brutus up. And what a Brutus! A perfect Girondin, mirrored in Shakespeare's art two hundred years before the real thing came to maturity and talked and stalked and had its head duly cut off by the coarser

Antonys and Octaviuses of its time, who at least knew the difference between life and rhetoric.

It will be said that these remarks can bear no other construction than an offer of my Caesar to the public as an improvement on Shakespeare's. And in fact, that is their precise purport. But here let me give a friendly warning to those scribes who have so often exclaimed against my criticisms of Shakespeare as blasphemies against a hitherto unquestioned Perfection and Infallibility. Such criticisms are no more new than the creed of my Diabolonian Puritan or my revival of the humors of Cool as a Cucumber. Too much surprise at them betrays an acquaintance with Shakespeare criticism so limited as not to include even the prefaces of Dr. Johnson and the utterances of Napoleon. I have merely repeated in the dialect of my own time and in the light of its philosophy what they said in the dialect and light of theirs. Do not be misled by the Shakespeare fanciers who, ever since his own time, have delighted in his plays just as they might have delighted in a particular breed of pigeons if they had never learnt to read. His genuine critics, from Ben Jonson to Mr. Frank Harris, have always kept as far on this side idolatry as I.

As to our ordinary uncritical citizens, they have been slowly trudging forward these three centuries to the point which Shakespeare reached at a bound in Elizabeth's time. Today most of them have arrived there or thereabouts, with the result that his plays are at last beginning to be performed as he wrote them; and the long line of disgraceful farces, melodramas, and stage pageants which actor-managers, from Garrick and Cibber to our own contemporaries, have hacked out of his plays as peasants have hacked huts out of the Coliseum, are beginning to vanish from the stage. It is a significant fact that the mutilators of Shakespeare, who never could be persuaded that Shakespeare knew his business better than they, have ever been the most fanatical of his worshippers. The late Augustin Daly thought no price too extravagant for an addition to his collection of Shakespeare relics; but in arranging Shakespeare's plays for the stage he proceeded on the assumption that Shakespeare was a botcher and he an artist. I am far too good a Shakespearean ever to forgive Sir Henry Irving for producing a version of *King Lear* so mutilated that the numerous critics who had never read the play could not follow the story of Gloster. Both these idolators of the Bard must have thought Mr. Forbes Robertson mad because he restored Fortinbras to the stage and played as much of Hamlet as there was time for instead of as little. And the instant success of the experiment probably altered their minds no further than to make them think the public mad. Mr. Benson actually gives the play complete at two sittings, causing the aforesaid numerous critics to remark with naïve surprise that Polonius is a complete and interesting character. It was the age of gross ignorance of Shakespeare and incapacity for his works that produced the indiscriminate eulogies with which we are familiar. It was the revival of genuine criticism of those works that coincided with the movement for giving genuine instead of spurious and silly representations of his plays. So much for Bardolatry!

It does not follow, however, that the right to criticize Shakespeare involves the power of writing better plays. And in fact—do not be surprised at my modesty—I do not profess to write better plays. The writing of practicable stage plays does not present an infinite scope to human talent; and the dramatists who magnify its difficulties are humbugs. The summit of their art has been attained again and again. No man will ever write a better tragedy than *Lear*, a better comedy than *Le Festin de Pierre* or *Peer Gynt*, a better opera than *Don Giovanni*, a better music drama than *The Nibelung's Ring*, or, for the matter of that, better fashionable plays and melodramas than are now being turned out by writers whom nobody dreams of mocking with the word immortal. It is the philosophy, the outlook on life, that changes, not the craft of the playwright. A generation that is thoroughly moralized and patriotized, that conceives virtuous indignation as spiritually nutritious, that murders the murderer and robs the thief, that grovels before all sorts of ideals, social, military, ecclesiastical, royal and divine, may be, from my point of view, steeped in error; but it need not want for as good plays as the hand of man can produce. Only, those plays will be neither written nor relished by men in whose philosophy guilt and innocence, and consequently revenge and idolatry, have no meaning. Such men must rewrite all the old plays in terms of their own philosophy; and that is why, as Mr. Stuart-Glennie has pointed out, there can be no new drama without a new philosophy. To which I may add that there can be no Shakespeare or Goethe without one either, nor two Shakespeares in one philosophic epoch, since, as I have said, the first great comer in that epoch reaps the whole harvest and reduces those who come after to the rank of mere gleaners, or, worse than that, fools who go laboriously through all the motions of the reaper and binder in an empty field. What is the use of writing plays or painting frescoes if you have nothing more to say or shew than was said and shewn by Shakespeare, Michael Angelo, and Raphael? If these had not seen things differently, for better or worse, from the dramatic poets of the Townley mysteries, or from Giotto, they could not have produced their works: no, not though their skill of pen and hand had been double what it was. After them there was no need (and *need* alone nerves men to face the persecution in the teeth of which new art is brought to birth) to redo the already done, until in due time, when their philosophy wore itself out, a new race of nineteenth century poets and critics, from Byron to William Morris, began, first to speak coldly of Shakespeare and Raphael, and then to rediscover, in the medieval art which these Renascence masters had superseded, certain forgotten elements which were germinating again for the new harvest. What is more, they began to discover that the technical skill of the masters was by no means superlative. Indeed, I defy anyone to prove that the great epoch makers in fine art have owed their position to their technical skill. It is true that when we search for examples of a prodigious command of language and of graphic line, we can think of nobody better than Shakespeare and Michael Angelo. But both of them laid their arts waste for centuries by leading later artists to seek greatness in copying their technique. The technique was acquired, refined on, and surpassed over and over again; but the supremacy of the two great exemplars remained undisputed. As a matter of easily observable fact, every generation produces men of extraordinary special faculty, artistic, mathematical, and linguistic, who for lack of new ideas, or indeed of any ideas worth mentioning, achieve no distinction outside music halls and class rooms, although they can do things easily that the great epoch makers did clumsily or not at all. The contempt of the academic pedant for the original artist is often founded on a genuine superiority of technical knowledge and aptitude; he is sometimes a better anatomical draughtsman than Raphael, a better hand at triple counterpoint than Beethoven, a better versifier than Byron. Nay, this is true not merely of pedants, but of men who have produced works of art of some note. If technical facility were the secret of greatness in art, Mr. Swinburne would be greater than Browning and Byron rolled into one, Stevenson greater than Scott or Dickens, Mendelssohn than Wagner, Maclise than Madox Brown. Besides, new ideas make their technique as water makes its channel; and the technician without ideas is as useless as the canal constructor without water, though he may do very skilfully what the Mississippi does very rudely. To clinch the argument, you have only to observe that the epoch maker himself has generally begun working professionally before his new ideas have mastered him sufficiently to insist on constant expression by his art. In such cases you are compelled to admit that if he had by chance died earlier, his greatness would have remained unachieved, although his technical qualifications would have been well enough established. The early imitative works of great men are usually conspicuously inferior to the best works of their forerunners. Imagine Wagner dying after composing *Rienzi*, or Shelley after *Zastrozzi*! Would any competent critic then have rated

Wagner's technical aptitude as high as Rossini's, Spontini's, or Meyerbeer's; or Shelley's as high as Moore's? Turn the problem another way: does anyone suppose that if Shakespeare had conceived Goethe's or Ibsen's ideas, he would have expressed them any worse than Goethe or Ibsen? Human faculty being what it is, is it likely that in our time any advance, except in external conditions, will take place in the arts of expression sufficient to enable an author, without making himself ridiculous, to undertake to say what he has to say better than Homer or Shakespeare? But the humblest author, and much more a rather arrogant one like myself, may profess to have something to say by this time that neither Homer nor Shakespeare said. And the playgoer may reasonably ask to have historical events and persons presented to him in the light of his own time, even though Homer and Shakespeare have already shewn them in the light of their time. For example, Homer presented Achilles and Ajax as heroes to the world in the Iliads. In due time came Shakespeare, who said, virtually: I really cannot accept this selfish hound and this brawny brute as great men merely because Homer flattered them in playing to the Greek gallery. Consequently we have, in *Troilus and Cressida*, the verdict of Shakespeare's epoch (our own) on the pair. This did not in the least involve any pretense on Shakespeare's part to be a greater poet than Homer.

When Shakespeare in turn came to deal with Henry V and Julius Caesar, he did so according to his own essentially knightly conception of a great statesman-commander. But in the XIX century comes the German historian Mommsen, who also takes Caesar for his hero, and explains the immense difference in scope between the perfect knight Vercingetorix and his great conqueror Julius Caesar. In this country, Carlyle, with his vein of peasant inspiration, apprehended the sort of greatness that places the true hero of history so far beyond the mere *preux chevalier,* whose fanatical personal honor, gallantry and self-sacrifice, are founded on a passion for death born of inability to bear the weight of a life that will not grant ideal conditions to the liver. This one ray of perception became Carlyle's whole stock-in-trade; and it sufficed to make a literary master of him. In due time, when Mommsen is an old man, and Carlyle dead, come I, and dramatize the by-this-time familiar distinction in *Arms and the Man*, with its comedic conflict between the knightly Bulgarian and the Mommsenite Swiss captain. Whereupon a great many playgoers who have not yet read Shakespeare, much less Mommsen and Carlyle, raise a shriek of concern for their knightly ideal as if nobody had ever questioned its sufficiency since the middle ages. Let them thank me for educating them so far. And let them allow me to set forth Caesar in the same modern light, taking the same liberty with Shakespeare as he with Homer, and with no thought of pretending to express the Mommsenite view of Caesar any better than Shakespeare expressed a view which was not even Plutarchian, and must, I fear, be referred to the tradition in stage conquerors established by Marlowe's *Tamburlaine* as much as to even the chivalrous conception of heroism dramatized in *Henry V*.

For my own part, I can avouch that such powers of invention, humor and stage ingenuity as I have been able to exercise in *Plays, Pleasant and Unpleasant*, and in these *Three Plays for Puritans*, availed me not at all until I saw the old facts in a new light. Technically, I do not find myself able to proceed otherwise than as former playwrights have done. True, my plays have the latest mechanical improvements: the action is not carried on by impossible soliloquys and asides; and my people get on and off the stage without requiring four doors to a room which in real life would have only one. But my stories are the old stories; my characters are the familiar harlequin and columbine, clown and pantaloon (note the harlequin's leap in the third act of *Caesar and Cleopatra*); my stage tricks and suspenses and thrills and jests are the ones in vogue when I was a boy, by which time my grandfather was tired of them. To the young people who make their acquaintance for the first time in my plays, they may be as novel as Cyrano's nose to those who have never seen Punch; whilst to older playgoers the unexpectedness of my attempt to substitute natural history for conventional ethics and roman-tic logic may so transfigure the eternal stage puppets and their inevitable dilemmas as to make their identification impossible for the moment. If so, so much the better for me: I shall perhaps enjoy a few years of immortality. But the whirligig of time will soon bring my audiences to my own point of view; and then the next Shakespeare that comes along will turn these petty tentatives of mine into masterpieces final for their epoch. By that time my twentieth century characteristics will pass unnoticed as a matter of course, whilst the eighteenth century artificiality that marks the work of every literary Irishman of my generation will seem antiquated and silly. It is a dangerous thing to be hailed at once, as a few rash admirers have hailed me, as above all things original: what the world calls originality is only an unaccustomed method of tickling it. Meyerbeer seemed prodigiously original to the Parisians when he first burst on them. To-day, he is only the crow who followed Beethoven's plough. I am a crow who has followed many ploughs. No doubt I seem prodigiously clever to those who have never hopped, hungry and curious, across the fields of philosophy, politics and art. Karl Marx said of Stuart Mill that his eminence was due to the flatness of the surrounding country. In these days of Board Schools, universal reading, cheap newspapers, and the inevitable ensuing demand for notabilities of all sorts, literary, military, political and fashionable, to write paragraphs about, that sort of eminence is within the reach of very moderate ability. Reputations are cheap nowadays. Even were they dear, it would still be impossible for any public-spirited citizen of the world to hope that his reputation might endure; for this would be to hope that the flood of general enlightenment may never rise above his miserable high-water mark. I hate to think that Shakespeare has lasted 300 years, though he got no further than Koheleth the Preacher, who died many centuries before him; or that Plato, more than 2,000 years old, is still ahead of our voters. We must hurry on: we must get rid of reputations: they are weeds in the soil of ignorance. Cultivate that soil, and they will flower more beautifully, but only as annuals. If this preface will at all help to get rid of mine, the writing of it will have been well worth the pains.

SURREY, 1900.

# Act I

*An October night on the Syrian border of Egypt towards the end of the XXXIII Dynasty, in the year 706 by Roman computation, afterwards reckoned by Christian computation as 48 B.C. A great radiance of silver fire, the dawn of a moonlit night, is rising in the east. The stars and the cloudless sky are our own contemporaries, nineteen and a half centuries younger than we know them; but you would not guess that from their appearance. Below them are two notable drawbacks of civilization: a palace, and soldiers. The palace, an old, low, Syrian building of whitened mud, is not so ugly as Buckingham Palace; and the officers in the courtyard are more highly civilized than modern English officers: for example, they do not dig up the corpses of their dead enemies and mutilate them, as we dug up Cromwell and the Mahdi. They are in two groups: one intent on the gambling of their captain Belzanor, a warrior of fifty, who, with his spear on the ground beside his knee, is stooping to throw dice with a sly-looking young Persian recruit; the other gathered about a guardsman who has just finished telling a naughty story (still current in English barracks) at which they are laughing uproariously. They are about a dozen in number, all highly aristocratic young Egyptian guardsmen, handsomely equipped with weapons and armor, very unEnglish in point of not being ashamed of and uncomfortable in their professional dress; on the contrary, rather ostentatiously and arrogantly warlike, as valuing themselves on their military caste.*

*Belzanor is a typical veteran, tough and wilful; prompt, capable and crafty where brute force will serve; helpless and boyish when it will not: an effective sergeant, an incompetent general, a deplorable dictator. Would, if influentially connected, be employed in the two last capacities by a modern European State on the strength of his success in the first. Is rather to be pitied just now in view of the fact that Julius Caesar is invading his country. Not knowing this, is intent on his game with the Persian, whom, as a foreigner, he considers quite capable of cheating him.*

*His subalterns are mostly handsome young fellows whose interest in the game and the story symbolizes with tolerable completeness the main interests in life of which they are conscious. Their spears are leaning against the walls, or lying on the ground ready to their hands. The corner of the courtyard forms a triangle of which one side is the front of the palace, with a doorway, the other a wall with a gateway. The storytellers are on the palace side: the gamblers, on the gateway side. Close to the gateway, against the wall, is a stone block high enough to enable a Nubian sentinel, standing on it, to look over the wall. The yard is lighted by a torch stuck in the wall. As the laughter from the group round the storyteller dies away, the kneeling Persian, winning the throw, snatches up the stake from the ground.*

BELZANOR:

By Apis, Persian, thy gods are good to thee.

THE PERSIAN:

Try yet again, O captain. Double or quits!

BELZANOR:

No more. I am not in the vein.

THE SENTINEL (*poising his javelin as he peers over the wall*):

Stand. Who goes there?

*They all start, listening. A strange voice replies from without.*

VOICE:

The bearer of evil tidings.

BELZANOR (*calling to the sentry*):

Pass him.

THE SENTINEL (*grounding his javelin*):

Draw near, O bearer of evil tidings.

BELZANOR (*pocketing the dice and picking up his spear*):

Let us receive this man with honor. He bears evil tidings.

*The guardsmen seize their spears and gather about the gate, leaving a way through for the new comer.*

PERSIAN (*rising from his knee*):

Are evil tidings, then, so honorable?

BELZANOR:

O barbarous Persian, hear my instruction. In Egypt the bearer of good tidings is sacrificed to the gods as a thank offering; but no god will accept the blood of the messenger of evil. When we have good tidings, we are careful to send them in the mouth of the cheapest slave we can find. Evil tidings are borne by young noblemen who desire to bring themselves into notice. (*They join the rest at the gate.*)

THE SENTINEL:

Pass, O young captain; and bow the head in the House of the Queen.

VOICE:

Go anoint thy javelin with fat of swine, O Blackamoor; for before morning the Romans will make thee eat it to the very butt.

*The owner of the voice, a fairhaired dandy, dressed in a different fashion to that affected by* the guardsmen, *but no less extravagantly, comes through the gateway laughing. He is somewhat battlestained; and his left forearm, bandaged, comes through a torn sleeve. In his right hand he carries a Roman sword in its sheath. He swaggers down the courtyard,* the Persian *on his right,* Belzanor *on his left, and* the guardsmen *crowding down behind him.*

BELZANOR:

Who art thou that laughest in the House of Cleopatra the Queen, and in the teeth of Belzanor, the captain of her guard?

THE NEW COMER:

I am Bel Affris, descended from the gods.

BELZANOR (*ceremoniously*):

Hail, cousin!

ALL (*except* the Persian):

Hail, cousin!

PERSIAN:

All the Queen's guards are descended from the gods, O stranger, save myself. I am Persian, and descended from many kings.

BEL AFFRIS (*to* the guardsmen):

Hail, cousins! (*To the Persian, condescendingly*) Hail, mortal!

BELZANOR:

You have been in battle, Bel Affris; and you are a soldier among soldiers. You will not let the Queen's women have the first of your tidings.

BEL AFFRIS:

I have no tidings, except that we shall have our throats cut presently, women, soldiers, and all.

PERSIAN (*to* Belzanor):

I told you so.

THE SENTINEL (*who has been listening*):

Woe, alas!

BEL AFFRIS (*calling to him*):

Peace, peace, poor Ethiop: destiny is with the gods who painted thee black. (*To* Belzanor) What has this mortal (*indicating* the Persian) told you?

BELZANOR:

He says that the Roman Julius Caesar, who has landed on our shores with a handful of followers, will make himself master of Egypt. He is afraid of the Roman soldiers. (*The guardsmen laugh with boisterous scorn.*) Peasants, brought up to scare crows and follow the plough. Sons of smiths and millers and tanners! And we nobles, consecrated to arms, descended from the gods!

PERSIAN:

Belzanor: the gods are not always good to their poor relations.

BELZANOR (*hotly, to* the Persian):

Man to man, are we worse than the slaves of Caesar?

BEL AFFRIS (*stepping between them*):

Listen, cousin. Man to man, we Egyptians are as gods above the Romans.

THE GUARDSMEN (*exultingly*):

Aha!

BEL AFFRIS:

But this Caesar does not pit man against man: he throws a legion at you where you are weakest as he throws a stone from a catapult; and that legion is as a man with one head, a thousand arms, and no religion. I have fought against them; and I know.

BELZANOR (*derisively*):

Were you frightened, cousin?

The guardsmen *roar with laughter, their eyes sparkling at the wit of their captain.*

BEL AFFRIS:

No, cousin; but I was beaten. They were frightened (perhaps); but they scattered us like chaff.

The guardsmen, *much damped, utter a growl of contemptuous disgust.*

BELZANOR:

Could you not die?

BEL AFFRIS:

No: that was too easy to be worthy of a descendant of the gods. Besides, there was no time: all was over in a moment. The attack came just where we least expected it.

BELZANOR:

That shews that the Romans are cowards.

BEL AFFRIS:

They care nothing about cowardice, these Romans: they fight to win. The pride and honor of war are nothing to them.

PERSIAN:

Tell us the tale of the battle. What befell?

THE GUARDSMEN (*gathering eagerly round* Bel Affris):

Ay: the tale of the battle.

BEL AFFRIS:

Know then, that I am a novice in the guard of the temple of Ra in Memphis, serving neither Cleopatra nor her brother Ptolemy, but only the high gods. We went a journey to inquire of Ptolemy why he had driven Cleopatra into Syria, and how we of Egypt should deal with the Roman Pompey, newly come to our shores after his defeat by Caesar at Pharsalia. What, think ye, did we learn? Even that Caesar is coming also in hot pursuit of his foe, and that Ptolemy has slain Pompey, whose severed head he holds in readiness to present to the conqueror. (*Sensation among* the guardsmen.) Nay, more: we found that Caesar is already come; for we had not made half a day's journey on our way back when we came upon a city rabble flying from his legions, whose landing they had gone out to withstand.

BELZANOR:

And ye, the temple guard! did ye not withstand these legions?

BEL AFFRIS:

What man could, that we did. But there came the sound of a trumpet whose voice was as the cursing of a black mountain. Then saw we a moving wall of shields coming towards us. You know how the heart burns when you charge a fortified wall; but how if the fortified wall were to charge you?

THE PERSIAN (*exulting in having told them so*):

Did I not say it?

BEL AFFRIS:

When the wall came nigh, it changed into a line of men—common fellows enough, with helmets, leather tunics, and breastplates. Every man of them flung his javelin: the one that came my way drove through my shield as through a papyrus—lo there! (*he points to the bandage on his left arm*) and would have gone through my neck had I not stooped. They were charging at the double then, and were upon us with short swords almost as soon as their javelins. When a man is close to you with such a sword, you can do nothing with our weapons: they are all too long.

THE PERSIAN:

What did you do?

BEL AFFRIS:

Doubled my fist and smote my Roman on the sharpness of his jaw. He was but mortal after all: he lay down in a stupor; and

I took his sword and laid it on. (*Drawing the sword*) Lo! a Roman sword with Roman blood on it!

THE GUARDSMEN (*approvingly*):

Good! (*They take the sword and hand it round, examining it curiously.*)

THE PERSIAN:

And your men?

BEL AFFRIS:

Fled. Scattered like sheep.

BELZANOR (*furiously*):

The cowardly slaves! Leaving the descendants of the gods to be butchered!

BEL AFFRIS (*with acid coolness*):

The descendants of the gods did not stay to be butchered, cousin. The battle was not to the strong; but the race was to the swift. The Romans, who have no chariots, sent a cloud of horsemen in pursuit, and slew multitudes. Then our high priest's captain rallied a dozen descendants of the gods and exhorted us to die fighting. I said to myself: surely it is safer to stand than to lose my breath and be stabbed in the back; so I joined our captain and stood. Then the Romans treated us with respect; for no man attacks a lion when the field is full of sheep, except for the pride and honor of war, of which these Romans know nothing. So we escaped with our lives; and I am come to warn you that you must open your gates to Caesar; for his advance guard is scarce an hour behind me; and not an Egyptian warrior is left standing between you and his legions.

THE SENTINEL:

Woe, alas! (*He throws down his javelin and flies into the palace.*)

BELZANOR:

Nail him to the door, quick! (The guardsmen *rush for him with their spears; but he is too quick for them.*) Now this news will run through the palace like fire through stubble.

BEL AFFRIS:

What shall we do to save the women from the Romans?

BELZANOR:

Why not kill them?

PERSIAN:

Because we should have to pay blood money for some of them. Better let the Romans kill them: it is cheaper.

BELZANOR (*awestruck at his brain power*):

O subtle one! O serpent!

BEL AFFRIS:

> But your Queen?

BELZANOR:

> True: we must carry off Cleopatra.

BEL AFFRIS:

> Will ye not await her command?

BELZANOR:

> Command! a girl of sixteen! Not we. At Memphis ye deem her a Queen: here we know better. I will take her on the crupper of my horse. When we soldiers have carried her out of Caesar's reach, then the priests and the nurses and the rest of them can pretend she is a queen again, and put their commands into her mouth.

PERSIAN:

> Listen to me, Belzanor.

BELZANOR:

> Speak, O subtle beyond thy years.

THE PERSIAN:

> Cleopatra's brother Ptolemy is at war with her. Let us sell her to him.

THE GUARDSMEN:

> O subtle one! O serpent!

BELZANOR:

> We dare not. We are descended from the gods; but Cleopatra is descended from the river Nile; and the lands of our fathers will grow no grain if the Nile rises not to water them. Without our father's gifts we should live the lives of dogs.

PERSIAN:

> It is true: the Queen's guard cannot live on its pay. But hear me further, O ye kinsmen of Osiris.

THE GUARDSMEN:

> Speak, O subtle one. Hear the serpent begotten!

PERSIAN:

> Have I heretofore spoken truly to you of Caesar, when you thought I mocked you?

GUARDSMEN:

> Truly, truly.

BELZANOR (*reluctantly admitting it*):

> So Bel Affris says.

PERSIAN:

> Hear more of him, then. This Caesar is a great lover of women: he makes them his friends and counsellors.

BELZANOR:

Faugh! This rule of women will be the ruin of Egypt.

THE PERSIAN:

Let it rather be the ruin of Rome! Caesar grows old now: he is past fifty and full of labors and battles. He is too old for the young women; and the old women are too wise to worship him.

BEL AFFRIS:

Take heed, Persian. Caesar is by this time almost within earshot.

PERSIAN:

Cleopatra is not yet a woman: neither is she wise. But she already troubles men's wisdom.

BELZANOR:

Ay: that is because she is descended from the river Nile and a black kitten of the sacred White Cat. What then?

PERSIAN:

Why, sell her secretly to Ptolemy, and then offer ourselves to Caesar as volunteers to fight for the overthrow of her brother and the rescue of our Queen, the Great Granddaughter of the Nile.

THE GUARDSMEN:

O serpent!

PERSIAN:

He will listen to us if we come with her picture in our mouths. He will conquer and kill her brother, and reign in Egypt with Cleopatra for his Queen. And we shall be her guard.

GUARDSMEN:

O subtlest of all the serpents! O admiration! O wisdom!

BEL AFFRIS:

He will also have arrived before you have done talking, O word spinner.

BELZANOR:

That is true. (*An affrighted uproar in the palace interrupts him.*) Quick: the flight has begun: guard the door. (*They rush to the door and form a cordon before it with their spears. A mob of women-servants and nurses surges out. Those in front recoil from the spears, screaming to those behind to keep back. Belzanor's voice dominates the disturbance as he shouts*) Back there. In again, unprofitable cattle.

THE GUARDSMEN:

Back, unprofitable cattle.

BELZANOR:

Send us out Ftatateeta, the Queen's chief nurse.

THE WOMEN (*calling into the palace*):

Ftatateeta, Ftatateeta. Come, come. Speak to Belzanor.

A WOMAN:

Oh, keep back. You are thrusting me on the spearheads.

*A huge grim woman, her face covered with a network of tiny wrinkles, and her eyes old, large, and wise; sinewy handed, very tall, very strong; with the mouth of a bloodhound and the jaws of a bulldog, appears on the threshold. She is dressed like a person of consequence in the palace, and confronts* the guardsmen *insolently.*

FTATATEETA:

Make way for the Queen's chief nurse.

BELZANOR (*with solemn arrogance*):

Ftatateeta: I am Belzanor, the captain of the Queen's guard, descended from the gods.

FTATATEETA (*retorting his arrogance with interest*):

Belzanor: I am Ftatateeta, the Queen's chief nurse; and your divine ancestors were proud to be painted on the wall in the pyramids of the kings whom my fathers served.

The women *laugh triumphantly.*

BELZANOR (*with grim humor*):

Ftatateeta: daughter of a long-tongued, swivel-eyed cha-meleon, the Romans are at hand. (*A cry of terror from the* women: *they would fly but for the spears.*) Not even the descen-dants of the gods can resist them; for they have each man seven arms, each carrying seven spears. The blood in their veins is boiling quicksilver; and their wives become mothers in three hours, and are slain and eaten the next day.

*A shudder of horror from* the women. Ftatateeta, *despising them and scorning the soldiers, pushes her way through the crowd and confronts the spear points undismayed.*

FTATATEETA:

Then fly and save yourselves, O cowardly sons of the cheap clay gods that are sold to fish porters; and leave us to shift for ourselves.

BELZANOR:

Not until you have first done our bidding, O terror of man-hood. Bring out Cleopatra the Queen to us and then go whither you will.

FTATATEETA (*with a derisive laugh*):

Now I know why the gods have taken her out of our hands.
(The guardsmen *start and look at one another.*) Know, thou foolish soldier, that the Queen has been missing since an hour past
sun down.

BELZANOR (*furiously*):

Hag: you have hidden her to sell to Caesar or her brother. (*He
grasps her by the left wrist, and drags her, helped by a few of the
guard, to the middle of the courtyard, where, as they fling her on her
knees, he draws a murderous looking knife.*) Where is she? Where
is she? or— (*He threatens to cut her throat.*)

FTATATEETA (*savagely*):

Touch me, dog; and the Nile will not rise on your fields for
seven times seven years of famine.

BELZANOR (*frightened, but desperate*):

I will sacrifice: I will pay. Or stay. (*To* the Persian) You, O subtle one: your father's lands lie far from the Nile. Slay her.

PERSIAN (*threatening her with his knife*):

Persia has but one god; yet he loves the blood of old women.
Where is Cleopatra?

FTATATEETA:

Persian: as Osiris lives, I do not know. I chid her for bringing
evil days upon us by talking to the sacred cats of the priests,
and carrying them in her arms. I told her she would be left
alone here when the Romans came as a punishment for her dis-
obedience. And now she is gone—run away—hidden. I speak
the truth. I call Osiris to witness——

THE WOMEN (*protesting officiously*):

She speaks the truth, Belzanor.

BELZANOR:

You have frightened the child: she is hiding. Search—quick—
into the palace—search every corner.

*The guards, led by* Belzanor, *shoulder their way into the palace through
the flying crowd of women, who escape through the courtyard gate.*

FTATATEETA (*screaming*):

Sacrilege! Men in the Queen's chambers! Sa— (*Her voice dies
away as* the Persian *puts his knife to her throat.*)

BEL AFFRIS (*laying a hand on* Ftatateeta's *left shoulder*):

Forbear her yet a moment, Persian. (*To* Ftatateeta, *very significantly*) Mother: your gods are asleep or away hunting; and the
sword is at your throat. Bring us to where the Queen is hid,
and you shall live.

FTATATEETA (*contemptuously*):

Who shall stay the sword in the hand of a fool, if the high gods put it there? Listen to me, ye young men without understanding. Cleopatra fears me; but she fears the Romans more. There is but one power greater in her eyes than the wrath of the Queen's nurse and the cruelty of Caesar; and that is the power of the Sphinx that sits in the desert watching the way to the sea. What she would have it know, she tells into the ears of the sacred cats; and on her birthday she sacrifices to it and decks it with poppies. Go ye therefore into the desert and seek Cleopatra in the shadow of the Sphinx; and on your heads see to it that no harm comes to her.

BEL AFFRIS (*to* the Persian):

May we believe this, O subtle one?

PERSIAN:

Which way come the Romans?

BEL AFFRIS:

Over the desert, from the sea, by this very Sphinx.

PERSIAN (*to* Ftatateeta):

O mother of guile! O aspic's tongue! You have made up this tale so that we two may go into the desert and perish on the spears of the Romans. (*Lifting his knife*) Taste death.

FTATATEETA:

Not from thee, baby. (*She snatches his ankle from under him and flies stooping along the palace wall, vanishing in the darkness within its precinct. Bel Affris roars with laughter as the Persian tumbles. The guardsmen rush out of the palace with Belzanor and a mob of fugitives, mostly carrying bundles.*)

PERSIAN:

Have you found Cleopatra?

BELZANOR:

She is gone. We have searched every corner.

THE NUBIAN SENTINEL (*appearing at the door of the palace*):

Woe! Alas! Fly, fly!

BELZANOR:

What is the matter now?

THE NUBIAN SENTINEL:

The sacred white cat has been stolen.

ALL:

Woe! Woe!

*General panic. They all fly with cries of consternation. The torch is thrown down and extinguished in the rush. Darkness. The noise of the fugitives dies away. Dead silence. Suspense. Then the blackness and stillness breaks softly into silver mist and strange airs as the windswept harp of Memnon plays at the dawning of the moon. It rises full over the desert; and a vast horizon comes into relief, broken by a huge shape which soon reveals itself in the spreading radiance as a Sphinx pedestalled on the sands. The light still clears, until the upraised eyes of the image are distinguished looking straight forward and upward in infinite fearless vigil, and a mass of color between its great paws defines itself as a heap of red poppies on which a girl lies motionless, her silken vest heaving gently and regularly with the breathing of a dreamless sleeper, and her braided hair glittering in a shaft of moonlight like a bird's wing.*

*Suddenly there comes from afar a vaguely fearful sound (it might be the bellow of a Minotaur softened by great distance) and Memnon's music stops. Silence: then a few faint high-ringing trumpet notes. Then silence again. Then a man comes from the south with stealing steps, ravished by the mystery of the night, all wonder, and halts, lost in contemplation, opposite the left flank of the Sphinx, whose bosom, with its burden, is hidden from him by its massive shoulder.*

THE MAN:

Hail, Sphinx: salutation from Julius Caesar! I have wandered in many lands, seeking the lost regions from which my birth into this world exiled me, and the company of creatures such as I myself. I have found flocks and pastures, men and cities, but no other Caesar, no air native to me, no man kindred to me, none who can do my day's deed, and think my night's thought. In the little world yonder, Sphinx, my place is as high as yours in this great desert; only I wander, and you sit still; I conquer, and you endure; I work and wonder, you watch and wait; I look up and am dazzled, look down and am darkened, look round and am puzzled, whilst your eyes never turn from looking out—out of the world—to the lost region—the home from which we have strayed. Sphinx, you and I, strangers to the race of men, are no strangers to one another: have I not been conscious of you and of this place since I was born? Rome is a madman's dream: this is my Reality. These starry lamps of yours I have seen from afar in Gaul, in Britain, in Spain, in Thessaly, signalling great secrets to some eternal sentinel below, whose post I never could find. And here at last is their sentinel—an image of the constant and immortal part of my life, silent, full of thoughts, alone in the silver desert. Sphinx, Sphinx: I have climbed mountains at night to hear in the distance the stealthy footfall of the winds that chase your sands in forbidden play—our invisible children, O Sphinx, laughing in whispers. My way hither was the way of destiny; for I am he of whose genius you are the symbol: part brute, part woman, and part God—nothing of man in me at all. Have I read your riddle, Sphinx?

THE GIRL (*who has wakened, and peeped cautiously from her nest to see who is speaking*):

Old gentleman.

CAESAR (*starting violently, and clutching his sword*):

Immortal gods!

THE GIRL:

Old gentleman: don't run away.

CAESAR (*stupefied*):

"Old gentleman: don't run away!!!" This! to Julius Caesar!

THE GIRL (*urgently*):

Old gentleman.

CAESAR:

Sphinx: you presume on your centuries. I am younger than you, though your voice is but a girl's voice as yet.

THE GIRL:

Climb up here, quickly; or the Romans will come and eat you.

CAESAR (*running forward past the Sphinx's shoulder, and seeing her*):

A child at its breast! a divine child!

THE GIRL:

Come up quickly. You must get up at its side and creep round.

CAESAR (*amazed*):

Who are you?

THE GIRL:

Cleopatra, Queen of Egypt.

CAESAR:

Queen of the Gypsies, you mean.

CLEOPATRA:

You must not be disrespectful to me, or the Sphinx will let the Romans eat you. Come up. It is quite cosy here.

CAESAR (*to himself*):

What a dream! What a magnificent dream! Only let me not wake, and I will conquer ten continents to pay for dreaming it out to the end. (*He climbs to the Sphinx's flank, and presently reappears to her on the pedestal, stepping round its right shoulder.*)

CLEOPATRA:

Take care. That's right. Now sit down: you may have its other paw. (*She seats herself comfortably on its left paw.*) It is very powerful and will protect us; but (*shivering, and with plaintive loneliness*) it would not take any notice of me or keep me company. I am glad you have come: I was very lonely. Did you happen to see a white cat anywhere?

CAESAR (*sitting slowly down on the right paw in extreme wonderment*):
Have you lost one?

CLEOPATRA:
Yes: the sacred white cat: is it not dreadful? I brought him here to sacrifice him to the Sphinx; but when we got a little way from the city a black cat called him, and he jumped out of my arms and ran away to it. Do you think that the black cat can have been my great-great-great-grandmother?

CAESAR (*staring at her*):
Your great-great-great-grandmother! Well, why not? Nothing would surprise me on this night of nights.

CLEOPATRA:
I think it must have been. My great-grandmother's great-grandmother was a black kitten of the sacred white cat; and the river Nile made her his seventh wife. That is why my hair is so wavy. And I always want to be let do as I like, no matter whether it is the will of the gods or not: that is because my blood is made with Nile water.

CAESAR:
What are you doing here at this time of night? Do you live here?

CLEOPATRA:
Of course not: I am the Queen; and I shall live in the palace at Alexandria when I have killed my brother, who drove me out of it. When I am old enough I shall do just what I like. I shall be able to poison the slaves and see them wriggle, and pretend to Ftatateeta that she is going to be put into the fiery furnace.

CAESAR:
Hm! Meanwhile why are you not at home and in bed?

CLEOPATRA:
Because the Romans are coming to eat us all. You are not at home and in bed either.

CAESAR (*with conviction*):
Yes I am. I live in a tent; and I am now in that tent, fast asleep and dreaming. Do you suppose that I believe you are real, you impossible little dream witch?

CLEOPATRA (*giggling and leaning trustfully towards him*):
You are a funny old gentleman. I like you.

CAESAR:
Ah, that spoils the dream. Why don't you dream that I am young?

CLEOPATRA:
I wish you were; only I think I should be more afraid of you. I like men, especially young men with round strong arms; but I

am afraid of them. You are old and rather thin and stringy; but you have a nice voice; and I like to have somebody to talk to, though I think you are a little mad. It is the moon that makes you talk to yourself in that silly way.

CAESAR:

What! you heard that, did you? I was saying my prayers to the great Sphinx.

CLEOPATRA:

But this isn't the great Sphinx.

CAESAR (*much disappointed, looking up at the statue*):

What!

CLEOPATRA:

This is only a dear little kitten of the Sphinx. Why, the great Sphinx is so big that it has a temple between its paws. This is my pet Sphinx. Tell me: do you think the Romans have any sorcerers who could take us away from the Sphinx by magic?

CAESAR:

Why? Are you afraid of the Romans?

CLEOPATRA (*very seriously*):

Oh, they would eat us if they caught us. They are barbarians. Their chief is called Julius Caesar. His father was a tiger and his mother a burning mountain; and his nose is like an elephant's trunk. (Caesar *involuntarily rubs his nose.*) They all have long noses, and ivory tusks, and little tails, and seven arms with a hundred arrows in each; and they live on human flesh.

CAESAR:

Would you like me to show you a real Roman?

CLEOPATRA (*terrified*):

No. You are frightening me.

CAESAR:

No matter: this is only a dream——

CLEOPATRA (*excitedly*):

It is not a dream: it is not a dream. See, see. (*She plucks a pin from her hair and jabs it repeatedly into his arm.*)

CAESAR:

Ffff—Stop. (*Wrathfully*) How dare you?

CLEOPATRA (*abashed*):

You said you were dreaming. (*Whimpering*) I only wanted to shew you——

CAESAR (*gently*):

Come, come: don't cry. A queen mustn't cry. (*He rubs his arm, wondering at the reality of the smart.*) Am I awake? (*He strikes his hand against the Sphinx to test its solidity. It feels so real that he begins to be alarmed, and says perplexedly*) Yes, I—(*quite panic-*

*stricken*) no: impossible: madness, madness! (*Desperately*) Back to camp—to camp. (*He rises to spring down from the pedestal.*)

CLEOPATRA (*flinging her arms in terror round him*):

No: you shan't leave me. No, no, no: don't go. I'm afraid— afraid of the Romans.

CAESAR (*as the conviction that he is really awake forces itself on him*):

Cleopatra: can you see my face well?

CLEOPATRA:

Yes. It is so white in the moonlight.

CAESAR:

Are you sure it is the moonlight that makes me look whiter than an Egyptian? (*Grimly*) Do you notice that I have a rather long nose?

CLEOPATRA (*recoiling, paralyzed by a terrible suspicion*):

Oh!

CAESAR:

It is a Roman nose, Cleopatra.

CLEOPATRA:

Ah! (*With a piercing scream she springs up; darts round the left shoulder of the Sphinx; scrambles down to the sand; and falls on her knees in frantic supplication, shrieking*) Bite him in two, Sphinx: bite him in two. I meant to sacrifice the white cat—I did indeed—I (Caesar, *who has slipped down from the pedestal, touches her on the shoulder*) Ah! (*She buries her head in her arms.*)

CAESAR:

Cleopatra: shall I teach you a way to prevent Caesar from eating you?

CLEOPATRA (*clinging to him piteously*):

Oh do, do, do. I will steal Ftatateeta's jewels and give them to you. I will make the river Nile water your lands twice a year.

CAESAR:

Peace, peace, my child. Your gods are afraid of the Romans: you see the Sphinx dare not bite me, nor prevent me carrying you off to Julius Caesar.

CLEOPATRA (*in pleading murmurings*):

You won't, you won't. You said you wouldn't.

CAESAR:

Caesar never eats women.

CLEOPATRA (*springing up full of hope*):

What!

CAESAR (*impressively*):

But he eats girls (*she relapses*) and cats. Now you are a silly little girl; and you are descended from the black kitten. You are both a girl and a cat.

CLEOPATRA (*trembling*):

And will he eat me?

CAESAR:

Yes; unless you make him believe that you are a woman.

CLEOPATRA:

Oh, you must get a sorcerer to make a woman of me. Are you a sorcerer?

CAESAR:

Perhaps. But it will take a long time; and this very night you must stand face to face with Caesar in the palace of your fathers.

CLEOPATRA:

No, no. I daren't.

CAESAR:

Whatever dread may be in your soul—however terrible Caesar may be to you—you must confront him as a brave woman and a great queen; and you must feel no fear. If your hand shakes: if your voice quavers; then—night and death! (*She moans.*) But if he thinks you worthy to rule, he will set you on the throne by his side and make you the real ruler of Egypt.

CLEOPATRA (*despairingly*):

No: he will find me out: he will find me out.

CAESAR (*rather mournfully*):

He is easily deceived by women. Their eyes dazzle him; and he sees them not as they are, but as he wishes them to appear to him.

CLEOPATRA (*hopefully*):

Then we will cheat him. I will put on Ftatateeta's head-dress; and he will think me quite an old woman.

CAESAR:

If you do that he will eat you at one mouthful.

CLEOPATRA:

But I will give him a cake with my magic opal and seven hairs of the white cat baked in it; and——

CAESAR (*abruptly*):

Pah! you are a little fool. He will eat your cake and you too. (*He turns contemptuously from her.*)

CLEOPATRA (*running after him and clinging to him*):

Oh, please, please! I will do whatever you tell me. I will be good! I will be your slave. (*Again the terrible bellowing note sounds across the desert, now closer at hand. It is the bucina, the Roman war trumpet.*)

CAESAR:

Hark!

CLEOPATRA (*trembling*):

What was that?

CAESAR:

Caesar's voice.

CLEOPATRA (*pulling at his hand*):

Let us run away. Come. Oh, come.

CAESAR:

You are safe with me until you stand on your throne to receive Caesar. Now lead me thither.

CLEOPATRA (*only too glad to get away*):

I will, I will. (*Again the bucina.*) Oh, come, come, come: the gods are angry. Do you feel the earth shaking?

CAESAR:

It is the tread of Caesar's legions.

CLEOPATRA (*drawing him away*):

This way, quickly. And let us look for the white cat as we go. It is he that has turned you into a Roman.

CAESAR:

Incorrigible, oh, incorrigible! Away! (*He follows her, the bucina sounding louder as they steal across the desert. The moonlight wanes: the horizon again shows black against the sky, broken only by the fantastic silhouette of the Sphinx. The sky itself vanishes in darkness, from which there is no relief until the gleam of a distant torch falls on great Egyptian pillars supporting the roof of a majestic corridor. At the further end of this corridor a* Nubian slave *appears carrying the torch. Caesar, still led by* Cleopatra, *follows him. They come down the corridor,* Caesar *peering keenly about at the strange architecture, and at the pillar shadows between which, as the passing torch makes them hurry noiselessly backwards, figures of men with wings and hawks' heads, and vast black marble cats, seem to flit in and out of ambush. Further along, the wall turns a corner and makes a spacious transept in which* Caesar *sees, on his right, a throne, and behind the throne a door. On each side of the throne is a slender pillar with a lamp on it.*)

CAESAR:

What place is this?

CLEOPATRA:

This is where I sit on the throne when I am allowed to wear my crown and robes. (*The slave holds his torch to shew the throne.*)

CAESAR:

Order the slave to light the lamps.

CLEOPATRA (*shyly*):

Do you think I may?

CAESAR:

Of course. You are the Queen. (*She hesitates.*) Go on.

CLEOPATRA (*timidly, to the* slave):

Light all the lamps.

FTATATEETA (*suddenly coming from behind the throne*):

Stop. (*The* slave *stops. She turns sternly to* Cleopatra, *who quails like a naughty child.*) Who is this you have with you; and how dare you order the lamps to be lighted without my permission? (Cleopatra *is dumb with apprehension.*)

CAESAR:

Who is she?

CLEOPATRA:

Ftatateeta.

FTATATEETA (*arrogantly*):

Chief nurse to——

CAESAR (*cutting her short*):

I speak to the Queen. Be silent. (*To* Cleopatra) Is this how your servants know their places? Send her away; and do you (*to the* slave) do as the Queen has bidden. (*The* slave *lights the lamps. Meanwhile* Cleopatra *stands hesitating, afraid of* Ftatateeta.) You are the Queen: send her away.

CLEOPATRA (*cajoling*):

Ftatateeta, dear: you must go away—just for a little.

CAESAR:

You are not commanding her to go away: you are begging her. You are no Queen. You will be eaten. Farewell. (*He turns to go.*)

CLEOPATRA (*clutching him*):

No, no, no. Don't leave me.

CAESAR:

A Roman does not stay with queens who are afraid of their slaves.

CLEOPATRA:

I am not afraid. Indeed I am not afraid.

FTATATEETA:

We shall see who is afraid here. (*Menacingly*) Cleopatra——

CAESAR:

On your knees, woman: am I also a child that you dare trifle with me? (*He points to the floor at* Cleopatra's *feet.* Ftatateeta, *half cowed, half savage, hesitates.* Caesar *calls to the* Nubian) Slave. (*The* Nubian *comes to him.*) Can you cut off a head? (*The* Nubian *nods and grins ecstatically, showing all his teeth.* Caesar *takes his sword by the scabbard, ready to offer the hilt to the* Nubian, *and turns again to* Ftatateeta, *repeating his gesture.*) Have you remembered yourself, mistress?

Ftatateeta, *crushed, kneels before* Cleopatra, *who can hardly believe her eyes.*

FTATATEETA (*hoarsely*):

O Queen, forget not thy servant in the days of thy greatness.

CLEOPATRA (*blazing with excitement*):

Go. Begone. Go away. (Ftatateeta *rises with stooped head, and moves backwards towards the door.* Cleopatra *watches her submission eagerly, almost clapping her hands, which are trembling. Suddenly she cries*) Give me something to beat her with. (*She snatches a snake-skin from the throne and dashes after* Ftatateeta, *whirling it like a scourge in the air.* Caesar *makes a bound and manages to catch her and hold her while* Ftatateeta *escapes.*)

CAESAR:

You scratch, kitten, do you?

CLEOPATRA (*breaking from him*):

I will beat somebody. I will beat him. (*She attacks the* slave.) There, there, there! (*The* slave *flies for his life up the corridor and vanishes. She throws the snake-skin away and jumps on the step of the throne with her arms waving, crying*) I am a real Queen at last—a real, real Queen! Cleopatra the Queen! (Caesar *shakes his head dubiously, the advantage of the change seeming open to question from the point of view of the general welfare of Egypt. She turns and looks at him exultantly. Then she jumps down from the step, runs to him, and flings her arms round him rapturously, crying*) Oh, I love you for making me a Queen.

CAESAR:

But queens love only kings.

CLEOPATRA:

I will make all the men I love kings. I will make you a king. I will have many young kings, with round, strong arms; and when I am tired of them I will whip them to death; but you shall always be my king: my nice, kind, wise, good old king.

CAESAR:

Oh, my wrinkles, my wrinkles! And my child's heart! You will be the most dangerous of all Caesar's conquests.

CLEOPATRA (*appalled*):

Caesar! I forgot Caesar. (*Anxiously*) You will tell him that I am a Queen, will you not?—a real Queen. Listen! (*stealthily coaxing him*) let us run away and hide until Caesar is gone.

CAESAR:

If you fear Caesar, you are no true Queen; and though you were to hide beneath a pyramid, he would go straight to it and lift it with one hand. And then—! (*He chops his teeth together.*)

CLEOPATRA (*trembling*):

    Oh!

CAESAR:

    Be afraid if you dare. (*The note of the bucina resounds again in the distance. She moans with fear. Caesar exults in it, exclaiming*) Aha! Caesar approaches the throne of Cleopatra. Come: take your place. (*He takes her hand and leads her to the throne. She is too downcast to speak.*) Ho, there, Teetatota. How do you call your slaves?

CLEOPATRA (*spiritlessly, as she sinks on the throne and cowers there, shaking*):

    Clap your hands.

        *He claps his hands.* Ftatateeta *returns.*

CAESAR:

    Bring the Queen's robes, and her crown, and her women; and prepare her.

CLEOPATRA (*eagerly—recovering herself a little*):

    Yes, the crown, Ftatateeta: I shall wear the crown.

FTATATEETA:

    For whom must the Queen put on her state?

CAESAR:

    For a citizen of Rome. A king of kings, Totateeta.

CLEOPATRA (*stamping at her*):

    How dare you ask questions? Go and do as you are told. (*Ftatateeta goes out with a grim smile. Cleopatra goes on eagerly, to Caesar*) Caesar will know that I am a Queen when he sees my crown and robes, will he not?

CAESAR:

    No. How shall he know that you are not a slave dressed up in the Queen's ornaments?

CLEOPATRA:

    You must tell him.

CAESAR:

    He will not ask me. He will know Cleopatra by her pride, her courage, her majesty, and her beauty. (*She looks very doubtful.*) Are you trembling?

CLEOPATRA (*shivering with dread*):

    No, I—I—(*in a very sickly voice*) No.

    Ftatateeta *and three women* come in with the regalia.

FTATATEETA:

> Of all the Queen's women, these three alone are left. The rest are fled. (*They begin to deck* Cleopatra, *who submits, pale and motionless.*)

CAESAR:

> Good, good. Three are enough. Poor Caesar generally has to dress himself.

FTATATEETA (*contemptuously*):

> The Queen of Egypt is not a Roman barbarian. (*To* Cleopatra) Be brave, my nursling. Hold up your head before this stranger.

CAESAR (*admiring* Cleopatra, *and placing the crown on her head*):

> Is it sweet or bitter to be a Queen, Cleopatra?

CLEOPATRA:

> Bitter.

CAESAR:

> Cast our fear; and you will conquer Caesar. Tota: are the Romans at hand?

FTATATEETA:

> They are at hand; and the guard has fled.

THE WOMEN (*wailing subduedly*):

> Woe to us!

*The* Nubian *comes running down the hall.*

NUBIAN:

> The Romans are in the courtyard. (*He bolts through the door. With a shriek, the women fly after him. Ftatateeta's jaw expresses savage resolution: she does not budge.* Cleopatra *can hardly restrain herself from following them.* Caesar *grips her wrist, and looks steadfastly at her. She stands like a martyr.*)

CAESAR:

> The Queen must face Caesar alone. Answer "So be it."

CLEOPATRA (*white*):

> So be it.

CAESAR (*releasing her*):

> Good.

*A tramp and tumult of armed men is heard.* Cleopatra's *terror increases. The bucina sounds close at hand, followed by a formidable clangor of trumpets. This is too much for* Cleopatra: *she utters a cry and darts towards the door.* Ftatateeta *stops her ruthlessly.*

FTATATEETA:

> You are my nursling. You have said "So be it"; and if you die for it, you must make the Queen's word good. (*She hands*

Cleopatra *to Caesar, who takes her back, almost beside herself with apprehension, to the throne.*)

CAESAR:

Now, if you quail—! (*He seats himself on the throne.*)

*She stands on the step, all but unconscious, waiting for death. The Roman soldiers troop in tumultuously through the corridor, headed by their ensign with his eagle, and their bucinator, a burly fellow with his instrument coiled round his body, its brazen bell shaped like the head of a howling wolf. When they reach the transept, they stare in amazement at the throne; dress into ordered rank opposite it; draw their swords and lift them in the air with a shout of* Hail, Caesar. Cleopatra *turns and stares wildly at* Caesar; *grasps the situation; and, with a great sob of relief, falls into his arms.*

# Act II

*Alexandria. A hall on the first floor of the Palace, ending in a loggia approached by two steps. Through the arches of the loggia the Mediterranean can be seen, bright in the morning sun. The clean lofty walls, painted with a procession of the Egyptian theocracy, presented in profile as flat ornament, and the absence of mirrors, sham perspectives, stuffy upholstery and textiles, make the place handsome, wholesome, simple and cool, or, as a rich English manufacturer would express it, poor, bare, ridiculous and unhomely. For Tottenham Court Road civilization is to this Egyptian civilization as glass bead and tattoo civilization is to Tottenham Court Road.*

*The young king* Ptolemy Dionysus (*aged ten*) *is at the top of the steps, on his way in through the loggia, led by his guardian* Pothinus, *who has him by the hand. The court is assembled to receive him. It is made up of men and women (some of the women being officials) of various complexions and races, mostly Egyptian; some of them, comparatively fair, from lower Egypt; some, much darker, from upper Egypt; with a few Greeks and Jews. Prominent in a group on* Ptolemy's *right hand is* Theodotus, Ptolemy's *tutor. Another group, on* Ptolemy's *left, is headed by* Achillas, *the general of* Ptolemy's *troops.* Theodotus *is a little old man, whose features are as cramped and wizened as his limbs, except his tall straight forehead, which occupies more space than all the rest of his face. He maintains an air of magpie keenness and profundity, listening to what the others say with the sarcastic vigilance of a philosopher listening to the exercises of his disciples.* Achillas *is a tall handsome man of thirty-five, with a fine black beard curled like the coat of a poodle. Apparently not a clever man, but distinguished and dignified.* Pothinus *is a vigorous man of fifty, a eunuch, passionate, energetic and quick witted, but of common mind and character; impatient and unable to control his temper. He has fine tawny hair, like fur. Ptolemy, the King, looks much older than an English boy of ten; but he has the childish air, the habit of being in leading strings, the mixture of impotence and petulance, the appearance of being excessively washed, combed and dressed by other hands, which is exhibited by court-bred princes of all ages.*

*All receive the King with reverences. He comes down the steps to a chair of state which stands a little to his right, the only seat in the hall. Taking his place before it, he looks nervously for instructions to Pothinus, who places himself at his left hand.*

POTHINUS:
    The King of Egypt has a word to speak.

THEODOTUS (*in a squeak which he makes impressive by sheer self-opinionativeness*):
    Peace for the King's word!

PTOLEMY (*without any vocal inflexions: he is evidently repeating a lesson*):
    Take notice of this all of you. I am the firstborn son of Auletes the Flute Blower who was your King. My sister Berenice drove him from his throne and reigned in his stead but—but (*he hesitates*)——

POTHINUS (*stealthily prompting*):
    —but the gods would not suffer——

PTOLEMY:
    Yes—the gods would not suffer—not suffer—(*he stops; then, crestfallen*) I forget what the gods would not suffer.

THEODOTUS:
    Let Pothinus, the King's guardian, speak for the King.

POTHINUS (*suppressing his impatience with difficulty*):
    The King wished to say that the gods would not suffer the impiety of his sister to go unpunished.

PTOLEMY (*hastily*):
    Yes: I remember the rest of it. (*He resumes his monotone.*) Therefore the gods sent a stranger, one Mark Antony, a Roman captain of horsemen, across the sands of the desert and he set my father again upon the throne. And my father took Berenice my sister and struck her head off. And now that my father is dead yet another of his daughters, my sister Cleopatra, would snatch the kingdom from me and reign in my place. But the gods would not suffer (Pothinus *coughs admonitorily*)—the gods—the gods would not suffer——

POTHINUS (*prompting*):
    —will not maintain——

PTOLEMY:

    Oh yes—will not maintain such iniquity, they will give her head to the axe even as her sister's. But with the help of the witch Ftatateeta she hath cast a spell on the Roman Julius Caesar to make him uphold her false pretence to rule in Egypt. Take notice then that I will not suffer—that I will not suffer— (*pettishly, to* Pothinus) What is it that I will not suffer?

POTHINUS (*suddenly exploding with all the force and emphasis of political passion*):

    The King will not suffer a foreigner to take from him the throne of our Egypt. (*A shout of applause.*) Tell the King, Achillas, how many soldiers and horsemen follow the Roman?

THEODOTUS:

    Let the King's general speak!

ACHILLAS:

    But two Roman legions, O King. Three thousand soldiers and scarce a thousand horsemen.

*The court breaks into derisive laughter; and a great chattering begins, amid which* Rufio, *a Roman officer, appears in the loggia. He is a burly, black-bearded man of middle age, very blunt, prompt and rough, with small clear eyes, and plump nose and cheeks, which, however, like the rest of his flesh, are in ironhard condition.*

RUFIO (*from the steps*):

    Peace, ho! (*The laughter and chatter cease abruptly.*) Caesar approaches.

THEODOTUS (*with much presence of mind*):

    The King permits the Roman commander to enter!

Caesar, *plainly dressed, but wearing an oak wreath to conceal his baldness, enters from the loggia, attended by* Britannus, *his secretary, a Briton, about forty, tall, solemn, and already slightly bald, with a heavy, drooping, hazel-colored moustache trained so as to lose its ends in a pair of trim whiskers. He is carefully dressed in blue, with portfolio, inkhorn, and reed pen at his girdle. His serious air and sense of the importance of the business in hand is in marked contrast to the kindly interest of* Caesar, *who looks at the scene, which is new to him, with the frank curiosity of a child, and then turns to the King's chair:* Britannus *and* Rufio *posting themselves near the steps at the other side.*

CAESAR (*looking at* Pothinus *and* Ptolemy):

    Which is the King? the man or the boy?

POTHINUS:

>I am Pothinus, the guardian of my lord the King.

CAESAR (*patting* Ptolemy *kindly on the shoulder*):

>So you are the King. Dull work at your age, eh? (*To* Pothinus)
>Your servant, Pothinus. (*He turns away unconcernedly and comes
>slowly along the middle of the hall, looking from side to side at the
>courtiers until he reaches* Achillas.) And this gentleman?

THEODOTUS:

>Achillas, the King's general.

CAESAR (*to* Achillas, *very friendly*):

>A general, eh? I am a general myself. But I began too old, too
>old. Health and many victories, Achillas!

ACHILLAS:

>As the gods will, Caesar.

CAESAR (*turning to* Theodotus):

>And you, sir, are——?

THEODOTUS:

>Theodotus, the King's tutor.

CAESAR:

>You teach men how to be kings, Theodotus. That is very
>clever of you. (*Looking at the gods on the walls as he turns
>away from* Theodotus *and goes up again to* Pothinus). And
>this place?

POTHINUS:

>The council chamber of the chancellors of the King's treasury,
>Caesar.

CAESAR:

>Ah! that reminds me. I want some money.

POTHINUS:

>The King's treasury is poor, Caesar.

CAESAR:

>Yes: I notice that there is but one chair in it.

RUFIO (*shouting gruffly*):

>Bring a chair there, some of you, for Caesar.

PTOLEMY (*rising shyly to offer his chair*):

>Caesar——

CAESAR (*kindly*):

>No, no, my boy: that is your chair of state. Sit down.

*He makes* Ptolemy *sit down again. Meanwhile* Rufio, *looking about
him, sees in the nearest corner an image of the god Ra, represented as a
seated man with the head of a hawk. Before the image is a bronze tripod,
about as large as a three-legged stool, with a stick of incense burning on it.*
Rufio, *with Roman resourcefulness and indifference to foreign supersti-*

*tions, promptly seizes the tripod; shakes off the incense; blows away the ash; and dumps it down behind* Caesar, *nearly in the middle of the hall.*

RUFIO:

Sit on that, Caesar.

*A shiver runs through the court, followed by a hissing whisper of* Sacrilege!

CAESAR (*seating himself*):

Now, Pothinus, to business. I am badly in want of money.

BRITANNUS (*disapproving of these informal expressions*):

My master would say that there is a lawful debt due to Rome by Egypt, contracted by the King's deceased father to the Triumvirate; and that it is Caesar's duty to his country to require immediate payment.

CAESAR (*blandly*):

Ah, I forgot. I have not made my companions known here. Pothinus: this is Britannus, my secretary. He is an islander from the western end of the world, a day's voyage from Gaul. (*Britannus bows stiffly.*) This gentleman is Rufio, my comrade in arms. (Rufio *nods.*) Pothinus: I want 1,600 talents.

*The courtiers, appalled, murmur loudly, and* Theodotus *and* Achillas *appeal mutely to one another against so monstrous a demand.*

POTHINUS (*aghast*):

Forty million sesterces! Impossible. There is not so much money in the King's treasury.

CAESAR (*encouragingly*):

Only sixteen hundred talents, Pothinus. Why count it in sesterces? A sestertius is only worth a loaf of bread.

POTHINUS:

And a talent is worth a racehorse. I say it is impossible. We have been at strife here, because the King's sister Cleopatra falsely claims his throne. The King's taxes have not been collected for a whole year.

CAESAR:

Yes they have, Pothinus. My officers have been collecting them all the morning. (*Renewed whisper and sensation, not without some stifled laughter, among the courtiers.*)

RUFIO (*bluntly*):

You must pay, Pothinus. Why waste words? You are getting off cheaply enough.

POTHINUS (*bitterly*):

> Is it possible that Caesar, the conqueror of the world, has time to occupy himself with such a trifle as our taxes?

CAESAR:

> My friend: taxes are the chief business of a conqueror of the world.

POTHINUS:

> Then take warning, Caesar. This day, the treasures of the temples and the gold of the King's treasury shall be sent to the mint to be melted down for our ransom in the sight of the people. They shall see us sitting under bare walls and drinking from wooden cups. And their wrath be on your head, Caesar, if you force us to this sacrilege!

CAESAR:

> Do not fear, Pothinus: the people know how well wine tastes in wooden cups. In return for your bounty, I will settle this dispute about the throne for you, if you will. What say you?

POTHINUS:

> If I say no, will that hinder you?

RUFIO (*defiantly*):

> No.

CAESAR:

> You say the matter has been at issue for a year, Pothinus. May I have ten minutes at it?

POTHINUS:

> You will do your pleasure, doubtless.

CAESAR:

> Good! But first, let us have Cleopatra here.

THEODOTUS:

> She is not in Alexandria: she is fled into Syria.

CAESAR:

> I think not. (*To* Rufio) Call Totateeta.

RUFIO (*calling*):

> Ho there, Teetatota.

Ftatateeta *enters the loggia, and stands arrogantly at the top of the steps.*

FTATATEETA:

> Who pronounces the name of Ftatateeta, the Queen's chief nurse?

CAESAR:

> Nobody can pronounce it, Tota, except yourself. Where is your mistress?

Cleopatra, *who is hiding behind* Ftatateeta, *peeps out at them, laughing.* Caesar *rises.*

CAESAR:
Will the Queen favor us with her presence for a moment?

CLEOPATRA (*pushing* Ftatateeta *aside and standing haughtily on the brink of the steps*):
Am I to behave like a Queen?

CAESAR:
Yes.

Cleopatra *immediately comes down to the chair of state; seizes* Ptolemy *and drags him out of his seat; then takes his place in the chair.* Ftatateeta *seats herself on the step of the loggia, and sits there, watching the scene with sybilline intensity.*

PTOLEMY (*mortified, and struggling with his tears*):
Caesar: this is how she treats me always. If I am a king why is she allowed to take everything from me?

CLEOPATRA:
You are not to be King, you little cry-baby. You are to be eaten by the Romans.

CAESAR (*touched by* Ptolemy's *distress*):
Come here, my boy, and stand by me.

Ptolemy *goes over to* Caesar, *who, resuming his seat on the tripod, takes the boy's hand to encourage him.* Cleopatra, *furiously jealous, rises and glares at them.*

CLEOPATRA (*with flaming cheeks*):
Take your throne: I don't want it. (*She flings away from the chair, and approaches* Ptolemy, *who shrinks from her.*) Go this instant and sit down in your place.

CAESAR:
Go, Ptolemy. Always take a throne when it is offered to you.

RUFIO:
I hope you will have the good sense to follow your own advice when we return to Rome, Caesar.

Ptolemy *slowly goes back to the throne, giving* Cleopatra *a wide berth, in evident fear of her hands. She takes his place beside* Caesar.

CAESAR:
Pothinus——

CLEOPATRA (*interrupting him*):

> Are you not going to speak to me?

CAESAR:

> Be quiet. Open your mouth again before I give you leave; and you shall be eaten.

CLEOPATRA:

> I am not afraid. A queen must not be afraid. Eat my husband there, if you like: he is afraid.

CAESAR (*starting*):

> Your husband! What do you mean?

CLEOPATRA (*pointing to* Ptolemy):

> That little thing.

*The two Romans and the Briton stare at one another in amazement.*

THEODOTUS:

> Caesar: you are a stranger here, and not conversant with our laws. The kings and queens of Egypt may not marry except with their own royal blood. Ptolemy and Cleopatra are born king and consort just as they are born brother and sister.

BRITANNUS (*shocked*):

> Caesar: this is not proper.

THEODOTUS (*outraged*):

> How!

CAESAR (*recovering his self-possession*):

> Pardon him, Theodotus: he is a barbarian, and thinks that the customs of his tribe and island are the laws of nature.

BRITANNUS:

> On the contrary, Caesar, it is these Egyptians who are barbarians; and you do wrong to encourage them. I say it is a scandal.

CAESAR:

> Scandal or not, my friend, it opens the gate of peace. (*He rises and addresses* Pothinus *seriously*) Pothinus: hear what I propose.

RUFIO:

> Hear Caesar there.

CAESAR:

> Ptolemy and Cleopatra shall reign jointly in Egypt.

ACHILLAS:

> What of the King's younger brother and Cleopatra's younger sister?

RUFIO (*explaining*):

> There is another little Ptolemy, Caesar: so they tell me.

CAESAR:

> Well, the little Ptolemy can marry the other sister; and we will make them both a present of Cyprus.

POTHINUS (*impatiently*):

> Cyprus is of no use to anybody.

CAESAR:

> No matter: you shall have it for the sake of peace.

BRITANNUS (*unconsciously anticipating a later statesman*):

> Peace with honor, Pothinus.

POTHINUS (*mutinously*):

> Caesar: be honest. The money you demand is the price of our freedom. Take it; and leave us to settle our own affairs.

THE BOLDER COURTIERS (*encouraged by* Pothinus's *tone and* Caesar's *quietness*):

> Yes, yes. Egypt for the Egyptians!

*The conference now becomes an altercation, the Egyptians becoming more and more heated.* Caesar *remains unruffled; but* Rufio *grows fiercer and doggeder, and* Britannus *haughtily indignant.*

RUFIO (*contemptuously*):

> Egypt for the Egyptians! Do you forget that there is a Roman army of occupation here, left by Aulus Gabinius when he set up your toy king for you?

ACHILLAS (*suddenly asserting himself*):

> And now under my command. *I* am the Roman general here, Caesar.

CAESAR (*tickled by the humor of the situation*):

> And also the Egyptian general, eh?

POTHINUS (*triumphantly*):

> That is so, Caesar.

CAESAR (*to* Achillas):

> So you can make war on the Egyptians in the name of Rome, and on the Romans—on me, if necessary—in the name of Egypt?

ACHILLAS:

> That is so, Caesar.

CAESAR:

> And which side are you on at present, if I may presume to ask, general?

ACHILLAS:

> On the side of the right and of the gods.

CAESAR:

> Hm! How many men have you?

ACHILLAS:

That will appear when I take the field.

RUFIO (*truculently*):

Are your men Romans? If not, it matters not how many there are, provided you are no stronger than 500 to ten.

POTHINUS:

It is useless to try to bluff us, Rufio. Caesar has been defeated before and may be defeated again. A few weeks ago Caesar was flying for his life before Pompey: a few months hence he may be flying for his life before Cato and Juba of Numidia, the African King.

ACHILLAS (*following up* Pothinus's *speech menacingly*):

What can you do with 4,000 men?

THEODOTUS (*following up* Achillas's *speech with a raucous squeak*):

And without money? Away with you.

ALL THE COURTIERS (*shouting fiercely and crowding towards* Caesar):

Away with you. Egypt for the Egyptians! Begone.

Rufio *bites his beard, too angry to speak.* Caesar *sits as comfortably as if he were at breakfast, and the cat were clamoring for a piece of Finnan-haddie.*

CLEOPATRA:

Why do you let them talk to you like that, Caesar? Are you afraid?

CAESAR:

Why, my dear, what they say is quite true.

CLEOPATRA:

But if you go away, I shall not be Queen.

CAESAR:

I shall not go away until you are Queen.

POTHINUS:

Achillas: if you are not a fool, you will take that girl whilst she is under your hand.

RUFIO (*daring them*):

Why not take Caesar as well, Achillas?

POTHINUS (*retorting the defiance with interest*):

Well said, Rufio. Why not?

RUFIO:

Try, Achillas. (*Calling*) Guard there.

*The loggia immediately fills with* Caesar's *soldiers, who stand, sword in hand, at the top of the steps, waiting the word to charge from their centurion, who carries a cudgel. For a moment the Egyptians face them proudly: then they retire sullenly to their former places.*

BRITANNUS:

You are Caesar's prisoners, all of you.

CAESAR (*benevolently*):

Oh no, no, no. By no means. Caesar's guests, gentlemen.

CLEOPATRA:

Won't you cut their heads off?

CAESAR:

What! Cut off your brother's head?

CLEOPATRA:

Why not? He would cut off mine, if he got the chance. Wouldn't you, Ptolemy?

PTOLEMY (*pale and obstinate*):

I would. I will, too, when I grow up.

Cleopatra *is rent by a struggle between her newly-acquired dignity as a queen, and a strong impulse to put out her tongue at him. She takes no part in the scene which follows, but watches it with curiosity and wonder, fidgeting with the restlessness of a child, and sitting down on* Caesar's *tripod when he rises.*

POTHINUS:

Caesar: if you attempt to detain us——

RUFIO:

He will succeed, Egyptian: make up your mind to that. We hold the palace, the beach, and the eastern harbor. The road to Rome is open; and you shall travel it if Caesar chooses.

CAESAR (*courteously*):

I could do no less, Pothinus, to secure the retreat of my own soldiers. I am accountable for every life among them. But you are free to go. So are all here, and in the palace.

RUFIO (*aghast at this clemency*):

What! Renegades and all?

CAESAR (*softening the expression*):

Roman army of occupation and all, Rufio.

POTHINUS (*desperately*):

Then I make a last appeal to Caesar's justice. I shall call a witness to prove that but for us, the Roman army of occupation, led by the greatest soldier in the world, would now have Caesar at its mercy. (*Calling through the loggia*) Ho, there, Lucius Septimius (Caesar *starts, deeply moved*): if my voice can reach you, come forth and testify before Caesar.

CAESAR (*shrinking*):

No, no.

THEODOTUS:

Yes, I say. Let the military tribune bear witness.

Lucius Septimius, *a clean shaven, trim athlete of about 40, with sym-metrical features, resolute mouth, and handsome, thin Roman nose, in the dress of a Roman officer, comes in through the loggia and confronts Caesar, who hides his face with his robe for a moment; then, mastering himself, drops it, and confronts the tribune with dignity.*

POTHINUS:

Bear witness, Lucius Septimius. Caesar came hither in pursuit of his foe. Did we shelter his foe?

LUCIUS:

As Pompey's foot touched the Egyptian shore, his head fell by the stroke of my sword.

THEODOTUS (*with viperish relish*):

Under the eyes of his wife and child! Remember that, Caesar! They saw it from the ship he had just left. We have given you a full and sweet measure of vengeance.

CAESAR (*with horror*):

Vengeance!

POTHINUS:

Our first gift to you, as your galley came into the roadstead, was the head of your rival for the empire of the world. Bear witness, Lucius Septimius: is it not so?

LUCIUS:

It is so. With this hand, that slew Pompey, I placed his head at the feet of Caesar.

CAESAR:

Murderer! So would you have slain Caesar, had Pompey been victorious at Pharsalia.

LUCIUS:

Woe to the vanquished, Caesar! When I served Pompey, I slew as good men as he, only because he conquered them. His turn came at last.

THEODOTUS (*flatteringly*):

The deed was not yours, Caesar, but ours—nay, mine; for it was done by my counsel. Thanks to us, you keep your reputa-tion for clemency, and have your vengeance too.

CAESAR:

Vengeance! Vengeance!! Oh, if I could stoop to vengeance, what would I not exact from you as the price of this murdered man's blood. (*They shrink back, appalled and disconcerted.*) Was he not my son-in-law, my ancient friend, for 20 years the master of great Rome, for 30 years the compeller of victory? Did not I, as a Roman, share his glory? Was the Fate that forced us to fight for the mastery of the world, of our making? Am I Julius Caesar, or am I a wolf, that you fling to me the grey head of the old soldier, the laurelled conqueror, the mighty Roman, treacherously struck down by this callous ruffian, and then claim my gratitude for it! (*To* Lucius Septimius) Begone: you fill me with horror.

LUCIUS (*cold and undaunted*):

Pshaw! you have seen severed heads before, Caesar, and severed right hands too, I think; some thousands of them, in Gaul, after you vanquished Vercingetorix. Did you spare him, with all your clemency? Was that vengeance?

CAESAR:

No, by the gods! would that it had been! Vengeance at least is human. No, I say: those severed right hands, and the brave Vercingetorix basely strangled in a vault beneath the Capitol, were (*with shuddering satire*) a wise severity, a necessary protection to the commonwealth, a duty of statesmanship—follies and fictions ten times bloodier than honest vengeance! What a fool was I then! To think that men's lives should be at the mercy of such fools! (*Humbly*) Lucius Septimius, pardon me: why should the slayer of Vercingetorix rebuke the slayer of Pompey? You are free to go with the rest. Or stay if you will: I will find a place for you in my service.

LUCIUS:

The odds are against you, Caesar. I go. (*He turns to go out through the loggia.*)

RUFIO (*full of wrath at seeing his prey escaping*):

That means that he is a Republican.

LUCIUS (*turning defiantly on the loggia steps*):

And what are you?

RUFIO:

A Caesarian, like all Caesar's soldiers.

CAESAR (*courteously*):

Lucius: believe me, Caesar is no Caesarian. Were Rome a true republic, then were Caesar the first of Republicans. But you have made your choice. Farewell.

LUCIUS:

Farewell. Come, Achillas, whilst there is yet time.

Caesar, *seeing that* Rufio's *temper threatens to get the worse of him, puts his hand on his shoulder and brings him down the hall out of harm's way,* Britannus *accompanying them and posting himself on*

*Caesar's right hand. This movement brings the three in a little group to the place occupied by* Achillas, *who moves haughtily away and joins* Theodotus *on the other side.* Lucius Septimius *goes out through the soldiers in the loggia.* Pothinus, Theodotus *and* Achillas *follow him with the courtiers, very mistrustful of the soldiers, who close up in their rear and go out after them, keeping them moving without much ceremony. The* King *is left in his chair, piteous, obstinate, with twitching face and fingers. During these movements* Rufio *maintains an energetic grumbling, as follows:—*

RUFIO (*as* Lucius *departs*):
Do you suppose he would let us go if he had our heads in his hands?

CAESAR:
I have no right to suppose that his ways are any baser than mine.

RUFIO:
Psha!

CAESAR:
Rufio: if I take Lucius Septimius for my model, and become exactly like him, ceasing to be Caesar, will you serve me still?

BRITANNUS:
Caesar: this is not good sense. Your duty to Rome demands that her enemies should be prevented from doing further mischief. (Caesar, *whose delight in the moral eye-to-business of his British secretary is inexhaustible, smiles indulgently.*)

RUFIO:
It is no use talking to him, Britannus: you may save your breath to cool your porridge. But mark this, Caesar. Clemency is very well for you; but what is it for your soldiers, who have to fight to-morrow the men you spared yesterday? You may give what orders you please; but I tell you that your next victory will be a massacre, thanks to your clemency. *I,* for one, will take no prisoners. I will kill my enemies in the field; and then you can preach as much clemency as you please: I shall never have to fight them again. And now, with your leave, I will see these gentry off the premises. (*He turns to go.*)

CAESAR (*turning also and seeing* Ptolemy):
What! have they left the boy alone! Oh shame, shame!

RUFIO (*taking* Ptolemy's *hand and making him rise*):
Come, your majesty!

PTOLEMY (*to* Caesar, *drawing away his hand from* Rufio):
Is he turning me out of my palace?

RUFIO (*grimly*):

> You are welcome to stay if you wish.

CAESAR (*kindly*):

> Go, my boy. I will not harm you; but you will be safer away, among your friends. Here you are in the lion's mouth.

PTOLEMY (*turning to go*):

> It is not the lion I fear, but (*looking at* Rufio) the jackal. (*He goes out through the loggia.*)

CAESAR (*laughing approvingly*):

> Brave boy!

CLEOPATRA (*jealous of* Caesar's *approbation, calling after* Ptolemy):

> Little silly. You think that very clever.

CAESAR:

> Britannus: attend the King. Give him in charge to that Pothinus fellow. (Britannus *goes out after* Ptolemy.)

RUFIO (*pointing to* Cleopatra):

> And this piece of goods? What is to be done with her? However, I suppose I may leave that to you. (*He goes out through the loggia.*)

CLEOPATRA (*flushing suddenly and turning on* Caesar):

> Did you mean me to go with the rest?

CAESAR (*a little preoccupied, goes with a sigh to* Ptolemy's *chair, whilst she waits for his answer with red cheeks and clenched fists*):

> You are free to do just as you please, Cleopatra.

CLEOPATRA:

> Then you do not care whether I stay or not?

CAESAR (*smiling*):

> Of course I had rather you stayed.

CLEOPATRA:

> Much, much rather?

CAESAR (*nodding*):

> Much, much rather.

CLEOPATRA:

> Then I consent to stay, because I am asked. But I do not want to, mind.

CAESAR:

> That is quite understood. (*Calling*) Totateeta.

Ftatateeta, *still seated, turns her eyes on him with a sinister expression, but does not move.*

CLEOPATRA (*with a splutter of laughter*):

> Her name is not Totateeta: it is Ftatateeta. (*Calling*) Ftatateeta. (Ftatateeta *instantly rises and comes to* Cleopatra.)

CAESAR (*stumbling over the name*):

> Tfatafeeta will forgive the erring tongue of a Roman. Tota: the Queen will hold her state here in Alexandria. Engage women to attend upon her; and do all that is needful.

FTATATEETA:

> Am I then the mistress of the Queen's household?

CLEOPATRA (*sharply*):

> No: *I* am the mistress of the Queen's household. Go and do as you are told, or I will have you thrown into the Nile this very afternoon, to poison the poor crocodiles.

CAESAR (*shocked*):

> Oh no, no.

CLEOPATRA:

> Oh yes, yes. You are very sentimental, Caesar; but you are clever; and if you do as I tell you, you will soon learn to govern.

Caesar, *quite dumbfounded by this impertinence, turns in his chair and stares at her.*

Ftatateeta, *smiling grimly, and showing a splendid set of teeth, goes, leaving them alone together.*

CAESAR:

> Cleopatra: I really think I must eat you, after all.

CLEOPATRA (*kneeling beside him and looking at him with eager interest, half real, half affected to shew how intelligent she is*):

> You must not talk to me now as if I were a child.

CAESAR:

> You have been growing up since the Sphinx introduced us the other night; and you think you know more than I do already.

CLEOPATRA (*taken down, and anxious to justify herself*):

> No: that would be very silly of me: of course I know that. But—(*suddenly*) are you angry with me?

CAESAR:

> No.

CLEOPATRA (*only half believing him*):

> Then why are you so thoughtful?

CAESAR (*rising*):

> I have work to do, Cleopatra.

CLEOPATRA (*drawing back*):

> Work! (*Offended*) You are tired of talking to me; and that is your excuse to get away from me.

CAESAR (*sitting down again to appease her*):

> Well, well: another minute. But then—work!

CLEOPATRA:

> Work! what nonsense! You must remember that you are a king now: I have made you one. Kings don't work.

CAESAR:

> Oh! Who told you that, little kitten? Eh?

CLEOPATRA:

> My father was King of Egypt; and he never worked. But he was a great king, and cut off my sister's head because she rebelled against him and took the throne from him.

CAESAR:

> Well; and how did he get his throne back again?

CLEOPATRA (*eagerly, her eyes lighting up*):

> I will tell you. A beautiful young man, with strong round arms, came over the desert with many horsemen, and slew my sister's husband and gave my father back his throne. (*Wistfully*) I was only twelve then. Oh, I wish he would come again, now that I am a queen. I would make him my husband.

CAESAR:

> It might be managed, perhaps: for it was I who sent that beautiful young man to help your father.

CLEOPATRA (*enraptured*):

> You know him!

CAESAR (*nodding*):

> I do.

CLEOPATRA:

> Has he come with you? (Caesar *shakes his head: she is cruelly disappointed.*) Oh, I wish he had, I wish he had. If only I were a little older; so that he might not think me a mere kitten, as you do! But perhaps that is because you are old. He is many, many years younger than you, is he not?

CAESAR (*as if swallowing a pill*):

> He is somewhat younger.

CLEOPATRA:

> Would he be my husband, do you think, if I asked him?

CAESAR:

> Very likely.

CLEOPATRA:

> But I should not like to ask him. Could you not persuade him to ask me—without knowing that I wanted him to?

CAESAR (*touched by her innocence of the beautiful young man's character*):

> My poor child!

CLEOPATRA:

> Why do you say that as if you were sorry for me? Does he love anyone else?

CAESAR:

I am afraid so.

CLEOPATRA (*tearfully*):

Then I shall not be his first love.

CAESAR:

Not quite the first. He is greatly admired by women.

CLEOPATRA:

I wish I could be the first. But if he loves me, I will make him kill all the rest. Tell me: is he still beautiful? Do his strong round arms shine in the sun like marble?

CAESAR:

He is in excellent condition—considering how much he eats and drinks.

CLEOPATRA:

Oh, you must not say common, earthly things about him; for I love him. He is a god.

CAESAR:

He is a great captain of horsemen, and swifter of foot than any other Roman.

CLEOPATRA:

What is his real name?

CAESAR (*puzzled*):

His real name?

CLEOPATRA:

Yes. I always call him Horus, because Horus is the most beautiful of our gods. But I want to know his real name.

CAESAR:

His name is Mark Antony.

CLEOPATRA (*musically*):

Mark Antony, Mark Antony, Mark Antony! What a beautiful name! (*She throws her arms round* Caesar's *neck.*) Oh, how I love you for sending him to help my father! Did you love my father very much?

CAESAR:

No, my child; but your father, as you say, never worked. I always work. So when he lost his crown he had to promise me 16,000 talents to get it back for him.

CLEOPATRA:

Did he ever pay you?

CAESAR:

Not in full.

CLEOPATRA:

He was quite right: it was too dear. The whole world is not worth 16,000 talents.

CAESAR:

That is perhaps true, Cleopatra. Those Egyptians who work paid as much of it as he could drag from them. The rest is still due. But as I most likely shall not get it, I must go back to my work. So you must run away for a little and send my secretary to me.

CLEOPATRA (*coaxing*):

No: I want to stay and hear you talk about Mark Antony.

CAESAR:

But if I do not get to work, Pothinus and the rest of them will cut us off from the harbor; and then the way from Rome will be blocked.

CLEOPATRA:

No matter: I don't want you to go back to Rome.

CAESAR:

But you want Mark Antony to come from it.

CLEOPATRA (*springing up*):

Oh yes, yes, yes: I forgot. Go quickly and work, Caesar; and keep the way over the sea open for my Mark Antony. (*She runs out through the loggia, kissing her hand to Mark Antony across the sea.*)

CAESAR (*going briskly up the middle of the hall to the loggia steps*):

Ho, Britannus. (*He is startled by the entry of a wounded Roman soldier, who confronts him from the upper step.*) What now?

SOLDIER (*pointing to his bandaged head*):

This, Caesar; and two of my comrades killed in the market place.

CAESAR (*quiet, but attending*):

Ay. Why?

SOLDIER:

There is an army come to Alexandria, calling itself the Roman army.

CAESAR:

The Roman army of occupation. Ay?

SOLDIER:

Commanded by one Achillas.

CAESAR:

Well?

SOLDIER:

The citizens rose against us when the army entered the gates. I was with two others in the market place when the news came. They set upon us. I cut my way out; and here I am.

CAESAR:

> Good. I am glad to see you alive. (Rufio *enters the loggia hastily, passing behind the* soldier *to look out through one of the arches at the quay beneath*.) Rufio, we are besieged.

RUFIO:

> What! Already?

CAESAR:

> Now or to-morrow: what does it matter? We shall be besieged.

Britannus *runs in.*

BRITANNUS:

> Caesar——

CAESAR (*anticipating him*):

> Yes: I know. (Rufio *and* Britannus *come down the hall from the loggia at opposite sides, past* Caesar, *who waits for a moment near the step to say to the* soldier) Comrade: give the word to turn out on the beach and stand by the boats. Get your wound attended to. Go. (*The* soldier *hurries out.* Caesar *comes down the hall between* Rufio *and* Britannus) Rufio: we have some ships in the west harbor. Burn them.

RUFIO (*staring*):

> Burn them!!

CAESAR:

> Take every boat we have in the east harbor, and seize the Pharos—that island with the lighthouse. Leave half our men behind to hold the beach and the quay outside this palace: that is the way home.

RUFIO (*disapproving strongly*):

> Are we to give up the city?

CAESAR:

> We have not got it, Rufio. This palace we have; and—what is that building next door?

RUFIO:

> The theatre.

CAESAR:

> We will have that too: it commands the strand. For the rest, Egypt for the Egyptians!

RUFIO:

> Well, you know best, I suppose. Is that all?

CAESAR:

> That is all. Are those ships burnt yet?

RUFIO:

> Be easy: I shall waste no more time. (*He runs out.*)

BRITANNUS:

Caesar: Pothinus demands speech of you. In my opinion he needs a lesson. His manner is most insolent.

CAESAR:

Where is he?

BRITANNUS:

He waits without.

CAESAR:

Ho there! admit Pothinus.

Pothinus *appears in the loggia, and comes down the hall very haughtily to Caesar's left hand.*

CAESAR:

Well, Pothinus?

POTHINUS:

I have brought you our ultimatum, Caesar.

CAESAR:

Ultimatum! The door was open: you should have gone out through it before you declared war. You are my prisoner now. (*He goes to the chair and loosens his toga.*)

POTHINUS (*scornfully*):

I your prisoner! Do you know that you are in Alexandria, and that King Ptolemy, with an army outnumbering your little troop a hundred to one, is in possession of Alexandria?

CAESAR (*unconcernedly taking off his toga and throwing it on the chair*):

Well, my friend, get out if you can. And tell your friends not to kill any more Romans in the market place. Otherwise my soldiers, who do not share my celebrated clemency, will probably kill you. Britannus: pass the word to the guard; and fetch my armor. (Britannus *runs out.* Rufio *returns.*) Well?

RUFIO (*pointing from the loggia to a cloud of smoke drifting over the harbor*):

See there! (Pothinus *runs eagerly up the steps to look out.*)

CAESAR:

What, ablaze already! Impossible!

RUFIO:

Yes, five good ships, and a barge laden with oil grappled to each. But it is not my doing: the Egyptians have saved me the trouble. They have captured the west harbor.

CAESAR (*anxiously*):

And the east harbor? The lighthouse, Rufio?

RUFIO (*with a sudden splutter of raging ill usage, coming down to* Caesar *and scolding him*):

Can I embark a legion in five minutes? The first cohort is already on the beach. We can do no more. If you want faster work, come and do it yourself?

CAESAR (*soothing him*):

Good, good. Patience, Rufio, patience.

RUFIO:

Patience! Who is impatient here, you or I? Would I be here, if I could not oversee them from that balcony?

CAESAR:

Forgive me, Rufio; and (*anxiously*) hurry them as much as——

*He is interrupted by an outcry as of an old man in the extremity of misfortune. It draws near rapidly; and* Theodotus *rushes in, tearing his hair, and squeaking the most lamentable exclamations.* Rufio *steps back to stare at him, amazed at his frantic condition.* Pothinus *turns to listen.*

THEODOTUS (*on the steps, with uplifted arms*):

Horror unspeakable! Woe, alas! Help!

RUFIO:

What now?

CAESAR (*frowning*):

Who is slain?

THEODOTUS:

Slain! Oh, worse than the death of ten thousand men! Loss irreparable to mankind!

RUFIO:

What has happened, man?

THEODOTUS (*rushing down the hall between them*):

The fire has spread from your ships. The first of the seven wonders of the world perishes. The library of Alexandria is in flames.

RUFIO:

Psha! (*Quite relieved, he goes up to the loggia and watches the preparations of the troops on the beach.*)

CAESAR:

Is that all?

THEODOTUS (*unable to believe his senses*):

All! Caesar: will you go down to posterity as a barbarous soldier too ignorant to know the value of books?

CAESAR:

Theodotus: I am an author myself; and I tell you it is better that the Egyptians should live their lives than dream them away with the help of books.

THEODOTUS (*kneeling, with genuine literary emotion: the passion of the pedant*):

Caesar: once in ten generations of men, the world gains an immortal book.

CAESAR (*inflexible*):

If it did not flatter mankind, the common executioner would burn it.

THEODOTUS:

Without history, death would lay you beside your meanest soldier.

CAESAR:

Death will do that in any case. I ask no better grave.

THEODOTUS:

What is burning there is the memory of mankind.

CAESAR:

A shameful memory. Let it burn.

THEODOTUS (*wildly*):

Will you destroy the past?

CAESAR:

Ay, and build the future with its ruins. (Theodotus, *in despair, strikes himself on the temples with his fists.*) But harken, Theodotus, teacher of kings: you who valued Pompey's head no more than a shepherd values an onion, and who now kneel to me, with tears in your old eyes, to plead for a few sheepskins scrawled with errors. I cannot spare you a man or a bucket of water just now; but you shall pass freely out of the palace. Now, away with you to Achillas; and borrow his legions to put out the fire. (*He hurries him to the steps.*)

POTHINUS (*significantly*):

You understand, Theodotus: I remain a prisoner.

THEODOTUS:

A prisoner!

CAESAR:

Will you stay to talk whilst the memory of mankind is burning? (*Calling through the loggia*) Ho there! Pass Theodotus out. (*To* Theodotus) Away with you.

THEODOTUS (*to* Pothinus):

I must go to save the library. (*He hurries out.*)

CAESAR:

Follow him to the gate, Pothinus. Bid him urge your people to kill no more of my soldiers, for your sake.

POTHINUS:

My life will cost you dear if you take it, Caesar. (*He goes out after* Theodotus.)

Rufio, *absorbed in watching the embarkation, does not notice the departure of the two Egyptians.*

RUFIO (*shouting from the loggia to the beach*):
> All ready, there?

A CENTURION (*from below*):
> All ready. We wait for Caesar.

CAESAR:
> Tell them Caesar is coming—the rogues! (*Calling*) Britannicus. (*This magniloquent version of his secretary's name is one of* Caesar's *jokes. In later years it would have meant, quite seriously and officially, Conqueror of Britain.*)

RUFIO (*calling down*):
> Push off, all except the longboat. Stand by it to embark, Caesar's guard there. (*He leaves the balcony and comes down into the hall.*) Where are those Egyptians? Is this more clemency? Have you let them go?

CAESAR (*chuckling*):
> I have let Theodotus go to save the library. We must respect literature, Rufio.

RUFIO (*raging*):
> Folly on folly's head! I believe if you could bring back all the dead of Spain, Gaul and Thessaly to life, you would do it that we might have the trouble of fighting them over again.

CAESAR:
> Might not the gods destroy the world if their only thought were to be at peace next year? (Rufio, *out of all patience, turns away in anger.* Caesar *suddenly grips his sleeve, and adds slyly in his ear*) Besides, my friend: every Egyptian we imprison means imprisoning two Roman soldiers to guard him. Eh?

RUFIO:
> Agh! I might have known there was some fox's trick behind your fine talking. (*He gets away from* Caesar *with an ill-humored shrug, and goes to the balcony for another look at the preparations; finally goes out.*)

CAESAR:
> Is Britannus asleep? I sent him for my armor an hour ago. (*Calling*) Britannicus, thou British islander. Britannicus!

Cleopatra *runs in through the loggia with* Caesar's *helmet and sword, snatched from* Britannus, *who follows her with a cuirass and greaves. They come down to* Caesar, *she to his left hand,* Britannus *to his right.*

CLEOPATRA:

>I am going to dress you, Caesar. Sit down. (*He obeys.*) These Roman helmets are so becoming! (*She takes off his wreath.*) Oh! (*She bursts out laughing at him.*)

CAESAR:

>What are you laughing at?

CLEOPATRA:

>You're bald (*beginning with a big B, and ending with a splutter*).

CAESAR (*almost annoyed*):

>Cleopatra! (*He rises, for the convenience of* Britannus, *who puts the cuirass on him.*)

CLEOPATRA:

>So that is why you wear the wreath—to hide it.

BRITANNUS:

>Peace, Egyptian: they are the bays of the conqueror. (*He buckles the cuirass.*)

CLEOPATRA:

>Peace, thou: islander! (*To* Caesar) You should rub your head with strong spirits of sugar, Caesar. That will make it grow.

CAESAR (*with a wry face*):

>Cleopatra: do you like to be reminded that you are very young?

CLEOPATRA (*pouting*):

>No.

CAESAR (*sitting down again, and setting out his leg for* Britannus, *who kneels to put on his greaves*):

>Neither do I like to be reminded that I am—middle aged. Let me give you ten of my superfluous years. That will make you 26, and leave me only—no matter. Is it a bargain?

CLEOPATRA:

>Agreed. 26, mind. (*She puts the helmet on him.*) Oh! How nice! You look only about 50 in it!

BRITANNUS (*looking up severely at* Cleopatra):

>You must not speak in this manner to Caesar.

CLEOPATRA:

>Is it true that when Caesar caught you on that island, you were painted all over blue?

BRITANNUS:

>Blue is the color worn by all Britons of good standing. In war we stain our bodies blue; so that though our enemies may strip us of our clothes and our lives, they cannot strip us of our respectability. (*He rises.*)

CLEOPATRA (*with* Caesar's *sword*):

Let me hang this on. Now you look splendid. Have they made any statues of you in Rome?

CAESAR:

Yes, many statues.

CLEOPATRA:

You must send for one and give it to me.

RUFIO (*coming back into the loggia, more impatient than ever*):

Now Caesar: have you done talking? The moment your foot is aboard there will be no holding our men back: the boats will race one another for the lighthouse.

CAESAR (*drawing his sword and trying the edge*):

Is this well set to-day, Britannicus? At Pharsalia it was as blunt as a barrel-hoop.

BRITANNUS:

It will split one of the Egyptian's hairs to-day, Caesar. I have set it myself.

CLEOPATRA (*suddenly throwing her arms in terror round* Caesar):

Oh, you are not really going into battle to be killed?

CAESAR:

No, Cleopatra. No man goes to battle to be killed.

CLEOPATRA:

But they do get killed. My sister's husband was killed in battle. You must not go. Let him go (*pointing to* Rufio. *They all laugh at her*). Oh please, please don't go. What will happen to me if you never come back?

CAESAR (*gravely*):

Are you afraid?

CLEOPATRA (*shrinking*):

No.

CAESAR (*with quiet authority*):

Go to the balcony; and you shall see us take the Pharos. You must learn to look on battles. Go. (*She goes, downcast, and looks out from the balcony.*) That is well. Now, Rufio. March.

CLEOPATRA (*suddenly clapping her hands*):

Oh, you will not be able to go!

CAESAR:

Why? What now?

CLEOPATRA:

They are drying up the harbor with buckets—a multitude of soldiers—over there (*pointing out across the sea to her left*)—they are dipping up the water.

RUFIO (*hastening to look*):

It is true. The Egyptian army! Crawling over the edge of the west harbor like locusts. (*With sudden anger he strides down to Caesar.*) This is your accursed clemency, Caesar. Theodotus has brought them.

CAESAR (*delighted at his own cleverness*):

I meant him to, Rufio. They have come to put out the fire. The library will keep them busy whilst we seize the lighthouse. Eh? (*He rushes out buoyantly through the loggia, followed by* Britannus.)

RUFIO (*disgustedly*):

More foxing! Agh! (*He rushes off. A shout from the soldiers announces the appearance of* Caesar *below.*)

CENTURION (*below*):

All aboard. Give way there. (*Another shout.*)

CLEOPATRA (*waving her scarf through the loggia arch*):

Goodbye, goodbye, dear Caesar. Come back safe. Goodbye!

# Act III

*The edge of the quay in front of the palace, looking out west over the east harbor of Alexandria to Pharos island, just off the end of which, and connected with it by a narrow mole, is the famous lighthouse, a gigantic square tower of white marble diminishing in size storey by storey to the top, on which stands a cresset beacon. The island is joined to the main land by the Heptastadium, a great mole or causeway five miles long bounding the harbor on the south.*

*In the middle of the quay a Roman sentinel stands on guard, pilum in hand, looking out to the lighthouse with strained attention, his left hand shading his eyes. The pilum is a stout wooden shaft 4½ feet long, with an iron spit about three feet long fixed in it. The sentinel is so absorbed that he does not notice the approach from the north end of the quay of four Egyptian market porters carrying rolls of carpet, preceded by* Ftatateeta *and* Apollodorus *the Sicilian. Apollodorus is a dashing young man of about 24, handsome and debonair, dressed with deliberate aestheticism in the most delicate purples and dove greys, with ornaments of bronze, oxydized silver, and stones of jade and agate. His sword, designed as carefully as a medieval cross, has a blued blade showing through an openwork scabbard of purple leather and filagree. The porters, conducted by* Ftatateeta, *pass along the quay behind the sentinel to the steps of the palace, where they put down their bales and squat on the ground. Apollodorus does not pass along with them: he halts, amused by the preoccupation of the sentinel.*

APOLLODORUS (*calling to the* sentinel):

Who goes there, eh?

SENTINEL (*starting violently and turning with his pilum at the charge, revealing himself as a small, wiry, sandy-haired, conscientious young man with an elderly face*):

What's this? Stand. Who are you?

APOLLODORUS:

I am Apollodorus the Sicilian. Why, man, what are you dreaming of? Since I came through the lines beyond the theatre there, I have brought my caravan past three sentinels, all so busy staring at the lighthouse that not one of them challenged me. Is this Roman discipline?

SENTINEL:

We are not here to watch the land but the sea. Caesar has just landed on the Pharos. (*Looking at* Ftatateeta) What have you here? Who is this piece of Egyptian crockery?

FTATATEETA:

Apollodorus: rebuke this Roman dog; and bid him bridle his tongue in the presence of Ftatateeta, the mistress of the Queen's household.

APOLLODORUS:

My friend: this is a great lady, who stands high with Caesar.

SENTINEL (*not at all impressed, pointing to the carpets*):

And what is all this truck?

APOLLODORUS:

Carpets for the furnishing of the Queen's apartments in the palace. I have picked them from the best carpets in the world; and the Queen shall choose the best of my choosing.

SENTINEL:

So you are the carpet merchant?

APOLLODORUS (*hurt*):

My friend: I am a patrician.

SENTINEL:

A patrician! A patrician keeping a shop instead of following arms!

APOLLODORUS:

I do not keep a shop. Mine is a temple of the arts. I am a worshipper of beauty. My calling is to choose beautiful things for beautiful Queens. My motto is Art for Art's sake.

SENTINEL:

That is not the password.

APOLLODORUS:

It is a universal password.

SENTINEL:

I know nothing about universal passwords. Either give me the password for the day or get back to your shop.

Ftatateeta, *roused by his hostile tone, steals towards the edge of the quay with the step of a panther, and gets behind him.*

APOLLODORUS:

How if I do neither?

SENTINEL:

Then I will drive this pilum through you.

APOLLODORUS:

At your service, my friend. (*He draws his sword, and springs to his guard with unruffled grace.*)

FTATATEETA (*suddenly seizing the sentinel's arms from behind*):

Thrust your knife into the dog's throat, Apollodorus. (*The chivalrous* Apollodorus *laughingly shakes his head; breaks ground away from the sentinel towards the palace; and lowers his point.*)

SENTINEL (*struggling vainly*):

Curse on you! Let me go. Help ho!

FTATATEETA (*lifting him from the ground*):

Stab the little Roman reptile. Spit him on your sword.

*A couple of Roman soldiers, with a centurion, come running along the edge of the quay from the north end. They rescue their comrade, and throw off* Ftatateeta, *who is sent reeling away on the left hand of the sentinel.*

CENTURION (*an unattractive man of fifty, short in his speech and manners, with a vine wood cudgel in his hand*):

How now? What is all this?

FTATATEETA (*to* Apollodorus):

Why did you not stab him? There was time!

APOLLODORUS:

Centurion: I am here by order of the Queen to——

CENTURION (*interrupting him*):

The Queen! Yes, yes: (*to the* sentinel) pass him in. Pass all these bazaar people in to the Queen, with their goods. But mind you pass no one out that you have not passed in—not even the Queen herself.

SENTINEL:

This old woman is dangerous: she is as strong as three men. She wanted the merchant to stab me.

APOLLODORUS:

Centurion: I am not a merchant. I am a patrician and a votary of art.

CENTURION:

Is the woman your wife?

APOLLODORUS (*horrified*):

No, no! (*Correcting himself politely*) Not that the lady is not a striking figure in her own way. But (*emphatically*) she is not my wife.

FTATATEETA (*to the* Centurion):

Roman: I am Ftatateeta, the mistress of the Queen's household.

CENTURION:

Keep your hands off our men, mistress; or I will have you pitched into the harbor, though you were as strong as ten men. (*To his men*) To your posts: march! (*He returns with his men the way they came.*)

FTATATEETA (*looking malignantly after him*):

We shall see whom Isis loves best: her servant Ftatateeta or a dog of a Roman.

SENTINEL (*to* Apollodorus, *with a wave of his pilum towards the palace*):

Pass in there; and keep your distance. (*Turning to* Ftatateeta) Come within a yard of me, you old crocodile; and I will give you this (*the pilum*) in your jaws.

CLEOPATRA (*calling from the palace*):

Ftatateeta, Ftatateeta.

FTATATEETA (*looking up, scandalized*):

Go from the window, go from the window. There are men here.

CLEOPATRA:

I am coming down.

FTATATEETA (*distracted*):

No, no. What are you dreaming of? O ye gods, ye gods! Apollodorus: bid your men pick up your bales; and in with me quickly.

APOLLODORUS:

Obey the mistress of the Queen's household.

FTATATEETA (*impatiently, as the porters stoop to lift the bales*):

Quick, quick: she will be out upon us. (Cleopatra *comes from the palace and runs across the quay to* Ftatateeta.) Oh that ever I was born!

CLEOPATRA (*eagerly*):

Ftatateeta: I have thought of something. I want a boat—at once.

FTATATEETA:

A boat! No, no: you cannot. Apollodorus: speak to the Queen.

APOLLODORUS (*gallantly*):

Beautiful queen: I am Apollodorus the Sicilian, your servant, from the bazaar. I have brought you the three most beautiful Persian carpets in the world to choose from.

CLEOPATRA:

I have no time for carpets to-day. Get me a boat.

FTATATEETA:

What whim is this? You cannot go on the water except in the royal barge.

APOLLODORUS:

Royalty, Ftatateeta, lies not in the barge but in the Queen. (*To Cleopatra*) The touch of your majesty's foot on the gunwale of the meanest boat in the harbor will make it royal. (*He turns to the harbor and calls seaward*) Ho there, boatman! Pull in to the steps.

CLEOPATRA:

Apollodorus: you are my perfect knight; and I will always buy my carpets through you. (Apollodorus *bows joyously. An oar appears above the quay; and the* boatman, *a bullet-headed, vivacious, grinning fellow, burnt almost black by the sun, comes up a flight of steps from the water on the* sentinel's *right, oar in hand, and waits at the top.*) Can you row, Apollodorus?

APOLLODORUS:

My oars shall be your majesty's wings. Whither shall I row my Queen?

CLEOPATRA:

To the lighthouse. Come. (*She makes for the steps.*)

SENTINEL (*opposing her with his pilum at the charge*):

Stand. You cannot pass.

CLEOPATRA (*flushing angrily*):

How dare you? Do you know that I am the Queen?

SENTINEL:

I have my orders. You cannot pass.

CLEOPATRA:

I will make Caesar have you killed if you do not obey me.

SENTINEL:

He will do worse to me if I disobey my officer. Stand back.

CLEOPATRA:

Ftatateeta: strangle him.

SENTINEL (*alarmed—looking apprehensively at* Ftatateeta, *and brandishing his pilum*):

Keep off, there.

CLEOPATRA (*running to* Apollodorus):

Apollodorus: make your slaves help us.

APOLLODORUS:

I shall not need their help, lady. (*He draws his sword.*) Now, soldier: choose which weapon you will defend yourself with. Shall it be sword against pilum, or sword against sword?

SENTINEL:

Roman against Sicilian, curse you. Take that. (*He hurls his pilum at* Apollodorus, *who drops expertly on one knee. The pilum passes whizzing over his head and falls harmless.* Apollodorus, *with a cry of triumph, springs up and attacks the sentinel, who draws his sword and defends himself, crying*) Ho there, guard. Help!

Cleopatra, *half frightened, half delighted, takes refuge near the palace, where the porters are squatting among the bales. The boatman, alarmed, hurries down the steps out of harm's way, but stops, with his head just visible above the edge of the quay, to watch the fight. The sentinel is handicapped by his fear of an attack in the rear from* Ftatateeta. *His swordsmanship, which is of a rough and ready sort, is heavily taxed, as he has occasionally to strike at her to keep her off between a blow and a guard with* Apollodorus. *The* Centurion *returns with several soldiers.* Apollodorus *springs back towards* Cleopatra *as this reinforcement confronts him.*

CENTURION (*coming to the* sentinel's *right hand*):

What is this? What now?

SENTINEL (*panting*):

I could do well enough by myself if it weren't for the old woman. Keep her off me: that is all the help I need.

CENTURION:

Make your report, soldier. What has happened?

FTATATEETA:

Centurion: he would have slain the Queen.

SENTINEL (*bluntly*):

I would, sooner than let her pass. She wanted to take boat, and go—so she said—to the lighthouse. I stopped her, as I was ordered to; and she set this fellow on me. (*He goes to pick up his pilum and returns to his place with it.*)

CENTURION (*turning to* Cleopatra):

Cleopatra: I am loth to offend you; but without Caesar's express order we dare not let you pass beyond the Roman lines.

APOLLODORUS:

Well, Centurion; and has not the lighthouse been within the Roman lines since Caesar landed there?

CLEOPATRA:

Yes, yes. Answer that, if you can.

CENTURION (*to* Apollodorus):

As for you, Apollodorus, you may thank the gods that you are not nailed to the palace door with a pilum for your meddling.

APOLLODORUS (*urbanely*):

My military friend, I was not born to be slain by so ugly a weapon. When I fall, it will be (*holding up his sword*) by this white queen of arms, the only weapon fit for an artist. And now that you are convinced that we do not want to go beyond the lines, let me finish killing your sentinel and depart with the Queen.

CENTURION (*as the* sentinel *makes an angry demonstration*):

Peace there. Cleopatra. I must abide by my orders, and not by the subtleties of this Sicilian. You must withdraw into the palace and examine your carpets there.

CLEOPATRA (*pouting*):

I will not: I am the Queen. Caesar does not speak to me as you do. Have Caesar's centurions changed manners with his scullions?

CENTURION (*sulkily*):

I do my duty. That is enough for me.

APOLLODORUS:

Majesty: when a stupid man is doing something he is ashamed of, he always declares that it is his duty.

CENTURION (*angry*):

Apollodorus——

APOLLODORUS (*interrupting him with defiant elegance*):

I will make amends for that insult with my sword at fitting time and place. Who says artist, says duellist. (*To* Cleopatra) Hear my counsel, star of the east. Until word comes to these soldiers from Caesar himself, you are a prisoner. Let me go to him with a message from you, and a present; and before the sun has stooped half way to the arms of the sea, I will bring you back Caesar's order of release.

CENTURION (*sneering at him*):

And you will sell the Queen the present, no doubt.

APOLLODORUS:

Centurion: the Queen shall have from me, without payment, as the unforced tribute of Sicilian taste to Egyptian beauty, the richest of these carpets for her present to Caesar.

CLEOPATRA (*exultantly, to the* Centurion):

Now you see what an ignorant common creature you are!

CENTURION (*curtly*):

Well, a fool and his wares are soon parted. (*He turns to his men.*) Two more men to this post here; and see that no one leaves the palace but this man and his merchandize. If he draws his sword again inside the lines, kill him. To your posts. March.

*He goes out, leaving two auxiliary sentinels with the other.*

APOLLODORUS (*with polite goodfellowship*):

My friends: will you not enter the palace and bury our quarrel in a bowl of wine? (*He takes out his purse, jingling the coins in it.*) The Queen has presents for you all.

SENTINEL (*very sulky*):

You heard our orders. Get about your business.

FIRST AUXILIARY:

Yes: you ought to know better. Off with you.

SECOND AUXILIARY (*looking longingly at the purse—this* sentinel *is a hooknosed man, unlike his comrade, who is squab faced*):

Do not tantalize a poor man.

APOLLODORUS (*to* Cleopatra):

Pearl of Queens: the Centurion is at hand; and the Roman soldier is incorruptible when his officer is looking. I must carry your word to Caesar.

CLEOPATRA (*who has been meditating among the carpets*):

Are these carpets very heavy?

APOLLODORUS:

It matters not how heavy. There are plenty of porters.

CLEOPATRA:

How do they put the carpets into boats? Do they throw them down?

APOLLODORUS:

Not into small boats, majesty. It would sink them.

CLEOPATRA:

Not into that man's boat, for instance? (*Pointing to the* boatman.)

APOLLODORUS:

No. Too small.

CLEOPATRA:

But you can take a carpet to Caesar in it if I send one?

APOLLODORUS:

Assuredly.

CLEOPATRA:

And you will have it carried gently down the steps and take great care of it?

APOLLODORUS:

Depend on me.

CLEOPATRA:

Great, great care?

APOLLODORUS:

More than of my own body.

CLEOPATRA:

You will promise me not to let the porters drop it or throw it about?

APOLLODORUS:

Place the most delicate glass goblet in the palace in the heart of the roll, Queen; and if it be broken, my head shall pay for it.

CLEOPATRA:

Good. Come, Ftatateeta. (Ftatateeta *comes to her.* Apollodorus *offers to squire them into the palace.*) No, Apollodorus, you must not come. I will choose a carpet for myself. You must wait here. (*She runs into the palace.*)

APOLLODORUS (*to the porters*):

Follow this lady (*indicating* Ftatateeta); and obey her.

*The porters rise and take up their bales.*

FTATATEETA (*addressing the porters as if they were vermin*):

This way. And take your shoes off before you put your feet on those stairs.

*She goes in, followed by the porters with the carpets. Meanwhile Apollodorus goes to the edge of the quay and looks out over the harbor. The sentinels keep their eyes on him malignantly.*

APOLLODORUS (*addressing the* sentinel):

My friend——

SENTINEL (*rudely*):

Silence there.

FIRST AUXILIARY:

Shut your muzzle, you.

SECOND AUXILIARY (*in a half whisper, glancing apprehensively towards the north end of the quay*):

Can't you wait a bit?

APOLLODORUS:

Patience, worthy three-headed donkey. (*They mutter ferociously; but he is not at all intimidated.*) Listen: were you set here to watch me, or to watch the Egyptians?

SENTINEL:

We know our duty.

APOLLODORUS:

Then why don't you do it? There is something going on over there. (*Pointing southwestward to the mole.*)

SENTINEL (*sulkily*):

I do not need to be told what to do by the like of you.

APOLLODORUS:

Blockhead. (*He begins shouting*) Ho there, Centurion. Hoiho!

SENTINEL:

Curse your meddling. (*Shouting*) Hoiho! Alarm! Alarm!

FIRST AND SECOND AUXILIARIES:

Alarm! alarm! Hoiho!

*The* Centurion *comes running in with his guard.*

CENTURION:

What now? Has the old woman attacked you again? (*Seeing* Apollodorus) Are you here still?

APOLLODORUS (*pointing as before*):

See there. The Egyptians are moving. They are going to recapture the Pharos. They will attack by sea and land: by land along the great mole; by sea from the west harbor. Stir yourselves, my military friends: the hunt is up. (*A clangor of trumpets from several points along the quay.*) Aha! I told you so.

CENTURION (*quickly*):

The two extra men pass the alarm to the south posts. One man keep guard here. The rest with me—quick.

*The two auxiliary sentinels run off to the south. The* Centurion *and his guard run off northward; and immediately afterwards the bucina sounds. The four porters come from the palace carrying a carpet, followed by* Ftatateeta.

SENTINEL (*handling his pilum apprehensively*):

You again! (*The porters stop.*)

FTATATEETA:

Peace, Roman fellow: you are now singlehanded. Apollodorus: this carpet is Cleopatra's present to Caesar. It has rolled up in it ten precious goblets of the thinnest Iberian crystal, and a hundred eggs of the sacred blue pigeon. On your honor, let not one of them be broken.

APOLLODORUS:

On my head be it. (*To the porters*) Into the boat with them carefully.

*The porters carry the carpet to the steps.*

FIRST PORTER (*looking down at the boat*):

Beware what you do, sir. Those eggs of which the lady speaks must weigh more than a pound apiece. This boat is too small for such a load.

BOATMAN (*excitedly rushing up the steps*):

Oh thou injurious porter! Oh thou unnatural son of a she-camel! (*To* Apollodorus) My boat, sir, hath often carried five men. Shall it not carry your lordship and a bale of pigeons' eggs? (*To the porter*) Thou mangey dromedary, the gods shall punish thee for this envious wickedness.

FIRST PORTER (*stolidly*):

I cannot quit this bale now to beat thee; but another day I will lie in wait for thee.

APOLLODORUS (*going between them*):

Peace there. If the boat were but a single plank, I would get to Caesar on it.

FTATATEETA (*anxiously*):

In the name of the gods, Apollodorus, run no risks with that bale.

APOLLODORUS:

Fear not, thou venerable grotesque: I guess its great worth. (*To the porters*) Down with it, I say; and gently; or ye shall eat nothing but stick for ten days.

*The boatman goes down the steps, followed by the porters with the bale:* Ftatateeta *and* Apollodorus *watching from the edge.*

APOLLODORUS:

Gently, my sons, my children—(*with sudden alarm*) gently, ye dogs. Lay it level in the stern—so—'tis well.

FTATATEETA (*screaming down at one of the porters*):

Do not step on it, do not step on it. Oh thou brute beast!

FIRST PORTER (*ascending*):

Be not excited, mistress: all is well.

FTATATEETA (*panting*):

All well! Oh, thou hast given my heart a turn! (*She clutches her side, gasping.*)

*The four porters have now come up and are waiting at the stairhead to be paid.*

APOLLODORUS:

Here, ye hungry ones. (*He gives money to the first porter, who holds it in his hand to shew to the others. They crowd greedily to see how much it is, quite prepared, after the Eastern fashion, to protest to heaven against their patron's stinginess. But his liberality overpowers them.*)

FIRST PORTER:

O bounteous prince!

SECOND PORTER:

O lord of the bazaar!

THIRD PORTER:

O favored of the gods!

FOURTH PORTER:

O father to all the porters of the market!

SENTINEL (*enviously, threatening them fiercely with his pilum*):

Hence, dogs: off. Out of this. (*They fly before him northward along the quay.*)

APOLLODORUS:

Farewell, Ftatateeta. I shall be at the lighthouse before the Egyptians. (*He descends the steps.*)

FTATATEETA:

The gods speed thee and protect my nursling!

*The sentry returns from chasing the porters and looks down at the boat, standing near the stairhead lest* Ftatateeta *should attempt to escape.*

APOLLODORUS (*from beneath, as the boat moves off*):

Farewell, valiant pilum pitcher.

SENTINEL:

Farewell, shopkeeper.

APOLLODORUS:

Ha, ha! Pull, thou brave boatman, pull. Soho-o-o-o-o! (*He begins to sing in barcarolle measure to the rhythm of the oars*)

> My heart, my heart, spread out thy wings:
> Shake off thy heavy load of love—

Give me the oars, O son of a snail.

SENTINEL (*threatening* Ftatateeta):

Now mistress: back to your henhouse. In with you.

FTATATEETA (*falling on her knees and stretching her hands over the waters*):

Gods of the seas, bear her safely to the shore!

SENTINEL:

Bear who safely? What do you mean?

FTATATEETA (*looking darkly at him*):

Gods of Egypt and of Vengeance, let this Roman fool be beaten like a dog by his captain for suffering her to be taken over the waters.

SENTINEL:

Accursed one: is she then in the boat? (*He calls over the sea*) Hoiho, there, boatman! Hoiho!

APOLLODORUS (*singing in the distance*):

> My heart, my heart, be whole and free:
> Love is thine only enemy.

*Meanwhile* Rufio, *the morning's fighting done, sits munching dates on a faggot of brushwood outside the door of the lighthouse, which towers gigantic to the clouds on his left. His helmet, full of dates, is between his knees; and a leathern bottle of wine is by his side. Behind him the great stone pedestal of the lighthouse is shut in from the open sea by a low stone parapet, with a couple of steps in the middle to the broad coping. A huge chain with a hook hangs down from the lighthouse crane above his head. Faggots like the one he sits on lie beneath it ready to be drawn up to feed the beacon.*

    Caesar *is standing on the step at the parapet looking out anxiously, evidently ill at ease.* Britannus *comes out of the lighthouse door.*

RUFIO:

Well, my British islander. Have you been up to the top?

BRITANNUS:

I have. I reckon it at 200 feet high.

RUFIO:

Anybody up there?

BRITANNUS:

One elderly Tyrian to work the crane; and his son, a well conducted youth of 14.

RUFIO (*looking at the chain*):

What! An old man and a boy work that! Twenty men, you mean.

BRITANNUS:

Two only, I assure you. They have counterweights, and a machine with boiling water in it which I do not understand: it is not of British design. They use it to haul up barrels of oil and faggots to burn in the brazier on the roof.

RUFIO:

But——

BRITANNUS:

Excuse me: I came down because there are messengers coming along the mole to us from the island. I must see what their business is. (*He hurries out past the lighthouse.*)

CAESAR (*coming away from the parapet, shivering and out of sorts*):

Rufio: this has been a mad expedition. We shall be beaten. I wish I knew how our men are getting on with that barricade across the great mole.

RUFIO (*angrily*):

Must I leave my food and go starving to bring you a report?

CAESAR (*soothing him nervously*):

No, Rufio, no. Eat, my son, eat. (*He takes another turn,* Rufio *chewing dates meanwhile.*) The Egyptians cannot be such fools as not to storm the barricade and swoop down on us here before it is finished. It is the first time I have ever run an avoidable risk. I should not have come to Egypt.

RUFIO:

An hour ago you were all for victory.

CAESAR (*apologetically*):

Yes: I was a fool—rash, Rufio—boyish.

RUFIO:

Boyish! Not a bit of it. Here. (*Offering him a handful of dates.*)

CAESAR:

What are these for?

RUFIO:

To eat. That's what's the matter with you. When a man comes to your age, he runs down before his midday meal. Eat and drink; and then have another look at our chances.

CAESAR (*taking the dates*):

My age! (*He shakes his head and bites a date.*) Yes, Rufio: I am an old man—worn out now—true, quite true. (*He gives way to melancholy contemplation, and eats another date.*) Achillas is still in his prime: Ptolemy is a boy. (*He eats another date, and plucks up a little.*) Well, every dog has his day; and I have had mine: I cannot complain. (*With sudden cheerfulness*) These dates are not bad, Rufio. (Britannus *returns, greatly excited, with a leathern bag.* Caesar *is himself again in a moment.*) What now?

BRITANNUS (*triumphantly*):

Our brave Rhodian mariners have captured a treasure. There! (*He throws the bag down at* Caesar's *feet.*) Our enemies are delivered into our hands.

CAESAR:

In that bag?

BRITANNUS:

Wait till you hear, Caesar. This bag contains all the letters which have passed between Pompey's party and the army of occupation here.

CAESAR:

Well?

BRITANNUS (*impatient of* Caesar's *slowness to grasp the situation*):

Well, we shall now know who your foes are. The name of every man who has plotted against you since you crossed the Rubicon may be in these papers, for all we know.

CAESAR:

Put them in the fire.

BRITANNUS:

Put them—(*he gasps*)!!!!

CAESAR:

In the fire. Would you have me waste the next three years of my life in proscribing and condemning men who will be my friends when I have proved that my friendship is worth more than Pompey's was—than Cato's is. O incorrigible British islander: am I a bull dog, to seek quarrels merely to shew how stubborn my jaws are?

BRITANNUS:

But your honor—the honor of Rome——

CAESAR:

I do not make human sacrifices to my honor, as your Druids do. Since you will not burn these, at least I can drown them. (*He picks up the bag and throws it over the parapet into the sea.*)

BRITANNUS:

Caesar: this is mere eccentricity. Are traitors to be allowed to go free for the sake of a paradox?

RUFIO (*rising*):

Caesar: when the islander has finished preaching, call me again. I am going to have a look at the boiling water machine. (*He goes into the lighthouse.*)

BRITANNUS (*with genuine feeling*):

O Caesar, my great master, if I could but persuade you to regard life seriously, as men do in my country!

CAESAR:

Do they truly do so, Britannus?

BRITANNUS:

Have you not been there? Have you not seen them? What Briton speaks as you do in your moments of levity? What Briton neglects to attend the services at the sacred grove? What Briton wears clothes of many colors as you do, instead

of plain blue, as all solid, well esteemed men should? These are
moral questions with us.

CAESAR:

Well, well, my friend: some day I shall settle down and have a
blue toga, perhaps. Meanwhile, I must get on as best I can in
my flippant Roman way. (Apollodorus *comes past the lighthouse.*) What now?

BRITANNUS (*turning quickly, and challenging the stranger with official
haughtiness*):

What is this? Who are you? How did you come here?

APOLLODORUS:

Calm yourself, my friend: I am not going to eat you. I have
come by boat, from Alexandria, with precious gifts for Caesar.

CAESAR:

From Alexandria!

BRITANNUS (*severely*):

That is Caesar, sir.

RUFIO (*appearing at the lighthouse door*):

What's the matter now?

APOLLODORUS:

Hail, great Caesar! I am Apollodorus the Sicilian, an artist.

BRITANNUS:

An artist! Why have they admitted this vagabond?

CAESAR:

Peace, man. Apollodorus is a famous patrician amateur.

BRITANNUS (*disconcerted*):

I crave the gentleman's pardon. (*To* Caesar) I understood him
to say that he was a professional. (*Somewhat out of countenance,
he allows* Apollodorus *to approach* Caesar, *changing places with
him.* Rufio, *after looking* Apollodorus *up and down with marked
disparagement, goes to the other side of the platform.*)

CAESAR:

You are welcome, Apollodorus. What is your business?

APOLLODORUS:

First, to deliver to you a present from the Queen of Queens.

CAESAR:

Who is that?

APOLLODORUS:

Cleopatra of Egypt.

CAESAR (*taking him into his confidence in his most winning manner*):

Apollodorus: this is no time for playing with presents. Pray
you, go back to the Queen, and tell her that if all goes well I
shall return to the palace this evening.

APOLLODORUS:

Caesar: I cannot return. As I approached the lighthouse, some fool threw a great leathern bag into the sea. It broke the nose of my boat; and I had hardly time to get myself and my charge to the shore before the poor little cockleshell sank.

CAESAR:

I am sorry, Apollodorus. The fool shall be rebuked. Well, well: what have you brought me? The Queen will be hurt if I do not look at it.

RUFIO:

Have we time to waste on this trumpery? The Queen is only a child.

CAESAR:

Just so: that is why we must not disappoint her. What is the present, Apollodorus?

APOLLODORUS:

Caesar: it is a Persian carpet—a beauty! And in it are—so I am told—pigeons' eggs and crystal goblets and fragile precious things. I dare not for my head have it carried up that narrow ladder from the causeway.

RUFIO:

Swing it up by the crane, then. We will send the eggs to the cook; drink our wine from the goblets; and the carpet will make a bed for Caesar.

APOLLODORUS:

The crane! Caesar: I have sworn to tender this bale of carpet as I tender my own life.

CAESAR (*cheerfully*):

Then let them swing you up at the same time; and if the chain breaks, you and the pigeons' eggs will perish together. (*He goes to the chain and looks up along it, examining it curiously.*)

APOLLODORUS (*to* Britannus):

Is Caesar serious?

BRITANNUS:

His manner is frivolous because he is an Italian; but he means what he says.

APOLLODORUS:

Serious or not, he spake well. Give me a squad of soldiers to work the crane.

BRITANNUS:

Leave the crane to me. Go and await the descent of the chain.

APOLLODORUS:

> Good. You will presently see me there (*turning to them all and pointing with an eloquent gesture to the sky above the parapet*) rising like the sun with my treasure.

*He goes back the way he came. Britannus goes into the lighthouse.*

RUFIO (*ill-humoredly*):

> Are you really going to wait here for this foolery, Caesar?

CAESAR (*backing away from the crane as it gives signs of working*):

> Why not?

RUFIO:

> The Egyptians will let you know why not if they have the sense to make a rush from the shore end of the mole before our barricade is finished. And here we are waiting like children to see a carpet full of pigeons' eggs.

*The chain rattles, and is drawn up high enough to clear the parapet. It then swings round out of sight behind the lighthouse.*

CAESAR:

> Fear not, my son Rufio. When the first Egyptian takes his first step along the mole, the alarm will sound; and we two will reach the barricade from our end before the Egyptians reach it from their end—we two, Rufio: I, the old man, and you, his biggest boy. And the old man will be there first. So peace; and give me some more dates.

APOLLODORUS (*from the causeway below*):

> Soho, haul away. So-ho-o-o-o! (*The chain is drawn up and comes round again from behind the lighthouse. Apollodorus is swinging in the air with his bale of carpet at the end of it. He breaks into song as he soars above the parapet*)

> > Aloft, aloft, behold the blue
> > That never shone in woman's eyes—

> Easy there: stop her. (*He ceases to rise.*) Further round! (*The chain comes forward above the platform.*)

RUFIO (*calling up*):

> Lower away there. (*The chain and its load begin to descend.*)

APOLLODORUS (*calling up*):

> Gently—slowly—mind the eggs.

RUFIO (*calling up*):

> Easy there—slowly—slowly.

Apollodorus *and the bale are deposited safely on the flags in the middle of the platform.* Rufio *and* Caesar *help* Apollodorus *to cast off the chain from the bale.*

RUFIO:

Haul up.

*The chain rises clear of their heads with a rattle.* Britannus *comes from the lighthouse and helps them to uncord the carpet.*

APOLLODORUS (*when the cords are loose*):

Stand off, my friends: let Caesar see. (*He throws the carpet open.*)

RUFIO:

Nothing but a heap of shawls. Where are the pigeons' eggs?

APOLLODORUS:

Approach, Caesar; and search for them among the shawls.

RUFIO (*drawing his sword*):

Ha, treachery! Keep back, Caesar: I saw the shawl move: there is something alive there.

BRITANNUS (*drawing his sword*):

It is a serpent.

APOLLODORUS:

Dares Caesar thrust his hand into the sack where the serpent moves?

RUFIO (*turning on him*):

Treacherous dog——

CAESAR:

Peace. Put up your swords. Apollodorus: your serpent seems to breathe very regularly. (*He thrusts his hand under the shawls and draws out a bare arm.*) This is a pretty little snake.

RUFIO (*drawing out the other arm*):

Let us have the rest of you.

*They pull* Cleopatra *up by the wrists into a sitting position.* Britannus, *scandalized, sheathes his sword with a drive of protest.*

CLEOPATRA (*gasping*):

Oh, I'm smothered. Oh, Caesar; a man stood on me in the boat; and a great sack of something fell upon me out of the sky; and then the boat sank, and then I was swung up into the air and bumped down.

CAESAR (*petting her as she rises and takes refuge on his breast*):

Well, never mind: here you are safe and sound at last.

RUFIO:

Ay; and now that she is here, what are we to do with her?

BRITANNUS:

She cannot stay here, Caesar, without the companionship of some matron.

CLEOPATRA (*jealously, to* Caesar, *who is obviously perplexed*):

Aren't you glad to see me?

CAESAR:

Yes, yes; *I* am very glad. But Rufio is very angry; and Britannus is shocked.

CLEOPATRA (*contemptuously*):

You can have their heads cut off, can you not?

CAESAR:

They would not be so useful with their heads cut off as they are now, my sea bird.

RUFIO (*to* Cleopatra):

We shall have to go away presently and cut some of your Egyptians' heads off. How will you like being left here with the chance of being captured by that little brother of yours if we are beaten?

CLEOPATRA:

But you mustn't leave me alone. Caesar you will not leave me alone, will you?

RUFIO:

What! not when the trumpet sounds and all our lives depend on Caesar's being at the barricade before the Egyptians reach it? Eh?

CLEOPATRA:

Let them lose their lives: they are only soldiers.

CAESAR (*gravely*):

Cleopatra: when that trumpet sounds, we must take every man his life in his hand, and throw it in the face of Death. And of my soldiers who have trusted me there is not one whose hand I shall not hold more sacred than your head. (Cleopatra *is overwhelmed. Her eyes fill with tears.*) Apollodorus: you must take her back to the palace.

APOLLODORUS:

Am I a dolphin, Caesar, to cross the seas with young ladies on my back? My boat is sunk: all yours are either at the barricade or have returned to the city. I will hail one if I can: that is all I can do. (*He goes back to the causeway.*)

CLEOPATRA (*struggling with her tears*):

It does not matter. I will not go back. Nobody cares for me.

CAESAR:

Cleopatra——

CLEOPATRA:

You want me to be killed.

CAESAR (*still more gravely*):

My poor child: your life matters little here to anyone but your-self. (*She gives way altogether at this, casting herself down on the faggots weeping. Suddenly a great tumult is heard in the distance, bucinas and trumpets sounding through a storm of shouting.* Britannus *rushes to the parapet and looks along the mole.* Caesar *and* Rufio *turn to one another with quick intelligence.*)

CAESAR:

Come, Rufio.

CLEOPATRA (*scrambling to her knees and clinging to him*):

No, no. Do not leave me, Caesar. (*He snatches his skirt from her clutch.*) Oh!

BRITANNUS (*from the parapet*):

Caesar: we are cut off. The Egyptians have landed from the west harbor between us and the barricade!!!

RUFIO (*running to see*):

Curses! It is true. We are caught like rats in a trap.

CAESAR (*ruthfully*):

Rufio, Rufio: my men at the barricade are between the sea party and the shore party. I have murdered them.

RUFIO (*coming back from the parapet to* Caesar's *right hand*):

Ay: that comes of fooling with this girl here.

APOLLODORUS (*coming up quickly from the causeway*):

Look over the parapet, Caesar.

CAESAR:

We have looked, my friend. We must defend ourselves here.

APOLLODORUS:

I have thrown the ladder into the sea. They cannot get in with-out it.

RUFIO:

Ay; and we cannot get out. Have you thought of that?

APOLLODORUS:

Not get out! Why not? You have ships in the east harbor.

BRITANNUS (*hopefully, at the parapet*):

The Rhodian galleys are standing in towards us already. (*Cae-sar quickly joins* Britannus *at the parapet.*)

RUFIO (*to* Apollodorus, *impatiently*):

And by what road are we to walk to the galleys, pray?

APOLLODORUS (*with gay, defiant rhetoric*):

By the road that leads everywhere—the diamond path of the sun and moon. Have you never seen the child's shadow play

of *The Broken Bridge?* "Ducks and geese with ease get over"—
eh? (*He throws away his cloak and cap, and binds his sword on his
back.*)

RUFIO:

What are you talking about?

APOLLODORUS:

I will shew you. (*Calling to* Britannus) How far off is the nearest galley?

BRITANNUS:

Fifty fathom.

CAESAR:

No, no: they are further off than they seem in this clear air to
your British eyes. Nearly quarter of a mile, Apollodorus.

APOLLODORUS:

Good. Defend yourselves here until I send you a boat from that
galley.

RUFIO:

Have you wings, perhaps?

APOLLODORUS:

Water wings, soldier. Behold!

*He runs up the steps between* Caesar *and* Britannus *to the coping of the
parapet; springs into the air; and plunges head foremost into the sea.*

CAESAR (*like a schoolboy—wildly excited*):

Bravo, bravo! (*Throwing off his cloak*) By Jupiter, I will do that
too.

RUFIO (*seizing him*):

You are mad. You shall not.

CAESAR:

Why not? Can I not swim as well as he?

RUFIO (*frantic*):

Can an old fool dive and swim like a young one? He is twenty-
five and you are fifty.

CAESAR (*breaking loose from* Rufio):

Old!!!

BRITANNUS (*shocked*):

Rufio: you forget yourself.

CAESAR:

I will race you to the galley for a week's pay, father Rufio.

CLEOPATRA:

But me! me!! me!!! what is to become of me?

CAESAR:

    I will carry you on my back to the galley like a dolphin. Rufio: when you see me rise to the surface, throw her in: I will answer for her. And then in with you after her, both of you.

CLEOPATRA:

    No, no, NO. I shall be drowned.

BRITANNUS:

    Caesar: I am a man and a Briton, not a fish. I must have a boat. I cannot swim.

CLEOPATRA:

    Neither can I.

CAESAR (*to* Britannus):

    Stay here, then, alone, until I recapture the lighthouse: I will not forget you. Now, Rufio.

RUFIO:

    You have made up your mind to this folly?

CAESAR:

    The Egyptians have made it up for me. What else is there to do? And mind where you jump: I do not want to get your fourteen stone in the small of my back as I come up. (*He runs up the steps and stands on the coping.*)

BRITANNUS (*anxiously*):

    One last word, Caesar. Do not let yourself be seen in the fashionable part of Alexandria until you have changed your clothes.

CAESAR (*calling over the sea*):

    Ho, Apollodorus: (*he points skyward and quotes the barcarolle*)

    The white upon the blue above—

APOLLODORUS (*swimming in the distance*):

    Is purple on the green below—

CAESAR (*exultantly*):

    Aha! (*He plunges into the sea.*)

CLEOPATRA (*running excitedly to the steps*):

    Oh, let me see. He will be drowned. (Rufio *seizes her.*) Ah—ah—ah—ah! (*He pitches her screaming into the sea.* Rufio *and* Britannus *roar with laughter.*)

RUFIO (*looking down after her*):

    He has got her. (*To* Britannus) Hold the fort, Briton. Caesar will not forget you. (*He springs off.*)

BRITANNUS (*running to the steps to watch them as they swim*):

    All safe, Rufio?

RUFIO (*swimming*):

   All safe.

CAESAR (*swimming further off*):

   Take refuge up there by the beacon; and pile the fuel on the trap door, Britannus.

BRITANNUS (*calling in reply*):

   I will first do so, and then commend myself to my country's gods. (*A sound of cheering from the sea. Britannus gives full vent to his excitement*) The boat has reached him: Hip, hip, hip, hurrah!

# Act IV

*Cleopatra's sousing in the east harbor of Alexandria was in October 48 B.C. In March 47 she is passing the afternoon in her boudoir in the palace, among a bevy of her ladies, listening to a slave girl who is playing the harp in the middle of the room. The harpist's master, an old musician, with a lined face, prominent brows, white beard, moustache and eyebrows twisted and horned at the ends, and a consciously keen and pretentious expression, is squatting on the floor close to her on her right, watching her performance. Ftatateeta is in attendance near the door, in front of a group of female slaves. Except the harp player all are seated: Cleopatra in a chair opposite the door on the other side of the room; the rest on the ground. Cleopatra's ladies are all young, the most conspicuous being Charmian and Iras, her favorites. Charmian is a hatchet faced, terra cotta colored little goblin, swift in her movements, and neatly finished at the hands and feet. Iras is a plump, goodnatured creature, rather fatuous, with a profusion of red hair, and a tendency to giggle on the slightest provocation.*

CLEOPATRA:

   Can I——

FTATATEETA (*insolently, to the player*):

   Peace, thou! The Queen speaks. (*The player stops.*)

CLEOPATRA (*to the old musician*):

   I want to learn to play the harp with my own hands. Caesar loves music. Can you teach me?

MUSICIAN:

   Assuredly I and no one else can teach the Queen. Have I not discovered the lost method of the ancient Egyptians, who could make a pyramid tremble by touching a bass string? All the other teachers are quacks: I have exposed them repeatedly.

CLEOPATRA:

   Good: you shall teach me. How long will it take?

MUSICIAN:

> Not very long: only four years. Your Majesty must first become proficient in the philosophy of Pythagoras.

CLEOPATRA:

> Has she (*indicating the slave*) become proficient in the philosophy of Pythagoras?

MUSICIAN:

> Oh, she is but a slave. She learns as a dog learns.

CLEOPATRA:

> Well, then, I will learn as a dog learns; for she plays better than you. You shall give me a lesson every day for a fortnight. (*The musician hastily scrambles to his feet and bows profoundly.*) After that, whenever I strike a false note you shall be flogged; and if I strike so many that there is not time to flog you, you shall be thrown into the Nile to feed the crocodiles. Give the girl a piece of gold; and send them away.

MUSICIAN (*much taken aback*):

> But true art will not be thus forced.

FTATATEETA (*pushing him out*):

> What is this? Answering the Queen, forsooth. Out with you.

*He is pushed out by* Ftatateeta, *the girl following with her harp, amid the laughter of the ladies and slaves.*

CLEOPATRA:

> Now, can any of you amuse me? Have you any stories or any news?

IRAS:

> Ftatateeta——

CLEOPATRA:

> Oh, Ftatateeta, Ftatateeta, always Ftatateeta. Some new tale to set me against her.

IRAS:

> No: this time Ftatateeta has been virtuous. (*All the ladies laugh—not the slaves.*) Pothinus has been trying to bribe her to let him speak with you.

CLEOPATRA (*wrathfully*):

> Ha! you all sell audiences with me, as if I saw whom you please, and not whom I please. I should like to know how much of her gold piece that harp girl will have to give up before she leaves the palace.

IRAS:

> We can easily find out that for you.

*The ladies laugh.*

CLEOPATRA (*frowning*):

You laugh; but take care, take care. I will find out some day how to make myself served as Caesar is served.

CHARMIAN:

Old hooknose! (*They laugh again.*)

CLEOPATRA (*revolted*):

Silence. Charmian: do not you be a silly little Egyptian fool. Do you know why I allow you all to chatter impertinently just as you please, instead of treating you as Ftatateeta would treat you if she were Queen?

CHARMIAN:

Because you try to imitate Caesar in everything; and he lets everybody say what they please to him.

CLEOPATRA:

No; but because I asked him one day why he did so; and he said "Let your women talk; and you will learn something from them." What have I to learn from them? I said. "What they are," said he; and oh! you should have seen his eye as he said it. You would have curled up, you shallow things. (*They laugh. She turns fiercely on* Iras) At whom are you laughing—at me or at Caesar?

IRAS:

At Caesar.

CLEOPATRA:

If you were not a fool, you would laugh at me; and if you were not a coward you would not be afraid to tell me so. (Ftatateeta *returns.*) Ftatateeta: they tell me that Pothinus has offered you a bribe to admit him to my presence.

FTATATEETA (*protesting*):

Now by my father's gods——

CLEOPATRA (*cutting her short despotically*):

Have I not told you not to deny things? You would spend the day calling your father's gods to witness to your virtues if I let you. Go take the bribe; and bring in Pothinus. (Ftatateeta *is about to reply.*) Don't answer me. Go.

Ftatateeta *goes out; and* Cleopatra *rises and begins to prowl to and fro between her chair and the door, meditating. All rise and stand.*

IRAS (*as she reluctantly rises*):

Heigho! I wish Caesar were back in Rome.

CLEOPATRA (*threateningly*):

It will be a bad day for you all when he goes. Oh, if I were not ashamed to let him see that I am as cruel at heart as my father, I would make you repent that speech! Why do you wish him away?

CHARMIAN:

He makes you so terribly prosy and serious and learned and philosophical. It is worse than being religious, at our ages. (*The ladies laugh.*)

CLEOPATRA:

Cease that endless cackling, will you. Hold your tongues.

CHARMIAN (*with mock resignation*):

Well, well: we must try to live up to Caesar.

*They laugh again.* Cleopatra *rages silently as she continues to prowl to and fro.* Ftatateeta *comes back with* Pothinus, *who halts on the threshold.*

FTATATEETA (*at the door*):

Pothinus craves the ear of the——

CLEOPATRA:

There, there: that will do: let him come in. (*She resumes her seat. All sit down except* Pothinus, *who advances to the middle of the room.* Ftatateeta *takes her former place.*) Well, Pothinus: what is the latest news from your rebel friends?

POTHINUS (*haughtily*):

I am no friend of rebellion. And a prisoner does not receive news.

CLEOPATRA:

You are no more a prisoner than I am—than Caesar is. These six months we have been besieged in this palace by my subjects. You are allowed to walk on the beach among the soldiers. Can I go further myself, or can Caesar?

POTHINUS:

You are but a child, Cleopatra, and do not understand these matters.

*The ladies laugh.* Cleopatra *looks inscrutably at him.*

CHARMIAN:

I see you do not know the latest news, Pothinus.

POTHINUS:

What is that?

CHARMIAN:

That Cleopatra is no longer a child. Shall I tell you how to grow much older, and much, much wiser in one day?

POTHINUS:

I should prefer to grow wiser without growing older.

CHARMIAN:

Well, go up to the top of the lighthouse; and get somebody to take you by the hair and throw you into the sea. (*The ladies laugh.*)

CLEOPATRA:

She is right, Pothinus: you will come to the shore with much conceit washed out of you. (*The ladies laugh.* Cleopatra *rises impatiently.*) Begone, all of you. I will speak with Pothinus alone. Drive them out, Ftatateeta. (*They run out laughing.* Ftatateeta *shuts the door on them.*) What are you waiting for?

FTATATEETA:

It is not meet that the Queen remain alone with——

CLEOPATRA (*interrupting her*):

Ftatateeta: must I sacrifice you to your father's gods to teach you that *I* am Queen of Egypt, and not you?

FTATATEETA (*indignantly*):

You are like the rest of them. You want to be what these Romans call a New Woman. (*She goes out, banging the door.*)

CLEOPATRA (*sitting down again*):

Now, Pothinus: why did you bribe Ftatateeta to bring you hither?

POTHINUS (*studying her gravely*):

Cleopatra: what they tell me is true. You are changed.

CLEOPATRA:

Do you speak with Caesar every day for six months: and you will be changed.

POTHINUS:

It is the common talk that you are infatuated with this old man.

CLEOPATRA:

Infatuated? What does that mean? Made foolish, is it not? Oh no: I wish I were.

POTHINUS:

You wish you were made foolish! How so?

CLEOPATRA:

When I was foolish, I did what I liked, except when Ftatateeta beat me; and even then I cheated her and did it by stealth. Now that Caesar has made me wise, it is no use my liking or disliking; I do what must be done, and have no time to attend to myself. That is not happiness; but it is greatness. If Caesar were gone, I think I could govern the Egyptians; for what Caesar is to me, I am to the fools around me.

POTHINUS (*looking hard at her*):

Cleopatra: this may be the vanity of youth.

CLEOPATRA:

No, no: it is not that I am so clever, but that the others are so stupid.

POTHINUS (*musingly*):

Truly, that is the great secret.

CLEOPATRA:

Well, now tell me what you came to say?

POTHINUS (*embarrassed*):

I! Nothing.

CLEOPATRA:

Nothing!

POTHINUS:

At least—to beg for my liberty: that is all.

CLEOPATRA:

For that you would have knelt to Caesar. No, Pothinus: you came with some plan that depended on Cleopatra being a little nursery kitten. Now that Cleopatra is a Queen, the plan is upset.

POTHINUS (*bowing his head submissively*):

It is so.

CLEOPATRA (*exultant*):

Aha!

POTHINUS (*raising his eyes keenly to hers*):

Is Cleopatra then indeed a Queen, and no longer Caesar's prisoner and slave?

CLEOPATRA:

Pothinus: we are all Caesar's slaves—all we in this land of Egypt—whether we will or no. And she who is wise enough to know this will reign when Caesar departs.

POTHINUS:

You harp on Caesar's departure.

CLEOPATRA:

What if I do?

POTHINUS:

Does he not love you?

CLEOPATRA:

Love me! Pothinus: Caesar loves no one. Who are those we love? Only those whom we do not hate: all people are strangers and enemies to us except those we love. But it is not so with Caesar. He has no hatred in him: he makes friends with everyone as he does with dogs and children. His kindness to me is a wonder: neither mother, father, nor nurse have ever taken so much care for me, or thrown open their thoughts to me so freely.

POTHINUS:

Well: is not this love?

CLEOPATRA:

What! When he will do as much for the first girl he meets on his way back to Rome? Ask his slave, Britannus: he has been just as good to him. Nay, ask his very horse! His kindness is not for anything in me: it is in his own nature.

POTHINUS:

But how can you be sure that he does not love you as men love women?

CLEOPATRA:

Because I cannot make him jealous. I have tried.

POTHINUS:

Hm! Perhaps I should have asked, then, do you love him?

CLEOPATRA:

Can one love a god? Besides, I love another Roman: one whom I saw long before Caesar—no god, but a man—one who can love and hate—one whom I can hurt and who would hurt me.

POTHINUS:

Does Caesar know this?

CLEOPATRA:

Yes.

POTHINUS:

And he is not angry.

CLEOPATRA:

He promises to send him to Egypt to please me!

POTHINUS:

I do not understand this man?

CLEOPATRA (*with superb contempt*):

You understand Caesar! How could you? (*Proudly*) I do—by instinct.

POTHINUS (*deferentially, after a moment's thought*):

Your Majesty caused me to be admitted to-day. What message has the Queen for me?

CLEOPATRA:

This. You think that by making my brother king, you will rule in Egypt, because you are his guardian and he is a little silly.

POTHINUS:

The Queen is pleased to say so.

CLEOPATRA:

The Queen is pleased to say this also. That Caesar will eat up you, and Achillas, and my brother, as a cat eats up mice; and that he will put on this land of Egypt as a shepherd puts on his garment. And when he has done that, he will return to Rome, and leave Cleopatra here as his viceroy.

POTHINUS (*breaking out wrathfully*):

That he will never do. We have a thousand men to his ten; and we will drive him and his beggarly legions into the sea.

CLEOPATRA (*with scorn, getting up to go*):

You rant like any common fellow. Go, then, and marshal your thousands; and make haste; for Mithridates of Pergamos is at hand with reinforcements for Caesar. Caesar has held you at bay with two legions: we shall see what he will do with twenty.

POTHINUS:

Cleopatra——

CLEOPATRA:

Enough, enough: Caesar has spoiled me for talking to weak things like you. (*She goes out*. Pothinus, *with a gesture of rage, is following, when Ftatateeta enters and stops him*.)

POTHINUS:

Let me go forth from this hateful place.

FTATATEETA:

What angers you?

POTHINUS:

The curse of all the gods of Egypt be upon her! She has sold her country to the Roman, that she may buy it back from him with her kisses.

FTATATEETA:

Fool: did she not tell you that she would have Caesar gone?

POTHINUS:

You listened?

FTATATEETA:

I took care that some honest woman should be at hand whilst you were with her.

POTHINUS:

Now by the gods——

FTATATEETA:

Enough of your gods! Caesar's gods are all powerful here. It is no use you coming to Cleopatra: you are only an Egyptian. She will not listen to any of her own race: she treats us all as children.

POTHINUS:

May she perish for it!

FTATATEETA (*balefully*):

May your tongue wither for that wish! Go! send for Lucius Septimius, the slayer of Pompey. He is a Roman: may be she will listen to him. Begone!

POTHINUS (*darkly*):

I know to whom I must go now.

FTATATEETA (*suspiciously*):

To whom, then?

POTHINUS:

To a greater Roman than Lucius. And mark this, mistress. You thought, before Caesar came, that Egypt should presently be ruled by you and your crew in the name of Cleopatra. I set myself against it——

FTATATEETA (*interrupting him—wrangling*):

Ay; that it might be ruled by you and your crew in the name of Ptolemy.

POTHINUS:

Better me, or even you, than a woman with a Roman heart; and that is what Cleopatra is now become. Whilst I live, she shall never rule. So guide yourself accordingly. (*He goes out.*)

*It is by this time drawing on to dinner time. The table is laid on the roof of the palace; and thither* Rufio *is now climbing, ushered by a majestic palace official, wand of office in hand, and followed by a slave carrying an inlaid stool. After many stairs they emerge at last into a massive colonnade on the roof. Light curtains are drawn between the columns on the north and east to soften the westering sun. The official* leads Rufio *to one of these shaded sections. A cord for pulling the curtains apart hangs down between the pillars.*

THE OFFICIAL (*bowing*):

The Roman commander will await Caesar here.

*The slave sets down the stool near the southernmost column, and slips out through the curtains.*

RUFIO (*sitting down, a little blown*):

Pouf! That was a climb. How high have we come?

THE OFFICIAL:

We are on the palace roof, O Beloved of Victory!

RUFIO:

Good! the Beloved of Victory has no more stairs to get up.

*A second official enters from the opposite end, walking backwards.*

THE SECOND OFFICIAL:

Caesar approaches.

Caesar, *fresh from the bath, clad in a new tunic of purple silk, comes in, beaming and festive, followed by two slaves carrying a light couch, which is hardly more than an elaborately designed bench. They place it near the northmost of the two curtained columns. When this is done they slip out through the curtains; and the two officials, formally bowing, follow them.* Rufio *rises to receive* Caesar.

CAESAR (*coming over to him*):

Why, Rufio! (*Surveying his dress with an air of admiring astonishment*) A new baldrick! A new golden pommel to your sword! And you have had your hair cut! But not your beard—? impossible! (*He sniffs at* Rufio's *beard.*) Yes, perfumed, by Jupiter Olympus!

RUFIO (*growling*):

Well: is it to please myself?

CAESAR (*affectionately*):

No, my son Rufio, but to please me—to celebrate my birthday.

RUFIO (*contemptuously*):

Your birthday! You always have a birthday when there is a pretty girl to be flattered or an ambassador to be conciliated. We had seven of them in ten months last year.

CAESAR (*contritely*):

It is true, Rufio! I shall never break myself of these petty deceits.

RUFIO:

Who is to dine with us—besides Cleopatra?

CAESAR:

Apollodorus the Sicilian.

RUFIO:

That popinjay!

CAESAR:

Come! the popinjay is an amusing dog—tells a story; sings a song; and saves us the trouble of flattering the Queen. What does she care for old politicians and camp-fed bears like us? No: Apollodorus is good company, Rufio, good company.

RUFIO:

Well, he can swim a bit and fence a bit: he might be worse, if he only knew how to hold his tongue.

CAESAR:

The gods forbid he should ever learn! Oh, this military life! this tedious, brutal life of action! That is the worst of us Romans: we are mere doers and drudgers: a swarm of bees turned into men. Give me a good talker—one with wit and imagination enough to live without continually doing something!

RUFIO:

Ay! a nice time he would have of it with you when dinner was over! Have you noticed that I am before my time?

CAESAR:

Aha! I thought that meant something. What is it?

RUFIO:

Can we be overheard here?

CAESAR:

Our privacy invites eavesdropping. I can remedy that. (*He claps his hands twice. The curtains are drawn, revealing the roof garden with a banqueting table set across in the middle for four persons, one at each end, and two side by side. The side next* Caesar *and* Rufio *is blocked with golden wine vessels and basins. A gorgeous major-domo is superintending the laying of the table by a staff of slaves. The colonnade goes round the garden at both sides to the further end, where a gap in it, like a great gateway, leaves the view open to the sky beyond the western edge of the roof, except in the middle, where a life size image of Ra, seated on a huge plinth, towers up, with hawk head and crown of asp and disk. His altar, which stands at his feet, is a single white stone.*) Now everybody can see us, nobody will think of listening to us. (*He sits down on the bench left by the two slaves.*)

RUFIO (*sitting down on his stool*):

Pothinus wants to speak to you. I advise you to see him: there is some plotting going on here among the women.

CAESAR:

Who is Pothinus?

RUFIO:

The fellow with hair like squirrel's fur—the little King's bear leader, whom you kept prisoner.

CAESAR (*annoyed*):

And has he not escaped?

RUFIO:

No.

CAESAR (*rising imperiously*):

Why not? You have been guarding this man instead of watching the enemy. Have I not told you always to let prisoners escape unless there are special orders to the contrary? Are there not enough mouths to be fed without him?

RUFIO:

Yes; and if you would have a little sense and let me cut his throat, you would save his rations. Anyhow, he won't escape. Three sentries have told him they would put a pilum through him if they saw him again. What more can they do? He prefers to stay and spy on us. So would I if I had to do with generals subject to fits of clemency.

CAESAR (*resuming his seat, argued down*):

Hm! And so he wants to see me.

RUFIO:

Ay. I have brought him with me. He is waiting there (*jerking his thumb over his shoulder*) under guard.

CAESAR:

And you want me to see him?

RUFIO (*obstinately*):

I don't want anything. I daresay you will do what you like. Don't put it on to me.

CAESAR (*with an air of doing it expressly to indulge* Rufio):

Well, well: let us have him.

RUFIO (*calling*):

Ho there, guard! Release your man and send him up. (*Beckoning*) Come along!

Pothinus *enters and stops mistrustfully between the two, looking from one to the other.*

CAESAR (*graciously*):

Ah, Pothinus! You are welcome. And what is the news this afternoon?

POTHINUS:

Caesar: I come to warn you of a danger, and to make you an offer.

CAESAR:

Never mind the danger. Make the offer.

RUFIO:

Never mind the offer. What's the danger?

POTHINUS:

Caesar: you think that Cleopatra is devoted to you.

CAESAR (*gravely*):

My friend: I already know what I think. Come to your offer.

POTHINUS:

I will deal plainly. I know not by what strange gods you have been enabled to defend a palace and a few yards of beach against a city and an army. Since we cut you off from Lake Mareotis, and you dug wells in the salt sea sand and brought up buckets of fresh water from them, we have known that your gods are irresistible, and that you are a worker of miracles. I no longer threaten you——

RUFIO (*sarcastically*):

Very handsome of you, indeed.

POTHINUS:

So be it: you are the master. Our gods sent the north west winds to keep you in our hands; but you have been too strong for them.

CAESAR (*gently urging him to come to the point*):

Yes, yes, my friend. But what then?

RUFIO:

Spit it out, man. What have you to say?

POTHINUS:

I have to say that you have a traitress in your camp. Cleopa-tra——

THE MAJOR-DOMO (*at the table, announcing*):

The Queen! (Caesar *and* Rufio *rise.*)

RUFIO (*aside to* Pothinus):

You should have spat it out sooner, you fool. Now it is too late.

Cleopatra, *in gorgeous raiment, enters in state through the gap in the colonnade, and comes down past the image of Ra and past the table to* Caesar. *Her retinue, headed by* Ftatateeta, *joins the staff at the table.* Caesar *gives* Cleopatra *his seat, which she takes.*

CLEOPATRA (*quickly, seeing* Pothinus):

What is he doing here?

CAESAR (*seating himself beside her, in the most amiable of tempers*):

Just going to tell me something about you. You shall hear it. Proceed, Pothinus.

POTHINUS (*disconcerted*):

Caesar— (*He stammers.*)

CAESAR:

Well, out with it.

POTHINUS:

What I have to say is for your ear, not for the Queen's.

CLEOPATRA (*with subdued ferocity*):

There are means of making you speak. Take care.

POTHINUS (*defiantly*):

Caesar does not employ those means.

CAESAR:

My friend: when a man has anything to tell in this world, the difficulty is not to make him tell it, but to prevent him from telling it too often. Let me celebrate my birthday by setting you free. Farewell: we shall not meet again.

CLEOPATRA (*angrily*):

Caesar: this mercy is foolish.

POTHINUS (*to* Caesar):

Will you not give me a private audience? Your life may depend on it. (Caesar *rises loftily.*)

RUFIO (*aside to* Pothinus):

Ass! Now we shall have some heroics.

CAESAR (*oratorically*):

Pothinus——

RUFIO (*interrupting him*):

Caesar: the dinner will spoil if you begin preaching your favourite sermon about life and death.

CLEOPATRA (*priggishly*):

Peace, Rufio. I desire to hear Caesar.

RUFIO (*bluntly*):

Your Majesty has heard it before. You repeated it to Apollodorus last week; and he thought it was all your own. (*Caesar's dignity collapses. Much tickled, he sits down again and looks roguishly at* Cleopatra, *who is furious.* Rufio *calls as before*) Ho there, guard! Pass the prisoner out. He is released. (*To* Pothinus) Now off with you. You have lost your chance.

POTHINUS (*his temper overcoming his prudence*):

I will speak.

CAESAR (*to* Cleopatra):

You see. Torture would not have wrung a word from him.

POTHINUS:

Caesar: you have taught Cleopatra the arts by which the Romans govern the world.

CAESAR:

Alas! they cannot even govern themselves. What then?

POTHINUS:

What then? Are you so besotted with her beauty that you do not see that she is impatient to reign in Egypt alone, and that her heart is set on your departure?

CLEOPATRA (*rising*):

Liar!

CAESAR (*shocked*):

What! Protestations! Contradictions!

CLEOPATRA (*ashamed, but trembling with suppressed rage*):

No. I do not deign to contradict. Let him talk. (*She sits down again.*)

POTHINUS:

From her own lips I have heard it. You are to be her catspaw: you are to tear the crown from her brother's head and set it on her own, delivering us all into her hand—delivering yourself also. And then Caesar can return to Rome, or depart through the gate of death, which is nearer and surer.

CAESAR (*calmly*):

Well, my friend; and is not this very natural?

POTHINUS (*astonished*):

Natural! Then you do not resent treachery?

CAESAR:

Resent! O thou foolish Egyptian, what have I to do with resentment? Do I resent the wind when it chills me, or the night when it makes me stumble in the darkness? Shall I resent youth when it turns from age, and ambition when it turns from servitude? To tell me such a story as this is but to tell me that the sun will rise to-morrow.

CLEOPATRA (*unable to contain herself*):

But it is false—false. I swear it.

CAESAR:

It is true, though you swore it a thousand times, and believed all you swore. (*She is convulsed with emotion. To screen her, he rises and takes* Pothinus *to* Rufio, *saying*) Come, Rufio: let us see Pothinus past the guard. I have a word to say to him. (*Aside to them*) We must give the Queen a moment to recover herself. (*Aloud*) Come. (*He takes* Pothinus *and* Rufio *out with him, conversing with them meanwhile.*) Tell your friends, Pothinus, that they must not think I am opposed to a reasonable settlement of the country's affairs— (*They pass out of hearing.*)

CLEOPATRA (*in a stifled whisper*):

Ftatateeta, Ftatateeta.

FTATATEETA (*hurrying to her from the table and petting her*):

Peace, child: be comforted——

CLEOPATRA (*interrupting her*):

Can they hear us?

FTATATEETA:

No, dear heart, no.

CLEOPATRA:

Listen to me. If he leaves the Palace alive, never see my face again.

FTATATEETA:

He? Poth——

CLEOPATRA (*striking her on the mouth*):

Strike his life out as I strike his name from your lips. Dash him down from the wall. Break him on the stones. Kill, kill, kill him.

FTATATEETA (*shewing all her teeth*):

The dog shall perish.

CLEOPATRA:

Fail in this, and you go out from before me for ever.

FTATATEETA (*resolutely*):

So be it. You shall not see my face until his eyes are darkened.

Caesar *comes back, with* Apollodorus, *exquisitely dressed, and* Rufio.

CLEOPATRA (*to* Ftatateeta):

Come soon—soon. (Ftatateeta *turns her meaning eyes for a moment on her mistress; then goes grimly away past Ra and out.* Cleopatra *runs like a gazelle to* Caesar) So you have come back to me, Caesar. (*Caressingly*) I thought you were angry. Welcome, Apollodorus. (*She gives him her hand to kiss, with her other arm about* Caesar.)

APOLLODORUS:

Cleopatra grows more womanly beautiful from week to week.

CLEOPATRA:

Truth, Apollodorus?

APOLLODORUS:

Far, far short of the truth! Friend Rufio threw a pearl into the sea: Caesar fished up a diamond.

CAESAR:

Caesar fished up a touch of rheumatism, my friend. Come: to dinner! to dinner! (*They move towards the table.*)

CLEOPATRA (*skipping like a young fawn*):

Yes, to dinner. I have ordered such a dinner for you, Caesar!

CAESAR:

Ay? What are we to have?

CLEOPATRA:

Peacocks' brains.

CAESAR (*as if his mouth watered*):

Peacocks' brains, Apollodorus!

APOLLODORUS:

Not for me. I prefer nightingales' tongues. (*He goes to one of the two covers set side by side.*)

CLEOPATRA:

Roast boar, Rufio!

RUFIO (*gluttonously*):

Good! (*He goes to the seat next to* Apollodorus, *on his left.*)

CAESAR (*looking at his seat, which is at the end of the table, to Ra's left hand*):

What has become of my leathern cushion?

CLEOPATRA (*at the opposite end*):

I have got new ones for you.

THE MAJOR-DOMO:

> These cushions, Caesar, are of Maltese gauze, stuffed with rose leaves.

CAESAR:

> Rose leaves! Am I a caterpillar? (*He throws the cushions away and seats himself on the leather mattress underneath.*)

CLEOPATRA:

> What a shame! My new cushions!

THE MAJOR-DOMO (*at* Caesar's *elbow*):

> What shall we serve to whet Caesar's appetite?

CAESAR:

> What have you got?

THE MAJOR-DOMO:

> Sea hedgehogs, black and white sea acorns, sea nettles, beccaficoes, purple shellfish——

CAESAR:

> Any oysters?

THE MAJOR-DOMO:

> Assuredly.

CAESAR:

> British oysters?

THE MAJOR-DOMO (*assenting*):

> British oysters, Caesar.

CAESAR:

> Oysters, then. (The Major-Domo *signs to a slave at each order; and the slave goes out to execute it.*) I have been in Britain—that western land of romance—the last piece of earth on the edge of the ocean that surrounds the world. I went there in search of its famous pearls. The British pearl was a fable; but in searching for it I found the British oyster.

APOLLODORUS:

> All posterity will bless you for it. (*To* the Major-Domo) Sea hedgehogs for me.

RUFIO:

> Is there nothing solid to begin with?

THE MAJOR-DOMO:

> Fieldfares with asparagus——

CLEOPATRA (*interrupting*):

> Fattened fowls! have some fattened fowls, Rufio.

RUFIO:

> Ay, that will do.

CLEOPATRA (*greedily*):

> Fieldfares for me.

THE MAJOR-DOMO:

Caesar will deign to choose his wine? Sicilian, Lesbian, Chian——

RUFIO (*contemptuously*):

All Greek.

APOLLODORUS:

Who would drink Roman wine when he could get Greek? Try the Lesbian, Caesar.

CAESAR:

Bring me my barley water.

RUFIO (*with intense disgust*):

Ugh! Bring me my Falernian. (*The Falernian is presently brought to him.*)

CLEOPATRA (*pouting*):

It is waste of time giving you dinners, Caesar. My scullions would not condescend to your diet.

CAESAR (*relenting*):

Well, well: let us try the Lesbian. (The Major-Domo *fills* Caesar's *goblet; then* Cleopatra's *and* Apollodorus's.) But when I return to Rome, I will make laws against these extravagances. I will even get the laws carried out.

CLEOPATRA (*coaxingly*):

Never mind. To-day you are to be like other people: idle, luxurious, and kind. (*She stretches her hand to him along the table.*)

CAESAR:

Well, for once I will sacrifice my comfort—(*kissing her hand*) there! (*He takes a draught of wine.*) Now are you satisfied?

CLEOPATRA:

And you no longer believe that I long for your departure for Rome?

CAESAR:

I no longer believe anything. My brains are asleep. Besides, who knows whether I shall return to Rome?

RUFIO (*alarmed*):

How? Eh? What?

CAESAR:

What has Rome to shew me that I have not seen already? One year of Rome is like another, except that I grow older, whilst the crowd in the Appian Way is always the same age.

APOLLODORUS:

It is no better here in Egypt. The old men, when they are tired of life, say "We have seen everything except the source of the Nile."

CAESAR (*his imagination catching fire*):

And why not see that? Cleopatra: will you come with me and track the flood to its cradle in the heart of the regions of mystery? Shall we leave Rome behind us—Rome, that has achieved greatness only to learn how greatness destroys nations of men who are not great! Shall I make you a new kingdom, and build you a holy city there in the great unknown?

CLEOPATRA (*rapturously*):

Yes, yes. You shall.

RUFIO:

Ay: now he will conquer Africa with two legions before we come to the roast boar.

APOLLODORUS:

Come: no scoffing. This is a noble scheme: in it Caesar is no longer merely the conquering soldier, but the creative poet-artist. Let us name the holy city, and consecrate it with Lesbian wine.

CAESAR:

Cleopatra shall name it herself.

CLEOPATRA:

It shall be called Caesar's Gift to his Beloved.

APOLLODORUS:

No, no. Something vaster than that—something universal, like the starry firmament.

CAESAR (*prosaically*):

Why not simply The Cradle of the Nile?

CLEOPATRA:

No: the Nile is my ancestor; and he is a god. Oh! I have thought of something. The Nile shall name it himself. Let us call upon him. (*To the Major-Domo*) Send for him. (*The three men stare at one another; but the Major-Domo goes out as if he had received the most matter-of-fact order.*) And (*to the retinue*) away with you all.

*The retinue withdraws, making obeisance.*

*A priest enters, carrying a miniature sphinx with a tiny tripod before it. A morsel of incense is smoking in the tripod. The priest comes to the table and places the image in the middle of it. The light begins to change to the magenta purple of the Egyptian sunset, as if the god had brought a strange colored shadow with him. The three men are determined not to be impressed; but they feel curious in spite of themselves.*

CAESAR:

What hocus-pocus is this?

CLEOPATRA:

You shall see. And it is not hocus-pocus. To do it properly, we should kill something to please him; but perhaps he will answer Caesar without that if we spill some wine to him.

APOLLODORUS (*turning his head to look up over his shoulder at Ra*):

Why not appeal to our hawkheaded friend here?

CLEOPATRA (*nervously*):

Sh! He will hear you and be angry.

RUFIO (*phlegmatically*):

The source of the Nile is out of his district, I expect.

CLEOPATRA:

No: I will have my city named by nobody but my dear little sphinx, because it was in its arms that Caesar found me asleep. (*She languishes at* Caesar; *then turns curtly to the priest*) Go. I am a priestess, and have power to take your charge from you. (*The priest makes a reverence and goes out.*) Now let us call on the Nile all together. Perhaps he will rap on the table.

CAESAR:

What! table rapping! Are such superstitions still believed in this year 707 of the Republic?

CLEOPATRA:

It is no superstition: our priests learn lots of things from the tables. Is it not so, Apollodorus?

APOLLODORUS:

Yes: I profess myself a converted man. When Cleopatra is priestess, Apollodorus is devotee. Propose the conjuration.

CLEOPATRA:

You must say with me "Send us thy voice, Father Nile."

ALL FOUR (*holding their glasses together before the idol*):

Send us thy voice, Father Nile.

*The death cry of a man in mortal terror and agony answers them. Appalled, the men set down their glasses, and listen. Silence. The purple deepens in the sky.* Caesar, *glancing at* Cleopatra, *catches her pouring out her wine before the god, with gleaming eyes, and mute assurances of gratitude and worship.* Apollodorus *springs up and runs to the edge of the roof to peer down and listen.*

CAESAR (*looking piercingly at* Cleopatra):

What was that?

CLEOPATRA (*petulantly*):

Nothing. They are beating some slave.

CAESAR:

Nothing!

RUFIO:

A man with a knife in him, I'll swear.

CAESAR (*rising*):

A murder!

APOLLODORUS (*at the back, waving his hand for silence*):

S-sh! Silence. Did you hear that?

CAESAR:

Another cry?

APOLLODORUS (*returning to the table*):

No, a thud. Something fell on the beach, I think.

RUFIO (*grimly, as he rises*):

Something with bones in it, eh?

CAESAR (*shuddering*):

Hush, hush, Rufio. (*He leaves the table and returns to the colon-nade: Rufio following at his left elbow, and Apollodorus at the other side.*)

CLEOPATRA (*still in her place at the table*):

Will you leave me, Caesar? Apollodorus: are you going?

APOLLODORUS:

Faith, dearest Queen, my appetite is gone.

CAESAR:

Go down to the courtyard, Apollodorus; and find out what has happened.

Apollodorus *nods and goes out, making for the staircase by which* Rufio *ascended.*

CLEOPATRA:

Your soldiers have killed somebody, perhaps. What does it matter?

*The murmur of a crowd rises from the beach below.* Caesar *and* Rufio *look at one another.*

. CAESAR:

This must be seen to. (*He is about to follow* Apollodorus *when* Rufio *stops him with a hand on his arm as* Ftatateeta *comes back by the far end of the roof, with dragging steps, a drowsy satiety in her eyes and in the corners of the bloodhound lips. For a moment* Caesar *suspects that she is drunk with wine. Not so* Rufio: *he knows well the red vintage that has inebriated her.*)

RUFIO (*in a low tone*):

There is some mischief between those two.

FTATATEETA:

> The Queen looks again on the face of her servant.

Cleopatra *looks at her for a moment with an exultant reflection of her murderous expression. Then she flings her arms round her; kisses her repeatedly and savagely; and tears off her jewels and heaps them on her. The two men turn from the spectacle to look at one another.* Ftatateeta *drags herself sleepily to the altar; kneels before Ra; and remains there in prayer.* Caesar *goes to* Cleopatra, *leaving* Rufio *in the colonnade.*

CAESAR (*with searching earnestness*):

> Cleopatra: what has happened?

CLEOPATRA (*in mortal dread of him, but with her utmost cajolery*):

> Nothing, dearest Caesar. (*With sickly sweetness, her voice almost failing*) Nothing. I am innocent. (*She approaches him affectionately*) Dear Caesar: are you angry with me? Why do you look at me so? I have been here with you all the time. How can I know what has happened?

CAESAR (*reflectively*):

> That is true.

CLEOPATRA (*greatly relieved, trying to caress him*):

> Of course it is true. (*He does not respond to the caress.*) You know it is true, Rufio.

> *The murmur without suddenly swells to a roar and subsides.*

RUFIO:

> I shall know presently. (*He makes for the altar in the burly trot that serves him for a stride, and touches* Ftatateeta *on the shoulder.*) Now, mistress: I shall want you. (*He orders her, with a gesture, to go before him.*)

FTATATEETA (*rising and glowering at him*):

> My place is with the Queen.

CLEOPATRA:

> She has done no harm, Rufio.

CAESAR (*to* Rufio):

> Let her stay.

RUFIO (*sitting down on the altar*):

> Very well. Then my place is here too; and you can see what is the matter for yourself. The city is in a pretty uproar, it seems.

CAESAR (*with grave displeasure*):

> Rufio: there is a time for obedience.

RUFIO:

> And there is a time for obstinacy. (*He folds his arms doggedly.*)

CAESAR (*to* Cleopatra):

Send her away.

CLEOPATRA (*whining in her eagerness to propitiate him*):

Yes, I will. I will do whatever you ask me, Caesar, always, because I love you. Ftatateeta: go away.

FTATATEETA:

The Queen's word is my will. I shall be at hand for the Queen's call. (*She goes out past Ra, as she came.*)

RUFIO (*following her*):

Remember, Caesar, your bodyguard also is within call. (*He follows her out.*)

Cleopatra, *presuming upon* Caesar's *submission to* Rufio, *leaves the table and sits down on the bench in the colonnade.*

CLEOPATRA:

Why do you allow Rufio to treat you so? You should teach him his place.

CAESAR:

Teach him to be my enemy, and to hide his thoughts from me as you are now hiding yours.

CLEOPATRA (*her fears returning*):

Why do you say that, Caesar? Indeed, indeed, I am not hiding anything. You are wrong to treat me like this. (*She stifles a sob.*) I am only a child; and you turn into stone because you think some one has been killed. I cannot bear it. (*She purposely breaks down and weeps. He looks at her with profound sadness and complete coldness. She looks up to see what effect she is producing. Seeing that he is unmoved, she sits up, pretending to struggle with her emotion and to put it bravely away.*) But there: I know you hate tears: you shall not be troubled with them. I know you are not angry, but only sad; only I am so silly, I cannot help being hurt when you speak coldly. Of course you are quite right: it is dreadful to think of anyone being killed or even hurt; and I hope nothing really serious has— (*Her voice dies away under his contemptuous penetration.*)

CAESAR:

What has frightened you into this? What have you done? (*A trumpet sounds on the beach below.*) Aha! that sounds like the answer.

CLEOPATRA (*sinking back trembling on the bench and covering her face with her hands*):

I have not betrayed you, Caesar: I swear it.

CAESAR:

> I know that. I have not trusted you. (*He turns from her, and is about to go out when* Apollodorus *and* Britannus *drag in* Lucius Septimius *to him.* Rufio *follows.* Caesar *shudders.*) Again, Pompey's murderer!

RUFIO:

> The town has gone mad, I think. They are for tearing the palace down and driving us into the sea straight away. We laid hold of this renegade in clearing them out of the courtyard.

CAESAR:

> Release him. (*They let go his arms.*) What has offended the citizens, Lucius Septimius?

LUCIUS:

> What did you expect, Caesar? Pothinus was a favorite of theirs.

CAESAR:

> What has happened to Pothinus? I set him free, here, not half an hour ago. Did they not pass him out?

LUCIUS:

> Ay, through the gallery arch sixty feet above ground, with three inches of steel in his ribs. He is as dead as Pompey. We are quits now, as to killing—you and I.

CAESAR (*shocked*):

> Assassinated!—our prisoner, our guest! (*He turns reproachfully on* Rufio) Rufio——

RUFIO (*emphatically—anticipating the question*):

> Whoever did it was a wise man and a friend of yours (Cleopatra *is greatly emboldened*); but none of us had a hand in it. So it is no use to frown at me. (Caesar *turns and looks at* Cleopatra.)

CLEOPATRA (*violently—rising*):

> He was slain by order of the Queen of Egypt. I am not Julius Caesar the dreamer, who allows every slave to insult him. Rufio has said I did well: now the others shall judge me too. (*She turns to the others*) This Pothinus sought to make me conspire with him to betray Caesar to Achillas and Ptolemy. I refused; and he cursed me and came privily to Caesar to accuse me of his own treachery. I caught him in the act; and he insulted me—me, the Queen! to my face. Caesar would not avenge me: he spoke him fair and set him free. Was I right to avenge myself? Speak, Lucius.

LUCIUS:

> I do not gainsay it. But you will get little thanks from Caesar for it.

CLEOPATRA:

> Speak, Apollodorus. Was I wrong?

APOLLODORUS:

I have only one word of blame, most beautiful. You should have called upon me, your knight; and in fair duel I should have slain the slanderer.

CLEOPATRA (*passionately*):

I will be judged by your very slave, Caesar. Britannus: speak. Was I wrong?

BRITANNUS:

Were treachery, falsehood, and disloyalty left unpunished, society must become like an arena full of wild beasts, tearing one another to pieces. Caesar is in the wrong.

CAESAR (*with quiet bitterness*):

And so the verdict is against me, it seems.

CLEOPATRA (*vehemently*):

Listen to me, Caesar. If one man in all Alexandria can be found to say that I did wrong, I swear to have myself crucified on the door of the palace by my own slaves.

CAESAR:

If one man in all the world can be found, now or forever, to know that you did wrong, that man will have either to conquer the world as I have, or be crucified by it. (*The uproar in the streets again reaches them.*) Do you hear? These knockers at your gate are also believers in vengeance and in stabbing. You have slain their leader: it is right that they shall slay you. If you doubt it, ask your four counsellors here. And then in the name of that right (*he emphasizes the word with great scorn*) shall I not slay them for murdering their Queen, and be slain in my turn by their countrymen as the invader of their fatherland? Can Rome do less then than slay these slayers too, to shew the world how Rome avenges her sons and her honor? And so, to the end of history, murder shall breed murder, always in the name of right and honor and peace, until the gods are tired of blood and create a race that can understand. (*Fierce uproar. Cleopatra becomes white with terror.*) Hearken, you who must not be insulted. Go near enough to catch their words: you will find them bitterer than the tongue of Pothinus. (*Loftily wrapping himself up in an impenetrable dignity.*) Let the Queen of Egypt now give her orders for vengeance, and take her measures for defence; for she has renounced Caesar. (*He turns to go.*)

CLEOPATRA (*terrified, running to him and falling on her knees*):

You will not desert me, Caesar. You will defend the palace.

CAESAR:

You have taken the powers of life and death upon you. I am only a dreamer.

CLEOPATRA:

But they will kill me.

CAESAR:

And why not?

CLEOPATRA:

In pity——

CAESAR:

Pity! What! has it come to this so suddenly, that nothing can save you now but pity? Did it save Pothinus?

*She rises, wringing her hands, and goes back to the bench in despair. Apollodorus shews his sympathy with her by quietly posting himself behind the bench. The sky has by this time become the most vivid purple, and soon begins to change to a glowing pale orange, against which the colonnade and the great image show darklier and darklier.*

RUFIO:

Caesar: enough of preaching. The enemy is at the gate.

CAESAR (*turning on him and giving way to his wrath*):

Ay; and what has held him baffled at the gate all these months? Was it my folly, as you deem it, or your wisdom? In this Egyptian Red Sea of blood, whose hand has held all your heads above the waves? (*Turning on* Cleopatra) And yet, when Caesar says to such an one, "Friend, go free," you, clinging for your little life to my sword, dare steal out and stab him in the back? And you, soldiers and gentlemen, and honest servants as you forget that you are, applaud this assassination, and say "Caesar is in the wrong." By the gods, I am tempted to open my hand and let you all sink into the flood.

CLEOPATRA (*with a ray of cunning hope*):

But, Caesar, if you do, you will perish yourself.

*Caesar's eyes blaze.*

RUFIO (*greatly alarmed*):

Now, by great Jove, you filthy little Egyptian rat, that is the very word to make him walk out alone into the city and leave us here to be cut to pieces. (*Desperately, to* Caesar) Will you desert us because we are a parcel of fools? I mean no harm by killing: I do it as a dog kills a cat, by instinct. We are all dogs at your heels; but we have served you faithfully.

CAESAR (*relenting*):

Alas, Rufio, my son, my son: as dogs we are like to perish now in the streets.

APOLLODORUS (*at his post behind* Cleopatra*'s seat*):

Caesar, what you say has an Olympian ring in it: it must be right; for it is fine art. But I am still on the side of Cleopatra. If we must die, she shall not want the devotion of a man's heart nor the strength of a man's arm.

CLEOPATRA (*sobbing*):

But I don't want to die.

CAESAR (*sadly*):

Oh, ignoble, ignoble!

LUCIUS (*coming forward between* Caesar *and* Cleopatra):

Hearken to me, Caesar. It may be ignoble; but I also mean to live as long as I can.

CAESAR:

Well, my friend, you are likely to outlive Caesar. Is it any magic of mine, think you, that has kept your army and this whole city at bay for so long? Yesterday, what quarrel had they with me that they should risk their lives against me? But to-day we have flung them down their hero, murdered; and now every man of them is set upon clearing out this nest of assassins—for such we are and no more. Take courage then; and sharpen your sword. Pompey's head has fallen; and Caesar's head is ripe.

APOLLODORUS:

Does Caesar despair?

CAESAR (*with infinite pride*):

He who has never hoped can never despair. Caesar, in good or bad fortune, looks his fate in the face.

LUCIUS:

Look it in the face, then; and it will smile as it always has on Caesar.

CAESAR (*with involuntary haughtiness*):

Do you presume to encourage me?

LUCIUS:

I offer you my services. I will change sides if you will have me.

CAESAR (*suddenly coming down to earth again, and looking sharply at him, divining that there is something behind the offer*):

What! At this point?

LUCIUS (*firmly*):

At this point.

RUFIO:

Do you suppose Caesar is mad, to trust you?

LUCIUS:

I do not ask him to trust me until he is victorious. I ask for my life, and for a command in Caesar's army. And since Caesar is a fair dealer, I will pay in advance.

CAESAR:

Pay! How?

LUCIUS:

With a piece of good news for you.

Caesar *divines the news in a flash*.

RUFIO:

What news?

CAESAR (*with an elate and buoyant energy which makes* Cleopatra *sit up and stare*):

What news! What news, did you say, my son Rufio? The relief has arrived: what other news remains for us? Is it not so, Lucius Septimius? Mithridates of Pergamos is on the march.

LUCIUS:

He has taken Pelusium.

CAESAR (*delighted*):

Lucius Septimius: you are henceforth my officer. Rufio: the Egyptians must have sent every soldier from the city to prevent Mithridates crossing the Nile. There is nothing in the streets now but mob—mob!

LUCIUS:

It is so. Mithridates is marching by the great road to Memphis to cross above the Delta. Achillas will fight him there.

CAESAR (*all audacity*):

Achillas shall fight Caesar there. See, Rufio. (*He runs to the table; snatches a napkin; and draws a plan on it with his finger dipped in wine, whilst* Rufio *and* Lucius Septimius *crowd about him to watch, all looking closely, for the light is now almost gone.*) Here is the palace (*pointing to his plan*): here is the theatre. You (*to* Rufio) take twenty men and pretend to go by that street (*pointing it out*); and whilst they are stoning you, out go the cohorts by this and this. My streets are right, are they, Lucius?

LUCIUS:

Ay, that is the fig market——

CAESAR (*too much excited to listen to him*):

I saw them the day we arrived. Good! (*He throws the napkin on the table and comes down again into the colonnade.*) Away, Britannus: tell Petronius that within an hour half our forces must take ship for the western lake. See to my horse and armor. (*Britannus runs out.*) With the rest, *I* shall march round the lake and up the Nile to meet Mithridates. Away, Lucius; and give the word.

Lucius *hurries out after* Britannus.

RUFIO:

Come: this is something like business.

CAESAR (*buoyantly*):

Is it not, my only son? (*He claps his hands. The slaves hurry in to the table.*) No more of this mawkish revelling: away with all this stuff: shut it out of my sight and be off with you. (*The slaves begin to remove the table; and the curtains are drawn, shutting in the colonnade.*) You understand about the streets, Rufio?

RUFIO:

Ay, I think I do. I will get through them, at all events.

> *The bucina sounds busily in the courtyard beneath.*

CAESAR:

Come, then: we must talk to the troops and hearten them. You down to the beach: I to the courtyard. (*He makes for the staircase.*)

CLEOPATRA (*rising from her seat, where she has been quite neglected all this time, and stretching out her hands timidly to him*):

Caesar.

CAESAR (*turning*):

Eh?

CLEOPATRA:

Have you forgotten me?

CAESAR (*indulgently*):

I am busy now, my child, busy. When I return your affairs shall be settled. Farewell; and be good and patient.

*He goes, preoccupied and quite indifferent. She stands with clenched fists, in speechless rage and humiliation.*

RUFIO:

That game is played and lost, Cleopatra. The woman always gets the worst of it.

CLEOPATRA (*haughtily*):

Go. Follow your master.

RUFIO (*in her ear, with rough familiarity*):

A word first. Tell your executioner that if Pothinus had been properly killed—in the throat—he would not have called out. Your man bungled his work.

CLEOPATRA (*enigmatically*):

How do you know it was a man?

RUFIO (*startled, and puzzled*):

It was not you: you were with us when it happened. (*She turns her back scornfully on him. He shakes his head, and draws the curtains to go out. It is now a magnificent moonlit night. The table has been removed.* Ftatateeta *is seen in the light of the moon and stars, again in prayer before the white altar-stone of Ra.* Rufio *starts; closes the curtains again softly; and says in a low voice to* Cleopatra) Was it she? with her own hand?

CLEOPATRA (*threateningly*):

Whoever it was, let my enemies beware of her. Look to it, Rufio, you who dare make the Queen of Egypt a fool before Caesar.

RUFIO (*looking grimly at her*):

I will look to it, Cleopatra. (*He nods in confirmation of the promise, and slips out through the curtains, loosening his sword in its sheath as he goes.*)

ROMAN SOLDIERS (*in the courtyard below*):

Hail, Caesar! Hail, hail!

Cleopatra *listens. The bucina sounds again, followed by several trumpets.*

CLEOPATRA (*wringing her hands and calling*):

Ftatateeta. Ftatateeta. It is dark; and I am alone. Come to me. (*Silence.*) Ftatateeta. (*Louder.*) Ftatateeta. (*Silence. In a panic she snatches the cord and pulls the curtains apart.*)

Ftatateeta *is lying dead on the altar of Ra, with her throat cut. Her blood deluges the white stone.*

# Act V

*High noon. Festival and military pageant on the esplanade before the palace. In the east harbor Caesar's galley, so gorgeously decorated that it seems to be rigged with flowers, is alongside the quay, close to the steps Apollodorus descended when he embarked with the carpet. A Roman guard is posted there in charge of a gangway, whence a red floorcloth is laid down the middle of the esplanade, turning off to the north opposite the central gate in the palace front, which shuts in the esplanade on the south side. The broad steps of the gate, crowded with Cleopatra's ladies, all in their gayest attire, are like a flower garden. The façade is lined by her guard, officered by the same gallants to whom Bel Affris announced the coming of Caesar six months before in the old palace on the Syrian border. The north side is lined by Roman soldiers, with the townsfolk on tiptoe*

*behind them, peering over their heads at the cleared esplanade, in which
the officers stroll about, chatting. Among these are* Belzanor *and the Persian; also the* Centurion, *vinewood cudgel in hand, battle worn, thick-
booted, and much outshone, both socially and decoratively, by the Egyptian
officers.*

Apollodorus *makes his way through the townsfolk and calls to the officers from behind the Roman line.*

APOLLODORUS:

Hullo! May I pass?

CENTURION:

Pass Apollodorus the Sicilian there! (*The soldiers let him
through.*)

BELZANOR:

Is Caesar at hand?

APOLLODORUS:

Not yet. He is still in the market place. I could not stand any
more of the roaring of the soldiers! After half an hour of the
enthusiasm of an army, one feels the need of a little sea air.

PERSIAN:

Tell us the news. Hath he slain the priests?

APOLLODORUS:

Not he. They met him in the market place with ashes on their
heads and their gods in their hands. They placed the gods at his
feet. The only one that was worth looking at was Apis: a miracle of gold and ivory work. By my advice he offered the chief
priest two talents for it.

BELZANOR (*appalled*):

Apis the all-knowing for two talents! What said the chief
priest?

APOLLODORUS:

He invoked the mercy of Apis, and asked for five.

BELZANOR:

There will be famine and tempest in the land for this.

PERSIAN:

Pooh! Why did not Apis cause Caesar to be vanquished by
Achillas? Any fresh news from the war, Apollodorus?

APOLLODORUS:

The little King Ptolemy was drowned.

BELZANOR:

Drowned! How?

APOLLODORUS:

With the rest of them. Caesar attacked them from three sides at
once and swept them into the Nile. Ptolemy's barge sank.

BELZANOR:

A marvelous man, this Caesar! Will he come soon, think you?

APOLLODORUS:

He was settling the Jewish question when I left.

*A flourish of trumpets from the north, and commotion among the towns-folk, announces the approach of* Caesar.

PERSIAN:

He has made short work of them. Here he comes. (*He hurries to his post in front of the Egyptian lines.*)

BELZANOR (*following him*):

Ho there! Caesar comes.

*The soldiers stand at attention, and dress their lines.* Apollodorus *goes to the Egyptian line.*

CENTURION (*hurrying to the gangway guard*):

Attention there! Caesar comes.

Caesar *arrives in state with* Rufio: Britannus *following. The soldiers receive him with enthusiastic shouting.*

CAESAR:

I see my ship awaits me. The hour of Caesar's farewell to Egypt has arrived. And now, Rufio, what remains to be done before I go?

RUFIO (*at his left hand*):

You have not yet appointed a Roman governor for this province.

CAESAR (*looking whimsically at him, but speaking with perfect gravity*):

What say you to Mithridates of Pergamos, my reliever and res-cuer, the great son of Eupator?

RUFIO:

Why, that you will want him elsewhere. Do you forget that you have some three or four armies to conquer on your way home?

CAESAR:

Indeed! Well, what say you to yourself?

RUFIO (*incredulously*):

I! I a governor! What are you dreaming of? Do you not know that I am only the son of a freedman?

CAESAR (*affectionately*):

Has not Caesar called you his son? (*Calling to the whole assem-bly*) Peace awhile there; and hear me.

THE ROMAN SOLDIERS:

Hear Caesar.

CAESAR:

Hear the service, quality, rank and name of the Roman governor. By service, Caesar's shield; by quality, Caesar's friend; by rank, a Roman soldier. (*The Roman soldiers give a triumphant shout.*) By name, Rufio. (*They shout again.*)

RUFIO (*kissing* Caesar's *hand*):

Ay: I am Caesar's shield; but of what use shall I be when I am no longer on Caesar's arm? Well, no matter— (*He becomes husky, and turns away to recover himself.*)

CAESAR:

Where is that British Islander of mine?

BRITANNUS (*coming forward on* Caesar's *right hand*):

Here, Caesar.

CAESAR:

Who bade you, pray, thrust yourself into the battle of the Delta, uttering the barbarous cries of your native land, and affirming yourself a match for any four of the Egyptians, to whom you applied unseemly epithets?

BRITANNUS:

Caesar: I ask you to excuse the language that escaped me in the heat of the moment.

CAESAR:

And how did you, who cannot swim, cross the canal with us when we stormed the camp?

BRITANNUS:

Caesar: I clung to the tail of your horse.

CAESAR:

These are not the deeds of a slave, Britannicus, but of a free man.

BRITANNUS:

Caesar: I was born free.

CAESAR:

But they call you Caesar's slave.

BRITANNUS:

Only as Caesar's slave have I found real freedom.

CAESAR (*moved*):

Well said. Ungrateful that I am, I was about to set you free; but now I will not part from you for a million talents. (*He claps him friendly on the shoulder. Britannus, gratified, but a trifle shamefaced, takes his hand and kisses it sheepishly.*)

BELZANOR (*to the Persian*):

This Roman knows how to make men serve him.

PERSIAN:

Ay: men too humble to become dangerous rivals to him.

BELZANOR:

O subtle one! O cynic!

CAESAR (*seeing* Apollodorus *in the Egyptian corner and calling to him*):

Apollodorus: I leave the art of Egypt in your charge. Remember: Rome loves art and will encourage it ungrudgingly.

APOLLODORUS:

I understand, Caesar. Rome will produce no art itself; but it will buy up and take away whatever the other nations produce.

CAESAR:

What! Rome produce no art! Is peace not an art? is war not an art? is government not an art? is civilization not an art? All these we give you in exchange for a few ornaments. You will have the best of the bargain. (*Turning to* Rufio) And now, what else have I to do before I embark? (*Trying to recollect*) There is something I cannot remember: what can it be? Well, well: it must remain undone: we must not waste this favorable wind. Farewell, Rufio.

RUFIO:

Caesar: I am loth to let you go to Rome without your shield. There are too many daggers there.

CAESAR:

It matters not: I shall finish my life's work on my way back; and then I shall have lived long enough. Besides: I have always disliked the idea of dying: I had rather be killed. Farewell.

RUFIO (*with a sigh, raising his hands and giving* Caesar *up as incorrigible*):

Farewell. (*They shake hands.*)

CAESAR (*waving his hand to* Apollodorus):

Farewell, Apollodorus, and my friends, all of you. Aboard!

*The gangway is run out from the quay to the ship. As* Caesar *moves towards it,* Cleopatra, *cold and tragic, cunningly dressed in black, without ornaments or decoration of any kind, and thus making a striking figure among the brilliantly dressed bevy of ladies as she passes through it, comes from the palace and stands on the steps.* Caesar *does not see her until she speaks.*

CLEOPATRA:

Has Cleopatra no part in this leave taking?

CAESAR (*enlightened*):

Ah, I knew there was something. (*To* Rufio) How could you let me forget her, Rufio? (*Hastening to her*) Had I gone without seeing you, I should never have forgiven myself. (*He takes her hands, and brings her into the middle of the esplanade. She submits stonily.*) Is this mourning for me?

CLEOPATRA:

No.

CAESAR (*remorsefully*):

Ah, that was thoughtless of me! It is for your brother.

CLEOPATRA:

No.

CAESAR (*remorsefully*):

For whom, then?

CLEOPATRA:

Ask the Roman governor whom you have left us.

CAESAR:

Rufio?

CLEOPATRA:

Yes: Rufio. (*She points at him with deadly scorn.*) He who is to rule here in Caesar's name, in Caesar's way, according to Caesar's boasted laws of life.

CAESAR (*dubiously*):

He is to rule as he can, Cleopatra. He has taken the work upon him, and will do it in his own way.

CLEOPATRA:

Not in your way, then?

CAESAR (*puzzled*):

What do you mean by my way?

CLEOPATRA:

Without punishment. Without revenge. Without judgment.

CAESAR (*approvingly*):

Ay: that is the right way, the great way, the only possible way in the end. (*To Rufio*) Believe it, Rufio, if you can.

RUFIO:

Why, I believe it, Caesar. You have convinced me of it long ago. But look you. You are sailing for Numidia to-day. Now tell me: if you meet a hungry lion there, you will not punish it for wanting to eat you?

CAESAR (*wondering what he is driving at*):

No.

RUFIO:

Nor revenge upon it the blood of those it has already eaten.

CAESAR:

No.

RUFIO:

Nor judge it for its guiltiness.

CAESAR:

No.

RUFIO:

What, then, will you do to save your life from it?

CAESAR (*promptly*):

Kill it, man, without malice, just as it would kill me. What does this parable of the lion mean?

RUFIO:

Why, Cleopatra had a tigress that killed men at her bidding. I thought she might bid it kill you some day. Well, had I not been Caesar's pupil, what pious things might I not have done to that tigress? I might have punished it. I might have revenged Pothinus on it.

CAESAR (*interjects*):

Pothinus!

RUFIO (*continuing*):

I might have judged it. But I put all these follies behind me; and, without malice, only cut its throat. And that is why Cleopatra comes to you in mourning.

CLEOPATRA (*vehemently*):

He has shed the blood of my servant Ftatateeta. On your head be it as upon his, Caesar, if you hold him free of it.

CAESAR (*energetically*):

On my head be it, then; for it was well done. Rufio: had you set yourself in the seat of the judge, and with hateful ceremonies and appeals to the gods handed that woman over to some hired executioner to be slain before the people in the name of justice, never again would I have touched your hand without a shudder. But this was natural slaying: I feel no horror at it.

Rufio, *satisfied, nods at* Cleopatra, *mutely inviting her to mark that.*

CLEOPATRA (*pettish and childish in her impotence*):

No: not when a Roman slays an Egyptian. All the world will now see how unjust and corrupt Caesar is.

CAESAR (*taking her hands coaxingly*):

Come: do not be angry with me. I am sorry for that poor Totateeta. (*She laughs in spite of herself.*) Aha! you are laughing. Does that mean reconciliation?

CLEOPATRA (*angry with herself for laughing*):

No, no, NO!! But it is so ridiculous to hear you call her Totateeta.

CAESAR:

What! As much a child as ever, Cleopatra! Have I not made a woman of you after all?

CLEOPATRA:

Oh, it is you who are a great baby: you make me seem silly because you will not behave seriously. But you have treated me badly; and I do not forgive you.

CAESAR:

Bid me farewell.

CLEOPATRA:

I will not.

CAESAR (*coaxing*):

I will send you a beautiful present from Rome.

CLEOPATRA (*proudly*):

Beauty from Rome to Egypt indeed! What can Rome give me that Egypt cannot give me?

APOLLODORUS:

That is true, Caesar. If the present is to be really beautiful, I shall have to buy it for you in Alexandria.

CAESAR:

You are forgetting the treasures for which Rome is most famous, my friend. You cannot buy them in Alexandria.

APOLLODORUS:

What are they, Caesar?

CAESAR:

Her sons. Come, Cleopatra: forgive me and bid me farewell; and I will send you a man, Roman from head to heel and Roman of the noblest; not old and ripe for the knife; not lean in the arms and cold in the heart; not hiding a bald head under his conqueror's laurels; not stooped with the weight of the world on his shoulders; but brisk and fresh, strong and young, hoping in the morning, fighting in the day, and revelling in the evening. Will you take such an one in exchange for Caesar?

CLEOPATRA (*palpitating*):

His name, his name?

CAESAR:

Shall it be Mark Antony? (*She throws herself into his arms.*)

RUFIO:

You are a bad hand at a bargain, mistress, if you will swap Caesar for Antony.

CAESAR:

So now you are satisfied.

CLEOPATRA:

You will not forget.

CAESAR:
> I will not forget. Farewell: I do not think we shall meet again. Farewell. (*He kisses her on the forehead. She is much affected and begins to sniff. He embarks.*)

THE ROMAN SOLDIERS (*as he sets his foot on the gangway*):
> Hail, Caesar; and farewell!

*He reaches the ship and returns* Rufio's *wave of the hand.*

APOLLODORUS (*to* Cleopatra):
> No tears, dearest Queen: they stab your servant to the heart. He will return some day.

CLEOPATRA:
> I hope not. But I can't help crying, all the same. (*She waves her handkerchief to* Caesar; *and the ship begins to move.*)

THE ROMAN SOLDIERS (*drawing their swords and raising them in the air*):
> Hail, Caesar!

# Notes to Caesar and Cleopatra

## Cleopatra's Cure for Baldness

For the sake of conciseness in a hurried situation I have made Cleopatra recommend rum. This, I am afraid, is an anachronism: the only real one in the play. To balance it, I give a couple of the remedies she actually believed in. They are quoted by Galen from Cleopatra's book on Cosmetic.

"For bald patches, powder red sulphuret of arsenic and take it up with oak gum, as much as it will bear. Put on a rag and apply, having soaped the place well first. I have mixed the above with a foam of nitre, and it worked well."

Several other receipts follow, ending with: "The following is the best of all, acting for fallen hairs, when applied with oil or pomatum; acts also for falling off of eyelashes or for people getting bald all over. It is wonderful. Of domestic mice burnt, one part; of vine rag burnt, one part; of horse's teeth burnt, one part; of bear's grease one; of deer's marrow one; of reed bark one. To be pounded when dry, and mixed with plenty of honey till it gets the consistency of honey; then the bear's grease and marrow to be mixed (when melted), the medicine to be put in a brass flask, and the bald part rubbed till it sprouts."

Concerning these ingredients, my fellow-dramatist, Gilbert Murray, who, as a Professor of Greek, has applied to classical antiquity the methods of high scholarship (my own method is pure divination), writes to me as follows: "Some of this I don't understand, and possibly Galen did not, as he quotes your heroine's own language. Foam of nitre is, I think, something like soapsuds. Reed bark is an odd expression. It might mean the outside membrane of a reed: I do not know what it ought to be called. In the burnt mice receipt I take it that you first mixed the solid powders with honey, and then added the grease. I expect Cleopatra preferred it because in most of the others you have to lacerate the skin, prick it, or rub it till it bleeds. I do not know what vine rag is. I translate literally."

## Apparent Anachronisms

The only way to write a play which shall convey to the general public an impression of antiquity is to make the characters speak blank verse and abstain from reference to steam, telegraphy, or any of the material conditions of their existence. The more ignorant men are, the more convinced are they that their little parish and their little chapel is an apex to which civilization and philosophy have painfully struggled up the pyramid of time from a desert of savagery. Savagery, they think, became barbarism; barbarism became ancient civilization; ancient civilization became Pauline Christianity; Pauline Christianity became Roman Catholicism; Roman Catholicism became the Dark Ages; and the Dark Ages were finally enlightened by the Protestant instincts of the English race. The whole process is summed up as Progress with a capital P. And any elderly gentleman of Progressive temperament will testify that the improvement since he was a boy is enormous.

Now if we count the generations of Progressive elderly gentlemen since, say, Plato, and add together the successive enormous improvements to which each of them has testified, it will strike us at once as an unaccountable fact that the world, instead of having been improved in 67 generations out of all recognition, presents, on the whole, a rather less dignified appearance in Ibsen's *Enemy of the People* than in Plato's *Republic*. And in truth, the period of time covered by history is far too short to allow of any perceptible progress in the popular sense of Evolution of the Human Species. The notion that there has been any such Progress since Caesar's time (less than 20 centuries) is too absurd for discussion. All the savagery, barbarism, dark ages and the rest of it of which we have any record as existing in the past, exists at the present moment. A British carpenter or stonemason may point out that he gets twice as much money for his labor as his father did in the same trade, and that his suburban house, with its bath, its cottage piano, its drawing-room suite, and its album of photographs, would have shamed the plainness of his grandmother's. But the descendants of feudal barons, living in squalid lodgings on a salary of fifteen shillings a week instead of in castles on princely revenues, do not congratulate the world on the change. Such changes, in fact, are not to the point. It has been known, as far back as our records go, that man running wild in the woods is different to man kennelled in a city slum; that a dog seems to understand a shepherd better than a hewer of wood and drawer of water can understand an astronomer; and that breeding, gentle nurture and luxurious food and shelter will produce a kind of man with whom the common laborer is socially incompatible. The same thing is true of horses and dogs. Now there is clearly room for great changes in the world by increasing the percentage of individuals who are carefully bred and gently nurtured, even to finally making the most of every man and woman born. But that possibility existed in the days of the Hittites as much as it does to-day. It does not give the slightest real support to the common assumption that the civilized contemporaries of the Hittites were unlike their civilized descendants to-day.

This would appear the tritest commonplace if it were not that the ordinary citizen's ignorance of the past combines with his idealization of the present to mislead and flatter him. Our latest book on the new railway across Asia describes the dulness of the Siberian farmer and the vulgar pursepride of the Siberian man of business without the least consciousness that the sting of contemptuous instances given might have been saved by writing simply "Farmers and provincial plutocrats in Siberia are exactly what they are in England." The latest professor descanting on the civilization of the Western Empire in the fifth century feels bound to assume, in the teeth of his own researches, that the Christian was one sort of animal and the Pagan another. It might as well be assumed, as indeed it generally is assumed by implication, that a murder committed with a poisoned arrow is different to a murder committed with a Mauser rifle. All such notions are illusions. Go back to the first syllable of recorded time, and there you will find your Christian and your Pagan, your yokel and your poet, helot and hero, Don Quixote and Sancho, Tamino and Papageno, Newton and bushman unable to count eleven, all alive and contemporaneous, and all convinced that they are the heirs of all the ages and the privileged recipients of THE truth (all others damnable heresies), just as you have them to-day, flourishing in countries each of which is the bravest and best that ever sprang at Heaven's command from out the azure main.

Again, there is the illusion of "increased command over Nature," meaning that cotton is cheap and that ten miles of country road on a bicycle have replaced four on foot. But even if man's increased command over Nature included any increased command over himself (the only sort of command relevant to his evolution into a higher being), the fact remains that it is only by running away from the increased command over Nature to country places where Nature is still in primitive command over Man that he can recover from the effects of the smoke, the stench, the foul air, the overcrowding, the racket, the ugliness, the dirt which the cheap cotton costs us. If manufacturing activity means Progress, the town must be more advanced than the country; and the field laborers and village artizans of to-day must be much less changed from the servants of Job than the proletariat of modern London from the proletariat of Caesar's Rome. Yet the cockney proletarian is so inferior to the village laborer that it is only by steady recruiting from the country that London is kept alive. This does not seem as if the change since Job's time were Progress in the popular sense: quite the reverse. The common stock of discoveries in physics has accumulated a little: that is all.

One more illustration. Is the Englishman prepared to admit that the American is his superior as a human being? I ask this question because the scarcity of labor in America relatively to the demand for it has led to a development of machinery there, and a consequent "increase of command over Nature" which makes many of our English methods appear almost medieval to the up-to-date Chicagoan. This means that the American has an advantage over the Englishman of exactly the same nature that the Englishman has over the contemporaries of Cicero. Is the Englishman prepared to draw the same conclusion in both cases? I think not. The American, of course, will draw it cheerfully; but I must then ask him whether, since a modern negro has a greater "command over Nature" than Washington had, we are also to accept the conclusion, involved in his former one, that humanity has progressed from Washington to the *fin de siècle* negro.

Finally, I would point out that if life is crowned by its success and devotion in industrial organization and ingenuity, we had better worship the ant and the bee (as moralists urge us to do in our childhood), and humble ourselves before the arrogance of the birds of Aristophanes.

My reason then for ignoring the popular conception of Progress in Caesar and Cleopatra is that there is no reason to suppose that any Progress has taken place since their time. But even if I shared the popular delusion, I do not see that I could have made any essential difference in the play. I can only imitate humanity as I know it. Nobody knows whether Shakespeare thought that ancient Athenian joiners, weavers, or bellows menders were any different from Elizabethan ones; but it is quite certain that he could not have made them so, unless, indeed, he had played the literary man and made Quince say, not "Is all our company here?" but "Bottom: was not that Socrates that passed us at the Piræus with Glaucon and Polemarchus on his way to the house of Kephalus." And so on.

## Cleopatra

Cleopatra was only sixteen when Caesar went to Egypt; but in Egypt sixteen is a riper age than it is in England. The childishness I have ascribed to her, as far as it is childishness of character and not lack of experience, is not a matter of years. It may be observed in our own climate at the present day in many women of fifty. It is a mistake to suppose that the difference between wisdom and folly has anything to do with the difference between physical age and physical youth. Some women are younger at seventy than most women at seventeen.

It must be borne in mind, too, that Cleopatra was a queen, and was therefore not the typical Greek-cultured, educated Egyptian lady of her time. To represent her by any such type would be as absurd as to represent George IV by a type founded on the attainments of Sir Isaac Newton. It is true that an ordinarily well educated Alexandrian girl of her time would no more have believed bogey stories about the Romans than the daughter of a modern Oxford professor would believe them about the Germans (though, by the way, it is possible to talk great nonsense at Oxford about foreigners when we are at war with them). But I do not feel bound to believe that Cleopatra was well educated. Her father, the illustrious Flute Blower, was not at all a parent of the Oxford professor type. And Cleopatra was a chip of the old block.

## Britannus

I find among those who have read this play in manuscript a strong conviction that an ancient Briton could not possibly have been like a modern one. I see no reason to adopt this curious view. It is true that the Roman and Norman conquests must have for a time disturbed the normal British type produced by the climate. But Britannus, born before these events, represents the unadulterated Briton who fought Caesar and impressed Roman observers much as we should expect the ancestors of Mr. Podsnap to impress the cultivated Italians of their time.

I am told that it is not scientific to treat national character as a product of climate. This only shews the wide difference between common knowledge and the intellectual game called science. We have men of exactly the same stock, and speaking the same language, growing in Great Britain, in Ireland, and in America. The result is three of the most distinctly marked nationalities under the sun. Racial characteristics are quite another matter. The difference between a Jew and a Gentile has nothing to do with the difference between an Englishman and a German. The characteristics of Britannus are local characteristics, not race characteristics. In an ancient Briton they would, I take it, be exaggerated, since modern Britain, disforested, drained, urbanified and consequently cosmopolized, is presumably less characteristically British than Caesar's Britain.

And again I ask does anyone who, in the light of a competent knowledge of his own age, has studied history from contemporary documents, believe that 67 generations of promiscuous marriage have made any appreciable difference in the human fauna of these isles? Certainly I do not.

## Julius Caesar

As to Caesar himself, I have purposely avoided the usual anachronism of going to Caesar's books, and concluding that the style is the man. That is only true of authors who have the specific literary genius, and have practised long enough to attain complete self-expression in letters. It is not true even on these conditions in an age when literature is conceived as a game of style, and not as a vehicle of self-expression by the author. Now Caesar was an amateur stylist writing books of travel and campaign histories in a style so impersonal that the authenticity of the later volumes is disputed. They reveal some of his qualities just as the *Voyage of a Naturalist Round the World* reveals some of Darwin's, without expressing his private personality. An Englishman reading them would say that Caesar was a man of great common sense and good taste, meaning thereby a man without originality or moral courage.

In exhibiting Caesar as a much more various person than the historian of the Gallic wars, I hope I have not succumbed unconsciously to the dramatic illusion to which all great men owe part of their reputation and some the whole of it. I admit that reputations gained in war are specially questionable. Able civilians taking up the profession of arms, like Caesar and Cromwell, in middle age, have snatched all its laurels from opponent commanders bred to it, apparently because capable persons engaged in military pursuits are so scarce that the existence of two of them at the same time in the same hemisphere is extremely rare. The capacity of any conqueror is therefore more likely than not to be an illusion produced by the incapacity of his adversary. At all events, Caesar might have won his battles without being wiser than Charles XII or Nelson or Joan of Arc, who were, like most modern "self-made" millionaires, half-witted geniuses, enjoying the worship accorded by all races to certain forms of insanity. But Caesar's victories were only advertisements for an eminence that would never have become popular without them. Caesar is greater off the battle field than on it. Nelson off his quarterdeck was so quaintly out of the question that when his head was injured at the battle of the Nile, and his conduct became for some years openly scandalous, the difference was not important enough to be noticed. It may, however, be said that peace hath her illusory reputations no less than war. And it is certainly true that in civil life mere capacity for work—the power of killing a dozen secretaries under you, so to speak, as a life-or-death courier kills horses—enables men with common ideas and superstitions to distance all competitors in the strife of political ambition. It was this power of work that astonished Cicero as the most prodigious of Caesar's gifts, as it astonished later observers in Napoleon before it wore him out. How if Caesar were nothing but a Nelson and a Gladstone combined! a prodigy of vitality without any special quality of mind! nay, with ideas that were worn out before he was born, as Nelson's and Gladstone's were! I have considered that possibility too, and rejected it. I cannot cite all the stories about Caesar which seem to me to shew that he was genuinely original; but let me at least point out that I have been careful to attribute nothing but originality to him. Originality gives a man an air of frankness, generosity, and magnanimity by enabling him to estimate the value of truth, money, or success in any particular instance quite independently of convention and moral generalization. He therefore will not, in the ordinary Treasury bench fashion, tell a lie which everybody knows to be a lie (and consequently expects him as a matter of good taste to tell). His lies are not found out: they pass for candors. He understands the paradox of money, and gives it away when he can get most for it: in other words, when its value is least, which is just when a common man tries hardest to get it. He knows that the real moment of success is not the moment apparent to the crowd. Hence, in order to produce an impression of complete disinterestedness and magnanimity, he has only to act with entire selfishness; and this is perhaps the only sense in which a man can be said to be *naturally* great. It is in this sense that I have represented Caesar as great. Having virtue, he has no need of goodness. He is neither forgiving, frank, nor generous, because a man who is too great to resent has nothing to forgive; a man who says things that other people are afraid to say need be no more frank than Bismarck was; and there is no generosity in giving things you do not want to people of whom you intend to make use. This distinction between virtue and goodness is not understood in England: hence the poverty of our drama in heroes. Our stage attempts at them are mere goody-goodies. Goodness, in its popular British sense of self-denial, implies that man is vicious by nature, and that supreme goodness is supreme martyrdom. Not sharing that pious opinion, I have not given countenance to it in any of my plays. In this I follow the precedent of the ancient myths, which represent the hero as vanquishing his enemies, not in fair fight, but with enchanted sword, superequine horse and magical invulnerability, the possession of which, from the vulgar moralistic point of view, robs his exploits of any merit whatever.

As to Caesar's sense of humor, there is no more reason to assume that he lacked it than to assume that he was deaf or blind. It is said that on the occasion of his assassination by a conspiracy of moralists (it is always your moralist who makes assassination a duty, on the scaffold or off it), he defended himself until the good Brutus struck him, when he exclaimed "What! you too, Brutus!" and disdained further fight. If this be true, he must have been an incorrigible comedian. But even if we waive this story, or accept the traditional sentimental interpretation of it, there is still abundant evidence of his lightheartedness and adventurousness. Indeed it is clear from his whole history that what has been called his ambition was an instinct for exploration. He had much more of Columbus and Franklin in him than of Henry V.

However, nobody need deny Caesar a share, at least, of the qualities I have attributed to him. All men, much more Julius Caesars, possess all qualities in some degree. The really interesting question is whether I am right in assuming that the way to produce an impression of greatness is by exhibiting a man, not as mortifying his nature by doing his duty, in the manner which our system of putting little men into great positions (not having enough great men in our influential families to go round) forces us to inculcate, but as simply doing what he naturally wants to do. For this raises the question whether our world has not been wrong in its moral theory for the last 2,500 years or so. It must be a constant puzzle to many of us that the Christian era, so excellent in its intentions, should have been practically such a very discreditable episode in the history of the race. I doubt if this is altogether due to the vulgar and sanguinary sensationalism of our religious legends, with their substitution of gross physical torments and public executions for the passion of humanity. Islam, substituting voluptuousness for torment (a merely superficial difference, it is true), has done no better. It may have been the failure of Christianity to emancipate itself from expiatory theories of moral responsibility, guilt, innocence, reward, punishment, and the rest of it, that baffled its intention of changing the world. But these are bound up in all philosophies of creation as opposed to cosmism. They may therefore be regarded as the price we pay for popular religion.

# MAN AND SUPERMAN

## A COMEDY AND
## A PHILOSOPHY

# Act I

Roebuck Ramsden *is in his study, opening the morning's letters. The study, handsomely and solidly furnished, proclaims the man of means. Not a speck of dust is visible: it is clear that there are at least two housemaids and a parlormaid downstairs, and a housekeeper upstairs who does not let them spare elbow-grease. Even the top of* Roebuck's *head is polished: on a sunshiny day he could heliograph his orders to distant camps by merely nodding. In no other respect, however, does he suggest the military man. It is in active civil life that men get his broad air of importance, his dignified expectation of deference, his determinate mouth disarmed and refined since the hour of his success by the withdrawal of opposition and the concession of comfort and precedence and power. He is more than a highly respectable man: he is marked out as a president of highly respectable men, a chairman among directors, an alderman among councillors, a mayor among aldermen. Four tufts of iron-grey hair, which will soon be as white as isinglass, and are in other respects not at all unlike it, grow in two symmetrical pairs above his ears and at the angles of his spreading jaws. He wears a black frock coat, a white waistcoat (it is bright spring weather), and trousers, neither black nor perceptibly blue, of one of those indefinitely mixed hues which the modern clothier has produced to harmonize with the religions of respectable men. He has not been out of doors yet to-day; so he still wears his slippers, his boots being ready for him on the hearthrug. Surmising that he has no valet, and seeing that he has no secretary with a shorthand notebook and a typewriter, one meditates on how little our great burgess domesticity has been disturbed by new fashions and methods, or by the enterprise of the railway and hotel companies which sell you a Saturday to Monday of life at Folkestone as a real gentleman for two guineas, first class fares both ways included.*

*How old is* Roebuck? *The question is important on the threshold of a drama of ideas; for under such circumstances everything depends on whether his adolescence belonged to the sixties or to the eighties. He was born, as a matter of fact, in 1839, and was a Unitarian and Free Trader from his boyhood, and an Evolutionist from the publication of the* Origin of Species. *Consequently he has always classed himself as an advanced thinker and fearlessly outspoken reformer.*

*Sitting at his writing table, he has on his right the windows giving on Portland Place. Through these, as through a proscenium, the curious spec-*

205

*tator may contemplate his profile as well as the blinds will permit. On his
left is the inner wall, with a stately bookcase, and the door not quite in the
middle, but somewhat further from him. Against the wall opposite him
are two busts on pillars: one, to his left, of John Bright; the other, to his
right, of Mr Herbert Spencer. Between them hang an engraved portrait of
Richard Cobden; enlarged photographs of Martineau, Huxley, and
George Eliot; autotypes of allegories by Mr G. F. Watts (for Roebuck
believes in the fine arts with all the earnestness of a man who does not
understand them), and an impression of Dupont's engraving of
Delaroche's Beaux Arts hemicycle, representing the great men of all ages.
On the wall behind him, above the mantelshelf, is a family portrait of
impenetrable obscurity.*

*A chair stands near the writing table for the convenience of business
visitors. Two other chairs are against the wall between the busts.*

*A parlormaid enters with a visitor's card. Roebuck takes it, and nods,
pleased. Evidently a welcome caller:*

RAMSDEN:
　　Shew him up.

　　　　*The parlormaid goes out and returns with the visitor.*

THE MAID:
　　Mr Robinson.

*Mr Robinson is really an uncommonly nice looking young fellow. He
must, one thinks, be the jeune premier; for it is not in reason to suppose
that a second such attractive male figure should appear in one story. The
slim, shapely frame, the elegant suit of new mourning, the small head and
regular features, the pretty little moustache, the frank clear eyes, the
wholesome bloom on the youthful complexion, the well brushed glossy hair,
not curly, but of fine texture and good dark color, the arch of good nature
in the eyebrows, the erect forehead and neatly pointed chin, all announce
the man who will love and suffer later on. And that he will not do so without sympathy is guaranteed by an engaging sincerity and eager modest
serviceableness which stamp him as a man of amiable nature. The
moment he appears, Ramsden's face expands into fatherly liking and welcome, an expression which drops into one of decorous grief as the young
man approaches him with sorrow in his face as well as in his black clothes.
Ramsden seems to know the nature of the bereavement. As the visitor
advances silently to the writing table, the old man rises and shakes his
hand across it without a word: a long, affectionate shake which tells the
story of a recent sorrow common to both.*

RAMSDEN (*concluding the handshake and cheering up*):

Well, well, Octavius, it's the common lot. We must all face it some day. Sit down.

Octavius *takes the visitor's chair.* Ramsden *replaces himself in his own.*

OCTAVIUS:

Yes: we must face it, Mr Ramsden. But I owed him a great deal. He did everything for me that my father could have done if he had lived.

RAMSDEN:

He had no son of his own, you see.

OCTAVIUS:

But he had daughters; and yet he was as good to my sister as to me. And his death was so sudden! I always intended to thank him—to let him know that I had not taken all his care of me as a matter of course, as any boy takes his father's care. But I waited for an opportunity; and now he is dead—dropped without a moment's warning. He will never know what I felt. (*He takes out his handkerchief and cries unaffectedly.*)

RAMSDEN:

How do we know that, Octavius? He may know it: we cannot tell. Come! don't grieve. (Octavius *masters himself and puts up his handkerchief.*) That's right. Now let me tell you something to console you. The last time I saw him—it was in this very room—he said to me: "Tavy is a generous lad and the soul of honor; and when I see how little consideration other men get from their sons, I realize how much better than a son he's been to me." There! Doesn't that do you good?

OCTAVIUS:

Mr Ramsden: he used to say to me that he had met only one man in the world who was the soul of honor, and that was Roebuck Ramsden.

RAMSDEN:

Oh, that was his partiality: we were very old friends, you know. But there was something else he used to say about you. I wonder whether I ought to tell you or not!

OCTAVIUS:

You know best.

RAMSDEN:

It was something about his daughter.

OCTAVIUS (*eagerly*):

About Ann! Oh, do tell me that, Mr Ramsden.

RAMSDEN:

Well, he said he was glad, after all, you were not his son, because he thought that someday Annie and you—(*Octavius blushes vividly*). Well, perhaps I shouldn't have told you. But he was in earnest.

OCTAVIUS:

Oh, if only I thought I had a chance! You know, Mr Ramsden, I don't care about money or about what people call position; and I can't bring myself to take an interest in the business of struggling for them. Well, Ann has a most exquisite nature; but she is so accustomed to be in the thick of that sort of thing that she thinks a man's character incomplete if he is not ambitious. She knows that if she married me she would have to reason herself out of being ashamed of me for not being a big success of some kind.

RAMSDEN (*getting up and planting himself with his back to the fireplace*):

Nonsense, my boy, nonsense! You're too modest. What does she know about the real value of men at her age? (*More seriously*) Besides, she's a wonderfully dutiful girl. Her father's wish would be sacred to her. Do you know that since she grew up to years of discretion, I don't believe she has ever once given her own wish as a reason for doing anything or not doing it. It's always "Father wishes me to," or "Mother wouldn't like it." It's really almost a fault in her. I have often told her she must learn to think for herself.

OCTAVIUS (*shaking his head*):

I couldn't ask her to marry me because her father wished it, Mr Ramsden.

RAMSDEN:

Well, perhaps not. No: of course not. I see that. No: you certainly couldn't. But when you win her on your own merits, it will be a great happiness to her to fulfil her father's desire as well as her own. Eh? Come! you'll ask her, won't you?

OCTAVIUS (*with sad gaiety*):

At all events I promise you I shall never ask anyone else.

RAMSDEN:

Oh, you shan't need to. She'll accept you, my boy—although (*here he suddenly becomes very serious indeed*) you have one great drawback.

OCTAVIUS (*anxiously*):

What drawback is that, Mr Ramsden? I should rather say which of my many drawbacks?

RAMSDEN:

I'll tell you, Octavius. (*He takes from the table a book bound in red cloth*). I have in my hand a copy of the most infamous, the most scandalous, the most mischievous, the most blackguardly book that ever escaped burning at the hands of the common hangman. I have not read it: I would not soil my mind with such filth; but I have read what the papers say of it. The title is quite enough for me. (*He reads it*). The Revolutionist's Handbook and Pocket Companion. By John Tanner, M.I.R.C., Member of the Idle Rich Class.

OCTAVIUS (*smiling*):

But Jack—

RAMSDEN (*testily*):

For goodness' sake, don't call him Jack under my roof (*he throws the book violently down on the table. Then, somewhat relieved, he comes past the table to* Octavius, *and addresses him at close quarters with impressive gravity*). Now, Octavius, I know that my dead friend was right when he said you were a generous lad. I know that this man was your schoolfellow, and that you feel bound to stand by him because there was a boyish friendship between you. But I ask you to consider the altered circumstances. You were treated as a son in my friend's house. You lived there; and your friends could not be turned from the door. This man Tanner was in and out there on your account almost from his childhood. He addresses Annie by her Christian name as freely as you do. Well, while her father was alive, that was her father's business, not mine. This man Tanner was only a boy to him: his opinions were something to be laughed at, like a man's hat on a child's head. But now Tanner is a grown man and Annie a grown woman. And her father is gone. We don't as yet know the exact terms of his will; but he often talked it over with me; and I have no more doubt than I have that you're sitting there that the will appoints me Annie's trustee and guardian. (*Forcibly*) Now I tell you, once for all, I can't and I won't have Annie placed in such a position that she must, out of regard for you, suffer the intimacy of this fellow Tanner. It's not fair: it's not right: it's not kind. What are you going to do about it?

OCTAVIUS:

But Ann herself has told Jack that whatever his opinions are, he will always be welcome because he knew her dear father.

RAMSDEN (*out of patience*):

That girl's mad about her duty to her parents. (*He starts off like a goaded ox in the direction of John Bright, in whose expression there is no sympathy for him. As he speaks he fumes down to Herbert Spencer, who receives him still more coldly.*) Excuse me, Octavius; but there are limits to social toleration. You know that I am not a bigoted or prejudiced man. You know that I am plain Roebuck Ramsden when other men who have done less have got handles to their names, because I have stood for equality and liberty of conscience while they were truckling to the Church and to the aristocracy. Whitefield and I lost chance after chance through our advanced opinions. But I draw the line at Anarchism and Free Love and that sort of thing. If I am to be Annie's guardian, she will have to learn that she has a duty to me. I won't have it: I will not have it. She must forbid John Tanner the house; and so must you.

*The parlormaid returns.*

OCTAVIUS:
 But—
RAMSDEN (*calling his attention to the servant*):
 Ssh! Well?
THE MAID:
 Mr Tanner wishes to see you, sir.
RAMSDEN:
 Mr Tanner!
OCTAVIUS:
 Jack!
RAMSDEN:
 How dare Mr Tanner call on me! Say I cannot see him.
OCTAVIUS (*hurt*):
 I am sorry you are turning my friend from your door like that.
THE MAID (*calmly*):
 He's not at the door, sir. He's upstairs in the drawingroom with Miss Ramsden. He came with Mrs Whitefield and Miss Ann and Miss Robinson, sir.

*Ramsden's feelings are beyond words.*

OCTAVIUS (*grinning*):
 That's very like Jack, Mr Ramsden. You must see him, even if it's only to turn him out.
RAMSDEN (*hammering out his words with suppressed fury*):
 Go upstairs and ask Mr Tanner to be good enough to step down here. (*The parlormaid goes out; and* Ramsden *returns to the fireplace, as to a fortified position*). I must say that of all the

confounded pieces of impertinence—well, if these are Anarchist manners, I hope you like them. And Annie with him! Annie! A—(*he chokes*).

OCTAVIUS:

Yes: that's what surprises me. He's so desperately afraid of Ann. There must be something the matter.

Mr John Tanner *suddenly opens the door and enters. He is too young to be described simply as a big man with a beard. But it is already plain that middle life will find him in that category. He has still some of the slimness of youth; but youthfulness is not the effect he aims at: his frock coat would befit a prime minister; and a certain high chested carriage of the shoulders, a lofty pose of the head, and the Olympian majesty with which a mane, or rather a huge wisp, of hazel colored hair is thrown back from an imposing brow, suggest Jupiter rather than Apollo. He is prodigiously fluent of speech, restless, excitable (mark the snorting nostril and the restless blue eye, just the thirty-secondth of an inch too wide open), possibly a little mad. He is carefully dressed, not from the vanity that cannot resist finery, but from a sense of the importance of everything he does which leads him to make as much of paying a call as other men do of getting married or laying a foundation stone. A sensitive, susceptible, exaggerative, earnest man: a megalomaniac, who would be lost without a sense of humor.*

*Just at present the sense of humor is in abeyance. To say that he is excited is nothing: all his moods are phases of excitement. He is now in the panic-stricken phase; and he walks straight up to* Ramsden *as if with the fixed intention of shooting him on his own hearthrug. But what he pulls from his breast pocket is not a pistol, but a foolscap document which he thrusts under the indignant nose of* Ramsden *as he exclaims—*

TANNER:

Ramsden: do you know what this is?

RAMSDEN (*loftily*):

No, sir.

TANNER:

It's a copy of Whitefield's will. Ann got it this morning.

RAMSDEN:

When you say Ann, you mean, I presume, Miss Whitefield.

TANNER:

I mean our Ann, your Ann, Tavy's Ann, and now, Heaven help me, my Ann!

OCTAVIUS (*rising, very pale*):

What do you mean?

TANNER:

Mean! (*He holds up the will*). Do you know who is appointed Ann's guardian by this will?

RAMSDEN (*coolly*):

I believe I am.

TANNER:

You! You and I, man. I! I!! I!!! Both of us! (*He flings the will down on the writing table*).

RAMSDEN:

You! Impossible.

TANNER:

It's only too hideously true. (*He throws himself into* Octavius's *chair*). Ramsden: get me out of it somehow. You don't know Ann as well as I do. She'll commit every crime a respectable woman can; and she'll justify everyone of them by saying that it was the wish of her guardians. She'll put everything on us; and we shall have no more control over her than a couple of mice over a cat.

OCTAVIUS:

Jack: I wish you wouldn't talk like that about Ann.

TANNER:

This chap's in love with her: that's another complication. Well, she'll either jilt him and say I didn't approve of him, or marry him and say you ordered her to. I tell you, this is the most staggering blow that has ever fallen on a man of my age and temperament.

RAMSDEN:

Let me see that will, sir. (*He goes to the writing table and picks it up*). I cannot believe that my old friend Whitefield would have shewn such a want of confidence in me as to associate me with—(*His countenance falls as he reads*).

TANNER:

It's all my own doing: that's the horrible irony of it. He told me one day that you were to be Ann's guardian; and like a fool I began arguing with him about the folly of leaving a young woman under the control of an old man with obsolete ideas.

RAMSDEN (*stupended*):

My ideas obsolete!!!!!!!

TANNER:

Totally. I had just finished an essay called Down with Government by the Greyhaired; and I was full of arguments and illustrations. I said the proper thing was to combine the experience of an old hand with the vitality of a young one. Hang me if he didn't take me at my word and alter his will—it's dated only a fortnight after that conversation—appointing me as joint guardian with you!

RAMSDEN (*pale and determined*):

I shall refuse to act.

TANNER:

What's the good of that? I've been refusing all the way from Richmond; but Ann keeps on saying that of course she's only an orphan; and that she can't expect the people who were glad to come to the house in her father's time to trouble much about her now. That's the latest game. An orphan! It's like hearing an ironclad talk about being at the mercy of the winds and waves.

OCTAVIUS:

This is not fair, Jack. She is an orphan. And you ought to stand by her.

TANNER:

Stand by her! What danger is she in? She has the law on her side; she has popular sentiment on her side; she has plenty of money and no conscience. All she wants with me is to load up all her moral responsibilities on me, and do as she likes at the expense of my character. I can't control her; and she can compromise me as much as she likes. I might as well be her husband.

RAMSDEN:

You can refuse to accept the guardianship. *I* shall certainly refuse to hold it jointly with you.

TANNER:

Yes; and what will she say to that? what does she say to it? Just that her father's wishes are sacred to her, and that she shall always look up to me as her guardian whether I care to face the responsibility or not. Refuse! You might as well refuse to accept the embraces of a boa constrictor when once it gets round your neck.

OCTAVIUS:

This sort of talk is not kind to me, Jack.

TANNER (*rising and going to* Octavius *to console him, but still lamenting*):

If he wanted a young guardian, why didn't he appoint Tavy?

RAMSDEN:

Ah! why indeed?

OCTAVIUS:

I will tell you. He sounded me about it; but I refused the trust because I loved her. I had no right to let myself be forced on her as a guardian by her father. He spoke to her about it; and she said I was right. You know I love her, Mr Ramsden; and Jack knows it too. If Jack loved a woman, I would not compare her to a boa constrictor in his presence, however much I might dislike her (*he sits down between the busts and turns his face to the wall*).

RAMSDEN:

I do not believe that Whitefield was in his right senses when he made that will. You have admitted that he made it under your influence.

TANNER:

You ought to be pretty well obliged to me for my influence. He leaves you two thousand five hundred for your trouble. He leaves Tavy a dowry for his sister and five thousand for himself.

OCTAVIUS (*his tears flowing afresh*):

Oh, I can't take it. He was too good to us.

TANNER:

You won't get it, my boy, if Ramsden upsets the will.

RAMSDEN:

Ha! I see. You have got me in a cleft stick.

TANNER:

He leaves me nothing but the charge of Ann's morals, on the ground that I have already more money than is good for me. That shews that he had his wits about him, doesn't it?

RAMSDEN (*grimly*):

I admit that.

OCTAVIUS (*rising and coming from his refuge by the wall*):

Mr Ramsden: I think you are prejudiced against Jack. He is a man of honor, and incapable of abusing—

TANNER:

Don't, Tavy: you'll make me ill. I am not a man of honor: I am a man struck down by a dead hand. Tavy: you must marry her after all and take her off my hands. And I had set my heart on saving you from her!

OCTAVIUS:

Oh, Jack, you talk of saving me from my highest happiness.

TANNER:

Yes, a lifetime of happiness. If it were only the first half hour's happiness, Tavy, I would buy it for you with my last penny. But a lifetime of happiness! No man alive could bear it: it would be hell on earth.

RAMSDEN (*violently*):

Stuff, sir. Talk sense; or else go and waste someone else's time: I have something better to do than listen to your fooleries (*he positively kicks his way to his table and resumes his seat*).

TANNER:

> You hear him, Tavy! Not an idea in his head later than eighteensixty. We can't leave Ann with no other guardian to turn to.

RAMSDEN:

> I am proud of your contempt for my character and opinions, sir. Your own are set forth in that book, I believe.

TANNER (*eagerly going to the table*):

> What! You've got my book! What do you think of it?

RAMSDEN:

> Do you suppose I would read such a book, sir?

TANNER:

> Then why did you buy it?

RAMSDEN:

> I did not buy it, sir. It has been sent me by some foolish lady who seems to admire your views. I was about to dispose of it when Octavius interrupted me. I shall do so now, with your permission. (*He throws the book into the waste paper basket with such vehemence that* Tanner *recoils under the impression that it is being thrown at his head.*)

TANNER:

> You have no more manners than I have myself. However, that saves ceremony between us. (*He sits down again*). What do you intend to do about this will?

OCTAVIUS:

> May I make a suggestion?

RAMSDEN:

> Certainly, Octavius.

OCTAVIUS:

> Arn't we forgetting that Ann herself may have some wishes in this matter?

RAMSDEN:

> I quite intend that Annie's wishes shall be consulted in every reasonable way. But she is only a woman, and a young and inexperienced woman at that.

TANNER:

> Ramsden: I begin to pity you.

RAMSDEN (*hotly*):

> I don't want to know how you feel towards me, Mr Tanner.

TANNER:

> Ann will do just exactly what she likes. And what's more, she'll force us to advise her to do it; and she'll put the blame on us if it turns out badly. So, as Tavy is longing to see her—

OCTAVIUS (*shyly*):

> I am not, Jack.

TANNER:

You lie, Tavy: you are. So let's have her down from the drawingroom and ask her what she intends us to do. Off with you, Tavy, and fetch her. (Tavy *turns to go*). And don't be long; for the strained relations between myself and Ramsden will make the interval rather painful (Ramsden *compresses his lips, but says nothing*).

OCTAVIUS:

Never mind him, Mr Ramsden. He's not serious. (*He goes out*).

RAMSDEN (*very deliberately*):

Mr Tanner: you are the most impudent person I have ever met.

TANNER (*seriously*):

I know it, Ramsden. Yet even I cannot wholly conquer shame. We live in an atmosphere of shame. We are ashamed of everything that is real about us; ashamed of ourselves, of our relatives, of our incomes, of our accents, of our opinions, of our experience, just as we are ashamed of our naked skins. Good Lord, my dear Ramsden, we are ashamed to walk, ashamed to ride in an omnibus, ashamed to hire a hansom instead of keeping a carriage, ashamed of keeping one horse instead of two and a groom-gardener instead of a coachman and footman. The more things a man is ashamed of, the more respectable he is. Why, you're ashamed to buy my book, ashamed to read it: the only thing you're not ashamed of is to judge me for it without having read it; and even that only means that you're ashamed to have heterodox opinions. Look at the effect I produce because my fairy godmother withheld from me this gift of shame. I have every possible virtue that a man can have except—

RAMSDEN:

I am glad you think so well of yourself.

TANNER:

All you mean by that is that you think I ought to be ashamed of talking about my virtues. You don't mean that I haven't got them: you know perfectly well that I am as sober and honest a citizen as yourself, as truthful personally, and much more truthful politically and morally.

RAMSDEN (*touched on his most sensitive point*):

I deny that. I will not allow you or any man to treat me as if I were a mere member of the British public. I detest its prejudices; I scorn its narrowness; I demand the right to think for myself. You pose as an advanced man. Let me tell you that I was an advanced man before you were born.

TANNER:

I knew it was a long time ago.

RAMSDEN:

> I am as advanced as ever I was. I defy you to prove that I have ever hauled down the flag. I am more advanced than ever I was. I grow more advanced every day.

TANNER:

> More advanced in years, Polonius.

RAMSDEN:

> Polonius! So you are Hamlet, I suppose.

TANNER:

> No: I am only the most impudent person you've ever met. That's your notion of a thoroughly bad character. When you want to give me a piece of your mind, you ask yourself, as a just and upright man, what is the worst you can fairly say of me. Thief, liar, forger, adulterer, perjurer, glutton, drunkard? Not one of these names fit me. You have to fall back on my deficiency in shame. Well, I admit it. I even congratulate myself; for if I were ashamed of my real self, I should cut as stupid a figure as any of the rest of you. Cultivate a little impudence, Ramsden; and you will become quite a remarkable man.

RAMSDEN:

> I have no—

TANNER:

> You have no desire for that sort of notoriety. Bless you, I knew that answer would come as well as I know that a box of matches will come out of an automatic machine when I put a penny in the slot: you would be ashamed to say anything else.

*The crushing retort for which* Ramsden *has been visibly collecting his forces is lost for ever; for at this point* Octavius *returns with* Miss Ann Whitefield *and her mother; and* Ramsden *springs up and hurries to the door to receive them. Whether* Ann *is good-looking or not depends upon your taste; also and perhaps chiefly on your age and sex. To* Octavius *she is an enchantingly beautiful woman, in whose presence the world becomes transfigured, and the puny limits of individual consciousness are suddenly made infinite by a mystic memory of the whole life of the race to its beginnings in the east, or even back to the paradise from which it fell. She is to him the reality of romance, the inner good sense of nonsense, the unveiling of his eyes, the freeing of his soul, the abolition of time, place and circumstance, the etherealization of his blood into rapturous rivers of the very water of life itself, the revelation of all the mysteries and the sanctification of all the dogmas. To her mother she is, to put it as moderately as possible, nothing whatever of the kind. Not that* Octavius's *admiration is in any way ridiculous or discreditable.* Ann *is a well formed creature, as far as that goes; and she is perfectly ladylike, graceful, and comely, with ensnar-*

*ing eyes and hair. Besides, instead of making herself an eyesore, like her mother, she has devised a mourning costume of black and violet silk which does honor to her late father and reveals the family tradition of brave unconventionality by which* Ramsden *sets such store.*

*But all this is beside the point as an explanation of Ann's charm. Turn up her nose, give a cast to her eye, replace her black and violet confection by the apron and feathers of a flower girl, strike all the aitches out of her speech, and* Ann *would still make men dream. Vitality is as common as humanity; but, like humanity, it sometimes rises to genius; and* Ann *is one of the vital geniuses. Not at all, if you please, an oversexed person: that is a vital defect, not a true excess. She is a perfectly respectable, perfectly self-controlled woman, and looks it; though her pose is fashionably frank and impulsive. She inspires confidence as a person who will do nothing she does not mean to do; also some fear, perhaps, as a woman who will probably do everything she means to do without taking more account of other people than may be necessary and what she calls right. In short, what the weaker of her own sex sometimes call a cat.*

*Nothing can be more decorous than her entry and her reception by* Ramsden, *whom she kisses. The late Mr Whitefield would be gratified almost to impatience by the long faces of the men (except* Tanner, *who is fidgety), the silent handgrasps, the sympathetic placing of chairs, the sniffing of the widow, and the liquid eye of the daughter, whose heart, apparently, will not let her control her tongue to speech.* Ramsden *and* Octavius *take the two chairs from the wall, and place them for the two ladies; but* Ann *comes to* Tanner *and takes his chair, which he offers with a brusque gesture, subsequently relieving his irritation by sitting down on the corner of the writing table with studied indecorum.* Octavius *gives* Mrs Whitefield *a chair next* Ann, *and himself takes the vacant one which* Ramsden *has placed under the nose of the effigy of Mr Herbert Spencer.*

*Mrs Whitefield, by the way, is a little woman, whose faded flaxen hair looks like straw on an egg. She has an expression of muddled shrewdness, a squeak of protest in her voice, and an odd air of continually elbowing away some larger person who is crushing her into a corner. One guesses her as one of those women who are conscious of being treated as silly and negligible, and who, without having strength enough to assert themselves effectually, at any rate never submit to their fate. There is a touch of chivalry in* Octavius's *scrupulous attention to her, even whilst his whole soul is absorbed by* Ann.

Ramsden *goes solemnly back to his magisterial seat at the writing table, ignoring* Tanner, *and opens the proceedings.*

RAMSDEN:

I am sorry, Annie, to force business on you at a sad time like the present. But your poor dear father's will has raised a very serious question. You have read it, I believe?

Ann *assents with a nod and a catch of her breath, too much affected to speak.*

I must say I am surprised to find Mr Tanner named as joint guardian and trustee with myself of you and Rhoda. (*A pause. They all look portentous; but they have nothing to say.* Ramsden, *a little ruffled by the lack of any response, continues*) I don't know that I can consent to act under such conditions. Mr Tanner has, I understand, some objection also; but I do not profess to understand its nature: he will no doubt speak for himself. But we are agreed that we can decide nothing until we know your views. I am afraid I shall have to ask you to choose between my sole guardianship and that of Mr Tanner; for I fear it is impossible for us to undertake a joint arrangement.

ANN (*in a low musical voice*):

Mamma—

MRS WHITEFIELD (*hastily*):

Now, Ann, I do beg you not to put it on me. I have no opinion on the subject; and if I had, it would probably not be attended to. I am quite content with whatever you three think best.

Tanner *turns his head and looks fixedly at* Ramsden, *who angrily refuses to receive this mute communication.*

ANN (*resuming in the same gentle voice, ignoring her mother's bad taste*)

Mamma knows that she is not strong enough to bear the whole responsibility for me and Rhoda without some help and advice. Rhoda must have a guardian; and though I am older, I do not think any young unmarried woman should be left quite to her own guidance. I hope you agree with me, Granny?

TANNER (*starting*):

Granny! Do you intend to call your guardians Granny?

ANN:

Don't be foolish, Jack. Mr Ramsden has always been Grandpapa Roebuck to me: I am Granny's Annie; and he is Annie's Granny. I christened him so when I first learned to speak.

RAMSDEN (*sarcastically*):

I hope you are satisfied, Mr Tanner. Go on, Annie: I quite agree with you.

ANN:

Well, if I am to have a guardian, can I set aside anybody whom my dear father appointed for me?

RAMSDEN (*biting his lip*):

You approve of your father's choice, then?

ANN:

It is not for me to approve or disapprove. I accept it. My father loved me and knew best what was good for me.

RAMSDEN:

Of course I understand your feeling, Annie. It is what I should have expected of you; and it does you credit. But it does not settle the question so completely as you think. Let me put a case to you. Suppose you were to discover that I had been guilty of some disgraceful action—that I was not the man your poor dear father took me for! Would you still consider it right that I should be Rhoda's guardian?

ANN:

I can't imagine you doing anything disgraceful, Granny.

TANNER (*to* Ramsden):

You haven't done anything of the sort, have you?

RAMSDEN (*indignantly*):

No sir.

MRS WHITEFIELD (*placidly*):

Well, then, why suppose it?

ANN:

You see, Granny, Mamma would not like me to suppose it.

RAMSDEN (*much perplexed*):

You are both so full of natural and affectionate feeling in these family matters that it is very hard to put the situation fairly before you.

TANNER:

Besides, my friend, you are not putting the situation fairly before them.

RAMSDEN (*sulkily*):

Put it yourself, then.

TANNER:

I will. Ann: Ramsden thinks I am not fit to be your guardian; and I quite agree with him. He considers that if your father had read my book, he wouldn't have appointed me. That book is the disgraceful action he has been talking about. He thinks it's your duty for Rhoda's sake to ask him to act alone and to make me withdraw. Say the word; and I will.

ANN:

But I haven't read your book, Jack.

TANNER (*diving at the waste-paper basket and fishing the book out for her*):

Then read it at once and decide.

RAMSDEN (*vehemently*):

If I am to be your guardian, I positively forbid you to read that book, Annie. (*He smites the table with his fist and rises.*)

ANN:

Of course not if you don't wish it. (*She puts the book on the table.*)

TANNER:

If one guardian is to forbid you to read the other guardian's book, how are we to settle it? Suppose I order you to read it! What about your duty to me?

ANN (*gently*):

I am sure you would never purposely force me into a painful dilemma, Jack.

RAMSDEN (*irritably*):

Yes, yes, Annie: this is all very well, and, as I said, quite natural and becoming. But you must make a choice one way or the other. We are as much in a dilemma as you.

ANN:

I feel that I am too young, too inexperienced, to decide. My father's wishes are sacred to me.

MRS WHITEFIELD:

If you two men won't carry them out I must say it is rather hard that you should put the responsibility on Ann. It seems to me that people are always putting things on other people in this world.

RAMSDEN:

I am sorry you take it in that way.

ANN (*touchingly*):

Do you refuse to accept me as your ward, Granny?

RAMSDEN:

No: I never said that. I greatly object to act with Mr Tanner: that's all.

MRS WHITEFIELD:

Why? What's the matter with poor Jack?

TANNER:

My views are too advanced for him.

RAMSDEN (*indignantly*):

They are not. I deny it.

ANN:

Of course not. What nonsense! Nobody is more advanced than Granny. I am sure it is Jack himself who has made all the difficulty. Come, Jack! be kind to me in my sorrow. You don't refuse to accept me as your ward, do you?

TANNER (*gloomily*):

No. I let myself in for it; so I suppose I must face it. (*He turns away to the bookcase, and stands there, moodily studying the titles of the volumes.*)

ANN (*rising and expanding with subdued but gushing delight*):

Then we are all agreed; and my dear father's will is to be carried out. You don't know what a joy that is to me and to my mother! (*She goes to* Ramsden *and presses both his hands, saying*) And I shall have my dear Granny to help and advise me. (*She casts a glance at* Tanner *over her shoulder*). And Jack the Giant Killer. (*She goes past her mother to* Octavius) And Jack's inseparable friend Ricky-ticky-tavy (*he blushes and looks inexpressibly foolish*).

MRS WHITEFIELD (*rising and shaking her widow's weeds straight*):

Now that you are Ann's guardian, Mr Ramsden, I wish you would speak to her about her habit of giving people nick-names. They can't be expected to like it. (*She moves towards the door.*)

ANN:

How can you say such a thing, Mamma! (*Glowing with affectionate remorse*) Oh, I wonder can you be right! Have I been inconsiderate? (*She turns to* Octavius, *who is sitting astride his chair with his elbows on the back of it. Putting her hand on his forehead she turns his face up suddenly.*) Do you want to be treated like a grown up man? Must I call you Mr Robinson in future?

OCTAVIUS (*earnestly*):

Oh please call me Ricky-ticky-tavy. "Mr Robinson" would hurt me cruelly. (*She laughs and pats his cheek with her finger; then comes back to* Ramsden.) You know I'm beginning to think that Granny is rather a piece of impertinence. But I never dreamt of its hurting you.

RAMSDEN (*breezily, as he pats her affectionately on the back*):

My dear Annie, nonsense. I insist on Granny. I won't answer to any other name than Annie's Granny.

ANN (*gratefully*):

You all spoil me, except Jack.

TANNER (*over his shoulder, from the bookcase*):

I think you ought to call me Mr Tanner.

ANN (*gently*):

No you don't, Jack. That's like the things you say on purpose to shock people: those who know you pay no attention to them. But, if you like, I'll call you after your famous ancestor Don Juan.

RAMSDEN:

Don Juan!

ANN (*innocently*):

Oh, is there any harm in it? I didn't know. Then I certainly won't call you that. May I call you Jack until I can think of something else?

TANNER:

Oh, for Heaven's sake don't try to invent anything worse. I capitulate. I consent to Jack. I embrace Jack. Here endeth my first and last attempt to assert my authority.

ANN:

You see, Mamma, they all really like to have pet names.

MRS WHITEFIELD:

Well, I think you might at least drop them until we are out of mourning.

ANN (*reproachfully, stricken to the soul*):

Oh, how could you remind me, mother? (*She hastily leaves the room to conceal her emotion.*)

MRS WHITEFIELD:

Of course. My fault as usual! (*She follows* Ann.)

TANNER (*coming from the bookcase*):

Ramsden: we're beated—smashed—nonentitized, like her mother.

RAMSDEN:

Stuff, sir. (*He follows* Mrs Whitefield *out of the room.*)

TANNER (*left alone with* Octavius, *stares whimsically at him*):

Tavy: do you want to count for something in the world?

OCTAVIUS:

I want to count for something as a poet: I want to write a great play.

TANNER:

With Ann as the heroine?

OCTAVIUS:

Yes: I confess it.

TANNER:

Take care, Tavy. The play with Ann as the heroine is all right; but if you're not very careful, by Heaven she'll marry you.

OCTAVIUS (*sighing*):

No such luck, Jack!

TANNER:

Why, man, your head is in the lioness's mouth: you are half swallowed already—in three bites—Bite One, Ricky; Bite Two, Ticky; Bite Three, Tavy; and down you go.

OCTAVIUS:

She is the same to everybody, Jack: you know her ways.

TANNER:

Yes: she breaks everybody's back with the stroke of her paw; but the question is, which of us will she eat? My own opinion is that she means to eat you.

OCTAVIUS (*rising, pettishly*):

It's horrible to talk like that about her when she is upstairs crying for her father. But I do so want her to eat me that I can bear your brutalities because they give me hope.

TANNER:

Tavy; that's the devilish side of a woman's fascination: she makes you will your own destruction.

OCTAVIUS:

But it's not destruction: it's fulfilment.

TANNER:

Yes, of her purpose; and that purpose is neither her happiness nor yours, but Nature's. Vitality in a woman is a blind fury of creation. She sacrifices herself to it: do you think she will hesitate to sacrifice you?

OCTAVIUS:

Why, it is just because she is self-sacrificing that she will not sacrifice those she loves.

TANNER:

That is the profoundest of mistakes, Tavy. It is the self-sacrificing women that sacrifice others most recklessly. Because they are unselfish, they are kind in little things. Because they have a purpose which is not their own purpose, but that of the whole universe, a man is nothing to them but an instrument of that purpose.

OCTAVIUS:

Don't be ungenerous, Jack. They take the tenderest care of us.

TANNER:

Yes, as a soldier takes care of his rifle or a musician of his violin. But do they allow us any purpose or freedom of our own? Will they lend us to one another? Can the strongest man escape from them when once he is appropriated? They tremble when we are in danger, and weep when we die; but the tears are not for us, but for a father wasted, a son's breeding thrown away. They accuse us of treating them as a mere means to our pleasure; but how can so feeble and transient a folly as a man's selfish pleasure enslave a woman as the whole purpose of Nature embodied in a woman can enslave a man?

OCTAVIUS:

What matter, if the slavery makes us happy?

TANNER:

No matter at all if you have no purpose of your own, and are, like most men, a mere breadwinner. But you, Tavy, are an artist: that is, you have a purpose as absorbing and as unscrupulous as a woman's purpose.

OCTAVIUS:

Not unscrupulous.

TANNER:

Quite unscrupulous. The true artist will let his wife starve, his children go barefoot, his mother drudge for his living at seventy, sooner than work at anything but his art. To women he is half vivisector, half vampire. He gets into intimate relations with them to study them, to strip the mask of convention from them, to surprise their inmost secrets, knowing that they have the power to rouse his deepest creative energies, to rescue him from his cold reason, to make him see visions and dream dreams, to inspire him, as he calls it. He persuades women that they may do this for their own purpose whilst he really means them to do it for his. He steals the mother's milk and blackens it to make printer's ink to scoff at her and glorify ideal women with. He pretends to spare her the pangs of child-bearing so that he may have for himself the tenderness and fostering that belong of right to her children. Since marriage began, the great artist has been known as a bad husband. But he is worse: he is a child-robber, a blood-sucker, a hypocrite and a cheat. Perish the race and wither a thousand women if only the sacrifice of them enable him to act Hamlet better, to paint a finer picture, to write a deeper poem, a greater play, a profounder philosophy! For mark you, Tavy, the artist's work is to shew us ourselves as we really are. Our minds are nothing but this knowledge of ourselves; and he who adds a jot to such knowledge creates new minds as surely as any woman creates new men. In the rage of that creation he is as ruthless as the woman, as dangerous to her as she to him, and as horribly fascinating. Of all human struggles there is none so treacherous and remorseless as the struggle between the artist man and the mother woman. Which shall use up the other? that is the issue between them. And it is all the deadlier because, in your romanticist cant, they love one another.

OCTAVIUS:

Even if it were so—and I don't admit it for a moment—it is out of the deadliest struggles that we get the noblest characters.

TANNER:

Remember that the next time you meet a grizzly bear or a Bengal tiger, Tavy.

OCTAVIUS:

I meant where there is love, Jack.

TANNER:

Oh, the tiger will love you. There is no love sincerer than the love of food. I think Ann loves you that way: she patted your cheek as if it were a nicely underdone chop.

OCTAVIUS:

You know, Jack, I should have to run away from you if I did not make it a fixed rule not to mind anything you say. You come out with perfectly revolting things sometimes.

Ramsden *returns, followed by* Ann. *They come in quickly, with their former leisurely air of decorous grief changed to one of genuine concern, and, on* Ramsden's *part, of worry. He comes between the two men, intending to address* Octavius, *but pulls himself up abruptly as he sees* Tanner.

RAMSDEN:

I hardly expected to find you still here, Mr Tanner.

TANNER:

Am I in the way? Good morning, fellow guardian (*he goes towards the door*).

ANN:

Stop, Jack. Granny: he must know, sooner or later.

RAMSDEN:

Octavius: I have a very serious piece of news for you. It is of the most private and delicate nature—of the most painful nature too, I am sorry to say. Do you wish Mr Tanner to be present whilst I explain?

OCTAVIUS (*turning pale*):

I have no secrets from Jack.

RAMSDEN:

Before you decide that finally, let me say that the news concerns your sister, and that it is terrible news.

OCTAVIUS:

Violet! What has happened? Is she—dead?

RAMSDEN:

I am not sure that it is not even worse than that.

OCTAVIUS:

Is she badly hurt? Has there been an accident?

RAMSDEN:

No: nothing of that sort.

TANNER:

Ann: will you have the common humanity to tell us what the matter is?

ANN (*half whispering*):

> I can't. Violet has done something dreadful. We shall have to get her away somewhere. (*She flutters to the writing table and sits in* Ramsden's *chair, leaving the three men to fight it out between them.*)

OCTAVIUS (*enlightened*):

> Is that what you meant, Mr Ramsden?

RAMSDEN:

> Yes. (Octavius *sinks upon a chair, crushed.*) I am afraid there is no doubt that Violet did not really go to Eastbourne three weeks ago when we thought she was with the Parry Whitefields. And she called on a strange doctor yesterday with a wedding ring on her finger. Mrs Parry Whitefield met her there by chance; and so the whole thing came out.

OCTAVIUS (*rising with his fists clenched*):

> Who is the scoundrel?

ANN:

> She won't tell us.

OCTAVIUS (*collapsing into the chair again*):

> What a frightful thing!

TANNER (*with angry sarcasm*):

> Dreadful. Appalling. Worse than death, as Ramsden says. (*He comes to* Octavius.) What would you not give, Tavy, to turn it into a railway accident, with all her bones broken, or something equally respectable and deserving of sympathy?

OCTAVIUS:

> Don't be brutal, Jack.

TANNER:

> Brutal! Good Heavens, man, what are you crying for? Here is a woman whom we all supposed to be making bad water color sketches, practising Grieg and Brahms, gadding about to concerts and parties, wasting her life and her money. We suddenly learn that she has turned from these sillinesses to the fulfilment of her highest purpose and greatest function—to increase, multiply and replenish the earth. And instead of admiring her courage and rejoicing in her instinct; instead of crowning the completed womanhood and raising the triumphal strain of "Unto us a child is born: unto us a son is given," here you are—you who have been as merry as grigs in your mourning for the dead—all pulling long faces and looking as ashamed and disgraced as if the girl had committed the vilest of crimes.

RAMSDEN (*roaring with rage*):

> I will not have these abominations uttered in my house (*he smites the writing table with his fist*).

TANNER:

Look here: if you insult me again I'll take you at your word and leave your house. Ann: where is Violet now?

ANN:

Why? Are you going to her?

TANNER:

Of course I am going to her. She wants help; she wants money; she wants respect and congratulation; she wants every chance for her child. She does not seem likely to get it from you: she shall from me. Where is she?

ANN:

Don't be so headstrong, Jack. She's upstairs.

TANNER:

What! Under Ramsden's sacred roof! Go and do your miserable duty, Ramsden. Hunt her out into the street. Cleanse your threshold from her contamination. Vindicate the purity of your English home. I'll go for a cab.

ANN (*alarmed*):

Oh, Granny, you mustn't do that.

OCTAVIUS (*broken-heartedly, rising*):

I'll take her away, Mr Ramsden. She had no right to come to your house.

RAMSDEN (*indignantly*):

But I am only too anxious to help her. (*Turning on* Tanner) How dare you, sir, impute such monstrous intentions to me? I protest against it. I am ready to put down my last penny to save her from being driven to run to you for protection.

TANNER (*subsiding*):

It's all right, then. He's not going to act up to his principles. It's agreed that we all stand by Violet.

OCTAVIUS:

But who is the man? He can make reparation by marrying her; and he shall, or he shall answer for it to me.

RAMSDEN:

He shall, Octavius. There you speak like a man.

TANNER:

Then you don't think him a scoundrel, after all?

OCTAVIUS:

Not a scoundrel! He is a heartless scoundrel.

RAMSDEN:

A damned scoundrel. I beg your pardon, Annie; but I can say no less.

TANNER:

So we are to marry your sister to a damned scoundrel by way of reforming her character! On my soul, I think you are all mad.

ANN:

Don't be absurd, Jack. Of course you are quite right, Tavy; but we don't know who he is: Violet won't tell us.

TANNER:

What on earth does it matter who he is? He's done his part; and Violet must do the rest.

RAMSDEN (*beside himself*):

Stuff! lunacy! There is a rascal in our midst, a libertine, a villain worse than a murderer; and we are not to learn who he is! In our ignorance we are to shake him by the hand; to introduce him into our homes; to trust our daughters with him; to— to—

ANN (*coaxingly*):

There, Granny, don't talk so loud. It's most shocking: we must all admit that; but if Violet won't tell us, what can we do? Nothing. Simply nothing.

RAMSDEN:

Hmph! I'm not so sure of that. If any man has paid Violet any special attention, we can easily find that out. If there is any man of notoriously loose principles among us—

TANNER:

Ahem!

RAMSDEN (*raising his voice*):

Yes sir, I repeat, if there is any man of notoriously loose principles among us—

TANNER:

Or any man notoriously lacking in self-control.

RAMSDEN (*aghast*):

Do you dare to suggest that *I* am capable of such an act?

TANNER:

My dear Ramsden, this is an act of which every man is capable. That is what comes of getting at cross purposes with Nature. The suspicion you have just flung at me clings to us all. It's a sort of mud that sticks to the judge's ermine or the cardinal's robe as fast as to the rags of the tramp. Come, Tavy: don't look so bewildered: it might have been me: it might have been Ramsden; just as it might have been anybody. If it had, what could we do but lie and protest—as Ramsden is going to protest.

RAMSDEN (*choking*):

I—I—I—

TANNER:

Guilt itself could not stammer more confusedly. And yet you know perfectly well he's innocent, Tavy.

RAMSDEN (*exhausted*):

I am glad you admit that, sir. I admit, myself, that there is an element of truth in what you say, grossly as you may distort it to gratify your malicious humor. I hope, Octavius, no suspicion of me is possible in your mind.

OCTAVIUS:

Of you! No, not for a moment.

TANNER (*drily*):

I think he suspects me just a little.

OCTAVIUS:

Jack: you couldn't—you wouldn't—

TANNER:

Why not?

OCTAVIUS (*appalled*):

Why not!

TANNER:

Oh, well, I'll tell you why not. First, you would feel bound to quarrel with me. Second, Violet doesn't like me. Third, if I had the honor of being the father of Violet's child, I should boast of it instead of denying it. So be easy: our friendship is not in danger.

OCTAVIUS:

I should have put away the suspicion with horror if only you would think and feel naturally about it. I beg your pardon.

TANNER:

My pardon! nonsense! And now let's sit down and have a family council. (*He sits down. The rest follow his example, more or less under protest.*) Violet is going to do the State a service; consequently she must be packed abroad like a criminal until it's over. What's happening upstairs?

ANN:

Violet is in the housekeeper's room—by herself, of course.

TANNER:

Why not in the drawingroom?

ANN:

Don't be absurd, Jack. Miss Ramsden is in the drawingroom with my mother, considering what to do.

TANNER:

Oh! the housekeeper's room is the penitentiary, I suppose; and the prisoner is waiting to be brought before her judges. The old cats!

ANN:

Oh, Jack!

RAMSDEN:

You are at present a guest beneath the roof of one of the old cats, sir. My sister is the mistress of this house.

TANNER:

She would put me in the housekeeper's room, too, if she dared, Ramsden. However, I withdraw cats. Cats would have more sense. Ann: as your guardian, I order you to go to Violet at once and be particularly kind to her.

ANN:

I have seen her, Jack. And I am sorry to say I am afraid she is going to be rather obstinate about going abroad. I think Tavy ought to speak to her about it.

OCTAVIUS:

How can I speak to her about such a thing (*he breaks down*)?

ANN:

Don't break down, Ricky. Try to bear it for all our sakes.

RAMSDEN:

Life is not all plays and poems, Octavius. Come! face it like a man.

TANNER (*chafing again*):

Poor dear brother! Poor dear friends of the family! Poor dear Tabbies and Grimalkins! Poor dear everybody except the woman who is going to risk her life to create another life! Tavy: don't you be a selfish ass. Away with you and talk to Violet; and bring her down here if she cares to come. (*Octavius rises*). Tell her we'll stand by her.

RAMSDEN (*rising*):

No, sir—

TANNER (*rising also and interrupting him*):

Oh, we understand: it's against your conscience; but still you'll do it.

OCTAVIUS:

I assure you all, on my word, I never meant to be selfish. It's so hard to know what to do when one wishes earnestly to do right.

TANNER:

My dear Tavy, your pious English habit of regarding the world as a moral gymnasium built expressly to strengthen your character in, occasionally leads you to think about your own confounded principles when you should be thinking about other people's necessities. The need of the present hour is a happy mother and a healthy baby. Bend your energies on that; and you will see your way clearly enough.

Octavius, *much perplexed, goes out.*

RAMSDEN (*facing* Tanner *impressively*):

And Morality, sir? What is to become of that?

TANNER:

Meaning a weeping Magdalen and an innocent child branded with her shame. Not in our circle, thank you. Morality can go to its father the devil.

RAMSDEN:

I thought so, sir. Morality sent to the devil to please our libertines, male and female. That is to be the future of England, is it?

TANNER:

Oh, England will survive your disapproval. Meanwhile, I understand that you agree with me as to the practical course we are to take?

RAMSDEN:

Not in your spirit, sir. Not for your reasons.

TANNER:

You can explain that if anybody calls you to account, here or hereafter. (*He turns away, and plants himself in front of Mr Herbert Spencer, at whom he stares gloomily.*)

ANN (*rising and coming to* Ramsden):

Granny: hadn't you better go up to the drawingroom and tell them what we intend to do?

RAMSDEN (*looking pointedly at* Tanner):

I hardly like to leave you alone with this gentleman. Will you not come with me?

ANN:

Miss Ramsden would not like to speak about it before me, Granny. I ought not to be present.

RAMSDEN:

You are right: I should have thought of that. You are a good girl, Annie.

*He pats her on the shoulder. She looks up at him with beaming eyes; and he goes out, much moved. Having disposed of him, she looks at* Tanner. *His back being turned to her, she gives a moment's attention to her personal appearance, then softly goes to him and speaks almost into his ear.*

ANN:

Jack (*he turns with a start*): are you glad that you are my guardian? You don't mind being made responsible for me, I hope.

TANNER:

> The latest addition to your collection of scapegoats, eh?

ANN:

> Oh, that stupid old joke of yours about me! Do please drop it. Why do you say things that you know must pain me? I do my best to please you, Jack: I suppose I may tell you so now that you are my guardian. You will make me so unhappy if you refuse to be friends with me.

TANNER (*studying her as gloomily as he studied the bust*):

> You need not go begging for my regard. How unreal our moral judgments are! You seem to me to have absolutely no conscience—only hypocrisy; and you can't see the difference—yet there is a sort of fascination about you. I always attend to you, somehow. I should miss you if I lost you.

ANN (*tranquilly slipping her arm into his and walking about with him*):

> But isn't that only natural, Jack? We have known each other since we were children. Do you remember—

TANNER (*abruptly breaking loose*):

> Stop! I remember everything.

ANN:

> Oh, I daresay we were often very silly; but—

TANNER:

> I won't have it, Ann. I am no more that schoolboy now than I am the dotard of ninety I shall grow into if I live long enough. It is over: let me forget it.

ANN:

> Wasn't it a happy time? (*She attempts to take his arm again.*)

TANNER:

> Sit down and behave yourself. (*He makes her sit down in the chair next the writing table.*) No doubt it was a happy time for you. You were a good girl and never compromised yourself. And yet the wickedest child that ever was slapped could hardly have had a better time. I can understand the success with which you bullied the other girls: your virtue imposed on them. But tell me this: did you ever know a good boy?

ANN:

> Of course. All boys are foolish sometimes; but Tavy was always a really good boy.

TANNER (*struck by this*):

> Yes: you're right. For some reason you never tempted Tavy.

ANN:

> Tempted! Jack!

TANNER:

Yes, my dear Lady Mephistopheles, tempted. You were insatiably curious as to what a boy might be capable of, and diabolically clever at getting through his guard and surprising his inmost secrets.

ANN:

What nonsense! All because you used to tell me long stories of the wicked things you had done—silly boys' tricks! And you call such things inmost secrets! Boys' secrets are just like men's; and you know what they are!

TANNER (*obstinately*):

No I don't. What are they, pray?

ANN:

Why, the things they tell everybody, of course.

TANNER:

Now I swear I told you things I told no one else. You lured me into a compact by which we were to have no secrets from one another. We were to tell one another everything. I didn't notice that you never told me anything.

ANN:

You didn't want to talk about me, Jack. You wanted to talk about yourself.

TANNER:

Ah, true, horribly true. But what a devil of a child you must have been to know that weakness and to play on it for the satisfaction of your own curiosity! I wanted to brag to you, to make myself interesting. And I found myself doing all sorts of mischievous things simply to have something to tell you about. I fought with boys I didn't hate; I lied about things I might just as well have told the truth about; I stole things I didn't want; I kissed little girls I didn't care for. It was all bravado: passionless and therefore unreal.

ANN:

I never told of you, Jack.

TANNER:

No; but if you had wanted to stop me you would have told of me. You wanted me to go on.

ANN (*flashing out*):

Oh, that's not true: it's not true, Jack. I never wanted you to do those dull, disappointing, brutal, stupid, vulgar things. I always hoped that it would be something really heroic at last. (*Recovering herself*) Excuse me, Jack; but the things you did were never a bit like the things I wanted you to do. They often gave me great uneasiness; but I could not tell on you and get you into trouble. And you were only a boy. I knew you would grow out of them. Perhaps I was wrong.

TANNER (*sardonically*):

Do not give way to remorse, Ann. At least nineteen twentieths of the exploits I confessed to you were pure lies. I soon noticed that you didn't like the true stories.

ANN:

Of course I knew that some of the things couldn't have happened. But—

TANNER:

You are going to remind me that some of the most disgraceful ones did.

ANN (*fondly, to his great terror*):

I don't want to remind you of anything. But I knew the people they happened to, and heard about them.

TANNER:

Yes; but even the true stories were touched up for telling. A sensitive boy's humiliations may be very good fun for ordinary thickskinned grown-ups; but to the boy himself they are so acute, so ignominious, that he cannot confess them—cannot but deny them passionately. However, perhaps it was as well for me that I romanced a bit; for, on the one occasion when I told you the truth, you threatened to tell of me.

ANN:

Oh, never. Never once.

TANNER:

Yes, you did. Do you remember a dark-eyed girl named Rachel Rosetree? (Ann's *brows contract for an instant involuntarily.*) I got up a love affair with her; and we met one night in the garden and walked about very uncomfortably with our arms round one another, and kissed at parting, and were most conscientiously romantic. If that love affair had gone on, it would have bored me to death; but it didn't go on; for the next thing that happened was that Rachel cut me because she found out that I had told you. How did she find it out? From you. You went to her and held the guilty secret over her head, leading her a life of abject terror and humiliation by threatening to tell on her.

ANN:

And a very good thing for her, too. It was my duty to stop her misconduct; and she is thankful to me for it now.

TANNER:

Is she?

ANN:

She ought to be, at all events.

TANNER:

It was not your duty to stop my misconduct, I suppose.

ANN:

I did stop it by stopping her.

TANNER:

Are you sure of that? You stopped my telling you about my adventures; but how do you know that you stopped the adventures?

ANN:

Do you mean to say that you went on in the same way with other girls?

TANNER:

No. I had enough of that sort of romantic tom-foolery with Rachel.

ANN (*unconvinced*):

Then why did you break off our confidences and become quite strange to me?

TANNER (*enigmatically*):

It happened just then that I got something that I wanted to keep all to myself instead of sharing it with you.

ANN:

I am sure I shouldn't have asked for any of it if you had grudged it.

TANNER:

It wasn't a box of sweets, Ann. It was something you'd never have let me call my own.

ANN (*incredulously*):

What?

TANNER:

My soul.

ANN:

Oh, do be sensible, Jack. You know you're talking nonsense.

TANNER:

The most solemn earnest, Ann. You didn't notice at that time that you were getting a soul too. But you were. It was not for nothing that you suddenly found you had a moral duty to chastise and reform Rachel. Up to that time you had traded pretty extensively in being a good child; but you had never set up a sense of duty to others. Well, I set one up too. Up to that time I had played the boy buccaneer with no more conscience than a fox in a poultry farm. But now I began to have scruples, to feel obligations, to find that veracity and honor were no longer goody-goody expressions in the mouths of grown up people, but compelling principles in myself.

ANN (*quietly*):

Yes, I suppose you're right. You were beginning to be a man, and I to be a woman.

TANNER:

Are you sure it was not that we were beginning to be something more? What does the beginning of manhood and womanhood mean in most people's mouths? You know: it means the beginning of love. But love began long before that for me. Love played its part in the earliest dreams and follies and romances I can remember—may I say the earliest follies and romances we can remember?—though we did not understand it at the time. No: the change that came to me was the birth in me of moral passion; and I declare that according to my experience moral passion is the only real passion.

ANN:

All passions ought to be moral, Jack.

TANNER:

Ought! Do you think that anything is strong enough to impose oughts on a passion except a stronger passion still?

ANN:

Our moral sense controls passion, Jack. Don't be stupid.

TANNER:

Our moral sense! And is that not a passion? Is the devil to have all the passions as well as all the good tunes? If it were not a passion—if it were not the mightiest of the passions, all the other passions would sweep it away like a leaf before a hurricane. It is the birth of that passion that turns a child into a man.

ANN:

There are other passions, Jack. Very strong ones.

TANNER:

All the other passions were in me before; but they were idle and aimless—mere childish greedinesses and cruelties, curiosities and fancies, habits and superstitions, grotesque and ridiculous to the mature intelligence. When they suddenly began to shine like newly lit flames it was by no light of their own, but by the radiance of the dawning moral passion. That passion dignified them, gave them conscience and meaning, found them a mob of appetites and organized them into an army of purposes and principles. My soul was born of that passion.

ANN:

I noticed that you got more sense. You were a dreadfully destructive boy before that.

TANNER:

Destructive! Stuff! I was only mischievous.

ANN:

Oh Jack, you were very destructive. You ruined all the young fir trees by chopping off their leaders with a wooden sword. You broke all the cucumber frames with your catapult. You set fire to the common: the police arrested Tavy for it because he ran away when he couldn't stop you. You—

TANNER:

Pooh! pooh! pooh! these were battles, bombardments, strategems to save our scalps from the red Indians. You have no imagination, Ann. I am ten times more destructive now than I was then. The moral passion has taken my destructiveness in hand and directed it to moral ends. I have become a reformer, and, like all reformers, an iconoclast. I no longer break cucumber frames and burn gorse bushes: I shatter creeds and demolish idols.

ANN (*bored*):

I am afraid I am too feminine to see any sense in destruction. Destruction can only destroy.

TANNER:

Yes. That is why it is so useful. Construction cumbers the ground with institutions made by busybodies. Destruction clears it and gives us breathing space and liberty.

ANN:

It's no use, Jack. No woman will agree with you there.

TANNER:

That's because you confuse construction and destruction with creation and murder. They're quite different: I adore creation and abhor murder. Yes: I adore it in tree and flower, in bird and beast, even in you. (*A flush of interest and delight suddenly chases the growing perplexity and boredom from her face.*) It was the creative instinct that led you to attach me to you by bonds that have left their mark on me to this day. Yes, Ann: the old childish compact between us was an unconscious love compact—

ANN:

Jack!

TANNER:

Oh, don't be alarmed—

ANN:

I am not alarmed.

TANNER (*whimsically*):

Then you ought to be: where are your principles?

ANN:

Jack: are you serious or are you not?

TANNER:

> Do you mean about the moral passion?

ANN:

> No, no; the other one. (*Confused*) Oh! you are so silly: one never knows how to take you.

TANNER:

> You must take me quite seriously. I am your guardian; and it is my duty to improve your mind.

ANN:

> The love compact is over, then, is it? I suppose you grew tired of me?

TANNER:

> No; but the moral passion made our childish relations impossible. A jealous sense of my new individuality arose in me—

ANN:

> You hated to be treated as a boy any longer. Poor Jack!

TANNER:

> Yes, because to be treated as a boy was to be taken on the old footing. I had become a new person; and those who knew the old person laughed at me. The only man who behaved sensibly was my tailor: he took my measure anew every time he saw me, whilst all the rest went on with their old measurements and expected them to fit me.

ANN:

> You became frightfully self-conscious.

TANNER:

> When you go to heaven, Ann, you will be frightfully conscious of your wings for the first year or so. When you meet your relatives there, and they persist in treating you as if you were still a mortal, you will not be able to bear them. You will try to get into a circle which has never known you except as an angel.

ANN:

> So it was only your vanity that made you run away from us after all?

TANNER:

> Yes, only my vanity, as you call it.

ANN:

> You need not have kept away from me on that account.

TANNER:

> From you above all others. You fought harder than anybody against my emancipation.

ANN (*earnestly*):

> Oh, how wrong you are! I would have done anything for you.

TANNER:

> Anything except let me get loose from you. Even then you had acquired by instinct that damnable woman's trick of heaping obligations on a man, of placing yourself so entirely and helplessly at his mercy that at last he dare not take a step without running to you for leave. I know a poor wretch whose one desire in life is to run away from his wife. She prevents him by threatening to throw herself in front of the engine of the train he leaves her in. That is what all women do. If we try to go where you do not want us to go there is no law to prevent us; but when we take the first step your breasts are under our foot as it descends: your bodies are under our wheels as we start. No woman shall ever enslave me in that way.

ANN:

> But, Jack, you cannot get through life without considering other people a little.

TANNER:

> Ay; but what other people? It is this consideration of other people—or rather this cowardly fear of them which we call consideration—that makes us the sentimental slaves we are. To consider you, as you call it, is to substitute your will for my own. How if it be a baser will than mine? Are women taught better than men or worse? Are mobs of voters taught better than statesmen or worse? Worse, of course, in both cases. And then what sort of world are you going to get, with its public men considering its voting mobs, and its private men considering their wives? What does Church and State mean nowadays? The Woman and the Ratepayer.

ANN (*placidly*):

> I am so glad you understand politics, Jack: it will be most useful to you if you go into parliament (*he collapses like a pricked bladder*). But I am sorry you thought my influence a bad one.

TANNER:

> I don't say it was a bad one. But bad or good, I didn't choose to be cut to your measure. And I won't be cut to it.

ANN:

> Nobody wants you to, Jack. I assure you—really on my word—I don't mind your queer opinions one little bit. You know we have all been brought up to have advanced opinions. Why do you persist in thinking me so narrow minded?

TANNER:

> That's the danger of it. I know you don't mind, because you've found out that it doesn't matter. The boa constrictor doesn't

mind the opinions of a stag one little bit when once she has got her coils round it.

ANN (*rising in sudden enlightenment*):

O-o-o-o-oh! now I understand why you warned Tavy that I am a boa constrictor. Granny told me. (*She laughs and throws her boa round his neck.*) Doesn't it feel nice and soft, Jack?

TANNER (*in the toils*):

You scandalous woman, will you throw away even your hypocrisy?

ANN:

I am never hypocritical with you, Jack. Are you angry? (*She withdraws the boa and throws it on a chair.*) Perhaps I shouldn't have done that.

TANNER (*contemptuously*):

Pooh, prudery! Why should you not, if it amuses you?

ANN (*shyly*):

Well, because—because I suppose what you really meant by the boa constrictor was this (*she puts her arms round his neck*).

TANNER (*staring at her*):

Magnificent audacity! (*She laughs and pats his cheeks.*) Now just to think that if I mentioned this episode not a soul would believe me except the people who would cut me for telling, whilst if you accused me of it nobody would believe my denial!

ANN (*taking her arms away with perfect dignity*):

You are incorrigible, Jack. But you should not jest about our affection for one another. Nobody could possibly misunderstand it. You do not misunderstand it, I hope.

TANNER:

My blood interprets for me, Ann. Poor Ricky Ticky Tavy!

ANN (*looking quickly at him as if this were a new light*):

Surely you are not so absurd as to be jealous of Tavy.

TANNER:

Jealous! Why should I be? But I don't wonder at your grip of him. I feel the coils tightening round my very self, though you are only playing with me.

ANN:

Do you think I have designs on Tavy?

TANNER:

I know you have.

ANN (*earnestly*):

Take care, Jack. You may make Tavy very unhappy if you mislead him about me.

TANNER:

Never fear: he will not escape you.

ANN:

> I wonder are you really a clever man!

TANNER:

> Why this sudden misgiving on the subject?

ANN:

> You seem to understand all the things I don't understand; but you are a perfect baby in the things I do understand.

TANNER:

> I understand how Tavy feels for you, Ann: you may depend on that, at all events.

ANN:

> And you think you understand how I feel for Tavy, don't you?

TANNER:

> I know only too well what is going to happen to poor Tavy.

ANN:

> I should laugh at you, Jack, if it were not for poor papa's death. Mind! Tavy will be very unhappy.

TANNER:

> Yes; but he won't know it, poor devil. He is a thousand times too good for you. That's why he is going to make the mistake of his life about you.

ANN:

> I think men make more mistakes by being too clever than by being too good (*she sits down, with a trace of contempt for the whole male sex in the elegant carriage of her shoulders*).

TANNER:

> Oh, I know you don't care very much about Tavy. But there is always one who kisses and one who only allows the kiss. Tavy will kiss; and you will only turn the cheek. And you will throw him over if anybody better turns up.

ANN (*offended*):

> You have no right to say such things, Jack. They are not true, and not delicate. If you and Tavy choose to be stupid about me, that is not my fault.

TANNER (*remorsefully*):

> Forgive my brutalities, Ann. They are levelled at this wicked world, not at you. (*She looks up at him, pleased and forgiving. He becomes cautious at once.*) All the same, I wish Ramsden would come back. I never feel safe with you: there is a devilish charm—or no: not a charm, a subtle interest (*she laughs*)—Just so: you know it; and you triumph in it. Openly and shamelessly triumph in it!

ANN:

>   What a shocking flirt you are, Jack!

TANNER:

>   A flirt!! I!!!

ANN:

>   Yes, a flirt. You are always abusing and offending people; but you never really mean to let go your hold of them.

TANNER:

>   I will ring the bell. This conversation has already gone further than I intended.

Ramsden *and* Octavius *come back with* Miss Ramsden, *a hardheaded old maiden lady in a plain brown silk gown, with enough rings, chains and brooches to shew that her plainness of dress is a matter of principle, not of poverty. She comes into the room very determinedly: the two men, perplexed and downcast, following her.* Ann *rises and goes eagerly to meet her.* Tanner *retreats to the wall between the busts and pretends to study the pictures.* Ramsden *goes to his table as usual; and* Octavius *clings to the neighborhood of* Tanner.

MISS RAMSDEN (*almost pushing* Ann *aside as she comes to* Mrs Whitefield's *chair and plants herself there resolutely*):

>   I wash my hands of the whole affair.

OCTAVIUS (*very wretched*):

>   I know you wish me to take Violet away, Miss Ramsden. I will. (*He turns irresolutely to the door*).

RAMSDEN:

>   No no—

MISS RAMSDEN:

>   What is the use of saying no, Roebuck? Octavius knows that I would not turn any truly contrite and repentant woman from your doors. But when a woman is not only wicked, but intends to go on being wicked, she and I part company.

ANN:

>   Oh, Miss Ramsden, what do you mean? What has Violet said?

RAMSDEN:

>   Violet is certainly very obstinate. She won't leave London. I don't understand her.

MISS RAMSDEN:

>   I do. It's as plain as the nose on your face, Roebuck, that she won't go because she doesn't want to be separated from this man, whoever he is.

ANN:

>   Oh, surely, surely! Octavius: did you speak to her?

OCTAVIUS:

She won't tell us anything. She won't make any arrangement until she has consulted somebody. It can't be anybody else than the scoundrel who has betrayed her.

TANNER (*to* Octavius):

Well, let her consult him. He will be glad enough to have her sent abroad. Where is the difficulty?

MISS RAMSDEN (*taking the answer out of* Octavius's *mouth*):

The difficulty, Mr Jack, is that when I offered to help her I didn't offer to become her accomplice in her wickedness. She either pledges her word never to see that man again, or else she finds some new friends; and the sooner the better.

*The parlormaid appears at the door.* Ann *hastily resumes her seat, and looks as unconcerned as possible.* Octavius *instinctively imitates her.*

THE MAID:

The cab is at the door, ma'am.

MISS RAMSDEN:

What cab?

THE MAID:

For Miss Robinson.

MISS RAMSDEN:

Oh! (*Recovering herself*) All right. (*The maid withdraws.*) She has sent for a cab.

TANNER:

*I* wanted to send for that cab half an hour ago.

MISS RAMSDEN:

I am glad she understands the position she has placed herself in.

RAMSDEN:

I don't like her going away in this fashion, Susan. We had better not do anything harsh.

OCTAVIUS:

No: thank you again and again; but Miss Ramsden is quite right. Violet cannot expect to stay.

ANN:

Hadn't you better go with her, Tavy?

OCTAVIUS:

She won't have me.

MISS RAMSDEN:

Of course she won't. She's going straight to that man.

TANNER:

As a natural result of her virtuous reception here.

RAMSDEN (*much troubled*):

> There, Susan! You hear! and there's some truth in it. I wish you could reconcile it with your principles to be a little patient with this poor girl. She's very young; and there's a time for everything.

MISS RAMSDEN:

> Oh, she will get all the sympathy she wants from the men. I'm surprised at you, Roebuck.

TANNER:

> So am I, Ramsden, most favorably.

Violet *appears at the door. She is as impenitent and self-possessed a young lady as one would desire to see among the best behaved of her sex. Her small head and tiny resolute mouth and chin; her haughty crispness of speech and trimness of carriage; the ruthless elegance of her equipment, which includes a very smart hat with a dead bird in it, mark a personality which is as formidable as it is exquisitely pretty. She is not a siren, like* Ann: *admiration comes to her without any compulsion or even interest on her part; besides, there is some fun in* Ann, *but in this woman none, perhaps no mercy either: if anything restrains her, it is intelligence and pride, not compassion. Her voice might be the voice of a schoolmistress addressing a class of girls who had disgraced themselves, as she proceeds with complete composure and some disgust to say what she has come to say.*

VIOLET:

> I have only looked in to tell Miss Ramsden that she will find her birthday present to me, the filagree bracelet, in the housekeeper's room.

TANNER:

> Do come in, Violet, and talk to us sensibly.

VIOLET:

> Thank you: I have had quite enough of the family conversation this morning. So has your mother, Ann: she has gone home crying. But at all events, I have found out what some of my pretended friends are worth. Good-bye.

TANNER:

> No, no: one moment. I have something to say which I beg you to hear. (*She looks at him without the slightest curiosity, but waits, apparently as much to finish getting her glove on as to hear what he has to say.*) I am altogether on your side in this matter. I congratulate you, with the sincerest respect, on having the courage to do what you have done. You are entirely in the right; and the family is entirely in the wrong.

*Sensation.* Ann *and* Miss Ramsden *rise and turn towards the two.* Violet, *more surprised than any of the others, forgets her glove, and comes forward into the middle of the room, both puzzled and displeased.* Octavius *alone does not move or raise his head: he is overwhelmed with shame.*

ANN (*pleading to* Tanner *to be sensible*):
> Jack!

MISS RAMSDEN (*outraged*):
> Well, I must say!

VIOLET (*sharply to* Tanner):
> Who told you?

TANNER:
> Why, Ramsden and Tavy of course. Why should they not?

VIOLET:
> But they don't know.

TANNER:
> Don't know what?

VIOLET:
> They don't know that I am in the right, I mean.

TANNER:
> Oh, they know it in their hearts, though they think themselves bound to blame you by their silly superstitions about morality and propriety and so forth. But I know, and the whole world really knows, though it dare not say so, that you were right to follow your instinct; that vitality and bravery are the greatest qualities a woman can have, and motherhood her solemn initiation into womanhood; and that the fact of your not being legally married matters not one scrap either to your own worth or to our real regard for you.

VIOLET (*flushing with indignation*):
> Oh! You think me a wicked woman, like the rest. You think I have not only been vile, but that I share your abominable opinions. Miss Ramsden: I have borne your hard words because I knew you would be sorry for them when you found out the truth. But I won't bear such a horrible insult as to be complimented by Jack on being one of the wretches of whom he approves. I have kept my marriage a secret for my husband's sake. But now I claim my right as a married woman not to be insulted.

OCTAVIUS (*raising his head with inexpressible relief*):
> You are married!

VIOLET:

Yes; and I think you might have guessed it. What business had you all to take it for granted that I had no right to wear my wedding ring? Not one of you even asked me: I cannot forget that.

TANNER (*in ruins*):

I am utterly crushed. I meant well. I apologize—abjectly apologize.

VIOLET:

I hope you will be more careful in future about the things you say. Of course one does not take them seriously; but they are very disagreeable, and rather in bad taste, I think.

TANNER (*bowing to the storm*):

I have no defence: I shall know better in future than to take any woman's part. We have all disgraced ourselves in your eyes, I am afraid, except Ann. She befriended you. For Ann's sake, forgive us.

VIOLET:

Yes: Ann has been very kind; but then Ann knew.

TANNER:

Oh!

MISS RAMSDEN (*stiffly*):

And who, pray, is the gentleman who does not acknowledge his wife?

VIOLET (*promptly*):

That is my business, Miss Ramsden, and not yours. I have my reasons for keeping my marriage a secret for the present.

RAMSDEN:

All I can say is that we are extremely sorry, Violet. I am shocked to think of how we have treated you.

OCTAVIUS (*awkwardly*):

I beg your pardon, Violet. I can say no more.

MISS RAMSDEN (*still loth to surrender*):

Of course what you say puts a very different complexion on the matter. All the same, I owe it to myself—

VIOLET (*cutting her short*):

You owe me an apology, Miss Ramsden: that's what you owe both to yourself and to me. If you were a married woman you would not like sitting in the housekeeper's room and being treated like a naughty child by young girls and old ladies without any serious duties and responsibilities.

TANNER:

Don't hit us when we're down, Violet. We seem to have made fools of ourselves; but really it was you who made fools of us.

VIOLET:

It was no business of yours, Jack, in any case.

TANNER:

No business of mine! Why, Ramsden as good as accused me of being the unknown gentleman.

Ramsden *makes a frantic demonstration; but* Violet's *cool keen anger extinguishes it.*

VIOLET:

You! Oh, how infamous! how abominable! how disgracefully you have all been talking about me! If my husband knew it he would never let me speak to any of you again. (*To Ramsden*) I think you might have spared me that, at least.

RAMSDEN:

But I assure you I never—at least it is a monstrous perversion of something I said that—

MISS RAMSDEN:

You needn't apologize, Roebuck. She brought it all on herself. It is for her to apologize for having deceived us.

VIOLET:

I can make allowances for you, Miss Ramsden: you cannot understand how I feel on this subject, though I should have expected rather better taste from people of greater experience. However, I quite feel that you have all placed yourselves in a very painful position; and the most truly considerate thing for me to do is to go at once. Good morning.

*She goes, leaving them staring.*

MISS RAMSDEN:

Well, I must say!

RAMSDEN (*plaintively*):

I don't think she is quite fair to us.

TANNER:

You must cower before the wedding ring like the rest of us, Ramsden. The cup of our ignominy is full.

# Act II

*On the carriage drive in the park of a country house near Richmond a motor car has broken down. It stands in front of a clump of trees round which the drive sweeps to the house, which is partly visible through them:*

*indeed* Tanner, *standing in the drive with the car on his right hand, could get an unobstructed view of the west corner of the house on his left were he not far too much interested in a pair of supine legs in blue serge trousers which protrude from beneath the machine. He is watching them intently with bent back and hands supported on his knees. His leathern overcoat and peaked cap proclaim him one of the dismounted passengers.*

THE LEGS:

Aha! I got him.

TANNER:

All right now?

THE LEGS:

Aw right now.

Tanner *stoops and takes the legs by the ankles, drawing their owner forth like a wheelbarrow, walking on his hands, with a hammer in his mouth. He is a young man in a neat suit of blue serge, clean shaven, dark eyed, square fingered, with short well brushed black hair and rather irregular sceptically turned eyebrows. When he is manipulating the car his movements are swift and sudden, yet attentive and deliberate. With* Tanner *and* Tanner's *friends his manner is not in the least deferential, but cool and reticent, keeping them quite effectually at a distance whilst giving them no excuse for complaining of him. Nevertheless he has a vigilant eye on them always, and that, too, rather cynically, like a man who knows the world well from its seamy side. He speaks slowly and with a touch of sarcasm; and as he does not at all affect the gentleman in his speech, it may be inferred that his smart appearance is a mark of respect to himself and his own class, not to that which employs him.*

*He now gets into the car to test his machinery and put his cap and over-coat on again.* Tanner *takes off his leathern overcoat and pitches it into the car. The chauffeur (or automobilist or motoreer or whatever England may presently decide to call him) looks round inquiringly in the act of stowing away his hammer.*

THE CHAUFFEUR:

Had enough of it, eh?

TANNER:

I may as well walk to the house and stretch my legs and calm my nerves a little. (*Looking at his watch*) I suppose you know that we have come from Hyde Park Corner to Richmond in twenty-one minutes.

THE CHAUFFEUR:

I'd ha done it under fifteen if I'd had a clear road all the way.

TANNER:

Why do you do it? Is it for love of sport or for the fun of terrifying your unfortunate employer?

THE CHAUFFEUR:

What are you afraid of?

TANNER:

The police, and breaking my neck.

THE CHAUFFEUR:

Well, if you like easy going, you can take a bus, you know. It's cheaper. You pay me to save your time and give you the value of your thousand pound car. (*He sits down calmly.*)

TANNER:

I am the slave of that car and of you too. I dream of the accursed thing at night.

THE CHAUFFEUR:

You'll get over that. If you're going up to the house, may I ask how long you're goin to stay there? Because if you mean to put in the whole morning talkin to the ladies, I'll put the car in the stables and make myself comfortable. If not, I'll keep the car on the go about here till you come.

TANNER:

Better wait here. We shan't be long. There's a young American gentleman, a Mr Malone, who is driving Mr Robinson down in his new American steam car.

THE CHAUFFEUR (*springing up and coming hastily out of the car to* Tanner):

American steam car! Wot! racin us down from London!

TANNER:

Perhaps they're here already.

THE CHAUFFEUR:

If I'd known it! (*With deep reproach*) Why didn't you tell me, Mr Tanner?

TANNER:

Because I've been told that this car is capable of 84 miles an hour; and I already know what you are capable of when there is a rival car on the road. No, Henry: there are things it is not good for you to know; and this was one of them. However, cheer up: we are going to have a day after your own heart. The American is to take Mr Robinson and his sister and Miss Whitefield. We are to take Miss Rhoda.

THE CHAUFFEUR (*consoled, and musing on another matter*):

That's Miss Whitefield's sister, isn't it?

TANNER:

Yes.

THE CHAUFFEUR:

> And Miss Whitefield herself is goin in the other car? Not with you?

TANNER:

> Why the devil should she come with me? Mr Robinson will be in the other car. (The Chauffeur *looks at* Tanner *with cool incredulity, and turns to the car, whistling a popular air softly to himself.* Tanner, *a little annoyed, is about to pursue the subject when he hears the footsteps of* Octavius *on the gravel.* Octavius *is coming from the house, dressed for motoring, but without his overcoat*). We've lost the race, thank Heaven: here's Mr Robinson. Well, Tavy, is the steam car a success?

OCTAVIUS:

> I think so. We came from Hyde Park Corner here in seventeen minutes. (The Chauffeur, *furious, kicks the car with a groan of vexation.*) How long were you?

TANNER:

> Oh, about three quarters of an hour or so.

THE CHAUFFEUR (*remonstrating*):

> Now, now, Mr Tanner, come now! We could ha done it easy under fifteen.

TANNER:

> By the way, let me introduce you. Mr Octavius Robinson: Mr Enry Straker.

STRAKER:

> Pleased to meet you, sir. Mr Tanner is gittin at you with is Enry Straker, you know. You call it Henery. But I don't mind, bless you.

TANNER:

> You think it's simply bad taste in me to chaff him, Tavy. But you're wrong. This man takes more trouble to drop his aitches than ever his father did to pick them up. It's a mark of caste to him. I have never met anybody more swollen with the pride of class than Enry is.

STRAKER:

> Easy, easy! A little moderation, Mr Tanner.

TANNER:

> A little moderation, Tavy, you observe. You would tell me to draw it mild. But this chap has been educated. What's more, he knows that we haven't. What was that Board School of yours, Straker?

STRAKER:

> Sherbrooke Road.

TANNER:

> Sherbrooke Road! Would any of us say Rugby! Harrow! Eton! in that tone of intellectual snobbery? Sherbrooke Road is a place where boys learn something: Eton is a boy farm where we are sent because we are nuisances at home, and because in after life, whenever a Duke is mentioned, we can claim him as an old school-fellow.

STRAKER:

> You don't know nothing about it, Mr Tanner. It's not the Board School that does it: it's the Polytechnic.

TANNER:

> His university, Octavius. Not Oxford, Cambridge, Durham, Dublin or Glasgow. Not even those Nonconformist holes in Wales. No, Tavy. Regent Street, Chelsea, the Borough—I don't know half their confounded names: these are his universities, not mere shops for selling class limitations like ours. You despise Oxford, Enry, don't you?

STRAKER:

> No, I don't. Very nice sort of place, Oxford, I should think, for people that like that sort of place. They teach you to be a gentleman there. In the Polytechnic they teach you to be an engineer or such like. See?

TANNER:

> Sarcasm, Tavy, sarcasm! Oh, if you could only see into Enry's soul, the depth of his contempt for a gentleman, the arrogance of his pride in being an engineer, would appall you. He positively likes the car to break down because it brings out my gentlemanly helplessness and his workmanlike skill and resource.

STRAKER:

> Never you mind him, Mr Robinson. He likes to talk. We know him, don't we?

OCTAVIUS (*earnestly*):

> But there's a great truth at the bottom of what he says. I believe most intensely in the dignity of labor.

STRAKER (*unimpressed*):

> That's because you never done any, Mr Robinson. My business is to do away with labor. You'll get more out of me and a machine than you will out of twenty laborers, and not so much to drink either.

TANNER:

> For Heaven's sake, Tavy, don't start him on political economy. He knows all about it; and we don't. You're only a poetic Socialist, Tavy: he's a scientific one.

STRAKER (*unperturbed*):

Yes. Well, this conversation is very improvin; but I've got to look after the car; and you two want to talk about your ladies. I know. (*He retires to busy himself about the car; and presently saunters off towards the house.*)

TANNER:

That's a very momentous social phenomenon.

OCTAVIUS:

What is?

TANNER:

Straker is. Here have we literary and cultured persons been for years setting up a cry of the New Woman whenever some unusually old fashioned female came along; and never noticing the advent of the New Man. Straker's the New Man.

OCTAVIUS:

I see nothing new about him, except your way of chaffing him. But I don't want to talk about him just now. I want to speak to you about Ann.

TANNER:

Straker knew even that. He learnt it at the Polytechnic, probably. Well, what about Ann? Have you proposed to her?

OCTAVIUS (*self-reproachfully*):

I was brute enough to do so last night.

TANNER:

Brute enough! What do you mean?

OCTAVIUS (*dithyrambically*):

Jack: we men are all coarse: we never understand how exquisite a woman's sensibilities are. How could I have done such a thing!

TANNER:

Done what, you maudlin idiot?

OCTAVIUS:

Yes, I am an idiot. Jack: if you had heard her voice! if you had seen her tears! I have lain awake all night thinking of them. If she had reproached me, I could have borne it better.

TANNER:

Tears! that's dangerous. What did she say?

OCTAVIUS:

She asked me how she could think of anything now but her dear father. She stifled a sob—(*he breaks down*).

TANNER (*patting him on the back*):

Bear it like a man, Tavy, even if you feel it like an ass. It's the old game: she's not tired of playing with you yet.

OCTAVIUS (*impatiently*):

Oh, don't be a fool, Jack. Do you suppose this eternal shallow cynicism of yours has any real bearing on a nature like hers?

TANNER:

Hm! Did she say anything else?

OCTAVIUS:

Yes; and that is why I expose myself and her to your ridicule by telling you what passed.

TANNER (*remorsefully*):

No, dear Tavy, not ridicule, on my honor! However, no matter. Go on.

OCTAVIUS:

Her sense of duty is so devout, so perfect, so—

TANNER:

Yes: I know. Go on.

OCTAVIUS:

You see, under this new arrangement, you and Ramsden are her guardians; and she considers that all her duty to her father is now transferred to you. She said she thought I ought to have spoken to you both in the first instance. Of course she is right; but somehow it seems rather absurd that I am to come to you and formally ask to be received as a suitor for your ward's hand.

TANNER:

I am glad that love has not totally extinguished your sense of humor, Tavy.

OCTAVIUS:

That answer won't satisfy her.

TANNER:

My official answer is, obviously, Bless you, my children: may you be happy!

OCTAVIUS:

I wish you would stop playing the fool about this. If it is not serious to you, it is to me, and to her.

TANNER:

You know very well that she is as free to choose as you are.

OCTAVIUS:

She does not think so.

TANNER:

Oh, doesn't she! just! However, say what you want me to do?

OCTAVIUS:

I want you to tell her sincerely and earnestly what you think about me. I want you to tell her that you can trust her to me— that is, if you feel you can.

TANNER:

I have no doubt that I can trust her to you. What worries me is the idea of trusting you to her. Have you read Maeterlinck's book about the bee?

OCTAVIUS (*keeping his temper with difficulty*):

I am not discussing literature at present.

TANNER:

Be just a little patient with me. *I* am not discussing literature: the book about the bee is natural history. It's an awful lesson to mankind. You think that you are Ann's suitor; that you are the pursuer and she the pursued; that it is your part to woo, to persuade, to prevail, to overcome. Fool: it is you who are the pursued, the marked down quarry, the destined prey. You need not sit looking longingly at the bait through the wires of the trap: the door is open, and will remain so until it shuts behind you for ever.

OCTAVIUS:

I wish I could believe that, vilely as you put it.

TANNER:

Why, man, what other work has she in life but to get a husband? It is a woman's business to get married as soon as possible, and a man's to keep unmarried as long as he can. You have your poems and your tragedies to work at: Ann has nothing.

OCTAVIUS:

I cannot write without inspiration. And nobody can give me that except Ann.

TANNER:

Well, hadn't you better get it from her at a safe distance? Petrarch didn't see half as much of Laura, nor Dante of Beatrice, as you see of Ann now; and yet they wrote first-rate poetry—at least so I'm told. They never exposed their idolatry to the test of domestic familiarity; and it lasted them to their graves. Marry Ann; and at the end of a week you'll find no more inspiration in her than in a plate of muffins.

OCTAVIUS:

You think I shall tire of her!

TANNER:

Not at all: you don't get tired of muffins. But you don't find inspiration in them; and you won't in her when she ceases to be a poet's dream and becomes a solid eleven stone wife. You'll be forced to dream about somebody else; and then there will be a row.

OCTAVIUS:

This sort of talk is no use, Jack. You don't understand. You have never been in love.

TANNER:

I! I have never been out of it. Why, I am in love even with Ann. But I am neither the slave of love nor its dupe. Go to the bee, thou poet: consider her ways and be wise. By Heaven, Tavy, if women could do without our work, and we ate their children's bread instead of making it, they would kill us as the spider kills her mate or as the bees kill the drone. And they would be right if we were good for nothing but love.

OCTAVIUS:

Ah, if we were only good enough for Love! There is nothing like Love: there is nothing else but Love: without it the world would be a dream of sordid horror.

TANNER:

And this—this is the man who asks me to give him the hand of my ward! Tavy: I believe we were changed in our cradles, and that you are the real descendant of Don Juan.

OCTAVIUS:

I beg you not to say anything like that to Ann.

TANNER:

Don't be afraid. She has marked you for her own; and nothing will stop her now. You are doomed. (Straker *comes back with a newspaper.*) Here comes the New Man, demoralizing himself with a halfpenny paper as usual.

STRAKER:

Now would you believe it, Mr Robinson, when we're out motoring we take in two papers, the *Times* for him, the *Leader* or the *Echo* for me. And do you think I ever see my paper? Not much. He grabs the *Leader* and leaves me to stodge myself with his *Times*.

OCTAVIUS:

Are there no winners in the *Times*?

TANNER:

Enry don't old with bettin, Tavy. Motor records are his weakness. What's the latest?

STRAKER:

Paris to Biskra at forty mile an hour average, not countin the Mediterranean.

TANNER:

How many killed?

STRAKER:

> Two silly sheep. What does it matter? Sheep don't cost such a lot: they were glad to ave the price without the trouble o sellin em to the butcher. All the same, d'y'see, there'll be a clamor agin it presently; and then the French Government'll stop it; an our chance'll be gone, see? That what makes me fairly mad: Mr Tanner won't do a good run while he can.

TANNER:

> Tavy: do you remember my uncle James?

OCTAVIUS:

> Yes. Why?

TANNER:

> Uncle James had a first rate cook: he couldn't digest anything except what she cooked. Well, the poor man was shy and hated society. But his cook was proud of her skill, and wanted to serve up dinners to princes and ambassadors. To prevent her from leaving him, that poor old man had to give a big dinner twice a month, and suffer agonies of awkwardness. Now here am I; and here is this chap Enry Straker, the New Man. I loathe travelling; but I rather like Enry. He cares for nothing but tearing along in a leather coat and goggles, with two inches of dust all over him, at sixty miles an hour and the risk of his life and mine. Except, of course, when he is lying on his back in the mud under the machine trying to find out where it has given way. Well, if I don't give him a thousand mile run at least once a fortnight I shall lose him. He will give me the sack and go to some American millionaire; and I shall have to put up with a nice respectful groom-gardener-amateur, who will touch his hat and know his place. I am Enry's slave, just as Uncle James was his cook's slave.

STRAKER (*exasperated*):

> Garn! I wish I had a car that would go as fast as you can talk, Mr Tanner. What I say is that you lose money by a motor car unless you keep it workin. Might as well ave a pram and a nuss-maid to wheel you in it as that car and me if you don't git the last inch out of us both.

TANNER (*soothingly*):

> All right, Henry, all right. We'll go out for half an hour presently.

STRAKER (*in disgust*):

> Arf an ahr! (*He returns to his machine; seats himself in it; and turns up a fresh page of his paper in search of more news.*)

OCTAVIUS:

> Oh, that reminds me. I have a note for you from Rhoda. (*He gives Tanner a note.*)

TANNER (*opening it*):

I rather think Rhoda is heading for a row with Ann. As a rule there is only one person an English girl hates more than she hates her mother; and that's her eldest sister. But Rhoda positively prefers her mother to Ann. She—(*indignantly*) Oh, I say!

OCTAVIUS:

What's the matter?

TANNER:

Rhoda was to have come with me for a ride in the motor car. She says Ann has forbidden her to go out with me.

Straker *suddenly begins whistling his favorite air with remarkable deliberation. Surprised by this burst of larklike melody, and jarred by a sardonic note in its cheerfulness, they turn and look inquiringly at him. But he is busy with his paper; and nothing comes of their movement.*

OCTAVIUS (*recovering himself*):

Does she give any reason?

TANNER:

Reason! An insult is not a reason. Ann forbids her to be alone with me on any occasion. Says I am not a fit person for a young girl to be with. What do you think of your paragon now?

OCTAVIUS:

You must remember that she has a very heavy responsibility now that her father is dead. Mrs Whitefield is too weak to control Rhoda.

TANNER (*staring at him*):

In short, you agree with Ann.

OCTAVIUS:

No; but I think I understand her. You must admit that your views are hardly suited for the formation of a young girl's mind and character.

TANNER:

I admit nothing of the sort. I admit that the formation of a young lady's mind and character usually consists in telling her lies; but I object to the particular lie that I am in the habit of abusing the confidence of girls.

OCTAVIUS:

Ann doesn't say that, Jack.

TANNER:

What else does she mean?

STRAKER (*catching sight of* Ann *coming from the house*):

Miss Whitefield, gentlemen. (*He dismounts and strolls away down the avenue with the air of a man who knows he is no longer wanted.*)

ANN (*coming between* Octavius *and* Tanner):

>Good morning, Jack. I have come to tell you that poor Rhoda has got one of her headaches and cannot go out with you to-day in the car. It is a cruel disappointment to her, poor child!

TANNER:

>What do you say now, Tavy?

OCTAVIUS:

>Surely you cannot misunderstand, Jack. Ann is shewing you the kindest consideration, even at the cost of deceiving you.

ANN:

>What do you mean?

TANNER:

>Would you like to cure Rhoda's headache, Ann?

ANN:

>Of course.

TANNER:

>Then tell her what you said just now; and add that you arrived about two minutes after I had received her letter and read it.

ANN:

>Rhoda has written to you!

TANNER:

>With full particulars.

OCTAVIUS:

>Never mind him, Ann. You were right—quite right. Ann was only doing her duty, Jack; and you know it. Doing it in the kindest way, too.

ANN (*going to* Octavius):

>How kind you are, Tavy! How helpful! How well you understand!

>> *Octavius beams.*

TANNER:

>Ay: tighten the coils. You love her, Tavy, don't you?

OCTAVIUS:

>She knows I do.

ANN:

>Hush. For shame, Tavy!

TANNER:

>Oh, I give you leave. I am your guardian; and I commit you to Tavy's care for the next hour. I am off for a turn in the car.

ANN:

>No, Jack. I must speak to you about Rhoda. Ricky: will you go back to the house and entertain your American friend. He's rather on Mamma's hands so early in the morning. She wants to finish her housekeeping.

OCTAVIUS:

    I fly, dearest Ann (*he kisses her hand*).

ANN (*tenderly*):

    Ricky Ticky Tavy!

    *He looks at her with an eloquent blush, and runs off.*

TANNER (*bluntly*):

    Now look here, Ann. This time you've landed yourself; and if Tavy were not in love with you past all salvation he'd have found out what an incorrigible liar you are.

ANN:

    You misunderstand, Jack. I didn't dare tell Tavy the truth.

TANNER:

    No: your daring is generally in the opposite direction. What the devil do you mean by telling Rhoda that I am too vicious to associate with her? How can I ever have any human or decent relations with her again, now that you have poisoned her mind in that abominable way?

ANN:

    I know you are incapable of behaving badly—

TANNER:

    Then why did you lie to her?

ANN:

    I had to.

TANNER:

    Had to!

ANN:

    Mother made me.

TANNER (*his eye flashing*):

    Ha! I might have known it. The mother! Always the mother!

ANN:

    It was that dreadful book of yours. You know how timid mother is. All timid women are conventional: we must be conventional, Jack, or we are so cruelly, so vilely misunderstood. Even you, who are a man, cannot say what you think without being misunderstood and vilified—yes: I admit it: I have had to vilify you. Do you want to have poor Rhoda misunderstood and vilified in the same way? Would it be right for mother to let her expose herself to such treatment before she is old enough to judge for herself?

TANNER:

    In short, the way to avoid misunderstanding is for everybody to lie and slander and insinuate and pretend as hard as they can. That is what obeying your mother comes to.

ANN:

> I love my mother, Jack.

TANNER (*working himself up into a sociological rage*):

> Is that any reason why you are not to call your soul your own? Oh, I protest against this vile abjection of youth to age! Look at fashionable society as you know it. What does it pretend to be? An exquisite dance of nymphs. What is it? A horrible procession of wretched girls, each in the claws of a cynical, cunning, avaricious, disillusioned, ignorantly experienced, foul-minded old woman whom she calls mother, and whose duty it is to corrupt her mind and sell her to the highest bidder. Why do these unhappy slaves marry anybody, however old and vile, sooner than not marry at all? Because marriage is their only means of escape from these decrepit fiends who hide their selfish ambitions, their jealous hatreds of the young rivals who have supplanted them, under the mask of maternal duty and family affection. Such things are abominable: the voice of nature proclaims for the daughter a father's care and for the son a mother's. The law for father and son and mother and daughter is not the law of love: it is the law of revolution, of emancipation, of final supersession of the old and worn-out by the young and capable. I tell you, the first duty of manhood and womanhood is a Declaration of Independence: the man who pleads his father's authority is no man: the woman who pleads her mother's authority is unfit to bear citizens to a free people.

ANN (*watching him with quiet curiosity*):

> I suppose you will go in seriously for politics some day, Jack.

TANNER (*heavily let down*):

> Eh? What? Wh—? (*Collecting his scattered wits*) What has that got to do with what I have been saying?

ANN:

> You talk so well.

TANNER:

> Talk! Talk! It means nothing to you but talk. Well, go back to your mother, and help her to poison Rhoda's imagination as she has poisoned yours. It is the tame elephants who enjoy capturing the wild ones.

ANN:

> I am getting on. Yesterday I was a boa constrictor: to-day I am an elephant.

TANNER:

> Yes. So pack your trunk and begone: I have no more to say to you.

ANN:

> You are so utterly unreasonable and impracticable. What can I do?

TANNER:

> Do! Break your chains. Go your way according to your own conscience and not according to your mother's. Get your mind clean and vigorous; and learn to enjoy a fast ride in a motor car instead of seeing nothing in it but an excuse for a detestable intrigue. Come with me to Marseilles and across to Algiers and to Biskra, at sixty miles an hour. Come right down to the Cape if you like. That will be a Declaration of Independence with a vengeance. You can write a book about it afterwards. That will finish your mother and make a woman of you.

ANN (*thoughtfully*):

> I don't think there would be any harm in that, Jack. You are my guardian: you stand in my father's place, by his own wish. Nobody could say a word against our travelling together. It would be delightful: thank you a thousand times, Jack. I'll come.

TANNER (*aghast*):

> You'll come!!!

ANN:

> Of course.

TANNER:

> But—(*he stops, utterly appalled; then resumes feebly*) No: look here, Ann: if there's no harm in it there's no point in doing it.

ANN:

> How absurd you are! You don't want to compromise me, do you?

TANNER:

> Yes: that's the whole sense of my proposal.

ANN:

> You are talking the greatest nonsense; and you know it. You would never do anything to hurt me.

TANNER:

> Well, if you don't want to be compromised, don't come.

ANN (*with simple earnestness*):

> Yes, I will come, Jack, since you wish it. You are my guardian; and I think we ought to see more of one another and come to know one another better. (*Gratefully*) It's very thoughtful and very kind of you, Jack, to offer me this lovely holiday, especially after what I said about Rhoda. You really are good—much better than you think. When do we start?

TANNER:

> But——

*The conversation is interrupted by the arrival of* Mrs Whitefield *from the house. She is accompanied by the American gentleman, and followed by* Ramsden *and* Octavius.

Hector Malone *is an Eastern American; but he is not at all ashamed of his nationality. This makes English people of fashion think well of him, as of a young fellow who is manly enough to confess to an obvious disadvantage without any attempt to conceal or extenuate it. They feel that he ought not to be made to suffer for what is clearly not his fault, and make a point of being specially kind to him. His chivalrous manners to women, and his ele-vated moral sentiments, being both gratuitous and unusual, strike them as being a little unfortunate; and though they find his vein of easy humor rather amusing when it has ceased to puzzle them (as it does at first), they have had to make him understand that he really must not tell anecdotes unless they are strictly personal and scandalous, and also that oratory is an accomplishment which belongs to a cruder stage of civilization than that in which his migration has landed him. On these points* Hector *is not quite convinced: he still thinks that the British are apt to make merits of their stupidities, and to represent their various incapacities as points of good breeding. English life seems to him to suffer from a lack of edifying rhetoric (which he calls moral tone); English behavior to shew a want of respect for womanhood; English pronunciation to fail very vulgarly in tackling such words as world, girl, bird, etc.; English society to be plain spoken to an extent which stretches occasionally to intolerable coarseness; and English intercourse to need enlivening by games and stories and other pastimes; so he does not feel called upon to acquire these defects after taking great pains to cultivate himself in a first rate manner before venturing across the Atlantic. To this culture he finds English people either totally indifferent, as they very commonly are to all culture, or else politely evasive, the truth being that* Hector's *culture is nothing but a state of saturation with our literary exports of thirty years ago, reimported by him to be unpacked at a moment's notice and hurled at the head of English literature, science and art, at every conversational opportunity. The dismay set up by these sallies encour-ages him in his belief that he is helping to educate England. When he finds people chattering harmlessly about Anatole France and Nietzsche, he dev-astates them with Matthew Arnold, the Autocrat of the Breakfast Table, and even Macaulay; and as he is devoutly religious at bottom, he first leads the unwary, by humorous irreverences, to leave popular theology out of account in discussing moral questions with him, and then scatters them in confusion by demanding whether the carrying out of his ideals of conduct was not the manifest object of God Almighty in creating honest men and pure women. The engaging freshness of his personality and the dumb-foundering staleness of his culture make it extremely difficult to decide whether he is worth knowing; for whilst his company is undeniably pleasant and enlivening, there is intellectually nothing new to be got out of him, especially as he despises politics, and is careful not to talk commercial shop, in which department he is probably much in advance of his English capitalist friends. He gets on best with romantic Christians of the amoristic sect: hence the friendship which has sprung up between him and* Octavius.

*In appearance* Hector *is a neatly built young man of twenty-four, with a short, smartly trimmed black beard, clear, well shaped eyes, and an ingratiating vivacity of expression. He is, from the fashionable point of view, faultlessly dressed. As he comes along the drive from the house with* Mrs Whitefield *he is sedulously making himself agreeable and entertaining, and thereby placing on her slender wit a burden it is unable to bear. An Englishman would let her alone, accepting boredom and indifference as their common lot; and the poor lady wants to be either let alone or let prattle about the things that interest her.*

Ramsden *strolls over to inspect the motor car.* Octavius *joins* Hector.

ANN (*pouncing on her mother joyously*):

> Oh, mamma, what do you think! Jack is going to take me to Nice in his motor car. Isn't it lovely? I am the happiest person in London.

TANNER (*desperately*):

> Mrs Whitefield objects. I am sure she objects. Doesn't she, Ramsden?

RAMSDEN:

> I should think it very likely indeed.

ANN:

> You don't object, do you, mother?

MRS WHITEFIELD:

> *I* object! Why should I? I think it will do you good, Ann. (*Trotting over to* Tanner) I meant to ask you to take Rhoda out for a run occasionally: she is too much in the house; but it will do when you come back.

TANNER:

> Abyss beneath abyss of perfidy!

ANN (*hastily, to distract attention from this outburst*):

> Oh, I forgot: you have not met Mr Malone. Mr Tanner, my guardian: Mr Hector Malone.

HECTOR:

> Pleased to meet you, Mr Tanner. I should like to suggest an extension of the travelling party to Nice, if I may.

ANN:

> Oh, we're all coming. That's understood, isn't it?

HECTOR:

> I also am the modest possessor of a motor car. If Miss Robinson will allow me the privilege of taking her, my car is at her service.

OCTAVIUS:

Violet!

*General constraint.*

ANN (*subduedly*):

Come, mother: we must leave them to talk over the arrangements. I must see to my travelling kit.

Mrs Whitefield *looks bewildered; but* Ann *draws her discreetly away; and
they disappear round the corner towards the house.*

HECTOR:

I think I may go so far as to say that I can depend on Miss
Robinson's consent.

*Continued embarrassment.*

OCTAVIUS:

I'm afraid we must leave Violet behind. There are circumstances which make it impossible for her to come on such an
expedition.

HECTOR (*amused and not at all convinced*):

Too American, eh? Must the young lady have a chaperone?

OCTAVIUS:

It's not that, Malone—at least not altogether.

HECTOR:

Indeed! May I ask what other objection applies?

TANNER (*impatiently*):

Oh, tell him, tell him. We shall never be able to keep the secret
unless everybody knows what it is. Mr Malone: if you go to Nice
with Violet, you go with another man's wife. She is married.

HECTOR (*thunderstruck*):

You don't tell me so!

TANNER:

We do. In confidence.

RAMSDEN (*with an air of importance, lest* Malone *should suspect a misalliance*):

Her marriage has not yet been made known: she desires that it
shall not be mentioned for the present.

HECTOR:

I shall respect the lady's wishes. Would it be indiscreet to ask
who her husband is, in case I should have an opportunity of
consulting him about this trip?

TANNER:

We don't know who he is.

HECTOR (*retiring into his shell in a very marked manner*):

In that case, I have no more to say.

*They become more embarrassed than ever.*

OCTAVIUS:

You must think this very strange.

HECTOR:

A little singular. Pardon me for saying so.

RAMSDEN (*half apologetic, half huffy*):

The young lady was married secretly; and her husband has forbidden her, it seems, to declare his name. It is only right to tell you, since you are interested in Miss—er—in Violet.

OCTAVIUS (*sympathetically*):

I hope this is not a disappointment to you.

HECTOR (*softened, coming out of his shell again*):

Well: it is a blow. I can hardly understand how a man can leave his wife in such a position. Surely it's not customary. It's not manly. It's not considerate.

OCTAVIUS:

We feel that, as you may imagine, pretty deeply.

RAMSDEN (*testily*):

It is some young fool who has not enough experience to know what mystifications of this kind lead to.

HECTOR (*with strong symptoms of moral repugnance*):

I hope so. A man need be very young and pretty foolish too to be excused for such conduct. You take a very lenient view, Mr Ramsden. Too lenient to my mind. Surely marriage should ennoble a man.

TANNER (*sardonically*):

Ha!

HECTOR:

Am I to gather from that cacchination that you don't agree with me, Mr Tanner?

TANNER (*drily*):

Get married and try. You may find it delightful for a while: you certainly won't find it ennobling. The greatest common measure of a man and a woman is not necessarily greater than the man's single measure.

HECTOR:

Well, we think in America that a woman's moral number is higher than a man's, and that the purer nature of a woman lifts a man right out of himself, and makes him better than he was.

OCTAVIUS (*with conviction*):

So it does.

TANNER:

No wonder American women prefer to live in Europe! It's more comfortable than standing all their lives on an altar to be worshipped. Anyhow, Violet's husband has not been ennobled. So what's to be done?

HECTOR (*shaking his head*):

I can't dismiss that man's conduct as lightly as you do, Mr Tanner. However, I'll say no more. Whoever he is, he's Miss Robinson's husband; and I should be glad for her sake to think better of him.

OCTAVIUS (*touched; for he divines a secret sorrow*):

I'm very sorry, Malone. Very sorry.

HECTOR (*gratefully*):

You're a good fellow, Robinson. Thank you.

TANNER:

Talk about something else. Violet's coming from the house.

HECTOR:

I should esteem it a very great favor, gentlemen, if you would take the opportunity to let me have a few words with the lady alone. I shall have to cry off this trip; and it's rather a delicate—

RAMSDEN (*glad to escape*):

Say no more. Come, Tanner. Come, Tavy. (*He strolls away into the park with* Octavius *and* Tanner, *past the motor car.*)

Violet *comes down the avenue to* Hector.

VIOLET:

Are they looking?

HECTOR:

No.

*She kisses him.*

VIOLET:

Have you been telling lies for my sake?

HECTOR:

Lying! Lying hardly describes it. I overdo it. I get carried away in an ecstacy of mendacity. Violet: I wish you'd let me own up.

VIOLET (*instantly becoming serious and resolute*):

No, no, Hector: you promised me not to.

HECTOR:

I'll keep my promise until you release me from it. But I feel mean, lying to those men, and denying my wife. Just dastardly.

VIOLET:

I wish your father were not so unreasonable.

HECTOR:

He's not unreasonable. He's right from his point of view. He has a prejudice against the English middle class.

VIOLET:

It's too ridiculous. You know how I dislike saying such things to you, Hector; but if I were to—oh, well, no matter.

HECTOR:

I know. If you were to marry the son of an English manufacturer of office furniture, your friends would consider it a misalliance. And here's my silly old dad, who is the biggest office furniture man in the world, would shew me the door for marrying the most perfect lady in England merely because she has no handle to her name. Of course it's just absurd. But I tell you, Violet, I don't like deceiving him. I feel as if I was stealing his money. Why won't you let me own up?

VIOLET:

We can't afford it. You can be as romantic as you please about love, Hector; but you mustn't be romantic about money.

HECTOR (*divided between his uxoriousness and his habitual elevation of moral sentiment*):

That's very English. (*Appealing to her impulsively*) Violet: dad's bound to find us out someday.

VIOLET:

Oh yes, later on of course. But don't let's go over this every time we meet, dear. You promised—

HECTOR:

All right, all right, I—

VIOLET (*not to be silenced*):

It is I and not you who suffer by this concealment; and as to facing a struggle and poverty and all that sort of thing I simply will not do it. It's too silly.

HECTOR:

You shall not. I'll sort of borrow the money from my dad until I get on my own feet; and then I can own up and pay up at the same time.

VIOLET (*alarmed and indignant*):

Do you mean to work? Do you want to spoil our marriage?

HECTOR:

Well, I don't mean to let marriage spoil my character. Your friend Mr Tanner has got the laugh on me a bit already about that; and—

VIOLET:

    The beast! I hate Jack Tanner.

HECTOR (*magnanimously*):

    Oh, he's all right: he only needs the love of a good woman to ennoble him. Besides, he's proposed a motoring trip to Nice; and I'm going to take you.

VIOLET:

    How jolly!

HECTOR:

    Yes; but how are we going to manage? You see, they've warned me off going with you, so to speak. They've told me in confidence that you're married. That's just the most overwhelming confidence I've ever been honored with.

Tanner *returns with* Straker, *who goes to his car.*

TANNER:

    Your car is a great success, Mr Malone. Your engineer is showing it off to Mr Ramsden.

HECTOR (*eagerly—forgetting himself*):

    Let's come, Vi.

VIOLET (*coldly, warning him with her eyes*):

    I beg your pardon, Mr Malone, I did not quite catch—

HECTOR (*recollecting himself*):

    I ask to be allowed the pleasure of shewing you my little American steam car, Miss Robinson.

VIOLET:

    I shall be very pleased. (*They go off together down the avenue.*)

TANNER:

    About this trip, Straker.

STRAKER (*preoccupied with the car*):

    Yes?

TANNER:

    Miss Whitefield is supposed to be coming with me.

STRAKER:

    So I gather.

TANNER:

    Mr Robinson is to be one of the party.

STRAKER:

    Yes.

TANNER:

    Well, if you can manage so as to be a good deal occupied with me, and leave Mr Robinson a good deal occupied with Miss Whitefield, he will be deeply grateful to you.

STRAKER (*looking round at him*):

Evidently.

TANNER:

"Evidently"! Your grandfather would have simply winked.

STRAKER:

My grandfather would have touched his at.

TANNER:

And I should have given your good nice respectful grandfather a sovereign.

STRAKER:

Five shillins, more likely. (*He leaves the car and approaches* Tanner.) What about the lady's views?

TANNER:

She is just as willing to be left to Mr Robinson as Mr Robinson is to be left to her. (Straker *looks at his principal with cool scepticism; then turns to the car whistling his favorite air.*) Stop that aggravating noise. What do you mean by it? (Straker *calmly resumes the melody and finishes it.* Tanner *politely hears it out before he again addresses* Straker, *this time with elaborate seriousness.*) Enry: I have ever been a warm advocate of the spread of music among the masses; but I object to your obliging the company whenever Miss Whitefield's name is mentioned. You did it this morning, too.

STRAKER (*obstinately*):

It's not a bit o use. Mr Robinson may as well give it up first as last.

TANNER:

Why?

STRAKER:

Garn! You know why. Course it's not my business; but you needn't start kiddin me about it.

TANNER:

I am not kidding. I don't know why.

STRAKER (*cheerfully sulky*):

Oh, very well. All right. It ain't my business.

TANNER (*impressively*):

I trust, Enry, that, as between employer and engineer, I shall always know how to keep my proper distance, and not intrude my private affairs on you. Even our business arrangements are subject to the approval of your Trade Union. But don't abuse your advantages. Let me remind you that Voltaire said that what was too silly to be said could be sung.

STRAKER:

It wasn't Voltaire: it was Bow Mar Shay.

TANNER:

> I stand corrected: Beaumarchais of course. Now you seem to think that what is too delicate to be said can be whistled. Unfortunately your whistling, though melodious, is unintelligible. Come! there's nobody listening: neither my genteel relatives nor the secretary of your confounded Union. As man to man, Enry, why do you think that my friend has no chance with Miss Whitefield?

STRAKER:

> Cause she's arter summun else.

TANNER:

> Bosh! who else?

STRAKER:

> You.

TANNER:

> Me!!!

STRAKER:

> Mean to tell me you didn't know? Oh, come, Mr Tanner!

TANNER (*in fierce earnest*):

> Are you playing the fool, or do you mean it?

STRAKER (*with a flash of temper*):

> I'm not playin no fool. (*More coolly*) Why, it's as plain as the nose on your face. If you ain't spotted that, you don't know much about these sort of things. (*Serene again*) Ex-cuse me, you know, Mr Tanner; but you asked me as man to man; and I told you as man to man.

TANNER (*wildly appealing to the heavens*):

> Then I—*I* am the bee, the spider, the marked down victim, the destined prey.

STRAKER:

> I dunno about the bee and the spider. But the marked down victim, that's what you are and no mistake; and a jolly good job for you, too, I should say.

TANNER (*momentously*):

> Henry Straker: the golden moment of your life has arrived.

STRAKER:

> What d'y'mean?

TANNER:

> That record to Biskra.

STRAKER (*eagerly*):

> Yes?

TANNER:

> Break it.

STRAKER (*rising to the height of his destiny*):

    D'y'mean it?

TANNER:

    I do.

STRAKER:

    When?

TANNER:

    Now. Is that machine ready to start?

STRAKER (*quailing*):

    But you can't—

TANNER (*cutting him short by getting into the car*):

    Off we go. First to the bank for money; then to my rooms for my kit; then to your rooms for your kit; then break the record from London to Dover or Folkestone; then across the channel and away like mad to Marseilles, Gibraltar, Genoa, any port from which we can sail to a Mahometan country where men are protected from women.

STRAKER:

    Garn! you're kiddin.

TANNER (*resolutely*):

    Stay behind then. If you won't come I'll do it alone. (*He starts the motor.*)

STRAKER (*running after him*):

    Here! Mister! arf a mo! steady on! (*he scrambles in as the car plunges forward*).

# Act III

*Evening in the Sierra Nevada. Rolling slopes of brown, with olive trees instead of apple trees in the cultivated patches, and occasional prickly pears instead of gorse and bracken in the wilds. Higher up, tall stone peaks and precipices, all handsome and distinguished. No wild nature here: rather a most aristocratic mountain landscape made by a fastidious artist-creator. No vulgar profusion of vegetation: even a touch of aridity in the frequent patches of stones: Spanish magnificence and Spanish economy everywhere.*

*Not very far north of a spot at which the high road over one of the passes crosses a tunnel on the railway from Malaga to Granada, is one of the mountain amphitheatres of the Sierra. Looking at it from the wide end of the horse-shoe, one sees, a little to the right, in the face of the cliff, a romantic cave which is really an abandoned quarry, and towards the left a little hill, commanding a view of the road, which skirts the amphitheatre on the left, maintaining its higher level on embankments and an occasional stone* arch. On the hill, watching the road, is a man who is either a Spaniard or a Scotchman. Probably a Spaniard, since he wears the dress of a Spanish goatherd and seems at home in the Sierra Nevada, but very like a Scotchman for all that. In the hollow, on the slope leading to the quarry-cave, are about a dozen men who, as they recline at their ease round a heap of smouldering white ashes of dead leaf and brushwood, have an air of being conscious of themselves as picturesque scoundrels honoring the Sierra by using it as an effective pictorial background. As a matter of artistic fact they are not picturesque; and the mountains tolerate them as lions tolerate lice. An English policeman or Poor Law Guardian would recognize them as a selected band of tramps and ablebodied paupers.

This description of them is not wholly contemptuous. Whoever has intelligently observed the tramp, or visited the ablebodied ward of a workhouse, will admit that our social failures are not all drunkards and weaklings. Some of them are men who do not fit the class they were born into. Precisely the same qualities that make the educated gentleman an artist may make an uneducated manual laborer an ablebodied pauper. There are men who fall helplessly into the workhouse because they are good for nothing; but there are also men who are there because they are strongminded enough to disregard the social convention (obviously not a disinterested one on the part of the ratepayer) which bids a man live by heavy and badly paid drudgery when he has the alternative of walking into the workhouse, announcing himself as a destitute person, and legally compelling the Guardians to feed, clothe and house him better than he could feed, clothe and house himself without great exertion. When a man who is born a poet refuses a stool in a stockbroker's office, and starves in a garret, spunging on a poor landlady or on his friends and relatives sooner than work against his grain; or when a lady, because she is a lady, will face any extremity of parasitic dependence rather than take a situation as cook or parlormaid, we make large allowances for them. To such allowances the ablebodied pauper, and his nomadic variant the tramp, are equally entitled.

Further, the imaginative man, if his life is to be tolerable to him, must have leisure to tell himself stories, and a position which lends itself to imaginative decoration. The ranks of unskilled labor offer no such positions. We misuse our laborers horribly; and when a man refuses to be misused, we have no right to say that he is refusing honest work. Let us be frank in this matter before we go on with our play; so that we may enjoy it without hypocrisy. If we were reasoning, farsighted people, four fifths of us would go straight to the Guardians for relief, and knock the whole social system to pieces with most beneficial reconstructive results. The reason we do not do this is because we work like bees or ants, by instinct or habit, not reasoning about the matter at all. Therefore when a man comes along who can and does reason, and who, applying the Kantian test to his conduct, can truly say to us, If everybody did as I do, the world would be compelled to reform *itself industrially, and abolish slavery and squalor, which exist only because everybody does as you do, let us honor that man and seriously consider the advisability of following his example. Such a man is the able-bodied, able-minded pauper. Were he a gentleman doing his best to get a pension or a sinecure instead of sweeping a crossing, nobody would blame him for deciding that so long as the alternative lies between living mainly at the expense of the community and allowing the community to live mainly at his, it would be folly to accept what is to him personally the greater of the two evils.*

*We may therefore contemplate the tramps of the Sierra without prejudice, admitting cheerfully that our objects—briefly, to be gentlemen of fortune—are much the same as theirs, and the difference in our position and methods merely accidental. One or two of them, perhaps, it would be wiser to kill without malice in a friendly and frank manner; for there are bipeds, just as there are quadrupeds, who are too dangerous to be left unchained and unmuzzled; and these cannot fairly expect to have other men's lives wasted in the work of watching them. But as society has not the courage to kill them, and, when it catches them, simply wreaks on them some superstitious expiatory rites of torture and degradation, and then lets them loose with heightened qualifications for mischief, it is just as well that they are at large in the Sierra, and in the hands of a chief who looks as if he might possibly, on provocation, order them to be shot.*

*This chief, seated in the centre of the group on a squared block of stone from the quarry, is a tall strong man, with a striking cockatoo nose, glossy black hair, pointed beard, upturned moustache, and a Mephistophelean affectation which is fairly imposing, perhaps because the scenery admits of a larger swagger than Piccadilly, perhaps because of a certain sentimentality in the man which gives him that touch of grace which alone can excuse deliberate picturesquesness. His eyes and mouth are by no means rascally; he has a fine voice and a ready wit; and whether he is really the strongest man in the party or not, he looks it. He is certainly the best fed, the best dressed, and the best trained. The fact that he speaks English is not unexpected, in spite of the Spanish landscape; for with the exception of one man who might be guessed as a bullfighter ruined by drink, and one unmistakable Frenchman, they are all cockney or American; therefore, in a land of cloaks and sombreros, they mostly wear seedy overcoats, woollen mufflers, hard hemispherical hats, and dirty brown gloves. Only a very few dress after their leader, whose broad sombrero with a cock's feather in the band, and voluminous cloak descending to his high boots, are as un-English as possible. None of them are armed; and the ungloved ones keep their hands in their pockets because it is their national belief that it must be dangerously cold in the open air with the night coming on. (It is as warm an evening as any reasonable man could desire.)*

*Except the bullfighting inebriate there is only one person in the company who looks more than, say, thirty-three. He is a small man with reddish whiskers, weak eyes, and the anxious look of a small tradesman in difficulties. He wears the only tall hat visible: it shines in the sunset with the sticky glow of some sixpenny patent hat reviver, often applied and constantly tending to produce a worse state of the original surface than the ruin it was applied to remedy. He has a collar and cuffs of celluloid; and his brown Chesterfield overcoat, with velvet collar, is still presentable. He is pre-eminently the respectable man of the party, and is certainly over forty, possibly over fifty. He is the corner man on the leader's right, opposite three men in scarlet ties on his left. One of these three is the Frenchman. Of the remaining two, who are both English, one is argumentative, solemn, and obstinate; the other rowdy and mischievous.*

*The chief, with a magnificent fling of the end of his cloak across his left shoulder, rises to address them. The applause which greets him shews that he is a favorite orator.*

THE CHIEF:

Friends and fellow brigands. I have a proposal to make to this meeting. We have now spent three evenings in discussing the question Have Anarchists or Social-Democrats the most personal courage? We have gone into the principles of Anarchism and Social-Democracy at great length. The cause of Anarchy has been ably represented by our one Anarchist, who doesn't know what Anarchism means (*laughter*)—

THE ANARCHIST (*rising*):

A point of order, Mendoza—

MENDOZA (*forcibly*):

No, by thunder: your last point of order took half an hour. Besides, Anarchists don't believe in order.

THE ANARCHIST (*mild, polite but persistent: he is, in fact, the respectable looking elderly man in the celluloid collar and cuffs*):

That is a vulgar error. I can prove—

MENDOZA:

Order, order.

THE OTHERS (*shouting*):

Order, order. Sit down. Chair! Shut up.

The Anarchist *is suppressed.*

MENDOZA:

On the other hand we have three Social-Democrats among us. They are not on speaking terms; and they have put before us three distinct and incompatible views of Social-Democracy.

THE THREE MEN IN SCARLET TIES:

> 1. Mr Chairman, I protest. A personal explanation. 2. It's a lie. I never said so. Be fair, Mendoza. 3. Je demande la parole. C'est absolument faux. C'est faux! faux!! faux!!! Assas-s-s-s-sin!!!!!!

MENDOZA:

> Order, order.

THE OTHERS:

> Order, order, order! Chair!

*The* Social-Democrats *are suppressed.*

MENDOZA:

> Now, we tolerate all opinions here. But after all, comrades, the vast majority of us are neither Anarchists nor Socialists, but gentlemen and Christians.

THE MAJORITY (*shouting assent*):

> Hear, hear! So we are. Right.

THE ROWDY SOCIAL-DEMOCRAT (*smarting under suppression*):

> You ain't no Christian. You're a Sheeny, you are.

MENDOZA (*with crushing magnanimity*):

> My friend: *I* am an exception to all rules. It is true that I have the honor to be a Jew; and when the Zionists need a leader to reassemble our race on its historic soil of Palestine, Mendoza will not be the last to volunteer (*sympathetic applause—hear, hear, &c.*). But I am not a slave to any superstition. I have swallowed all the formulas, even that of Socialism; though, in a sense, once a Socialist, always a Socialist.

THE SOCIAL-DEMOCRATS:

> Hear, hear!

MENDOZA:

> But I am well aware that the ordinary man—even the ordinary brigand, who can scarcely be called an ordinary man (Hear, hear!)—is not a philosopher. Common sense is good enough for him; and in our business affairs common sense is good enough for me. Well, what is our business here in the Sierra Nevada, chosen by the Moors as the fairest spot in Spain? Is it to discuss abstruse questions of political economy? No: it is to hold up motor cars and secure a more equitable distribution of wealth.

THE SULKY SOCIAL-DEMOCRAT:

> All made by labor, mind you.

MENDOZA (*urbanely*):

> Undoubtedly. All made by labor, and on its way to be squandered by wealthy vagabonds in the dens of vice that disfigure the sunny shores of the Mediterranean. We intercept that

wealth. We restore it to circulation among the class that produced it and that chiefly needs it—the working class. We do
this at the risk of our lives and liberties, by the exercise of the
virtues of courage, endurance, foresight, and abstinence—
especially abstinence. I myself have eaten nothing but prickly
pears and broiled rabbit for three days.

THE SULKY SOCIAL-DEMOCRAT (*stubbornly*):
No more ain't we.

MENDOZA (*indignantly*):
Have I taken more than my share?

THE SULKY SOCIAL-DEMOCRAT (*unmoved*):
Why should you?

THE ANARCHIST:
Why should he not? To each according to his needs: from each
according to his means.

THE FRENCHMAN (*shaking his fist at* the Anarchist):
Fumiste!

MENDOZA (*diplomatically*):
I agree with both of you.

THE GENUINELY ENGLISH BRIGANDS:
Hear, hear! Bravo, Mendoza!

MENDOZA:
What I say is, let us treat one another as gentlemen, and strive
to excel in personal courage only when we take the field.

THE ROWDY SOCIAL-DEMOCRAT (*derisively*):
Shikespear.

*A whistle comes from* the goatherd *on the hill. He springs up and points
excitedly forward along the road to the north.*

THE GOATHERD:
Automobile! Automobile! (*He rushes down the hill and joins the
rest, who all scramble to their feet.*)

MENDOZA (*in ringing tones*):
To arms! Who has the gun?

THE SULKY SOCIAL-DEMOCRAT (*handing a rifle to* Mendoza):
Here.

MENDOZA:
Have the nails been strewn in the road?

THE ROWDY SOCIAL-DEMOCRAT:
Two ahnces of em.

MENDOZA:
Good! (*To* the Frenchman) With me, Duval. If the nails fail,
puncture their tires with a bullet. (*He gives the rifle to* Duval,

*who follows him up the hill.* Mendoza *produces an opera glass. The others hurry across to the road and disappear to the north.*)

MENDOZA (*on the hill, using his glass*):
Two only, a capitalist and his chauffeur. They look English.

DUVAL:
Angliche! Aoh yess. Cochons! (*Handling the rifle*) Faut tirer, n'est-ce-pas?

MENDOZA:
No: the nails have gone home. Their tire is down: they stop.

DUVAL (*shouting to the others*):
Fondez sur eux, nom de Dieu!

MENDOZA (*rebuking his excitement*):
Du calme, Duval: keep your hair on. They take it quietly. Let us descend and receive them.

Mendoza *descends, passing behind the fire and coming forward, whilst* Tanner *and* Straker, *in their motoring goggles, leather coats, and caps, are led in from the road by the brigands.*

TANNER:
Is this the gentleman you describe as your boss? Does he speak English?

THE ROWDY SOCIAL-DEMOCRAT:
Course he does. Y' down't suppowz we Hinglishmen lets ahr-selves be bossed by a bloomin Spenniard, do you?

MENDOZA (*with dignity*):
Allow me to introduce myself: Mendoza, President of the League of the Sierra! (*Posing loftily*) I am a brigand: I live by robbing the rich.

TANNER (*promptly*):
I am a gentleman: I live by robbing the poor. Shake hands.

THE ENGLISH SOCIAL-DEMOCRATS:
Hear, hear!

*General laughter and good humor.* Tanner *and* Mendoza *shake hands. The* Brigands *drop into their former places.*

STRAKER:
Ere! where do I come in?

TANNER (*introducing*):
My friend and chauffeur.

THE SULKY SOCIAL-DEMOCRAT (*suspiciously*):
Well, which is he? friend or show-foor? It makes all the differ-ence, you know.

MENDOZA (*explaining*):

We should expect ransom for a friend. A professional chauffeur is free of the mountains. He even takes a trifling percentage of his principal's ransom if he will honor us by accepting it.

STRAKER:

I see. Just to encourage me to come this way again. Well, I'll think about it.

DUVAL (*impulsively rushing across to* Straker):

Mon frère! (*He embraces him rapturously and kisses him on both cheeks.*)

STRAKER (*disgusted*):

Ere, git out: don't be silly. Who are you, pray?

DUVAL:

Duval: Social-Democrat.

STRAKER:

Oh, you're a Social-Democrat, are you?

THE ANARCHIST:

He means that he has sold out to the parliamentary humbugs and the bourgeoisie. Compromise! that is his faith.

DUVAL (*furiously*):

I understand what he say. He say Bourgeois. He say Compromise. Jamais de la vie! Misérable menteur—

STRAKER:

See here, Captain Mendoza, ow much o this sort o thing do you put up with here? Are we avin a pleasure trip in the mountains, or are we at a Socialist meetin?

THE MAJORITY:

Hear, hear! Shut up. Chuck it. Sit down, &c. &c. (*The* Social-Democrats *and the* Anarchist *are hustled into the background.* Straker, *after superintending this proceeding with satisfaction, places himself on* Mendoza's *left,* Tanner *being on his right.*)

MENDOZA:

Can we offer you anything? Broiled rabbit and prickly pears—

TANNER:

Thank you: we have dined.

MENDOZA (*to his followers*):

Gentlemen: business is over for the day. Go as you please until morning.

*The* Brigands *disperse into groups lazily. Some go into the cave. Others sit down or lie down to sleep in the open. A few produce a pack of cards and move off towards the road; for it is now starlight; and they know that motor cars have lamps which can be turned to account for lighting a card party.*

STRAKER (*calling after them*):

Don't none of you go fooling with that car, d'ye hear?

MENDOZA:

No fear, Monsieur le Chauffeur. The first one we captured cured us of that.

STRAKER (*interested*):

What did it do?

MENDOZA:

It carried three brave comrades of ours, who did not know how to stop it, into Granada, and capsized them opposite the police station. Since then we never touch one without sending for the chauffeur. Shall we chat at our ease?

TANNER:

By all means.

*Tanner, Mendoza, and Straker sit down on the turf by the fire. Mendoza delicately waives his presidential dignity, of which the right to sit on the squared stone block is the appanage, by sitting on the ground like his guests, and using the stone only as a support for his back.*

MENDOZA:

It is the custom in Spain always to put off business until to-morrow. In fact, you have arrived out of office hours. However, if you would prefer to settle the question of ransom at once, I am at your service.

TANNER:

To-morrow will do for me. I am rich enough to pay anything in reason.

MENDOZA (*respectfully, much struck by this admission*):

You are a remarkable man, sir. Our guests usually describe themselves as miserably poor.

TANNER:

Pooh! Miserably poor people don't own motor cars.

MENDOZA:

Precisely what we say to them.

TANNER:

Treat us well: we shall not prove ungrateful.

STRAKER:

No prickly pears and broiled rabbits, you know. Don't tell me you can't do us a bit better than that if you like.

MENDOZA:

Wine, kids, milk, cheese and bread can be procured for ready money.

STRAKER (*graciously*):

Now you're talking.

TANNER:

Are you all Socialists here, may I ask?

MENDOZA (*repudiating this humiliating misconception*):

Oh no, no, no: nothing of the kind, I assure you. We naturally have modern views as to the justice of the existing distribution of wealth: otherwise we should lose our self-respect. But nothing that you could take exception to, except two or three faddists.

TANNER:

I had no intention of suggesting anything discreditable. In fact, I am a bit of a Socialist myself.

STRAKER (*drily*):

Most rich men are, I notice.

MENDOZA:

Quite so. It has reached us, I admit. It is in the air of the century.

STRAKER:

Socialism must be looking up a bit if your chaps are taking to it.

MENDOZA:

That is true, sir. A movement which is confined to philosophers and honest men can never exercise any real political influence: there are too few of them. Until a movement shews itself capable of spreading among brigands, it can never hope for a political majority.

TANNER:

But are your brigands any less honest than ordinary citizens?

MENDOZA:

Sir: I will be frank with you. Brigandage is abnormal. Abnormal professions attract two classes: those who are not good enough for ordinary bourgeois life and those who are too good for it. We are dregs and scum, sir: the dregs very filthy, the scum very superior.

STRAKER:

Take care! some o the dregs'll hear you.

MENDOZA:

It does not matter: each brigand thinks himself scum, and likes to hear the others called dregs.

TANNER:

Come! you are a wit. (Mendoza *inclines his head, flattered*). May one ask you a blunt question?

MENDOZA:

As blunt as you please.

TANNER:

> How does it pay a man of your talent to shepherd such a flock
> as this on broiled rabbit and prickly pears? I have seen men less
> gifted, and I'll swear less honest, supping at the Savoy on foie
> gras and champagne.

MENDOZA:

> Pooh! they have all had their turn at the broiled rabbit, just as
> I shall have my turn at the Savoy. Indeed, I have had a turn
> there already—as waiter.

TANNER:

> A waiter! You astonish me!

MENDOZA (*reflectively*):

> Yes: I, Mendoza of the Sierra, was a waiter. Hence, perhaps,
> my cosmopolitanism. (*With sudden intensity*) Shall I tell you
> the story of my life?

STRAKER (*apprehensively*):

> If it ain't too long, old chap—

TANNER (*interrupting him*):

> Tsh-sh: you are a Philistine, Henry: you have no romance in
> you. (*To* Mendoza) You interest me extremely, President. Never
> mind Henry: he can go to sleep.

MENDOZA:

> The woman I loved—

STRAKER:

> Oh, this is a love story, is it? Right you are. Go on: I was only
> afraid you were going to talk about yourself.

MENDOZA:

> Myself! I have thrown myself away for her sake: that is why I am
> here. No matter: I count the world well lost for her. She had, I
> pledge you my word, the most magnificent head of hair I ever
> saw. She had humor; she had intellect; she could cook to perfec-
> tion; and her highly strung temperament made her uncertain,
> incalculable, variable, capricious, cruel, in a word, enchanting.

STRAKER:

> A six shillin novel sort o woman, all but the cookin. Er name
> was Lady Gladys Plantagenet, wasn't it?

MENDOZA:

> No, sir: she was not an earl's daughter. Photography, repro-
> duced by the half-tone process, has made me familiar with the
> appearance of the daughters of the English peerage; and I can
> honestly say that I would have sold the lot, faces, dowries,
> clothes, titles, and all, for a smile from this woman. Yet she was
> a woman of the people, a worker: otherwise—let me recipro-
> cate your bluntness—I should have scorned her.

TANNER:

Very properly. And did she respond to your love?

MENDOZA:

Should I be here if she did? She objected to marry a Jew.

TANNER:

On religious grounds?

MENDOZA:

No: she was a freethinker. She said that every Jew considers in his heart that English people are dirty in their habits.

TANNER (*surprised*):

Dirty!

MENDOZA:

It shewed her extraordinary knowledge of the world; for it is undoubtedly true. Our elaborate sanitary code makes us unduly contemptuous of the Gentile.

TANNER:

Did you ever hear that, Henry?

STRAKER:

I've heard my sister say so. She was cook in a Jewish family once.

MENDOZA:

I could not deny it; neither could I eradicate the impression it made on her mind. I could have got round any other objection; but no woman can stand a suspicion of indelicacy as to her person. My entreaties were in vain: she always retorted that she wasn't good enough for me, and recommended me to marry an accursed barmaid named Rebecca Lazarus, whom I loathed. I talked of suicide: she offered me a packet of beetle poison to do it with. I hinted at murder: she went into hysterics; and as I am a living man I went to America so that she might sleep without dreaming that I was stealing upstairs to cut her throat. In America I went out west and fell in with a man who was wanted by the police for holding up trains. It was he who had the idea of holding up motors cars in the South of Europe: a welcome idea to a desperate and disappointed man. He gave me some valuable introductions to capitalists of the right sort. I formed a syndicate; and the present enterprise is the result. I became leader, as the Jew always becomes leader, by his brains and imagination. But with all my pride of race I would give everything I possess to be an Englishman. I am like a boy: I cut her name on the trees and her initials on the sod. When I am alone I lie down and tear my wretched hair and cry Louisa—

STRAKER (*startled*):

Louisa!

MENDOZA:

It is her name—Louisa—Louisa Straker—

TANNER:

Straker!

STRAKER (*scrambling up on his knees most indignantly*):

Look here: Louisa Straker is my sister, see? Wot do you mean by gassin about her like this? Wotshe got to do with you?

MENDOZA:

A dramatic coincidence! You are Enry, her favorite brother!

STRAKER:

Oo are you callin Enry? What call have you to take a liberty with my name or with hers? For two pins I'd punch your fat ed, so I would.

MENDOZA (*with grandiose calm*):

If I let you do it, will you promise to brag of it afterwards to her? She will be reminded of her Mendoza: that is all I desire.

TANNER:

This is genuine devotion, Henry. You should respect it.

STRAKER (*fiercely*):

Funk, more likely.

MENDOZA (*springing to his feet*):

Funk! Young man: I come of a famous family of fighters; and as your sister well knows, you would have as much chance against me as a perambulator against your motor car.

STRAKER (*secretly daunted, but rising from his knees with an air of reckless pugnacity*):

I ain't afraid of you. With your Louisa! Louisa! Miss Straker is good enough for you, I should think.

MENDOZA:

I wish you could persuade her to think so.

STRAKER (*exasperated*):

Here—

TANNER (*rising quickly and interposing*):

Oh come, Henry: even if you could fight the President you can't fight the whole League of the Sierra. Sit down again and be friendly. A cat may look at a king; and even a President of brigands may look at your sister. All this family pride is really very old fashioned.

STRAKER (*subdued, but grumbling*):

Let him look at her. But wot does he mean by makin out that she ever looked at im? (*Reluctantly resuming his couch on the turf*) Ear him talk, one ud think she was keepin company with him. (*He turns his back on them and composes himself to sleep.*)

MENDOZA (*to* Tanner, *becoming more confidential as he finds himself virtually alone with a sympathetic listener in the still starlight of the mountains; for all the rest are asleep by this time*):

It was just so with her, sir. Her intellect reached forward into the twentieth century: her social prejudices and family affections reached back into the dark ages. Ah, sir, how the words of Shakespeare seem to fit every crisis in our emotions!

> I loved Louisa: 40,000 brothers
> Could not with all their quantity of love
> Make up my sum.

And so on. I forget the rest. Call it madness if you will—infatuation. I am an able man, a strong man: in ten years I should have owned a first-class hotel. I met her; and—you see!—I am a brigand, an outcast. Even Shakespeare cannot do justice to what I feel for Louisa. Let me read you some lines that I have written about her myself. However slight their literary merit may be, they express what I feel better than any casual words can. (*He produces a packet of hotel bills scrawled with manuscript, and kneels at the fire to decipher them, poking it with a stick to make it glow*).

TANNER (*slapping him rudely on the shoulder*):

Put them in the fire, President.

MENDOZA (*startled*):

Eh?

TANNER:

You are sacrificing your career to a monomania.

MENDOZA:

I know it.

TANNER:

No you don't. No man would commit such a crime against himself if he really knew what he was doing. How can you look round at these august hills, look up at this divine sky, taste this finely tempered air, and then talk like a literary hack on a second floor in Bloomsbury?

MENDOZA (*shaking his head*):

The Sierra is no better than Bloomsbury when once the novelty has worn off. Besides, these mountains make you dream of women—of women with magnificent hair.

TANNER:

Of Louisa, in short. They will not make me dream of women, my friend: I am heartwhole.

MENDOZA:

Do not boast until morning, sir. This is a strange country for dreams.

TANNER:

Well, we shall see. Goodnight. (*He lies down and composes himself to sleep.*)

Mendoza, *with a sigh, follows his example; and for a few moments there is peace in the Sierra. Then* Mendoza *sits up suddenly and says pleadingly to* Tanner—

MENDOZA:

Just allow me to read a few lines before you go to sleep. I should really like your opinion of them.

TANNER (*drowsily*):

Go on. I am listening.

MENDOZA:

> I saw thee first in Whitsun week
> Louisa, Louisa—

TANNER (*rousing himself*):

My dear President, Louisa is a very pretty name; but it really doesn't rhyme well to Whitsun week.

MENDOZA:

Of course not. Louisa is not the rhyme, but the refrain.

TANNER (*subsiding*):

Ah, the refrain. I beg your pardon. Go on.

MENDOZA:

Perhaps you do not care for that one: I think you will like this better. (*He recites, in rich soft tones, and in slow time*)

> Louisa, I love thee.
> I love thee, Louisa.
> Louisa, Louisa, Louisa, I love thee.
> One name and one phrase make my music, Louisa.
> Louisa, Louisa, Louisa, I love thee.

> Mendoza thy lover,
> Thy lover, Mendoza,
> Mendoza adoringly lives for Louisa.
> There's nothing but that in the world for Mendoza.
> Louisa, Louisa, Mendoza adores thee.

(*Affected*) There is no merit in producing beautiful lines upon such a name. Louisa is an exquisite name, is it not?

TANNER (*all but asleep, responds with a faint groan*).

MENDOZA:

> O wert thou, Louisa,
> The wife of Mendoza,
> Mendoza's Louisa, Louisa Mendoza,
> How blest were the life of Louisa's Mendoza!
> How painless his longing of love for Louisa!

That is real poetry—from the heart—from the heart of hearts. Don't you think it will move her?

*No answer.*

(*Resignedly*) Asleep, as usual. Doggrel to all the world: heavenly music to me! Idiot that I am to wear my heart on my sleeve! (*He composes himself to sleep, murmuring*) Louisa, I love thee; I love thee, Louisa; Louisa, Louisa, Louisa, I—

*Straker snores; rolls over on his side; and relapses into sleep. Stillness settles on the Sierra; and the darkness deepens. The fire has again buried itself in white ash and ceased to glow. The peaks shew unfathomably dark against the starry firmament; but now the stars dim and vanish; and the sky seems to steal away out of the universe. Instead of the Sierra there is nothing; omnipresent nothing. No sky, no peaks, no light, no sound, no time nor space, utter void. Then somewhere the beginning of a pallor, and with it a faint throbbing buzz as of a ghostly violoncello palpitating on the same note endlessly. A couple of ghostly violins presently take advantage of this bass*

*and therewith the pallor reveals a man in the void, an incorporeal but visible man, seated, absurdly enough, on nothing. For a moment he raises his head as the music passes him by. Then, with a heavy sigh, he droops in utter dejection; and the violins, discouraged, retrace their melody in despair and at last give it up, extinguished by wailings from uncanny wind instruments, thus:—*

*It is all very odd. One recognizes the Mozartian strain; and on this hint, and by the aid of certain sparkles of violet light in the pallor, the man's costume explains itself as that of a Spanish nobleman of the XV–XVI century. Don Juan, of course; but where? why? how? Besides, in the brief lifting of his face, now hidden by his hat brim, there was a curious suggestion of Tanner. A more critical, fastidious, handsome face, paler and colder, without Tanner's impetuous credulity and enthusiasm, and without a touch of his modern plutocratic vulgarity, but still a resemblance, even an identity. The name too: Don Juan Tenorio, John Tanner. Where on earth—or elsewhere—have we got to from the XX century and the Sierra?*

*Another pallor in the void, this time not violet, but a disagreeable smoky yellow. With it, the whisper of a ghostly clarionet turning this tune into infinite sadness:*

*The yellowish pallor moves: there is an old crone wandering in the void, bent and toothless; draped, as well as one can guess, in the coarse brown frock of some religious order. She wanders and wanders in her slow hopeless way, much as a wasp flies in its rapid busy way, until she blunders against the thing she seeks: companionship. With a sob of relief the poor old creature clutches at the presence of the man and addresses him in her dry unlovely voice, which can still express pride and resolution as well as suffering.*

THE OLD WOMAN:

　　Excuse me; but I am so lonely; and this place is so awful.

DON JUAN:

　　A new comer?

THE OLD WOMAN:

　　Yes: I suppose I died this morning. I confessed; I had extreme unction; I was in bed with my family about me and my eyes fixed on the cross. Then it grew dark; and when the light came back it was this light by which I walk seeing nothing. I have wandered for hours in horrible loneliness.

DON JUAN (*sighing*):

> Ah! you have not yet lost the sense of time. One soon does, in eternity.

THE OLD WOMAN:

> Where are we?

DON JUAN:

> In hell.

THE OLD WOMAN (*proudly*):

> Hell! I in hell! How dare you?

DON JUAN (*unimpressed*):

> Why not, Señora?

THE OLD WOMAN:

> You do not know to whom you are speaking. I am a lady, and a faithful daughter of the Church.

DON JUAN:

> I do not doubt it.

THE OLD WOMAN:

> But how then can I be in hell? Purgatory, perhaps: I have not been perfect: who has? But hell! oh, you are lying.

DON JUAN:

> Hell, Señora, I assure you; hell at its best: that is, its most solitary—though perhaps you would prefer company.

THE OLD WOMAN:

> But I have sincerely repented; I have confessed—

DON JUAN:

> How much?

THE OLD WOMAN:

> More sins than I really committed. I loved confession.

DON JUAN:

> Ah, that is perhaps as bad as confessing too little. At all events, Señora, whether by oversight or intention, you are certainly damned, like myself; and there is nothing for it now but to make the best of it.

THE OLD WOMAN (*indignantly*):

> Oh! and I might have been so much wickeder! All my good deeds wasted! It is unjust.

DON JUAN:

> No: you were fully and clearly warned. For your bad deeds, vicarious atonement, mercy without justice. For your good deeds, justice without mercy. We have many good people here.

THE OLD WOMAN:

> Were you a good man?

DON JUAN:

> I was a murderer.

THE OLD WOMAN:

A murderer! Oh, how dare they send me to herd with murderers! I was not as bad as that: I was a good woman. There is some mistake: where can I have it set right?

DON JUAN:

I do not know whether mistakes can be corrected here. Probably they will not admit a mistake even if they have made one.

THE OLD WOMAN:

But whom can I ask?

DON JUAN:

I should ask the Devil, Señora: he understands the ways of this place, which is more than I ever could.

THE OLD WOMAN:

The Devil! *I* speak to the Devil!

DON JUAN:

In hell, Señora, the Devil is the leader of the best society.

THE OLD WOMAN:

I tell you, wretch, I know I am not in hell.

DON JUAN:

How do you know?

THE OLD WOMAN:

Because I feel no pain.

DON JUAN:

Oh, then there is no mistake: you are intentionally damned.

THE OLD WOMAN:

Why do you say that?

DON JUAN:

Because hell, Señora, is a place for the wicked. The wicked are quite comfortable in it: it was made for them. You tell me you feel no pain. I conclude you are one of those for whom Hell exists.

THE OLD WOMAN:

Do you feel no pain?

DON JUAN:

I am not one of the wicked, Señora; therefore it bores me, bores me beyond description, beyond belief.

THE OLD WOMAN:

Not one of the wicked! You said you were a murderer.

DON JUAN:

Only a duel. I ran my sword through an old man who was trying to run his through me.

THE OLD WOMAN:

If you were a gentleman, that was not a murder.

DON JUAN:

The old man called it murder, because he was, he said, defending his daughter's honor. By this he meant that because I foolishly fell in love with her and told her so, she screamed; and he tried to assassinate me after calling me insulting names.

THE OLD WOMAN:

You were like all men. Libertines and murderers all, all, all!

DON JUAN:

And yet we meet here, dear lady.

THE OLD WOMAN:

Listen to me. My father was slain by just such a wretch as you, in just such a duel, for just such a cause. I screamed: it was my duty. My father drew on my assailant: his honor demanded it. He fell: that was the reward of honor. I am here: in hell, you tell me: that is the reward of duty. Is there justice in heaven?

DON JUAN:

No; but there is justice in hell: heaven is far above such idle human personalities. You will be welcome in hell, Señora. Hell is the home of honor, duty, justice, and the rest of the seven deadly virtues. All the wickedness on earth is done in their name: where else but in hell should they have their reward? Have I not told you that the truly damned are those who are happy in hell?

THE OLD WOMAN:

And are you happy here?

DON JUAN (*springing to his feet*):

No; and that is the enigma on which I ponder in darkness. Why am I here? I, who repudiated all duty, trampled honor underfoot, and laughed at justice!

THE OLD WOMAN:

Oh, what do I care why you are here? Why am *I* here? I, who sacrificed all my inclinations to womanly virtue and propriety!

DON JUAN:

Patience, lady: you will be perfectly happy and at home here. As saith the poet, "Hell is a city much like Seville."

THE OLD WOMAN:

Happy! here! where I am nothing! where I am nobody!

DON JUAN:

Not at all: you are a lady; and wherever ladies are is hell. Do not be surprised or terrified: you will find everything here that a lady can desire, including devils who will serve you from sheer love of servitude, and magnify your importance for the sake of dignifying their service—the best of servants.

THE OLD WOMAN:

My servants will be devils!

DON JUAN:

Have you ever had servants who were not devils?

THE OLD WOMAN:

Never: they were devils, perfect devils, all of them. But that is only a manner of speaking. I thought you meant that my servants here would be real devils.

DON JUAN:

No more real devils than you will be a real lady. Nothing is real here. That is the horror of damnation.

THE OLD WOMAN:

Oh, this is all madness. This is worse than fire and the worm.

DON JUAN:

For you, perhaps, there are consolations. For instance: how old were you when you changed from time to eternity?

THE OLD WOMAN:

Do not ask me how old I was—as if I were a thing of the past. I am 77.

DON JUAN:

A ripe age, Señora. But in hell old age is not tolerated. It is too real. Here we worship Love and Beauty. Our souls being entirely damned, we cultivate our hearts. As a lady of 77, you would not have a single acquaintance in hell.

THE OLD WOMAN:

How can I help my age, man?

DON JUAN:

You forget that you have left your age behind you in the realm of time. You are no more 77 than you are 7 or 17 or 27.

THE OLD WOMAN:

Nonsense!

DON JUAN:

Consider, Señora: was not this true even when you lived on earth? When you were 70, were you really older underneath your wrinkles and your grey hairs than when you were 30?

THE OLD WOMAN:

No, younger: at 30 I was a fool. But of what use is it to feel younger and look older?

DON JUAN:

You see, Señora, the look was only an illusion. Your wrinkles lied, just as the plump smooth skin of many a stupid girl of 17, with heavy spirits and decrepit ideas, lies about her age? Well, here we have no bodies: we see each other as bodies only because we learnt to think about one another under that aspect when we were alive; and we still think in that way, knowing no other. But we can appear to one another at what age we choose. You have but to will any of your old looks back, and back they will come.

THE OLD WOMAN:

It cannot be true.

DON JUAN:

Try.

THE OLD WOMAN:

Seventeen!

DON JUAN:

Stop. Before you decide, I had better tell you that these things are a matter of fashion. Occasionally we have a rage for 17; but it does not last long. Just at present the fashionable age is 40— or say 37; but there are signs of a change. If you were at all good-looking at 27, I should suggest your trying that, and setting a new fashion.

THE OLD WOMAN:

I do not believe a word you are saying. However, 27 be it. (*Whisk! the old woman becomes a young one, and so handsome that in the radiance into which her dull yellow halo has suddenly lightened one might almost mistake her for* Ann Whitefield.)

DON JUAN:

Doña Ana de Ulloa!

ANA:

What? You know me!

DON JUAN:

And you forget me!

ANA:

I cannot see your face. (*He raises his hat.*) Don Juan Tenorio! Monster! You who slew my father! even here you pursue me.

DON JUAN:

I protest I do not pursue you. Allow me to withdraw (*going*).

ANA (*seizing his arm*):

You shall not leave me alone in this dreadful place.

DON JUAN:

Provided my staying be not interpreted as pursuit.

ANA (*releasing him*):

You may well wonder how I can endure your presence. My dear, dear father!

DON JUAN:

Would you like to see him?

ANA:

My father here!!!

DON JUAN:

No: he is in heaven.

ANA:

I knew it. My noble father! He is looking down on us now.
What must he feel to see his daughter in this place, and in conversation with his murderer!

DON JUAN:

By the way, if we should meet him—

ANA:

How can we meet him? He is in heaven.

DON JUAN:

He condescends to look in upon us here from time to time.
Heaven bores him. So let me warn you that if you meet him he
will be mortally offended if you speak of me as his murderer!
He maintains that he was a much better swordsman than I, and
that if his foot had not slipped he would have killed me. No
doubt he is right: I was not a good fencer. I never dispute the
point; so we are excellent friends.

ANA:

It is no dishonor to a soldier to be proud of his skill in arms.

DON JUAN:

You would rather not meet him, probably.

ANA:

How dare you say that?

DON JUAN:

Oh, that is the usual feeling here. You may remember that on
earth—though of course we never confessed it—the death of
anyone we knew, even those we liked best, was always mingled
with a certain satisfaction at being finally done with them.

ANA:

Monster! Never, never.

DON JUAN (*placidly*):

I see you recognize the feeling. Yes: a funeral was always a fes-
tivity in black, especially the funeral of a relative. At all events,
family ties are rarely kept up here. Your father is quite accustomed to this: he will not expect any devotion from you.

ANA:

Wretch: I wore mourning for him all my life.

DON JUAN:

Yes: it became you. But a life of mourning is one thing: an eternity of it quite another. Besides, here you are as dead as he. Can
anything be more ridiculous than one dead person mourning
for another? Do not look shocked, my dear Ana; and do not be
alarmed: there is plenty of humbug in hell (indeed there is

hardly anything else); but the humbug of death and age and change is dropped because here we are all dead and all eternal. You will pick up our ways soon.

ANA:

And will all the men call me their dear Ana?

DON JUAN:

No. That was a slip of the tongue. I beg your pardon.

ANA (*almost tenderly*):

Juan: did you really love me when you behaved so disgracefully to me?

DON JUAN (*impatiently*):

Oh, I beg you not to begin talking about love. Here they talk of nothing else but love—its beauty, its holiness, its spirituality, its devil knows what!—excuse me; but it does so bore me. They don't know what they're talking about. I do. They think they have achieved the perfection of love because they have no bodies. Sheer imaginative debauchery! Faugh!

ANA:

Has even death failed to refine your soul, Juan? Has the terrible judgment of which my father's statue was the minister taught you no reverence?

DON JUAN:

How is that very flattering statue, by the way? Does it still come to supper with naughty people and cast them into this bottomless pit?

ANA:

It has been a great expense to me. The boys in the monastery school would not let it alone: the mischievous ones broke it; and the studious ones wrote their names on it. Three new noses in two years, and fingers without end. I had to leave it to its fate at last; and now I fear it is shockingly mutilated. My poor father!

DON JUAN:

Hush! Listen! (*Two great chords rolling on syncopated waves of sound break forth: D minor and its dominant: a sound of dreadful joy to all musicians.*) Ha! Mozart's statue music. It is your father. You had better disappear until I prepare him. (*She vanishes*).

*From the void comes a living statue of white marble, designed to represent a majestic old man. But he waives his majesty with infinite grace; walks with a feather-like step; and makes every wrinkle in his war worn visage brim over with holiday joyousness. To his sculptor he owes a perfectly trained figure, which he carries erect and trim; and the ends of his moustache curl up, elastic as watchsprings, giving him an air which, but for its Spanish dignity, would be called jaunty. He is on the pleasantest terms with* Don Juan. *His voice, save for a much more distinguished intonation, is so like the voice of* Roebuck Ramsden *that it calls attention to the fact that they are not unlike one another in spite of their very different fashions of shaving*).

DON JUAN:

Ah, here you are, my friend. Why don't you learn to sing the splendid music Mozart has written for you?

THE STATUE:

Unluckily he has written it for a bass voice. Mine is a counter tenor. Well: have you repented yet?

DON JUAN:

I have too much consideration for you to repent, Don Gonzalo. If I did, you would have no excuse for coming from Heaven to argue with me.

THE STATUE:

True. Remain obdurate, my boy. I wish I had killed you, as I should have done but for an accident. Then I should have come here; and you would have had a statue and a reputation for piety to live up to. Any news?

DON JUAN:

Yes: your daughter is dead.

THE STATUE (*puzzled*):

My daughter? (*Recollecting*) Oh! the one you were taken with. Let me see: what was her name?

DON JUAN:

Ana.

THE STATUE:

To be sure: Ana. A goodlooking girl, if I recollect aright. Have you warned Whatshisname—her husband?

DON JUAN:

My friend Ottavio? No: I have not seen him since Ana arrived.

Ana *comes indignantly to light.*

ANA:

What does this mean? Ottavio here and your friend! And you, father, have forgotten my name. You are indeed turned to stone.

THE STATUE:

My dear: I am so much more admired in marble than I ever was in my own person that I have retained the shape the sculptor gave me. He was one of the first men of his day: you must acknowledge that.

ANA:

> Father! Vanity! personal vanity! from you!

THE STATUE:

> Ah, you outlived that weakness, my daughter: you must be nearly 80 by this time. I was cut off (by an accident) in my 64th year, and am considerably your junior in consequence. Besides, my child, in this place, what our libertine friend here would call the farce of parental wisdom is dropped. Regard me, I beg, as a fellow creature, not as a father.

ANA:

> You speak as this villain speaks.

THE STATUE:

> Juan is a sound thinker, Ana. A bad fencer, but a sound thinker.

ANA (*horror creeping upon her*):

> I begin to understand. These are devils, mocking me. I had better pray.

THE STATUE (*consoling her*):

> No, no, no, my child: do not pray. If you do, you will throw away the main advantage of this place. Written over the gate here are the words "Leave every hope behind, ye who enter." Only think what a relief that is! For what is hope? A form of moral responsibility. Here there is no hope, and consequently no duty, no work, nothing to be gained by praying, nothing to be lost by doing what you like. Hell, in short, is a place where you have nothing to do but amuse yourself. (Don Juan *sighs deeply*). You sigh, friend Juan; but if you dwelt in heaven, as I do, you would realize your advantages.

DON JUAN:

> You are in good spirits to-day, Commander. You are positively brilliant. What is the matter?

THE STATUE:

> I have come to a momentous decision, my boy. But first, where is our friend the Devil? I must consult him in the matter. And Ana would like to make his acquaintance, no doubt.

ANA:

> You are preparing some torment for me.

DON JUAN:

> All that is superstition, Ana. Reassure yourself. Remember: the devil is not so black as he is painted.

THE STATUE:

> Let us give him a call.

*At the wave of the statue's hand the great chords roll out again; but this time Mozart's music gets grotesquely adulterated with Gounod's. A scarlet halo begins to glow; and into it the* Devil *rises, very Mephistophelean, and not at all unlike* Mendoza, *though not so interesting. He looks older; is getting prematurely bald; and, in spite of an effusion of goodnature and friendliness, is peevish and sensitive when his advances are not reciprocated. He does not inspire much confidence in his powers of hard work or endurance, and is, on the whole, a disagreeably self-indulgent looking person; but he is clever and plausible, though perceptibly less well bred than the two other men, and enormously less vital than the woman.*

THE DEVIL (*heartily*):

Have I the pleasure of again receiving a visit from the illustrious Commander of Calatrava? (*Coldly*) Don Juan, your servant. (*Politely*) And a strange lady? My respects, Señora.

ANA:

Are you—

THE DEVIL (*bowing*):

Lucifer, at your service.

ANA:

I shall go mad.

THE DEVIL (*gallantly*):

Ah, Señora, do not be anxious. You come to us from earth, full of the prejudices and terrors of that priest-ridden place. You have heard me ill spoken of; and yet, believe me, I have hosts of friends there.

ANA:

Yes: you reign in their hearts.

THE DEVIL (*shaking his head*):

You flatter me, Señora; but you are mistaken. It is true that the world cannot get on without me; but it never gives me credit for that: in its heart it mistrusts and hates me. Its sympathies are all with misery, with poverty, with starvation of the body and of the heart. I call on it to sympathize with joy, with love, with happiness, with beauty—

DON JUAN (*nauseated*):

Excuse me: I am going. You know I cannot stand this.

THE DEVIL (*angrily*):

Yes: I know that you are no friend of mine.

THE STATUE:

What harm is he doing you, Juan? It seems to me that he was talking excellent sense when you interrupted him.

THE DEVIL (*warmly shaking the* statue's *hand*):

Thank you, my friend: thank you. You have always understood me: he has always disparaged and avoided me.

DON JUAN:

I have treated you with perfect courtesy.

THE DEVIL:

Courtesy! What is courtesy? I care nothing for mere courtesy. Give me warmth of heart, true sincerity, the bond of sympathy with love and joy—

DON JUAN:

You are making me ill.

THE DEVIL:

There! (*Appealing to* the statue):

You hear, sir! Oh, by what irony of fate was this cold selfish egotist sent to my kingdom, and you taken to the icy mansions of the sky!

THE STATUE:

I can't complain. I was a hypocrite; and it served me right to be sent to heaven.

THE DEVIL:

Why, sir, do you not join us, and leave a sphere for which your temperament is too sympathetic, your heart too warm, your capacity for enjoyment too generous?

THE STATUE:

I have this day resolved to do so. In future, excellent Son of the Morning, I am yours. I have left Heaven for ever.

THE DEVIL (*again grasping his hand*):

Ah, what an honor for me! What a triumph for our cause! Thank you, thank you. And now, my friend—I may call you so at last—could you not persuade him to take the place you have left vacant above?

THE STATUE (*shaking his head*):

I cannot conscientiously recommend anybody with whom I am on friendly terms to deliberately make himself dull and uncomfortable.

THE DEVIL:

Of course not; but are you sure he would be uncomfortable? Of course you know best: you brought him here originally; and we had the greatest hopes of him. His sentiments were in the best taste of our best people. You remember how he sang? (*He begins to sing in a nasal operatic baritone, tremulous from an eternity of misuse in the French manner*)

Vivan le femmine!
Viva il buon vino!

THE STATUE (*taking up the tune an octave higher in his counter tenor*)

> Sostegno e gloria
> D'umanità.

THE DEVIL:

Precisely. Well, he never sings for us now.

DON JUAN:

Do you complain of that? Hell is full of musical amateurs: music is the brandy of the damned. May not one lost soul be permitted to abstain?

THE DEVIL:

You dare blaspheme against the sublimest of the arts!

DON JUAN (*with cold disgust*):

You talk like a hysterical woman fawning on a fiddler.

THE DEVIL:

I am not angry. I merely pity you. You have no soul; and you are unconscious of all that you lose. Now you, Señor Commander, are a born musician. How well you sing! Mozart would be delighted if he were still here; but he moped and went to heaven. Curious how these clever men, whom you would have supposed born to be popular here, have turned out social failures, like Don Juan!

DON JUAN:

I am really very sorry to be a social failure.

THE DEVIL:

Not that we don't admire your intellect, you know. We do. But I look at the matter from your own point of view. You don't get on with us. The place doesn't suit you. The truth is, you have— I won't say no heart; for we know that beneath all your affected cynicism you have a warm one—

DON JUAN (*shrinking*):

Don't, please don't.

THE DEVIL (*nettled*):

Well, you've no capacity for enjoyment. Will that satisfy you?

DON JUAN:

It is a somewhat less insufferable form of cant than the other. But if you'll allow me, I'll take refuge, as usual, in solitude.

THE DEVIL:

Why not take refuge in Heaven? That's the proper place for you. (*To* Ana) Come, Señora! could you not persuade him for his own good to try change of air?

ANA:

But can he go to Heaven if he wants to?

THE DEVIL:

What's to prevent him?

ANA:

Can anybody—can *I* go to Heaven if I want to?

THE DEVIL (*rather contemptuously*):

Certainly, if your taste lies that way.

ANA:

But why doesn't everybody go to Heaven, then?

THE STATUE (*chuckling*):

*I* can tell you that, my dear. It's because heaven is the most angelically dull place in all creation: that's why.

THE DEVIL:

His excellency the Commander puts it with military bluntness; but the strain of living in Heaven is intolerable. There is a notion that I was turned out of it; but as a matter of fact nothing could have induced me to stay there. I simply left it and organized this place.

THE STATUE:

I don't wonder at it. Nobody could stand an eternity of heaven.

THE DEVIL:

Oh, it suits some people. Let us be just, Commander: it is a question of temperament. I don't admire the heavenly temperament: I don't understand it: I don't know that I particularly want to understand it; but it takes all sorts to make a universe. There is no accounting for tastes: there are people who like it. I think Don Juan would like it.

DON JUAN:

But—pardon my frankness—could you really go back there if you desired to; or are the grapes sour?

THE DEVIL:

Back there! I often go back there. Have you never read the book of Job? Have you any canonical authority for assuming that there is any barrier between our circle and the other one?

ANA:

But surely there is a great gulf fixed.

THE DEVIL:

Dear lady: a parable must not be taken literally. The gulf is the difference between the angelic and the diabolic temperament. What more impassable gulf could you have? Think of what you have seen on earth. There is no physical gulf between the philosopher's class room and the bull ring; but the bull fighters do not come to the class room for all that. Have you ever been in the country where I have the largest following—England? There they have great racecourses, and also concert rooms where they play the classical compositions of his Excellency's friend Mozart. Those who go to the racecourses can stay away from them and go to the classical concerts instead if they like: there is no law against it; for Englishmen never will be slaves: they are free to do whatever the Government and public opinion allow them to do. And the classical concert is admitted to be a higher, more cultivated, poetic, intellectual, ennobling place than the racecourse. But do the lovers of racing desert their sport and flock to the concert room? Not they. They would suffer there all the weariness the Commander has suffered in heaven. There is the great gulf of the parable between the two places. A mere physical gulf they could bridge; or at least I could bridge it for them (the earth is full of Devil's Bridges); but the gulf of dislike is impassable and eternal. And that is the only gulf that separates my friends here from those who are invidiously called the blest.

ANA:

I shall go to heaven at once.

THE STATUE:

My child: one word of warning first. Let me complete my friend Lucifer's similitude of the classical concert. At every one of those concerts in England you will find rows of weary people who are there, not because they really like classical music, but because they think they ought to like it. Well, there is the same thing in heaven. A number of people sit there in glory, not because they are happy, but because they think they owe it to their position to be in heaven. They are almost all English.

THE DEVIL:

Yes: the Southerners give it up and join me just as you have done. But the English really do not seem to know when they are thoroughly miserable. An Englishman thinks he is moral when he is only uncomfortable.

THE STATUE:

In short, my daughter, if you go to Heaven without being naturally qualified for it, you will not enjoy yourself there.

ANA:

And who dares say that I am not naturally qualified for it? The most distinguished princes of the Church have never questioned it. I owe it to myself to leave this place at once.

THE DEVIL (*offended*):

As you please, Señora. I should have expected better taste from you.

ANA:

Father: I shall expect you to come with me. You cannot stay here. What will people say?

THE STATUE:

> People! Why, the best people are here—princes of the church and all. So few go to Heaven, and so many come here, that the blest, once called a heavenly host, are a continually dwindling minority. The saints, the fathers, the elect of long ago are the cranks, the faddists, the outsiders of to-day.

THE DEVIL:

> It is true. From the beginning of my career I knew that I should win in the long run by sheer weight of public opinion, in spite of the long campaign of misrepresentation and calumny against me. At bottom the universe is a constitutional one; and with such a majority as mine I cannot be kept permanently out of office.

DON JUAN:

> I think, Ana, you had better stay here.

ANA (*jealously*):

> You do not want me to go with you.

DON JUAN:

> Surely you do not want to enter Heaven in the company of a reprobate like me.

ANA:

> All souls are equally precious. You repent, do you not?

DON JUAN:

> My dear Ana, you are silly. Do you suppose heaven is like earth, where people persuade themselves that what is done can be undone by repentance; that what is spoken can be unspoken by withdrawing it; that what is true can be annihilated by a general agreement to give it the lie? No: heaven is the home of the masters of reality: that is why I am going thither.

ANA:

> Thank you: I am going to heaven for happiness. I have had quite enough of reality on earth.

DON JUAN:

> Then you must stay here; for hell is the home of the unreal and of the seekers for happiness. It is the only refuge from heaven, which is, as I tell you, the home of the masters of reality, and from earth, which is the home of the slaves of reality. The earth is a nursery in which men and women play at being heros and heroines, saints, and sinners; but they are dragged down from their fool's paradise by their bodies: hunger and cold and thirst, age and decay and disease, death above all, make them slaves of reality: thrice a day meals must be eaten and digested: thrice a century a new generation must be engendered: ages of faith, of romance, and of science are all driven at last to have but one

prayer "Make me a healthy animal." But here you escape this
tyranny of the flesh; for here you are not an animal at all: you are
a ghost, an appearance, an illusion, a convention, deathless, ageless: in a word, bodiless. There are no social questions here, no
political questions, no religious questions, best of all, perhaps,
no sanitary questions. Here you call your appearance beauty,
your emotions love, your sentiments heroism, your aspirations
virtue, just as you did on earth; but here there are no hard facts
to contradict you, no ironic contrast of your needs with your
pretensions, no human comedy, nothing but a perpetual
romance, a universal melodrama. As our German friend put it in
his poem, "the poetically nonsensical here is good sense; and the
Eternal Feminine draws us ever upward and on"—without getting us a step farther. And yet you want to leave this paradise!

ANA:

But if Hell be so beautiful as this, how glorious must heaven be!

The Devil, the Statue, *and* Don Juan *all begin to speak at once in violent protest; then stop, abashed.*

DON JUAN:

I beg your pardon.

THE DEVIL:

Not at all. I interrupted you.

THE STATUE:

You were going to say something.

DON JUAN:

After you, gentlemen.

THE DEVIL (*to* Don Juan):

You have been so eloquent on the advantages of my dominions
that I leave you to do equal justice to the drawbacks of the
alternative establishment.

DON JUAN:

In Heaven, as I picture it, dear lady, you live and work instead
of playing and pretending. You face things as they are; you
escape nothing but glamor; and your steadfastness and your
peril are your glory. If the play still goes on here and on earth,
and all the world is a stage, Heaven is at least behind the
scenes. But Heaven cannot be described by metaphor. Thither
I shall go presently, because there I hope to escape at last from
lies and from the tedious, vulgar pursuit of happiness, to spend
my eons in contemplation—

THE STATUE:

Ugh!

DON JUAN:

> Señor Commander: I do not blame your disgust: a picture gallery is a dull place for a blind man. But even as you enjoy the contemplation of such romantic mirages as beauty and pleasure; so would I enjoy the contemplation of that which interests me above all things: namely, Life: the force that ever strives to attain greater power of contemplating itself. What made this brain of mine, do you think? Not the need to move my limbs; for a rat with half my brains moves as well as I. Not merely the need to do, but the need to know what I do, lest in my blind efforts to live I should be slaying myself.

THE STATUE:

> You would have slain yourself in your blind efforts to fence but for my foot slipping, my friend.

DON JUAN:

> Audacious ribald: your laughter will finish in hideous boredom before morning.

THE STATUE:

> Ha ha! Do you remember how I frightened you when I said something like that to you from my pedestal in Seville? It sounds rather flat without my trombones.

DON JUAN:

> They tell me it generally sounds flat with them, Commander.

ANA:

> Oh, do not interrupt with these frivolities, father. Is there nothing in Heaven but contemplation, Juan?

DON JUAN:

> In the Heaven I seek, no other joy. But there is the work of helping Life in its struggle upward. Think of how it wastes and scatters itself, how it raises up obstacles to itself and destroys itself in its ignorance and blindness. It needs a brain, this irresistible force, lest in its ignorance it should resist itself. What a piece of work is man! says the poet. Yes: but what a blunderer! Here is the highest miracle of organization yet attained by life, the most intensely alive thing that exists, the most conscious of all the organisms; and yet, how wretched are his brains! Stupidity made sordid and cruel by the realities learnt from toil and poverty: Imagination resolved to starve sooner than face these realities, piling up illusions to hide them, and calling itself cleverness, genius! And each accusing the other of its own defect: Stupidity accusing Imagination of folly, and Imagination accusing Stupidity of ignorance: whereas, alas! Stupidity has all the knowledge, and Imagination all the intelligence.

THE DEVIL:

And a pretty kettle of fish they make of it between them. Did I not say, when I was arranging that affair of Faust's, that all Man's reason has done for him is to make him beastlier than any beast. One splendid body is worth the brains of a hundred dyspeptic, flatulent philosophers.

DON JUAN:

You forget that brainless magnificence of body has been tried. Things immeasurably greater than man in every respect but brain have existed and perished. The megatherium, the icthyosaurus have paced the earth with seven-league steps and hidden the day with cloud vast wings. Where are they now? Fossils in museums, and so few and imperfect at that, that a knuckle bone or a tooth of one of them is prized beyond the lives of a thousand soldiers. These things lived and wanted to live; but for lack of brains they did not know how to carry out their purpose, and so destroyed themselves.

THE DEVIL:

And is Man any the less destroying himself for all this boasted brain of his? Have you walked up and down upon the earth lately? I have; and I have examined Man's wonderful inventions. And I tell you that in the arts of life man invents nothing; but in the arts of death he outdoes Nature herself, and produces by chemistry and machinery all the slaughter of plague, pestilence and famine. The peasant I tempt to-day eats and drinks what was eaten and drunk by the peasants of ten thousand years ago; and the house he lives in has not altered as much in a thousand centuries as the fashion of a lady's bonnet in a score of weeks. But when he goes out to slay, he carries a marvel of mechanism that lets loose at the touch of his finger all the hidden molecular energies, and leaves the javelin, the arrow, the blowpipe of his fathers far behind. In the arts of peace Man is a bungler. I have seen his cotton factories and the like, with machinery that a greedy dog could have invented if it had wanted money instead of food. I know his clumsy typewriters and bungling locomotives and tedious bicycles: they are toys compared to the Maxim gun, the submarine torpedo boat. There is nothing in Man's industrial machinery but his greed and sloth: his heart is in his weapons. This marvellous force of Life of which you boast is a force of Death: Man measures his strength by his destructiveness. What is his religion? An excuse for hating me. What is his law? An excuse for hanging you. What is his morality? Gentility! an excuse for consuming without producing. What is his art? An excuse for gloating over pictures of slaughter. What are his politics? Either the worship of a despot because a despot can kill, or parliamentary cockfighting. I spent an evening lately in a certain celebrated legislature, and heard the pot lecturing the kettle for its blackness, and ministers answering questions. When I left I chalked up on the door the old nursery saying "Ask no questions and you will be told no lies." I bought a sixpenny family magazine, and found it full of pictures of young men shooting and stabbing one another. I saw a man die: he was a London bricklayer's laborer with seven children. He left seventeen pounds club money; and his wife spent it all on his funeral and went into the workhouse with the children next day. She would not have spent sevenpence on her children's schooling: the law had to force her to let them be taught gratuitously; but on death she spent all she had. Their imagination glows, their energies rise up at the idea of death, these people: they love it; and the more horrible it is the more they enjoy it. Hell is a place far above their comprehension: they derive their notion of it from two of the greatest fools that ever lived, an Italian and an Englishman. The Italian described it as a place of mud, frost, filth, fire, and venomous serpents: all torture. This ass, when he was not lying about me, was maundering about some woman whom he saw once in the street. The Englishman described me as being expelled from Heaven by cannons and gunpowder; and to this day every Briton believes that the whole of his silly story is in the Bible. What else he says I do not know; for it is all in a long poem which neither I nor anyone else ever succeeded in wading through. It is the same in everything. The highest form of literature is the tragedy, a play in which everybody is murdered at the end. In the old chronicles you read of earthquakes and pestilences, and are told that these shewed the power and majesty of God and the littleness of Man. Nowadays the chronicles describe battles. In a battle two bodies of men shoot at one another with bullets and explosive shells until one body runs away, when the others chase the fugitives on horseback and cut them to pieces as they fly. And this, the chronicle concludes, shews the greatness and majesty of empires, and the littleness of the vanquished. Over such battles the people run about the streets yelling with delight, and egg their Governments on to spend hundreds of millions of money in the slaughter, whilst the strongest Ministers dare not spend an extra penny in the pound against the poverty and pestilence through which they themselves daily walk. I could give you a thousand instances; but they all come to the same thing: the power that governs the earth is not the power of Life but of Death; and the inner need that has nerved Life to the effort of organizing itself into the human being is not the need for higher life but for a more efficient engine of destruction. The plague, the famine, the earthquake, the tempest were too spasmodic in their action; the tiger and crocodile were too easily satiated and not cruel enough: something more constantly, more ruthlessly, more ingeniously destructive was needed; and that something was Man, the inventor of the rack, the stake, the gallows, and the electrocutor; of the sword and gun; above all, of justice, duty, patriotism and all the other isms by which even those who are clever enough to be humanely disposed are persuaded to become the most destructive of all the destroyers.

DON JUAN:

Pshaw! all this is old. Your weak side, my diabolic friend, is that you have always been a gull: you take Man at his own valuation. Nothing would flatter him more than your opinion of him. He loves to think of himself as bold and bad. He is neither one nor the other: he is only a coward. Call him tyrant, murderer, pirate, bully; and he will adore you, and swagger about with the consciousness of having the blood of the old sea kings in his veins. Call him liar and thief; and he will only take an action against you for libel. But call him coward; and he will go mad with rage: he will face death to outface that stinging truth. Man gives every reason for his conduct save one, every excuse for his crimes save one, every plea for his safety save one; and that one is his cowardice. Yet all his civilization is founded on his cowardice, on his abject tameness, which he calls his respectability. There are limits to what a mule or an ass will stand; but Man will suffer himself to be degraded until his vileness becomes so loathsome to his oppressors that they themselves are forced to reform it.

THE DEVIL:

Precisely. And these are the creatures in whom you discover what you call a Life Force!

DON JUAN:

Yes; for now comes the most surprising part of the whole business.

THE STATUE:

What's that?

DON JUAN:

Why, that you can make any of these cowards brave by simply putting an idea into his head.

THE STATUE:

Stuff! As an old soldier I admit the cowardice: it's as universal as sea sickness, and matters just as little. But that about putting an idea into a man's head is stuff and nonsense. In a battle all you need to make you fight is a little hot blood and the knowledge that it's more dangerous to lose than to win.

DON JUAN:

That is perhaps why battles are so useless. But men never really overcome fear until they imagine they are fighting to further a universal purpose—fighting for an idea, as they call it. Why was the Crusader braver than the pirate? Because he fought, not for himself, but for the Cross. What force was it that met him with a valor as reckless as his own? The force of men who fought, not for themselves, but for Islam. They took Spain from us, though we were fighting for our very hearths and homes; but when we, too, fought for that mighty idea, a Catholic Church, we swept them back to Africa.

THE DEVIL (*ironically*):

What! you a Catholic, Señor Don Juan! A devotee! My congratulations.

THE STATUE (*seriously*):

Come come! as a soldier, I can listen to nothing against the Church.

DON JUAN:

Have no fear, Commander: this idea of a Catholic Church will survive Islam, will survive the Cross, will survive even that vulgar pageant of incompetent schoolboyish gladiators which you call the Army.

THE STATUE:

Juan: you will force me to call you to account for this.

DON JUAN:

Useless: I cannot fence. Every idea for which Man will die will be a Catholic idea. When the Spaniard learns at last that he is no better than the Saracen, and his prophet no better than Mahomet, he will arise, more Catholic than ever, and die on a barricade across the filthy slum he starves in, for universal liberty and equality.

THE STATUE:

Bosh!

DON JUAN:

What you call bosh is the only thing men dare die for. Later on, Liberty will not be Catholic enough: men will die for human perfection, to which they will sacrifice all their liberty gladly.

THE DEVIL:

Ay: they will never be at a loss for an excuse for killing one another.

DON JUAN:

What of that? It is not death that matters, but the fear of death. It is not killing and dying that degrades us, but base living, and accepting the wages and profits of degradation. Better ten dead men than one live slave or his master. Men shall yet rise up, father against son and brother against brother, and kill one another for the great Catholic idea of abolishing slavery.

THE DEVIL:

Yes, when the Liberty and Equality of which you prate shall have made free white Christians cheaper in the labor market than black heathen slaves sold by auction at the block.

DON JUAN:

Never fear! the white laborer shall have his turn too. But I am not now defending the illusory forms the great ideas take. I am giving you examples of the fact that this creature Man, who in his own selfish affairs is a coward to the backbone, will fight for an idea like a hero. He may be abject as a citizen; but he is dangerous as a fanatic. He can only be enslaved whilst he is spiritually weak enough to listen to reason. I tell you, gentlemen, if you can shew a man a piece of what he now calls God's work to do, and what he will later on call by many new names, you can make him entirely reckless of the consequences to himself personally.

ANA:

Yes: he shirks all his responsibilities, and leaves his wife to grapple with them.

THE STATUE:

Well said, daughter. Do not let him talk you out of your common sense.

THE DEVIL:

Alas! Señor Commander, now that we have got on to the subject of Woman, he will talk more than ever. However, I confess it is for me the one supremely interesting subject.

DON JUAN:

To a woman, Señora, man's duties and responsibilities begin and end with the task of getting bread for her children. To her, Man is only a means to the end of getting children and rearing them.

ANA:

Is that your idea of a woman's mind? I call it cynical and disgusting materialism.

DON JUAN:

> Pardon me, Ana: I said nothing about a woman's whole mind. I spoke of her view of Man as a separate sex. It is no more cynical than her view of herself as above all things a Mother. Sexually, Woman is Nature's contrivance for perpetuating its highest achievement. Sexually, Man is Woman's contrivance for fulfilling Nature's behest in the most economical way. She knows by instinct that far back in the evolutional process she invented him, differentiated him, created him in order to produce something better than the single-sexed process can produce. Whilst he fulfils the purpose for which she made him, he is welcome to his dreams, his follies, his ideals, his heroisms, provided that the keystone of them all is the worship of woman, of motherhood, of the family, of the hearth. But how rash and dangerous it was to invent a separate creature whose sole function was her own impregnation! For mark what has happened. First, Man has multiplied on her hands until there are as many men as women; so that she has been unable to employ for her purposes more than a fraction of the immense energy she has left at his disposal by saving him the exhausting labor of gestation. This superfluous energy has gone to his brain and to his muscle. He has become too strong to be controlled by her bodily, and too imaginative and mentally vigorous to be content with mere self-reproduction. He has created civilization without consulting her, taking her domestic labor for granted as the foundation of it.

ANA:

> That is true, at all events.

THE DEVIL:

> Yes; and this civilization! what is it, after all?

DON JUAN:

> After all, an excellent peg to hang your cynical commonplaces on; but before all, it is an attempt on Man's part to make himself something more than the mere instrument of Woman's purpose. So far, the result of Life's continual effort not only to maintain itself, but to achieve higher and higher organization and completer self-consciousness, is only, at best, a doubtful campaign between its forces and those of Death and Degeneration. The battles in this campaign are mere blunders, mostly won, like actual military battles, in spite of the commanders.

THE STATUE:

> That is a dig at me. No matter: go on, go on.

DON JUAN:

> It is a dig at a much higher power than you, Commander. Still, you must have noticed in your profession that even a stupid general can win battles when the enemy's general is a little stupider.

THE STATUE (*very seriously*):

> Most true, Juan, most true. Some donkeys have amazing luck.

DON JUAN:

> Well, the Life Force is stupid; but it is not so stupid as the forces of Death and Degeneration. Besides, these are in its pay all the time. And so Life wins, after a fashion. What mere copiousness of fecundity can supply and mere greed preserve, we possess. The survival of whatever form of civilization can produce the best rifle and the best fed riflemen is assured.

THE DEVIL:

> Exactly! the survival, not of the most effective means of Life but of the most effective means of Death. You always come back to my point, in spite of your wrigglings and evasions and sophistries, not to mention the intolerable length of your speeches.

DON JUAN:

> Oh come! who began making long speeches? However, if I overtax your intellect, you can leave us and seek the society of love and beauty and the rest of your favorite boredoms.

THE DEVIL (*much offended*):

> This is not fair, Don Juan, and not civil. I am also on the intellectual plane. Nobody can appreciate it more than I do. I am arguing fairly with you, and, I think, utterly refuting you. Let us go on for another hour if you like.

DON JUAN:

> Good: let us.

THE STATUE:

> Not that I see any prospect of your coming to any point in particular, Juan. Still, since in this place, instead of merely killing time we have to kill eternity, go ahead by all means.

DON JUAN (*somewhat impatiently*):

> My point, you marble-headed old masterpiece, is only a step ahead of you. Are we agreed that Life is a force which has made innumerable experiments in organizing itself; that the mammoth and the man, the mouse and the megatherium, the flies and the fleas and the Fathers of the Church, are all more or less successful attempts to build up that raw force into higher and higher individuals, the ideal individual being omnipotent, omniscient, infallible, and withal completely, unilludedly self-conscious: in short, a god?

THE DEVIL:

I agree, for the sake of argument.

THE STATUE:

I agree, for the sake of avoiding argument.

ANA:

I most emphatically disagree as regards the Fathers of the Church; and I must beg you not to drag them into the argument.

DON JUAN:

I did so purely for the sake of alliteration, Ana; and I shall make no further allusion to them. And now, since we are, with that exception, agreed so far, will you not agree with me further that Life has not measured the success of its attempts at godhead by the beauty or bodily perfection of the result, since in both these respects the birds, as our friend Aristophanes long ago pointed out, are so extraordinarily superior, with their power of flight and their lovely plumage, and, may I add, the touching poetry of their loves and nestings, that it is inconceivable that Life, having once produced them, should, if love and beauty were her object, start off on another line and labor at the clumsy elephant and the hideous ape, whose grandchildren we are?

ANA:

Aristophanes was a heathen; and you, Juan, I am afraid, are very little better.

THE DEVIL:

You conclude, then, that Life was driving at clumsiness and ugliness?

DON JUAN:

No, perverse devil that you are, a thousand times no. Life was driving at brains—at its darling object: an organ by which it can attain not only self-consciousness but self-understanding.

THE STATUE:

This is metaphysics, Juan. Why the devil should—(*to* The Devil) I beg your pardon.

THE DEVIL:

Pray don't mention it. I have always regarded the use of my name to secure additional emphasis as a high compliment to me. It is quite at your service, Commander.

THE STATUE:

Thank you: that's very good of you. Even in heaven, I never quite got out of my old military habits of speech. What I was going to ask Juan was why Life should bother itself about getting a brain. Why should it want to understand itself? Why not be content to enjoy itself?

DON JUAN:

> Without a brain, Commander, you would enjoy yourself with-
> out knowing it, and so lose all the fun.

THE STATUE:

> True, most true. But I am quite content with brain enough to
> know that I'm enjoying myself. I don't want to understand
> why. In fact, I'd rather not. My experience is that one's plea-
> sures don't bear thinking about.

DON JUAN:

> That is why intellect is so unpopular. But to Life, the force
> behind the Man, intellect is a necessity, because without it he
> blunders into death. Just as Life, after ages of struggle, evolved
> that wonderful bodily organ the eye, so that the living organ-
> ism could see where it was going and what was coming to help
> or threaten it, and thus avoid a thousand dangers that formerly
> slew it, so it is evolving to-day a mind's eye that shall see, not
> the physical world, but the purpose of Life, and thereby enable
> the individual to work for that purpose instead of thwarting
> and baffling it by setting up shortsighted personal aims as at
> present. Even as it is, only one sort of man has ever been happy,
> has ever been universally respected among all the conflicts of
> interests and illusions.

THE STATUE:

> You mean the military man.

DON JUAN:

> Commander: I do not mean the military man. When the mili-
> tary man approaches, the world locks up its spoons and packs
> off its womankind. No: I sing, not arms and the hero, but the
> philosophic man: he who seeks in contemplation to discover
> the inner will of the world, in invention to discover the means
> of fulfilling that will, and in action to do that will by the so-
> discovered means. Of all other sorts of men I declare myself
> tired. They are tedious failures. When I was on earth, profes-
> sors of all sorts prowled round me feeling for an unhealthy spot
> in me on which they could fasten. The doctors of medicine
> bade me consider what I must do to save my body, and offered
> me quack cures for imaginary diseases. I replied that I was not
> a hypochondriac; so they called me Ignoramus and went their
> way. The doctors of divinity bade me consider what I must do
> to save my soul; but I was not a spiritual hypochondriac any
> more than a bodily one, and would not trouble myself about
> that either; so they called me Atheist and went their way. After
> them came the politician, who said there was only one purpose
> in Nature, and that was to get him into parliament. I told him

I did not care whether he got into parliament or not; so he called me Mugwump and went his way. Then came the romantic man, the Artist, with his love songs and his paintings and his poems; and with him I had great delight for many years, and some profit; for I cultivated my senses for his sake; and his songs taught me to hear better, his paintings to see better, and his poems to feel more deeply. But he led me at last into the worship of Woman.

ANA:

Juan!

DON JUAN:

Yes: I came to believe that in her voice was all the music of the song, in her face all the beauty of the painting, and in her soul all the emotion of the poem.

ANA:

And you were disappointed, I suppose. Well, was it her fault that you attributed all these perfections to her?

DON JUAN:

Yes, partly. For with a wonderful instinctive cunning, she kept silent and allowed me to glorify her; to mistake my own visions, thoughts, and feelings for hers. Now my friend the romantic man was often too poor or too timid to approach those women who were beautiful or refined enough to seem to realize his ideal; and so he went to his grave believing in his dream. But I was more favored by nature and circumstance. I was of noble birth and rich; and when my person did not please, my conversation flattered, though I generally found myself fortunate in both.

THE STATUE:

Coxcomb!

DON JUAN:

Yes; but even my coxcombry pleased. Well, I found that when I had touched a woman's imagination, she would allow me to persuade myself that she loved me; but when my suit was granted she never said "I am happy: my love is satisfied": she always said, first, "At last, the barriers are down," and second, "When will you come again?"

ANA:

That is exactly what men say.

DON JUAN:

I protest I never said it. But all women say it. Well, these two speeches always alarmed me; for the first meant that the lady's impulse had been solely to throw down my fortifications and gain my citadel; and the second openly announced that henceforth she regarded me as her property, and counted my time as already wholly at her disposal.

THE DEVIL:

That is where your want of heart came in.

THE STATUE (*shaking his head*):

You shouldn't repeat what a woman says, Juan.

ANA (*severely*):

It should be sacred to you.

THE STATUE:

Still, they certainly do always say it. I never minded the barriers; but there was always a slight shock about the other, unless one was very hard hit indeed.

DON JUAN:

Then the lady, who had been happy and idle enough before, became anxious, preoccupied with me, always intriguing, conspiring, pursuing, watching, waiting, bent wholly on making sure of her prey—I being the prey, you understand. Now this was not what I had bargained for. It may have been very proper and very natural; but it was not music, painting, poetry and joy incarnated in a beautiful woman. I ran away from it. I ran away from it very often: in fact I became famous for running away from it.

ANA:

Infamous, you mean.

DON JUAN:

I did not run away from you. Do you blame me for running away from the others?

ANA:

Nonsense, man. You are talking to a woman of 77 now. If you had had the chance, you would have run away from me too—if I had let you. You would not have found it so easy with me as with some of the others. If men will not be faithful to their home and their duties, they must be made to be. I daresay you all want to marry lovely incarnations of music and painting and poetry. Well, you can't have them, because they don't exist. If flesh and blood is not good enough for you you must go without: that's all. Women have to put up with flesh-and-blood husbands—and little enough of that too, sometimes; and you will have to put up with flesh-and-blood wives. (The Devil *looks dubious*. The Statue *makes a wry face*.) I see you don't like that, any of you; but it's true, for all that; so if you don't like it you can lump it.

DON JUAN:

My dear lady, you have put my whole case against romance into a few sentences. That is just why I turned my back on the romantic man with the artist nature, as he called his infatuation. I thanked him for teaching me to use my eyes and ears; but I told him that his beauty worshipping and happiness hunting and woman idealizing was not worth a dump as a philosophy of life; so he called me Philistine and went his way.

ANA:

It seems that Woman taught you something, too, with all her defects.

DON JUAN:

She did more: she interpreted all the other teaching for me. Ah, my friends, when the barriers were down for the first time, what an astounding illumination! I had been prepared for infatuation, for intoxication, for all the illusions of love's young dream; and lo! never was my perception clearer, nor my criticism more ruthless. The most jealous rival of my mistress never saw every blemish in her more keenly than I. I was not duped: I took her without chloroform.

ANA:

But you did take her.

DON JUAN:

That was the revelation. Up to that moment I had never lost the sense of being my own master; never consciously taken a single step until my reason had examined and approved it. I had come to believe that I was a purely rational creature: a thinker! I said, with the foolish philosopher, "I think; therefore I am." It was Woman who taught me to say "I am; therefore I think." And also "I would think more; therefore I must be more."

THE STATUE:

This is extremely abstract and metaphysical, Juan. If you would stick to the concrete, and put your discoveries in the form of entertaining anecdotes about your adventures with women, your conversation would be easier to follow.

DON JUAN:

Bah! what need I add? Do you not understand that when I stood face to face with Woman, every fibre in my clear critical brain warned me to spare her and save myself. My morals said No. My conscience said No. My chivalry and pity for her said No. My prudent regard for myself said No. My ear, practised on a thousand songs and symphonies; my eye, exercised on a thousand paintings; tore her voice, her features, her color to shreds. I caught all those tell-tale resemblances to her father and mother by which I knew what she would be like in thirty years time. I noted the gleam of gold from a dead tooth in the laughing mouth: I made curious observations of the strange odors of the chemistry of the nerves. The visions of my romantic reveries, in which I had trod the plains of heaven with a deathless, ageless creature of coral and ivory, deserted me in that supreme hour. I remembered them and desperately strove to recover their illusion; but they now seemed the emptiest of inventions: my judgment was not to be corrupted: my brain still said No on every issue. And whilst I was in the act of framing my excuse to the lady, Life seized me and threw me into her arms as a sailor throws a scrap of fish into the mouth of a seabird.

THE STATUE:

You might as well have gone without thinking such a lot about it, Juan. You are like all the clever men: you have more brains than is good for you.

THE DEVIL:

And were you not the happier for the experience, Señor Don Juan?

DON JUAN:

The happier, no: the wiser, yes. That moment introduced me for the first time to myself, and, through myself, to the world. I saw then how useless it is to attempt to impose conditions on the irresistible force of Life; to preach prudence, careful selection, virtue, honor, chastity—

ANA:

Don Juan: a word against chastity is an insult to me.

DON JUAN:

I say nothing against your chastity, Señora, since it took the form of a husband and twelve children. What more could you have done had you been the most abandoned of women?

ANA:

I could have had twelve husbands and no children: that's what I could have done, Juan. And let me tell you that that would have made all the difference to the earth which I replenished.

THE STATUE:

Bravo Ana! Juan: you are floored, quelled, annihilated.

DON JUAN:

No; for though that difference is the true essential difference—Doña Ana has, I admit, gone straight to the real point—yet it is not a difference of love or chastity, or even constancy; for twelve children by twelve different husbands would have replenished the earth perhaps more effectively. Suppose my friend Ottavio had died when you were thirty, you would never have remained a widow: you were too beautiful. Suppose the successor of Ottavio had died when you were forty, you would still have been irresistible; and a woman who marries twice marries three times if she becomes free to do so. Twelve lawful children borne by one highly respectable lady to three different fathers is not impossible nor condemned by public opinion. That such a lady may be more law abiding than the poor girl whom we used to spurn into the gutter for bearing one unlawful infant is no doubt true; but dare you say she is less self-indulgent?

ANA:

She is less virtuous: that is enough for me.

DON JUAN:

In that case, what is virtue but the Trade Unionism of the married? Let us face the facts, dear Ana. The Life Force respects marriage only because marriage is a contrivance of its own to secure the greatest number of children and the closest care of them. For honor, chastity and all the rest of your moral figments it cares not a rap. Marriage is the most licentious of human institutions—

ANA:

Juan!

THE STATUE (*protesting*):

Really!—

DON JUAN (*determinedly*):

I say the most licentious of human institutions: that is the secret of its popularity. And a woman seeking a husband is the most unscrupulous of all the beasts of prey. The confusion of marriage with morality has done more to destroy the conscience of the human race than any other single error. Come, Ana! do not look shocked: you know better than any of us that marriage is a mantrap baited with simulated accomplishments and delusive idealizations. When your sainted mother, by dint of scoldings and punishments, forced you to learn how to play half a dozen pieces on the spinet—which she hated as much as you did—had she any other purpose than to delude your suitors into the belief that your husband would have in his home an angel who would fill it with melody, or at least play him to sleep after dinner? You married my friend Ottavio: well, did you ever open the spinet from the hour when the Church united him to you?

ANA:

You are a fool, Juan. A young married woman has something else to do than sit at the spinet without any support for her back; so she gets out of the habit of playing.

DON JUAN:

> Not if she loves music. No: believe me, she only throws away the bait when the bird is in the net.

ANA (*bitterly*):

> And men, I suppose, never throw off the mask when their bird is in the net. The husband never becomes negligent, selfish, brutal—oh never!

DON JUAN:

> What do these recriminations prove, Ana? Only that the hero is as gross an imposture as the heroine.

ANA:

> It is all nonsense: most marriages are perfectly comfortable.

DON JUAN:

> "Perfectly" is a strong expression, Ana. What you mean is that sensible people make the best of one another. Send me to the galleys and chain me to the felon whose number happens to be next before mine; and I must accept the inevitable and make the best of the companionship. Many such companionships, they tell me, are touchingly affectionate; and most are at least tolerably friendly. But that does not make a chain a desirable ornament nor the galleys an abode of bliss. Those who talk most about the blessings of marriage and the constancy of its vows are the very people who declare that if the chain were broken and the prisoners left free to choose, the whole social fabric would fly asunder. You cannot have the argument both ways. If the prisoner is happy, why lock him in? If he is not, why pretend that he is?

ANA:

> At all events, let me take an old woman's privilege again, and tell you flatly that marriage peoples the world and debauchery does not.

DON JUAN:

> How if a time come when this shall cease to be true? Do you not know that where there is a will there is a way—that whatever Man really wishes to do he will finally discover a means of doing? Well, you have done your best, you virtuous ladies, and others of your way of thinking, to bend Man's mind wholly towards honorable love as the highest good, and to understand by honorable love romance and beauty and happiness in the possession of beautiful, refined, delicate, affectionate women. You have taught women to value their own youth, health, shapeliness, and refinement above all things. Well, what place have squalling babies and household cares in this exquisite paradise of the senses and emotions? Is it not the inevitable end of it all that the human will shall say to the human brain: Invent me a means by which I can

have love, beauty, romance, emotion, passion without their wretched penalties, their expenses, their worries, their trials, their illnesses and agonies and risks of death, their retinue of servants and nurses and doctors and schoolmasters.

THE DEVIL:

All this, Señor Don Juan, is realized here in my realm.

DON JUAN:

Yes, at the cost of death. Man will not take it at that price: he demands the romantic delights of your hell whilst he is still on earth. Well, the means will be found: the brain will not fail when the will is in earnest. The day is coming when great nations will find their numbers dwindling from census to census; when the six roomed villa will rise in price above the family mansion; when the viciously reckless poor and the stupidly pious rich will delay the extinction of the race only by degrading it; whilst the boldly prudent, the thriftily sefish and ambitious, the imaginative and poetic, the lovers of money and solid comfort, the worshippers of success, of art, and of love, will all oppose to the Force of Life the device of sterility.

THE STATUE:

That is all very eloquent, my young friend; but if you had lived to Ana's age, or even to mine, you would have learned that the people who get rid of the fear of poverty and children and all the other family troubles, and devote themselves to having a good time of it, only leave their minds free for the fear of old age and ugliness and impotence and death. The childless laborer is more tormented by his wife's idleness and her constant demands for amusement and distraction than he could be by twenty children; and his wife is more wretched than he. I have had my share of vanity; for as a young man I was admired by women; and as a statue I am praised by art critics. But I confess that had I found nothing to do in the world but wallow in these delights I should have cut my throat. When I married Ana's mother—or perhaps, to be strictly correct, I should rather say when I at last gave in and allowed Ana's mother to marry me—I knew that I was planting thorns in my pillow, and that marriage for me, a swaggering young officer thitherto unvanquished, meant defeat and capture.

ANA (scandalized):

Father!

THE STATUE:

I am sorry to shock you, my love; but since Juan has stripped every rag of decency from the discussion I may as well tell the frozen truth.

ANA:

Hmf! I suppose I was one of the thorns.

THE STATUE:

By no means: you were often a rose. You see, your mother had most of the trouble you gave.

DON JUAN:

Then may I ask, Commander, why you have left Heaven to come here and wallow, as you express it, in sentimental beatitudes which you confess would once have driven you to cut your throat?

THE STATUE (*struck by this*):

Egad, that's true.

THE DEVIL (*alarmed*):

What! You are going back from your word! (*To* Don Juan) And all your philosophizing has been nothing but a mask for proselytizing! (*To* the Statue) Have you forgotten already the hideous dulness from which I am offering you a refuge here? (*To* Don Juan) And does your demonstration of the approaching sterilization and extinction of mankind lead to anything better than making the most of those pleasures of art and love which you yourself admit refined you, elevated you, developed you?

DON JUAN:

I never demonstrated the extinction of mankind. Life cannot will its own extinction either in its blind amorphous state or in any of the forms into which it has organized itself. I had not finished when His Excellency interrupted me.

THE STATUE:

I begin to doubt whether you ever will finish, my friend. You are extremely fond of hearing yourself talk.

DON JUAN:

True; but since you have endured so much, you may as well endure to the end. Long before this sterilization which I described becomes more than a clearly foreseen possibility, the reaction will begin. The great central purpose of breeding the race, ay, breeding it to heights now deemed superhuman: that purpose which is now hidden in a mephitic cloud of love and romance and prudery and fastidiousness, will break through into clear sunlight as a purpose no longer to be confused with the gratification of personal fancies, the impossible realization of boys' and girls' dreams of bliss, or the need of older people for companionship or money. The plain-spoken marriage services of the vernacular Churches will no longer be abbreviated and half suppressed as indelicate. The sober decency, earnestness and authority of their declaration of the real purpose of marriage will be honored and accepted, whilst their romantic vowings and pledgings and until-death-do-us-partings and the like will be expunged as unbearable frivolities. Do my sex the justice to admit, Señora, that we have always recognized that the sex relation is not a personal or friendly relation at all.

ANA:

Not a personal or friendly relation! What relation is more personal? more sacred? more holy?

DON JUAN:

Sacred and holy, if you like, Ana, but not personally friendly. Your relation to God is sacred and holy: dare you call it personally friendly? In the sex relation the universal creative energy, of which the parties are both the helpless agents, overrides and sweeps away all personal considerations and dispenses with all personal relations. The pair may be utter strangers to one another, speaking different languages, differing in race and color, in age and disposition, with no bond between them but a possibility of that fecundity for the sake of which the Life Force throws them into one another's arms at the exchange of a glance. Do we not recognize this by allowing marriages to be made by parents without consulting the woman? Have you not often expressed your disgust at the immorality of the English nation, in which women and men of noble birth become acquainted and court each other like peasants? And how much does even the peasant know of his bride or she of him before he engages himself? Why, you would not make a man your lawyer or your family doctor on so slight an acquaintance as you would fall in love with and marry him!

ANA:

Yes, Juan: we know the libertine's philosophy. Always ignore the consequences to the woman.

DON JUAN:

The consequences, yes: they justify her fierce grip of the man. But surely you do not call that attachment a sentimental one. As well call the policeman's attachment to his prisoner a love relation.

ANA:

You see you have to confess that marriage is necessary, though, according to you, love is the slightest of all the relations.

DON JUAN:

How do you know that it is not the greatest of all the relations? far too great to be a personal matter. Could your father have served his country if he had refused to kill any enemy of Spain unless he personally hated him? Can a woman serve her country if she refuses to marry any man she does not personally love? You know it is not so: the woman of noble birth marries as the man of noble birth fights, on political and family grounds, not on personal ones.

THE STATUE (*impressed*):

A very clever point that, Juan: I must think it over. You are really full of ideas. How did you come to think of this one?

DON JUAN:

I learnt it by experience. When I was on earth, and made those proposals to ladies which, though universally condemned, have made me so interesting a hero of legend, I was not infrequently met in some such way as this. The lady would say that she would countenance my advances, provided they were honorable. On inquiring what that proviso meant, I found that it meant that I proposed to get possession of her property if she had any, or to undertake her support for life if she had not; that I desired her continual companionship, counsel and conversation to the end of my days, and would bind myself under penalties to be always enraptured by them; and, above all, that I would turn my back on all other women for ever for her sake. I did not object to these conditions because they were exorbitant and inhuman: it was their extraordinary irrelevance that prostrated me. I invariably replied with perfect frankness that I had never dreamt of any of these things; that unless the lady's character and intellect were equal or superior to my own, her conversation must degrade and her counsel mislead me; that her constant companionship might, for all I knew, become intolerably tedious to me; that I could not answer for my feelings for a week in advance, much less to the end of my life; that to cut me off from all natural and unconstrained relations with the rest of my fellow creatures would narrow and warp me if I submitted to it, and, if not, would bring me under the curse of clandestinity; that, finally, my proposals to her were wholly unconnected with any of these matters, and were the outcome of a perfectly simple impulse of my manhood towards her womanhood.

ANA:

You mean that it was an immoral impulse.

DON JUAN:

Nature, my dear lady, is what you call immoral. I blush for it; but I cannot help it. Nature is a pandar, Time a wrecker, and Death a murderer. I have always preferred to stand up to those facts and build institutions on their recognition. You prefer to propitiate the three devils by proclaiming their chastity, their thrift, and their loving kindness; and to base your institutions on these flatteries. Is it any wonder that the institutions do not work smoothly?

THE STATUE:

What used the ladies to say, Juan?

DON JUAN:

Oh come! Confidence for confidence. First tell me what you used to say to the ladies.

THE STATUE:

I! Oh, I swore that I would be faithful to the death; that I should die if they refused me; that no woman could ever be to me what she was—

ANA:

She! Who?

THE STATUE:

Whoever it happened to be at the time, my dear. I had certain things I always said. One of them was that even when I was eighty, one white hair of the woman I loved would make me tremble more than the thickest gold tress from the most beautiful young head. Another was that I could not bear the thought of anyone else being the mother of my children.

DON JUAN (*revolted*):

You old rascal!

THE STATUE (*stoutly*):

Not a bit; for I really believed it with all my soul at the moment. I had a heart: not like you. And it was this sincerity that made me successful.

DON JUAN:

Sincerity! To be fool enough to believe a ramping, stamping, thumping lie: that is what you call sincerity! To be so greedy for a woman that you deceive yourself in your eagerness to deceive her: sincerity, you call it!

THE STATUE:

Oh, damn your sophistries! I was a man in love, not a lawyer. And the women loved me for it, bless them!

DON JUAN:

They made you think so. What will you say when I tell you that though I played the lawyer so callously, they made me think so too? I also had my moments of infatuation in which I gushed nonsense and believed it. Sometimes the desire to give pleasure by saying beautiful things so rose in me on the flood of emotion that I said them recklessly. At other times I argued against myself with a devilish coldness that drew tears. But I found it just as hard to escape in the one case as in the others. When the lady's instinct was set on me, there was nothing for it but life-long servitude or flight.

ANA:

You dare boast, before me and my father, that every woman found you irresistible.

DON JUAN:

Am I boasting? It seems to me that I cut the most pitiable of figures. Besides, I said "when the lady's instinct was set on me." It was not always so; and then, heavens! what transports of virtuous indignation! what overwhelming defiance to the dastardly seducer! what scenes of Imogen and Iachimo!

ANA:

I made no scenes. I simply called my father.

DON JUAN:

And he came, sword in hand, to vindicate outraged honor and morality by murdering me.

THE STATUE:

Murdering! What do you mean? Did I kill you or did you kill me?

DON JUAN:

Which of us was the better fencer?

THE STATUE:

I was.

DON JUAN:

Of course you were. And yet you, the hero of those scandalous adventures you have just been relating to us, you had the effrontery to pose as the avenger of outraged morality and con-demn me to death! You would have slain me but for an acci-dent.

THE STATUE:

I was expected to, Juan. That is how things were arranged on earth. I was not a social reformer; and I always did what it was customary for a gentleman to do.

DON JUAN:

That may account for your attacking me, but not for the revolt-ing hypocrisy of your subsequent proceedings as a statue.

THE STATUE:

That all came of my going to Heaven.

THE DEVIL:

I still fail to see, Señor Don Juan, that these episodes in your earthly career and in that of the Señor Commander in any way discredit my view of life. Here, I repeat, you have all that you sought without anything that you shrank from.

DON JUAN:

On the contrary, here I have everything that disappointed me without anything that I have not already tried and found wanting. I tell you that as long as I can conceive something better than myself I cannot be easy unless I am striving to bring it into existence or clearing the way for it. That is the law of my life. That is the working within me of Life's incessant aspiration to higher organization, wider, deeper, intenser self-consciousness, and clearer self-understanding. It was the supremacy of this purpose that reduced love for me to the mere pleasure of a moment, art for me to the mere schooling of my faculties, religion for me to a mere excuse for laziness, since it had set up a God who looked at the world and saw that it was good, against the instinct in me that looked through my eyes at the world and saw that it could be improved. I tell you that in the pursuit of my own pleasure, my own health, my own fortune, I have never known happiness. It was not love for Woman that delivered me into her hands: it was fatigue, exhaustion. When I was a child, and bruised my head against a stone, I ran to the nearest woman and cried away my pain against her apron. When I grew up, and bruised my soul against the brutalities and stupidities with which I had to strive, I did again just what I had done as a child. I have enjoyed, too, my rests, my recuperations, my breathing times, my very prostrations after strife; but rather would I be dragged through all the circles of the foolish Italian's Inferno than through the pleasures of Europe. That is what has made this place of eternal pleasures so deadly to me. It is the absence of this instinct in you that makes you that strange monster called a Devil. It is the success with which you have diverted the attention of men from their real purpose, which in one degree or another is the same as mine, to yours, that has earned you the name of The Tempter. It is the fact that they are doing your will, or rather drifting with your want of will, instead of doing their own, that makes them the uncomfortable, false, restless, artificial, petulant, wretched creatures they are.

THE DEVIL (*mortified*):

Señor Don Juan: you are uncivil to my friends.

DON JUAN:

Pooh! why should I be civil to them or to you? In this Palace of Lies a truth or two will not hurt you. Your friends are all the dullest dogs I know. They are not beautiful: they are only decorated. They are not clean: they are only shaved and starched. They are not dignified: they are only fashionably dressed. They are not educated: they are only college passmen. They are not religious: they are only pewrenters. They are not moral: they are only conventional. They are not virtuous: they are only cowardly. They are not even vicious: they are only "frail." They are not artistic: they are only lascivious. They are not prosperous: they are only rich. They are not loyal, they are only servile; not dutiful, only sheepish; not public spirited, only patriotic; not courageous, only quarrelsome; not determined, only obstinate; not masterful, only domineering; not self-controlled, only obtuse; not self-respecting, only vain; not kind, only sentimental; not social, only gregarious; not considerate, only polite; not intelligent, only opinionated; not progressive, only factious; not imaginative, only superstitious; not just, only vindictive; not generous, only propitiatory; not disciplined, only cowed; and not truthful at all—liars every one of them, to the very backbone of their souls.

THE STATUE:

Your flow of words is simply amazing, Juan. How I wish I could have talked like that to my soldiers.

THE DEVIL:

It is mere talk, though. It has all been said before; but what change has it ever made? What notice has the world ever taken of it?

DON JUAN:

Yes, it is mere talk. But why is it mere talk? Because, my friend, beauty, purity, respectability, religion, morality, art, patriotism, bravery and the rest are nothing but words which I or anyone else can turn inside out like a glove. Were they realities, you would have to plead guilty to my indictment; but fortunately for your self-respect, my diabolical friend, they are not realities. As you say, they are mere words, useful for duping barbarians into adopting civilization, or the civilized poor into submitting to be robbed and enslaved. That is the family secret of the governing caste; and if we who are of that caste aimed at more Life for the world instead of at more power and luxury for our miserable selves, that secret would make us great. Now, since I, being a nobleman, am in the secret too, think how tedious to me must be your unending cant about all these moralistic figments, and how squalidly disastrous your sacrifice of your lives to them! If you even believed in your moral game enough to play it fairly, it would be interesting to watch; but you don't: you cheat at every trick; and if your opponent outcheats you, you upset the table and try to murder him.

THE DEVIL:

> On earth there may be some truth in this, because the people are uneducated and cannot appreciate my religion of love and beauty; but here—

DON JUAN:

> Oh yes: I know. Here there is nothing but love and beauty. Ugh! it is like sitting for all eternity at the first act of a fashionable play, before the complications begin. Never in my worst moments of superstitious terror on earth did I dream that Hell was so horrible. I live, like a hairdresser, in the continual contemplation of beauty, toying with silken tresses. I breathe an atmosphere of sweetness, like a confectioner's shopboy. Commander: are there any beautiful women in Heaven?

THE STATUE:

> None. Absolutely none. All dowdies. Not two pennorth of jewellery among a dozen of them. They might be men of fifty.

DON JUAN:

> I am impatient to get there. Is the word beauty ever mentioned; and are there any artistic people?

THE STATUE:

> I give you my word they won't admire a fine statue even when it walks past them.

DON JUAN:

> I go.

THE DEVIL:

> Don Juan: shall I be frank with you?

DON JUAN:

> Were you not so before?

THE DEVIL:

> As far as I went, yes. But I will now go further, and confess to you that men get tired of everything, of heaven no less than of hell; and that all history is nothing but a record of the oscillations of the world between these two extremes. An epoch is but a swing of the pendulum; and each generation thinks the world is progressing because it is always moving. But when you are as old as I am; when you have a thousand times wearied of heaven, like myself and the Commander, and a thousand times wearied of hell, as you are wearied now, you will no longer imagine that every swing from heaven to hell is an emancipation, every swing from hell to heaven an evolution. Where you now see reform, progress, fulfilment of upward tendency, continual ascent by Man on the stepping stones of his dead selves to higher things, you will see nothing but an infinite comedy of illusion. You will discover the profound

truth of the saying of my friend Koheleth, that there is nothing new under the sun. Vanitas vanitatum—

DON JUAN (*out of all patience*):

By Heaven, this is worse than your cant about love and beauty. Clever dolt that you are, is a man no better than a worm, or a dog than a wolf, because he gets tired of everything? Shall he give up eating because he destroys his appetite in the act of gratifying it? Is a field idle when it is fallow? Can the Commander expend his hellish energy here without accumulating heavenly energy for his next term of blessedness? Granted that the great Life Force has hit on the device of the clockmaker's pendulum, and uses the earth for its bob; that the history of each oscillation, which seems so novel to us the actors, is but the history of the last oscillation repeated; nay more, that in the unthinkable infinitude of time the sun throws off the earth and catches it again a thousand times as a circus rider throws up a ball, and that the total of all our epochs is but the moment between the toss and the catch, has the colossal mechanism no purpose?

THE DEVIL:

None, my friend. You think, because you have a purpose, Nature must have one. You might as well expect it to have fingers and toes because you have them.

DON JUAN:

But I should not have them if they served no purpose. And I, my friend, am as much a part of Nature as my own finger is a part of me. If my finger is the organ by which I grasp the sword and the mandoline, my brain is the organ by which Nature strives to understand itself. My dog's brain serves only my dog's purposes; but my brain labors at a knowledge which does nothing for me personally but make my body bitter to me and my decay and death a calamity. Were I not possessed with a purpose beyond my own I had better be a ploughman than a philosopher; for the ploughman lives as long as the philosopher, eats more, sleeps better, and rejoices in the wife of his bosom with less misgiving. This is because the philosopher is in the grip of the Life Force. This Life Force says to him "I have done a thousand wonderful things unconsciously by merely willing to live and following the line of least resistance: now I want to know myself and my destination, and choose my path; so I have made a special brain—a philosopher's brain—to grasp this knowledge for me as the husbandman's hand grasps the plough for me. And this" says the Life Force to the philosopher "must thou strive to do for me until thou diest, when I will make another brain and another philosopher to carry on the work."

THE DEVIL:

What is the use of knowing?

DON JUAN:

Why, to be able to choose the line of greatest advantage instead of yielding in the direction of the least resistance. Does a ship sail to its destination no better than a log drifts nowhither? The philosopher is Nature's pilot. And there you have our difference: to be in hell is to drift: to be in heaven is to steer.

THE DEVIL:

On the rocks, most likely.

DON JUAN:

Pooh! which ship goes oftenest on the rocks or to the bottom—the drifting ship or the ship with a pilot on board?

THE DEVIL:

Well, well, go your way, Señor Don Juan. I prefer to be my own master and not the tool of any blundering universal force. I know that beauty is good to look at; that music is good to hear; that love is good to feel; and that they are all good to think about and talk about. I know that to be well exercised in these sensations, emotions, and studies is to be a refined and cultivated being. Whatever they may say of me in churches on earth, I know that it is universally admitted in good society that the Prince of Darkness is a gentleman; and that is enough for me. As to your Life Force, which you think irresistible, it is the most resistible thing in the world for a person of any character. But if you are naturally vulgar and credulous, as all reformers are, it will thrust you first into religion, where you will sprinkle water on babies to save their souls from me; then it will drive you from religion into science, where you will snatch the babies from the water sprinkling and inoculate them with disease to save them from catching it accidentally; then you will take to politics, where you will become the catspaw of corrupt functionaries and the henchman of ambitious humbugs; and the end will be despair and decrepitude, broken nerve and shattered hopes, vain regrets for that worst and silliest of wastes and sacrifices, the waste and sacrifice of the power of enjoyment: in a word, the punishment of the fool who pursues the better before he has secured the good.

DON JUAN:

But at least I shall not be bored. The service of the Life Force has that advantage, at all events. So fare you well, Señor Satan.

THE DEVIL (*amiably*):

Fare you well, Don Juan. I shall often think of our interesting chats about things in general. I wish you every happiness: Heaven, as I said before, suits some people. But if you should change your mind, do not forget that the gates are always open here to the repentant prodigal. If you feel at any time that warmth of heart, sincere unforced affection, innocent enjoyment, and warm, breathing, palpitating reality—

DON JUAN:

Why not say flesh and blood at once, though we have left those two greasy commonplaces behind us?

THE DEVIL (*angrily*):

You throw my friendly farewell back in my teeth, then, Don Juan?

DON JUAN:

By no means. But though there is much to be learnt from a cynical devil, I really cannot stand a sentimental one. Señor Commander: you know the way to the frontier of hell and heaven. Be good enough to direct me.

THE STATUE:

Oh, the frontier is only the difference between two ways of looking at things. Any road will take you across it if you really want to get there.

DON JUAN:

Good. (*Saluting* Doña Ana) Señora: your servant.

ANA:

But I am going with you.

DON JUAN:

I can find my own way to heaven, Ana; but I cannot find yours (*he vanishes*).

ANA:

How annoying!

THE STATUE (*calling after him*):

Bon voyage, Juan! (*He wafts a final blast of his great rolling chords after him as a parting salute. A faint echo of the first ghostly melody comes back in acknowledgment.*) Ah! there he goes. (*Puffing a long breath out through his lips*) Whew! How he does talk! They'll never stand it in heaven.

THE DEVIL (*gloomily*):

His going is a political defeat. I cannot keep these Life Worshippers: they all go. This is the greatest loss I have had since that Dutch painter went—a fellow who would paint a hag of 70 with as much enjoyment as a Venus of 20.

THE STATUE:

I remember: he came to heaven. Rembrandt.

THE DEVIL:

Ay, Rembrandt. There is something unnatural about these fellows. Do not listen to their gospel, Señor Commander: it is dangerous. Beware of the pursuit of the Superhuman: it leads to an indiscriminate contempt for the Human. To a man, horses and dogs and cats are mere species, outside the moral world. Well, to the Superman, men and women are a mere species too, also outside the moral world. This Don Juan was kind to women and courteous to men as your daughter here was kind to her pet cats and dogs; but such kindness is a denial of the exclusively human character of the soul.

THE STATUE:

And who the deuce is the Superman?

THE DEVIL:

Oh, the latest fashion among the Life Force fanatics. Did you not meet in Heaven, among the new arrivals, that German Polish madman—what was his name? Nietzsche?

THE STATUE:

Never heard of him.

THE DEVIL:

Well, he came here first, before he recovered his wits. I had some hopes of him; but he was a confirmed Life Force worshipper. It was he who raked up the Superman, who is as old as Prometheus; and the 20th century will run after this newest of the old crazes when it gets tired of the world, the flesh, and your humble servant.

THE STATUE:

Superman is a good cry; and a good cry is half the battle. I should like to see this Nietzsche.

THE DEVIL:

Unfortunately he met Wagner here, and had a quarrel with him.

THE STATUE:

Quite right, too. Mozart for me!

THE DEVIL:

Oh, it was not about music. Wagner once drifted into Life Force worship, and invented a Superman called Siegfried. But he came to his senses afterwards. So when they met here, Nietzsche denounced him as a renegade; and Wagner wrote a pamphlet to prove that Nietzsche was a Jew; and it ended in Nietzsche's going to heaven in a huff. And a good riddance too. And now, my friend, let us hasten to my palace and celebrate your arrival with a grand musical service.

THE STATUE:

> With pleasure: you're most kind.

THE DEVIL:

> This way, Commander. We go down the old trap (*he places himself on the grave trap*).

THE STATUE:

> Good. (*Reflectively*) All the same, the Superman is a fine conception. There is something statuesque about it. (*He places himself on the grave trap beside* The Devil. *It begins to descend slowly. Red glow from the abyss.*) Ah, this reminds me of old times.

THE DEVIL:

> And me also.

ANA:

> Stop! (*The trap stops.*)

THE DEVIL:

> You, Señora, cannot come this way. You will have an apotheosis. But you will be at the palace before us.

ANA:

> That is not what I stopped you for. Tell me: where can I find the Superman?

THE DEVIL:

> He is not yet created, Señora.

THE STATUE:

> And never will be, probably. Let us proceed: the red fire will make me sneeze. (*They descend.*)

ANA:

> Not yet created! Then my work is not yet done. (*Crossing herself devoutly*) I believe in the Life to Come. (*Crying to the universe*) A father—a father for the Superman!

*She vanishes into the void; and again there is nothing: all existence seems suspended infinitely. Then, vaguely, there is a live human voice crying somewhere. One sees, with a shock, a mountain peak shewing faintly against a lighter background. The sky has returned from afar; and we suddenly remember where we were. The cry becomes distinct and urgent: it says* Automobile, Automobile. *The complete reality comes back with a rush: in a moment it is full morning in the Sierra; and the* brigands *are scrambling to their feet and making for the road as the goatherd runs down from the hill, warning them of the approach of another motor.* Tanner *and* Mendoza *rise amazedly and stare at one another with scattered wits.* Straker *sits up to yawn for a moment before he gets on his feet, making it a point of honor not to shew any undue interest in the excitement of the bandits.* Mendoza *gives a quick look to see that his followers are attending to the alarm; then exchanges a private word with* Tanner.

MENDOZA:

Did you dream?

TANNER:

Damnably. Did you?

MENDOZA:

Yes. I forget what. You were in it.

TANNER:

So were you. Amazing!

MENDOZA:

I warned you. (*A shot is heard from the road.*) Dolts! they will play with that gun. (*The brigands come running back scared.*) Who fired that shot? (*to* Duval) was it you?

DUVAL (*breathless*):

I have not shoot. Dey shoot first.

ANARCHIST:

I told you to begin by abolishing the State. Now we are all lost.

THE ROWDY SOCIAL-DEMOCRAT (*stampeding across the amphitheatre*):

Run, everybody.

MENDOZA (*collaring him; throwing him on his back; and drawing a knife*):

I stab the man who stirs. (*He blocks the way. The stampede is checked.*) What has happened?

THE SULKY SOCIAL-DEMOCRAT.

A motor—

THE ANARCHIST.

Three men—

DUVAL:

Deux femmes—

MENDOZA:

Three men and two women! Why have you not brought them here? Are you afraid of them?

THE ROWDY ONE (*getting up*):

Thyve a hescort. Ow, de-ooh lut's ook it, Mendowza.

THE SULKY ONE:

Two armored cars full o soldiers at the ed o the valley.

ANARCHIST:

The shot was fired in the air. It was a signal.

Straker *whistles his favorite air, which falls on the ears of the* brigands *like a funeral march.*

TANNER:

It is not an escort, but an expedition to capture you. We were advised to wait for it; but I was in a hurry.

THE ROWDY ONE (*in an agony of apprehension*):

And Ow my good Lord, ere we are, wytin for em! Lut's tike to the mahntns.

MENDOZA:

Idiot, what do you know about the mountains? Are you a Spaniard? You would be given up by the first shepherd you met. Besides, we are already within range of their rifles.

THE ROWDY ONE:

Bat—

MENDOZA:

Silence. Leave this to me. (*To* Tanner) Comrade: you will not betray us.

STRAKER:

Oo are you callin comrade?

MENDOZA:

Last night the advantage was with me. The robber of the poor was at the mercy of the robber of the rich. You offered your hand: I took it.

TANNER:

I bring no charge against you, comrade. We have spent a pleasant evening with you: that is all.

STRAKER:

I gev my and to nobody, see?

MENDOZA (*turning on him impressively*):

Young man, if I am tried, I shall plead guilty, and explain what drove me from England, home and duty. Do you wish to have the respectable name of Straker dragged through the mud of a Spanish criminal court? The police will search me. They will find Louisa's portrait. It will be published in the illustrated papers. You blench. It will be your doing, remember.

STRAKER (*with baffled rage*):

I don't care about the court. It's avin our name mixed up with yours that I object to, you blackmailin swine, you.

MENDOZA:

Language unworthy of Louisa's brother! But no matter: you are muzzled: that is enough for us. (*He turns to face his own men, who back uneasily across the amphitheatre towards the cave to take refuge behind him, as a fresh party, muffled for motoring, comes from the road in riotous spirits. Ann, who makes straight for Tanner, comes first; then Violet, helped over the rough ground by Hector holding her right hand and Ramsden her left. Mendoza goes to his presidential block and seats himself calmly with his rank and file grouped behind him, and his Staff, consisting of Duval and the Anarchist on his right and the two Social-Democrats on his left, supporting him in flank.*)

ANN:

    It's Jack!

TANNER:

    Caught!

HECTOR:

    Why, certainly it is. I said it was you, Tanner. We've just been
stopped by a puncture: the road is full of nails.

VIOLET:

    What are you doing here with all these men?

ANN:

    Why did you leave us without a word of warning?

HECTOR:

    I want that bunch of roses, Miss Whitefield. (*To* Tanner) When
we found you were gone, Miss Whitefield bet me a bunch of
roses my car would not overtake yours before you reached
Monte Carlo.

TANNER:

    But this is not the road to Monte Carlo.

HECTOR:

    No matter. Miss Whitefield tracked you at every stopping
place: she is a regular Sherlock Holmes.

TANNER:

    The Life Force! I am lost.

OCTAVIUS (*bounding gaily down from the road into the amphitheatre,
and coming between* Tanner *and* Straker):

    I am so glad you are safe, old chap. We were afraid you had
been captured by brigands.

RAMSDEN (*who has been staring at* Mendoza):

    I seem to remember the face of your friend here. (Mendoza *rises
politely and advances with a smile between* Ann *and* Ramsden).

HECTOR:

    Why, so do I.

OCTAVIUS:

    I know you perfectly well, sir; but I can't think where I have
met you.

MENDOZA (*to* Violet):

    Do you remember me, madam?

VIOLET:

    Oh, quite well; but I am so stupid about names.

MENDOZA:

    It was at the Savoy Hotel. (*To* Hector) You, sir, used to come
with this lady (Violet) to lunch. (*To* Octavius) You, sir, often
brought this lady (Ann) and her mother to dinner on your way
to the Lyceum Theatre. (*To* Ramsden) You, sir, used to come to

supper, with (*dropping his voice to a confidential but perfectly audible whisper*) several different ladies.

RAMSDEN (*angrily*):

Well, what is that to you, pray?

OCTAVIUS:

Why, Violet, I thought you hardly knew one another before this trip, you and Malone!

VIOLET (*vexed*):

I suppose this person was the manager.

MENDOZA:

The waiter, madam. I have a grateful recollection of you all. I gathered from the bountiful way in which you treated me that you all enjoyed your visits very much.

VIOLET:

What impertinence! (*She turns her back on him, and goes up the hill with* Hector).

RAMSDEN:

That will do, my friend. You do not expect these ladies to treat you as an acquaintance, I suppose, because you have waited on them at table.

MENDOZA:

Pardon me: it was you who claimed my acquaintance. The ladies followed your example. However, this display of the unfortunate manners of your class closes the incident. For the future, you will please address me with the respect due to a stranger and fellow traveller. (*He turns haughtily away and resumes his presidential seat.*)

TANNER:

There! I have found one man on my journey capable of reasonable conversation; and you all instinctively insult him. Even the New Man is as bad as any of you. Enry: you have behaved just like a miserable gentleman.

STRAKER:

Gentleman! Not me.

RAMSDEN:

Really, Tanner, this tone—

ANN:

Don't mind him, Granny: you ought to know him by this time (*she takes his arm and coaxes him away to the hill to join* Violet *and* Hector. Octavius *follows her, dog-like*).

VIOLET (*calling from the hill*):

Here are the soldiers. They are getting out of their motors.

DUVAL (*panicstricken*):

Oh, nom de Dieu!

THE ANARCHIST:

> Fools: the State is about to crush you because you spared it at the prompting of the political hangers-on of the bourgeoisie.

THE SULKY SOCIAL-DEMOCRAT (*argumentative to the last*):

> On the contrary, only by capturing the State machine—

THE ANARCHIST:

> It is going to capture you.

THE ROWDY SOCIAL-DEMOCRAT (*his anguish culminating*):

> Ow, chack it. Wot are we ere for? Wot are we wytin for?

MENDOZA (*between his teeth*):

> Go on. Talk politics, you idiots: nothing sounds more respectable. Keep it up, I tell you.

*The soldiers line the road, commanding the amphitheatre with their rifles. The brigands, struggling with an overwhelming impulse to hide behind one another, look as unconcerned as they can.* Mendoza *rises superbly, with undaunted front. The officer in command steps down from the road into the amphitheatre; looks hard at the brigands; and then inquiringly at* Tanner.

THE OFFICER:

> Who are these men, Señor Ingles?

TANNER:

> My escort.

Mendoza, *with a Mephistophelean smile, bows profoundly. An irrepressible grin runs from face to face among the* brigands. *They touch their hats, except the* Anarchist, *who defies the State with folded arms.*

# Act IV

*The garden of a villa in Granada. Whoever wishes to know what it is like must go to Granada and see. One may prosaically specify a group of hills dotted with villas, the Alhambra on the top of one of the hills, and a considerable town in the valley, approached by dusty white roads in which the children, no matter what they are doing or thinking about, automatically whine for halfpence and reach out little clutching brown palms for them; but there is nothing in this description except the Alhambra, the begging, and the color of the roads, that does not fit Surrey as well as Spain. The difference is that the Surrey hills are comparatively small and ugly, and should properly be called the Surrey Protuberances; but these Spanish hills are of mountain stock: the amenity which conceals their size does not compromise their dignity.*

*This particular garden is on a hill opposite the Alhambra; and the villa is as expensive and pretentious as a villa must be if it is to be let furnished by the week to opulent American and English visitors. If we stand on the lawn at the foot of the garden and look uphill, our horizon is the stone balustrade of a flagged platform on the edge of infinite space at the top of the hill. Between us and this platform is a flower garden with a circular basin and fountain in the centre, surrounded by geometrical flower beds, gravel paths, and clipped yew trees in the genteelest order. The garden is higher than our lawn; so we reach it by a few steps in the middle of its embankment. The platform is higher again than the garden, from which we mount a couple more steps to look over the balustrade at a fine view of the town up the valley and of the hills that stretch away beyond it to where, in the remotest distance, they become mountains. On our left is the villa, accessible by steps from the left hand corner of the garden. Returning from the platform through the garden and down again to the lawn (a movement which leaves the villa behind us on our right) we find evidence of literary interests on the part of the tenants in the fact that there is no tennis net nor set of croquet hoops, but, on our left, a little iron garden table with books on it, mostly yellow-backed, and a chair beside it. A chair on the right has also a couple of open books upon it. There are no newspapers, a circumstance which, with the absence of games, might lead an intelligent spectator to the most far reaching conclusions as to the sort of people who live in the villa. Such speculations are checked, however, on this delightfully fine afternoon, by the appearance at a little gate in a paling on our left, of* Henry Straker *in his professional costume. He opens the gate for an elderly gentleman, and follows him on to the lawn.*

*This elderly gentleman defies the Spanish sun in a black frock coat, tall silk hat, trousers in which narrow stripes of dark grey and lilac blend into a highly respectable color, and a black necktie tied into a bow over spotless linen. Probably therefore a man whose social position needs constant and scrupulous affirmation without regard to climate: one who would dress thus for the middle of the Sahara or the top of Mont Blanc. And since he has not the stamp of the class which accepts as its life-mission the advertizing and maintenance of first rate tailoring and millinery, he looks vulgar in his finery, though in a working dress of any kind he would look dignified enough. He is a bullet cheeked man with a red complexion, stubbly hair, smallish eyes, a hard mouth that folds down at the corners, and a dogged chin. The looseness of skin that comes with age has attacked his throat and the laps of his cheeks; but he is still hard as an apple above the mouth; so that the upper half of his face looks younger than the lower. He has the self-confidence of one who has made money, and something of the truculence of one who has made it in a brutalizing struggle, his civility having under it a perceptible menace that he has other methods in reserve if necessary. Withal, a man to be rather pitied when he is not to be feared;*

*for there is something pathetic about him at times, as if the huge commercial machine which has worked him into his frock coat had allowed him very little of his own way and left his affections hungry and baffled. At the first word that falls from him it is clear that he is an Irishman whose native intonation has clung to him through many changes of place and rank. One can only guess that the original material of his speech was perhaps the surly Kerry brogue; but the degradation of speech that occurs in London, Glasgow, Dublin and big cities generally has been at work on it so long that nobody but an arrant cockney would dream of calling it a brogue now; for its music is almost gone, though its surliness is still perceptible. Straker, as a very obvious cockney, inspires him with implacable contempt, as a stupid Englishman who cannot even speak his own language properly. Straker, on the other hand, regards the old gentleman's accent as a joke thoughtfully provided by Providence expressly for the amusement of the British race, and treats him normally with the indulgence due to an inferior and unlucky species, but occasionally with indignant alarm when the old gentleman shews signs of intending his Irish nonsense to be taken seriously.*

STRAKER:

I'll go tell the young lady. She said you'd prefer to stay here (*he turns to go up through the garden to the villa*).

MALONE (*who has been looking round him with lively curiosity*):

The young lady? That's Miss Violet, eh?

STRAKER (*stopping on the steps with sudden suspicion*):

Well, you know, don't you?

MALONE:

Do I?

STRAKER (*his temper rising*):

Well, do you or don't you?

MALONE:

What business is that of yours?

Straker, *now highly indignant, comes back from the steps and confronts the visitor.*

STRAKER:

I'll tell you what business it is of mine. Miss Robinson—

MALONE (*interrupting*):

Oh, her name is Robinson, is it? Thank you.

STRAKER:

Why, you don't know even her name?

MALONE:

Yes I do, now that you've told me.

STRAKER (*after a moment of stupefaction at the old man's readiness in repartee*):

Look here: what do you mean by gittin into my car and lettin me bring you here if you're not the person I took that note to?

MALONE:

Who else did you take it to, pray?

STRAKER:

I took it to Mr Ector Malone, at Miss Robinson's request, see? Miss Robinson is not my principal: I took it to oblige her. I know Mr Malone; and he ain't you, not by a long chalk. At the hotel they told me that your name is Ector Malone—

MALONE:

*H*ector Malone.

STRAKER (*with calm superiority*):

Hector in your own country: that's what comes o livin in provincial places like Ireland and America. Over here you're Ector: if you avn't noticed it before you soon will.

*The growing strain of the conversation is here relieved by* Violet, *who has sallied from the villa and through the garden to the steps, which she now descends, coming very opportunely between* Malone *and* Straker.

VIOLET (*to* Straker):

Did you take my message?

STRAKER:

Yes, miss. I took it to the hotel and sent it up, expecting to see young Mr Malone. Then out walks this gent, and says it's all right and he'll come with me. So as the hotel people said he was Mr Ector Malone, I fetched him. And now he goes back on what he said. But if he isn't the gentleman you meant, say the word: it's easy enough to fetch him back again.

MALONE:

I should esteem it a great favor if I might have a short conversation with you, madam. I am Hector's father, as this bright Britisher would have guessed in the course of another hour or so.

STRAKER (*coolly defiant*):

No, not in another year or so. When we've ad you as long to polish up as we've ad im, perhaps you'll begin to look a little bit up to is mark. At present you fall a long way short. You've got too many aitches, for one thing. (*To* Violet, *amiably*) All right, Miss: you want to talk to him: I shan't intrude. (*He nods affably to* Malone *and goes out through the little gate in the paling.*)

VIOLET (*very civilly*):

I am so sorry, Mr Malone, if that man has been rude to you. But what can we do? He is our chauffeur.

MALONE:

Your hwat?

VIOLET:

The driver of our automobile. He can drive a motor car at seventy miles an hour, and mend it when it breaks down. We are dependent on our motor cars; and our motor cars are dependent on him; so of course we are dependent on him.

MALONE:

I've noticed, madam, that every thousand dollars an Englishman gets seems to add one to the number of people he's dependent on. However, you needn't apologize for your man: I made him talk on purpose. By doing so I learnt that you're staying here in Grannida with a party of English, including my son Hector.

VIOLET (*conversationally*):

Yes. We intended to go to Nice; but we had to follow a rather eccentric member of our party who started first and came here. Won't you sit down? (*She clears the nearest chair of the two books on it.*)

MALONE (*impressed by this attention*):

Thank you. (*He sits down, examining her curiously as she goes to the iron table to put down the books. When she turns to him again, he says*) Miss Robinson, I believe?

VIOLET (*sitting down*):

Yes.

MALONE (*taking a letter from his pocket*):

Your note to Hector runs as follows (Violet *is unable to repress a start. He pauses quietly to take out and put on his spectacles, which have gold rims*): "Dearest: they have all gone to the Alhambra for the afternoon. I have shammed headache and have the garden all to myself. Jump into Jack's motor: Straker will rattle you here in a jiffy. Quick, quick, quick. Your loving Violet." (*He looks at her; but by this time she has recovered herself, and meets his spectacles with perfect composure. He continues slowly*) Now I don't know on what terms young people associate in English society; but in America that note would be considered to imply a very considerable degree of affectionate intimacy between the parties.

VIOLET:

Yes: I know your son very well, Mr Malone. Have you any objection?

MALONE (*somewhat taken aback*):

No, no objection exactly. Provided it is understood that my son is altogether dependent on me, and that I have to be consulted in any important step he may propose to take.

VIOLET:

I am sure you would not be unreasonable with him, Mr Malone.

MALONE:

I hope not, Miss Robinson; but at your age you might think many things unreasonable that don't seem so to me.

VIOLET (*with a little shrug*):

Oh well, I suppose there's no use our playing at cross purposes, Mr Malone. Hector wants to marry me.

MALONE:

I inferred from your note that he might. Well, Miss Robinson, he is his own master; but if he marries you he shall not have a rap from me. (*He takes off his spectacles and pockets them with the note*).

VIOLET (*with some severity*):

That is not very complimentary to me, Mr Malone.

MALONE:

I say nothing against you, Miss Robinson: I daresay you are an amiable and excellent young lady. But I have other views for Hector.

VIOLET:

Hector may not have other views for himself, Mr Malone.

MALONE:

Possibly not. Then he does without me: that's all. I daresay you are prepared for that. When a young lady writes to a young man to come to her quick, quick, quick, money seems nothing and love seems everything.

VIOLET (*sharply*):

I beg your pardon, Mr Malone: I do not think anything so foolish. Hector must have money.

MALONE (*staggered*):

Oh, very well, very well. No doubt he can work for it.

VIOLET:

What is the use of having money if you have to work for it? (*She rises impatiently*). It's all nonsense, Mr Malone: you must enable your son to keep up his position. It is his right.

MALONE (*grimly*):

I should not advise you to marry him on the strength of that right, Miss Robinson.

*Violet, who has almost lost her temper, controls herself with an effort; unclenches her fingers; and resumes her seat with studied tranquillity and reasonableness.*

VIOLET:

What objection have you to me, pray? My social position is as good as Hector's, to say the least. He admits it.

MALONE (*shrewdly*):

You tell him so from time to time, eh? Hector's social position in England, Miss Robinson, is just what I choose to buy for him. I have made him a fair offer. Let him pick out the most historic house, castle or abbey that England contains. The day that he tells me he wants it for a wife worthy of its traditions, I buy it for him, and give him the means of keeping it up.

VIOLET:

What do you mean by a wife worthy of its traditions? Cannot any well bred woman keep such a house for him?

MALONE:

No: she must be born to it.

VIOLET:

Hector was not born to it, was he?

MALONE:

His granmother was a barefooted Irish girl that nursed me by a turf fire. Let him marry another such, and I will not stint her marriage portion. Let him raise himself socially with my money or raise somebody else: so long as there is a social profit somewhere, I'll regard my expenditure as justified. But there must be a profit for someone. A marriage with you would leave things just where they are.

VIOLET:

Many of my relations would object very much to my marrying the grandson of a common woman, Mr Malone. That may be prejudice; but so is your desire to have him marry a title prejudice.

MALONE (*rising, and approaching her with a scrutiny in which there is a good deal of reluctant respect*):

You seem a pretty straightforward downright sort of a young woman.

VIOLET:

I do not see why I should be made miserably poor because I cannot make profits for you. Why do you want to make Hector unhappy?

MALONE:

He will get over it all right enough. Men thrive better on disappointments in love than on disappointments in money. I daresay you think that sordid; but I know what I'm talking about. My father died of starvation in Ireland in the black 47. Maybe you've heard of it.

VIOLET:

The Famine?

MALONE (*with smouldering passion*):

No, the starvation. When a country is full of food, and exporting it, there can be no famine. My father was starved dead; and I was starved out to America in my mother's arms. English rule drove me and mine out of Ireland. Well, you can keep Ireland. I and my like are coming back to buy England; and we'll buy the best of it. I want no middle class properties and no middle class women for Hector. That's straightforward, isn't it, like yourself?

VIOLET (*icily pitying his sentimentality*):

Really, Mr Malone, I am astonished to hear a man of your age and good sense talking in that romantic way. Do you suppose English noblemen will sell their places to you for the asking?

MALONE:

I have the refusal of two of the oldest family mansions in England. One historic owner can't afford to keep all the rooms dusted: the other can't afford the death duties. What do you say now?

VIOLET:

Of course it is very scandalous; but surely you know that the Government will sooner or later put a stop to all these Socialistic attacks on property.

MALONE (*grinning*):

D'y' think they'll be able to get that done before I buy the house—or rather the abbey? They're both abbeys.

VIOLET (*putting that aside rather impatiently*):

Oh, well, let us talk sense, Mr Malone. You must feel that we havn't been talking sense so far.

MALONE:

I can't say I do. I mean all I say.

VIOLET:

Then you don't know Hector as I do. He is romantic and faddy—he gets it from you, I fancy—and he wants a certain sort of wife to take care of him. Not a faddy sort of person, you know.

MALONE:

Somebody like you, perhaps?

VIOLET (*quietly*):

> Well, yes. But you cannot very well ask me to undertake this with absolutely no means of keeping up his position.

MALONE (*alarmed*):

> Stop a bit, stop a bit. Where are we getting to? I'm not aware that I'm asking you to undertake anything.

VIOLET:

> Of course, Mr Malone, you can make it very difficult for me to speak to you if you choose to misunderstand me.

MALONE (*half bewildered*):

> I don't wish to take any unfair advantage; but we seem to have got off the straight track somehow.

Straker, *with the air of a man who has been making haste, opens the little gate, and admits* Hector, *who, snorting with indignation, comes upon the lawn, and is making for his father when* Violet, *greatly dismayed, springs up and intercepts him.* Straker *does not wait; at least he does not remain visibly within earshot.*

VIOLET:

> Oh, how unlucky! Now please, Hector, say nothing. Go away until I have finished speaking to your father.

HECTOR (*inexorably*):

> No, Violet: I mean to have this thing out, right away. (*He puts her aside; passes her by; and faces his father, whose cheeks darken as his Irish blood begins to simmer*). Dad: you've not played this hand straight.

MALONE:

> Hwat d'y'mean?

HECTOR:

> You've opened a letter addressed to me. You've impersonated me and stolen a march on this lady. That's dishonorable.

MALONE (*threateningly*):

> Now you take care what you're saying, Hector. Take care, I tell you.

HECTOR:

> I have taken care. I am taking care. I'm taking care of my honor and my position in English society.

MALONE (*hotly*):

> Your position has been got by my money: do you know that?

HECTOR:

> Well, you've just spoiled it all by opening that letter. A letter from an English lady, not addressed to you—a confidential letter! a delicate letter! a private letter! opened by my father!

That's a sort of thing a man can't struggle against in England. The sooner we go back together the better. (*He appeals mutely to the heavens to witness the shame and anguish of two outcasts*).

VIOLET (*snubbing him with an instinctive dislike for scene making*):

Don't be unreasonable, Hector. It was quite natural of Mr Malone to open my letter: his name was on the envelope.

MALONE:

There! You've no common sense, Hector. I thank you, Miss Robinson.

HECTOR:

I thank you, too. It's very kind of you. My father knows no better.

MALONE (*furiously clenching his fists*):

Hector—

HECTOR (*with undaunted moral force*):

Oh, it's no use hectoring me. A private letter's a private letter, dad: you can't get over that.

MALONE (*raising his voice*):

I won't be talked back to by you, d'y'hear?

VIOLET:

Ssh! please, please. Here they all come.

*Father and son, checked, glare mutely at one another as* Tanner *comes in through the little gate with* Ramsden, *followed by* Octavius *and* Ann.

VIOLET:

Back already!

TANNER:

The Alhambra is not open this afternoon.

VIOLET:

What a sell!

*Tanner passes on, and presently finds himself between* Hector *and a strange elder, both apparently on the verge of personal combat. He looks from one to the other for an explanation. They sulkily avoid his eye, and nurse their wrath in silence.*

RAMSDEN:

Is it wise for you to be out in the sunshine with such a headache, Violet?

TANNER:

Have you recovered too, Malone?

VIOLET:

    Oh, I forgot. We have not all met before. Mr Malone: won't you introduce your father?

HECTOR (*with Roman firmness*):

    No I will not. He is no father of mine.

MALONE (*very angry*):

    You disown your dad before your English friends, do you?

VIOLET:

    Oh please don't make a scene.

Ann *and* Octavius, *lingering near the gate, exchange an astonished glance, and discreetly withdraw up the steps to the garden, where they can enjoy the disturbance without intruding. On their way to the steps* Ann *sends a little grimace of mute sympathy to* Violet, *who is standing with her back to the little table, looking on in helpless annoyance as her husband soars to higher and higher moral eminences without the least regard to the old man's millions.*

HECTOR:

    I'm very sorry, Miss Robinson; but I'm contending for a principle. I am a son, and, I hope, a dutiful one; but before everything I'm a Man!!! And when dad treats my private letters as his own, and takes it on himself to say that I shan't marry you if I am happy and fortunate enough to gain your consent, then I just snap my fingers and go my own way.

TANNER:

    Marry Violet!

RAMSDEN:

    Are you in your senses?

TANNER:

    Do you forget what we told you?

HECTOR (*recklessly*):

    I don't care what you told me.

RAMSDEN (*scandalized*):

    Tut tut, sir! Monstrous! (*he flings away towards the gate, his elbows quivering with indignation*).

TANNER:

    Another madman! These men in love should be locked up. (*He gives* Hector *up as hopeless, and turns away towards the garden; but* Malone, *taking offence in a new direction, follows him and compels him, by the aggressiveness of his tone, to stop.*)

MALONE:

    I don't understand this. Is Hector not good enough for this lady, pray?

TANNER:

My dear sir, the lady is married already. Hector knows it; and yet he persists in his infatuation. Take him home and lock him up.

MALONE (*bitterly*):

So this is the high-born social tone I've spoilt be me ignorant, uncultivated behavior! Makin love to a married woman! (*He comes angrily between* Hector *and* Violet, *and almost bawls into* Hector's *left ear*) You've picked up that habit of the British aristocracy, have you?

HECTOR:

That's all right. Don't you trouble yourself about that. I'll answer for the morality of what I'm doing.

TANNER (*coming forward to* Hector's *right hand with flashing eyes*):

Well said, Malone! You also see that mere marriage laws are not morality! I agree with you; but unfortunately Violet does not.

MALONE:

I take leave to doubt that, sir. (*Turning on* Violet) Let me tell you, Mrs Robinson, or whatever your right name is, you had no right to send that letter to my son when you were the wife of another man.

HECTOR (*outraged*):

This is the last straw. Dad: you have insulted my wife.

MALONE:

Your wife!

TANNER:

You the missing husband! Another moral impostor! (*He smites his brow, and collapses into* Malone's *chair.*)

MALONE:

You've married without my consent!

RAMSDEN:

You have deliberately humbugged us, sir!

HECTOR:

Here: I have had just about enough of being badgered. Violet and I are married: that's the long and the short of it. Now what have you got to say—any of you?

MALONE:

I know what I've got to say. She's married a beggar.

HECTOR:

No; she's married a Worker (*his American pronunciation imparts an overwhelming intensity to this simple and unpopular word*). I start to earn my own living this very afternoon.

MALONE (*sneering angrily*):

Yes: you're very plucky now, because you got your remittance from me yesterday or this morning, I reckon. Wait til it's spent. You won't be so full of cheek then.

HECTOR (*producing a letter from his pocketbook*):

Here it is (*thrusting it on his father*). Now you just take your remittance and yourself out of my life. I'm done with remittances; and I'm done with you. I don't sell the privilege of insulting my wife for a thousand dollars.

MALONE (*deeply wounded and full of concern*):

Hector: you don't know what poverty is.

HECTOR (*fervidly*):

Well, I want to know what it is. I want'be a Man. Violet: you come along with me, to your own home: I'll see you through.

OCTAVIUS (*jumping down from the garden to the lawn and running to Hector's left hand*):

I hope you'll shake hands with me before you go, Hector. I admire and respect you more than I can say. (*He is affected almost to tears as they shake hands.*)

VIOLET (*also almost in tears, but of vexation*):

Oh don't be an idiot, Tavy. Hector's about as fit to become a workman as you are.

TANNER (*rising from his chair on the other side of* Hector):

Never fear: there's no question of his becoming a navvy, Mrs Malone. (*To* Hector) There's really no difficulty about capital to start with. Treat me as a friend: draw on me.

OCTAVIUS (*impulsively*):

Or on me.

MALONE (*with fierce jealousy*):

Who wants your durty money? Who should he draw on but his own father? (Tanner *and* Octavius *recoil,* Octavius *rather hurt,* Tanner *consoled by the solution of the money difficulty.* Violet *looks up hopefully.*) Hector: don't be rash, my boy. I'm sorry for what I said: I never meant to insult Violet: I take it all back. She's just the wife you want: there!

HECTOR (*patting him on the shoulder*):

Well, that's all right, dad. Say no more: we're friends again. Only, I take no money from anybody.

MALONE (*pleading abjectly*):

Don't be hard on me, Hector. I'd rather you quarrelled and took the money than made friends and starved. You don't know what the world is: I do.

HECTOR:

> No, no, NO. That's fixed: that's not going to change. (*He passes his father inexorably by, and goes to* Violet). Come, Mrs Malone: you've got to move to the hotel with me, and take your proper place before the world.

VIOLET:

> But I must go in, dear, and tell Davis to pack. Won't you go on and make them give you a room overlooking the garden for me? I'll join you in half an hour.

HECTOR:

> Very well. You'll dine with us, Dad, won't you?

MALONE (*eager to conciliate him*):

> Yes, yes.

HECTOR:

> See you all later. (*He waves his hand to* Ann, *who has now been joined by* Tanner, Octavius, *and* Ramsden *in the garden, and goes out through the little gate, leaving his father and* Violet *together on the lawn*).

MALONE:

> You'll try to bring him to his senses, Violet: I know you will.

VIOLET:

> I had no idea he could be so headstrong. If he goes on like that, what can I do?

MALONE:

> Don't be discurridged: domestic pressure may be slow; but it's sure. You'll wear him down. Promise me you will.

VIOLET:

> I will do my best. Of course I think it's the greatest nonsense deliberately making us poor like that.

MALONE:

> Of course it is.

VIOLET (*after a moment's reflection*):

> You had better give me the remittance. He will want it for his hotel bill. I'll see whether I can induce him to accept it. Not now, of course, but presently.

MALONE (*eagerly*):

> Yes, yes, yes: that's just the thing (*he hands her the thousand dollar bill, and adds cunningly*) Y'understand that this is only a bachelor allowance.

VIOLET (*coolly*):

> Oh, quite. (*She takes it*). Thank you. By the way, Mr Malone, those two houses you mentioned—the abbeys.

MALONE:

> Yes?

VIOLET:

> Don't take one of them until I've seen it. One never knows what may be wrong with these places.

MALONE:

> I won't. I'll do nothing without consulting you, never fear.

VIOLET (*politely, but without a ray of gratitude*):

> Thanks: that will be much the best way. (*She goes calmly back to the villa, escorted obsequiously by* Malone *to the upper end of the garden.*)

TANNER (*drawing* Ramsden's *attention to* Malone's *cringing attitude as he takes leave of* Violet):

> And that poor devil is a billionaire! one of the master spirits of the age! Led in a string like a pug dog by the first girl who takes the trouble to despise him. I wonder will it ever come to that with me. (*He comes down to the lawn*).

RAMSDEN (*following him*):

> The sooner the better for you.

MALONE (*slapping his hands as he returns through the garden*):

> That'll be a grand woman for Hector. I wouldn't exchange her for ten duchesses. (*He descends to the lawn and comes between* Tanner *and* Ramsden.)

RAMSDEN (*very civil to the billionaire*):

> It's an unexpected pleasure to find you in this corner of the world, Mr Malone. Have you come to buy up the Alhambra?

MALONE:

> Well, I don't say I mightn't. I think I could do better with it than the Spanish government. But that's not what I came about. To tell you the truth, about a month ago I overheard a deal between two men over a bundle of shares. They differed about the price: they were young and greedy, and didn't know that if the shares were worth what was bid for them they must be worth what was asked, the margin being too small to be of any account, you see. To amuse meself, I cut in and bought the shares. Well, to this day I havn't found out what the business is. The office is in this town; and the name is Mendoza, Limited. Now whether Mendoza's a mine, or a steamboat line, or a bank, or a patent article—

TANNER:

> He's a man. I know him: his principles are thoroughly commercial. Let us take you round the town in our motor, Mr Malone, and call on him on the way.

MALONE:

> If you'll be so kind, yes. And may I ask who—

TANNER:

Mr Roebuck Ramsden, a very old friend of your daughter-in-law.

MALONE:

Happy to meet you, Mr Ramsden.

RAMSDEN:

Thank you. Mr Tanner is also one of our circle.

MALONE:

Glad to know you also, Mr Tanner.

TANNER:

Thanks. (Malone *and* Ramsden *go out very amicably through the little gate.* Tanner *calls to* Octavius, *who is wandering in the garden with* Ann) Tavy! (Tavy *comes to the steps,* Tanner *whispers loudly to him*) Violet has married a financier of brigands. (Tanner *hurries away to overtake* Malone *and* Ramsden. Ann *strolls to the steps with an idle impulse to torment* Octavius).

ANN:

Won't you go with them, Tavy?

OCTAVIUS (*tears suddenly flushing his eyes*):

You cut me to the heart, Ann, by wanting me to go (*he comes down on the lawn to hide his face from her. She follows him caressingly*).

ANN:

Poor Ricky Ticky Tavy! Poor heart!

OCTAVIUS:

It belongs to you, Ann. Forgive me: I must speak of it. I love you. You know I love you.

ANN:

What's the good, Tavy? You know that my mother is determined that I shall marry Jack.

OCTAVIUS (*amazed*):

Jack!

ANN:

It seems absurd, doesn't it?

OCTAVIUS (*with growing resentment*):

Do you mean to say that Jack has been playing with me all this time? That he has been urging me not to marry you because he intends to marry you himself?

ANN (*alarmed*):

No no: you mustn't lead him to believe that I said that: I don't for a moment think that Jack knows his own mind. But it's clear from my father's will that he wished me to marry Jack. And my mother is set on it.

OCTAVIUS:

But you are not bound to sacrifice yourself always to the wishes of your parents.

ANN:

My father loved me. My mother loves me. Surely their wishes are a better guide than my own selfishness.

OCTAVIUS:

Oh, I know how unselfish you are, Ann. But believe me—though I know I am speaking in my own interest—there is another side to this question. Is it fair to Jack to marry him if you do not love him? Is it fair to destroy my happiness as well as your own if you can bring yourself to love me?

ANN (*looking at him with a faint impulse of pity*):

Tavy, my dear, you are a nice creature—a good boy.

OCTAVIUS (*humiliated*):

Is that all?

ANN (*mischievously in spite of her pity*):

That's a great deal, I assure you. You would always worship the ground I trod on, wouldn't you?

OCTAVIUS:

I do. It sounds ridiculous; but it's no exaggeration. I do; and I always shall.

ANN:

Always is a long word, Tavy. You see, I shall have to live up always to your idea of my divinity; and I don't think I could do that if we were married. But if I marry Jack, you'll never be disillusioned—at least not until I grow too old.

OCTAVIUS:

I too shall grow old, Ann. And when I am eighty, one white hair of the woman I love will make me tremble more than the thickest gold tress from the most beautiful young head.

ANN (*quite touched*):

Oh, that's poetry, Tavy, real poetry. It gives me that strange sudden sense of an echo from a former existence which always seems to me such a striking proof that we have immortal souls.

OCTAVIUS:

Do you believe that it is true?

ANN:

Tavy: if it is to come true, you must lose me as well as love me.

OCTAVIUS:

Oh! (*he hastily sits down at the little table and covers his face with his hands*).

ANN (*with conviction*):

Tavy: I wouldn't for worlds destroy your illusions. I can neither take you nor let you go. I can see exactly what will suit you. You must be a sentimental old bachelor for my sake.

OCTAVIUS (*desperately*):

Ann: I'll kill myself.

ANN:

Oh no you won't: that wouldn't be kind. You won't have a bad time. You will be very nice to women; and you will go a good deal to the opera. A broken heart is a very pleasant complaint for a man in London if he has a comfortable income.

OCTAVIUS (*considerably cooled, but believing that he is only recovering his self-control*):

I know you mean to be kind, Ann. Jack has persuaded you that cynicism is a good tonic for me. (*He rises with quiet dignity*).

ANN (*studying him slyly*):

You see, I'm disillusionizing you already. That's what I dread.

OCTAVIUS:

You do not dread disillusionizing Jack.

ANN (*her face lighting up with mischievous ecstasy—whispering*):

I can't: he has no illusions about me. I shall surprise Jack the other way. Getting over an unfavorable impression is ever so much easier than living up to an ideal. Oh, I shall enrapture Jack sometimes!

OCTAVIUS (*resuming the calm phase of despair, and beginning to enjoy his broken heart and delicate attitude without knowing it*):

I don't doubt that. You will enrapture him always. And he—the fool!—thinks you would make him wretched.

ANN:

Yes: that's the difficulty, so far.

OCTAVIUS (*heroically*):

Shall *I* tell him that you love him?

ANN (*quickly*):

Oh no: he'd run away again.

OCTAVIUS (*shocked*):

Ann: would you marry an unwilling man?

ANN:

What a queer creature you are, Tavy! There's no such thing as a willing man when you really go for him. (*She laughs naughtily.*) I'm shocking you, I suppose. But you know you are really getting a sort of satisfaction already in being out of danger yourself.

OCTAVIUS (*startled*):

Satisfaction! (*Reproachfully*) You say that to me!

ANN:

Well, if it were really agony, would you ask for more of it?

OCTAVIUS:

Have I asked for more of it?

ANN:

You have offered to tell Jack that I love him. That's self-sacrifice, I suppose; but there must be some satisfaction in it. Perhaps it's because you're a poet. You are like the bird that presses its breast against the sharp thorn to make itself sing.

OCTAVIUS:

It's quite simple. I love you; and I want you to be happy. You don't love me; so I can't make you happy myself; but I can help another man to do it.

ANN:

Yes: it seems quite simple. But I doubt if we ever know why we do things. The only really simple thing is to go straight for what you want and grab it. I suppose I don't love you, Tavy; but sometimes I feel as if I should like to make a man of you somehow. You are very foolish about women.

OCTAVIUS (*almost coldly*):

I am content to be what I am in that respect.

ANN:

Then you must keep away from them, and only dream about them. I wouldn't marry you for worlds, Tavy.

OCTAVIUS:

I have no hope, Ann: I accept my ill luck. But I don't think you quite know how much it hurts.

ANN:

You are so softhearted! It's queer that you should be so different from Violet. Violet's as hard as nails.

OCTAVIUS:

Oh no. I am sure Violet is thoroughly womanly at heart.

ANN (*with some impatience*):

Why do you say that? Is it unwomanly to be thoughtful and businesslike and sensible? Do you want Violet to be an idiot— or something worse, like me?

OCTAVIUS:

Something worse—like you! What do you mean, Ann?

ANN:

Oh well, I don't mean that, of course. But I have a great respect for Violet. She gets her own way always.

OCTAVIUS (*sighing*):

So do you.

ANN:

> Yes; but somehow she gets it without coaxing—without having to make people sentimental about her.

OCTAVIUS (*with brotherly callousness*):

> Nobody could get very sentimental about Violet, I think, pretty as she is.

ANN:

> Oh yes they could, if she made them.

OCTAVIUS:

> But surely no really nice woman would deliberately practise on men's instincts in that way.

ANN (*throwing up her hands*):

> Oh Tavy, Tavy, Ricky Ticky Tavy, heaven help the woman who marries you!

OCTAVIUS (*his passion reviving at the name*):

> Oh why, why, why do you say that? Don't torment me. I don't understand.

ANN:

> Suppose she were to tell fibs, and lay snares for men?

OCTAVIUS:

> Do you think *I* could marry such a woman—I, who have known and loved you?

ANN:

> Hm! Well, at all events, she wouldn't let you if she were wise. So that's settled. And now I can't talk any more. Say you forgive me, and that the subject is closed.

OCTAVIUS:

> I have nothing to forgive; and the subject is closed. And if the wound is open, at least you shall never see it bleed.

ANN:

> Poetic to the last, Tavy. Goodbye, dear. (*She pats his cheek; has an impulse to kiss him and then another impulse of distaste which prevents her; finally runs away through the garden and into the villa.*)

Octavius *again takes refuge at the table, bowing his head on his arms and sobbing softly. Mrs Whitefield, who has been pottering round the Granada shops, and has a net full of little parcels in her hand, comes in through the gate and sees him.*

MRS WHITEFIELD (*running to him and lifting his head*):

> What's the matter, Tavy? Are you ill?

OCTAVIUS:

> No, nothing, nothing.

MRS WHITEFIELD (*still holding his head, anxiously*):

But you're crying. Is it about Violet's marriage?

OCTAVIUS:

No, no. Who told you about Violet?

MRS WHITEFIELD (*restoring the head to its owner*):

I met Roebuck and that awful old Irishman. Are you sure you're not ill? What's the matter?

OCTAVIUS (*affectionately*):

It's nothing—only a man's broken heart. Doesn't that sound ridiculous?

MRS WHITEFIELD:

But what is it all about? Has Ann been doing anything to you?

OCTAVIUS:

It's not Ann's fault. And don't think for a moment that I blame you.

MRS WHITEFIELD (*startled*):

For what?

OCTAVIUS (*pressing her hand consolingly*):

For nothing. I said I didn't blame you.

MRS WHITEFIELD:

But I haven't done anything. What's the matter?

OCTAVIUS (*smiling sadly*):

Can't you guess? I daresay you are right to prefer Jack to me as a husband for Ann; but I love Ann; and it hurts rather. (*He rises and moves away from her towards the middle of the lawn*).

MRS WHITEFIELD (*following him hastily*):

Does Ann say that I want her to marry Jack?

OCTAVIUS:

Yes: she has told me.

MRS WHITEFIELD (*thoughtfully*):

Then I'm very sorry for you, Tavy. It's only her way of saying she wants to marry Jack. Little she cares what *I* say or what *I* want!

OCTAVIUS:

But she would not say it unless she believed it. Surely you don't suspect Ann of—of deceit!!

MRS WHITEFIELD:

Well, never mind, Tavy. I don't know which is best for a young man: to know too little, like you, or too much, like Jack.

Tanner *returns*.

TANNER:

Well, I've disposed of old Malone. I've introduced him to Mendoza, Limited; and left the two brigands together to talk it out. Hullo, Tavy! anything wrong?

OCTAVIUS:

> I must go wash my face, I see. (*To* Mrs Whitefield) Tell him what you wish. (*To* Tanner) You may take it from me, Jack, that Ann approves of it.

TANNER (*puzzled by his manner*):

> Approves of what?

OCTAVIUS:

> Of what Mrs Whitefield wishes. (*He goes his way with sad dignity to the villa.*)

TANNER (*to* Mrs Whitefield):

> This is very mysterious. What is it you wish? It shall be done, whatever it is.

MRS WHITEFIELD (*with snivelling gratitude*):

> Thank you, Jack. (*She sits down.* Tanner *brings the other chair from the table and sits close to her with his elbows on his knees, giving her his whole attention.*) I don't know why it is that other people's children are so nice to me, and that my own have so little consideration for me. It's no wonder I don't seem able to care for Ann and Rhoda as I do for you and Tavy and Violet. It's a very queer world. It used to be so straightforward and simple; and now nobody seems to think and feel as they ought. Nothing has been right since that speech that Professor Tyndall made at Belfast.

TANNER:

> Yes: life is more complicated than we used to think. But what am I to do for you?

MRS WHITEFIELD:

> That's just what I want to tell you. Of course you'll marry Ann whether I like it or not—

TANNER (*starting*):

> It seems to me that I shall presently be married to Ann whether I like it myself or not.

MRS WHITEFIELD (*peacefully*):

> Oh, very likely you will: you know what she is when she has set her mind on anything. But don't put it on me: that's all I ask. Tavy has just let out that she's been saying that I am making her marry you; and the poor boy is breaking his heart about it; for he is in love with her himself, though what he sees in her so wonderful, goodness knows: *I* don't. It's no use telling Tavy that Ann puts things into people's heads by telling them that I want them when the thought of them never crossed my mind. It only sets Tavy against me. But you know better than that. So if you marry her, don't put the blame on me.

TANNER (*emphatically*):

> I haven't the slightest intention of marrying her.

MRS WHITEFIELD (*slyly*):

>She'd suit you better than Tavy. She'd meet her match in you, Jack. I'd like to see her meet her match.

TANNER:

>No man is a match for a woman, except with a poker and a pair of hobnailed boots. Not always even then. Anyhow, *I* can't take the poker to her. I should be a mere slave.

MRS WHITEFIELD:

>No: she's afraid of you. At all events, you would tell her the truth about herself. She wouldn't be able to slip out of it as she does with me.

TANNER:

>Everybody would call me a brute if I told Ann the truth about herself in terms of her own moral code. To begin with, Ann says things that are not strictly true.

MRS WHITEFIELD:

>I'm glad somebody sees she is not an angel.

TANNER:

>In short—to put it as a husband would put it when exasperated to the point of speaking out—she is a liar. And since she has plunged Tavy head over ears in love with her without any intention of marrying him, she is a coquette, according to the standard definition of a coquette as a woman who rouses passions she has no intention of gratifying. And as she has now reduced you to the point of being willing to sacrifice me at the altar for the mere satisfaction of getting me to call her a liar to her face, I may conclude that she is a bully as well. She can't bully men as she bullies women; so she habitually and unscrupulously uses her personal fascination to make men give her whatever she wants. That makes her almost something for which I know no polite name.

MRS WHITEFIELD (*in mild expostulation*):

>Well, you can't expect perfection, Jack.

TANNER:

>I don't. But what annoys me is that Ann does. I know perfectly well that all this about her being a liar and a bully and a coquette and so forth is a trumped-up moral indictment which might be brought against anybody. We all lie; we all bully as much as we dare; we all bid for admiration without the least intention of earning it; we all get as much rent as we can out of our powers of fascination. If Ann would admit this I shouldn't quarrel with her. But she won't. If she has children she'll take advantage of their telling lies to amuse herself by whacking them. If another woman makes eyes at me, she'll refuse to

know a coquette. She will do just what she likes herself whilst insisting on everybody else doing what the conventional code prescribes. In short, I can stand everything except her confounded hypocrisy. That's what beats me.

MRS WHITEFIELD (*carried away by the relief of hearing her own opinion so eloquently expressed*):

Oh, she is a hypocrite. She is: she is. Isn't she?

TANNER:

Then why do you want to marry me to her?

MRS WHITEFIELD (*querulously*):

There now! put it on me, of course. I never thought of it until Tavy told me she said I did. But, you know, I'm very fond of Tavy: he's a sort of son to me; and I don't want him to be trampled on and made wretched.

TANNER:

Whereas I don't matter, I suppose.

MRS WHITEFIELD:

Oh, you are different, somehow: you are able to take care of yourself. You'd serve her out. And anyhow, she must marry somebody.

TANNER:

Aha! there speaks the life instinct. You detest her; but you feel that you must get her married.

MRS WHITEFIELD (*rising, shocked*):

Do you mean that I detest my own daughter! Surely you don't believe me to be so wicked and unnatural as that, merely because I see her faults.

TANNER (*cynically*):

You love her, then?

MRS WHITEFIELD:

Why, of course I do. What queer things you say, Jack! We can't help loving our own blood relations.

TANNER:

Well, perhaps it saves unpleasantness to say so. But for my part, I suspect that the tables of consanguinity have a natural basis in a natural repugnance (*he rises*).

MRS WHITEFIELD:

You shouldn't say things like that, Jack. I hope you won't tell Ann that I have been speaking to you. I only wanted to set myself right with you and Tavy. I couldn't sit mumchance and have everything put on me.

TANNER (*politely*):

Quite so.

MRS WHITEFIELD (*dissatisfied*):

And now I've only made matters worse. Tavy's angry with me because I don't worship Ann. And when it's been put into my head that Ann ought to marry you, what can I say except that it would serve her right?

TANNER:

Thank you.

MRS WHITEFIELD:

Now don't be silly and twist what I say into something I don't mean. I ought to have fair play—

Ann *comes from the villa, followed presently by* Violet, *who is dressed for driving.*

ANN (*coming to her mother's right hand with threatening suavity*):

Well, mamma darling, you seem to be having a delightful chat with Jack. We can hear you all over the place.

MRS WHITEFIELD (*appalled*):

Have you overheard—

TANNER:

Never fear: Ann is only—well, we were discussing that habit of hers just now. She hasn't heard a word.

MRS WHITEFIELD (*stoutly*):

I don't care whether she has or not: I have a right to say what I please.

VIOLET (*arriving on the lawn and coming between* Mrs Whitefield *and* Tanner):

I've come to say goodbye. I'm off for my honeymoon.

MRS WHITEFIELD (*crying*):

Oh don't say that, Violet. And no wedding, no breakfast, no clothes, nor anything.

VIOLET (*petting her*):

It won't be for long.

MRS WHITEFIELD:

Don't let him take you to America. Promise me that you won't.

VIOLET (*very decidedly*):

I should think not, indeed. Don't cry, dear: I'm only going to the hotel.

MRS WHITEFIELD:

But going in that dress, with your luggage, makes one realize— (*she chokes, and then breaks out again*) How I wish you were my daughter, Violet!

VIOLET (*soothing her*):

There, there: so I am. Ann will be jealous.

MRS WHITEFIELD:

>   Ann doesn't care a bit for me.

ANN:

>   Fie, mother! Come, now: you mustn't cry any more: you know Violet doesn't like it (Mrs Whitefield *dries her eyes, and subsides*).

VIOLET:

>   Goodbye, Jack.

TANNER:

>   Goodbye, Violet.

VIOLET:

>   The sooner you get married too, the better. You will be much less misunderstood.

TANNER (*restively*):

>   I quite expect to get married in the course of the afternoon. You all seem to have set your minds on it.

VIOLET:

>   You might do worse. (*To* Mrs Whitefield: *putting her arm round her*) Let me take you to the hotel with me: the drive will do you good. Come in and get a wrap. (*She takes her towards the villa.*)

MRS WHITEFIELD (*as they go up through the garden*):

>   I don't know what I shall do when you are gone, with no one but Ann in the house; and she always occupied with the men! It's not to be expected that your husband will care to be bothered with an old woman like me. Oh, you needn't tell me: politeness is all very well; but I know what people think—(*She talks herself and* Violet *out of sight and hearing*).

Ann, *musing on* Violet's *opportune advice, approaches* Tanner; *examines him humorously for a moment from toe to top; and finally delivers her opinion.*

ANN:

>   Violet is quite right. You ought to get married.

TANNER (*explosively*):

>   Ann: I will not marry you. Do you hear? I won't, won't, won't, won't, WON'T marry you.

ANN (*placidly*):

>   Well, nobody axd you, sir she said, sir she said, sir she said. So that's settled.

TANNER:

>   Yes, nobody has asked me; but everybody treats the thing as settled. It's in the air. When we meet, the others go away on absurd pretexts to leave us alone together. Ramsden no longer

scowls at me: his eye beams, as if he were already giving you away to me in church. Tavy refers me to your mother and gives me his blessing. Straker openly treats you as his future employer: it was he who first told me of it.

ANN:

Was that why you ran away?

TANNER:

Yes, only to be stopped by a lovesick brigand and run down like a truant schoolboy.

ANN:

Well, if you don't want to be married, you needn't be (*she turns away from him and sits down, much at her ease*).

TANNER (*following her*):

Does any man want to be hanged? Yet men let themselves be hanged without a struggle for life, though they could at least give the chaplain a black eye. We do the world's will, not our own. I have a frightful feeling that I shall let myself be married because it is the world's will that you should have a husband.

ANN:

I daresay I shall, someday.

TANNER:

But why me—me of all men? Marriage is to me apostasy, profanation of the sanctuary of my soul, violation of my manhood, sale of my birthright, shameful surrender, ignominious capitulation, acceptance of defeat. I shall decay like a thing that has served its purpose and is done with; I shall change from a man with a future to a man with a past; I shall see in the greasy eyes of all the other husbands their relief at the arrival of a new prisoner to share their ignominy. The young men will scorn me as one who has sold out: to the young women I, who have always been an enigma and a possibility, shall be merely somebody else's property—and damaged goods at that: a secondhand man at best.

ANN:

Well, your wife can put on a cap and make herself ugly to keep you in countenance, like my grandmother.

TANNER:

So that she may make her triumph more insolent by publicly throwing away the bait the moment the trap snaps on the victim!

ANN:

After all, though, what difference would it make? Beauty is all very well at first sight; but who ever looks at it when it has been in the house three days? I thought our pictures very lovely when papa bought them; but I haven't looked at them for years. You never bother about my looks: you are too well used to me. I might be the umbrella stand.

TANNER:

You lie, you vampire: you lie.

ANN:

Flatterer. Why are you trying to fascinate me, Jack, if you don't want to marry me?

TANNER:

The Life Force. I am in the grip of the Life Force.

ANN:

I don't understand in the least: it sounds like the Life Guards.

TANNER:

Why don't you marry Tavy? He is willing. Can you not be satisfied unless your prey struggles?

ANN (*turning to him as if to let him into a secret*):

Tavy will never marry. Haven't you noticed that that sort of man never marries?

TANNER:

What! a man who idolizes women! who sees nothing in nature but romantic scenery for love duets! Tavy, the chivalrous, the faithful, the tenderhearted and true! Tavy never marry! Why, he was born to be swept up by the first pair of blue eyes he meets in the street.

ANN:

Yes, I know. All the same, Jack, men like that always live in comfortable bachelor lodgings with broken hearts, and are adored by their landladies, and never get married. Men like you always get married.

TANNER (*smiting his brow*):

How frightfully, horribly true! It has been staring me in the face all my life; and I never saw it before.

ANN:

Oh, it's the same with women. The poetic temperament's a very nice temperament, very amiable, very harmless and poetic, I daresay; but it's an old maid's temperament.

TANNER:

Barren. The Life Force passes it by.

ANN:

If that's what you mean by the Life Force, yes.

TANNER:

You don't care for Tavy?

ANN (*looking round carefully to make sure that* Tavy *is not within earshot*):

No.

TANNER:

And you do care for me?

ANN (*rising quietly and shaking her finger at him*):

Now Jack! Behave yourself.

TANNER:

Infamous, abandoned woman! Devil!

ANN:

Boa-constrictor! Elephant!

TANNER:

Hypocrite!

ANN (*softly*):

I must be, for my future husband's sake.

TANNER:

For mine! (*Correcting himself savagely*) I mean for his.

ANN (*ignoring the correction*):

Yes, for yours. You had better marry what you call a hypocrite, Jack. Women who are not hypocrites go about in rational dress and are insulted and get into all sorts of hot water. And then their husbands get dragged in too, and live in continual dread of fresh complications. Wouldn't you prefer a wife you could depend on?

TANNER:

No, a thousand times no: hot water is the revolutionist's element. You clean men as you clean milkpails, by scalding them.

ANN:

Cold water has its uses too. It's healthy.

TANNER (*despairingly*):

Oh, you are witty: at the supreme moment the Life Force endows you with every quality. Well, I too can be a hypocrite. Your father's will appointed me your guardian, not your suitor. I shall be faithful to my trust.

ANN (*in low siren tones*):

He asked me who would I have as my guardian before he made that will. I chose you!

TANNER:

The will is yours then! The trap was laid from the beginning.

ANN (*concentrating all her magic*):

From the beginning—from our childhood—for both of us— by the Life Force.

TANNER:

I will not marry you. I will not marry you.

ANN:

Oh, you will, you will.

TANNER:

I tell you, no, no, no.

ANN:

> I tell you, yes, yes, yes.

TANNER:

> No.

ANN (*coaxing—imploring—almost exhausted*):

> Yes. Before it is too late for repentance. Yes.

TANNER (*struck by the echo from the past*):

> When did all this happen to me before? Are we two dreaming?

ANN (*suddenly losing her courage, with an anguish that she does not conceal*):

> No. We are awake; and you have said no: that is all.

TANNER (*brutally*):

> Well?

ANN:

> Well, I made a mistake: you do not love me.

TANNER (*seizing her in his arms*):

> It is false: I love you. The Life Force enchants me: I have the whole world in my arms when I clasp you. But I am fighting for my freedom, for my honor, for my self, one and indivisible.

ANN:

> Your happiness will be worth them all.

TANNER:

> You would sell freedom and honor and self for happiness?

ANN:

> It will not be all happiness for me. Perhaps death.

TANNER (*groaning*):

> Oh, that clutch holds and hurts. What have you grasped in me? Is there a father's heart as well as a mother's?

ANN:

> Take care, Jack: if anyone comes while we are like this, you will have to marry me.

TANNER:

> If we two stood now on the edge of a precipice, I would hold you tight and jump.

ANN (*panting, failing more and more under the strain*):

> Jack: let me go. I have dared so frightfully—it is lasting longer than I thought. Let me go: I can't bear it.

TANNER:

> Nor I. Let it kill us.

ANN:

> Yes: I don't care. I am at the end of my forces. I don't care. I think I am going to faint.

*At this moment* Violet *and* Octavius *come from the villa with* Mrs Whitefield, *who is wrapped up for driving. Simultaneously* Malone *and* Ramsden, *followed by* Mendoza *and* Straker, *come in through the little gate in the paling.* Tanner *shamefacedly releases* Ann, *who raises her hand giddily to her forehead.*

MALONE:

Take care. Something's the matter with the lady.

RAMSDEN:

What does this mean?

VIOLET (*running between* Ann *and* Tanner):

Are you ill?

ANN (*reeling, with a supreme effort*):

I have promised to marry Jack. (*She swoons.* Violet *kneels by her and chafes her hand.* Tanner *runs round to her other hand, and tries to lift her head.* Octavius *goes to* Violet's *assistance, but does not know what to do.* Mrs Whitefield *hurries back into the villa.* Octavius, Malone *and* Ramsden *run to* Ann *and crowd round her, stooping to assist.* Straker *coolly comes to* Ann's *feet, and* Mendoza *to her head, both upright and self-possessed*).

STRAKER:

Now then, ladies and gentlemen: she don't want a crowd round her: she wants air—all the air she can git. If you please, gents—(Malone *and* Ramsden *allow him to drive them gently past* Ann *and up the lawn towards the garden, where* Octavius, *who has already become conscious of his uselessness, joins them.* Straker, *following them up, pauses for a moment to instruct* Tanner). Don't lift er ed, Mr Tanner: let it go flat so's the blood can run back into it.

MENDOZA:

He is right, Mr Tanner. Trust to the air of the Sierra. (*He withdraws delicately to the garden steps.*)

TANNER (*rising*):

I yield to your superior knowledge of physiology, Henry. (*He withdraws to the corner of the lawn; and* Octavius *immediately hurries down to him.*)

TAVY (*aside to* Tanner, *grasping his hand*):

Jack: be very happy.

TANNER (*aside to* Tavy):

I never asked her. It is a trap for me. (*He goes up the lawn towards the garden.* Octavius *remains petrified.*)

MENDOZA (*intercepting* Mrs Whitefield, *who comes from the villa with a glass of brandy*):

What is this, madam (*he takes it from her*)?

MRS WHITEFIELD:

A little brandy.

MENDOZA:

The worst thing you could give her. Allow me. (*He swallows it.*) Trust to the air of the Sierra, madam.

*For a moment the men all forget* Ann *and stare at* Mendoza.

ANN (*in* Violet's *ear, clutching her round the neck*):

Violet: did Jack say anything when I fainted?

VIOLET:

No.

ANN:

Ah! (*with a sigh of intense relief she relapses*).

MRS WHITEFIELD:

Oh, she's fainted again.

*They are about to rush back to her; but* Mendoza *stops them with a warning gesture.*

ANN (*supine*):

No I havn't. I'm quite happy.

TANNER (*suddenly walking determinedly to her, and snatching her hand from* Violet *to feel her pulse*):

Why, her pulse is positively bounding. Come, get up. What nonsense! Up with you. (*He gets her up summarily.*)

ANN:

Yes: I feel strong enough now. But you very nearly killed me, Jack, for all that.

MALONE:

A rough wooer, eh? They're the best sort, Miss Whitefield. I congratulate Mr Tanner; and I hope to meet you and him as frequent guests at the Abbey.

ANN:

Thank you. (*She goes past* Malone *to* Octavius) Ricky Ticky Tavy: congratulate me. (*Aside to him*) I want to make you cry for the last time.

TAVY (*steadfastly*):

No more tears. I am happy in your happiness. And I believe in you in spite of everything.

RAMSDEN (*coming between* Malone *and* Tanner):

You are a happy man, Jack Tanner. I envy you.

MENDOZA (*advancing between* Violet *and* Tanner):

Sir: there are two tragedies in life. One is not to get your heart's desire. The other is to get it. Mine and yours, sir.

TANNER:

Mr Mendoza: I have no heart's desires. Ramsden: it is very easy for you to call me a happy man: you are only a spectator. I am one of the principals; and I know better. Ann: stop tempting Tavy, and come back to me.

ANN (*complying*):

You are absurd, Jack. (*She takes his proffered arm.*)

TANNER (*continuing*):

I solemnly say that I am not a happy man. Ann looks happy; but she is only triumphant, successful, victorious. That is not happiness, but the price for which the strong sell their happiness. What we have both done this afternoon is to renounce happiness, renounce freedom, renounce tranquillity, above all, renounce the romantic possibilities of an unknown future, for the cares of a household and a family. I beg that no man may seize the occasion to get half drunk and utter imbecile speeches and coarse pleasantries at my expense. We propose to furnish our own house according to our own taste; and I hereby give notice that the seven or eight travelling clocks, the four or five dressing cases, the salad bowls, the carvers and fish slices, the copy of Tennyson in extra morocco, and all the other articles you are preparing to heap upon us, will be instantly sold, and the proceeds devoted to circulating free copies of the Revolutionist's Handbook. The wedding will take place three days after our return to England, by special license, at the office of the district superintendent registrar, in the presence of my solicitor and his clerk, who, like his clients, will be in ordinary walking dress—

VIOLET (*with intense conviction*):

You are a brute, Jack.

ANN (*looking at him with fond pride and caressing his arm*):

Never mind her, dear. Go on talking.

TANNER:

Talking!

*Universal laughter.*

# Major Barbara

## A DISCUSSION
## IN THREE ACTS

*N.B.* The Euripidean verses in the second act of Major Barbara are not by me, nor even directly by Euripides. They are by Professor Gilbert Murray, whose English version of The Bacchae came into our dramatic literature with all the impulsive power of an original work shortly before Major Barbara was begun. The play, indeed, stands indebted to him in more ways than one.

G.B.S.

# Act I

*It is after dinner in January 1906, in the library in* Lady Britomart
Undershaft's *house in Wilton Crescent. A large and comfortable settee is
in the middle of the room, upholstered in dark leather. A person sitting on
it (it is vacant at present) would have, on his right,* Lady Britomart's
*writing table, with the lady herself busy at it; a smaller writing table
behind him on his left; the door behind him on* Lady Britomart's *side;
and a window with a window seat directly on his left. Near the window is
an armchair.*

Lady Britomart *is a woman of fifty or thereabouts, well dressed and yet
careless of her dress, well bred and quite reckless of her breeding, well man-
nered and yet appallingly outspoken and indifferent to the opinion of her
interlocutors, amiable and yet peremptory, arbitrary, and high-tempered
to the last bearable degree, and withal a very typical managing matron of
the upper class, treated as a naughty child until she grew into a scolding
mother, and finally settling down with plenty of practical ability and
worldly experience, limited in the oddest way with domestic and class lim-
itations, conceiving the universe exactly as if it were a large house in
Wilton Crescent, though handling her corner of it very effectively on that
assumption, and being quite enlightened and liberal as to the books in the
library, the pictures on the walls, the music in the portfolios, and the articles in the papers.*

*Her son,* Stephen, *comes in. He is a gravely correct young man under 25,
taking himself very seriously, but still in some awe of his mother, from childish habit and bachelor shyness rather than from any weakness of character.*

STEPHEN:
> What's the matter?

LADY BRITOMART:
> Presently, Stephen.

Stephen *submissively walks to the settee and sits down. He takes up a Liberal weekly called The Speaker.*

LADY BRITOMART:
> Don't begin to read, Stephen. I shall require all your attention.

STEPHEN:

It was only while I was waiting—

LADY BRITOMART:

Don't make excuses, Stephen. (*He puts down The Speaker*). Now! (*She finishes her writing; rises; and comes to the settee*). I have not kept you waiting very long, I think.

STEPHEN:

Not at all, mother.

LADY BRITOMART:

Bring me my cushion. (*He takes the cushion from the chair at the desk and arranges it for her as she sits down on the settee*). Sit down. (*He sits down and fingers his tie nervously*). Don't fiddle with your tie, Stephen: there is nothing the matter with it.

STEPHEN:

I beg your pardon. (*He fiddles with his watch chain instead*).

LADY BRITOMART:

Now are you attending to me, Stephen?

STEPHEN:

Of course, mother.

LADY BRITOMART:

No: it's not of course. I want something much more than your everyday matter-of-course attention. I am going to speak to you very seriously, Stephen. I wish you would let that chain alone.

STEPHEN (*hastily relinquishing the chain*):

Have I done anything to annoy you, mother? If so, it was quite unintentional.

LADY BRITOMART (*astonished*):

Nonsense! (*With some remorse*) My poor boy, did you think I was angry with you?

STEPHEN:

What is it, then, mother? You are making me very uneasy.

LADY BRITOMART (*squaring herself at him rather aggressively*):

Stephen: may I ask how soon you intend to realize that you are a grown-up man, and that I am only a woman?

STEPHEN (*amazed*):

Only a—

LADY BRITOMART:

Don't repeat my words, please: it is a most aggravating habit. You must learn to face life seriously, Stephen. I really cannot bear the whole burden of our family affairs any longer. You must advise me: you must assume the responsibility.

STEPHEN:

I!

LADY BRITOMART:

Yes, you, of course. You were 24 last June. You've been at Harrow and Cambridge. You've been to India and Japan. You must know a lot of things, now; unless you have wasted your time most scandalously. Well, advise me.

STEPHEN (*much perplexed*):

You know I have never interfered in the household—

LADY BRITOMART:

No: I should think not. I don't want you to order the dinner.

STEPHEN:

I mean in our family affairs.

LADY BRITOMART:

Well, you must interfere now; for they are getting quite beyond me.

STEPHEN (*troubled*):

I have thought sometimes that perhaps I ought; but really, mother, I know so little about them; and what I do know is so painful! it is so impossible to mention some things to you—(*he stops, ashamed*).

LADY BRITOMART:

I suppose you mean your father.

STEPHEN (*almost inaudibly*):

Yes.

LADY BRITOMART:

My dear: we can't go on all our lives not mentioning him. Of course you were quite right not to open the subject until I asked you to; but you are old enough now to be taken into my confidence, and to help me to deal with him about the girls.

STEPHEN:

But the girls are all right. They are engaged.

LADY BRITOMART (*complacently*):

Yes: I have made a very good match for Sarah. Charles Lomax will be a millionaire at 35. But that is ten years ahead; and in the meantime his trustees cannot under the terms of his father's will allow him more than £800 a year.

STEPHEN:

But the will says also that if he increases his income by his own exertions, they may double the increase.

LADY BRITOMART:

Charles Lomax's exertions are much more likely to decrease his income than to increase it. Sarah will have to find at least another £800 a year for the next ten years; and even then they will be as poor as church mice. And what about Barbara? I thought Barbara was going to make the most brilliant career of all of you. And what does she do? Joins the Salvation Army; discharges her maid; lives on a pound a week; and walks in one evening with a professor of Greek whom she has picked up in the street, and who pretends to be a Salvationist, and actually plays the big drum for her in public because he has fallen head over ears in love with her.

STEPHEN:

I was certainly rather taken aback when I heard they were engaged. Cusins is a very nice fellow, certainly: nobody would ever guess that he was born in Australia; but—

LADY BRITOMART:

Oh, Adolphus Cusins will make a very good husband. After all, nobody can say a word against Greek: it stamps a man at once as an educated gentleman. And my family, thank Heaven, is not a pig-headed Tory one. We are Whigs, and believe in liberty. Let snobbish people say what they please: Barbara shall marry, not the man they like, but the man *I* like.

STEPHEN:

Of course I was thinking only of his income. However, he is not likely to be extravagant.

LADY BRITOMART:

Don't be too sure of that, Stephen. I know your quiet, simple, refined, poetic people like Adolphus: quite content with the best of everything! They cost more than your extravagant people, who are always as mean as they are second rate. No: Barbara will need at least £2000 a year. You see it means two additional households. Besides, my dear, you must marry soon. I don't approve of the present fashion of philandering bachelors and late marriages; and I am trying to arrange something for you.

STEPHEN:

It's very good of you, mother; but perhaps I had better arrange that for myself.

LADY BRITOMART:

Nonsense! you are much too young to begin matchmaking: you would be taken in by some pretty little nobody. Of course I don't mean that you are not to be consulted: you know that as well as I do. (Stephen *closes his lips and is silent*). Now don't sulk, Stephen.

STEPHEN:

I am not sulking, mother. What has all this got to do with—with—with my father?

LADY BRITOMART:

My dear Stephen: where is the money to come from? It is easy enough for you and the other children to live on my income as long as we are in the same house; but I can't keep four families in four separate houses. You know how poor my father is: he has barely seven thousand a year now; and really, if he were not the Earl of Stevenage, he would have to give up society. He can do nothing for us. He says, naturally enough, that it is absurd that he should be asked to provide for the children of a man who is rolling in money. You see, Stephen, your father must be fabulously wealthy, because there is always a war going on somewhere.

STEPHEN:

You need not remind me of that, mother. I have hardly ever opened a newspaper in my life without seeing our name in it. The Undershaft torpedo! The Undershaft quick firers! The Undershaft ten inch! the Undershaft disappearing rampart gun! the Undershaft submarine! and now the Undershaft aerial battleship! At Harrow they called me the Woolwich Infant. At Cambridge it was the same. A little brute at King's who was always trying to get up revivals, spoilt my Bible— your first birthday present to me—by writing under my name, "Son and heir to Undershaft and Lazarus, Death and Destruction Dealers: address, Christendom and Judea." But that was not so bad as the way I was kowtowed to everywhere because my father was making millions by selling cannons.

LADY BRITOMART:

It is not only the cannons, but the war loans that Lazarus arranges under cover of giving credit for the cannons. You know, Stephen, it's perfectly scandalous. Those two men, Andrew Undershaft and Lazarus, positively have Europe under their thumbs. That is why your father is able to behave as he does. He is above the law. Do you think Bismarck or Gladstone or Disraeli could have openly defied every social and moral obligation all their lives as your father has? They simply wouldn't have dared. I asked Gladstone to take it up. I asked The Times to take it up. I asked the Lord Chamberlain to take it up. But it was just like asking them to declare war on the Sultan. They wouldn't. They said they couldn't touch him. I believe they were afraid.

STEPHEN:

What could they do? He does not actually break the law.

LADY BRITOMART:

Not break the law! He is always breaking the law. He broke the law when he was born: his parents were not married.

STEPHEN:

Mother! Is that true?

LADY BRITOMART:

Of course it's true: that was why we separated.

STEPHEN:

He married without letting you know this!

LADY BRITOMART (*rather taken aback by this inference*):

Oh no. To do Andrew justice, that was not the sort of thing he did. Besides, you know the Undershaft motto: Unashamed. Everybody knew.

STEPHEN:

But you said that was why you separated.

LADY BRITOMART:

Yes, because he was not content with being a foundling himself: he wanted to disinherit you for another foundling. That was what I couldn't stand.

STEPHEN (*ashamed*):

Do you mean for—for—for—

LADY BRITOMART:

Don't stammer, Stephen. Speak distinctly.

STEPHEN:

But this is so frightful to me, mother. To have to speak to you about such things!

LADY BRITOMART:

It's not pleasant for me, either, especially if you are still so childish that you must make it worse by a display of embarrassment. It is only in the middle classes, Stephen, that people get into a state of dumb helpless horror when they find that there are wicked people in the world. In our class, we have to decide what is to be done with wicked people; and nothing should disturb our self-possession. Now ask your question properly.

STEPHEN:

Mother: have you no consideration for me? For Heaven's sake either treat me as a child, as you always do, and tell me nothing at all; or tell me everything and let me take it as best I can.

LADY BRITOMART:

Treat you as a child! What do you mean? It is most unkind and ungrateful of you to say such a thing. You know I have never treated any of you as children. I have always made you my companions and friends, and allowed you perfect freedom to do and say whatever you liked, so long as you liked what I could approve of.

STEPHEN (*desperately*):

I daresay we have been the very imperfect children of a very perfect mother; but I do beg you to let me alone for once, and tell me about this horrible business of my father wanting to set me aside for another son.

LADY BRITOMART (*amazed*):

Another son! I never said anything of the kind. I never dreamt of such a thing. This is what comes of interrupting me.

STEPHEN:

But you said—

LADY BRITOMART (*cutting him short*):

Now be a good boy, Stephen, and listen to me patiently. The Undershafts are descended from a foundling in the parish of St Andrew Undershaft in the city. That was long ago, in the reign of James the First. Well, this foundling was adopted by an armorer and gun-maker. In the course of time the foundling succeeded to the business; and from some notion of gratitude, or some vow or something, he adopted another foundling, and left the business to him. And that foundling did the same. Ever since that, the cannon business has always been left to an adopted foundling named Andrew Undershaft.

STEPHEN:

But did they never marry? Were there no legitimate sons?

LADY BRITOMART:

Oh yes: they married just as your father did; and they were rich enough to buy land for their own children and leave them well provided for. But they always adopted and trained some foundling to succeed them in the business; and of course they always quarrelled with their wives furiously over it. Your father was adopted in that way; and he pretends to consider himself bound to keep up the tradition and adopt somebody to leave the business to. Of course I was not going to stand that. There may have been some reason for it when the Undershafts could only marry women in their own class, whose sons were not fit to govern great estates. But there could be no excuse for passing over my son.

STEPHEN (*dubiously*):

I am afraid I should make a poor hand of managing a cannon foundry.

LADY BRITOMART:

Nonsense! you could easily get a manager and pay him a salary.

STEPHEN:

My father evidently had no great opinion of my capacity.

LADY BRITOMART:

Stuff, child! you were only a baby: it had nothing to do with your capacity. Andrew did it on principle, just as he did every perverse and wicked thing on principle. When my father remonstrated, Andrew actually told him to his face that history tells us of only two successful institutions: one the Undershaft firm, and the other the Roman Empire under the Antonines. That was because the Antonine emperors all adopted their successors. Such rubbish! The Stevenages are as good as the Antonines, I hope; and you are a Stevenage. But that was Andrew all over. There you have the man! Always clever and unanswerable when he was defending nonsense and wickedness: always awkward and sullen when he had to behave sensibly and decently!

STEPHEN:

Then it was on my account that your home life was broken up, mother. I am sorry.

LADY BRITOMART:

Well, dear, there were other differences. I really cannot bear an immoral man. I am not a Pharisee, I hope; and I should not have minded his merely doing wrong things: we are none of us perfect. But your father didn't exactly do wrong things: he said them and thought them: that was what was so dreadful. He really had a sort of religion of wrongness. Just as one doesn't mind men practising immorality so long as they own that they are in the wrong by preaching morality; so I couldn't forgive Andrew for preaching immorality while he practised morality. You would all have grown up without principles, without any knowledge of right and wrong, if he had been in the house. You know, my dear, your father was a very attractive man in some ways. Children did not dislike him; and he took advantage of it to put the wickedest ideas into their heads, and make them quite unmanageable. I did not dislike him myself: very far from it; but nothing can bridge over moral disagreement.

STEPHEN:

All this simply bewilders me, mother. People may differ about matters of opinion, or even about religion; but how can they differ about right and wrong? Right is right; and wrong is wrong; and if a man cannot distinguish them properly, he is either a fool or a rascal: that's all.

LADY BRITOMART (*touched*):

That's my own boy (*she pats his cheek*)! Your father could never answer that: he used to laugh and get out of it under cover of some affectionate nonsense. And now that you understand the situation, what do you advise me to do?

STEPHEN:

Well, what can you do?

LADY BRITOMART:

I must get the money somehow.

STEPHEN:

We cannot take money from him. I had rather go and live in some cheap place like Bedford Square or even Hampstead than take a farthing of his money.

LADY BRITOMART:

But after all, Stephen, our present income comes from Andrew.

STEPHEN (*shocked*):

I never knew that.

LADY BRITOMART:

Well, you surely didn't suppose your grandfather had anything to give me. The Stevenages could not do everything for you. We gave you social position. Andrew had to contribute something. He had a very good bargain, I think.

STEPHEN (*bitterly*):

We are utterly dependent on him and his cannons, then?

LADY BRITOMART:

Certainly not: the money is settled. But he provided it. So you see it is not a question of taking money from him or not: it is simply a question of how much. I don't want any more for myself.

STEPHEN:

Nor do I.

LADY BRITOMART:

But Sarah does; and Barbara does. That is, Charles Lomax and Adolphus Cusins will cost them more. So I must put my pride in my pocket and ask for it, I suppose. That is your advice, Stephen, is it not?

STEPHEN:

No.

LADY BRITOMART (*sharply*):

Stephen!

STEPHEN:

Of course if you are determined—

LADY BRITOMART:

I am not determined: I ask your advice; and I am waiting for it. I will not have all the responsibility thrown on my shoulders.

STEPHEN (*obstinately*):

I would die sooner than ask him for another penny.

LADY BRITOMART (*resignedly*):

You mean that *I* must ask him. Very well, Stephen: it shall be as you wish. You will be glad to know that your grandfather concurs. But he thinks I ought to ask Andrew to come here and see the girls. After all, he must have some natural affection for them.

STEPHEN:

Ask him here!!!

LADY BRITOMART:

Do not repeat my words, Stephen. Where else can I ask him?

STEPHEN:

I never expected you to ask him at all.

LADY BRITOMART:

Now don't tease, Stephen. Come! you see that it is necessary that he should pay us a visit, don't you?

STEPHEN (*reluctantly*):

I suppose so, if the girls cannot do without his money.

LADY BRITOMART:

Thank you, Stephen: I knew you would give me the right advice when it was properly explained to you. I have asked your father to come this evening. (Stephen *bounds from his seat*) Don't jump, Stephen: it fidgets me.

STEPHEN (*in utter consternation*):

Do you mean to say that my father is coming here tonight—that he may be here at any moment?

LADY BRITOMART (*looking at her watch*):

I said nine. (*He gasps. She rises*). Ring the bell, please. (Stephen *goes to the smaller writing table; presses a button on it; and sits at it with his elbows on the table and his head in his hands, outwitted and overwhelmed*). It is ten minutes to nine yet; and I have to prepare the girls. I asked Charles Lomax and Adolphus to dinner on purpose that they might be here. Andrew had better see them in case he should cherish any delusions as to their being capable of supporting their wives. (*The butler enters:* Lady Britomart *goes behind the settee to speak to him*). Morrison: go up to the drawing room and tell everybody to come down here at once. (Morrison *withdraws*. Lady Britomart *turns to* Stephen). Now remember, Stephen: I shall need all your countenance and authority. (*He rises and tries to recover some vestige of these attributes*). Give me a chair, dear. (*He pushes a chair forward from the wall to where she stands, near the smaller writing table. She sits down; and he goes to the armchair, into which he throws himself*). I don't know how Barbara will take it. Ever since they made her a major in the Salvation Army she has developed a propensity to have her own way and order people about which quite cows me sometimes. It's not ladylike: I'm sure I don't know where she picked it up. Anyhow, Barbara shan't bully me; but still it's

just as well that your father should be here before she has time
to refuse to meet him or make a fuss. Don't look nervous,
Stephen: it will only encourage Barbara to make difficulties. *I*
am nervous enough, goodness knows; but I don't shew it.

Sarah *and* Barbara *come in with their respective young men,* Charles
Lomax *and* Adolphus Cusins. Sarah *is slender, bored, and mundane.*
Barbara *is robuster, jollier, much more energetic.* Sarah *is fashionably
dressed:* Barbara *is in Salvation Army uniform.* Lomax, *a young man
about town, is like many other young men about town. He is afflicted with
a frivolous sense of humor which plunges him at the most inopportune
moments into paroxysms of imperfectly suppressed laughter.* Cusins *is a
spectacled student, slight, thin haired, and sweet voiced, with a more com-
plex form of* Lomax's *complaint. His sense of humor is intellectual and subtle, and is complicated by an appalling temper. The lifelong struggle of a
benevolent temperament and a high conscience against impulses of inhuman ridicule and fierce impatience has set up a chronic strain which has
visibly wrecked his constitution. He is a most implacable, determined, tena-
cious, intolerant person who by mere force of character presents himself as—
and indeed actually is—considerate, gentle, explanatory, even mild and
apologetic, capable possibly of murder, but not of cruelty or coarseness. By the
operation of some instinct which is not merciful enough to blind him with
the illusions of love, he is obstinately bent on marrying* Barbara. Lomax
*likes* Sarah *and thinks it will be rather a lark to marry her. Consequently
he has not attempted to resist* Lady Britomart's *arrangements to that end.*

*All four look as if they had been having a good deal of fun in the draw-
ing room. The girls enter first, leaving the swains outside.* Sarah *comes to
the settee.* Barbara *comes in after her and stops at the door.*

BARBARA:
Are Cholly and Dolly to come in?
LADY BRITOMART (*forcibly*):
Barbara: I will not have Charles called Cholly: the vulgarity of
it positively makes me ill.
BARBARA:
It's all right, mother: Cholly is quite correct nowadays. Are
they to come in?
LADY BRITOMART:
Yes, if they will behave themselves.
BARBARA (*through the door*):
Come in, Dolly; and behave yourself.

Barbara *comes to her mother's writing table.* Cusins *enters smiling, and
wanders towards* Lady Britomart.

SARAH (*calling*):

Come in, Cholly. (Lomax *enters, controlling his features very imperfectly, and places himself vaguely between* Sarah *and* Barbara).

LADY BRITOMART (*peremptorily*):

Sit down, all of you. (*They sit.* Cusins *crosses to the window and seats himself there.* Lomax *takes a chair.* Barbara *sits at the writing table and* Sarah *on the settee*). I don't in the least know what you are laughing at, Adolphus. I am surprised at you, though I expected nothing better from Charles Lomax.

CUSINS (*in a remarkably gentle voice*):

Barbara has been trying to teach me the West Ham Salvation March.

LADY BRITOMART:

I see nothing to laugh at in that; nor should you if you are really converted.

CUSINS (*sweetly*):

You were not present. It was really funny, I believe.

LOMAX:

Ripping.

LADY BRITOMART:

Be quiet, Charles. Now listen to me, children. Your father is coming here this evening.

*General stupefaction.* Lomax, Sarah, *and* Barbara *rise:* Sarah *scared, and* Barbara *amused and expectant.*

LOMAX (*remonstrating*):

Oh I say!

LADY BRITOMART:

You are not called on to say anything, Charles.

SARAH:

Are you serious, mother?

LADY BRITOMART:

Of course I am serious. It is on your account, Sarah, and also on Charles's. (*Silence.* Sarah *sits, with a shrug.* Charles *looks painfully unworthy*). I hope you are not going to object, Barbara.

BARBARA:

I! why should I? My father has a soul to be saved like anybody else. He's quite welcome as far as I am concerned. (*She sits on the table, and softly whistles "Onward, Christian Soldiers"*).

LOMAX (*still remonstrant*):

But really, don't you know! Oh I say!

LADY BRITOMART (*frigidly*):

What do you wish to convey, Charles?

LOMAX:

Well, you must admit that this is a bit thick.

LADY BRITOMART (*turning with ominous suavity to* Cusins):

Adolphus: you are a professor of Greek. Can you translate Charles Lomax's remarks into reputable English for us?

CUSINS (*cautiously*):

If I may say so, Lady Brit, I think Charles has rather happily expressed what we all feel. Homer, speaking of Autolycus, uses the same phrase. πυκινὸν δόμον ἐλθεῖν means a bit thick.

LOMAX (*handsomely*):

Not that I mind, you know, if Sarah don't. (*He sits*).

LADY BRITOMART (*crushingly*):

Thank you. Have I your permission, Adolphus, to invite my own husband to my own house?

CUSINS (*gallantly*):

You have my unhesitating support in everything you do.

LADY BRITOMART:

Tush! Sarah: have you nothing to say?

SARAH:

Do you mean that he is coming regularly to live here?

LADY BRITOMART:

Certainly not. The spare room is ready for him if he likes to stay for a day or two and see a little more of you; but there are limits.

SARAH:

Well, he can't eat us, I suppose. *I* don't mind.

LOMAX (*chuckling*):

I wonder how the old man will take it.

LADY BRITOMART:

Much as the old woman will, no doubt, Charles.

LOMAX (*abashed*):

I didn't mean—at least—

LADY BRITOMART:

You didn't think, Charles. You never do; and the result is, you never mean anything. And now please attend to me, children. Your father will be quite a stranger to us.

LOMAX:

I suppose he hasn't seen Sarah since she was a little kid.

LADY BRITOMART:

Not since she was a little kid, Charles, as you express it with that elegance of diction and refinement of thought that seem never to desert you. Accordingly—er—(*impatiently*) Now I have forgotten what I was going to say. That comes of your provoking me to be sarcastic, Charles. Adolphus: will you kindly tell me where I was.

CUSINS (*sweetly*):

You were saying that as Mr Undershaft has not seen his children since they were babies, he will form his opinion of the way you have brought them up from their behavior tonight, and that therefore you wish us all to be particularly careful to conduct ourselves well, especially Charles.

LADY BRITOMART (*with emphatic approval*):

Precisely.

LOMAX:

Look here, Dolly: Lady Brit didn't say that.

LADY BRITOMART (*vehemently*):

I did, Charles. Adolphus's recollection is perfectly correct. It is most important that you should be good; and I do beg you for once not to pair off into opposite corners and giggle and whisper while I am speaking to your father.

BARBARA:

All right, mother. We'll do you credit. (*She comes off the table, and sits in her chair with ladylike elegance*).

LADY BRITOMART:

Remember, Charles, that Sarah will want to feel proud of you instead of ashamed of you.

LOMAX:

Oh I say! there's nothing to be exactly proud of, don't you know.

LADY BRITOMART:

Well, try and look as if there was.

Morrison, *pale and dismayed, breaks into the room in unconcealed disorder.*

MORRISON:

Might I speak a word to you, my lady?

LADY BRITOMART:

Nonsense! Shew him up.

MORRISON:

Yes, my lady. (*He goes*).

LOMAX:

Does Morrison know who it is?

LADY BRITOMART:

Of course. Morrison has always been with us.

LOMAX:

It must be a regular corker for him, don't you know.

LADY BRITOMART:

Is this a moment to get on my nerves, Charles, with your out-
rageous expressions?

LOMAX:

But this is something out of the ordinary, really—

MORRISON (*at the door*):

The—er—Mr Undershaft. (*He retreats in confusion*).

*Andrew Undershaft comes in. All rise. Lady Britomart meets him in the middle of the room behind the settee.*

*Andrew is, on the surface, a stoutish, easygoing elderly man, with kindly patient manners, and an engaging simplicity of character. But he has a watchful, deliberate, waiting, listening face, and formidable reserves of power, both bodily and mental, in his capacious chest and long head. His gentleness is partly that of a strong man who has learnt by experience that his natural grip hurts ordinary people unless he handles them very care-
fully, and partly the mellowness of age and success. He is also a little shy in his present very delicate situation.*

LADY BRITOMART:

Good evening, Andrew.

UNDERSHAFT:

How d'ye do, my dear.

LADY BRITOMART:

You look a good deal older.

UNDERSHAFT (*apologetically*):

I am somewhat older. (*Taking her hand with a touch of courtship*)
Time has stood still with you.

LADY BRITOMART (*throwing away his hand*):

Rubbish! This is your family.

UNDERSHAFT (*surprised*):

Is it so large? I am sorry to say my memory is failing very badly
in some things. (*He offers his hand with paternal kindness to*
Lomax).

LOMAX (*jerkily shaking his hand*):

Ahdedoo.

UNDERSHAFT:

I can see you are my eldest. I am very glad to meet you again,
my boy.

LOMAX (*remonstrating*):

No, but look here don't you know—(*Overcome*) Oh I say!

LADY BRITOMART (*recovering from momentary speechlessness*):

Andrew: do you mean to say that you don't remember how
many children you have?

UNDERSHAFT:

Well, I am afraid I—. They have grown so much—er. Am I making any ridiculous mistake? I may as well confess: I recollect only one son. But so many things have happened since, of course—er—

LADY BRITOMART (*decisively*):

Andrew: you are talking nonsense. Of course you have only one son.

UNDERSHAFT:

Perhaps you will be good enough to introduce me, my dear.

LADY BRITOMART:

That is Charles Lomax, who is engaged to Sarah.

UNDERSHAFT:

My dear sir, I beg your pardon.

LOMAX:

Notatall. Delighted, I assure you.

LADY BRITOMART:

This is Stephen.

UNDERSHAFT (*bowing*):

Happy to make your acquaintance, Mr Stephen. Then (*going to* Cusins) you must be my son. (*Taking* Cusins' *hands in his*) How are you, my young friend? (*To* Lady Britomart) He is very like you, my love.

CUSINS:

You flatter me, Mr Undershaft. My name is Cusins: engaged to Barbara. (*Very explicitly*) That is Major Barbara Undershaft, of the Salvation Army. That is Sarah, your second daughter. This is Stephen Undershaft, your son.

UNDERSHAFT:

My dear Stephen, I beg your pardon.

STEPHEN:

Not at all.

UNDERSHAFT:

Mr Cusins: I am much indebted to you for explaining so precisely. (*Turning to* Sarah) Barbara, my dear—

SARAH (*prompting him*):

Sarah.

UNDERSHAFT:

Sarah, of course. (*They shake hands. He goes over to* Barbara) Barbara—I am right this time, I hope?

BARBARA:

Quite right. (*They shake hands*).

LADY BRITOMART (*resuming command*):

Sit down, all of you. Sit down, Andrew. (*She comes forward and*

*sits on the settee.* Cusins *also brings his chair forward on her left.*
Barbara *and* Stephen *resume their seats.* Lomax *gives his chair to*
Sarah *and goes for another*).

UNDERSHAFT:

Thank you, my love.

LOMAX (*conversationally, as he brings a chair forward between the writing table and the settee, and offers it to* Undershaft):

Takes you some time to find out exactly where you are, don't it?

UNDERSHAFT (*accepting the chair, but remaining standing*):

That is not what embarrasses me, Mr Lomax. My difficulty is
that if I play the part of a father, I shall produce the effect of an
intrusive stranger; and if I play the part of a discreet stranger, I
may appear a callous father.

LADY BRITOMART:

There is no need for you to play any part at all, Andrew. You
had much better be sincere and natural.

UNDERSHAFT (*submissively*):

Yes, my dear: I daresay that will be best. (*He sits down comfortably*). Well, here I am. Now what can I do for you all?

LADY BRITOMART:

You need not do anything, Andrew. You are one of the family.
You can sit with us and enjoy yourself.

*A painfully conscious pause.* Barbara *makes a face at* Lomax, *whose too
long suppressed mirth immediately explodes in agonized neighings.*

LADY BRITOMART (*outraged*):

Charles Lomax: if you can behave yourself, behave yourself. If
not, leave the room.

LOMAX:

I'm awfully sorry, Lady Brit; but really you know, upon my
soul! (*He sits on the settee between* Lady Britomart *and* Undershaft, *quite overcome*).

BARBARA:

Why don't you laugh if you want to, Cholly? It's good for your
inside.

LADY BRITOMART:

Barbara: you have had the education of a lady. Please let your
father see that; and don't talk like a street girl.

UNDERSHAFT:

Never mind me, my dear. As you know, I am not a gentleman;
and I was never educated.

LOMAX (*encouragingly*):

Nobody'd know it, I assure you. You look all right, you know.

CUSINS:

Let me advise you to study Greek, Mr Undershaft. Greek scholars are privileged men. Few of them know Greek; and none of them know anything else; but their position is unchallengeable. Other languages are the qualifications of waiters and commercial travellers: Greek is to a man of position what the hallmark is to silver.

BARBARA:

Dolly: don't be insincere. Cholly: fetch your concertina and play something for us.

LOMAX (*jumps up eagerly, but checks himself to remark doubtfully to* Undershaft):

Perhaps that sort of thing isn't in your line, eh?

UNDERSHAFT:

I am particularly fond of music.

LOMAX (*delighted*):

Are you? Then I'll get it. (*He goes upstairs for the instrument*).

UNDERSHAFT:

Do you play, Barbara?

BARBARA:

Only the tambourine. But Cholly's teaching me the concertina.

UNDERSHAFT:

Is Cholly also a member of the Salvation Army?

BARBARA:

No: he says it's bad form to be a dissenter. But I don't despair of Cholly. I made him come yesterday to a meeting at the dock gates, and take the collection in his hat.

UNDERSHAFT (*looks whimsically at his wife*)!!

LADY BRITOMART:

It is not my doing, Andrew. Barbara is old enough to take her own way. She has no father to advise her.

BARBARA:

Oh yes she has. There are no orphans in the Salvation Army.

UNDERSHAFT:

Your father there has a great many children and plenty of experience, eh?

BARBARA (*looking at him with quick interest and nodding*):

Just so. How did you come to understand that? (Lomax *is heard at the door trying the concertina*).

LADY BRITOMART:

Come in, Charles. Play us something at once.

LOMAX:

Righto! (*He sits down in his former place, and preludes*).

UNDERSHAFT:

One moment, Mr Lomax. I am rather interested in the Salvation Army. Its motto might be my own: Blood and Fire.

LOMAX (*shocked*):

But not your sort of blood and fire, you know.

UNDERSHAFT:

My sort of blood cleanses: my sort of fire purifies.

BARBARA:

So do ours. Come down tomorrow to my shelter—the West Ham shelter—and see what we're doing. We're going to march to a great meeting in the Assembly Hall at Mile End. Come and see the shelter and then march with us: it will do you a lot of good. Can you play anything?

UNDERSHAFT:

In my youth I earned pennies, and even shillings occasionally, in the streets and in public house parlors by my natural talent for stepdancing. Later on, I became a member of the Undershaft orchestral society, and performed passably on the tenor trombone.

LOMAX (*scandalized—putting down the concertina*):

Oh I say!

BARBARA:

Many a sinner has played himself into heaven on the trombone, thanks to the Army.

LOMAX (*to* Barbara, *still rather shocked*):

Yes; but what about the cannon business, don't you know? (*To* Undershaft) Getting into heaven is not exactly in your line, is it?

LADY BRITOMART:

Charles!!!

LOMAX:

Well; but it stands to reason, don't it? The cannon business may be necessary and all that: we can't get on without cannons; but it isn't right, you know. On the other hand, there may be a certain amount of tosh about the Salvation Army—I belong to the Established Church myself—but still you can't deny that it's religion; and you can't go against religion, can you? At least unless you're downright immoral, don't you know.

UNDERSHAFT:

You hardly appreciate my position, Mr Lomax—

LOMAX (*hastily*):

I'm not saying anything against you personally—

UNDERSHAFT:

Quite so, quite so. But consider for a moment. Here I am, a profiteer in mutilation and murder. I find myself in a specially amiable humor just now because, this morning, down at the foundry, we blew twenty-seven dummy soldiers into fragments with a gun which formerly destroyed only thirteen.

LOMAX (*leniently*):

Well, the more destructive war becomes, the sooner it will be abolished, eh?

UNDERSHAFT:

Not at all. The more destructive war becomes the more fascinating we find it. No, Mr Lomax: I am obliged to you for making the usual excuse for my trade; but I am not ashamed of it. I am not one of those men who keep their morals and their business in water-tight compartments. All the spare money my trade rivals spend on hospitals, cathedrals, and other receptacles for conscience money, I devote to experiments and researches in improved methods of destroying life and property. I have always done so; and I always shall. Therefore your Christmas card moralities of peace on earth and goodwill among men are of no use to me. Your Christianity, which enjoins you to resist not evil, and to turn the other cheek, would make me a bankrupt. My morality—my religion—must have a place for cannons and torpedoes in it.

STEPHEN (*coldly—almost sullenly*):

You speak as if there were half a dozen moralities and religions to choose from, instead of one true morality and one true religion.

UNDERSHAFT:

For me there is only one true morality; but it might not fit you, as you do not manufacture aerial battleships. There is only one true morality for every man; but every man has not the same true morality.

LOMAX (*overtaxed*):

Would you mind saying that again? I didn't quite follow it.

CUSINS:

It's quite simple. As Euripides says, one man's meat is another man's poison morally as well as physically.

UNDERSHAFT:

Precisely.

LOMAX:

Oh, that! Yes, yes, yes. True. True.

STEPHEN:

In other words, some men are honest and some are scoundrels.

BARBARA:

Bosh! There are no scoundrels.

UNDERSHAFT:

Indeed? Are there any good men?

BARBARA:

No. Not one. There are neither good men nor scoundrels: there are just children of one Father; and the sooner they stop calling one another names the better. You needn't talk to me: I know them. I've had scores of them through my hands: scoundrels, criminals, infidels, philanthropists, missionaries, county councillors, all sorts. They're all just the same sort of sinner; and there's the same salvation ready for them all.

UNDERSHAFT:

May I ask have you ever saved a maker of cannons?

BARBARA:

No. Will you let me try?

UNDERSHAFT:

Well, I will make a bargain with you. If I go to see you tomorrow in your Salvation Shelter, will you come the day after to see me in my cannon works?

BARBARA:

Take care. It may end in your giving up the cannons for the sake of the Salvation Army.

UNDERSHAFT:

Are you sure it will not end in your giving up the Salvation Army for the sake of the cannons?

BARBARA:

I will take my chance of that.

UNDERSHAFT:

And I will take my chance of the other. (*They shake hands on it*). Where is your shelter?

BARBARA:

In West Ham. At the sign of the cross. Ask anybody in Canning Town. Where are your works?

UNDERSHAFT:

In Perivale St Andrews. At the sign of the sword. Ask anybody in Europe.

LOMAX:

Hadn't I better play something?

BARBARA:

Yes. Give us Onward, Christian Soldiers.

LOMAX:

Well, that's rather a strong order to begin with, don't you

know. Suppose I sing Thou'rt passing hence, my brother. It's much the same tune.

BARBARA:

It's too melancholy. You get saved, Cholly; and you'll pass hence, my brother, without making such a fuss about it.

LADY BRITOMART:

Really, Barbara, you go on as if religion were a pleasant subject. Do have some sense of propriety.

UNDERSHAFT:

I do not find it an unpleasant subject, my dear. It is the only one that capable people really care for.

LADY BRITOMART (*looking at her watch*):

Well, if you are determined to have it, I insist on having it in a proper and respectable way. Charles: ring for prayers.

*General amazement.* Stephen *rises in dismay.*

LOMAX (*rising*):

Oh I say!

UNDERSHAFT (*rising*):

I am afraid I must be going.

LADY BRITOMART:

You cannot go now, Andrew: it would be most improper. Sit down. What will the servants think?

UNDERSHAFT:

My dear: I have conscientious scruples. May I suggest a compromise? If Barbara will conduct a little service in the drawing room, with Mr Lomax as organist, I will attend it willingly. I will even take part, if a trombone can be procured.

LADY BRITOMART:

Don't mock, Andrew.

UNDERSHAFT (*shocked—to* Barbara):

You don't think I am mocking, my love, I hope.

BARBARA:

No, of course not; and it wouldn't matter if you were: half the Army came to their first meeting for a lark. (*Rising*) Come along. (*She throws her arm round her father and sweeps him out, calling to the others from the threshold*) Come, Dolly. Come, Cholly.

Cusins *rises.*

LADY BRITOMART:

I will not be disobeyed by everybody. Adolphus: sit down. (*He does not*). Charles: you may go. You are not fit for prayers: you cannot keep your countenance.

LOMAX:

Oh I say! (*He goes out*).

LADY BRITOMART (*continuing*):

But you, Adolphus, can behave yourself if you choose to. I insist on your staying.

CUSINS:

My dear Lady Brit: there are things in the family prayer book that I couldn't bear to hear you say.

LADY BRITOMART:

What things, pray?

CUSINS:

Well, you would have to say before all the servants that we have done things we ought not to have done, and left undone things we ought to have done, and that there is no health in us. I cannot bear to hear you doing yourself such an injustice, and Barbara such an injustice. As for myself, I flatly deny it: I have done my best. I shouldn't dare to marry Barbara—I couldn't look you in the face—if it were true. So I must go to the drawing room.

LADY BRITOMART (*offended*):

Well, go. (*He starts for the door*). And remember this, Adolphus (*he turns to listen*): I have a very strong suspicion that you went to the Salvation Army to worship Barbara and nothing else. And I quite appreciate the very clever way in which you systematically humbug me. I have found you out. Take care Barbara doesn't. That's all.

CUSINS (*with unruffled sweetness*):

Don't tell on me. (*He steals out*).

LADY BRITOMART:

Sarah: if you want to go, go. Anything's better than to sit there as if you wished you were a thousand miles away.

SARAH (*languidly*):

Very well, mamma. (*She goes*).

Lady Britomart, *with a sudden flounce, gives way to a little gust of tears.*

STEPHEN (*going to her*):

Mother: what's the matter?

LADY BRITOMART (*swishing away her tears with her handkerchief*):

Nothing. Foolishness. You can go with him, too, if you like, and leave me with the servants.

STEPHEN:

Oh, you mustn't think that, mother. I—I don't like him.

LADY BRITOMART:

The others do. That is the injustice of a woman's lot. A woman has to bring up her children; and that means to restrain them, to deny them things they want, to set them tasks, to punish them when they do wrong, to do all the unpleasant things. And then the father, who has nothing to do but pet them and spoil them, comes in when all her work is done and steals their affection from her.

STEPHEN:

He has not stolen our affection from you. It is only curiosity.

LADY BRITOMART (*violently*):

I won't be consoled, Stephen. There is nothing the matter with me. (*She rises and goes towards the door*).

STEPHEN:

Where are you going, mother?

LADY BRITOMART:

To the drawing room, of course. (*She goes out. Onward, Christian Soldiers, on the concertina, with tambourine accompaniment, is heard when the door opens*). Are you coming, Stephen?

STEPHEN:

No. Certainly not. (*She goes. He sits down on the settee, with compressed lips and an expression of strong dislike*).


# Act II

*The yard of the West Ham shelter of the Salvation Army is a cold place on a January morning. The building itself, an old warehouse, is newly whitewashed. Its gabled end projects into the yard in the middle, with a door on the ground floor, and another in the loft above it without any balcony or ladder, but with a pulley rigged over it for hoisting sacks. Those who come from this central gable end into the yard have the gateway leading to the street on their left, with a stone horse-trough just beyond it, and, on the right, a penthouse shielding a table from the weather. There are forms at the table; and on them are seated a man and a woman, both much down on their luck, finishing a meal of bread (one thick slice each, with margarine and golden syrup) and diluted milk.*

*The man, a workman out of employment, is young, agile, a talker, a poser, sharp enough to be capable of anything in reason except honesty or altruistic considerations of any kind. The woman is a commonplace old bundle of poverty and hard-worn humanity. She looks sixty and probably is forty-five. If they were rich people, gloved and muffed and well wrapped up in furs and overcoats, they would be numbed and miserable; for it is a grindingly cold raw January day; and a glance at the background of grimy warehouses and leaden sky visible over the whitewashed walls of the yard would drive any idle rich person straight to the Mediterranean. But these two, being no more troubled with visions of the Mediterranean than of the moon, and being compelled to keep more of their clothes in the pawn-shop, and less on their persons, in winter than in summer, are not depressed by the cold: rather are they stung into vivacity, to which their meal has just now given an almost jolly turn. The man takes a pull at his mug, and then gets up and moves about the yard with his hands deep in his pockets, occasionally breaking into a stepdance.*

THE WOMAN:

Feel better arter your meal, sir?

THE MAN:

No. Call that a meal! Good enough for you, praps; but wot is it to me, an intelligent workin man.

THE WOMAN:

Workin man! Wot are you?

THE MAN:

Painter.

THE WOMAN (*sceptically*):

Yus, I dessay.

THE MAN:

Yus, you dessay! I know. Every loafer that can't do nothink calls isself a painter. Well, I'm a real painter: grainer, finisher, thirty-eight bob a week when I can get it.

THE WOMAN:

Then why don't you go and get it?

THE MAN:

I'll tell you why. Fust: I'm intelligent—fffff! it's rotten cold here (*he dances a step or two*)—yes: intelligent beyond the station o life into which it has pleased the capitalists to call me; and they don't like a man that sees through em. Second, an intelligent bein needs a doo share of appiness; so I drink somethink cruel when I get the chawnce. Third, I stand by my class and do as little as I can so's to leave arf the job for me fellow workers. Fourth, I'm fly enough to know wots inside the law and wots outside it; and inside it I do as the capitalists do: pinch wot I can lay me ands on. In a proper state of society I am sober, industrious and honest: in Rome, so to speak, I do as the Romans do. Wot's the consequence? When trade is bad—and it's rotten bad just now—and the employers az to sack arf their men, they generally start on me.

THE WOMAN:

What's your name?

THE MAN:

Price. Bronterre O'Brien Price. Usually called Snobby Price, for short.

THE WOMAN:

Snobby's a carpenter, ain't it? You said you was a painter.

PRICE:

Not that kind of snob, but the genteel sort. I'm too uppish, owing to my intelligence, and my father being a Chartist and a reading, thinking man: a stationer, too. I'm none of your common hewers of wood and drawers of water; and don't you forget it. (*He returns to his seat at the table, and takes up his mug*). Wot's your name?

THE WOMAN:

Rummy Mitchens, sir.

PRICE (*quaffing the remains of his milk to her*):

Your elth, Miss Mitchens.

RUMMY (*correcting him*):

Missis Mitchens.

PRICE:

Wot! Oh Rummy, Rummy! Respectable married woman, Rummy, gittin rescued by the Salvation Army by pretendin to be a bad un. Same old game!

RUMMY:

What am I to do? I can't starve. Them Salvation lasses is dear good girls; but the better you are, the worse they likes to think you were before they rescued you. Why shouldn't they av a bit o credit, poor loves? they're worn to rags by their work. And where would they get the money to rescue us if we was to let on we're no worse than other people? You know what ladies and gentlemen are.

PRICE:

Thievin swine! Wish I ad their job, Rummy, all the same. Wot does Rummy stand for? Pet name praps?

RUMMY:

Short for Romola.

PRICE:

For wot!?

RUMMY:

Romola. It was out of a new book. Somebody me mother wanted me to grow up like.

PRICE:

> We're companions in misfortune, Rummy. Both on us got names that nobody cawnt pronounce. Consequently I'm Snobby and you're Rummy because Bill and Sally wasn't good enough for our parents. Such is life!

RUMMY:

> Who saved you, Mr Price? Was it Major Barbara?

PRICE:

> No: I come here on my own. I'm going to be Bronterre O'Brien Price, the converted painter. I know wot they like. I'll tell em how I blasphemed and gambled and wopped my poor old mother—

RUMMY (*shocked*):

> Used you to beat your mother?

PRICE:

> Not likely. She used to beat me. No matter: you come and listen to the converted painter, and you'll hear how she was a pious woman that taught me me prayers at er knee, an how I used to come home drunk and drag her out o bed be er snow white airs, an lam into er with the poker.

RUMMY:

> That's what's so unfair to us women. Your confessions is just as big lies as ours: you don't tell what you really done no more than us; but you men can tell your lies right out at the meetins and be made much of for it; while the sort o confessions we az to make az to be wispered to one lady at a time. It ain't right, spite of all their piety.

PRICE:

> Right! Do you spose the Army'd be allowed if it went and did right? Not much. It combs our air and makes us good little blokes to be robbed and put upon. But I'll play the game as good as any of em. I'll see somebody struck by lightnin, or hear a voice sayin "Snobby Price: where will you spend eternity?" I'll av a time of it, I tell you.

RUMMY:

> You won't be let drink, though.

PRICE:

> I'll take it out in gorspellin, then. I don't want to drink if I can get fun enough any other way.

Jenny Hill, *a pale, overwrought, pretty Salvation lass of 18, comes in through the yard gate, leading* Peter Shirley, *a half hardened, half worn-out elderly man, weak with hunger.*

JENNY (*supporting him*):

> Come! pluck up. I'll get you something to eat. You'll be all right then.

PRICE (*rising and hurrying officiously to take the old man off* Jenny's hands):

> Poor old man! Cheer up, brother: you'll find rest and peace and appiness ere. Hurry up with the food, miss: e's fair done. (Jenny *hurries into the shelter*). Ere, buck up, daddy! she's fetchin y'a thick slice o breadn treacle, an a mug o skyblue. (*He seats him at the corner of the table*).

RUMMY (*gaily*):

> Keep up your old art! Never say die!

SHIRLEY:

> I'm not an old man. I'm ony 46. I'm as good as ever I was. The grey patch come in my hair before I was thirty. All it wants is three pennorth o hair dye: am I to be turned on the streets to starve for it? Holy God! I've worked ten to twelve hours a day since I was thirteen, and paid my way all through; and now am I to be thrown into the gutter and my job given to a young man that can do it no better than me because I've black hair that goes white at the first change?

PRICE (*cheerfully*):

> No good jawrin about it. You're ony a jumped-up, jerked-off, orspittle-turned-out incurable of an ole workin man: who cares about you? Eh? Make the thievin swine give you a meal: they've stole many a one from you. Get a bit o your own back. (Jenny *returns with the usual meal*). There you are, brother. Awsk a blessin an tuck that into you.

SHIRLEY (*looking at it ravenously but not touching it, and crying like a child*):

> I never took anything before.

JENNY (*petting him*):

> Come, come! the Lord sends it to you: he wasn't above taking bread from his friends; and why should you be? Besides, when we find you a job you can pay us for it if you like.

SHIRLEY (*eagerly*):

> Yes, yes: that's true. I can pay you back: it's only a loan. (*Shivering*) Oh Lord! oh Lord! (*He turns to the table and attacks the meal ravenously*).

JENNY:

> Well, Rummy, are you more comfortable now?

RUMMY:

> God bless you, lovey! you've fed my body and saved my soul,

havn't you? (Jenny, *touched, kisses her*). Sit down and rest a bit: you must be ready to drop.

JENNY:

I've been going hard since morning. But there's more work than we can do. I mustn't stop.

RUMMY:

Try a prayer for just two minutes. You'll work all the better after.

JENNY (*her eyes lighting up*):

Oh isn't it wonderful how a few minutes prayer revives you! I was quite lightheaded at twelve o'clock, I was so tired; but Major Barbara just sent me to pray for five minutes; and I was able to go on as if I had only just begun. (*To* Price) Did you have a piece of bread?

PRICE (*with unction*):

Yes, miss; but I've got the piece that I value more; and that's the peace that passeth hall hannerstennin.

RUMMY (*fervently*):

Glory Hallelujah!

Bill Walker, *a rough customer of about 25, appears at the yard gate and looks malevolently at* Jenny.

JENNY:

That makes me so happy. When you say that, I feel wicked for loitering here. I must get to work again.

*She is hurrying to the shelter, when the new-comer moves quickly up to the door and intercepts her. His manner is so threatening that she retreats as he comes at her truculently, driving her down the yard.*

BILL:

Aw knaow you. You're the one that took awy maw girl. You're the one that set er agen me. Well, I'm gowin to ev er aht. Not that Aw care a carse for er or you: see? Bat Aw'll let er knaow; and Aw'll let you knaow. Aw'm gowing to give her a doin that'll teach er to cat awy from me. Nah in wiv you and tell er to cam aht afore Aw cam in and kick er aht. Tell er Bill Walker wants er. She'll knaow wot thet means; and if she keeps me witin it'll be worse. You stop to jawr beck at me; and Aw'll stawt on you: d'ye eah? There's your wy. In you gow. (*He takes her by the arm and slings her towards the door of the shelter. She falls on her hand and knee.* Rummy *helps her up again*).

PRICE (*rising, and venturing irresolutely towards* Bill):

Easy there, mate. She ain't doin you no arm.

BILL:

Oo are you callin mite? (*Standing over him threateningly*) You're gowin to stend ap for er, aw yer? Put ap your ends.

RUMMY (*running indignantly to him to scold him*):

Oh, you great brute—(*He instantly swings his left hand back against her face. She screams and reels back to the trough, where she sits down, covering her bruised face with her hands and rocking herself and moaning with pain*).

JENNY (*going to her*):

Oh, God forgive you! How could you strike an old woman like that?

BILL (*seizing her by the hair so violently that she also screams, and tearing her away from the old woman*):

You Gawd forgimme again an Aw'll Gawd forgive you one on the jawr thet'll stop you pryin for a week. (*Holding her and turning fiercely on* Price) Ev you ennything to sy agen it?

PRICE (*intimidated*):

No, matey: she ain't anything to do with me.

BILL:

Good job for you! Aw'd pat two meals into you and fawt you with one finger arter, you stawved cur. (*To* Jenny) Nah are you gowin to fetch aht Mog Ebbijem; or em Aw to knock your fice off you and fetch her meself?

JENNY (*writhing in his grasp*):

Oh please someone go in and tell Major Barbara—(*she screams again as he wrenches her head down; and* Price *and* Rummy *flee into the shelter*).

BILL:

You want to gow in and tell your Mijor of me, do you?

JENNY:

Oh please don't drag my hair. Let me go.

BILL:

Do you or down't you? (*She stifles a scream*). Yus or nao?

JENNY:

God give me strength—

BILL (*striking her with his fist in the face*):

Gow an shaow her thet, and tell her if she wants one lawk it to cam and interfere with me. (Jenny, *crying with pain, goes into the shed. He goes to the form and addresses the old man*). Eah: finish your mess; an git aht o maw wy.

SHIRLEY (*springing up and facing him fiercely, with the mug in his hand*):

You take a liberty with me, and I'll smash you over the face with the mug and cut your eye out. Ain't you satisfied—young whelps like you—with takin the bread out o the mouths of your elders that have brought you up and slaved for you, but you must come shovin and cheekin and bullyin in here, where the bread o charity is sickenin in our stummicks?

BILL (*contemptuously, but backing a little*):

Wot good are you, you aold palsy mag? Wot good are you?

SHIRLEY:

As good as you and better. I'll do a day's work agen you or any fat young soaker of your age. Go and take my job at Horrockses, where I worked for ten year. They want young men there: they can't afford to keep men over forty-five. They're very sorry—give you a character and happy to help you to get anything suited to your years—sure a steady man won't be long out of a job. Well, let em try you. They'll find the differ. What do you know? Not as much as how to beeyave yourself—layin your dirty fist across the mouth of a respectable woman!

BILL:

Downt provowk me to ly it acrost yours: d'ye eah?

SHIRLEY (*with blighting contempt*):

Yes: you like an old man to hit, don't you, when you've finished with the women. I ain't seen you hit a young one yet.

BILL (*stung*):

You loy, you aold soupkitchener, you. There was a yang menn eah. Did Aw offer to itt him or did Aw not?

SHIRLEY:

Was he starvin or was he not? Was he a man or only a crosseyed thief an a loafer? Would you hit my son-in-law's brother?

BILL:

Oo's ee?

SHIRLEY:

Todger Fairmile o Balls Pond. Him that won £20 off the Japanese wrastler at the music hall by standin out 17 minutes 4 seconds agen him.

BILL (*sullenly*):

Aw'm nao music awl wrastler. Ken he box?

SHIRLEY:

Yes: an you can't.

BILL:

Wot! Aw cawn't, cawn't Aw? Wot's thet you sy (*threatening him*)?

SHIRLEY (*not budging an inch*):

Will you box Todger Fairmile if I put him on to you? Say the word.

BILL (*subsiding with a slouch*):

Aw'll stend ap to enny menn alawv, if he was ten Todger Fair-mawls. But Aw don't set ap to be a perfeshnal.

SHIRLEY (*looking down on him with unfathomable disdain*):

You box! Slap an old woman with the back o your hand! You hadn't even the sense to hit her where a magistrate couldn't see the mark of it, you silly young lump of conceit and ignorance. Hit a girl in the jaw and ony make her cry! If Todger Fairmile'd done it, she wouldn't a got up inside o ten minutes, no more than you would if he got on to you. Yah! I'd set about you myself if I had a week's feedin in me instead o two months' starvation. (*He turns his back on him and sits down moodily at the table*).

BILL (*following him and stooping over him to drive the taunt in*):

You loy! you've the bread and treacle in you that you cam eah to beg.

SHIRLEY (*bursting into tears*):

Oh God! it's true: I'm only an old pauper on the scrap heap. (*Furiously*) But you'll come to it yourself; and then you'll know. You'll come to it sooner than a teetotaller like me, fillin yourself with gin at this hour o the mornin!

BILL:

Aw'm nao gin drinker, you oald lawr; bat wen Aw want to give my girl a bloomin good awdin Aw lawk to ev a bit o devil in me: see? An eah Aw emm, talkin to a rotten aold blawter like you sted o givin her wot for. (*Working himself into a rage*) Aw'm gowin in there to fetch her aht. (*He makes vengefully for the shelter door*).

SHIRLEY:

You're goin to the station on a stretcher, more likely; and they'll take the gin and the devil out of you there when they get you inside. You mind what you're about: the major here is the Earl o Stevenage's granddaughter.

BILL (*checked*):

Garn!

SHIRLEY:

You'll see.

BILL (*his resolution oozing*):

Well, Aw ain't dan nathin to er.

SHIRLEY:

S'pose she said you did! who'd believe you?

BILL (*very uneasy, skulking back to the corner of the penthouse*):

Gawd! there's no jastice in this cantry. To think wot them people can do! Aw'm as good as er.

SHIRLEY:

Tell her so. It's just what a fool like you would do.

Barbara, *brisk and businesslike, comes from the shelter with a note book, and addresses herself to* Shirley. Bill, *cowed, sits down in the corner on a form, and turns his back on them.*

BARBARA:

Good morning.

SHIRLEY (*standing up and taking off his hat*):

Good morning, miss.

BARBARA:

Sit down: make yourself at home. (*He hesitates; but she puts a friendly hand on his shoulder and makes him obey*). Now then! since you've made friends with us, we want to know all about you. Names and addresses and trades.

SHIRLEY:

Peter Shirley. Fitter. Chucked out two months ago because I was too old.

BARBARA (*not at all surprised*):

You'd pass still. Why didn't you dye your hair?

SHIRLEY:

I did. Me age come out at a coroner's inquest on me daughter.

BARBARA:

Steady?

SHIRLEY:

Teetotaller. Never out of a job before. Good worker. And sent to the knackers like an old horse!

BARBARA:

No matter: if you did your part God will do his.

SHIRLEY (*suddenly stubborn*):

My religion's no concern of anybody but myself.

BARBARA (*guessing*):

*I* know. Secularist?

SHIRLEY (*hotly*):

Did I offer to deny it?

BARBARA:

Why should you? My own father's a Secularist, I think. Our Father—yours and mine—fulfils himself in many ways; and I daresay he knew what he was about when he made a Secularist of you. So buck up, Peter! we can always find a job for a steady man like you. (Shirley, *disarmed and a little bewildered, touches his hat. She turns from him to* Bill). What's your name?

BILL (*insolently*):

Wot's thet to you?

BARBARA (*calmly making a note*):

Afraid to give his name. Any trade?

BILL:

Oo's afride to give is nime? (*Doggedly, with a sense of heroically defying the House of Lords in the person of* Lord Stevenage) If you want to bring a chawge agen me, bring it. (*She waits, unruffled*). Moy nime's Bill Walker.

BARBARA (*as if the name were familiar: trying to remember how*):

Bill Walker? (*Recollecting*) Oh, I know: you're the man that Jenny Hill was praying for inside just now. (*She enters his name in her note book*).

BILL:

Oo's Jenny Ill? And wot call as she to pry for me?

BARBARA:

I don't know. Perhaps it was you that cut her lip.

BILL (*defiantly*):

Yus, it was me that cat her lip. Aw ain't afride o you.

BARBARA:

How could you be, since you're not afraid of God? You're a brave man, Mr Walker. It takes some pluck to do our work here; but none of us dare lift our hand against a girl like that, for fear of her father in heaven.

BILL (*sullenly*):

I want nan o your kentin jawr. I spowse you think Aw cam eah to beg from you, like this demmiged lot eah. Not me. Aw down't want your bread and scripe and ketlep. Aw don't blieve in your Gawd, no more than you do yourself.

BARBARA (*sunnily apologetic and ladylike, as on a new footing with him*):

Oh, I beg your pardon for putting your name down, Mr Walker. I didn't understand. I'll strike it out.

BILL (*taking this as a slight, and deeply wounded by it*):

Eah! you let maw nime alown. Ain't it good enaff to be in your book?

BARBARA (*considering*):

Well, you see, there's no use putting down your name unless I can do something for you, is there? What's your trade?

BILL (*still smarting*):

Thet's nao concern o yours.

BARBARA:

Just so. (*Very businesslike*) I'll put you down as (*writing*) the man who—struck—poor little Jenny Hill—in the mouth.

BILL (*rising threateningly*):

> See eah. Aw've ed enaff o this.

BARBARA (*quite sunny and fearless*):

> What did you come to us for?

BILL:

> Aw cam for maw gel, see? Aw cam to tike her aht o this and to brike er jawr for er.

BARBARA (*complacently*):

> You see I was right about your trade. (Bill, *on the point of retorting furiously, finds himself, to his great shame and terror, in danger of crying instead. He sits down again suddenly*). What's her name?

BILL (*dogged*):

> Er nime's Mog Ebbijem: thet's wot her nime is.

BARBARA:

> Mog Habbijam! Oh, she's gone to Canning Town, to our barracks there.

BILL (*fortified by his resentment of* Mog's *perfidy*):

> Is she? (*Vindictively*) Then Aw'm gowin to Kennintahn arter her. (*He crosses to the gate; hesitates; finally comes back at* Barbara). Are you loyin to me to git shat o me?

BARBARA:

> I don't want to get shut of you. I want to keep you here and save your soul. You'd better stay: you're going to have a bad time today, Bill.

BILL:

> Oo's gowin to give it to me? You, preps?

BARBARA:

> Someone you don't believe in. But you'll be glad afterwards.

BILL (*slinking off*):

> Aw'll gow to Kennintahn to be aht o reach o your tangue. (*Suddenly turning on her with intense malice*) And if Aw down't fawnd Mog there, Aw'll cam beck and do two years for you, selp me Gawd if Aw down't!

BARBARA (*a shade kindlier, if possible*):

> It's no use, Bill. She's got another bloke.

BILL:

> Wot!

BARBARA:

> One of her own converts. He fell in love with her when he saw her with her soul saved, and her face clean, and her hair washed.

BILL (*surprised*):

> Wottud she wash it for, the carroty slat? It's red.

BARBARA:

It's quite lovely now, because she wears a new look in her eyes with it. It's a pity you're too late. The new bloke has put your nose out of joint, Bill.

BILL:

Aw'll put his nowse aht o joint for him. Not that Aw care a carse for er, mawnd thet. But Aw'll teach her to drop me as if Aw was dirt. And Aw'll teach him to meddle with maw judy. Wots iz bleedin nime?

BARBARA:

Sergeant Todger Fairmile.

SHIRLEY (*rising with grim joy*):

I'll go with him, miss. I want to see them two meet. I'll take him to the infirmary when it's over.

BILL (*to* Shirley, *with undissembled misgiving*):

Is thet im you was speakin on?

SHIRLEY:

That's him.

BILL:

Im that wrastled in the music awl?

SHIRLEY:

The competitions at the National Sportin Club was worth nigh a hundred a year to him. He's gev em up now for religion; so he's a bit fresh for want of the exercise he was accustomed to. He'll be glad to see you. Come along.

BILL:

Wot's is wight?

SHIRLEY:

Thirteen four. (Bill's *last hope expires*).

BARBARA:

Go and talk to him, Bill. He'll convert you.

SHIRLEY:

He'll convert your head into a mashed potato.

BILL (*sullenly*):

Aw ain't afride of im. Aw ain't afride of ennybody Bat e can lick me. She's dan me. (*He sits down moodily on the edge of the horse trough*).

SHIRLEY:

You ain't goin. I thought not. (*He resumes his seat*).

BARBARA (*calling*):

Jenny!

JENNY (*appearing at the shelter door with a plaster on the corner of her mouth*):

Yes, Major.

BARBARA:

> Send Rummy Mitchens out to clear away here.

JENNY:

> I think she's afraid.

BARBARA (*her resemblance to her mother flashing out for a moment*):

> Nonsense! she must do as she's told.

JENNY (*calling into the shelter*):

> Rummy: the Major says you must come.

Jenny *comes to* Barbara, *purposely keeping on the side next* Bill, *lest he should suppose that she shrank from him or bore malice.*

BARBARA:

> Poor little Jenny! Are you tired? (*Looking at the wounded cheek*) Does it hurt?

JENNY:

> No: it's all right now. It was nothing.

BARBARA (*critically*):

> It was as hard as he could hit, I expect. Poor Bill! You don't feel angry with him, do you?

JENNY:

> Oh no, no, no: indeed I don't, Major, bless his poor heart! (Barbara *kisses her; and she runs away merrily into the shelter. Bill writhes with an agonizing return of his new and alarming symptoms, but says nothing.* Rummy Mitchens *comes from the shelter*).

BARBARA (*going to meet Rummy*):

> Now Rummy, bustle. Take in those mugs and plates to be washed; and throw the crumbs about for the birds.

Rummy *takes the three plates and mugs; but* Shirley *takes back his mug from her, as there is still some milk left in it.*

RUMMY:

> There ain't any crumbs. This ain't a time to waste good bread on birds.

PRICE (*appearing at the shelter door*):

> Gentleman come to see the shelter, Major. Says he's your father.

BARBARA:

> All right. Coming. (Snobby *goes back into the shelter, followed by* Barbara).

RUMMY (*stealing across to* Bill *and addressing him in a subdued voice, but with intense conviction*):

> I'd av the lor of you, you flat eared pignosed potwalloper, if

she'd let me. You're no gentleman, to hit a lady in the face. (Bill, *with greater things moving in him, takes no notice*).

SHIRLEY (*following her*):

Here! in with you and don't get yourself into more trouble by talking.

RUMMY (*with hauteur*):

I ain't ad the pleasure o being hintroduced to you, as I can remember. (*She goes into the shelter with the plates*).

SHIRLEY:

That's the—

BILL (*savagely*):

Down't you talk to me, d'ye eah? You lea me alown, or Aw'll do you a mischief. Aw'm not dirt under your feet, ennywy.

SHIRLEY (*calmly*):

Don't you be afeerd. You ain't such prime company that you need expect to be sought after. (*He is about to go into the shelter when* Barbara *comes out, with* Undershaft *on her right*).

BARBARA:

Oh, there you are, Mr Shirley! (*Between them*) This is my father: I told you he was a Secularist, didn't I? Perhaps you'll be able to comfort one another.

UNDERSHAFT (*startled*):

A Secularist! Not the least in the world: on the contrary, a confirmed mystic.

BARBARA:

Sorry, I'm sure. By the way, papa, what is your religion? in case I have to introduce you again.

UNDERSHAFT:

My religion? Well, my dear, I am a Millionaire. That is my religion.

BARBARA:

Then I'm afraid you and Mr Shirley won't be able to comfort one another after all. You're not a Millionaire, are you, Peter?

SHIRLEY:

No; and proud of it.

UNDERSHAFT (*gravely*):

Poverty, my friend, is not a thing to be proud of.

SHIRLEY (*angrily*):

Who made your millions for you? Me and my like. What's kep us poor? Keepin you rich. I wouldn't have your conscience, not for all your income.

UNDERSHAFT:

I wouldn't have your income, not for all your conscience, Mr Shirley. (*He goes to the penthouse and sits down on a form*).

BARBARA (*stopping* Shirley *adroitly as he is about to retort*):

You wouldn't think he was my father, would you, Peter? Will you go into the shelter and lend the lasses a hand for a while: we're worked off our feet.

SHIRLEY (*bitterly*):

Yes: I'm in their debt for a meal, ain't I?

BARBARA:

Oh, not because you're in their debt, but for love of them, Peter, for love of them. (*He cannot understand, and is rather scandalized*) There! don't stare at me. In with you; and give that conscience of yours a holiday (*bustling him into the shelter*).

SHIRLEY (*as he goes in*):

Ah! it's a pity you never was trained to use your reason, miss. You'd have been a very taking lecturer on Secularism.

Barbara *turns to her father.*

UNDERSHAFT:

Never mind me, my dear. Go about your work; and let me watch it for a while.

BARBARA:

All right.

UNDERSHAFT:

For instance, what's the matter with that outpatient over there?

BARBARA (*looking at* Bill, *whose attitude has never changed, and whose expression of brooding wrath has deepened*):

Oh, we shall cure him in no time. Just watch. (*She goes over to Bill and waits. He glances up at her and casts his eyes down again, uneasy, but grimmer than ever*). It would be nice to just stamp on Mog Habbijam's face, wouldn't it, Bill?

BILL (*starting up from the trough in consternation*):

It's a loy: Aw never said so. (*She shakes her head*). Oo taold you wot was in moy mawnd?

BARBARA:

Only your new friend.

BILL:

Wot new friend?

BARBARA:

The devil, Bill. When he gets round people they get miserable, just like you.

BILL (*with a heartbreaking attempt at devil-may-care cheerfulness*):

Aw ain't miserable. (*He sits down again, and stretches his legs in an attempt to seem indifferent*).

BARBARA:

Well, if you're happy, why don't you look happy, as we do?

BILL (*his legs curling back in spite of him*):

Aw'm eppy enaff, Aw tell you. Woy cawn't you lea me alown? Wot ev I dan to you? Aw ain't smashed your fice, ev Aw?

BARBARA (*softly: wooing his soul*):

It's not me that's getting at you, Bill.

BILL:

Oo else is it?

BARBARA:

Somebody that doesn't intend you to smash women's faces, I suppose. Somebody or something that wants to make a man of you.

BILL (*blustering*):

Mike a menn o me! Ain't Aw a menn? eh? Oo sez Aw'm not a menn?

BARBARA:

There's a man in you somewhere, I suppose. But why did he let you hit poor little Jenny Hill? That wasn't very manly of him, was it?

BILL (*tormented*):

Ev dan wiv it, Aw tell you. Chack it. Aw'm sick o your Jenny Ill and er silly little fice.

BARBARA:

Then why do you keep thinking about it? Why does it keep coming up against you in your mind? You're not getting converted, are you?

BILL (*with conviction*):

Not ME. Not lawkly.

BARBARA:

That's right, Bill. Hold out against it. Put out your strength. Don't let's get you cheap. Todger Fairmile said he wrestled for three nights against his salvation harder than he ever wrestled with the Jap at the music hall. He gave in to the Jap when his arm was going to break. But he didn't give in to his salvation until his heart was going to break. Perhaps you'll escape that. You havn't any heart, have you?

BILL:

Wot d'ye mean? Woy ain't Aw got a awt the sime as ennybody else?

BARBARA:

A man with a heart wouldn't have bashed poor little Jenny's face, would he?

BILL (*almost crying*):

Ow, will you lea me alown? Ev Aw ever offered to meddle with you, that you cam neggin and provowkin me lawk this? (*He writhes convulsively from his eyes to his toes*).

BARBARA (*with a steady soothing hand on his arm and a gentle voice that never lets him go*):

It's your soul that's hurting you, Bill, and not me. We've been through it all ourselves. Come with us, Bill. (*He looks wildly round*). To brave manhood on earth and eternal glory in heaven. (*He is on the point of breaking down*). Come. (*A drum is heard in the shelter; and* Bill, *with a gasp, escapes from the spell as* Barbara *turns quickly.* Adolphus *enters from the shelter with a big drum*). Oh! there you are, Dolly. Let me introduce a new friend of mine, Mr Bill Walker. This is my bloke, Bill: Mr Cusins. (Cusins *salutes with his drumstick*).

BILL:

Gowin to merry im?

BARBARA:

Yes.

BILL (*fervently*):

Gawd elp im! Gaw-aw-aw-awd elp im!

BARBARA:

Why? Do you think he won't be happy with me?

BILL:

Aw've aony ed to stend it for a mawnin: e'll ev to stend it for a lawftawm.

CUSINS:

That is a frightful reflection, Mr Walker. But I can't tear myself away from her.

BILL:

Well, Aw ken. (*To* Barbara) Eah! do you knaow where Aw'm gowin to, and wot Aw'm gowin to do?

BARBARA:

Yes: you're going to heaven; and you're coming back here before the week's out to tell me so.

BILL:

You loy. Aw'm gowin to Kennintahn, to spit in Todger Fairmawl's eye. Aw beshed Jenny Ill's fice; an nar Aw'll git me aown fice beshed and cam beck and shaow it to er. Ee'll itt me ardern Aw itt er. That'll mike us square. (*To* Adolphus) Is thet fair or is it not? You're a genlmn: you oughter knaow.

BARBARA:

Two black eyes won't make one white one, Bill.

BILL:

Aw didn't awst you. Cawnt you never keep your mahth shat? Oy awst the genlmn.

CUSINS (*reflectively*):

Yes: I think you're right, Mr Walker. Yes: I should do it. It's curious: it's exactly what an ancient Greek would have done.

BARBARA:

But what good will it do?

CUSINS:

Well, it will give Mr Fairmile some exercise; and it will satisfy Mr Walker's soul.

BILL:

Rot! there ain't nao sach a thing as a saoul. Ah kin you tell wevver Aw've a saoul or not? You never seen it.

BARBARA:

I've seen it hurting you when you went against it.

BILL (*with compressed aggravation*):

If you was maw gel and took the word aht o me mahth'lawk thet, Aw'd give you sathink you'd feel urtin, Aw would. (*To* Adolphus) You tike maw tip, mite. Stop er jawr; or you'll doy afoah your tawm (*With intense expression*) Wore aht: thet's wot you'll be: wore aht. (*He goes away through the gate*).

CUSINS (*looking after him*):

I wonder!

BARBARA:

Dolly! (*indignant, in her mother's manner*).

CUSINS:

Yes, my dear, it's very wearing to be in love with you. If it lasts, I quite think I shall die young.

BARBARA:

Should you mind?

CUSINS:

Not at all. (*He is suddenly softened, and kisses her over the drum, evidently not for the first time, as people cannot kiss over a big drum without practice.* Undershaft *coughs*).

BARBARA:

It's all right, papa, we've not forgotten you. Dolly: explain the place to papa: I haven't time. (*She goes busily into the shelter*).

Undershaft *and* Adolphus *now have the yard to themselves.* Undershaft, *seated on a form, and still keenly attentive, looks hard at* Adolphus. Adolphus *looks hard at him.*

UNDERSHAFT:

I fancy you guess something of what is in my mind, Mr Cusins. (Cusins *flourishes his drumsticks as if in the act of beating a lively rataplan, but makes no sound*). Exactly so. But suppose Barbara finds you out!

CUSINS:

You know, I do not admit that I am imposing on Barbara. I am quite genuinely interested in the views of the Salvation Army. The fact is, I am a sort of collector of religions; and the curious thing is that I find I can believe them all. By the way, have you any religion?

UNDERSHAFT:

Yes.

CUSINS:

Anything out of the common?

UNDERSHAFT:

Only that there are two things necessary to Salvation.

CUSINS (*disappointed, but polite*):

Ah, the Church Catechism. Charles Lomax also belongs to the Established Church.

UNDERSHAFT:

The two things are—

CUSINS:

Baptism and—

UNDERSHAFT:

No. Money and gunpowder.

CUSINS (*surprised, but interested*):

That is the general opinion of our governing classes. The novelty is in hearing any man confess it.

UNDERSHAFT:

Just so.

CUSINS:

Excuse me: is there any place in your religion for honor, justice, truth, love, mercy and so forth?

UNDERSHAFT:

Yes: they are the graces and luxuries of a rich, strong, and safe life.

CUSINS:

Suppose one is forced to choose between them and money or gunpowder?

UNDERSHAFT:

Choose money and gunpowder; for without enough of both you cannot afford the others.

CUSINS:

That is your religion?

UNDERSHAFT:

Yes.

*The cadence of this reply makes a full close in the conversation.* Cusins *twists his face dubiously and contemplates Undershaft. Undershaft contemplates him.*

CUSINS:

Barbara won't stand that. You will have to choose between your religion and Barbara.

UNDERSHAFT:

So will you, my friend. She will find out that that drum of yours is hollow.

CUSINS:

Father Undershaft: you are mistaken: I am a sincere Salvationist. You do not understand the Salvation Army. It is the army of joy, of love, of courage: it has banished the fear and remorse and despair of the old hell-ridden evangelical sects: it marches to fight the devil with trumpet and drum, with music and dancing, with banner and palm, as becomes a sally from heaven by its happy garrison. It picks the waster out of the public house and makes a man of him: it finds a worm wriggling in a back kitchen, and lo! a woman! Men and women of rank too, sons and daughters of the Highest. It takes the poor professor of Greek, the most artificial and self-suppressed of human creatures, from his meal of roots, and lets loose the rhapsodist in him; reveals the true worship of Dionysos to him; sends him down the public street drumming dithyrambs (*he plays a thundering flourish on the drum*).

UNDERSHAFT:

You will alarm the shelter.

CUSINS:

Oh, they are accustomed to these sudden ecstasies. However, if the drum worries you—(*he pockets the drumsticks; unhooks the drum; and stands it on the ground opposite the gateway*).

UNDERSHAFT:

Thank you.

CUSINS:

You remember what Euripides says about your money and gunpowder?

UNDERSHAFT:

No.

CUSINS (*declaiming*):

One and another
In money and guns may outpass his brother;
And men in their millions float and flow
And seethe with a million hopes as leaven;
And they win their will; or they miss their will;
And their hopes are dead or are pined for still;
But who'er can know
As the long days go
That to live is happy, has found his heaven.

My translation: what do you think of it?

UNDERSHAFT:

I think, my friend, that if you wish to know, as the long days go, that to live is happy, you must first acquire money enough for a decent life, and power enough to be your own master.

CUSINS:

You are damnably discouraging. (*He resumes his declamation*).

Is it so hard a thing to see
That the spirit of God—whate'er it be—
The law that abides and changes not, ages long,
The Eternal and Nature-born: these things be strong?
What else is Wisdom? What of Man's endeavor,
Or God's high grace so lovely and so great?
To stand from fear set free? to breathe and wait?
To hold a hand uplifted over Fate?
And shall not Barbara be loved for ever?

UNDERSHAFT:

Euripides mentions Barbara, does he?

CUSINS:

It is a fair translation. The word means Loveliness.

UNDERSHAFT:

May I ask—as Barbara's father—how much a year she is to be loved for ever on?

CUSINS:

As Barbara's father, that is more your affair than mine. I can feed her by teaching Greek: that is about all.

UNDERSHAFT:

Do you consider it a good match for her?

CUSINS (*with polite obstinacy*):

Mr Undershaft: I am in many ways a weak, timid, ineffectual person; and my health is far from satisfactory. But whenever I feel that I must have anything, I get it, sooner or later. I feel that way about Barbara. I don't like marriage: I feel intensely afraid of it; and I don't know what I shall do with Barbara or what she will do with me. But I feel that I and nobody else must marry her. Please regard that as settled.—Not that I wish to be arbitrary; but why should I waste your time in discussing what is inevitable?

UNDERSHAFT:

You mean that you will stick at nothing: not even the conversion of the Salvation Army to the worship of Dionysos.

CUSINS:

The business of the Salvation Army is to save, not to wrangle about the name of the pathfinder. Dionysos or another: what does it matter?

UNDERSHAFT (*rising and approaching him*):

Professor Cusins: you are a young man after my own heart.

CUSINS:

Mr Undershaft: you are, as far as I am able to gather, a most infernal old rascal; but you appeal very strongly to my sense of ironic humor.

Undershaft *mutely offers his hand. They shake.*

UNDERSHAFT (*suddenly concentrating himself*):

And now to business.

CUSINS:

Pardon me. We are discussing religion. Why go back to such an uninteresting and unimportant subject as business?

UNDERSHAFT:

Religion is our business at present, because it is through religion alone that we can win Barbara.

CUSINS:

Have you, too, fallen in love with Barbara?

UNDERSHAFT:

Yes, with a father's love.

CUSINS:

A father's love for a grown-up daughter is the most dangerous of all infatuations. I apologize for mentioning my own pale, coy, mistrustful fancy in the same breath with it.

UNDERSHAFT:

Keep to the point. We have to win her; and we are neither of us Methodists.

CUSINS:

That doesn't matter. The power Barbara wields here—the

power that wields Barbara herself—is not Calvinism, not Pres-
byterianism, not Methodism—

UNDERSHAFT:

Not Greek Paganism either, eh?

CUSINS:

I admit that. Barbara is quite original in her religion.

UNDERSHAFT (*triumphantly*):

Aha! Barbara Undershaft would be. Her inspiration comes
from within herself.

CUSINS:

How do you suppose it got there?

UNDERSHAFT (*in towering excitement*):

It is the Undershaft inheritance. I shall hand on my torch to my
daughter. She shall make my converts and preach my gospel—

CUSINS:

What! Money and gunpowder!

UNDERSHAFT:

Yes, money and gunpowder. Freedom and power. Command
of life and command of death.

CUSINS (*urbanely: trying to bring him down to earth*):

That is extremely interesting, Mr Undershaft. Of course you
know that you are mad.

UNDERSHAFT (*with redoubled force*):

And you?

CUSINS:

Oh, mad as a hatter. You are welcome to my secret since I have
discovered yours. But I am astonished. Can a madman make
cannons?

UNDERSHAFT:

Would anyone else than a madman make them? And now (*with
surging energy*) question for question. Can a sane man translate
Euripides?

CUSINS:

No.

UNDERSHAFT (*seizing him by the shoulder*):

Can a sane woman make a man of a waster or a woman of a
worm?

CUSINS (*reeling before the storm*):

Father Colossus—Mammoth Millionaire—

UNDERSHAFT (*pressing him*):

Are there two mad people or three in this Salvation shelter
today?

CUSINS:

You mean Barbara is as mad as we are?

UNDERSHAFT (*pushing him lightly off and resuming his equanimity suddenly and completely*):

Pooh, Professor! let us call things by their proper names. I am a millionaire; you are a poet; Barbara is a savior of souls. What have we three to do with the common mob of slaves and idolaters? (*He sits down again with a shrug of contempt for the mob*).

CUSINS:

Take care! Barbara is in love with the common people. So am I. Have you never felt the romance of that love?

UNDERSHAFT (*cold and sardonic*):

Have you ever been in love with Poverty, like St Francis? Have you ever been in love with Dirt, like St Simeon! Have you ever been in love with disease and suffering, like our nurses and philanthropists? Such passions are not virtues, but the most unnatural of all the vices. This love of the common people may please an earl's granddaughter and a university professor; but I have been a common man and a poor man; and it has no romance for me. Leave it to the poor to pretend that poverty is a blessing: leave it to the coward to make a religion of his cowardice by preaching humility: we know better than that. We three must stand together above the common people: how else can we help their children to climb up beside us? Barbara must belong to us, not to the Salvation Army.

CUSINS:

Well, I can only say that if you think you will get her away from the Salvation Army by talking to her as you have been talking to me, you don't know Barbara.

UNDERSHAFT:

My friend: I never ask for what I can buy.

CUSINS (*in a white fury*):

Do I understand you to imply that you can buy Barbara?

UNDERSHAFT:

No; but I can buy the Salvation Army.

CUSINS:

Quite impossible.

UNDERSHAFT:

You shall see. All religious organizations exist by selling themselves to the rich.

CUSINS:

Not the Army. That is the Church of the poor.

UNDERSHAFT:

All the more reason for buying it.

CUSINS:

I don't think you quite know what the Army does for the poor.

UNDERSHAFT:

Oh yes I do. It draws their teeth: that is enough for me as a man of business.

CUSINS:

Nonsense! It makes them sober—

UNDERSHAFT:

I prefer sober workmen. The profits are larger.

CUSINS:

—honest—

UNDERSHAFT:

Honest workmen are the most economical.

CUSINS:

—attached to their homes—

UNDERSHAFT:

So much the better: they will put up with anything sooner than change their shop.

CUSINS:

—happy—

UNDERSHAFT:

An invaluable safeguard against revolution.

CUSINS:

—unselfish—

UNDERSHAFT:

Indifferent to their own interests, which suits me exactly.

CUSINS:

—with their thoughts on heavenly things—

UNDERSHAFT (*rising*):

And not on Trade Unionism nor Socialism. Excellent.

CUSINS (*revolted*):

You really are an infernal old rascal.

UNDERSHAFT (*indicating* Peter Shirley, *who has just come from the shelter and strolled dejectedly down the yard between them*):

And this is an honest man!

SHIRLEY:

Yes; and what av I got by it? (*he passes on bitterly and sits on the form, in the corner of the penthouse*).

Snobby Price, *beaming sanctimoniously, and* Jenny Hill, *with a tambourine full of coppers, come from the shelter and go to the drum, on which* Jenny *begins to count the money.*

UNDERSHAFT (*replying to* Shirley):

Oh, your employers must have got a good deal by it from first to last. (*He sits on the table, with one foot on the side form,* Cusins, *overwhelmed, sits down on the same form nearer the shelter. Barbara comes from the shelter to the middle of the yard. She is excited and a little overwrought).*

BARBARA:

We've just had a splendid experience meeting at the other gate in Cripps's lane. I've hardly ever seen them so much moved as they were by your confession, Mr Price.

PRICE:

I could almost be glad of my past wickedness if I could believe that it would elp to keep hathers stright.

BARBARA:

So it will, Snobby. How much, Jenny?

JENNY:

Four and tenpence, Major.

BARBARA:

Oh Snobby, if you had given your poor mother just one more kick, we should have got the whole five shillings!

PRICE:

If she heard you say that, miss, she'd be sorry I didn't. But I'm glad. Oh what a joy it will be to her when she hears I'm saved!

UNDERSHAFT:

Shall I contribute the odd twopence, Barbara? The million-aire's mite, eh? (*He takes a couple of pennies from his pocket*).

BARBARA:

How did you make that twopence?

UNDERSHAFT:

As usual. By selling cannons, torpedoes, submarines, and my new patent Grand Duke hand grenade.

BARBARA:

Put it back in your pocket. You can't buy your salvation here for twopence: you must work it out.

UNDERSHAFT:

Is twopence not enough? I can afford a little more, if you press me.

BARBARA:

Two million millions would not be enough. There is bad blood on your hands; and nothing but good blood can cleanse them. Money is no use. Take it away. (*She turns to* Cusins). Dolly: you must write another letter for me to the papers. (*He makes a wry face*). Yes: I know you don't like it; but it must be done. The starvation this winter is beating us: everybody is unemployed. The General says we must close this shelter if we can't get more money. I force the collections at the meetings until I am ashamed: don't I, Snobby?

PRICE:

It's a fair treat to see you work it, miss. The way you got them up from three-and-six to four-and-ten with that hymn, penny by penny and verse by verse, was a caution. Not a Cheap Jack on Mile End Waste could touch you at it.

BARBARA:

Yes; but I wish we could do without it. I am getting at last to think more of the collection than of the people's souls. And what are those hatfuls of pence and halfpence? We want thousands! tens of thousands! hundreds of thousands! I want to convert people, not to be always begging for the Army in a way I'd die sooner than beg for myself.

UNDERSHAFT (*in profound irony*):

Genuine unselfishness is capable of anything, my dear.

BARBARA (*unsuspectingly, as she turns away to take the money from the drum and put it in a cash bag she carries*):

Yes, isn't it? (Undershaft *looks sardonically at* Cusins).

CUSINS (*aside to* Undershaft):

Mephistopheles! Machiavelli!

BARBARA (*tears coming into her eyes as she ties the bag and pockets it*):

How are we to feed them? I can't talk religion to a man with bodily hunger in his eyes. (*Almost breaking down*) It's frightful.

JENNY (*running to her*):

Major, dear—

BARBARA (*rebounding*):

No: don't comfort me. It will be all right. We shall get the money.

UNDERSHAFT:

How?

JENNY:

By praying for it, of course. Mrs Baines says she prayed for it last night; and she has never prayed for it in vain: never once. (*She goes to the gate and looks out into the street*).

BARBARA (*who has dried her eyes and regained her composure*):

By the way, dad, Mrs Baines has come to march with us to our big meeting this afternoon; and she is very anxious to meet you, for some reason or other. Perhaps she'll convert you.

UNDERSHAFT:

I shall be delighted, my dear.

JENNY (*at the gate: excitedly*):

Major! Major! here's that man back again.

JENNY:

> The man that hit me. Oh, I hope he's coming back to join us.

Bill Walker, *with frost on his jacket, comes through the gate, his hands deep in his pockets and his chin sunk between his shoulders, like a cleaned-out gambler. He halts between* Barbara *and the drum.*

BARBARA:

> Hullo, Bill! Back already!

BILL (*nagging at her*):

> Bin talkin ever sence, ev you?

BARBARA:

> Pretty nearly. Well, has Todger paid you out for poor Jenny's jaw?

BILL:

> Nao e ain't.

BARBARA:

> I thought your jacket looked a bit snowy.

BILL:

> Sao it is snaowy. You want to knaow where the snaow cam from, down't you?

BARBARA:

> Yes.

BILL:

> Well, it cam from orf the grahnd in Pawkinses Corner in Kennintahn. It got rabbed orf be maw shaoulders: see?

BARBARA:

> Pity you didn't rub some off with your knees, Bill! That would have done you a lot of good.

BILL (*with sour mirthless humor*):

> Aw was sivin anather menn's knees at the tawm. E was kneelin on moy ed, e was.

JENNY:

> Who was kneeling on your head?

BILL:

> Todger was. E was pryin for me: pryin camfortable wiv me as a cawpet. Sow was Mog. Sao was the aol bloomin meetin. Mog she sez "Ow Lawd brike is stabborn sperrit; bat down't urt is dear art." Thet was wot she said. "Down't urt is dear art"! An er blowk—thirteen stun four!—kneelin wiv all is wight on me. Fanny, ain't it?

JENNY:

> Oh no. We're so sorry, Mr Walker.

BARBARA (*enjoying it frankly*):

Nonsense! of course it's funny. Served you right, Bill! You must have done something to him first.

BILL (*doggedly*):

Aw did wot Aw said Aw'd do. Aw spit in is eye. E looks ap at the skoy and sez, "Ow that Aw should be fahnd worthy to be spit upon for the gospel's sike!" e sez; an Mog sez "Glaory Allelloolier!"; an then e called me Braddher, an dahned me as if Aw was a kid and e was me mather worshin me a Setterda nawt. Aw edn't jast nao shaow wiv im at all. Arf the street pryed; an the tather arf larfed fit to split theirselves. (*To Barbara*) There! are you settisfawd nah?

BARBARA (*her eyes dancing*):

Wish I'd been there, Bill.

BILL:

Yus: you'd a got in a hextra bit o talk on me, wouldn't you?

JENNY:

I'm so sorry, Mr Walker.

BILL (*fiercely*):

Down't you gow bein sorry for me: you've no call. Listen eah. Aw browk your jawr.

JENNY:

No, it didn't hurt me: indeed it didn't, except for a moment. It was only that I was frightened.

BILL:

Aw down't want to be forgive be you, or be ennybody. Wot Aw did Aw'll py for. Aw trawd to gat me aown jawr browk to settisfaw you—

JENNY (*distressed*):

Oh no—

BILL (*impatiently*):

Tell y' Aw did: cawn't you listen to wot's bein taold you? All Aw got be it was bein mide a sawt of in the pablic street for me pines. Well, if Aw cawn't settisfaw you one wy, Aw ken anather. Listen eah! Aw ed two quid sived agen the frost; an Aw've a pahnd of it left. A mite o mawn last week ed words with the judy e's gowin to merry. E give er wot-for; an e's bin fawnd fifteen bob. E ed a rawt to itt er cause they was gowin to be merrid; but Aw edn't nao rawt to itt you; sao put anather fawv bob on an call it a pahnd's worth. (*He produces a sovereign*). Eah's the manney. Tike it; and let's ev no more o your forgivin an pryin and your Mijor jawrin me. Let wot Aw dan be dan an pide for; and let there be a end of it.

JENNY:

Oh, I couldn't take it, Mr Walker. But if you would give a shilling or two to poor Rummy Mitchens! you really did hurt her; and she's old.

BILL (*contemptuously*):

Not lawkly. Aw'd give her anather as soon as look at er. Let her ev the lawr o me as she threatened! She ain't forgiven me: not mach. Wot Aw dan to er is not on me mawnd—wot she (*indicating* Barbara) mawt call on me conscience—no more than stickin a pig. It's this Christian gime o yours that Aw wown't ev plyed agen me: this bloomin forgivin an neggin an jawrin that mikes a menn thet sore that iz lawf's a burdn to im. Aw wown't ev it, Aw tell you; sao tike your manney and stop thraowin your silly beshed fice hap agen me.

JENNY:

Major: may I take a little of it for the Army?

BARBARA:

No: the Army is not to be bought. We want your soul, Bill; and we'll take nothing less.

BILL (*bitterly*):

Aw knaow. Me an maw few shillins is not good enaff for you. You're a earl's grendorter, you are. Nathink less than a anderd pahnd for you.

UNDERSHAFT:

Come, Barbara! you could do a great deal of good with a hundred pounds. If you will set this gentleman's mind at ease by taking his pound, I will give the other ninety-nine.

Bill, *dazed by such opulence, instinctively touches his cap.*

BARBARA:

Oh, you're too extravagant, papa. Bill offers twenty pieces of silver. All you need offer is the other ten. That will make the standard price to buy anybody who's for sale. I'm not; and the Army's not. (*To* Bill) You'll never have another quiet moment, Bill, until you come round to us. You can't stand out against your salvation.

BILL (*sullenly*):

Aw cawn't stend aht agen music awl wrastlers and awtful tangued women. Awve offered to py. Aw can do no more. Tike it or leave it. There it is. (*He throws the sovereign on the drum, and sits down on the horse-trough. The coin fascinates* Snobby Price, *who takes an early opportunity of dropping his cap on it*).

Mrs Baines *comes from the shelter. She is dressed as a Salvation Army Commissioner. She is an earnest looking woman of about 40, with a caressing, urgent voice, and an appealing manner.*

BARBARA:

This is my father, Mrs Baines. (Undershaft *comes from the table, taking his hat off with marked civility*). Try what you can do with him. He won't listen to me, because he remembers what a fool I was when I was a baby. (*She leaves them together and chats with Jenny*).

MRS BAINES:

Have you been shewn over the shelter, Mr Undershaft? You know the work we're doing, of course.

UNDERSHAFT (*very civilly*):

The whole nation knows it, Mrs Baines.

MRS BAINES:

No, sir: the whole nation does not know it, or we should not be crippled as we are for want of money to carry our work through the length and breadth of the land. Let me tell you that there would have been rioting this winter in London but for us.

UNDERSHAFT:

You really think so?

MRS BAINES:

I know it. I remember 1886, when you rich gentlemen hardened your hearts against the cry of the poor. They broke the windows of your clubs in Pall Mall.

UNDERSHAFT (*gleaming with approval of their method*):

And the Mansion House Fund went up next day from thirty thousand pounds to seventy-nine thousand! I remember quite well.

MRS BAINES:

Well, won't you help me to get at the people? They won't break windows then. Come here, Price. Let me shew you to this gentleman (Price *comes to be inspected*). Do you remember the window breaking?

PRICE:

My ole father thought it was the revolution, ma'am.

MRS BAINES:

Would you break windows now?

PRICE:

Oh no, ma'am. The windows of eaven av bin opened to me. I know now that the rich man is a sinner like myself.

RUMMY (*appearing above at the loft door*):

 Snobby Price!

SNOBBY:

 Wot is it?

RUMMY:

 Your mother's askin for you at the other gate in Cripps's Lane.
 She's heard about your confession (Price *turns pale*),

MRS BAINES:

 Go, Mr Price; and pray with her.

JENNY:

 You can go through the shelter, Snobby.

PRICE (*to* Mrs Baines):

 I couldn't face her now, ma'am, with all the weight of my sins
 fresh on me. Tell her she'll find her son at ome, waitin for her
 in prayer. (*He skulks off through the gate, incidentally stealing the
 sovereign on his way out by picking up his cap from the drum*).

MRS BAINES (*with swimming eyes*):

 You see how we take the anger and the bitterness against you
 out of their hearts, Mr Undershaft.

UNDERSHAFT:

 It is certainly most convenient and gratifying to all large
 employers of labor, Mrs Baines.

MRS BAINES:

 Barbara: Jenny: I have good news: most wonderful news.
 (Jenny *runs to her*). My prayers have been answered. I told you
 they would, Jenny, didn't I?

JENNY:

 Yes, yes.

BARBARA (*moving nearer to the drum*):

 Have we got money enough to keep the shelter open?

MRS BAINES:

 I hope we shall have enough to keep all the shelters open. Lord
 Saxmundham has promised us five thousand pounds—

BARBARA:

 Hooray!

JENNY:

 Glory!

MRS BAINES:

 —if—

BARBARA:

 "If!" If what?

MRS BAINES:

 —if five other gentlemen will give a thousand each to make it
 up to ten thousand.

BARBARA:

Who is Lord Saxmundham? I never heard of him.

UNDERSHAFT (*who has pricked up his ears at the peer's name, and is now watching* Barbara *curiously*):

A new creation, my dear. You have heard of Sir Horace Bodger?

BARBARA:

Bodger! Do you mean the distiller? Bodger's whisky!

UNDERSHAFT:

That is the man. He is one of the greatest of our public bene-factors. He restored the cathedral at Hakington. They made him a baronet for that. He gave half a million to the funds of his party: they made him a baron for that.

SHIRLEY:

What will they give him for the five thousand?

UNDERSHAFT:

There is nothing left to give him. So the five thousand, I should think, is to save his soul.

MRS BAINES:

Heaven grant it may! Oh Mr Undershaft, you have some very rich friends. Can't you help us towards the other five thou-sand? We are going to hold a great meeting this afternoon at the Assembly Hall in the Mile End Road. If I could only announce that one gentleman had come forward to support Lord Saxmundham, others would follow. Don't you know somebody? couldn't you? wouldn't you? (*her eyes fill with tears*) oh, think of those poor people, Mr Undershaft: think of how much it means to them, and how little to a great man like you.

UNDERSHAFT (*sardonically gallant*):

Mrs Baines: you are irresistible. I can't disappoint you; and I can't deny myself the satisfaction of making Bodger pay up. You shall have your five thousand pounds.

MRS BAINES:

Thank God!

UNDERSHAFT:

You don't thank me?

MRS BAINES:

Oh sir, don't try to be cynical: don't be ashamed of being a good man. The Lord will bless you abundantly; and our prayers will be like a strong fortification round you all the days of your life. (*With a touch of caution*) You will let me have the cheque to shew at the meeting, won't you? Jenny: go in and fetch a pen and ink. (Jenny *runs to the shelter door*).

UNDERSHAFT:

Do not disturb Miss Hill: I have a fountain pen (Jenny *halts. He sits at the table and writes the cheque.* Cusins *rises to make room for him. They all watch him silently*).

BILL (*cynically, aside to* Barbara, *his voice and accent horribly debased*):

Wot prawce selvytion nah?

BARBARA:

Stop. (Undershaft *stops writing: they all turn to her in surprise*). Mrs Baines: are you really going to take this money?

MRS BAINES (*astonished*):

Why not, dear?

BARBARA:

Why not! Do you know what my father is? Have you forgotten that Lord Saxmundham is Bodger the whisky man? Do you remember how we implored the County Council to stop him from writing Bodger's Whisky in letters of fire against the sky; so that the poor drink-ruined creatures on the Embankment could not wake up from their snatches of sleep without being reminded of their deadly thirst by that wicked sky sign? Do you know that the worst thing I have had to fight here is not the devil, but Bodger, Bodger, Bodger, with his whisky, his distilleries, and his tied houses? Are you going to make our shelter another tied house for him, and ask me to keep it?

BILL:

Rotten dranken whisky it is too.

MRS BAINES:

Dear Barbara: Lord Saxmundham has a soul to be saved like any of us. If heaven has found the way to make a good use of his money, are we to set ourselves up against the answer to our prayers?

BARBARA:

I know he has a soul to be saved. Let him come down here; and I'll do my best to help him to his salvation. But he wants to send his cheque down to buy us, and go on being as wicked as ever.

UNDERSHAFT (*with a reasonableness which* Cusins *alone perceives to be ironical*):

My dear Barbara: alcohol is a very necessary article. It heals the sick—

BARBARA:

It does nothing of the sort.

UNDERSHAFT:

Well, it assists the doctor: that is perhaps a less questionable way of putting it. It makes life bearable to millions of people who could not endure their existence if they were quite sober. It enables Parliament to do things at eleven at night that no sane person would do at eleven in the morning. Is it Bodger's fault that this inestimable gift is deplorably abused by less than one per cent of the poor? (*He turns again to the table; signs the cheque; and crosses it*).

MRS BAINES:

Barbara: will there be less drinking or more if all those poor souls we are saving come tomorrow and find the doors of our shelters shut in their faces? Lord Saxmundham gives us the money to stop drinking—to take his own business from him.

CUSINS (*impishly*):

Pure self-sacrifice on Bodger's part, clearly! Bless dear Bodger! (Barbara *almost breaks down as* Adolphus, *too, fails her*).

UNDERSHAFT (*tearing out the cheque and pocketing the book as he rises and goes past* Cusins *to* Mrs Baines):

I also, Mrs Baines, may claim a little disinterestedness. Think of my business! think of the widows and orphans! the men and lads torn to pieces with shrapnel and poisoned with lyddite! (Mrs Baines *shrinks; but he goes on remorselessly*) the oceans of blood, not one drop of which is shed in a really just cause! the ravaged crops! the peaceful peasants forced, women and men, to till their fields under the fire of opposing armies on pain of starvation! the bad blood of the fierce little cowards at home who egg on others to fight for the gratification of their national vanity! All this makes money for me: I am never richer, never busier than when the papers are full of it. Well, it is your work to preach peace on earth and goodwill to men. (Mrs Baines's *face lights up again*). Every convert you make is a vote against war. (*Her lips move in prayer*). Yet I give you this money to help you to hasten my own commercial ruin. (*He gives her the cheque*).

CUSINS (*mounting the form in an ecstasy of mischief*):

The millennium will be inaugurated by the unselfishness of Undershaft and Bodger. Oh be joyful! (*He takes the drum-sticks from his pocket and flourishes them*).

MRS BAINES (*taking the cheque*):

The longer I live the more proof I see that there is an Infinite Goodness that turns everything to the work of salvation sooner or later. Who would have thought that any good could have come out of war and drink? And yet their profits are brought today to the feet of salvation to do its blessed work. (*She is affected to tears*).

JENNY (*running to* Mrs Baines *and throwing her arms round her*):

Oh dear! how blessed, how glorious it all is!

CUSINS (*in a convulsion of irony*):

Let us seize this unspeakable moment. Let us march to the great meeting at once. Excuse me just an instant. (*He rushes into the shelter.* Jenny *takes her tambourine from the drum head*).

MRS BAINES:

Mr Undershaft: have you ever seen a thousand people fall on their knees with one impulse and pray? Come with us to the meeting. Barbara shall tell them that the Army is saved, and saved through you.

CUSINS (*returning impetuously from the shelter with a flag and a trombone, and coming between* Mrs Baines *and* Undershaft):

You shall carry the flag down the first street, Mrs Baines (*he gives her the flag*). Mr Undershaft is a gifted trombonist: he shall intone an Olympian diapason to the West Ham Salvation March. (*Aside to* Undershaft, *as he forces the trombone on him*) Blow, Machiavelli, blow.

UNDERSHAFT (*aside to him, as he takes the trombone*):

The trumpet in Zion! (Cusins *rushes to the drum, which he takes up and puts on.* Undershaft *continues, aloud*) I will do my best. I could vamp a bass if I knew the tune.

CUSINS:

It is a wedding chorus from one of Donizetti's operas; but we have converted it. We convert everything to good here, including Bodger. You remember the chorus. "For thee immense rejoicing—immenso giubilo—immenso giubilo." (*With drum obbligato*) Rum tum ti tum tum, tum tum ti ta—

BARBARA:

Dolly: you are breaking my heart.

CUSINS:

What is a broken heart more or less here? Dionysos Undershaft has descended. I am possessed.

MRS BAINES:

Come, Barbara: I must have my dear Major to carry the flag with me.

JENNY:

Yes, yes, Major darling.

CUSINS (*snatches the tambourine out of* Jenny's *hand and mutely offers it to* Barbara).

BARBARA (*coming forward a little as she puts the offer behind her with a shudder, whilst* Cusins *recklessly tosses the tambourine back to* Jenny *and goes to the gate*):

I can't come.

JENNY:

Not come!

MRS BAINES (*with tears in her eyes*):

Barbara: do you think I am wrong to take the money?

BARBARA (*impulsively going to her and kissing her*):

No, no: God help you, dear, you must: you are saving the Army. Go; and may you have a great meeting!

JENNY:

But arn't you coming?

BARBARA:

No. (*She begins taking off the silver S brooch from her collar*).

MRS BAINES:

Barbara: what are you doing?

JENNY:

Why are you taking your badge off? You can't be going to leave us, Major.

BARBARA (*quietly*):

Father: come here.

UNDERSHAFT (*coming to her*):

My dear! (*Seeing that she is going to pin the badge on his collar, he retreats to the penthouse in some alarm*).

BARBARA (*following him*):

Don't be frightened. (*She pins the badge on and steps back towards the table, shewing him to the others*) There! It's not much for £5000, is it?

MRS BAINES:

Barbara: if you won't come and pray with us, promise me you will pray for us.

BARBARA:

I can't pray now. Perhaps I shall never pray again.

MRS. BAINES:

Barbara!

JENNY:

Major!

BARBARA (*almost delirious*):

I can't bear any more. Quick march!

CUSINS (*calling to the procession in the street outside*):

Off we go. Play up, there! Immenso giubilo. (*He gives the time with his drum; and the band strikes up the march, which rapidly becomes more distant as the procession moves briskly away*).

MRS BAINES:

I must go, dear. You're overworked: you will be all right tomorrow. We'll never lose you. Now Jenny: step out with the old flag. Blood and Fire! (*She marches out through the gate with her flag*).

JENNY:

Glory Hallelujah! (*flourishing her tambourine and marching*).

UNDERSHAFT (*to* Cusins, *as he marches out past him easing the slide of his trombone*):

"My ducats and my daughter"!

CUSINS (*following him out*):

Money and gunpowder!

BARBARA:

Drunkenness and Murder! My God: why hast thou forsaken me?

*She sinks on the form with her face buried in her hands. The march passes away into silence.* Bill Walker *steals across to her.*

BILL (*taunting*):

Wot prawce selvytion nah?

SHIRLEY:

Don't you hit her when she's down.

BILL:

She itt me wen aw wiz dahn. Waw shouldn't Aw git a bit o me aown beck?

BARBARA (*raising her head*):

I didn't take your money, Bill. (*She crosses the yard to the gate and turns her back on the two men to hide her face from them*).

BILL (*sneering after her*):

Naow, it warn't enaff for you. (*Turning to the drum, he misses the money*) Ellow! If you ain't took it sammun else ez. Were's it gorn? Bly me if Jenny Ill didn't tike it arter all!

RUMMY (*screaming at him from the loft*):

You lie, you dirty blackguard! Snobby Price pinched it off the drum when he took up his cap. I was up here all the time an see im do it.

BILL:

Wot! Stowl maw manney! Waw didn't you call thief on him, you silly aold macker you?

RUMMY:

To serve you aht for ittin me acrost the fice. It's cost y'pahnd, that az. (*Raising a pœan of squalid triumph*) I done you. I'm even with you. I've ad it aht o y—(Bill *snatches up* Shirley's *mug and hurls it at her. She slams the loft door and vanishes. The mug smashes against the door and falls in fragments*).

BILL (*beginning to chuckle*):

Tell us, aol menn, wot o'clock this mawnin was it wen im as they call Snobby Prawce was sived?

BARBARA (*turning to him more composedly, and with unspoiled sweetness*):

About half past twelve, Bill. And he pinched your pound at a quarter to two. *I* know. Well, you can't afford to lose it. I'll send it to you.

BILL (*his voice and accent suddenly improving*):

Not if Aw wiz to stawve for it. Aw ain't to be bought.

SHIRLEY:

Ain't you? You'd sell yourself to the devil for a pint o beer; ony there ain't no devil to make the offer.

BILL (*unshamed*)

Sao Aw would, mite, and often ev, cheerful. But she cawn't baw me. (*Approaching* Barbara) You wanted maw saoul, did you? Well, you ain't got it.

BARBARA:

I nearly got it, Bill. But we've sold it back to you for ten thousand pounds.

SHIRLEY:

And dear at the money!

BARBARA:

No, Peter: it was worth more than money.

BILL (*salvationproof*):

It's nao good: you cawn't get rahnd me nah. Aw down't blieve in it; and Aw've seen tody that Aw was rawt. (*Going*) Sao long, aol soupkitchener! Ta, ta, Mijor Earl's Grendorter! (*Turning at the gate*) Wot prawce selvytion nah? Snobby Prawce! Ha! ha!

BARBARA (*offering her hand*):

Goodbye, Bill.

BILL (*taken aback, half plucks his cap off; then shoves it on again defiantly*):

Git aht. (Barbara *drops her hand, discouraged. He has a twinge of remorse*). But thets aw rawt, you knaow. Nathink pasnl. Naow mellice. Sao long, Judy. (*He goes*).

BARBARA:

No malice. So long, Bill.

SHIRLEY (*shaking his head*):

You make too much of him, miss, in your innocence.

BARBARA (*going to him*):

Peter: I'm like you now. Cleaned out, and lost my job.

SHIRLEY:

You've youth an hope. That's two better than me.

BARBARA:

I'll get you a job, Peter. That's hope for you: the youth will have to be enough for me. (*She counts her money*). I have just enough left for two teas at Lockharts, a Rowton doss for you, and my tram and bus home. (*He frowns and rises with offended pride. She takes his arm*). Don't be proud, Peter: it's sharing between friends. And promise me you'll talk to me and not let me cry. (*She draws him towards the gate*).

SHIRLEY:

Well, I'm not accustomed to talk to the like of you—

BARBARA (*urgently*):

Yes, yes: you must talk to me. Tell me about Tom Paine's books and Bradlaugh's lectures. Come along.

SHIRLEY:

Ah, if you would only read Tom Paine in the proper spirit, miss! (*They go out through the gate together*).

# Act III

*Next day after lunch* Lady Britomart *is writing in the library in Wilton Crescent.* Sarah *is reading in the armchair near the window.* Barbara, *in ordinary fashionable dress, pale and brooding, is on the settee.* Charles Lomax *enters. He starts on seeing* Barbara *fashionably attired and in low spirits.*

LOMAX:

You've left off your uniform!

Barbara *says nothing; but an expression of pain passes over her face.*

LADY BRITOMART (*warning him in low tones to be careful*):

Charles!

LOMAX (*much concerned, coming behind the settee and bending sympathetically over* Barbara)

I'm awfully sorry, Barbara. You know I helped you all I could with the concertina and so forth. (*Momentously*) Still, I have never shut my eyes to the fact that there is a certain amount of tosh about the Salvation Army. Now the claims of the Church of England—

LADY BRITOMART:

That's enough, Charles. Speak of something suited to your mental capacity.

LOMAX:

But surely the Church of England is suited to all our capacities.

BARBARA (*pressing his hand*):

Thank you for your sympathy, Cholly. Now go and spoon with Sarah.

LOMAX (*dragging a chair from the writing table and seating himself affectionately by* Sarah's *side*)

How is my ownest today?

SARAH:

I wish you wouldn't tell Cholly to do things, Barbara. He always comes straight and does them. Cholly: we're going to the works this afternoon.

LOMAX:

What works?

SARAH:

The cannon works.

LOMAX:

What? your governor's shop!

SARAH:

Yes.

LOMAX:

Oh I say!

Cusins *enters in poor condition. He also starts visibly when he sees* Barbara *without her uniform.*

BARBARA:

I expected you this morning, Dolly. Didn't you guess that?

CUSINS (*sitting down beside her*)

I'm sorry. I have only just breakfasted.

SARAH:

But we've just finished lunch.

BARBARA:

Have you had one of your bad nights?

CUSINS:

No: I had rather a good night: in fact, one of the most remarkable nights I have ever passed.

BARBARA:

The meeting?

CUSINS:

No: after the meeting.

LADY BRITOMART:

You should have gone to bed after the meeting. What were you doing?

CUSINS:

Drinking.

| LADY BRITOMART: | Adolphus! |
| SARAH: | Dolly! |
| BARBARA: | Dolly! |
| LOMAX: | Oh I say! |

LADY BRITOMART:

What were you drinking, may I ask?

CUSINS:

A most devilish kind of Spanish burgundy, warranted free from added alcohol: a Temperance burgundy in fact. Its richness in natural alcohol made any addition superfluous.

BARBARA:

Are you joking, Dolly?

CUSINS (*patiently*):

No. I have been making a night of it with the nominal head of this household: that is all.

LADY BRITOMART:

Andrew made you drunk!

CUSINS:

No: he only provided the wine. I think it was Dionysos who made me drunk. (*To* Barbara) I told you I was possessed.

LADY BRITOMART:

You're not sober yet. Go home to bed at once.

CUSINS:

I have never before ventured to reproach you, Lady Brit; but how could you marry the Prince of Darkness?

LADY BRITOMART:

It was much more excusable to marry him than to get drunk with him. That is a new accomplishment of Andrew's, by the way. He usen't to drink.

CUSINS:

He doesn't now. He only sat there and completed the wreck of my moral basis, the rout of my convictions, the purchase of my soul. He cares for you, Barbara. That is what makes him so dangerous to me.

BARBARA:

That has nothing to do with it, Dolly. There are larger loves and diviner dreams than the fireside ones. You know that, don't you?

CUSINS:

Yes: that is our understanding. I know it. I hold to it. Unless he can win me on that holier ground he may amuse me for a while; but he can get no deeper hold, strong as he is.

BARBARA:

Keep to that; and the end will be right. Now tell me what happened at the meeting?

CUSINS:

It was an amazing meeting. Mrs Baines almost died of emotion. Jenny Hill simply gibbered with hysteria. The Prince of

Darkness played his trombone like a madman: its brazen roarings were like the laughter of the damned. 117 conversions took place then and there. They prayed with the most touching sincerity and gratitude for Bodger, and for the anonymous donor of the £5000. Your father would not let his name be given.

LOMAX:

That was rather fine of the old man, you know. Most chaps would have wanted the advertisement.

CUSINS:

He said all the charitable institutions would be down on him like kites on a battle-field if he gave his name.

LADY BRITOMART:

That's Andrew all over. He never does a proper thing without giving an improper reason for it.

CUSINS:

He convinced me that I have all my life been doing improper things for proper reasons.

LADY BRITOMART:

Adolphus: now that Barbara has left the Salvation Army, you had better leave it too. I will not have you playing that drum in the streets.

CUSINS:

Your orders are already obeyed, Lady Brit.

BARBARA:

Dolly: were you ever really in earnest about it? Would you have joined if you had never seen me?

CUSINS (*disingenuously*):

Well—er—well, possibly, as a collector of religions—

LOMAX (*cunningly*):

Not as a drummer, though, you know. You are a very clear-headed brainy chap, Dolly; and it must have been apparent to you that there is a certain amount of tosh about—

LADY BRITOMART:

Charles: if you must drivel, drivel like a grown-up man and not like a schoolboy.

LOMAX (*out of countenance*):

Well, drivel is drivel, don't you know, whatever a man's age.

LADY BRITOMART:

In good society in England, Charles, men drivel at all ages by repeating silly formulas with an air of wisdom. Schoolboys make their own formulas out of slang, like you. When they reach your age, and get political private secretaryships and things of that sort, they drop slang and get their formulas out of The Spectator or The Times. You had better confine yourself to The Times. You will find that there is a certain amount of tosh about The Times; but at least its language is reputable.

LOMAX (*overwhelmed*):

You are so awfully strong-minded, Lady Brit—

LADY BRITOMART:

Rubbish! (Morrison *comes in*). What is it?

MORRISON:

If you please, my lady, Mr Undershaft has just drove up to the door.

LADY BRITOMART:

Well, let him in. (Morrison *hesitates*). What's the matter with you?

MORRISON:

Shall I announce him, my lady; or is he at home here, so to speak, my lady?

LADY BRITOMART:

Announce him.

MORRISON:

Thank you, my lady. You won't mind my asking, I hope. The occasion is in a manner of speaking new to me.

LADY BRITOMART:

Quite right. Go and let him in.

MORRISON:

Thank you, my lady. (*He withdraws*).

LADY BRITOMART:

Children: go and get ready. (Sarah *and* Barbara *go upstairs for their out-of-door wraps*). Charles: go and tell Stephen to come down here in five minutes: you will find him in the drawing room. (Charles *goes*). Adolphus: tell them to send round the carriage in about fifteen minutes. (Adolphus *goes*).

MORRISON (*at the door*):

Mr Undershaft.

Undershaft *comes in*. Morrison *goes out*.

UNDERSHAFT:

Alone! How fortunate!

LADY BRITOMART (*rising*):

Don't be sentimental, Andrew. Sit down. (*She sits on the settee: he sits beside her, on her left. She comes to the point before he has time to breathe*). Sarah must have £800 a year until Charles Lomax comes into his property. Barbara will need more, and need it permanently, because Adolphus hasn't any property.

UNDERSHAFT (*resignedly*):

Yes, my dear: I will see to it. Anything else? for yourself, for instance?

LADY BRITOMART:

I want to talk to you about Stephen.

UNDERSHAFT (*rather wearily*):

Don't my dear. Stephen doesn't interest me.

LADY BRITOMART:

He does interest me. He is our son.

UNDERSHAFT:

Do you really think so? He has induced us to bring him into the world; but he chose his parents very incongruously, I think. I see nothing of myself in him, and less of you.

LADY BRITOMART:

Andrew: Stephen is an excellent son, and a most steady, capable, highminded young man. You are simply trying to find an excuse for disinheriting him.

UNDERSHAFT:

My dear Biddy: the Undershaft tradition disinherits him. It would be dishonest of me to leave the cannon foundry to my son.

LADY BRITOMART:

It would be most unnatural and improper of you to leave it to anyone else, Andrew. Do you suppose this wicked and immoral tradition can be kept up for ever? Do you pretend that Stephen could not carry on the foundry just as well as all the other sons of the big business houses?

UNDERSHAFT:

Yes: he could learn the office routine without understanding the business, like all the other sons; and the firm would go on by its own momentum until the real Undershaft—probably an Italian or a German—would invent a new method and cut him out.

LADY BRITOMART:

There is nothing that any Italian or German could do that Stephen could not do. And Stephen at least has breeding.

UNDERSHAFT:

The son of a foundling! Nonsense!

LADY BRITOMART:

My son, Andrew! And even you may have good blood in your veins for all you know.

UNDERSHAFT:

True. Probably I have. That is another argument in favor of a foundling.

LADY BRITOMART:

> Andrew: don't be aggravating. And don't be wicked. At present you are both.

UNDERSHAFT:

> This conversation is part of the Undershaft tradition, Biddy. Every Undershaft's wife has treated him to it ever since the house was founded. It is mere waste of breath. If the tradition be ever broken it will be for an abler man than Stephen.

LADY BRITOMART (*pouting*):

> Then go away.

UNDERSHAFT (*deprecatory*):

> Go away!

LADY BRITOMART:

> Yes: go away. If you will do nothing for Stephen, you are not wanted here. Go to your foundling, whoever he is; and look after him.

UNDERSHAFT:

> The fact is, Biddy—

LADY BRITOMART:

> Don't call me Biddy. I don't call you Andy.

UNDERSHAFT:

> I will not call my wife Britomart: it is not good sense. Seriously, my love, the Undershaft tradition has landed me in a difficulty. I am getting on in years; and my partner Lazarus has at last made a stand and insisted that the succession must be settled one way or the other; and of course he is quite right. You see, I haven't found a fit successor yet.

LADY BRITOMART (*obstinately*):

> There is Stephen.

UNDERSHAFT:

> That's just it: all the foundlings I can find are exactly like Stephen.

LADY BRITOMART:

> Andrew!!

UNDERSHAFT:

> I want a man with no relations and no schooling: that is, a man who would be out of the running altogether if he were not a strong man. And I can't find him. Every blessed foundling nowadays is snapped up in his infancy by Barnardo homes, or School Board officers, or Boards of Guardians; and if he shews the least ability he is fastened on by schoolmasters; trained to win scholarships like a racehorse; crammed with secondhand ideas; drilled and disciplined in docility and what they call good taste; and lamed for life so that he is fit for nothing but

teaching. If you want to keep the foundry in the family, you
had better find an eligible foundling and marry him to Barbara.

LADY BRITOMART:

Ah! Barbara! Your pet! You would sacrifice Stephen to Barbara.

UNDERSHAFT:

Cheerfully. And you, my dear, would boil Barbara to make
soup for Stephen.

LADY BRITOMART:

Andrew: this is not a question of our likings and dislikings: it
is a question of duty. It is your duty to make Stephen your successor.

UNDERSHAFT:

Just as much as it is your duty to submit to your husband.
Come, Biddy! these tricks of the governing class are of no use
with me. I am one of the governing class myself; and it is waste
of time giving tracts to a missionary. I have the power in this
matter; and I am not to be humbugged into using it for your
purposes.

LADY BRITOMART:

Andrew: you can talk my head off; but you can't change wrong
into right. And your tie is all on one side. Put it straight.

UNDERSHAFT (*disconcerted*):

It won't stay unless it's pinned (*he fumbles at it with childish gri-
maces*)—

Stephen *comes in.*

STEPHEN (*at the door*):

I beg your pardon (*about to retire*).

LADY BRITOMART:

No: come in, Stephen. (Stephen *comes forward to his mother's
writing table*).

UNDERSHAFT (*not very cordially*):

Good afternoon.

STEPHEN (*coldly*)

Good afternoon.

UNDERSHAFT (*to* Lady Britomart)

He knows all about the tradition, I suppose?

LADY BRITOMART:

Yes. (*To* Stephen) It is what I told you last night, Stephen.

UNDERSHAFT (*sulkily*):

I understand you want to come into the cannon business.

STEPHEN:

*I* go into trade! Certainly not.

UNDERSHAFT (*opening his eyes, greatly eased in mind and manner*):

Oh! in that case—

LADY BRITOMART:

Cannons are not trade, Stephen. They are enterprise.

STEPHEN:

I have no intention of becoming a man of business in any sense. I have no capacity for business and no taste for it. I intend to devote myself to politics.

UNDERSHAFT (*rising*):

My dear boy: this is an immense relief to me. And I trust it may prove an equally good thing for the country. I was afraid you would consider yourself disparaged and slighted. (*He moves toward* Stephen *as if to shake hands with him*).

LADY BRITOMART (*rising and interposing*):

Stephen: I cannot allow you to throw away an enormous property like this.

STEPHEN (*stiffly*)

Mother: there must be an end of treating me as a child, if you please. (Lady Britomart *recoils, deeply wounded by his tone*). Until last night I did not take your attitude seriously, because I did not think you meant it seriously. But I find now that you left me in the dark as to matters which you should have explained to me years ago. I am extremely hurt and offended. Any further discussion of my intentions had better take place with my father, as between one man and another.

LADY BRITOMART:

Stephen! (*She sits down again, her eyes filling with tears*).

UNDERSHAFT (*with grave compassion*):

You see, my dear, it is only the big men who can be treated as children.

STEPHEN:

I am sorry, mother, that you have forced me—

UNDERSHAFT (*stopping him*):

Yes, yes, yes, yes: that's all right, Stephen. She won't interfere with you any more: your independence is achieved: you have won your latchkey. Don't rub it in; and above all, don't apologize. (*He resumes his seat*). Now what about your future, as between one man and another—I beg your pardon, Biddy: as between two men and a woman.

LADY BRITOMART (*who has pulled herself together strongly*):

I quite understand, Stephen. By all means go your own way if you feel strong enough. (Stephen *sits down magisterially in the chair at the writing table with an air of affirming his majority*).

UNDERSHAFT:

It is settled that you do not ask for the succession to the cannon business.

STEPHEN:

I hope it is settled that I repudiate the cannon business.

UNDERSHAFT:

Come, come! don't be so devilishly sulky: it's boyish. Freedom should be generous. Besides, I owe you a fair start in life in exchange for disinheriting you. You can't become prime minister all at once. Haven't you a turn for something? What about literature, art, and so forth?

STEPHEN:

I have nothing of the artist about me, either in faculty or character, thank Heaven!

UNDERSHAFT:

A philosopher, perhaps? Eh?

STEPHEN:

I make no such ridiculous pretension.

UNDERSHAFT:

Just so. Well, there is the army, the navy, the Church, the Bar. The Bar requires some ability. What about the Bar?

STEPHEN:

I have not studied law. And I am afraid I have not the necessary push—I believe that is the name barristers give to their vulgarity—for success in pleading.

UNDERSHAFT:

Rather a difficult case, Stephen. Hardly anything left but the stage, is there? (Stephen *makes an impatient movement*). Well, come! is there anything you know or care for?

STEPHEN (*rising and looking at him steadily*)

I know the difference between right and wrong.

UNDERSHAFT (*hugely tickled*):

You don't say so! What! no capacity for business, no knowledge of law, no sympathy with art, no pretension to philosophy; only a simple knowledge of the secret that has puzzled all the philosophers, baffled all the lawyers, muddled all the men of business, and ruined most of the artists: the secret of right and wrong. Why, man, you're a genius, a master of masters, a god! At twentyfour, too!

STEPHEN (*keeping his temper with difficulty*):

You are pleased to be facetious. I pretend to nothing more than any honorable English gentleman claims as his birthright (*he sits down angrily*).

UNDERSHAFT:

Oh, that's everybody's birthright. Look at poor little Jenny Hill, the Salvation lassie! she would think you were laughing at her if you asked her to stand up in the street and teach grammar or geography or mathematics or even drawing room dancing; but it never occurs to her to doubt that she can teach morals and religion. You are all alike, you respectable people. You can't tell me the bursting strain of a ten-inch gun, which is a very simple matter; but you all think you can tell me the bursting strain of a man under temptation. You daren't handle high explosives; but you're all ready to handle honesty and truth and justice and the whole duty of man, and kill one another at that game. What a country! What a world!

LADY BRITOMART (*uneasily*):

What do you think he had better do, Andrew?

UNDERSHAFT:

Oh, just what he wants to do. He knows nothing and he thinks he knows everything. That points clearly to a political career. Get him a private secretaryship to someone who can get him an Under Secretaryship; and then leave him alone. He will find his natural and proper place in the end on the Treasury Bench.

STEPHEN (*springing up again*):

I am sorry, sir, that you force me to forget the respect due to you as my father. I am an Englishman and I will not hear the Government of my country insulted. (*He thrusts his hands in his pockets, and walks angrily across to the window*).

UNDERSHAFT (*with a touch of brutality*):

The government of your country! *I* am the government of your country: I, and Lazarus. Do you suppose that you and half a dozen amateurs like you, sitting in a row in that foolish gabble shop, can govern Undershaft and Lazarus? No, my friend: you will do what pays us. You will make war when it suits us, and keep peace when it doesn't. You will find out that trade requires certain measures when we have decided on those measures. When I want anything to keep my dividends up, you will discover that my want is a national need. When other people want something to keep my dividends down, you will call out the police and military. And in return you shall have the support and applause of my newspapers, and the delight of imagining that you are a great statesman. Government of your country! Be off with you, my boy, and play with your caucuses and leading articles and historic parties and great leaders and burning questions and the rest of your toys. *I* am going back to my counting-house to pay the piper and call the tune.

STEPHEN (*actually smiling, and putting his hand on his father's shoulder with indulgent patronage*):

Really, my dear father, it is impossible to be angry with you. You don't know how absurd all this sounds to me. You are very properly proud of having been industrious enough to make money; and it is greatly to your credit that you have made so much of it. But it has kept you in circles where you are valued for your money and deferred to for it, instead of in the doubtless very old-fashioned and behind-the-times public school and university where I formed my habits of mind. It is natural for you to think that money governs England; but you must allow me to think I know better.

UNDERSHAFT:

And what does govern England, pray?

STEPHEN:

Character, father, character.

UNDERSHAFT:

Whose character? Yours or mine?

STEPHEN:

Neither yours nor mine, father, but the best elements in the English national character.

UNDERSHAFT:

Stephen: I've found your profession for you. You're a born journalist. I'll start you with a high-toned weekly review. There!

*Before* Stephen *can reply* Sarah, Barbara, Lomax, *and* Cusins *come in ready for walking.* Barbara *crosses the room to the window and looks out.* Cusins *drifts amiably to the armchair.* Lomax *remains near the door, whilst* Sarah *comes to her mother.*

Stephen *goes to the smaller writing table and busies himself with his letters.*

SARAH:

Go and get ready, mamma: the carriage is waiting. (Lady Britomart *leaves the room*).

UNDERSHAFT (*to* Sarah):

Good day, my dear. Good afternoon, Mr Lomax.

LOMAX (*vaguely*):

Ahdedoo.

UNDERSHAFT (*to* Cusins):

Quite well after last night, Euripides, eh?

CUSINS:

As well as can be expected.

UNDERSHAFT:

> That's right. (*To* Barbara) So you are coming to see my death and devastation factory, Barbara?

BARBARA (*at the window*):

> You came yesterday to see my salvation factory. I promised you a return visit.

LOMAX (*coming forward between* Sarah *and* Undershaft):

> You'll find it awfully interesting. I've been through the Woolwich Arsenal; and it gives you a ripping feeling of security, you know, to think of the lot of beggars we could kill if it came to fighting. (*To* Undershaft, *with sudden solemnity*) Still, it must be rather an awful reflection for you, from the religious point of view as it were. You're getting on, you know, and all that.

SARAH:

> You don't mind Cholly's imbecility, papa, do you?

LOMAX (*much taken aback*):

> Oh I say!

UNDERSHAFT:

> Mr Lomax looks at the matter in a very proper spirit, my dear.

LOMAX:

> Just so. That's all I meant, I assure you.

SARAH:

> Are you coming, Stephen?

STEPHEN:

> Well, I am rather busy—er—(*Magnanimously*) Oh well, yes: I'll come. That is, if there is room for me.

UNDERSHAFT:

> I can take two with me in a little motor I am experimenting with for field use. You won't mind its being rather unfashionable. It's not painted yet; but it's bullet proof.

LOMAX (*appalled at the prospect of confronting Wilton Crescent in an unpainted motor*):

> Oh I say!

SARAH:

> The carriage for me, thank you. Barbara doesn't mind what she's seen in.

LOMAX:

> I say, Dolly, old chap: do you really mind the car being a guy? Because of course if you do I'll go in it. Still—

CUSINS:

> I prefer it.

LOMAX:

> Thanks awfully, old man. Come, my ownest. (*He hurries out to secure his seat in the carriage.* Sarah *follows him*).

CUSINS (*moodily walking across to* Lady Britomart*'s writing table*):

Why are we two coming to this Works Department of Hell? that is what I ask myself.

BARBARA:

I have always thought of it as a sort of pit where lost creatures with blackened faces stirred up smoky fires and were driven and tormented by my father. Is it like that, dad?

UNDERSHAFT (*scandalized*):

My dear! It is a spotlessly clean and beautiful hillside town.

CUSINS:

With a Methodist chapel? Oh do say there's a Methodist chapel.

UNDERSHAFT:

There are two: a Primitive one and a sophisticated one. There is even an Ethical Society; but it is not much patronized, as my men are all strongly religious. In the High Explosives Sheds they object to the presence of Agnostics as unsafe.

CUSINS:

And yet they don't object to you!

BARBARA:

Do they obey all your orders?

UNDERSHAFT:

I never give them any orders. When I speak to one of them it is "Well, Jones, is the baby doing well? and has Mrs Jones made a good recovery?" "Nicely, thank you, sir." And that's all.

CUSINS:

But Jones has to be kept in order. How do you maintain discipline among your men?

UNDERSHAFT:

I don't. They do. You see, the one thing Jones won't stand is any rebellion from the man under him, or any assertion of social equality between the wife of the man with 4 shillings a week less than himself, and Mrs Jones! Of course they all rebel against me, theoretically. Practically, every man of them keeps the man just below him in his place. I never meddle with them. I never bully them. I don't even bully Lazarus. I say that certain things are to be done; but I don't order anybody to do them. I don't say, mind you, that there is no ordering about and snubbing and even bullying. The men snub the boys and order them about; the carmen snub the sweepers; the artisans snub the unskilled laborers; the foremen drive and bully both the laborers and artisans; the assistant engineers find fault with the foremen; the chief engineers drop on the assistants; the departmental managers worry the chiefs; and the clerks have tall hats and hymnbooks and keep up the social tone by refusing to associate on equal terms with any-body. The result is a colossal profit, which comes to me.

CUSINS (*revolted*):

You really are a—well, what I was saying yesterday.

BARBARA:

What was he saying yesterday?

UNDERSHAFT:

Never mind, my dear. He thinks I have made you unhappy. Have I?

BARBARA:

Do you think I can be happy in this vulgar silly dress? I! who have worn the uniform. Do you understand what you have done to me? Yesterday I had a man's soul in my hand. I set him in the way of life with his face to salvation. But when we took your money he turned back to drunkenness and derision. (*With intense conviction*) I will never forgive you that. If I had a child, and you destroyed its body with your explosives—if you murdered Dolly with your horrible guns—I could forgive you if my forgiveness would open the gates of heaven to you. But to take a human soul from me, and turn it into the soul of a wolf! that is worse than any murder.

UNDERSHAFT:

Does my daughter despair so easily? Can you strike a man to the heart and leave no mark on him?

BARBARA (*her face lighting up*):

Oh, you are right: he can never be lost now: where was my faith?

CUSINS:

Oh, clever clever devil!

BARBARA:

You may be a devil; but God speaks through you sometimes. (*She takes her father's hands and kisses them*). You have given me back my happiness: I feel it deep down now, though my spirit is troubled.

UNDERSHAFT:

You have learnt something. That always feels at first as if you had lost something.

BARBARA:

Well, take me to the factory of death; and let me learn some-thing more. There must be some truth or other behind all this frightful irony. Come, Dolly. (*She goes out*).

CUSINS:

My guardian angel! (*To* Undershaft) Avaunt! (*He follows* Barbara).

STEPHEN (*quietly, at the writing table*):

> You must not mind Cusins, father. He is a very amiable good
> fellow; but he is a Greek scholar and naturally a little eccentric.

UNDERSHAFT:

> Ah, quite so. Thank you, Stephen. Thank you. (*He goes out*).

Stephen *smiles patronizingly; buttons his coat responsibly; and crosses the
room to the door.* Lady Britomart, *dressed for out-of-doors, opens it before
he reaches it. She looks round for the others; looks at* Stephen; *and turns
to go without a word.*

STEPHEN (*embarrassed*)

> Mother—

LADY BRITOMART:

> Don't be apologetic, Stephen. And don't forget that you have
> outgrown your mother. (*She goes out*).

*Perivale St Andrews lies between two Middlesex hills, half climbing the
northern one. It is an almost smokeless town of white walls, roofs of narrow
green slates or red tiles, tall trees, domes, campaniles, and slender chimney
shafts, beautifully situated and beautiful in itself. The best view of it is
obtained from the crest of a slope about half a mile to the east, where the
high explosives are dealt with. The foundry lies hidden in the depths
between, the tops of its chimneys sprouting like huge skittles into the middle distance. Across the crest runs an emplacement of concrete, with a
firestep, and a parapet which suggests a fortification, because there is a
huge cannon of the obsolete Woolwich Infant pattern peering across it at
the town. The cannon is mounted on an experimental gun carriage: possibly the original model of the Undershaft disappearing rampart gun
alluded to by Stephen. The firestep, being a convenient place to sit, is furnished here and there with straw disc cushions; and at one place there is
the additional luxury of a fur rug.*

Barbara *is standing on the firestep, looking over the parapet towards
the town. On her right is the cannon; on her left the end of a shed raised
on piles, with a ladder of three or four steps up to the door, which opens out-
wards and has a little wooden landing at the threshold, with a fire bucket
in the corner of the landing. Several dummy soldiers more or less mutilated, with straw protruding from their gashes, have been shoved out of the
way under the landing. A few others are nearly upright against the shed;
and one has fallen forward and lies, like a grotesque corpse, on the
emplacement. The parapet stops short of the shed, leaving a gap which is
the beginning of the path down the hill through the foundry to the town.
The rug is on the firestep near this gap. Down on the emplacement behind
the cannon is a trolley carrying a huge conical bombshell with a red band*

*painted on it. Further to the right is the door of an office, which, like the sheds, is of the lightest possible construction.*

Cusins *arrives by the path from the town.*

BARBARA:

Well?

CUSINS:

Not a ray of hope. Everything perfect! wonderful! real! It only needs a cathedral to be a heavenly city instead of a hellish one.

BARBARA:

Have you found out whether they have done anything for old Peter Shirley?

CUSINS:

They have found him a job as gatekeeper and time-keeper. He's frightfully miserable. He calls the time-keeping brain-work, and says he isn't used to it; and his gate lodge is so splendid that he's ashamed to use the rooms, and skulks in the scullery.

BARBARA:

Poor Peter!

Stephen *arrives from the town. He carries a fieldglass.*

STEPHEN (*enthusiastically*):

Have you two seen the place? Why did you leave us?

CUSINS:

I wanted to see everything I was not intended to see; and Barbara wanted to make the men talk.

STEPHEN:

Have you found anything discreditable?

CUSINS:

No. They call him Dandy Andy and are proud of his being a cunning old rascal; but it's all horribly, frightfully, immorally, unanswerably perfect.

Sarah *arrives.*

SARAH:

Heavens! what a place! (*She crosses to the trolley*). Did you see the nursing home!? (*She sits down on the shell*).

STEPHEN:

Did you see the libraries and schools!?

SARAH:

Did you see the ball room and the banqueting chamber in the Town Hall!?

STEPHEN:
> Have you gone into the insurance fund, the pension fund, the building society, the various applications of co-operation!?

Undershaft *comes from the office, with a sheaf of telegrams in his hand.*

UNDERSHAFT:
> Well, have you seen everything? I'm sorry I was called away. (*Indicating the telegrams*) Good news from Manchuria.

STEPHEN:
> Another Japanese victory?

UNDERSHAFT:
> Oh, I don't know. Which side wins does not concern us here. No: the good news is that the aerial battleship is a tremendous success. At the first trial it has wiped out a fort with three hundred soldiers in it.

CUSINS (*from the platform*):
> Dummy soldiers?

UNDERSHAFT (*striding across to* Stephen *and kicking the prostrate dummy brutally out of his way*):
> No: the real thing.

Cusins *and* Barbara *exchange glances. Then* Cusins *sits on the step and buries his face in his hands.* Barbara *gravely lays her hand on his shoulder. He looks up at her in whimsical desperation.*

UNDERSHAFT:
> Well, Stephen, what do you think of the place?

STEPHEN:
> Oh, magnificent. A perfect triumph of modern industry, Frankly, my dear father, I have been a fool: I had no idea of what it all meant: of the wonderful forethought, the power of organization, the administrative capacity, the financial genius, the colossal capital it represents. I have been repeating to myself as I came through your streets "Peace hath her victories no less renowned than War." I have only one misgiving about it all.

UNDERSHAFT:
> Out with it.

STEPHEN:
> Well, I cannot help thinking that all this provision for every want of your workmen may sap their independence and weaken their sense of responsibility. And greatly as we enjoyed our tea at that splendid restaurant—how they gave us all that

luxury and cake and jam and cream for threepence I really cannot imagine!—still you must remember that restaurants break
up home life. Look at the continent, for instance! Are you sure
so much pampering is really good for the men's characters?

UNDERSHAFT:

Well you see, my dear boy, when you are organizing civilization
you have to make up your mind whether trouble and anxiety
are good things or not. If you decide that they are, then, I take
it, you simply don't organize civilization; and there you are,
with trouble and anxiety enough to make us all angels! But if
you decide the other way, you may as well go through with it.
However, Stephen, our characters are safe here. A sufficient
dose of anxiety is always provided by the fact that we may be
blown to smithereens at any moment.

SARAH:

By the way, papa, where do you make the explosives?

UNDERSHAFT:

In separate little sheds, like that one. When one of them blows
up, it costs very little; and only the people quite close to it are
killed.

Stephen, *who is quite close to it, looks at it rather scaredly, and moves
away quickly to the cannon. At the same moment the door of the shed is
thrown abruptly open; and a foreman in overalls and list slippers comes out
on the little landing and holds the door for* Lomax, *who appears in the
doorway.*

LOMAX (*with studied coolness*):

My good fellow: you needn't get into a state of nerves.
Nothing's going to happen to you; and I suppose it wouldn't
be the end of the world if anything did. A little bit of British
pluck is what you want, old chap. (*He descends and strolls across
to* Sarah).

UNDERSHAFT (*to the foreman*):

Anything wrong, Bilton?

BILTON (*with ironic calm*):

Gentleman walked into the high explosives shed and lit a
cigaret, sir: that's all.

UNDERSHAFT:

Ah, quite so. (*Going over to* Lomax) Do you happen to remember what you did with the match?

LOMAX:

Oh come! I'm not a fool. I took jolly good care to blow it out
before I chucked it away.

BILTON:

The top of it was red hot inside, sir.

LOMAX:

Well, suppose it was! I didn't chuck it into any of your messes.

UNDERSHAFT:

Think no more of it, Mr Lomax. By the way, would you mind lending me your matches.

LOMAX (*offering his box*):

Certainly.

UNDERSHAFT:

Thanks. (*He pockets the matches*).

LOMAX (*lecturing to the company generally*):

You know, these high explosives don't go off like gunpowder, except when they're in a gun. When they're spread loose, you can put a match to them without the least risk: they just burn quietly like a bit of paper. (*Warming to the scientific interest of the subject*) Did you know that, Undershaft? Have you ever tried?

UNDERSHAFT:

Not on a large scale, Mr Lomax. Bilton will give you a sample of gun cotton when you are leaving if you ask him. You can experiment with it at home. (Bilton *looks puzzled*).

SARAH:

Bilton will do nothing of the sort, papa. I suppose it's your business to blow up the Russians and Japs; but you might really stop short of blowing up poor Cholly. (Bilton *gives it up and retires into the shed*).

LOMAX:

My ownest, there is no danger. (*He sits beside her on the shell*).

*Lady Britomart arrives from the town with a bouquet.*

LADY BRITOMART (*impetuously*)

Andrew: you shouldn't have let me see this place.

UNDERSHAFT:

Why, my dear?

LADY BRITOMART:

Never mind why: you shouldn't have: that's all. To think of all that (*indicating the town*) being yours! and that you have kept it to yourself all these years!

UNDERSHAFT:

It does not belong to me. I belong to it. It is the Undershaft inheritance.

LADY BRITOMART:

It is not. Your ridiculous cannons and that noisy banging foundry may be the Undershaft inheritance; but all that plate and linen, all that furniture and those houses and orchards and gardens belong to us. They belong to me: they are not a man's business. I won't give them up. You must be out of your senses to throw them all away; and if you persist in such folly, I will call in a doctor.

UNDERSHAFT (*stooping to smell the bouquet*):

Where did you get the flowers, my dear?

LADY BRITOMART:

Your men presented them to me in your William Morris Labor Church.

CUSINS:

Oh! It needed only that. A Labor Church! (*he mounts the firestep distractedly, and leans with his elbows on the parapet, turning his back to them*).

LADY BRITOMART:

Yes, with Morris's words in mosaic letters ten feet high round the dome. NO MAN IS GOOD ENOUGH TO BE ANOTHER MAN'S MASTER. The cynicism of it!

UNDERSHAFT:

It shocked the men at first, I am afraid. But now they take no more notice of it than of the ten commandments in church.

LADY BRITOMART:

Andrew: you are trying to put me off the subject of the inheritance by profane jokes. Well, you shan't. I don't ask it any longer for Stephen: he has inherited far too much of your perversity to be fit for it. But Barbara has rights as well as Stephen. Why should not Adolphus succeed to the inheritance? I could manage the town for him; and he can look after the cannons, if they are really necessary.

UNDERSHAFT:

I should ask nothing better if Adolphus were a foundling. He is exactly the sort of new blood that is wanted in English business. But he's not a foundling; and there's an end of it. (*He makes for the office door*).

CUSINS (*turning to them*):

Not quite. (*They all turn and stare at him*). I think—Mind! I am not committing myself in any way as to my future course—but I think the foundling difficulty can be got over. (*He jumps down to the emplacement*).

UNDERSHAFT (*coming back to him*):

What do you mean?

CUSINS:

Well, I have something to say which is in the nature of a confession.

SARAH:
LADY BRITOMART:
BARBARA:                } Confession!
STEPHEN:

LOMAX:                   Oh I say!
CUSINS:

> Yes, a confession. Listen, all. Until I met Barbara I thought myself in the main an honorable, truthful man, because I wanted the approval of my conscience more than I wanted anything else. But the moment I saw Barbara, I wanted her far more than the approval of my conscience.

LADY BRITOMART:
> Adolphus!

CUSINS:
> It is true. You accused me yourself, Lady Brit, of joining the Army to worship Barbara; and so I did. She bought my soul like a flower at a street corner; but she bought it for herself.

UNDERSHAFT:
> What! Not for Dionysos or another?

CUSINS:
> Dionysos and all the others are in herself. I adored what was divine in her, and was therefore a true worshipper. But I was romantic about her too. I thought she was a woman of the people, and that a marriage with a professor of Greek would be far beyond the wildest social ambitions of her rank.

LADY BRITOMART:
> Adolphus!!

LOMAX:
> Oh I say!!!

CUSINS:
> When I learnt the horrible truth—

LADY BRITOMART:
> What do you mean by the horrible truth, pray?

CUSINS:
> That she was enormously rich; that her grandfather was an earl; that her father was the Prince of Darkness—

UNDERSHAFT:
> Chut!

CUSINS:
> —and that I was only an adventurer trying to catch a rich wife, then I stooped to deceive her about my birth.

BARBARA: (*rising*)
> Dolly!

LADY BRITOMART:

Your birth! Now Adolphus, don't dare to make up a wicked story for the sake of these wretched cannons. Remember: I have seen photographs of your parents; and the Agent General for South Western Australia knows them personally and has assured me that they are most respectable married people.

CUSINS:

So they are in Australia; but here they are outcasts. Their marriage is legal in Australia, but not in England. My mother is my father's deceased wife's sister; and in this island I am consequently a foundling. (*Sensation*).

BARBARA:

Silly! (*She climbs to the cannon, and leans, listening, in the angle it makes with the parapet*).

CUSINS:

Is the subterfuge good enough, Machiavelli?

UNDERSHAFT (*thoughtfully*):

Biddy: this may be a way out of the difficulty.

LADY BRITOMART:

Stuff! A man can't make cannons any the better for being his own cousin instead of his proper self (*she sits down on the rug with a bounce that expresses her downright contempt for their casuistry*).

UNDERSHAFT (*to* Cusins):

You are an educated man. That is against the tradition.

CUSINS:

Once in ten thousand times it happens that the schoolboy is a born master of what they try to teach him. Greek has not destroyed my mind: it has nourished it. Besides, I did not learn it at an English public school.

UNDERSHAFT:

Hm! Well, I cannot afford to be too particular: you have cornered the foundling market. Let it pass. You are eligible, Euripides: you are eligible.

BARBARA:

Dolly: yesterday morning, when Stephen told us all about the tradition, you became very silent; and you have been strange and excited ever since. Were you thinking of your birth then?

CUSINS:

When the finger of Destiny suddenly points at a man in the middle of his breakfast, it makes him thoughtful.

UNDERSHAFT:

Aha! You have had your eye on the business, my young friend, have you?

CUSINS:

Take care! There is an abyss of moral horror between me and your accursed aerial battleships.

UNDERSHAFT:

Never mind the abyss for the present. Let us settle the practical details and leave your final decision open. You know that you will have to change your name. Do you object to that?

CUSINS:

Would any man named Adolphus—any man called Dolly!—object to be called something else?

UNDERSHAFT:

Good. Now, as to money! I propose to treat you handsomely from the beginning. You shall start at a thousand a year.

CUSINS (*with sudden heat, his spectacles twinkling with mischief*):

A thousand! You dare offer a miserable thousand to the son-in-law of a millionaire! No, by Heavens, Machiavelli! you shall not cheat me. You cannot do without me; and I can do without you. I must have two thousand five hundred a year for two years. At the end of that time, if I am a failure, I go. But if I am a success, and stay on, you must give me the other five thousand.

UNDERSHAFT:

What other five thousand?

CUSINS:

To make the two years up to five thousand a year. The two thousand five hundred is only half pay in case I should turn out a failure. The third year I must have ten per cent on the profits.

UNDERSHAFT (*taken aback*):

Ten per cent! Why, man, do you know what my profits are?

CUSINS:

Enormous, I hope: otherwise I shall require twentyfive per cent.

UNDERSHAFT:

But, Mr Cusins, this is a serious matter of business. You are not bringing any capital into the concern.

CUSINS:

What! no capital! Is my mastery of Greek no capital? Is my access to the subtlest thought, the loftiest poetry yet attained by humanity, no capital? My character! my intellect! my life! my career! what Barbara calls my soul! are these no capital? Say another word; and I double my salary.

UNDERSHAFT:

Be reasonable—

CUSINS (*peremptorily*):

Mr Undershaft: you have my terms. Take them or leave them.

UNDERSHAFT (*recovering himself*):

Very well. I note your terms; and I offer you half.

CUSINS (*disgusted*):

Half!

UNDERSHAFT (*firmly*):

Half.

CUSINS:

You call yourself a gentleman; and you offer me half!!

UNDERSHAFT:

I do not call myself a gentleman; but I offer you half.

CUSINS:

This to your future partner! your successor! your son-in-law!

BARBARA:

You are selling your own soul, Dolly, not mine. Leave me out of the bargain, please.

UNDERSHAFT:

Come! I will go a step further for Barbara's sake. I will give you three fifths; but that is my last word.

CUSINS:

Done!

LOMAX:

Done in the eye! Why, *I* get only eight hundred, you know.

CUSINS:

By the way, Mac, I am a classical scholar, not an arithmetical one. Is three fifths more than half or less?

UNDERSHAFT:

More, of course.

CUSINS:

I would have taken two hundred and fifty. How you can succeed in business when you are willing to pay all that money to a University don who is obviously not worth a junior clerk's wages!—well! What will Lazarus say?

UNDERSHAFT:

Lazarus is a gentle romantic Jew who cares for nothing but string quartets and stalls at fashionable theatres. He will be blamed for your rapacity in money matters, poor fellow! as he has hitherto been blamed for mine. You are a shark of the first order, Euripides. So much the better for the firm!

BARBARA:

Is the bargain closed, Dolly? Does your soul belong to him now?

CUSINS:

No: the price is settled: that is all. The real tug of war is still to come. What about the moral question?

LADY BRITOMART:

> There is no moral question in the matter at all, Adolphus. You must simply sell cannons and weapons to people whose cause is right and just, and refuse them to foreigners and criminals.

UNDERSHAFT (*determinedly*):

> No: none of that. You must keep the true faith of an Armorer, or you don't come in here.

CUSINS:

> What on earth is the true faith of an Armorer?

UNDERSHAFT:

> To give arms to all men who offer an honest price for them, without respect of persons or principles: to aristocrat and republican, to Nihilist and Tsar, to Capitalist and Socialist, to Protestant and Catholic, to burglar and policeman, to black man, white man and yellow man, to all sorts and conditions, all nationalities, all faiths, all follies, all causes and all crimes. The first Undershaft wrote up in his shop IF GOD GAVE THE HAND, LET NOT MAN WITHHOLD THE SWORD. The second wrote up ALL HAVE THE RIGHT TO FIGHT: NONE HAVE THE RIGHT TO JUDGE. The third wrote up TO MAN THE WEAPON: TO HEAVEN THE VICTORY. The fourth had no literary turn; so he did not write up anything; but he sold cannons to Napoleon under the nose of George the Third. The fifth wrote up PEACE SHALL NOT PREVAIL SAVE WITH A SWORD IN HER HAND. The sixth, my master, was the best of all. He wrote up NOTHING IS EVER DONE IN THIS WORLD UNTIL MEN ARE PREPARED TO KILL ONE ANOTHER IF IT IS NOT DONE. After that, there was nothing left for the seventh to say. So he wrote up, simply, UNASHAMED.

CUSINS:

> My good Machiavelli, I shall certainly write something up on the wall; only, as I shall write it in Greek, you won't be able to read it. But as to your Armorer's faith, if I take my neck out of the noose of my own morality I am not going to put it into the noose of yours. I shall sell cannons to whom I please and refuse them to whom I please. So there!

UNDERSHAFT:

> From the moment when you become Andrew Undershaft, you will never do as you please again. Don't come here lusting for power, young man.

CUSINS:

> If power were my aim I should not come here for it. You have no power.

UNDERSHAFT:

> None of my own, certainly.

CUSINS:

> I have more power than you, more will. You do not drive this place: it drives you. And what drives the place?

UNDERSHAFT (*enigmatically*):

> A will of which I am a part.

BARBARA (*startled*):

> Father! Do you know what you are saying; or are you laying a snare for my soul?

CUSINS:

> Don't listen to his metaphysics, Barbara. The place is driven by the most rascally part of society, the money hunters, the pleasure hunters, the military promotion hunters; and he is their slave.

UNDERSHAFT:

> Not necessarily. Remember the Armorer's Faith. I will take an order from a good man as cheerfully as from a bad one. If you good people prefer preaching and shirking to buying my weapons and fighting the rascals, don't blame me. I can make cannons: I cannot make courage and conviction. Bah! you tire me, Euripides, with your morality mongering. Ask Barbara: she understands. (*He suddenly reaches up and takes Barbara's hands, looking powerfully into her eyes*) Tell him, my love, what power really means.

BARBARA (*hypnotized*):

> Before I joined the Salvation Army, I was in my own power; and the consequence was that I never knew what to do with myself. When I joined it, I had not time enough for all the things I had to do.

UNDERSHAFT (*approvingly*):

> Just so. And why was that, do you suppose?

BARBARA:

> Yesterday I should have said, because I was in the power of God. (*She resumes her self-possession, withdrawing her hands from his with a power equal to his own*). But you came and shewed me that I was in the power of Bodger and Undershaft. Today I feel—oh! how can I put it into words? Sarah: do you remember the earthquake at Cannes, when we were little children?— how little the surprise of the first shock mattered compared to the dread and horror of waiting for the second? That is how I feel in this place today. I stood on the rock I thought eternal; and without a word of warning it reeled and crumbled under me. I was safe with an infinite wisdom watching me, an army marching to Salvation with me; and in a moment, at a stroke of your pen in a cheque book, I stood alone; and the heavens

were empty. That was the first shock of the earthquake: I am waiting for the second.

UNDERSHAFT:

Come, come, my daughter! don't make too much of your little tinpot tragedy. What do we do here when we spend years of work and thought and thousands of pounds of solid cash on a new gun or an aerial battleship that turns out just a hairsbreadth wrong after all? Scrap it. Scrap it without wasting another hour or another pound on it. Well, you have made for yourself something that you call a morality or a religion or what not. It doesn't fit the facts. Well, scrap it. Scrap it and get one that does fit. That is what is wrong with the world at present. It scraps its obsolete steam engines and dynamos; but it won't scrap its old prejudices and its old moralities and its old religions and its old political constitutions. What's the result? In machinery it does very well; but in morals and religion and politics it is working at a loss that brings it nearer bankruptcy every year. Don't persist in that folly. If your old religion broke down yesterday, get a newer and a better one for tomorrow.

BARBARA:

Oh how gladly I would take a better one to my soul! But you offer me a worse one. (*Turning on him with sudden vehemence*). Justify yourself: shew me some light through the darkness of this dreadful place, with its beautifully clean workshops, and respectable workmen, and model homes.

UNDERSHAFT:

Cleanliness and respectability do not need justification, Barbara: they justify themselves. I see no darkness here, no dreadfulness. In your Salvation shelter I saw poverty, misery, cold and hunger. You gave them bread and treacle and dreams of heaven. I give thirty shillings a week to twelve thousand a year. They find their own dreams; but I look after the drainage.

BARBARA:

And their souls?

UNDERSHAFT:

I save their souls just as I saved yours.

BARBARA (*revolted*):

You saved my soul! What do you mean?

UNDERSHAFT:

I fed you and clothed you and housed you. I took care that you should have money enough to live handsomely—more than enough; so that you could be wasteful, careless, generous. That saved your soul from the seven deadly sins.

BARBARA (*bewildered*):

The seven deadly sins!

UNDERSHAFT:

Yes, the deadly seven. (*Counting on his fingers*) Food, clothing, firing, rent, taxes, respectability and children. Nothing can lift those seven millstones from Man's neck but money; and the spirit cannot soar until the millstones are lifted. I lifted them from your spirit. I enabled Barbara to become Major Barbara; and I saved her from the crime of poverty.

CUSINS:

Do you call poverty a crime?

UNDERSHAFT:

The worst of crimes. All the other crimes are virtues beside it: all the other dishonors are chivalry itself by comparison. Poverty blights whole cities; spreads horrible pestilences; strikes dead the very souls of all who come within sight, sound, or smell of it. What you call crime is nothing: a murder here and a theft there, a blow now and a curse then: what do they matter? they are only the accidents and illnesses of life: there are not fifty genuine professional criminals in London. But there are millions of poor people, abject people, dirty people, ill fed, ill clothed people. They poison us morally and physically: they kill the happiness of society: they force us to do away with our own liberties and to organize unnatural cruelties for fear they should rise against us and drag us down into their abyss. Only fools fear crime: we all fear poverty. Pah! (*turning on* Barbara) you talk of your half-saved ruffian in West Ham: you accuse me of dragging his soul back to perdition. Well, bring him to me here; and I will drag his soul back again to salvation for you. Not by words and dreams; but by thirtyeight shillings a week, a sound house in a handsome street, and a permanent job. In three weeks he will have a fancy waistcoat; in three months a tall hat and a chapel sitting; before the end of the year he will shake hands with a duchess at a Primrose League meeting, and join the Conservative Party.

BARBARA:

And will he be the better for that?

UNDERSHAFT:

You know he will. Don't be a hypocrite, Barbara. He will be better fed, better housed, better clothed, better behaved; and his children will be pounds heavier and bigger. That will be better than an American cloth mattress in a shelter, chopping firewood, eating bread and treacle, and being forced to kneel down from time to time to thank heaven for it: knee drill, I think you call it. It is cheap work converting starving men with a Bible in one hand and a slice of bread in the other. I will undertake to convert West Ham to Mahometanism on the same terms. Try your hand on my men: their souls are hungry because their bodies are full.

BARBARA:

And leave the east end to starve?

UNDERSHAFT (*his energetic tone dropping into one of bitter and brooding remembrance*):

*I* was an east ender. I moralized and starved until one day I swore that I would be a full-fed free man at all costs; that nothing should stop me except a bullet, neither reason nor morals nor the lives of other men. I said "Thou shalt starve ere I starve"; and with that word I became free and great. I was a dangerous man until I had my will: now I am a useful, beneficent, kindly person. That is the history of most self-made millionaires, I fancy. When it is the history of every Englishman we shall have an England worth living in.

LADY BRITOMART:

Stop making speeches, Andrew. This is not the place for them.

UNDERSHAFT (*punctured*):

My dear: I have no other means of conveying my ideas.

LADY BRITOMART:

Your ideas are nonsense. You got on because you were selfish and unscrupulous.

UNDERSHAFT:

Not at all. I had the strongest scruples about poverty and starvation. Your moralists are quite unscrupulous about both: they make virtues of them. I had rather be a thief than a pauper. I had rather be a murderer than a slave. I don't want to be either; but if you force the alternative on me, then, by Heaven, I'll choose the braver and more moral one. I hate poverty and slavery worse than any other crimes whatsoever. And let me tell you this. Poverty and slavery have stood up for centuries to your sermons and leading articles: they will not stand up to my machine guns. Don't preach at them: don't reason with them. Kill them.

BARBARA:

Killing. Is that your remedy for everything?

UNDERSHAFT:

It is the final test of conviction, the only lever strong enough to overturn a social system, the only way of saying Must. Let six hundred and seventy fools loose in the streets; and three policemen can scatter them. But huddle them together in a certain

house in Westminster; and let them go through certain ceremonies and call themselves certain names until at last they get
the courage to kill; and your six hundred and seventy fools
become a government. Your pious mob fills up ballot papers and
imagines it is governing its masters; but the ballot paper that
really governs is the paper that has a bullet wrapped up in it.

CUSINS:

That is perhaps why, like most intelligent people, I never vote.

UNDERSHAFT:

Vote! Bah! When you vote, you only change the names of the
cabinet. When you shoot, you pull down governments, inau-
gurate new epochs, abolish old orders and set up new. Is that
historically true, Mr Learned Man, or is it not?

CUSINS:

It is historically true. I loathe having to admit it. I repudiate
your sentiments. I abhor your nature. I defy you in every possible way. Still, it is true. But it ought not to be true.

UNDERSHAFT:

Ought! ought! ought! ought! ought! Are you going to spend
your life saying ought, like the rest of our moralists? Turn your
oughts into shalls, man. Come and make explosives with me.
Whatever can blow men up can blow society up. The history of
the world is the history of those who had courage enough to
embrace this truth. Have you the courage to embrace it, Barbara?

LADY BRITOMART:

Barbara: I positively forbid you to listen to your father's abominable wickedness. And you, Adolphus, ought to know better
than to go about saying that wrong things are true. What does
it matter whether they are true if they are wrong?

UNDERSHAFT:

What does it matter whether they are wrong if they are true?

LADY BRITOMART (*rising*):

Children: come home instantly. Andrew: I am exceedingly
sorry I allowed you to call on us. You are wickeder than ever.
Come at once.

BARBARA (*shaking her head*):

It's no use running away from wicked people, mamma.

LADY BRITOMART:

It is every use. It shews your disapprobation of them.

BARBARA:

It does not save them.

LADY BRITOMART:

I can see that you are going to disobey me. Sarah: are you coming home or are you not?

SARAH:

> I daresay it's very wicked of papa to make cannons; but I don't think I shall cut him on that account.

LOMAX (*pouring oil on the troubled waters*):

> The fact is, you know, there is a certain amount of tosh about this notion of wickedness. It doesn't work. You must look at facts. Not that I would say a word in favor of anything wrong; but then, you see, all sorts of chaps are always doing all sorts of things; and we have to fit them in somehow, don't you know. What I mean is that you can't go cutting everybody; and that's about what it comes to. (*Their rapt attention to his eloquence makes him nervous*). Perhaps I don't make myself clear.

LADY BRITOMART:

> You are lucidity itself, Charles. Because Andrew is successful and has plenty of money to give to Sarah, you will flatter him and encourage him in his wickedness.

LOMAX (*unruffled*):

> Well, where the carcase is, there will the eagles be gathered, don't you know. (*To* Undershaft) Eh? What?

UNDERSHAFT:

> Precisely. By the way, may I call you Charles?

LOMAX:

> Delighted. Cholly is the usual ticket.

UNDERSHAFT (*to* Lady Britomart):

> Biddy—

LADY BRITOMART (*violently*):

> Don't dare call me Biddy. Charles Lomax: you are a fool. Adolphus Cusins: you are a Jesuit. Stephen: you are a prig. Barbara: you are a lunatic. Andrew: you are a vulgar tradesman. Now you all know my opinion; and my conscience is clear, at all events (*she sits down with a vehemence that the rug fortunately softens*).

UNDERSHAFT:

> My dear: you are the incarnation of morality. (*She snorts*). Your conscience is clear and your duty done when you have called everybody names. Come, Euripides! it is getting late; and we all want to go home. Make up your mind.

CUSINS:

> Understand this, you old demon—

LADY BRITOMART:

> Adolphus!

UNDERSHAFT:

> Let him alone, Biddy. Proceed, Euripides.

CUSINS:

> You have me in a horrible dilemma. I want Barbara.

UNDERSHAFT:

Like all young men, you greatly exaggerate the difference between one young woman and another.

BARBARA:

Quite true, Dolly.

CUSINS:

I also want to avoid being a rascal.

UNDERSHAFT (*with biting contempt*):

You lust for personal righteousness, for self-approval, for what you call a good conscience, for what Barbara calls salvation, for what I call patronizing people who are not so lucky as yourself.

CUSINS:

I do not: all the poet in me recoils from being a good man. But there are things in me that I must reckon with. Pity—

UNDERSHAFT:

Pity! The scavenger of misery.

CUSINS:

Well, love.

UNDERSHAFT:

I know. You love the needy and the outcast: you love the oppressed races, the negro, the Indian ryot, the underdog everywhere. Do you love the Japanese? Do you love the French? Do you love the English?

CUSINS:

No. Every true Englishman detests the English. We are the wickedest nation on earth; and our success is a moral horror.

UNDERSHAFT:

That is what comes of your gospel of love, is it?

CUSINS:

May I not love even my father-in-law?

UNDERSHAFT:

Who wants your love, man? By what right do you take the liberty of offering it to me? I will have your due heed and respect, or I will kill you. But your love! Damn your impertinence!

CUSINS (*grinning*):

I may not be able to control my affections, Mac.

UNDERSHAFT:

You are fencing, Euripides. You are weakening: your grip is slipping. Come! try your last weapon. Pity and love have broken in your hand: forgiveness is still left.

CUSINS:

No: forgiveness is a beggar's refuge. I am with you there: we must pay our debts.

UNDERSHAFT:

Well said. Come! you will suit me. Remember the words of Plato.

CUSINS (*starting*):

Plato! You dare quote Plato to me!

UNDERSHAFT:

Plato says, my friend, that society cannot be saved until either the Professors of Greek take to making gunpowder, or else the makers of gunpowder become Professors of Greek.

CUSINS:

Oh, tempter, cunning tempter!

UNDERSHAFT:

Come! choose, man, choose.

CUSINS:

But perhaps Barbara will not marry me if I make the wrong choice.

BARBARA:

Perhaps not.

CUSINS (*desperately perplexed*):

You hear!

BARBARA:

Father: do you love nobody?

UNDERSHAFT:

I love my best friend.

LADY BRITOMART:

And who is that, pray?

UNDERSHAFT:

My bravest enemy. That is the man who keeps me up to the mark.

CUSINS:

You know, the creature is really a sort of poet in his way. Suppose he is a great man, after all!

UNDERSHAFT:

Suppose you stop talking and make up your mind, my young friend.

CUSINS:

But you are driving me against my nature. I hate war.

UNDERSHAFT:

Hatred is the coward's revenge for being intimidated. Dare you make war on war? Here are the means: my friend Mr Lomax is sitting on them.

LOMAX (*springing up*):

Oh I say! You don't mean that this thing is loaded, do you? My ownest: come off it.

SARAH (*sitting placidly on the shell*):

If I am to be blown up, the more thoroughly it is done the better. Don't fuss, Cholly.

LOMAX (*to* Undershaft, *strongly remonstrant*):

Your own daughter, you know!

UNDERSHAFT:

So I see. (*To* Cusins) Well, my friend, may we expect you here at six tomorrow morning?

CUSINS (*firmly*):

Not on any account. I will see the whole establishment blown up with its own dynamite before I will get up at five. My hours are healthy, rational hours: eleven to five.

UNDERSHAFT:

Come when you please: before a week you will come at six and stay until I turn you out for the sake of your health. (*Calling*) Bilton! (*He turns to* Lady Britomart, *who rises*). My dear: let us leave these two young people to themselves for a moment. (Bilton *comes from the shed*). I am going to take you through the gun cotton shed.

BILTON (*barring the way*):

You can't take anything explosive in here, sir.

LADY BRITOMART:

What do you mean? Are you alluding to me?

BILTON (*unmoved*):

No, ma'am. Mr Undershaft has the other gentleman's matches in his pocket.

LADY BRITOMART (*abruptly*):

Oh! I beg your pardon. (*She goes into the shed*).

UNDERSHAFT:

Quite right, Bilton, quite right: here you are. (*He gives* Bilton *the box of matches*). Come, Stephen. Come, Charles. Bring Sarah. (*He passes into the shed*).

Bilton *opens the box and deliberately drops the matches into the firebucket.*

LOMAX:

Oh! I say (Bilton *stolidly hands him the empty box*). Infernal nonsense! Pure scientific ignorance! (*He goes in*).

SARAH:

Am I all right, Bilton?

BILTON:

You'll have to put on list slippers, miss: that's all. We've got em inside. (*She goes in*).

STEPHEN (*very seriously to* Cusins):

Dolly, old fellow, think. Think before you decide. Do you feel that you are a sufficiently practical man? It is a huge undertaking, an enormous responsibility. All this mass of business will be Greek to you.

CUSINS:

Oh, I think it will be much less difficult than Greek.

STEPHEN:

Well, I just want to say this before I leave you to yourselves. Don't let anything I have said about right and wrong prejudice you against this great chance in life. I have satisfied myself that the business is one of the highest character and a credit to our country. (*Emotionally*) I am very proud of my father. I—(*Unable to proceed, he presses* Cusins' *hand and goes hastily into the shed, followed by* Bilton).

Barbara *and* Cusins, *left alone together, look at one another silently.*

CUSINS:

Barbara: I am going to accept this offer.

BARBARA:

I thought you would.

CUSINS:

You understand, don't you, that I had to decide without consulting you. If I had thrown the burden of the choice on you, you would sooner or later have despised me for it.

BARBARA:

Yes: I did not want you to sell your soul for me any more than for this inheritance.

CUSINS:

It is not the sale of my soul that troubles me: I have sold it too often to care about that. I have sold it for a professorship. I have sold it for an income. I have sold it to escape being imprisoned for refusing to pay taxes for hangmen's ropes and unjust wars and things that I abhor. What is all human conduct but the daily and hourly sale of our souls for trifles? What I am now selling it for is neither money nor position nor comfort, but for reality and for power.

BARBARA:

You know that you will have no power, and that he has none.

CUSINS:

I know. It is not for myself alone. I want to make power for the world.

BARBARA:

I want to make power for the world too; but it must be spiritual power.

CUSINS:

I think all power is spiritual: these cannons will not go off by themselves. I have tried to make spiritual power by teaching Greek. But the world can never be really touched by a dead language and a dead civilization. The people must have power; and the people cannot have Greek. Now the power that is made here can be wielded by all men.

BARBARA:

Power to burn women's houses down and kill their sons and tear their husbands to pieces.

CUSINS:

You cannot have power for good without having power for evil too. Even mother's milk nourishes murderers as well as heroes. This power which only tears men's bodies to pieces has never been so horribly abused as the intellectual power, the imaginative power, the poetic, religious power that can enslave men's souls. As a teacher of Greek I gave the intellectual man weapons against the common man. I now want to give the common man weapons against the intellectual man. I love the common people. I want to arm them against the lawyers, the doctors, the priests, the literary men, the professors, the artists, and the politicians, who, once in authority, are more disastrous and tyrannical than all the fools, rascals, and impostors. I want a power simple enough for common men to use, yet strong enough to force the intellectual oligarchy to use its genius for the general good.

BARBARA:

Is there no higher power than that (*pointing to the shell*)?

CUSINS:

Yes; but that power can destroy the higher powers just as a tiger can destroy a man: therefore Man must master that power first. I admitted this when the Turks and Greeks were last at war. My best pupil went out to fight for Hellas. My parting gift to him was not a copy of Plato's Republic, but a revolver and a hundred Undershaft cartridges. The blood of every Turk he shot—if he shot any—is on my head as well as on Undershaft's. That act committed me to this place for ever. Your father's challenge has beaten me. Dare I make war on war? I dare. I must. I will. And now, is it all over between us?

BARBARA (*touched by his evident dread of her answer*):

Silly baby Dolly! How could it be!

CUSINS (*overjoyed*):

Then you—you—you—Oh for my drum! (*He flourishes imaginary drumsticks*).

BARBARA (*angered by his levity*):

Take care, Dolly, take care. Oh, if only I could get away from you and from father and from it all! if I could have the wings of a dove and fly away to heaven!

CUSINS:

And leave me!

BARBARA:

Yes, you, and all the other naughty mischievous children of men. But I can't. I was happy in the Salvation Army for a moment. I escaped from the world into a paradise of enthusiasm and prayer and soul saving; but the moment our money ran short, it all came back to Bodger: it was he who saved our people: he, and the Prince of Darkness, my papa. Undershaft and Bodger: their hands stretch everywhere: when we feed a starving fellow creature, it is with their bread, because there is no other bread; when we tend the sick, it is in the hospitals they endow; if we turn from the churches they build, we must kneel on the stones of the streets they pave. As long as that lasts, there is no getting away from them. Turning our backs on Bodger and Undershaft is turning our backs on life.

CUSINS:

I thought you were determined to turn your back on the wicked side of life.

BARBARA:

There is no wicked side: life is all one. And I never wanted to shirk my share in whatever evil must be endured, whether it be sin or suffering. I wish I could cure you of middle-class ideas, Dolly.

CUSINS (*gasping*):

Middle cl—! A snub! A social snub to me! from the daughter of a foundling!

BARBARA:

That is why I have no class, Dolly: I come straight out of the heart of the whole people. If I were middle-class I should turn my back on my father's business; and we should both live in an artistic drawing room, with you reading the reviews in one corner, and I in the other at the piano, playing Schumann: both very superior persons, and neither of us a bit of use. Sooner than that, I would sweep out the guncotton shed, or be one of Bodger's barmaids. Do you know what would have happened if you had refused papa's offer?

CUSINS:

I wonder!

BARBARA:

I should have given you up and married the man who accepted it. After all, my dear old mother has more sense than any of you. I felt like her when I saw this place—felt that I must have it—that never, never, never could I let it go; only she thought it was the houses and the kitchen ranges and the linen and china, when it was really all the human souls to be saved: not weak souls in starved bodies, sobbing with gratitude for a scrap of bread and treacle, but fullfed, quarrelsome, snobbish, uppish creatures, all standing on their little rights and dignities, and thinking that my father ought to be greatly obliged to them for making so much money for him—and so he ought. That is where salvation is really wanted. My father shall never throw it in my teeth again that my converts were bribed with bread. (*She is transfigured*). I have got rid of the bribe of bread. I have got rid of the bribe of heaven. Let God's work be done for its own sake: the work he had to create us to do because it cannot be done except by living men and women. When I die, let him be in my debt, not I in his; and let me forgive him as becomes a woman of my rank.

CUSINS:

Then the way of life lies through the factory of death?

BARBARA:

Yes, through the raising of hell to heaven and of man to God, through the unveiling of an eternal light in the Valley of The Shadow. (*Seizing him with both hands*) Oh, did you think my courage would never come back? did you believe that I was a deserter? that I, who have stood in the streets, and taken my people to my heart, and talked of the holiest and greatest things with them, could ever turn back and chatter foolishly to fashionable people about nothing in a drawing room? Never, never, never, never: Major Barbara will die with the colors. Oh! and I have my dear little Dolly boy still; and he has found me my place and my work. Glory Hallelujah! (*She kisses him*).

CUSINS:

My dearest: consider my delicate health. I cannot stand as much happiness as you can.

BARBARA:

Yes: it is not easy work being in love with me, is it? But it's good for you. (*She runs to the shed, and calls, childlike*) Mamma! Mamma! (Bilton *comes out of the shed, followed by* Undershaft). I want Mamma.

UNDERSHAFT:

She is taking off her list slippers, dear. (*He passes on to* Cusins). Well? What does she say?

CUSINS:

She has gone right up into the skies.

LADY BRITOMART (*coming from the shed and stopping on the steps, obstructing* Sarah, *who follows with* Lomax. Barbara *clutches like a baby at her mother's skirt*) Barbara: when will you learn to be independent and to act and think for yourself? I know as well as possible what that cry of "Mamma, Mamma," means. Always running to me!

SARAH (*touching* Lady Britomart's *ribs with her finger tips and imitating a bicycle horn*) Pip! pip!

LADY BRITOMART (*highly indignant*):

How dare you say Pip! pip! to me, Sarah? You are both very naughty children. What do you want, Barbara?

BARBARA:

I want a house in the village to live in with Dolly. (*Dragging at the skirt*) Come and tell me which one to take.

UNDERSHAFT (*to* Cusins):

Six o'clock tomorrow morning, Euripides.

# Pygmalion

A ROMANCE IN FIVE ACTS

# Preface to Pygmalion.

## A Professor of Phonetics.

As will be seen later on, Pygmalion needs, not a preface, but a sequel, which I have supplied in its due place.

The English have no respect for their language, and will not teach their children to speak it. They spell it so abominably that no man can teach himself what it sounds like. It is impossible for an Englishman to open his mouth without making some other Englishman hate or despise him. German and Spanish are accessible to foreigners: English is not accessible even to Englishmen. The reformer England needs today is an energetic phonetic enthusiast: that is why I have made such a one the hero of a popular play. There have been heroes of that kind crying in the wilderness for many years past. When I became interested in the subject towards the end of the eighteen-seventies, Melville Bell was dead; but Alexander J. Ellis was still a living patriarch, with an impressive head always covered by a velvet skull cap, for which he would apologize to public meetings in a very courtly manner. He and Tito Pagliardini, another phonetic veteran, were men whom it was impossible to dislike. Henry Sweet, then a young man, lacked their sweetness of character: he was about as conciliatory to conventional mortals as Ibsen or Samuel Butler. His great ability as a phonetician (he was, I think, the best of them all at his job) would have entitled him to high official recognition, and perhaps enabled him to popularize his subject, but for his Satanic contempt for all academic dignitaries and persons in general who thought more of Greek than of phonetics. Once, in the days when the Imperial Institute rose in South Kensington, and Joseph Chamberlain was booming the Empire, I induced the editor of a leading monthly review to commission an article from Sweet on the imperial importance of his subject. When it arrived, it contained nothing but a savagely derisive attack on a professor of language and literature whose chair Sweet regarded as proper to a phonetic expert only. The article, being libelous, had to be returned as impossible; and I had to renounce my dream of dragging its author into the limelight. When I met him afterwards, for the first time for many years, I found to my astonishment that he, who had been a quite tolerably presentable young man, had actually managed by sheer scorn to alter his personal appearance until he had become a sort of walking repudiation of Oxford and all its traditions. It must have been largely in his own despite that he was squeezed into something called a Readership of phonetics there. The future of phonetics rests probably with his pupils, who all swore by him; but nothing could bring the man himself into any sort of compliance with the university, to which he nevertheless clung by divine right in an intensely Oxonian way. I daresay his papers, if he has left any, include some satires that may be published without too destructive results fifty years hence. He was, I believe, not in the least an illnatured man: very much the opposite, I should say; but he would not suffer fools gladly.

Those who knew him will recognize in my third act the allusion to the patent shorthand in which he used to write postcards, and which may be acquired from a four and six-penny manual published by the Clarendon Press. The postcards which Mrs Higgins describes are such as I have received from Sweet. I would decipher a sound which a cockney would represent by *zerr,* and a Frenchman by *seu,* and then write demanding with some heat what on earth it meant. Sweet, with boundless contempt for my stupidity, would reply that it not only meant but obviously was the word Result, as no other word containing that sound, and capable of making sense with the context, existed in any language spoken on earth. That less expert mortals should require fuller indications was beyond Sweet's patience. Therefore, though the whole point of his "Current Shorthand" is that it can express every sound in the language perfectly, vowels as well as consonants, and that your hand has to make no stroke except the easy and current ones with which you write m, n, and u, l, p, and q, scribbling them at whatever angle comes easiest to you, his unfortunate determination to make this remarkable and quite legible script serve also as a shorthand reduced it in his own practice to the most inscrutable of cryptograms. His true objective was the provision of a full, accurate, legible script for our noble but ill-dressed language; but he was led past that by his contempt for the popular Pitman system of shorthand, which he called the Pitfall system. The triumph of Pitman was a triumph of business organization: there was a weekly paper to persuade you to learn Pitman: there were cheap textbooks and exercise books and transcripts of speeches for you to copy, and schools where experienced teachers coached you up to the necessary proficiency. Sweet could not organize his market in that fashion. He might as well have been the Sybil who tore up the leaves of prophecy that nobody would attend to. The four and six-penny manual, mostly in his lithographed handwriting, that was never vulgarly advertized, may perhaps some day be taken up by a syndicate and pushed upon the public as The Times pushed the Encyclopædia Britannica; but until then it will certainly not prevail against Pitman. I have bought three copies of it during my lifetime; and I am informed by the publishers that its cloistered existence is still a steady and healthy one. I actually learned the system two several times; and yet the shorthand in which I am writing these lines is Pitman's. And the reason is, that my secretary cannot transcribe Sweet, having been perforce taught in the schools of Pitman. Therefore, Sweet railed at Pitman as vainly as Thersites railed at Ajax: his raillery, however it may have eased his soul, gave no popular vogue to Current Shorthand.

Pygmalion Higgins is not a portrait of Sweet, to whom the adventure of Eliza Doolittle would have been impossible; still, as will be seen, there are touches of Sweet in the play. With Higgins's physique and temperament Sweet might have set the Thames on fire. As it was, he impressed himself professionally on Europe to an extent that made his comparative personal obscurity, and the failure of Oxford to do justice to his eminence, a puzzle to foreign specialists in his subject. I do not blame Oxford, because I think Oxford is quite right in demanding a certain social amenity from its nurslings (heaven knows it is not exorbitant in its requirements!); for although I well know how hard it is for a man of genius with a seriously underrated subject to maintain serene and kindly relations with the men who underrate it, and who keep all the best places for less important subjects which they profess without originality and sometimes without much capacity for them, still, if he overwhelms them with wrath and disdain, he cannot expect them to heap honors on him.

Of the later generations of phoneticians I know little. Among them towers the Poet Laureate, to whom perhaps Higgins may owe his Miltonic sympathies, though here again I must disclaim all portraiture. But if the play makes the public aware that there are such people as phoneticians, and that they are among the most important people in England at present, it will serve its turn.

I wish to boast that Pygmalion has been an extremely successful play all over Europe and North America as well as at home. It is so intensely and deliberately didactic, and its subject is esteemed so dry, that I delight in throwing it at the heads of the wiseacres who repeat the parrot cry that art should never be didactic. It goes to prove my contention that art should never be anything else.

Finally, and for the encouragement of people troubled with accents that cut them off from all high employment, I may add that the change wrought by Professor Higgins in the flower girl is neither impossible nor uncommon. The modern concierge's daughter who fulfils her ambition by playing the Queen of Spain in Ruy Blas at the Théâtre Français is only one of many thousands of men and women who have sloughed off their native dialects and acquired a new tongue. But the thing has to be done scientifically, or the last state of the aspirant may be worse than the first. An honest and natural slum dialect is more tolerable than the attempt of a phonetically untaught person to imitate the vulgar dialect of the golf club; and I am sorry to say that in spite of the efforts of our Academy of Dramatic Art, there is still too much sham golfing English on our stage, and too little of the noble English of Forbes Robertson.

# Act I

*Covent Garden at 11.15 p.m. Torrents of heavy summer rain. Cab whistles blowing frantically in all directions. Pedestrians running for shelter into the market and under the portico of St Paul's Church, where there are already several people, among them a lady and her daughter in evening dress. They are all peering out gloomily at the rain, except one man with his back turned to the rest, who seems wholly preoccupied with a notebook in which he is writing busily.*

*The church clock strikes the first quarter.*

THE DAUGHTER (*in the space between the central pillars, close to the one on her left*):
> I'm getting chilled to the bone. What can Freddy be doing all this time? He's been gone twenty minutes.

THE MOTHER (*on her daughter's right*):
> Not so long. But he ought to have got us a cab by this.

A BYSTANDER (*on the lady's right*):
> He won't get no cab not until half-past eleven, missus, when they come back after dropping their theatre fares.

THE MOTHER:
> But we must have a cab. We can't stand here until half-past eleven. It's too bad.

THE BYSTANDER:
> Well, it ain't my fault, missus.

THE DAUGHTER:
> If Freddy had a bit of gumption, he would have got one at the theatre door.

THE MOTHER:
> What could he have done, poor boy?

THE DAUGHTER:
> Other people got cabs. Why couldn't he?

*Freddy rushes in out of the rain from the Southampton Street side, and comes between them closing a dripping umbrella. He is a young man of twenty, in evening dress, very wet round the ankles.*

THE DAUGHTER:

Well, haven't you got a cab?

FREDDY:

There's not one to be had for love or money.

THE MOTHER:

Oh, Freddy, there must be one. You can't have tried.

THE DAUGHTER:

It's too tiresome. Do you expect us to go and get one ourselves?

FREDDY:

I tell you they're all engaged. The rain was so sudden: nobody
was prepared; and everybody had to take a cab. I've been to
Charing Cross one way and nearly to Ludgate Circus the
other; and they were all engaged.

THE MOTHER:

Did you try Trafalgar Square?

FREDDY:

There wasn't one at Trafalgar Square.

THE DAUGHTER:

Did you try?

FREDDY:

I tried as far as Charing Cross Station. Did you expect me to
walk to Hammersmith?

THE DAUGHTER:

You haven't tried at all.

THE MOTHER:

You really are very helpless, Freddy. Go again; and don't come
back until you have found a cab.

FREDDY:

I shall simply get soaked for nothing.

THE DAUGHTER:

And what about us? Are we to stay here all night in this
draught, with next to nothing on? You selfish pig—

FREDDY:

Oh, very well: I'll go, I'll go. (*He opens his umbrella and dashes
off Strandwards, but comes into collision with a flower girl, who is
hurrying in for shelter, knocking her basket out of her hands. A
blinding flash of lightning, followed instantly by a rattling peal of
thunder, orchestrates the incident*).

THE FLOWER GIRL:

Nah then, Freddy: look wh' y' gowin, deah.

FREDDY:

Sorry (*he rushes off*).

THE FLOWER GIRL (*picking up her scattered flowers and replacing them in the basket*):

There's menners f' yer! Te-oo banches o voylets trod into the mad. (*She sits down on the plinth of the column, sorting her flowers, on the lady's right. She is not at all an attractive person. She is perhaps eighteen, perhaps twenty, hardly older. She wears a little sailor hat of black straw that has long been exposed to the dust and soot of London and has seldom if ever been brushed. Her hair needs washing rather badly: its mousy color can hardly be natural. She wears a shoddy black coat that reaches nearly to her knees and is shaped to her waist. She has a brown skirt with a coarse apron. Her boots are much the worse for wear. She is no doubt as clean as she can afford to be; but compared to the ladies she is very dirty. Her features are no worse than theirs; but their condition leaves something to be desired; and she needs the services of a dentist*).

THE MOTHER:

How do you know that my son's name is Freddy, pray?

THE FLOWER GIRL:

Ow, eez ye-ooa san, is e? Wal, fewd dan y' de-ooty bawmz a mather should, eed now bettern to spawl a pore gel's flahrzn than ran awy athaht pyin. Will ye-oo py me f'them? (*Here, with apologies, this desperate attempt to represent her dialect without a phonetic alphabet must be abandoned as unintelligible outside London*).

THE DAUGHTER:

Do nothing of the sort, mother. The idea!

THE MOTHER:

Please allow me, Clara. Have you any pennies?

THE DAUGHTER:

No. I've nothing smaller than sixpence.

THE FLOWER GIRL (*hopefully*):

I can give you change for a tanner, kind lady.

THE MOTHER (*to* Clara):

Give it to me. (Clara *parts reluctantly*). Now (*to the girl*) this is for your flowers.

THE FLOWER GIRL:

Thank you kindly, lady.

THE DAUGHTER:

Make her give you the change. These things are only a penny a bunch.

THE MOTHER:

Do hold your tongue, Clara. (*To the girl*) You can keep the change.

THE FLOWER GIRL:

Oh, thank you, lady.

THE MOTHER:

Now tell me how you know that young gentleman's name.

THE FLOWER GIRL:

I didn't.

THE MOTHER:

I heard you call him by it. Don't try to deceive me.

THE FLOWER GIRL (*protesting*):

Who's trying to deceive you? I called him Freddy or Charlie same as you might yourself if you was talking to a stranger and wished to be pleasant. (*She sits down beside her basket*).

THE DAUGHTER:

Sixpence thrown away! Really, mamma, you might have spared Freddy that. (*She retreats in disgust behind the pillar*).

*An elderly gentleman of the amiable military type rushes into the shelter, and closes a dripping umbrella. He is in the same plight as* Freddy, *very wet about the ankles. He is in evening dress, with a light overcoat. He takes the place left vacant by* The Daughter's *retirement.*

THE GENTLEMAN:

Phew!

THE MOTHER (*to* The Gentleman):

Oh, sir, is there any sign of its stopping?

THE GENTLEMAN:

I'm afraid not. It started worse than ever about two minutes ago (*he goes to the plinth beside* The Flower Girl; *puts up his foot on it; and stoops to turn down his trouser ends*).

THE MOTHER:

Oh dear! (*She retires sadly and joins her daughter*).

THE FLOWER GIRL (*taking advantage of the military gentleman's proximity to establish friendly relations with him*):

If it's worse, it's a sign it's nearly over. So cheer up, Captain; and buy a flower off a poor girl.

THE GENTLEMAN:

I'm sorry. I haven't any change.

THE FLOWER GIRL:

I can give you change, Captain.

THE GENTLEMAN:

For a sovereign? I've nothing less.

THE FLOWER GIRL:

Garn! Oh do buy a flower off me, Captain. I can change half-a-crown. Take this for tuppence.

THE GENTLEMAN:

Now don't be troublesome: there's a good girl. (*Trying his pockets*) I really haven't any change—Stop: here's three hapence, if that's any use to you (*he retreats to the other pillar*).

THE FLOWER GIRL (*disappointed, but thinking three half-pence better than nothing*):

Thank you, sir.

THE BYSTANDER (*to the girl*):

You be careful: give him a flower for it. There's a bloke here behind taking down every blessed word you're saying. (*All turn to the man who is taking notes*).

THE FLOWER GIRL (*springing up terrified*):

I ain't done nothing wrong by speaking to the gentleman. I've a right to sell flowers if I keep off the kerb. (*Hysterically*) I'm a respectable girl: so help me, I never spoke to him except to ask him to buy a flower off me. (*General hubbub, mostly sympathetic to* The Flower Girl, *but deprecating her excessive sensibility. Cries of* Don't start hollerin'. Who's hurting you? Nobody's going to touch you. What's the good of fussing? Steady on. Easy easy, etc., *come from the elderly staid spectators, who pat her comfortingly. Less patient ones bid her shut her head, or ask her roughly what is wrong with her. A remoter group, not knowing what the matter is, crowd in and increase the noise with question and answer:* What's the row? What she do? Where is he? A tec taking her down. What! him? Yes: him over there: Took money off the gentleman, etc. The Flower Girl, *distraught and mobbed, breaks through them to* The Gentleman, *crying wildly*) Oh, sir, don't let him charge me. You dunno what it means to me. They'll take away my character and drive me on the streets for speaking to gentlemen. They—

THE NOTE TAKER (*coming forward on her right, the rest crowding after him*):

There, there, there, there! who's hurting you, you silly girl? What do you take me for?

THE BYSTANDER:

It's all right: he's a gentleman: look at his boots. (*Explaining to* The Note Taker) She thought you was a copper's nark, sir.

THE NOTE TAKER (*with quick interest*):

What's a copper's nark?

THE BYSTANDER (*inapt at definition*):

It's a—well, it's a copper's nark, as you might say. What else would you call it? A sort of informer.

THE FLOWER GIRL (*still hysterical*):

I take my Bible oath I never said a word—

THE NOTE TAKER (*overbearing but good-humored*):
Oh, shut up, shut up. Do I look like a policeman?

THE FLOWER GIRL (*far from reassured*):
Then what did you take down my words for? How do I know whether you took me down right? You just show me what you've wrote about me. (The Note Taker *opens his book and holds it steadily under her nose, though the pressure of the mob trying to read it over his shoulders would upset a weaker man*). What's that? That ain't proper writing. I can't read that.

THE NOTE TAKER:
I can. (*Reads, reproducing her pronunciation exactly*) "Cheer ap, Keptin; n' baw ya flahr orf a pore gel."

THE FLOWER GIRL (*much distressed*):
It's because I called him Captain. I meant no harm. (*To* The Gentleman) Oh, sir, don't let him lay a charge agen me for a word like that. You—

THE GENTLEMAN:
Charge! I make no charge. (*To* The Note Taker) Really, sir, if you are a detective, you need not begin protecting me against molestation by young women until I ask you. Anybody could see that the girl meant no harm.

THE BYSTANDERS GENERALLY (*demonstrating against police espionage*):
Course they could. What business is it of yours? You mind your own affairs. He wants promotion, he does. Taking down people's words! Girl never said a word to him. What harm if she did? Nice thing a girl can't shelter from the rain without being insulted, etc., etc., etc. (*She is conducted by the more sympathetic demonstrators back to her plinth, where she resumes her seat and struggles with her emotion*).

THE BYSTANDER:
He ain't a tec. He's a blooming busybody: that's what he is. I tell you, look at his boots.

THE NOTE TAKER (*turning on him genially*):
And how are all your people down at Selsey?

THE BYSTANDER (*suspiciously*):
Who told you my people come from Selsey?

THE NOTE TAKER:
Never you mind. They did. (*To the girl*) How do you come to be up so far east? You were born in Lisson Grove.

THE FLOWER GIRL (*appalled*):
Oh, what harm is there in my leaving Lisson Grove? It wasn't fit for a pig to live in; and I had to pay four-and-six a week. (*In tears*) Oh, boo—hoo—oo—

THE NOTE TAKER:

Live where you like; but stop that noise.

THE GENTLEMAN (*to the girl*):

Come, come! he can't touch you: you have a right to live where you please.

A SARCASTIC BYSTANDER (*thrusting himself between* The Note Taker *and* The Gentleman):

Park Lane, for instance. I'd like to go into the Housing Question with you, I would.

THE FLOWER GIRL (*subsiding into a brooding melancholy over her basket, and talking very low-spiritedly to herself*):

I'm a good girl, I am.

THE SARCASTIC BYSTANDER (*not attending to her*):

Do you know where *I* come from?

THE NOTE TAKER (*promptly*):

Hoxton.

*Titterings. Popular interest in* The Note Taker's *performance increases.*

THE SARCASTIC ONE (*amazed*):

Well, who said I didn't? Bly me! You know everything, you do.

THE FLOWER GIRL (*still nursing her sense of injury*):

Ain't no call to meddle with me, he ain't.

THE BYSTANDER (*to her*):

Of course he ain't. Don't you stand it from him. (*To* The Note Taker) See here: what call have you to know about people what never offered to meddle with you? Where's your warrant?

SEVERAL BYSTANDERS (*encouraged by this seeming point of law*):

Yes: where's your warrant?

THE FLOWER GIRL:

Let him say what he likes. I don't want to have no truck with him.

THE BYSTANDER:

You take us for dirt under your feet, don't you? Catch you taking liberties with a gentleman!

THE SARCASTIC BYSTANDER:

Yes: tell him where he come from if you want to go fortune-telling.

THE NOTE TAKER:

Cheltenham, Harrow, Cambridge, and India.

THE GENTLEMAN:

Quite right. (*Great laughter. Reaction in* The Note Taker's *favor. Exclamations of* He knows all about it. Told him proper. Hear him tell the toff where he come from? etc.). May I ask, sir, do you do this for your living at a music hall?

THE NOTE TAKER:

I've thought of that. Perhaps I shall some day.

*The rain has stopped; and the persons on the outside of the crowd begin to drop off.*

THE FLOWER GIRL (*resenting the reaction*):

He's no gentleman, he ain't, to interfere with a poor girl.

THE DAUGHTER (*out of patience, pushing her way rudely to the front and displacing* The Gentleman, *who politely retires to the other side of the pillar*):

What on earth is Freddy doing? I shall get pneumonia if I stay in this draught any longer.

THE NOTE TAKER (*to himself, hastily making a note of her pronunciation of "monia"*):

Earlscourt.

THE DAUGHTER (*violently*):

Will you please keep your impertinent remarks to yourself.

THE NOTE TAKER:

Did I say that out loud? I didn't mean to. I beg your pardon. Your mother's Epsom, unmistakeably.

THE MOTHER (*advancing between her daughter and* The Note Taker):

How very curious! I was brought up in Largelady Park, near Epsom.

THE NOTE TAKER (*uproariously amused*):

Ha! ha! What a devil of a name! Excuse me. (*To* The Daughter) You want a cab, do you?

THE DAUGHTER:

Don't dare speak to me.

THE MOTHER:

Oh please, please, Clara. (*Her daughter repudiates her with an angry shrug and retires haughtily*). We should be so grateful to you, sir, if you found us a cab. (The Note Taker *produces a whistle*). Oh, thank you. (*She joins her daughter*).

The Note Taker *blows a piercing blast.*

THE SARCASTIC BYSTANDER:

There! I knowed he was a plain-clothes copper.

THE BYSTANDER:

That ain't a police whistle: that's a sporting whistle.

THE FLOWER GIRL (*still preoccupied with her wounded feelings*):

He's no right to take away my character. My character is the same to me as any lady's.

THE NOTE TAKER:

I don't know whether you've noticed it; but the rain stopped about two minutes ago.

THE BYSTANDER:

So it has. Why didn't you say so before? and us losing our time listening to your silliness! (*He walks off towards the Strand*).

THE SARCASTIC BYSTANDER:

I can tell where you come from. You come from Anwell. Go back there.

THE NOTE TAKER (*helpfully*):

Hanwell.

THE SARCASTIC BYSTANDER (*affecting great distinction of speech*):

Thenk you, teacher. Haw haw! So long (*he touches his hat with mock respect and strolls off*).

THE FLOWER GIRL:

Frightening people like that! How would he like it himself?

THE MOTHER:

It's quite fine now, Clara. We can walk to a motor bus. Come. (*She gathers her skirts above her ankles and hurries off towards the Strand*).

THE DAUGHTER:

But the cab—(*her mother is out of hearing*). Oh, how tiresome! (*She follows angrily*).

*All the rest have gone except* The Note Taker, The Gentleman, *and* The Flower Girl, *who sits arranging her basket and still pitying herself in murmurs.*

THE FLOWER GIRL:

Poor girl! Hard enough for her to live without being worrited and chivied.

THE GENTLEMAN (*returning to his former place on* The Note Taker's *left*):

How do you do it, if I may ask?

THE NOTE TAKER:

Simply phonetics. The science of speech. That's my profession: also my hobby. Happy is the man who can make a living by his hobby! You can spot an Irishman or a Yorkshireman by his brogue. *I* can place any man within six miles. I can place him within two miles in London. Sometimes within two streets.

THE FLOWER GIRL:

Ought to be ashamed of himself, unmanly coward!

THE GENTLEMAN:

But is there a living in that?

THE NOTE TAKER:

Oh yes. Quite a fat one. This is an age of upstarts. Men begin in Kentish Town with £80 a year, and end in Park Lane with a hundred thousand. They want to drop Kentish Town; but they give themselves away every time they open their mouths. Now I can teach them—

THE FLOWER GIRL:

Let him mind his own business and leave a poor girl—

THE NOTE TAKER (*explosively*):

Woman: cease this detestable boohooing instantly; or else seek the shelter of some other place of worship.

THE FLOWER GIRL (*with feeble defiance*):

I've a right to be here if I like, same as you.

THE NOTE TAKER:

A woman who utters such depressing and disgusting sounds has no right to be anywhere—no right to live. Remember that you are a human being with a soul and the divine gift of articulate speech: that your native language is the language of Shakespeare and Milton and The Bible: and don't sit there crooning like a bilious pigeon.

THE FLOWER GIRL (*quite overwhelmed, looking up at him in mingled wonder and deprecation without daring to raise her head*):

Ah-ah-ah-ow-ow-ow-oo!

THE NOTE TAKER (*whipping out his book*):

Heavens! what a sound! (*He writes; then holds out the book and reads, reproducing her vowels exactly*) Ah-ah-ah-ow-ow-ow-oo!

THE FLOWER GIRL (*tickled by the performance, and laughing in spite of herself*):

Garn!

THE NOTE TAKER:

You see this creature with her kerbstone English: the English that will keep her in the gutter to the end of her days. Well, sir, in three months I could pass that girl off as a duchess at an ambassador's garden party. I could even get her a place as lady's maid or shop assistant, which requires better English. That's the sort of thing I do for commercial millionaires. And on the profits of it I do genuine scientific work in phonetics, and a little as a poet on Miltonic lines.

THE GENTLEMAN:

I am myself a student of Indian dialects; and—

THE NOTE TAKER (*eagerly*):

Are you? Do you know Colonel Pickering, the author of *Spoken Sanscrit*?

THE GENTLEMAN:

I am Colonel Pickering. Who are you?

THE NOTE TAKER:

Henry Higgins, author of *Higgins's Universal Alphabet*.

PICKERING (*with enthusiasm*):

I came from India to meet you.

HIGGINS:

I was going to India to meet you.

PICKERING:

Where do you live?

HIGGINS:

27A Wimpole Street. Come and see me tomorrow.

PICKERING:

I'm at the Carlton. Come with me now and let's have a jaw over some supper.

HIGGINS:

Right you are.

THE FLOWER GIRL (*to* Pickering, *as he passes her*):

Buy a flower, kind gentleman. I'm short for my lodging.

PICKERING:

I really haven't any change. I'm sorry (*he gets away*).

HIGGINS (*shocked at the girl's mendacity*):

Liar. You said you could change half-a-crown.

THE FLOWER GIRL (*rising in desperation*):

You ought to be stuffed with nails, you ought. (*Flinging the basket at his feet*) Take the whole blooming basket for sixpence.

*The church clock strikes the second quarter.*

HIGGINS (*hearing in it the voice of God, rebuking him for his Pharisaic want of charity to the poor girl*):

A reminder. (*He raises his hat solemnly; then throws a handful of money into the basket and follows* Pickering).

THE FLOWER GIRL (*picking up a half-crown*):

Ah-ow-ooh! (*Picking up a couple of florins*) Aaaaah-ow-ooh! (*Picking up several coins*) Aaaaaah-ow-ooh! (*Picking up a half-sovereign*) Aaaaaaaaaaaah-ow-ooh!!!

FREDDY (*springing out of a taxicab*):

Got one at last. Hallo! (*To the girl*) Where are the two ladies that were here?

THE FLOWER GIRL:

They walked to the bus when the rain stopped.

FREDDY:

And left me with a cab on my hands! Damnation!

THE FLOWER GIRL (*with grandeur*):

Never mind, young man. I'm going home in a taxi. (*She sails off to the cab. The driver puts his hand behind him and holds the door firmly shut against her. Quite understanding his mistrust, she shows him her handful of money*). Eightpence ain't no object to me, Charlie. (*He grins and opens the door*). Angel Court, Drury Lane, round the corner of Micklejohn's oil shop. Let's see how fast you can make her hop it. (*She gets in and pulls the door to with a slam as the taxicab starts*).

FREDDY:

Well, I'm dashed!

# Act II

*Next day at 11 a.m. Higgins's laboratory in Wimpole Street. It is a room on the first floor, looking on the street, and was meant for the drawing room. The double doors are in the middle of the back wall; and persons entering find in the corner to their right two tall file cabinets at right angles to one another against the walls. In this corner stands a flat writing-table, on which are a phonograph, a laryngoscope, a row of tiny organ pipes with bellows, a set of lamp chimneys for singing flames with burners attached to a gas plug in the wall by an indiarubber tube, several tuning-forks of different sizes, a life-size image of half a human head, showing in section the vocal organs, and a box containing a supply of wax cylinders for the phonograph.*

*Further down the room, on the same side, is a fireplace, with a comfortable leather-covered easy-chair at the side of the hearth nearest the door, and a coal-scuttle. There is a clock on the mantelpiece. Between the fireplace and the phonograph table is a stand for newspapers.*

*On the other side of the central door, to the left of the visitor, is a cabinet of shallow drawers. On it is a telephone and the telephone directory. The corner beyond, and most of the side wall, is occupied by a grand piano, with the keyboard at the end furthest from the door, and a bench for the player extending the full length of the keyboard. On the piano is a dessert dish heaped with fruit and sweets, mostly chocolates.*

*The middle of the room is clear. Besides the easy-chair, the piano bench, and two chairs at the phonograph table, there is one stray chair. It stands near the fireplace. On the walls, engravings: mostly Piranesis and mezzotint portraits. No paintings.*

Pickering *is seated at the table, putting down some cards and a tuning-fork which he has been using.* Higgins *is standing up near him, closing two or three file drawers which are hanging out. He appears in the morning light as a robust, vital, appetizing sort of man of forty or thereabouts, dressed in a professional-looking black frock-coat with a white linen collar and black silk tie. He is of the energetic, scientific type, heartily, even violently interested in everything that can be studied as a scientific subject, and careless about himself and other people, including their feelings. He is, in fact, but for his years and size, rather like a very impetuous baby "taking notice" eagerly and loudly, and requiring almost as much watching to keep him out of unintended mischief. His manner varies from genial bullying when he is in a good humor to stormy petulance when anything goes wrong; but he is so entirely frank and void of malice that he remains likeable even in his least reasonable moments.*

HIGGINS (*as he shuts the last drawer*):
Well, I think that's the whole show.
PICKERING:
It's really amazing. I haven't taken half of it in, you know.
HIGGINS:
Would you like to go over any of it again?
PICKERING (*rising and coming to the fireplace, where he plants himself with his back to the fire*):
No, thank you; not now. I'm quite done up for this morning.
HIGGINS (*following him, and standing beside him on his left*):
Tired of listening to sounds?
PICKERING:
Yes. It's a fearful strain. I rather fancied myself because I can pronounce twenty-four distinct vowel sounds; but your hundred and thirty beat me. I can't hear a bit of difference between most of them.
HIGGINS (*chuckling, and going over to the piano to eat sweets*):
Oh, that comes with practice. You hear no difference at first; but you keep on listening, and presently you find they're all as different as A from B. (Mrs Pearce *looks in: she is* Higgins's *housekeeper*). What's the matter?
MRS PEARCE (*hesitating, evidently perplexed*):
A young woman wants to see you sir.
HIGGINS:
A young woman! What does she want?
MRS PEARCE:
Well, sir, she says you'll be glad to see her when you know what she's come about. She's quite a common girl, sir. Very common indeed. I should have sent her away, only I thought perhaps

you wanted her to talk into your machines. I hope I've not done wrong; but really you see such queer people sometimes— you'll excuse me, I'm sure, sir—

HIGGINS:

Oh, that's all right, Mrs Pearce. Has she an interesting accent?

MRS PEARCE:

Oh, something dreadful, sir, really. I don't know how you can take an interest in it.

HIGGINS (*to* Pickering):

Lets have her up. Show her up, Mrs Pearce (*he rushes across to his working table and picks out a cylinder to use on the phonograph*).

MRS PEARCE (*only half resigned to it*):

Very well, sir. It's for you to say. (*She goes downstairs*).

HIGGINS:

This is rather a bit of luck. I'll show you how I make records. We'll set her talking; and I'll take it down first in Bell's visible Speech; then in broad Romic; and then we'll get her on the phonograph so that you can turn her on as often as you like with the written transcript before you.

MRS PEARCE (*returning*):

This is the young woman, sir.

The Flower Girl *enters in state. She has a hat with three ostrich feathers, orange, sky-blue, and red. She has a nearly clean apron, and the shoddy coat has been tidied a little. The pathos of this deplorable figure, with its innocent vanity and consequential air, touches* Pickering, *who has already straightened himself in the presence of* Mrs Pearce. *But as to* Higgins, *the only distinction he makes between men and women is that when he is neither bullying nor exclaiming to the heavens against some feather-weight cross, he coaxes women as a child coaxes its nurse when it wants to get anything out of her.*

HIGGINS (*brusquely, recognizing her with unconcealed disappointment, and at once, babylike, making an intolerable grievance of it*):

Why, this is the girl I jotted down last night. She's no use: I've got all the records I want of the Lisson Grove lingo; and I'm not going to waste another cylinder on it. (*To the girl*) Be off with you: I don't want you.

THE FLOWER GIRL:

Don't you be so saucy. You ain't heard what I come for yet. (*To Mrs Pearce, who is waiting at the door for further instructions*) Did you tell him I come in a taxi?

MRS PEARCE:

> Nonsense, girl! what do you think a gentleman like Mr Higgins cares what you came in?

THE FLOWER GIRL:

> Oh, we are proud! He ain't above giving lessons, not him: I heard him say so. Well, I ain't come here to ask for any compliment; and if my money's not good enough I can go elsewhere.

HIGGINS:

> Good enough for what?

THE FLOWER GIRL:

> Good enough for ye-oo. Now you know, don't you? I'm come to have lessons, I am. And to pay for em too: make no mistake.

HIGGINS (*stupent*):

> Well!!! (*Recovering his breath with a gasp*) What do you expect me to say to you?

THE FLOWER GIRL:

> Well, if you was a gentleman, you might ask me to sit down, I think. Don't I tell you I'm bringing you business?

HIGGINS:

> Pickering: shall we ask this baggage to sit down, or shall we throw her out of the window?

THE FLOWER GIRL (*running away in terror to the piano, where she turns at bay*):

> Ah-ah-oh-ow-ow-ow-oo! (*Wounded and whimpering*) I won't be called a baggage when I've offered to pay like any lady.

*Motionless, the two men stare at her from the other side of the room, amazed.*

PICKERING (*gently*):

> What is it you want, my girl?

THE FLOWER GIRL:

> I want to be a lady in a flower shop stead of selling at the corner of Tottenham Court Road. But they won't take me unless I can talk more genteel. He said he could teach me. Well, here I am ready to pay him—not asking any favor—and he treats me as if I was dirt.

MRS PEARCE:

> How can you be such a foolish ignorant girl as to think you could afford to pay Mr Higgins?

THE FLOWER GIRL:

> Why shouldn't I? I know what lessons cost as well as you do; and I'm ready to pay.

HIGGINS:

How much?

THE FLOWER GIRL (*coming back to him, triumphant*):

Now you're talking! I thought you'd come off it when you saw a chance of getting back a bit of what you chucked at me last night. (*Confidentially*) You'd had a drop in, hadn't you?

HIGGINS (*peremptorily*):

Sit down.

THE FLOWER GIRL:

Oh, if you're going to make a compliment of it—

HIGGINS (*thundering at her*):

Sit down.

MRS PEARCE (*severely*):

Sit down, girl. Do as you're told. (*She places the stray chair near the hearthrug between* Higgins *and* Pickering, *and stands behind it waiting for the girl to sit down*).

THE FLOWER GIRL:

Ah-ah-ah-ow-ow-oo! (*She stands, half rebellious, half bewildered*).

PICKERING (*very courteous*):

Won't you sit down?

LIZA (*coyly*):

Don't mind if I do. (*She sits down.* Pickering *returns to the hearthrug*).

HIGGINS:

What's your name?

THE FLOWER GIRL:

Liza Doolittle.

HIGGINS (*declaiming gravely*):

Eliza, Elizabeth, Betsy and Bess,
They went to the woods to get a bird's nes':

PICKERING:

They found a nest with four eggs in it:

HIGGINS:

They took one apiece, and left three in it.

*They laugh heartily at their own wit.*

LIZA:

Oh, don't be silly.

MRS PEARCE:

You mustn't speak to the gentleman like that.

LIZA:

Well, why won't he speak sensible to me?

HIGGINS:

Come back to business. How much do you propose to pay me for the lessons?

LIZA:

Oh, I know what's right. A lady friend of mine gets French lessons for eighteenpence an hour from a real French gentleman. Well, you wouldn't have the face to ask me the same for teaching me my own language as you would for French; so I won't give more than a shilling. Take it or leave it.

HIGGINS (*walking up and down the room, rattling his keys and his cash in his pockets*):

You know, Pickering, if you consider a shilling, not as a simple shilling, but as a percentage of this girl's income, it works out as fully equivalent to sixty or seventy guineas from a millionaire.

PICKERING:

How so?

HIGGINS:

Figure it out. A millionaire has about £150 a day. She earns about half-a-crown.

LIZA (*haughtily*):

Who told you I only—

HIGGINS (*continuing*):

She offers me two-fifths of her day's income for a lesson. Two-fifths of a millionaire's income for a day would be somewhere about £60. It's handsome. By George, it's enormous! it's the biggest offer I ever had.

LIZA (*rising, terrified*):

Sixty pounds! What are you talking about? I never offered you sixty pounds. Where would I get—

HIGGINS:

Hold your tongue.

LIZA (*weeping*):

But I ain't got sixty pounds. Oh—

MRS PEARCE:

Don't cry, you silly girl. Sit down. Nobody is going to touch your money.

HIGGINS:

Somebody is going to touch you, with a broomstick, if you don't stop snivelling. Sit down.

LIZA (*obeying slowly*):

Ah-ah-ah-ow-oo-o! One would think you was my father.

HIGGINS:

If I decide to teach you, I'll be worse than two fathers to you. Here (*he offers her his silk handkerchief*)!

LIZA:

What's this for?

HIGGINS:

To wipe your eyes. To wipe any part of your face that feels moist. Remember: that's your handkerchief; and that's your sleeve. Don't mistake the one for the other if you wish to become a lady in a shop.

Liza, *utterly bewildered, stares helplessly at him.*

MRS PEARCE:

It's no use talking to her like that, Mr Higgins: she doesn't understand you. Besides, you're quite wrong: she doesn't do it that way at all (*she takes the handkerchief*).

LIZA (*snatching it*):

Here! You give me that handkerchief. He give it to me, not to you.

PICKERING (*laughing*):

He did. I think it must be regarded as her property, Mrs Pearce.

MRS PEARCE (*resigning herself*):

Serve you right, Mr Higgins.

PICKERING:

Higgins: I'm interested. What about the ambassador's garden party? I'll say you're the greatest teacher alive if you make that good. I'll bet you all the expenses of the experiment you can't do it. And I'll pay for the lessons.

LIZA:

Oh, you are real good. Thank you, Captain.

HIGGINS (*tempted, looking at her*):

It's almost irresistible. She's so deliciously low—so horribly dirty—

LIZA (*protesting extremely*):

Ah-ah-ah-ah-ow-ow-oo-oo!!! I ain't dirty: I washed my face and hands afore I come, I did.

PICKERING:

You're certainly not going to turn her head with flattery, Higgins.

MRS PEARCE (*uneasy*):

Oh, don't say that, sir: there's more ways than one of turning a girl's head; and nobody can do it better than Mr Higgins, though he may not always mean it. I do hope, sir, you won't encourage him to do anything foolish.

HIGGINS (*becoming excited as the idea grows on him*):

What is life but a series of inspired follies? The difficulty is to find them to do. Never lose a chance: it doesn't come every day. I shall make a duchess of this draggletailed guttersnipe.

LIZA (*strongly deprecating this view of her*):

Ah-ah-ah-ow-ow-oo!

HIGGINS (*carried away*):

Yes: in six months—in three if she has a good ear and a quick tongue—I'll take her anywhere and pass her off as anything. We'll start today: now! this moment! Take her away and clean her, Mrs Pearce. Monkey Brand, if it won't come off any other way. Is there a good fire in the kitchen?

MRS PEARCE (*protesting*):

Yes; but—

HIGGINS (*storming on*):

Take all her clothes off and burn them. Ring up Whiteley or somebody for new ones. Wrap her up in brown paper till they come.

LIZA:

You're no gentleman, you're not, to talk of such things. I'm a good girl, I am; and I know what the like of you are, I do.

HIGGINS:

We want none of your Lisson Grove prudery here, young woman. You've got to learn to behave like a duchess. Take her away, Mrs Pearce. If she gives you any trouble, wallop her.

LIZA (*springing up and running between* Pickering *and* Mrs Pearce *for protection*):

No! I'll call the police, I will.

MRS PEARCE:

But I've no place to put her.

HIGGINS:

Put her in the dustbin.

LIZA:

Ah-ah-ah-ow-ow-oo!

PICKERING:

Oh come, Higgins! be reasonable.

MRS PEARCE (*resolutely*):

You must be reasonable, Mr Higgins: really you must. You can't walk over everybody like this.

Higgins, *thus scolded, subsides. The hurricane is succeeded by a zephyr of amiable surprise.*

HIGGINS (*with professional exquisiteness of modulation*):

*I* walk over everybody! My dear Mrs Pearce, my dear Pickering, I never had the slightest intention of walking over anyone. All I propose is that we should be kind to this poor girl. We must help her to prepare and fit herself for her new station in life. If I did not express myself clearly it was because I did not wish to hurt her delicacy, or yours.

Liza, *reassured, steals back to her chair.*

MRS PEARCE (*to* Pickering):

Well, did you ever hear anything like that, sir?

PICKERING (*laughing heartily*):

Never, Mrs Pearce: never.

HIGGINS (*patiently*):

What's the matter?

MRS PEARCE:

Well, the matter is, sir, that you can't take a girl up like that as if you were picking up a pebble on the beach.

HIGGINS:

Why not?

MRS PEARCE:

Why not! But you don't know anything about her. What about her parents? She may be married.

LIZA:

Garn!

HIGGINS:

There! As the girl very properly says, Garn! Married indeed! Don't you know that a woman of that class looks a worn out drudge of fifty a year after she's married?

LIZA:

Who'od marry me?

HIGGINS (*suddenly resorting to the most thrillingly beautiful low tones in his best elocutionary style*):

By George, Eliza, the streets will be strewn with the bodies of men shooting themselves for your sake before I've done with you.

MRS PEARCE:

Nonsense, sir. You mustn't talk like that to her.

LIZA (*rising and squaring herself determinedly*):

I'm going away. He's off his chump, he is. I don't want no balmies teaching me.

HIGGINS (*wounded in his tenderest point by her insensibility to his elocution*):

Oh, indeed! I'm mad, am I? Very well, Mrs Pearce: you needn't order the new clothes for her. Throw her out.

LIZA (*whimpering*):

Nah-ow. You got no right to touch me.

MRS PEARCE:

You see now what comes of being saucy. (*Indicating the door*) This way, please.

LIZA (*almost in tears*):

I didn't want no clothes. I wouldn't have taken them (*she throws away the handkerchief*). I can buy my own clothes.

HIGGINS (*deftly retrieving the handkerchief and intercepting her on her reluctant way to the door*):

You're an ungrateful wicked girl. This is my return for offering to take you out of the gutter and dress you beautifully and make a lady of you.

MRS PEARCE:

Stop, Mr Higgins. I won't allow it. It's you that are wicked. Go home to your parents, girl; and tell them to take better care of you.

LIZA:

I ain't got no parents. They told me I was big enough to earn my own living and turned me out.

MRS PEARCE:

Where's your mother?

LIZA:

I ain't got no mother. Her that turned me out was my sixth stepmother. But I done without them. And I'm a good girl, I am.

HIGGINS:

Very well, then, what on earth is all this fuss about? The girl doesn't belong to anybody—is no use to anybody but me. (*He goes to* Mrs Pearce *and begins coaxing*). You can adopt her, Mrs Pearce: I'm sure a daughter would be a great amusement to you. Now don't make any more fuss. Take her downstairs; and—

MRS PEARCE:

But what's to become of her? Is she to be paid anything? Do be sensible, sir.

HIGGINS:

Oh, pay her whatever is necessary: put it down in the house-keeping book. (*Impatiently*) What on earth will she want with money? She'll have her food and her clothes. She'll only drink if you give her money.

LIZA (*turning on him*):

> Oh you are a brute. It's a lie: nobody ever saw the sign of liquor on me. (*She goes back to her chair and plants herself there defiantly*).

PICKERING (*in good-humored remonstrance*):

> Does it occur to you, Higgins, that the girl has some feelings?

HIGGINS (*looking critically at her*):

> Oh no, I don't think so. Not any feelings that we need bother about. (*Cheerily*) Have you, Eliza?

LIZA:

> I got my feelings same as anyone else.

HIGGINS (*to* Pickering, *reflectively*):

> You see the difficulty?

PICKERING:

> Eh? What difficulty?

HIGGINS:

> To get her to talk grammar. The mere pronunciation is easy enough.

LIZA:

> I don't want to talk grammar. I want to talk like a lady.

MRS PEARCE:

> Will you please keep to the point, Mr Higgins? I want to know on what terms the girl is to be here. Is she to have any wages? And what is to become of her when you've finished your teaching? You must look ahead a little.

HIGGINS (*impatiently*):

> What's to become of her if I leave her in the gutter? Tell me that, Mrs Pearce.

MRS PEARCE:

> That's her own business, not yours, Mr Higgins.

HIGGINS:

> Well, when I've done with her, we can throw her back into the gutter; and then it will be her own business again; so that's all right.

LIZA:

> Oh, you've no feeling heart in you: you don't care for nothing but yourself (*she rises and takes the floor resolutely*). Here! I've had enough of this. I'm going (*making for the door*). You ought to be ashamed of yourself, you ought.

HIGGINS (*snatching a chocolate cream from the piano, his eyes suddenly beginning to twinkle with mischief*):

> Have some chocolates, Eliza.

LIZA (*halting, tempted*):

How do I know what might be in them? I've heard of girls being drugged by the like of you.

Higgins *whips out his penknife; cuts a chocolate in two; puts one half into his mouth and bolts it; and offers her the other half.*

HIGGINS:

Pledge of good faith, Eliza. I eat one half: you eat the other. (Liza *opens her mouth to retort: he pops the half chocolate into it*). You shall have boxes of them, barrels of them, every day. You shall live on them. Eh?

LIZA (*who has disposed of the chocolate after being nearly choked by it*):

I wouldn't have ate it, only I'm too ladylike to take it out of my mouth.

HIGGINS:

Listen, Eliza. I think you said you came in a taxi.

LIZA:

Well, what if I did? I've as good a right to take a taxi as anyone else.

HIGGINS:

You have, Eliza; and in future you shall have as many taxis as you want. You shall go up and down and round the town in a taxi every day. Think of that, Eliza.

MRS PEARCE:

Mr Higgins: you're tempting the girl. It's not right. She should think of the future.

HIGGINS:

At her age! Nonsense! Time enough to think of the future when you haven't any future to think of. No, Eliza: do as this lady does: think of other people's futures; but never think of your own. Think of chocolates, and taxis, and gold, and diamonds.

LIZA:

No: I don't want no gold and no diamonds. I'm a good girl, I am. (*She sits down again, with an attempt at dignity*).

HIGGINS:

You shall remain so, Eliza, under the care of Mrs Pearce. And you shall marry an officer in the Guards, with a beautiful moustache: the son of a marquis, who will disinherit him for marrying you, but will relent when he sees your beauty and goodness—

PICKERING:

Excuse me, Higgins; but I really must interfere. Mrs Pearce is quite right. If this girl is to put herself in your hands for six months for an experiment in teaching, she must understand thoroughly what she's doing.

HIGGINS:

How can she? She's incapable of understanding anything. Besides, do any of us understand what we are doing? If we did, would we ever do it?

PICKERING:

Very clever, Higgins; but not sound sense. (*To* Eliza) Miss Doolittle—

LIZA (*overwhelmed*):

Ah-ah-ow-oo!

HIGGINS:

There! That's all you'll get out of Eliza. Ah-ah-ow-oo! No use explaining. As a military man you ought to know that. Give her her orders: that's what she wants. Eliza: you are to live here for the next six months, learning how to speak beautifully, like a lady in a florist's shop. If you're good and do whatever you're told, you shall sleep in a proper bedroom, and have lots to eat, and money to buy chocolates and take rides in taxis. If you're naughty and idle you will sleep in the back kitchen among the black beetles, and be walloped by Mrs Pearce with a broomstick. At the end of six months you shall go to Buckingham Palace in a carriage, beautifully dressed. If the King finds out you're not a lady, you will be taken by the police to the Tower of London, where your head will be cut off as a warning to other presumptuous flower girls. If you are not found out, you shall have a present of seven-and-sixpence to start life with as a lady in a shop. If you refuse this offer you will be a most ungrateful and wicked girl; and the angels will weep for you. (*To* Pickering) Now are you satisfied, Pickering? (*To* Mrs Pearce) Can I put it more plainly and fairly, Mrs Pearce?

MRS PEARCE (*patiently*):

I think you'd better let me speak to the girl properly in private. I don't know that I can take charge of her or consent to the arrangement at all. Of course I know you don't mean her any harm; but when you get what you call interested in people's accents, you never think or care what may happen to them or you. Come with me, Eliza.

HIGGINS:

That's all right. Thank you, Mrs Pearce. Bundle her off to the bath-room.

LIZA (*rising reluctantly and suspiciously*):

You're a great bully, you are. I won't stay here if I don't like. I won't let nobody wallop me. I never asked to go to Buck'n'am

Palace, I didn't. I was never in trouble with the police, not me. I'm a good girl—

MRS PEARCE:

Don't answer back, girl. You don't understand the gentleman. Come with me. (*She leads the way to the door, and holds it open for* Eliza).

LIZA (*as she goes out*):

Well, what I say is right. I won't go near the King, not if I'm going to have my head cut off. If I'd known what I was letting myself in for, I wouldn't have come here. I always been a good girl; and I never offered to say a word to him; and I don't owe him nothing; and I don't care; and I won't be put upon; and I have my feelings the same as anyone else—

Mrs Pearce *shuts the door; and* Eliza's *plaints are no longer audible.* Pickering *comes from the hearth to the chair and sits astride it with his arms on the back.*

PICKERING:

Excuse the straight question, Higgins. Are you a man of good character where women are concerned?

HIGGINS (*moodily*):

Have you ever met a man of good character where women are concerned?

PICKERING:

Yes: very frequently.

HIGGINS (*dogmatically, lifting himself on his hands to the level of the piano, and sitting on it with a bounce*):

Well, I haven't. I find that the moment I let a woman make friends with me, she becomes jealous, exacting, suspicious, and a damned nuisance. I find that the moment I let myself make friends with a woman, I become selfish and tyrannical. Women upset everything. When you let them into your life, you find that the woman is driving at one thing and you're driving at another.

PICKERING:

At what, for example?

HIGGINS (*coming off the piano restlessly*):

Oh, Lord knows! I suppose the woman wants to live her own life; and the man wants to live his; and each tries to drag the other on to the wrong track. One wants to go north and the other south; and the result is that both have to go east, though they both hate the east wind. (*He sits down on the bench at the keyboard*). So here I am, a confirmed old bachelor, and likely to remain so.

PICKERING (*rising and standing over him gravely*):

Come, Higgins! You know what I mean. If I'm to be in this business I shall feel responsible for that girl. I hope it's understood that no advantage is to be taken of her position.

HIGGINS:

What! That thing! Sacred, I assure you. (*Rising to explain*) You see, she'll be a pupil; and teaching would be impossible unless pupils were sacred. I've taught scores of American millionairesses how to speak English: the best looking women in the world. I'm seasoned. They might as well be blocks of wood. *I* might as well be a block of wood. It's—

Mrs Pearce *opens the door. She has* Eliza's *hat in her hand.* Pickering *retires to the easy-chair at the hearth and sits down.*

HIGGINS (*eagerly*):

Well, Mrs Pearce: is it all right?

MRS PEARCE (*at the door*):

I just wish to trouble you with a word, if I may, Mr Higgins.

HIGGINS:

Yes, certainly. Come in. (*She comes forward*). Don't burn that, Mrs Pearce. I'll keep it as a curiosity. (*He takes the hat*).

MRS PEARCE:

Handle it carefully, sir, please. I had to promise her not to burn it; but I had better put it in the oven for a while.

HIGGINS (*putting it down hastily on the piano*):

Oh! thank you. Well, what have you to say to me?

PICKERING:

Am I in the way?

MRS PEARCE:

Not at all, sir. Mr Higgins: will you please be very particular what you say before the girl?

HIGGINS (*sternly*):

Of course. I'm always particular about what I say. Why do you say this to me?

MRS PEARCE (*unmoved*):

No, sir: you're not at all particular when you've mislaid anything or when you get a little impatient. Now it doesn't matter before me: I'm used to it. But you really must not swear before the girl.

HIGGINS (*indignantly*):

> *I* swear! (*Most emphatically*) I never swear. I detest the habit.
> What the devil do you mean?

MRS PEARCE (*stolidly*):

> That's what I mean, sir. You swear a great deal too much. I
> don't mind your damning and blasting, and what the devil and
> where the devil and who the devil—

HIGGINS:

> Mrs Pearce: this language from your lips! Really!

MRS PEARCE (*not to be put off*):

> —but there is a certain word I must ask you not to use. The girl
> has just used it herself because the bath was too hot. It begins
> with the same letter as bath. She knows no better: she learnt it
> at her mother's knee. But she must not hear it from your lips.

HIGGINS (*loftily*):

> I cannot charge myself with having ever uttered it, Mrs Pearce.
> (*She looks at him steadfastly. He adds, hiding an uneasy conscience
> with a judicial air*) Except perhaps in a moment of extreme and
> justifiable excitement.

MRS PEARCE:

> Only this morning, sir, you applied it to your boots, to the but-
> ter, and to the brown bread.

HIGGINS:

> Oh, that! Mere alliteration, Mrs Pearce, natural to a poet.

MRS PEARCE:

> Well, sir, whatever you choose to call it, I beg you not to let the
> girl hear you repeat it.

HIGGINS:

> Oh, very well, very well. Is that all?

MRS PEARCE:

> No, sir. We shall have to be very particular with this girl as to
> personal cleanliness.

HIGGINS:

> Certainly. Quite right. Most important.

MRS PEARCE:

> I mean not to be slovenly about her dress or untidy in leaving
> things about.

HIGGINS (*going to her solemnly*):

> Just so. I intended to call your attention to that. (*He passes on to*
> Pickering, *who is enjoying the conversation immensely*). It is these
> little things that matter, Pickering. Take care of the pence and
> the pounds will take care of themselves is as true of personal

habits as of money. (*He comes to anchor on the hearthrug, with the air of a man in an unassailable position*).

MRS PEARCE:

Yes, sir. Then might I ask you not to come down to breakfast in your dressing-gown, or at any rate not to use it as a napkin to the extent you do, sir. And if you would be so good as not to eat everything off the same plate, and to remember not to put the porridge saucepan out of your hand on the clean table-cloth, it would be a better example to the girl. You know you nearly choked yourself with a fishbone in the jam only last week.

HIGGINS (*routed from the hearthrug and drifting back to the piano*):

I may do these things sometimes in absence of mind; but surely I don't do them habitually. (*Angrily*) By the way: my dressing-gown smells most damnably of benzine.

MRS PEARCE:

No doubt it does, Mr Higgins. But if you will wipe your fingers—

HIGGINS (*yelling*):

Oh very well, very well: I'll wipe them in my hair in future.

MRS PEARCE:

I hope you're not offended, Mr Higgins.

HIGGINS (*shocked at finding himself thought capable of an unamiable sentiment*):

Not at all, not at all. You're quite right, Mrs Pearce: I shall be particularly careful before the girl. Is that all?

MRS PEARCE:

No, sir. Might she use some of those Japanese dresses you brought from abroad? I really can't put her back into her old things.

HIGGINS:

Certainly. Anything you like. Is that all?

MRS PEARCE:

Thank you, sir. That's all. (*She goes out*).

HIGGINS:

You know, Pickering, that woman has the most extraordinary ideas about me. Here I am, a shy, diffident sort of man. I've never been able to feel really grown-up and tremendous, like other chaps. And yet she's firmly persuaded that I'm an arbitrary overbearing bossing kind of person. I can't account for it.

Mrs Pearce *returns*.

MRS PEARCE:

If you please, sir, the trouble's beginning already. There's a dustman downstairs, Alfred Doolittle, wants to see you. He says you have his daughter here.

PICKERING (*rising*):

Phew! I say! (*He retreats to the hearthrug*).

HIGGINS (*promptly*):

Send the blackguard up.

MRS PEARCE:

Oh, very well, sir. (*She goes out*).

PICKERING:

He may not be a blackguard, Higgins.

HIGGINS:

Nonsense. Of course he's a blackguard.

PICKERING:

Whether he is or not, I'm afraid we shall have some trouble with him.

HIGGINS (*confidently*):

Oh no: I think not. If there's any trouble he shall have it with me, not I with him. And we are sure to get something interesting out of him.

PICKERING:

About the girl?

HIGGINS:

No. I mean his dialect.

PICKERING:

Oh!

MRS PEARCE (*at the door*):

Doolittle, sir. (*She admits* Doolittle *and retires*).

Alfred Doolittle *is an elderly but vigorous dustman, clad in the costume of his profession, including a hat with a back brim covering his neck and shoulders. He has well marked and rather interesting features, and seems equally free from fear and conscience. He has a remarkably expressive voice, the result of a habit of giving vent to his feelings without reserve. His present pose is that of wounded honor and stern resolution.*

DOOLITTLE (*at the door, uncertain which of the two gentlemen is his man*):

Professor Higgins?

HIGGINS:

Here. Good morning. Sit down.

DOOLITTLE:

> Morning, Governor. (*He sits down magisterially*) I come about a very serious matter, Governor.

HIGGINS (*to* Pickering):

> Brought up in Hounslow. Mother Welsh, I should think. (Doolittle *opens his mouth, amazed.* Higgins *continues*) What do you want, Doolittle?

DOOLITTLE (*menacingly*):

> I want my daughter: that's what I want. See?

HIGGINS:

> Of course you do. You're her father, aren't you? You don't suppose anyone else wants her, do you? I'm glad to see you have some spark of family feeling left. She's upstairs. Take her away at once.

DOOLITTLE (*rising, fearfully taken aback*):

> What!

HIGGINS:

> Take her away. Do you suppose I'm going to keep your daughter for you?

DOOLITTLE (*remonstrating*):

> Now, now, look here, Governor. Is this reasonable? Is it fairity to take advantage of a man like this? The girl belongs to me. You got her. Where do I come in? (*He sits down again*).

HIGGINS:

> Your daughter had the audacity to come to my house and ask me to teach her how to speak properly so that she could get a place in a flower-shop. This gentleman and my housekeeper have been here all the time. (*Bullying him*) How dare you come here and attempt to blackmail me? You sent her here on purpose.

DOOLITTLE (*protesting*):

> No, Governor.

HIGGINS:

> You must have. How else could you possibly know that she is here?

DOOLITTLE:

> Don't take a man up like that, Governor.

HIGGINS:

> The police shall take you up. This is a plant—a plot to extort money by threats. I shall telephone for the police. (*He goes resolutely to the telephone and opens the directory*).

DOOLITTLE:

> Have I asked you for a brass farthing? I leave it to the gentleman here: have I said a word about money?

HIGGINS (*throwing the book aside and marching down on* Doolittle *with a poser*):

What else did you come for?

DOOLITTLE (*sweetly*):

Well, what would a man come for? Be human, Governor.

HIGGINS (*disarmed*):

Alfred: did you put her up to it?

DOOLITTLE:

So help me, Governor, I never did. I take my Bible oath I ain't seen the girl these two months past.

HIGGINS:

Then how did you know she was here?

DOOLITTLE ("*most musical, most melancholy*"):

I'll tell you, Governor, if you'll only let me get a word in. I'm willing to tell you. I'm wanting to tell you. I'm waiting to tell you.

HIGGINS:

Pickering: this chap has a certain natural gift of rhetoric. Observe the rhythm of his native woodnotes wild. "I'm willing to tell you: I'm wanting to tell you: I'm waiting to tell you." Sentimental rhetoric! that's the Welsh strain in him. It also accounts for his mendacity and dishonesty.

PICKERING:

Oh, please, Higgins: I'm west-country myself. (*To* Doolittle) How did you know the girl was here if you didn't send her?

DOOLITTLE:

It was like this, Governor. The girl took a boy in the taxi to give him a jaunt. Son of her landlady, he is. He hung about on the chance of her giving him another ride home. Well, she sent him back for her luggage when she heard you was willing for her to stop here. I met the boy at the corner of Long Acre and Endell Street.

HIGGINS:

Public house. Yes?

DOOLITTLE:

The poor man's club, Governor: why shouldn't I?

PICKERING:

Do let him tell his story, Higgins.

DOOLITTLE:

He told me what was up. And I ask you, what was my feelings and my duty as a father? I says to the boy, "You bring me the luggage," I says—

PICKERING:

Why didn't you go for it yourself?

DOOLITTLE:

Landlady wouldn't have trusted me with it, Governor. She's that kind of woman: you know. I had to give the boy a penny afore he trusted me with it, the little swine. I brought it to her just to oblige you like, and make myself agreeable. That's all.

HIGGINS:

How much luggage?

DOOLITTLE:

Musical instrument, Governor. A few pictures, a trifle of jewellery, and a bird-cage. She said she didn't want no clothes. What was I to think from that, Governor? I ask you as a parent what was I to think?

HIGGINS:

So you came to rescue her from worse than death, eh?

DOOLITTLE (*appreciatively: relieved at being so well understood*):

Just so, Governor. That's right.

PICKERING:

But why did you bring her luggage if you intended to take her away?

DOOLITTLE:

Have I said a word about taking her away? Have I now?

HIGGINS (*determinedly*):

You're going to take her away, double quick. (*He crosses to the hearth and rings the bell*).

DOOLITTLE (*rising*):

No, Governor. Don't say that. I'm not the man to stand in my girl's light. Here's a career opening for her, as you might say; and—

Mrs Pearce *opens the door and awaits orders.*

HIGGINS:

Mrs Pearce: this is Eliza's father. He has come to take her away. Give her to him. (*He goes back to the piano, with an air of washing his hands of the whole affair*).

DOOLITTLE:

No. This is a misunderstanding. Listen here—

MRS PEARCE:

He can't take her away, Mr Higgins: how can he? You told me to burn her clothes.

DOOLITTLE:

> That's right. I can't carry the girl through the streets like a blooming monkey, can I? I put it to you.

HIGGINS:

> You have put it to me that you want your daughter. Take your daughter. If she has no clothes go out and buy her some.

DOOLITTLE (*desperate*):

> Where's the clothes she come in? Did I burn them or did your missus here?

MRS PEARCE:

> I am the housekeeper, if you please. I have sent for some clothes for your girl. When they come you can take her away. You can wait in the kitchen. This way, please.

*Doolittle, much troubled, accompanies her to the door; then hesitates; finally turns confidentially to* Higgins.

DOOLITTLE:

> Listen here, Governor. You and me is men of the world, ain't we?

HIGGINS:

> Oh! Men of the world, are we? You'd better go, Mrs Pearce.

MRS PEARCE:

> I think so, indeed, sir. (*She goes, with dignity*).

PICKERING:

> The floor is yours, Mr Doolittle.

DOOLITTLE (*to* Pickering):

> I thank you, Governor. (*To* Higgins, *who takes refuge on the piano bench, a little overwhelmed by the proximity of his visitor; for* Doolittle *has a professional flavor of dust about him*). Well, the truth is, I've taken a sort of fancy to you, Governor; and if you want the girl, I'm not so set on having her back home again but what I might be open to an arrangement. Regarded in the light of a young woman, she's a fine handsome girl. As a daughter she's not worth her keep; and so I tell you straight. All I ask is my rights as a father; and you're the last man alive to expect me to let her go for nothing; for I can see you're one of the straight sort, Governor. Well, what's a five-pound note to you? And what's Eliza to me? (*He returns to his chair and sits down judicially*).

PICKERING:

> I think you ought to know, Doolittle, that Mr Higgins's intentions are entirely honorable.

DOOLITTLE:

Course they are, Governor. If I thought they wasn't, I'd ask fifty.

HIGGINS (*revolted*):

Do you mean to say, you callous rascal, that you would sell your daughter for £50?

DOOLITTLE:

Not in a general way I wouldn't; but to oblige a gentleman like you I'd do a good deal, I do assure you.

PICKERING:

Have you no morals, man?

DOOLITTLE (*unabashed*):

Can't afford them, Governor. Neither could you if you was as poor as me. Not that I mean any harm, you know. But if Liza is going to have a bit out of this, why not me too?

HIGGINS (*troubled*):

I don't know what to do, Pickering. There can be no question that as a matter of morals it's a positive crime to give this chap a farthing. And yet I feel a sort of rough justice in his claim.

DOOLITTLE:

That's it, Governor. That's all I say. A father's heart, as it were.

PICKERING:

Well, I know the feeling; but really it seems hardly right—

DOOLITTLE:

Don't say that, Governor. Don't look at it that way. What am I, Governors both? I ask you, what am I? I'm one of the undeserving poor: that's what I am. Think of what that means to a man. It means that he's up agen middle class morality all the time. If there's anything going, and I put in for a bit of it, it's always the same story: "You're undeserving; so you can't have it." But my needs is as great as the most deserving widow's that ever got money out of six different charities in one week for the death of the same husband. I don't need less than a deserving man: I need more. I don't eat less hearty than him; and I drink a lot more. I want a bit of amusement, cause I'm a thinking man. I want cheerfulness and a song and a band when I feel low. Well, they charge me just the same for everything as they charge the deserving. What is middle class morality? Just an excuse for never giving me anything. Therefore, I ask you, as two gentlemen, not to play that game on me. I'm playing straight with you. I ain't pretending to be deserving. I'm undeserving; and I mean to go on being undeserving. I like it; and that's the truth. Will you take advantage of a man's nature to do him out of the price of his own daughter what he's brought up and fed and clothed by the sweat of his brow until she's growed big enough to be interesting to you two gentlemen? Is five pounds unreasonable? I put it to you; and I leave it to you.

HIGGINS (*rising, and going over to* Pickering):

Pickering: if we were to take this man in hand for three months, he could choose between a seat in the Cabinet and a popular pulpit in Wales.

PICKERING:

What do you say to that, Doolittle?

DOOLITTLE:

Not me, Governor, thank you kindly. I've heard all the preachers and all the prime ministers—for I'm a thinking man and game for politics or religion or social reform same as all the other amusements—and I tell you it's a dog's life any way you look at it. Undeserving poverty is my line. Taking one station in society with another, it's—it's—well, it's the only one that has any ginger in it, to my taste.

HIGGINS:

I suppose we must give him a fiver.

PICKERING:

He'll make a bad use of it, I'm afraid.

DOOLITTLE:

Not me, Governor, so help me I won't. Don't you be afraid that I'll save it and spare it and live idle on it. There won't be a penny of it left by Monday: I'll have to go to work same as if I'd never had it. It won't pauperize me, you bet. Just one good spree for myself and the missus, giving pleasure to ourselves and employment to others, and satisfaction to you to think it's not been throwed away. You couldn't spend it better.

HIGGINS (*taking out his pocket book and coming between* Doolittle *and the piano*):

This is irresistible. Let's give him ten. (*He offers two notes to the dustman*).

DOOLITTLE:

No, Governor. She wouldn't have the heart to spend ten; and perhaps I shouldn't neither. Ten pounds is a lot of money: it makes a man feel prudent like; and then goodbye to happiness. You give me what I ask you, Governor: not a penny more, and not a penny less.

PICKERING:

Why don't you marry that missus of yours? I rather draw the line at encouraging that sort of immorality.

DOOLITTLE:

Tell her so, Governor: tell her so. I'm willing. It's me that suffers by it. I've no hold on her. I got to be agreeable to her. I got

to give her presents. I got to buy her clothes something sinful.
I'm a slave to that woman, Governor, just because I'm not her
lawful husband. And she knows it too. Catch her marrying me!
Take my advice, Governor: marry Eliza while she's young and
don't know no better. If you don't you'll be sorry for it after. If
you do, she'll be sorry for it after; but better her than you,
because you're a man, and she's only a woman and don't know
how to be happy anyhow.

HIGGINS:

Pickering: if we listen to this man another minute, we shall
have no convictions left. (*To* Doolittle) Five pounds I think you
said.

DOOLITTLE:

Thank you kindly, Governor.

HIGGINS:

You're sure you won't take ten?

DOOLITTLE:

Not now. Another time, Governor.

HIGGINS (*handing him a five-pound note*):

Here you are.

DOOLITTLE:

Thank you, Governor. Good morning. (*He hurries to the door,
anxious to get away with his booty. When he opens it he is confronted
with a dainty and exquisitely clean young* Japanese Lady *in a simple blue cotton kimono printed cunningly with small white jasmine
blossoms.* Mrs Pearce *is with her. He gets out of her way deferentially
and apologizes*). Beg pardon, miss.

THE JAPANESE LADY:

Garn! Don't you know your own daughter?

DOOLITTLE, HIGGINS *and* PICKERING (*exclaiming simultaneously*):

Bly me! it's Eliza! What's that! This! By Jove!

LIZA:

Don't I look silly?

HIGGINS:

Silly?

MRS PEARCE (*at the door*):

Now, Mr Higgins, please don't say anything to make the girl
conceited about herself.

HIGGINS (*conscientiously*):

Oh! Quite right, Mrs Pearce. (*To* Eliza) Yes: damned silly.

MRS PEARCE:

Please, sir.

HIGGINS (*correcting himself*):

I mean extremely silly.

LIZA:

I should look all right with my hat on. (*She takes up her hat; puts it on; and walks across the room to the fireplace with a fashionable air*).

HIGGINS:

A new fashion, by George! And it ought to look horrible!

DOOLITTLE (*with fatherly pride*):

Well, I never thought she'd clean up as good looking as that, Governor. She's a credit to me, ain't she?

LIZA:

I tell you, it's easy to clean up here. Hot and cold water on tap, just as much as you like, there is. Woolly towels, there is; and a towel horse so hot, it burns your fingers. Soft brushes to scrub yourself, and a wooden bowl of soap smelling like primroses. Now I know why ladies is so clean. Washing's a treat for them. Wish they saw what it is for the like of me!

HIGGINS:

I'm glad the bathroom met with your approval.

LIZA:

It didn't: not all of it; and I don't care who hears me say it. Mrs Pearce knows.

HIGGINS:

What was wrong, Mrs Pearce?

MRS PEARCE (*blandly*):

Oh, nothing, sir. It doesn't matter.

LIZA:

I had a good mind to break it. I didn't know which way to look. But I hung a towel over it, I did.

HIGGINS:

Over what?

MRS PEARCE:

Over the looking-glass, sir.

HIGGINS:

Doolittle: you have brought your daughter up too strictly.

DOOLITTLE:

Me! I never brought her up at all, except to give her a lick of a strap now and again. Don't put it on me, Governor. She ain't accustomed to it, you see: that's all. But she'll soon pick up your free-and-easy ways.

LIZA:

I'm a good girl, I am; and I won't pick up no free-and-easy ways.

HIGGINS:

Eliza: if you say again that you're a good girl, your father shall take you home.

LIZA:

Not him. You don't know my father. All he come here for was to touch you for some money to get drunk on.

DOOLITTLE:

Well, what else would I want money for? To put into the plate in church, I suppose. (*She puts out her tongue at him. He is so incensed by this that* Pickering *presently finds it necessary to step between them*). Don't you give me none of your lip; and don't let me hear you giving this gentleman any of it neither, or you'll hear from me about it. See?

HIGGINS:

Have you any further advice to give her before you go, Doolittle? Your blessing, for instance.

DOOLITTLE:

No, Governor: I ain't such a mug as to put up my children to all I know myself. Hard enough to hold them in without that. If you want Eliza's mind improved, Governor, you do it yourself with a strap. So long, gentlemen. (*He turns to go*).

HIGGINS (*impressively*):

Stop. You'll come regularly to see your daughter. It's your duty, you know. My brother is a clergyman; and he could help you in your talks with her.

DOOLITTLE (*evasively*):

Certainly. I'll come, Governor. Not just this week, because I have a job at a distance. But later on you may depend on me. Afternoon, gentlemen. Afternoon, ma'am. (*He takes off his hat to* Mrs Pearce, *who disdains the salutation and goes out. He winks at* Higgins, *thinking him probably a fellow-sufferer from* Mrs Pearce's *difficult disposition, and follows her*).

LIZA:

Don't you believe the old liar. He'd as soon you set a bull-dog on him as a clergyman. You won't see him again in a hurry.

HIGGINS:

I don't want to, Eliza. Do you?

LIZA:

Not me. I don't want never to see him again, I don't. He's a disgrace to me, he is, collecting dust, instead of working at his trade.

PICKERING:

What is his trade, Eliza?

LIZA:

Taking money out of other people's pockets into his own. His proper trade's a navvy; and he works at it sometimes too—for exercise—and earns good money at it. Ain't you going to call me Miss Doolittle any more?

PICKERING:

    I beg your pardon, Miss Doolittle. It was a slip of the tongue.

LIZA:

    Oh, I don't mind; only it sounded so genteel. I should just like to take a taxi to the corner of Tottenham Court Road and get out there and tell it to wait for me, just to put the girls in their place a bit. I wouldn't speak to them, you know.

PICKERING:

    Better wait till we get you something really fashionable.

HIGGINS:

    Besides, you shouldn't cut your old friends now that you have risen in the world. That's what we call snobbery.

LIZA:

    You don't call the like of them my friends now, I should hope. They've took it out of me often enough with their ridicule when they had the chance; and now I mean to get a bit of my own back. But if I'm to have fashionable clothes, I'll wait. I should like to have some. Mrs Pearce says you're going to give me some to wear in bed at night different to what I wear in the daytime; but it do seem a waste of money when you could get something to show. Besides, I never could fancy changing into cold things on a winter night.

MRS PEARCE (*coming back*):

    Now, Eliza. The new things have come for you to try on.

LIZA:

    Ah-ow-oo-ooh! (*She rushes out*).

MRS PEARCE (*following her*):

    Oh, don't rush about like that, girl. (*She shuts the door behind her*).

HIGGINS:

    Pickering: we have taken on a stiff job.

PICKERING (*with conviction*):

    Higgins: we have.

# Act III

*It is* Mrs Higgins's *at-home day. Nobody has yet arrived. Her drawing room, in a flat on Chelsea Embankment, has three windows looking on the river; and the ceiling is not so lofty as it would be in an older house of the same pretension. The windows are open, giving access to a balcony with flowers in pots. If you stand with your face to the windows, you have the fireplace on your left and the door in the right-hand wall close to the corner nearest the windows.*

*Mrs Higgins was brought up on Morris and Burne Jones; and her room, which is very unlike her son's room in Wimpole Street, is not crowded with furniture and little tables and nick-nacks. In the middle of the room there is a big ottoman; and this, with the carpet, the Morris wall-papers, and the Morris chintz window curtains and brocade covers of the ottoman and its cushions, supply all the ornament, and are much too handsome to be hidden by odds and ends of useless things. A few good oil-paintings from the exhibitions in the Grosvenor Gallery thirty years ago (the Burne Jones, not the Whistler side of them) are on the walls. The only landscape is a Cecil Lawson on the scale of a Rubens. There is a portrait of* Mrs Higgins *as she was when she defied fashion in her youth in one of the beautiful Rossettian costumes which, when caricatured by people who did not understand, led to the absurdities of popular estheticism in the eighteen-seventies.*

*In the corner diagonally opposite the door* Mrs Higgins, *now over sixty and long past taking the trouble to dress out of the fashion, sits writing at an elegantly simple writing-table with a bell button within reach of her hand. There is a Chippendale chair further back in the room between her and the window nearest her side. At the other side of the room, further forward, is an Elizabethan chair roughly carved in the taste of Inigo Jones. On the same side a piano in a decorated case. The corner between the fireplace and the window is occupied by a divan cushioned in Morris chintz.*

*It is between four and five in the afternoon.*

*The door is opened violently; and* Higgins *enters with his hat on.*

MRS HIGGINS (*dismayed*):

Henry (*scolding him*)! What are you doing here to-day? It is my at-home day: you promised not to come. (*As he bends to kiss her, she takes his hat off, and presents it to him*).

HIGGINS:

Oh bother! (*He throws the hat down on the table*).

MRS HIGGINS:

Go home at once.

HIGGINS (*kissing her*):

I know, mother. I came on purpose.

MRS HIGGINS:

But you mustn't. I'm serious, Henry. You offend all my friends: they stop coming whenever they meet you.

HIGGINS:

Nonsense! I know I have no small talk; but people don't mind. (*He sits on the settee*).

MRS HIGGINS:

Oh! don't they? Small talk indeed! What about your large talk? Really, dear, you mustn't stay.

HIGGINS:

I must. I've a job for you. A phonetic job.

MRS HIGGINS:

No use, dear. I'm sorry; but I can't get round your vowels; and though I like to get pretty postcards in your patent shorthand, I always have to read the copies in ordinary writing you so thoughtfully send me.

HIGGINS:

Well, this isn't a phonetic job.

MRS HIGGINS:

You said it was.

HIGGINS:

Not your part of it. I've picked up a girl.

MRS HIGGINS:

Does that mean that some girl has picked you up?

HIGGINS:

Not at all. I don't mean a love affair.

MRS HIGGINS:

What a pity!

HIGGINS:

Why?

MRS HIGGINS:

Well, you never fall in love with anyone under forty-five. When will you discover that there are some rather nice-looking young women about?

HIGGINS:

Oh, I can't be bothered with young women. My idea of a lovable woman is something as like you as possible. I shall never get into the way of seriously liking young women: some habits lie too deep to be changed. (*Rising abruptly and walking about, jingling his money and his keys in his trouser pockets*) Besides, they're all idiots.

MRS HIGGINS:

Do you know what you would do if you really loved me, Henry?

HIGGINS:

Oh bother! What? Marry, I suppose?

MRS HIGGINS:

No. Stop fidgeting and take your hands out of your pockets. (*With a gesture of despair, he obeys and sits down again.*) That's a good boy. Now tell me about the girl.

HIGGINS:

She's coming to see you.

MRS HIGGINS:

I don't remember asking her.

HIGGINS:

You didn't. *I* asked her. If you'd known her you wouldn't have asked her.

MRS HIGGINS:

Indeed! Why?

HIGGINS:

Well, it's like this. She's a common flower girl. I picked her off the kerbstone.

MRS HIGGINS:

And invited her to my at-home!

HIGGINS (*rising and coming to her to coax her*):

Oh, that'll be all right. I've taught her to speak properly; and she has strict orders as to her behavior. She's to keep to two subjects: the weather and everybody's health—Fine day and How do you do, you know—and not to let herself go on things in general. That will be safe.

MRS HIGGINS:

Safe! To talk about our health! about our insides! perhaps about our outsides! How could you be so silly, Henry?

HIGGINS (*impatiently*):

Well, she must talk about something. (*He controls himself and sits down again*). Oh, she'll be all right: don't you fuss. Pickering is in it with me. I've a sort of bet on that I'll pass her off as a duchess in six months. I started on her some months ago; and she's getting on like a house on fire. I shall win my bet. She has a quick ear; and she's been easier to teach than my middle-class pupils because she's had to learn a complete new language. She talks English almost as you talk French.

MRS HIGGINS:

That's satisfactory, at all events.

HIGGINS:

Well, it is and it isn't.

MRS HIGGINS:

What does that mean?

HIGGINS:

You see, I've got her pronunciation all right; but you have to consider not only how a girl pronounces, but what she pronounces; and that's where—

*They are interrupted by* The Parlor-Maid, *announcing guests.*

THE PARLOR-MAID:

Mrs and Miss Eynsford Hill. (*She withdraws*).

HIGGINS:

Oh Lord! (*He rises; snatches his hat from the table; and makes for the door; but before he reaches it his mother introduces him*).

Mrs *and Miss Eynsford Hill are the mother and daughter who sheltered from the rain in Covent Garden. The mother is well bred, quiet, and has the habitual anxiety of straitened means. The daughter has acquired a gay air of being very much at home in society: the bravado of genteel poverty.*

MRS EYNSFORD HILL (*to Mrs Higgins*):

How do you do? (*They shake hands*).

MISS EYNSFORD HILL:

How d'you do? (*She shakes*).

MRS HIGGINS (*introducing*):

My son Henry.

MRS EYNSFORD HILL:

Your celebrated son! I have so longed to meet you, Professor Higgins.

HIGGINS (*glumly, making no movement in her direction*):

Delighted. (*He backs against the piano and bows brusquely*).

MISS EYNSFORD HILL (*going to him with confident familiarity*):

How do you do?

HIGGINS (*staring at her*):

I've seen you before somewhere. I haven't the ghost of a notion where; but I've heard your voice. (*Drearily*) It doesn't matter. You'd better sit down.

MRS HIGGINS:

I'm sorry to say that my celebrated son has no manners. You mustn't mind him.

MISS EYNSFORD HILL (*gaily*):

I don't. (*She sits in the Elizabethan chair*).

MRS EYNSFORD HILL (*a little bewildered*):

Not at all. (*She sits on the ottoman between her daughter and Mrs Higgins, who has turned her chair away from the writing-table*).

HIGGINS:

Oh, have I been rude? I didn't mean to be.

*He goes to the central window, through which, with his back to the company, he contemplates the river and the flowers in Battersea Park on the opposite bank as if they were a frozen desert.*

The Parlor-Maid *returns, ushering in* Pickering.

THE PARLOR-MAID:

Colonel Pickering. (*She withdraws*).

PICKERING:

How do you do, Mrs Higgins?

MRS HIGGINS:

So glad you've come. Do you know Mrs Eynsford Hill—Miss Eynsford Hill? (*Exchange of bows. The Colonel brings the Chippendale chair a little forward between* Mrs Hill *and* Mrs Higgins, *and sits down*).

PICKERING:

Has Henry told you what we've come for?

HIGGINS (*over his shoulder*):

We were interrupted: damn it!

MRS HIGGINS:

Oh Henry, Henry, really!

MRS EYNSFORD HILL (*half rising*):

Are we in the way?

MRS HIGGINS (*rising and making her sit down again*):

No, no. You couldn't have come more fortunately: we want you to meet a friend of ours.

HIGGINS (*turning hopefully*):

Yes, by George! We want two or three people. You'll do as well as anybody else.

The Parlor-Maid *returns, ushering* Freddy.

THE PARLOR-MAID:

Mr Eynsford Hill.

HIGGINS (*almost audibly, past endurance*):

God of Heaven! another of them.

FREDDY (*shaking hands with* Mrs Higgins):

Ahdedo?

MRS HIGGINS:

Very good of you to come. (*Introducing*) Colonel Pickering.

FREDDY (*bowing*):

Ahdedo?

MRS HIGGINS:

I don't think you know my son, Professor Higgins.

FREDDY (*going to* Higgins):

Ahdedo?

HIGGINS (*looking at him much as if he were a pickpocket*):

I'll take my oath I've met you before somewhere. Where was it?

FREDDY:

I don't think so.

HIGGINS (*resignedly*):

It don't matter, anyhow. Sit down.

*He shakes* Freddy's *hand, and almost slings him on to the ottoman with his face to the windows; then comes round to the other side of it.*

HIGGINS:

Well, here we are, anyhow! (*He sits down on the ottoman next* Mrs Eynsford Hill, *on her left*). And now, what the devil are we going to talk about until Eliza comes?

MRS HIGGINS:

Henry: you are the life and soul of the Royal Society's soirées; but really you're rather trying on more commonplace occasions.

HIGGINS:

Am I? Very sorry. (*Beaming suddenly*) I suppose I am, you know. (*Uproariously*) Ha, ha!

MISS EYNSFORD HILL (*who considers* Higgins *quite eligible matrimonially*):

I sympathize. *I* haven't any small talk. If people would only be frank and say what they really think!

HIGGINS (*relapsing into gloom*):

Lord forbid!

MRS EYNSFORD HILL (*taking up her daughter's cue*):

But why?

HIGGINS:

What they think they ought to think is bad enough, Lord knows; but what they really think would break up the whole show. Do you suppose it would be really agreeable if I were to come out now with what *I* really think?

MISS EYNSFORD HILL (*gaily*):

Is it so very cynical?

HIGGINS:

Cynical! Who the dickens said it was cynical? I mean it wouldn't be decent.

MRS EYNSFORD HILL (*seriously*):

Oh! I'm sure you don't mean that, Mr Higgins.

HIGGINS:

You see, we're all savages, more or less. We're supposed to be civilized and cultured—to know all about poetry and philosophy and art and science, and so on; but how many of us know even the meanings of these names? (*To* Miss Hill) What do you know of poetry? (*To* Mrs Hill) What do you know of science? (*Indicating* Freddy) What does he know of art or science or anything else? What the devil do you imagine I know of philosophy?

MRS HIGGINS (*warningly*):
Or of manners, Henry?

THE PARLOR-MAID (*opening the door*):
Miss Doolittle. (*She withdraws*).

HIGGINS (*rising hastily and running to* Mrs Higgins):
Here she is, mother. (*He stands on tiptoe and makes signs over his mother's head to* Eliza *to indicate to her which lady is her hostess*).

Eliza, *who is exquisitely dressed, produces an impression of such remarkable distinction and beauty as she enters that they all rise, quite fluttered. Guided by* Higgins's *signals, she comes to* Mrs Higgins *with studied grace.*

LIZA (*speaking with pedantic correctness of pronunciation and great beauty of tone*):
How do you do, Mrs Higgins? (*She gasps slightly in making sure of the H in* Higgins, *but is quite successful*). Mr Higgins told me I might come.

MRS HIGGINS (*cordially*):
Quite right: I'm very glad indeed to see you.

PICKERING:
How do you do, Miss Doolittle?

LIZA (*shaking hands with him*):
Colonel Pickering, is it not?

MRS EYNSFORD HILL:
I feel sure we have met before, Miss Doolittle. I remember your eyes.

LIZA:
How do you do? (*She sits down on the ottoman gracefully in the place just left vacant by* Higgins).

MRS EYNSFORD HILL (*introducing*):
My daughter Clara.

LIZA:
How do you do?

CLARA (*impulsively*):
How do you do? (*She sits down on the ottoman beside* Eliza, *devouring her with her eyes*).

FREDDY (*coming to their side of the ottoman*):
> I've certainly had the pleasure.

MRS EYNSFORD HILL (*introducing*):
> My son Freddy.

LIZA:
> How do you do?

Freddy *bows and sits down in the Elizabethan chair, infatuated.*

HIGGINS (*suddenly*):
> By George, yes: it all comes back to me! (*They stare at him*).
> Covent Garden! (*Lamentably*) What a damned thing!

MRS HIGGINS:
> Henry, please! (*He is about to sit on the edge of the table*) Don't sit
> on my writing-table: you'll break it.

HIGGINS (*sulkily*):
> Sorry.

*He goes to the divan, stumbling into the fender and over the fire-irons on
his way; extricating himself with muttered imprecations; and finishing his
disastrous journey by throwing himself so impatiently on the divan that he
almost breaks it.* Mrs Higgins *looks at him, but controls herself and says
nothing.*

*A long and painful pause ensues.*

MRS HIGGINS (*at last, conversationally*):
> Will it rain, do you think?

LIZA:
> The shallow depression in the west of these islands is likely to
> move slowly in an easterly direction. There are no indications
> of any great change in the barometrical situation.

FREDDY:
> Ha! ha! how awfully funny!

LIZA:
> What is wrong with that, young man? I bet I got it right.

FREDDY:
> Killing!

MRS EYNSFORD HILL:
> I'm sure I hope it won't turn cold. There's so much influenza
> about. It runs right through our whole family regularly every
> spring.

LIZA (*darkly*):

My aunt died of influenza: so they said.

MRS EYNSFORD HILL (*clicks her tongue sympathetically*):

!!!

LIZA (*in the same tragic tone*):

But it's my belief they done the old woman in.

MRS HIGGINS (*puzzled*):

Done her in?

LIZA:

Y-e-e-e-es, Lord love you! Why should she die of influenza?
She come through diphtheria right enough the year before. I
saw her with my own eyes. Fairly blue with it, she was. They
all thought she was dead; but my father he kept ladling gin
down her throat till she came to so sudden that she bit the
bowl off the spoon.

MRS EYNSFORD HILL (*startled*):

Dear me!

LIZA (*piling up the indictment*):

What call would a woman with that strength in her have to die
of influenza? What become of her new straw hat that should
have come to me? Somebody pinched it; and what I say is,
them as pinched it done her in.

MRS EYNSFORD HILL:

What does doing her in mean?

HIGGINS (*hastily*):

Oh, that's the new small talk. To do a person in means to kill
them.

MRS EYNSFORD HILL (*to* Eliza, *horrified*):

You surely don't believe that your aunt was killed?

LIZA:

Do I not! Them she lived with would have killed her for a hat-
pin, let alone a hat.

MRS EYNSFORD HILL:

But it can't have been right for your father to pour spirits down
her throat like that. It might have killed her.

LIZA:

Not her. Gin was mother's milk to her. Besides, he'd poured so
much down his own throat that he knew the good of it.

MRS EYNSFORD HILL:

Do you mean that he drank?

LIZA:

Drank! My word! Something chronic.

MRS EYNSFORD HILL:

How dreadful for you!

LIZA:

> Not a bit. It never did him no harm what I could see. But then he did not keep it up regular. (*Cheerfully*) On the burst, as you might say, from time to time. And always more agreeable when he had a drop in. When he was out of work, my mother used to give him fourpence and tell him to go out and not come back until he'd drunk himself cheerful and loving-like. There's lots of women has to make their husbands drunk to make them fit to live with. (*Now quite at her ease*) You see, it's like this. If a man has a bit of a conscience, it always takes him when he's sober; and then it makes him low-spirited. A drop of booze just takes that off and makes him happy. (*To* Freddy, *who is in convulsions of suppressed laughter*) Here! what are you sniggering at?

FREDDY:

> The new small talk. You do it so awfully well.

LIZA:

> If I was doing it proper, what was you laughing at? (*To* Higgins) Have I said anything I oughtn't?

MRS HIGGINS (*interposing*):

> Not at all, Miss Doolittle.

LIZA:

> Well, that's a mercy, anyhow. (*Expansively*) What I always say is—

HIGGINS (*rising and looking at his watch*):

> Ahem!

LIZA (*looking round at him; taking the hint; and rising*):

> Well: I must go. (*They all rise.* Freddy *goes to the door*). So pleased to have met you. Goodbye. (*She shakes hands with* Mrs Higgins).

MRS HIGGINS:

> Goodbye.

LIZA:

> Goodbye, Colonel Pickering.

PICKERING:

> Goodbye, Miss Doolittle. (*They shake hands*).

LIZA (*nodding to the others*):

> Goodbye, all.

FREDDY (*opening the door for her*):

> Are you walking across the Park, Miss Doolittle? If so—

LIZA:

> Walk! Not bloody likely. (*Sensation*). I am going in a taxi. (*She goes out*).

Pickering *gasps and sits down.* Freddy *goes out on the balcony to catch another glimpse of* Eliza.

MRS EYNSFORD HILL (*suffering from shock*):

Well, I really can't get used to the new ways.

CLARA (*throwing herself discontentedly into the Elizabethan chair*):

Oh, it's all right, mamma, quite right. People will think we never go anywhere or see anybody if you are so old-fashioned.

MRS EYNSFORD HILL:

I daresay I am very old-fashioned; but I do hope you won't begin using that expression, Clara. I have got accustomed to hear you talking about men as rotters, and calling everything filthy and beastly; though I do think it horrible and unladylike. But this last is really too much. Don't you think so, Colonel Pickering?

PICKERING:

Don't ask me. I've been away in India for several years; and manners have changed so much that I sometimes don't know whether I'm at a respectable dinner-table or in a ship's forecastle.

CLARA:

It's all a matter of habit. There's no right or wrong in it. Nobody means anything by it. And it's so quaint, and gives such a smart emphasis to things that are not in themselves very witty. I find the new small talk delightful and quite innocent.

MRS EYNSFORD HILL (*rising*):

Well, after that, I think it's time for us to go.

Pickering *and* Higgins *rise*.

CLARA (*rising*):

Oh yes: we have three at-homes to go to still. Goodbye, Mrs Higgins. Goodbye, Colonel Pickering. Goodbye, Professor Higgins.

HIGGINS (*coming grimly at her from the divan, and accompanying her to the door*):

Goodbye. Be sure you try on that small talk at the three at-homes. Don't be nervous about it. Pitch it in strong.

CLARA (*all smiles*):

I will. Goodbye. Such nonsense, all this early Victorian prudery!

HIGGINS (*tempting her*):

Such damned nonsense!

CLARA:

Such bloody nonsense!

MRS EYNSFORD HILL (*convulsively*):

Clara!

CLARA:

Ha! ha! (*She goes out radiant, conscious of being thoroughly up to date, and is heard descending the stairs in a stream of silvery laughter*).

FREDDY (*to the heavens at large*):

Well, I ask you—(*He gives it up, and comes to* Mrs Higgins). Goodbye.

MRS HIGGINS (*shaking hands*):

Goodbye. Would you like to meet Miss Doolittle again?

FREDDY (*eagerly*):

Yes, I should, most awfully.

MRS HIGGINS:

Well, you know my days.

FREDDY:

Yes. Thanks awfully. Goodbye. (*He goes out*).

MRS EYNSFORD HILL:

Goodbye, Mr Higgins.

HIGGINS:

Goodbye. Goodbye.

MRS EYNSFORD HILL (*to* Pickering):

It's no use. I shall never be able to bring myself to use that word.

PICKERING:

Don't. It's not compulsory, you know. You'll get on quite well without it.

MRS EYNSFORD HILL:

Only, Clara is so down on me if I am not positively reeking with the latest slang. Goodbye.

PICKERING:

Goodbye (*They shake hands*).

MRS EYNSFORD HILL (*to* Mrs Higgins):

You mustn't mind Clara. (Pickering, *catching from her lowered tone that this is not meant for him to hear, discreetly joins* Higgins *at the window*). We're so poor! and she gets so few parties, poor child! She doesn't quite know. (Mrs Higgins, *seeing that her eyes are moist, takes her hand sympathetically and goes with her to the door*). But the boy is nice. Don't you think so?

MRS HIGGINS:

Oh, quite nice. I shall always be delighted to see him.

MRS EYNSFORD HILL:

Thank you, dear. Goodbye. (*She goes out*).

HIGGINS (*eagerly*):

Well? Is Eliza presentable? (*He swoops on his mother and drags her to the ottoman, where she sits down in* Eliza's *place with her son on her left*).

Pickering *returns to his chair on her right.*

MRS HIGGINS:

You silly boy, of course she's not presentable. She's a triumph of your art and of her dressmaker's; but if you suppose for a moment that she doesn't give herself away in every sentence she utters, you must be perfectly cracked about her.

PICKERING:

But don't you think something might be done? I mean something to eliminate the sanguinary element from her conversation.

MRS HIGGINS:

Not as long as she is in Henry's hands.

HIGGINS (*aggrieved*):

Do you mean that my language is improper?

MRS HIGGINS:

No, dearest: it would be quite proper—say on a canal barge; but it would not be proper for her at a garden party.

HIGGINS (*deeply injured*):

Well I must say—

PICKERING (*interrupting him*):

Come, Higgins: you must learn to know yourself. I haven't heard such language as yours since we used to review the volunteers in Hyde Park twenty years ago.

HIGGINS (*sulkily*):

Oh, well, if you say so, I suppose I don't always talk like a bishop.

MRS HIGGINS (*quieting Henry with a touch*):

Colonel Pickering: will you tell me what is the exact state of things in Wimpole Street?

PICKERING (*cheerfully: as if this completely changed the subject*):

Well, I have come to live there with Henry. We work together at my Indian Dialects; and we think it more convenient—

MRS HIGGINS:

Quite so. I know all about that: it's an excellent arrangement. But where does this girl live?

HIGGINS:

With us, of course. Where should she live?

MRS HIGGINS:

But on what terms? Is she a servant? If not, what is she?

PICKERING (*slowly*):

I think I know what you mean, Mrs Higgins.

HIGGINS:

Well, dash me if *I* do! I've had to work at the girl every day for months to get her to her present pitch. Besides, she's useful.

She knows where my things are, and remembers my appointments and so forth.

MRS HIGGINS:

How does your housekeeper get on with her?

HIGGINS:

Mrs Pearce? Oh, she's jolly glad to get so much taken off her hands; for before Eliza came, she used to have to find things and remind me of my appointments. But she's got some silly bee in her bonnet about Eliza. She keeps saying "You don't think, sir": doesn't she, Pick?

PICKERING:

Yes: that's the formula. "You don't think, sir." That's the end of every conversation about Eliza.

HIGGINS:

As if I ever stop thinking about the girl and her confounded vowels and consonants. I'm worn out, thinking about her, and watching her lips and her teeth and her tongue, not to mention her soul, which is the quaintest of the lot.

MRS HIGGINS:

You certainly are a pretty pair of babies, playing with your live doll.

HIGGINS:

Playing! The hardest job I ever tackled: make no mistake about that, mother. But you have no idea how frightfully interesting it is to take a human being and change her into a quite different human being by creating a new speech for her. It's filling up the deepest gulf that separates class from class and soul from soul.

PICKERING (*drawing his chair closer to* Mrs Higgins *and bending over to her eagerly*):

Yes: it's enormously interesting. I assure you, Mrs Higgins, we take Eliza very seriously. Every week—every day almost—there is some new change. (*Closer again*) We keep records of every stage—dozens of gramophone disks and photographs—

HIGGINS (*assailing her at the other ear*):

Yes, by George: it's the most absorbing experiment I ever tackled. She regularly fills our lives up: doesn't she, Pick?

PICKERING:

We're always talking Eliza.

HIGGINS:

Teaching Eliza.

PICKERING:

Dressing Eliza.

MRS HIGGINS:

What!

HIGGINS:
Inventing new Elizas.

| HIGGINS: | *(speaking together)* | You know, she has the most extraordinary quickness of ear: |
| PICKERING: | | I assure you, my dear Mrs Higgins, that girl |

| HIGGINS: | | just like a parrot. I've tried her with every |
| PICKERING: | | is a genius. She can play the piano quite beautifully. |

| HIGGINS: | | possible sort of sound that a human being can make— |
| PICKERING: | | We have taken her to classical concerts and to music |

| HIGGINS: | | Continental dialects, African dialects, Hottentot |
| PICKERING: | | halls; and it's all the same to her: she plays everything |

| HIGGINS: | | clicks, things it took me years to get hold of; and |
| PICKERING: | | she hears right off when she comes home, whether it's |

| HIGGINS: | | she picks them up like a shot, right away, as if she had |
| PICKERING: | | Beethoven and Brahms or Lehar and Lionel Monckton; |

| HIGGINS: | | been at it all her life. |
| PICKERING: | | though six months ago, she'd never as much as touched a piano— |

MRS HIGGINS (*putting her fingers in her ears, as they are by this time shouting one another down with an intolerable noise*):
Sh-sh-sh—sh! (*They stop*).

PICKERING:
I beg your pardon. (*He draws his chair back apologetically*).

HIGGINS:
Sorry. When Pickering starts shouting nobody can get a word in edgeways.

MRS HIGGINS:
Be quiet, Henry. Colonel Pickering: don't you realize that when Eliza walked into Wimpole Street, something walked in with her?

PICKERING:

Her father did. But Henry soon got rid of him.

MRS HIGGINS:

It would have been more to the point if her mother had. But as her mother didn't something else did.

PICKERING:

But what?

MRS HIGGINS (*unconsciously dating herself by the word*):

A problem.

PICKERING:

Oh, I see. The problem of how to pass her off as a lady.

HIGGINS:

I'll solve that problem. I've half solved it already.

MRS HIGGINS:

No, you two infinitely stupid male creatures: the problem of what is to be done with her afterwards.

HIGGINS:

I don't see anything in that. She can go her own way, with all the advantages I have given her.

MRS HIGGINS:

The advantages of that poor woman who was here just now! The manners and habits that disqualify a fine lady from earning her own living without giving her a fine lady's income! Is that what you mean?

PICKERING (*indulgently, being rather bored*):

Oh, that will be all right, Mrs Higgins. (*He rises to go*).

HIGGINS (*rising also*):

We'll find her some light employment.

PICKERING:

She's happy enough. Don't you worry about her. Goodbye. (*He shakes hands as if he were consoling a frightened child, and makes for the door*).

HIGGINS:

Anyhow, there's no good bothering now. The thing's done. Goodbye, mother. (*He kisses her, and follows* Pickering).

PICKERING (*turning for a final consolation*):

There are plenty of openings. We'll do what's right. Goodbye.

HIGGINS (*to* Pickering *as they go out together*):

Let's take her to the Shakespeare exhibition at Earls Court.

PICKERING:

Yes: let's. Her remarks will be delicious.

HIGGINS:

She'll mimic all the people for us when we get home.

PICKERING:

Ripping. (*Both are heard laughing as they go downstairs*).

MRS HIGGINS (*rises with an impatient bounce, and returns to her work at the writing-table. She sweeps a litter of disarranged papers out of her way; snatches a sheet of paper from her stationery case; and tries resolutely to write. At the third line she gives it up; flings down her pen; grips the table angrily and exclaims*):

Oh, men! men!! men!!!

# Act IV

*The Wimpole Street laboratory. Midnight. Nobody in the room. The clock on the mantelpiece strikes twelve. The fire is not alight: it is a summer night. Presently* Higgins *and* Pickering *are heard on the stairs.*

HIGGINS (*calling down to* Pickering):

I say, Pick: lock up, will you? I shan't be going out again.

PICKERING:

Right. Can Mrs Pearce go to bed? We don't want anything more, do we?

HIGGINS:

Lord, no!

Eliza *opens the door and is seen on the lighted landing in opera cloak, brilliant evening dress, and diamonds, with fan, flowers, and all accessories. She comes to the hearth, and switches on the electric lights there. She is tired: her pallor contrasts strongly with her dark eyes and hair; and her expression is almost tragic. She takes off her cloak; puts her fan and flowers on the piano; and sits down on the bench, brooding and silent. Higgins, in evening dress, with overcoat and hat, comes in, carrying a smoking jacket which he has picked up downstairs. He takes off the hat and overcoat; throws them carelessly on the newspaper stand; disposes of his coat in the same way; puts on the smoking jacket; and throws himself wearily into the easy-chair at the hearth. Pickering, similarly attired, comes in. He also takes off his hat and overcoat, and is about to throw them on* Higgins's *when he hesitates.*

PICKERING:

I say: Mrs Pearce will row if we leave these things lying about in the drawing room.

HIGGINS:

Oh, chuck them over the bannisters into the hall. She'll find them there in the morning and put them away all right. She'll think we were drunk.

PICKERING:

> We are, slightly. Are there any letters?

HIGGINS:

> I didn't look. (Pickering *takes the overcoats and hats and goes downstairs. Higgins begins half singing half yawning an air from "La Fanciulla del Golden West." Suddenly he stops and exclaims*) I wonder where the devil my slippers are!

Eliza *looks at him darkly; then rises suddenly and leaves the room.* Higgins *yawns again, and resumes his song.* Pickering *returns, with the contents of the letter-box in his hand.*

PICKERING:

> Only circulars, and this coroneted billet-doux for you. (*He throws the circulars into the fender, and posts himself on the hearthrug, with his back to the grate*).

HIGGINS (*glancing at the billet-doux*):

> Money-lender. (*He throws the letter after the circulars*).

Eliza *returns with a pair of large down-at-heel slippers. She places them on the carpet before* Higgins, *and sits as before without a word.*

HIGGINS (*yawning again*):

> Oh Lord! What an evening! What a crew! What a silly tom-foolery! (*He raises his shoe to unlace it, and catches sight of the slippers. He stops unlacing and looks at them as if they had appeared there of their own accord*). Oh! they're there, are they?

PICKERING (*stretching himself*):

> Well, I feel a bit tired. It's been a long day. The garden party, a dinner party, and the opera! Rather too much of a good thing. But you've won your bet, Higgins. Eliza did the trick, and something to spare, eh?

HIGGINS (*fervently*):

> Thank God it's over!

Eliza *flinches violently; but they take no notice of her; and she recovers herself and sits stonily as before.*

PICKERING:

> Were you nervous at the garden party? *I* was. Eliza didn't seem a bit nervous.

HIGGINS:

> Oh, she wasn't nervous. I knew she'd be all right. No: it's the strain of putting the job through all these months that has told

on me. It was interesting enough at first, while we were at the phonetics; but after that I got deadly sick of it. If I hadn't backed myself to do it I should have chucked the whole thing up two months ago. It was a silly notion: the whole thing has been a bore.

PICKERING:

Oh come! the garden party was frightfully exciting. My heart began beating like anything.

HIGGINS:

Yes, for the first three minutes. But when I saw we were going to win hands down, I felt like a bear in a cage, hanging about doing nothing. The dinner was worse: sitting gorging there for over an hour, with nobody but a damned fool of a fashionable woman to talk to! I tell you, Pickering, never again for me. No more artificial duchesses. The whole thing has been simple purgatory.

PICKERING:

You've never been broken in properly to the social routine. (*Strolling over to the piano*) I rather enjoy dipping into it occasionally myself: it makes me feel young again. Anyhow, it was a great success: an immense success. I was quite frightened once or twice because Eliza was doing it so well. You see, lots of the real people can't do it at all: they're such fools that they think style comes by nature to people in their position; and so they never learn. There's always something professional about doing a thing superlatively well.

HIGGINS:

Yes: that's what drives me mad: the silly people don't know their own silly business. (*Rising*) However, it's over and done with; and now I can go to bed at last without dreading tomorrow.

*Eliza's beauty becomes murderous.*

PICKERING:

I think I shall turn in too. Still, it's been a great occasion: a triumph for you. Goodnight. (*He goes*).

HIGGINS (*following him*):

Goodnight. (*Over his shoulder, at the door*) Put out the lights, Eliza; and tell Mrs Pearce not to make coffee for me in the morning: I'll take tea. (*He goes out*).

Eliza *tries to control herself and feel indifferent as she rises and walks across to the hearth to switch off the lights. By the time she gets there she is on the point of screaming. She sits down in* Higgins's *chair and holds on hard to the arms. Finally she gives way and flings herself furiously on the floor, raging.*

HIGGINS (*in despairing wrath outside*):

What the devil have I done with my slippers? (*He appears at the door*).

LIZA (*snatching up the slippers, and hurling them at him one after the other with all her force*):

There are your slippers. And there. Take your slippers; and may you never have a day's luck with them!

HIGGINS (*astounded*):

What on earth—! (*He comes to her*). What's the matter? Get up. (*He pulls her up*). Anything wrong?

LIZA (*breathless*):

Nothing wrong—with you. I've won your bet for you, haven't I? That's enough for you. *I* don't matter, I suppose.

HIGGINS:

You won my bet! You! Presumptuous insect! *I* won it. What did you throw those slippers at me for?

LIZA:

Because I wanted to smash your face. I'd like to kill you, you selfish brute. Why didn't you leave me where you picked me out of—in the gutter? You thank God it's all over, and that now you can throw me back again there, do you? (*She crisps her fingers frantically*).

HIGGINS (*looking at her in cool wonder*):

The creature is nervous, after all.

LIZA (*gives a suffocated scream of fury, and instinctively darts her nails at his face*):!!

HIGGINS (*catching her wrists*):

Ah! would you? Claws in, you cat. How dare you show your temper to me? Sit down and be quiet. (*He throws her roughly into the easy-chair*).

LIZA (*crushed by superior strength and weight*):

What's to become of me? What's to become of me?

HIGGINS:

How the devil do I know what's to become of you? What does it matter what becomes of you?

LIZA:

You don't care. I know you don't care. You wouldn't care if I was dead. I'm nothing to you—not so much as them slippers.

HIGGINS (*thundering*):

Those slippers.

LIZA (*with bitter submission*):

Those slippers. I didn't think it made any difference now.

*A pause.* Eliza *hopeless and crushed.* Higgins *a little uneasy.*

HIGGINS (*in his loftiest manner*):

Why have you begun going on like this? May I ask whether you complain of your treatment here?

LIZA:

No.

HIGGINS:

Has anybody behaved badly to you? Colonel Pickering? Mrs Pearce? Any of the servants?

LIZA:

No.

HIGGINS:

I presume you don't pretend that *I* have treated you badly?

LIZA:

No.

HIGGINS:

I am glad to hear it. (*He moderates his tone*). Perhaps you're tired after the strain of the day. Will you have a glass of champagne? (*He moves towards the door*).

LIZA:

No. (*Recollecting her manners*) Thank you.

HIGGINS (*good-humored again*):

This has been coming on you for some days. I suppose it was natural for you to be anxious about the garden party. But that's all over now. (*He pats her kindly on the shoulder. She writhes*). There's nothing more to worry about.

LIZA:

No. Nothing more for you to worry about. (*She suddenly rises and gets away from him by going to the piano bench, where she sits and hides her face*). Oh God! I wish I was dead.

HIGGINS (*staring after her in sincere surprise*):

Why? In heaven's name, why? (*Reasonably, going to her*) Listen to me, Eliza. All this irritation is purely subjective.

LIZA:

I don't understand. I'm too ignorant.

HIGGINS:

It's only imagination. Low spirits and nothing else. Nobody's hurting you. Nothing's wrong. You go to bed like a good girl and sleep it off. Have a little cry and say your prayers: that will make you comfortable.

LIZA:

I heard your prayers. "Thank God it's all over!"

HIGGINS (*impatiently*):

Well, don't you thank God it's all over? Now you are free and can do what you like.

LIZA (*pulling herself together in desperation*):

What am I fit for? What have you left me fit for? Where am I to go? What am I to do? What's to become of me?

HIGGINS (*enlightened, but not at all impressed*):

Oh that's what's worrying you, is it? (*He thrusts his hands into his pockets, and walks about in his usual manner, rattling the contents of his pockets, as if condescending to a trivial subject out of pure kindness*). I shouldn't bother about it if I were you. I should imagine you won't have much difficulty in settling yourself somewhere or other, though I hadn't quite realized that you were going away. (*She looks quickly at him: he does not look at her, but examines the dessert stand on the piano and decides that he will eat an apple*). You might marry, you know. (*He bites a large piece out of the apple and munches it noisily*). You see, Eliza, all men are not confirmed old bachelors like me and the Colonel. Most men are the marrying sort (poor devils!); and you're not bad-looking: it's quite a pleasure to look at you sometimes—not now, of course, because you're crying and looking as ugly as the very devil; but when you're all right and quite yourself, you're what I should call attractive. That is, to the people in the marrying line, you understand. You go to bed and have a good nice rest; and then get up and look at yourself in the glass; and you won't feel so cheap.

Eliza *again looks at him, speechless, and does not stir. The look is quite lost on him: he eats his apple with a dreamy expression of happiness, as it is quite a good one.*

HIGGINS (*a genial afterthought occurring to him*):

I daresay my mother could find some chap or other who would do very well.

LIZA:

We were above that at the corner of Tottenham Court Road.

HIGGINS (*waking up*):

What do you mean?

LIZA:

I sold flowers. I didn't sell myself. Now you've made a lady of me I'm not fit to sell anything else. I wish you'd left me where you found me.

HIGGINS (*slinging the core of the apple decisively into the grate*):

Tosh, Eliza. Don't you insult human relations by dragging all this can't about buying and selling into it. You needn't marry the fellow if you don't like him.

LIZA:

What else am I to do?

HIGGINS:

Oh, lots of things. What about your old idea of a florist's shop? Pickering could set you up in one: he's lots of money. (*Chuckling*) He'll have to pay for all those togs you have been wearing today; and that, with the hire of the jewellery, will make a big hole in two hundred pounds. Why, six months ago you would have thought it the millennium to have a flower shop of your own. Come! you'll be all right. I must clear off to bed: I'm devilish sleepy. By the way, I came down for something: I forget what it was.

LIZA:

Your slippers.

HIGGINS:

Oh yes, of course. You shied them at me. (*He picks them up, and is going out when she rises and speaks to him*).

LIZA:

Before you go, sir—

HIGGINS (*dropping the slippers in his surprise at her calling him Sir*): Eh?

LIZA:

Do my clothes belong to me or to Colonel Pickering?

HIGGINS (*coming back into the room as if her question were the very climax of unreason*):

What the devil use would they be to Pickering?

LIZA:

He might want them for the next girl you pick up to experiment on.

HIGGINS (*shocked and hurt*):

Is that the way you feel towards us?

LIZA:

I don't want to hear anything more about that. All I want to know is whether anything belongs to me. My own clothes were burnt.

HIGGINS:

But what does it matter? Why need you start bothering about that in the middle of the night?

LIZA:

> I want to know what I may take away with me. I don't want to be accused of stealing.

HIGGINS (*now deeply wounded*):

> Stealing! You shouldn't have said that, Eliza. That shows a want of feeling.

LIZA:

> I'm sorry. I'm only a common ignorant girl; and in my station I have to be careful. There can't be any feelings between the like of you and the like of me. Please will you tell me what belongs to me and what doesn't?

HIGGINS (*very sulky*):

> You may take the whole damned houseful if you like. Except the jewels. They're hired. Will that satisfy you? (*He turns on his heel and is about to go in extreme dudgeon*).

LIZA (*drinking in his emotion like nectar, and nagging him to provoke a further supply*):

> Stop, please. (*She takes off her jewels*). Will you take these to your room and keep them safe? I don't want to run the risk of their being missing.

HIGGINS (*furious*):

> Hand them over. (*She puts them into his hands*). If these belonged to me instead of to the jeweller, I'd ram them down your ungrateful throat. (*He perfunctorily thrusts them into his pockets, unconsciously decorating himself with the protruding ends of the chains*).

LIZA (*taking a ring off*):

> This ring isn't the jeweller's: it's the one you bought me in Brighton. I don't want it now. (Higgins *dashes the ring violently into the fireplace, and turns on her so threateningly that she crouches over the piano with her hands over her face, and exclaims*) Don't you hit me.

HIGGINS:

> Hit you! You infamous creature, how dare you accuse me of such a thing? It is you who have hit me. You have wounded me to the heart.

LIZA (*thrilling with hidden joy*):

> I'm glad. I've got a little of my own back, anyhow.

HIGGINS (*with dignity, in his finest professional style*):

> You have caused me to lose my temper: a thing that has hardly ever happened to me before. I prefer to say nothing more tonight. I am going to bed.

LIZA (*pertly*):

> You'd better leave a note for Mrs Pearce about the coffee; for she won't be told by me.

HIGGINS (*formally*):

Damn Mrs Pearce; and damn the coffee; and damn you; and damn my own folly in having lavished hard-earned knowledge and the treasure of my regard and intimacy on a heartless guttersnipe. (*He goes out with impressive decorum, and spoils it by slamming the door savagely*).

Eliza *smiles for the first time; expresses her feelings by a wild pantomime in which an imitation of* Higgins's *exit is confused with her own triumph; and finally goes down on her knees on the hearthrug to look for the ring.*

## Act V

Mrs Higgins's *drawing room. She is at her writing-table as before.* The Parlor-Maid *comes in.*

THE PARLOR-MAID (*at the door*):

Mr Henry, ma'am, is downstairs with Colonel Pickering.

MRS HIGGINS:

Well, show them up.

THE PARLOR-MAID:

They're using the telephone, ma'am. Telephoning to the police, I think.

MRS HIGGINS:

What!

THE PARLOR-MAID (*coming further in and lowering her voice*):

Mr Henry is in a state, ma'am. I thought I'd better tell you.

MRS HIGGINS:

If you had told me that Mr Henry was not in a state it would have been more surprising. Tell them to come up when they've finished with the police. I suppose he's lost something.

THE PARLOR-MAID:

Yes, ma'am (*going*).

MRS HIGGINS:

Go upstairs and tell Miss Doolittle that Mr Henry and the Colonel are here. Ask her not to come down till I send for her.

THE PARLOR-MAID:

Yes, ma'am.

Higgins *bursts in. He is, as* The Parlor-Maid *has said, in a state.*

HIGGINS:

Look here, mother: here's a confounded thing!

MRS HIGGINS:

Yes, dear. Good morning. (*He checks his impatience and kisses her, whilst* The Parlor-Maid *goes out*). What is it?

HIGGINS:

Eliza's bolted.

MRS HIGGINS (*calmly continuing her writing*):

You must have frightened her.

HIGGINS:

Frightened her! nonsense! She was left last night, as usual, to turn out the lights and all that; and instead of going to bed she changed her clothes and went right off: her bed wasn't slept in. She came in a cab for her things before seven this morning; and that fool Mrs Pearce let her have them without telling me a word about it. What am I to do?

MRS HIGGINS:

Do without, I'm afraid, Henry. The girl has a perfect right to leave if she chooses.

HIGGINS (*wandering distractedly across the room*):

But I can't find anything. I don't know what appointments I've got. I'm—(Pickering *comes in.* Mrs Higgins *puts down her pen and turns away from the writing-table*).

PICKERING (*shaking hands*):

Good morning, Mrs Higgins. Has Henry told you? (*He sits down on the ottoman*).

HIGGINS:

What does that ass of an inspector say? Have you offered a reward?

MRS HIGGINS (*rising in indignant amazement*):

You don't mean to say you have set the police after Eliza.

HIGGINS:

Of course. What are the police for? What else could we do? (*He sits in the Elizabethan chair*).

PICKERING:

The inspector made a lot of difficulties. I really think he suspected us of some improper purpose.

MRS HIGGINS:

Well, of course he did. What right have you to go to the police and give the girl's name as if she were a thief, or a lost umbrella, or something? Really! (*She sits down again, deeply vexed*).

HIGGINS:

But we want to find her.

PICKERING:

We can't let her go like this, you know, Mrs Higgins. What were we to do?

MRS HIGGINS:

You have no more sense, either of you, than two children. Why—

The Parlor-Maid *comes in and breaks off the conversation.*

THE PARLOR-MAID:

Mr Henry: a gentleman wants to see you very particular. He's been sent on from Wimpole Street.

HIGGINS:

Oh, bother! I can't see anyone now. Who is it?

THE PARLOR-MAID:

A Mr Doolittle, sir.

PICKERING:

Doolittle! Do you mean the dustman?

THE PARLOR-MAID:

Dustman! Oh no, sir: a gentleman.

HIGGINS (*springing up excitedly*):

By George, Pick, it's some relative of hers that she's gone to. Somebody we know nothing about. (*To* The Parlor-Maid) Send him up, quick.

THE PARLOR-MAID:

Yes, sir. (*She goes*).

HIGGINS (*eagerly, going to his mother*):

Genteel relatives! now we shall hear something. (*He sits down in the Chippendale chair*).

MRS HIGGINS:

Do you know any of her people?

PICKERING:

Only her father: the fellow we told you about.

THE PARLOR-MAID (*announcing*):

Mr Doolittle. (*She withdraws*).

Doolittle *enters. He is brilliantly dressed in a new fashionable frock-coat, with white waistcoat and grey trousers. A flower in his buttonhole, a daz-zling silk hat, and patent leather shoes complete the effect. He is too con-cerned with the business he has come on to notice Mrs Higgins. He walks straight to* Higgins, *and accosts him with vehement reproach.*

DOOLITTLE (*indicating his own person*):

See here! Do you see this? You done this.

HIGGINS:

Done what, man?

DOOLITTLE:

This, I tell you. Look at it. Look at this hat. Look at this coat.

PICKERING:

Has Eliza been buying you clothes?

DOOLITTLE:

Eliza! not she. Not half. Why would she buy me clothes?

MRS HIGGINS:

Good morning, Mr Doolittle. Won't you sit down?

DOOLITTLE (*taken aback as he becomes conscious that he has forgotten his hostess*):

Asking your pardon, ma'am. (*He approaches her and shakes her proffered hand*). Thank you. (*He sits down on the ottoman, on* Pickering*'s right*). I am that full of what has happened to me that I can't think of anything else.

HIGGINS:

What the dickens has happened to you?

DOOLITTLE:

I shouldn't mind if it had only happened to me: anything might happen to anybody and nobody to blame but Providence, as you might say. But this is something that you done to me: yes, you, Henry Higgins.

HIGGINS:

Have you found Eliza? that's the point.

DOOLITTLE:

Have you lost her?

HIGGINS:

Yes.

DOOLITTLE:

You have all the luck, you have. I ain't found her; but she'll find me quick enough now after what you done to me.

MRS HIGGINS:

But what has my son done to you, Mr Doolittle?

DOOLITTLE:

Done to me! Ruined me. Destroyed my happiness. Tied me up and delivered me into the hands of middle class morality.

HIGGINS (*rising intolerantly and standing over* Doolittle):

You're raving. You're drunk. You're mad. I gave you five pounds. After that I had two conversations with you, at half a-crown an hour. I've never seen you since.

DOOLITTLE:

Oh! Drunk! am I? Mad! am I? Tell me this. Did you or did you not write a letter to an old blighter in America that was giving five million to found Moral Reform Societies all over the world, and that wanted you to invent a universal language for him?

HIGGINS:

What! Ezra D. Wannafeller! He's dead. (*He sits down again carelessly*).

DOOLITTLE:

Yes: he's dead; and I'm done for. Now did you or did you not write a letter to him to say that the most original moralist at present in England, to the best of your knowledge, was Alfred Doolittle, a common dustman.

HIGGINS:

Oh, after your last visit I remember making some silly joke of the kind.

DOOLITTLE:

Ah! you may well call it a silly joke. It put the lid on me right enough. Just give him the chance he wanted to show that Americans is not like us: that they recognize and respect merit in every class of life, however humble. Them words is in his blooming will, in which, Henry Higgins, thanks to your silly joking, he leaves me a share in his Pre-digested Cheese Trust worth three thousand a year on condition that I lecture for his Wannafeller Moral Reform World League as often as they ask me up to six times a year.

HIGGINS:

The devil he does! Whew! (*Brightening suddenly*) What a lark!

PICKERING:

A safe thing for you, Doolittle. They won't ask you twice.

DOOLITTLE:

It ain't the lecturing I mind. I'll lecture them blue in the face, I will, and not turn a hair. It's making a gentleman of me that I object to. Who asked him to make a gentleman of me? I was happy. I was free. I touched pretty nigh everybody for money when I wanted it, same as I touched you, Henry Higgins. Now I am worrited; tied neck and heels; and everybody touches me for money. It's a fine thing for you, says my solicitor. Is it? says I. You mean it's a good thing for you, I says. When I was a poor man and had a solicitor once when they found a pram in the dust cart, he got me off, and got shut of me and got me shut of him as quick as he could. Same with the doctors: used to shove me out of the hospital before I could hardly stand on my legs, and nothing to pay. Now they finds out that I'm not a healthy man and can't live unless they looks after me twice a day. In the house I'm not let do a hand's turn for myself: somebody else must do it and touch me for it. A year ago I hadn't a relative in the world except two or three that wouldn't speak to me. Now I've fifty, and not a decent week's wages among the lot of them. I have to live for others and not for myself: that's middle class morality. You talk of losing Eliza. Don't you be anxious: I bet she's on my doorstep by this: she that could support herself easy by selling flowers if I wasn't respectable. And the next one to touch me will be you, Henry Higgins. I'll have to learn to speak middle class language from you, instead of speaking proper English. That's where you'll come in; and I daresay that's what you done it for.

MRS HIGGINS:

But, my dear Mr Doolittle, you need not suffer all this if you are really in earnest. Nobody can force you to accept this bequest. You can repudiate it. Isn't that so, Colonel Pickering?

PICKERING:

I believe so.

DOOLITTLE (*softening his manner in deference to her sex*):

That's the tragedy of it, ma'am. It's easy to say chuck it; but I haven't the nerve. Which of us has? We're all intimidated. Intimidated, ma'am: that's what we are. What is there for me if I chuck it but the workhouse in my old age? I have to dye my hair already to keep my job as a dustman. If I was one of the deserving poor, and had put by a bit, I could chuck it; but then why should I, acause the deserving poor might as well be millionaires for all the happiness they ever has. They don't know what happiness is. But I, as one of the undeserving poor, have nothing between me and the pauper's uniform but this here blasted three thousand a year that shoves me into the middle class. (Excuse the expression, ma'am: you'd use it yourself if you had my provocation.) They've got you every way you turn: it's a choice between the Skilly of the workhouse and the Char Bydis of the middle class; and I haven't the nerve for the workhouse. Intimidated: that's what I am. Broke. Bought up. Happier men than me will call for my dust, and touch me for their tip; and I'll look on helpless, and envy them. And that's what your son has brought me to. (*He is overcome by emotion*).

MRS HIGGINS:

Well, I'm very glad you're not going to do anything foolish, Mr Doolittle. For this solves the problem of Eliza's future. You can provide for her now.

DOOLITTLE (*with melancholy resignation*):

Yes, ma'am: I'm expected to provide for everyone now, out of three thousand a year.

HIGGINS (*jumping up*):

> Nonsense! he can't provide for her. He shan't provide for her. She doesn't belong to him. I paid him five pounds for her. Doolittle: either you're an honest man or a rogue.

DOOLITTLE (*tolerantly*):

> A little of both, Henry, like the rest of us: a little of both.

HIGGINS:

> Well, you took that money for the girl; and you have no right to take her as well.

MRS HIGGINS:

> Henry: don't be absurd. If you want to know where Eliza is, she is upstairs.

HIGGINS (*amazed*):

> Upstairs!!! Then I shall jolly soon fetch her downstairs. (*He makes resolutely for the door*).

MRS HIGGINS (*rising and following him*):

> Be quiet, Henry. Sit down.

HIGGINS:

> I—

MRS HIGGINS:

> Sit down, dear; and listen to me.

HIGGINS:

> Oh very well, very well, very well. (*He throws himself ungraciously on the ottoman, with his face towards the windows*). But I think you might have told us this half an hour ago.

MRS HIGGINS:

> Eliza came to me this morning. She passed the night partly walking about in a rage, partly trying to throw herself into the river and being afraid to, and partly in the Carlton Hotel. She told me of the brutal way you two treated her.

HIGGINS (*bounding up again*):

> What!

PICKERING (*rising also*):

> My dear Mrs Higgins, she's been telling you stories. We didn't treat her brutally. We hardly said a word to her; and we parted on particularly good terms. (*Turning on* Higgins). Higgins: did you bully her after I went to bed?

HIGGINS:

> Just the other way about. She threw my slippers in my face. She behaved in the most outrageous way. I never gave her the slightest provocation. The slippers came bang into my face the moment I entered the room—before I had uttered a word. And used perfectly awful language.

PICKERING (*astonished*):

> But why? What did we do to her?

MRS HIGGINS:

> I think I know pretty well what you did. The girl is naturally rather affectionate, I think. Isn't she, Mr Doolittle?

DOOLITTLE:

> Very tender-hearted, ma'am. Takes after me.

MRS HIGGINS:

> Just so. She had become attached to you both. She worked very hard for you, Henry! I don't think you quite realize what anything in the nature of brain work means to a girl like that. Well, it seems that when the great day of trial came, and she did this wonderful thing for you without making a single mistake, you two sat there and never said a word to her, but talked together of how glad you were that it was all over and how you had been bored with the whole thing. And then you were surprised because she threw your slippers at you! *I* should have thrown the fire-irons at you.

HIGGINS:

> We said nothing except that we were tired and wanted to go to bed. Did we, Pick?

PICKERING (*shrugging his shoulders*):

> That was all.

MRS HIGGINS (*ironically*):

> Quite sure?

PICKERING:

> Absolutely. Really, that was all.

MRS HIGGINS:

> You didn't thank her, or pet her, or admire her, or tell her how splendid she'd been.

HIGGINS (*impatiently*):

> But she knew all about that. We didn't make speeches to her, if that's what you mean.

PICKERING (*conscience stricken*):

> Perhaps we were a little inconsiderate. Is she very angry?

MRS HIGGINS (*returning to her place at the writing-table*):

> Well, I'm afraid she won't go back to Wimpole Street, especially now that Mr Doolittle is able to keep up the position you have thrust on her; but she says she is quite willing to meet you on friendly terms and to let bygones be bygones.

HIGGINS (*furious*):

> Is she, by George? Ho!

MRS HIGGINS:

> If you promise to behave yourself, Henry, I'll ask her to come down. If not, go home; for you have taken up quite enough of my time.

HIGGINS:

> Oh, all right. Very well. Pick: you behave yourself. Let us put on our best Sunday manners for this creature that we picked out of the mud. (*He flings himself sulkily into the Elizabethan chair*).

DOOLITTLE (*remonstrating*):

> Now, now, Henry Higgins! have some consideration for my feelings as a middle class man.

MRS HIGGINS:

> Remember your promise, Henry. (*She presses the bell-button on the writing-table*). Mr Doolittle: will you be so good as to step out on the balcony for a moment. I don't want Eliza to have the shock of your news until she has made it up with these two gentlemen. Would you mind?

DOOLITTLE:

> As you wish, lady. Anything to help Henry to keep her off my hands. (*He disappears through the window*).

The parlor-maid *answers the bell*. Pickering *sits down in* Doolittle's *place*.

MRS HIGGINS:

> Ask Miss Doolittle to come down, please.

THE PARLOR-MAID:

> Yes, ma'am. (*She goes out*).

MRS HIGGINS:

> Now, Henry: be good.

HIGGINS:

> I am behaving myself perfectly.

PICKERING:

> He is doing his best, Mrs Higgins.

*A pause.* Higgins *throws back his head; stretches out his legs; and begins to whistle*.

MRS HIGGINS:

> Henry, dearest, you don't look at all nice in that attitude.

HIGGINS (*pulling himself together*):

> I was not trying to look nice, mother.

MRS HIGGINS:

> It doesn't matter, dear. I only wanted to make you speak.

HIGGINS:

Why?

MRS HIGGINS:

Because you can't speak and whistle at the same time.

Higgins *groans. Another very trying pause.*

HIGGINS (*springing up, out of patience*):

Where the devil is that girl? Are we to wait here all day?

Eliza *enters, sunny, self-possessed, and giving a staggeringly convincing exhibition of ease of manner. She carries a little work-basket, and is very much at home.* Pickering *is too much taken aback to rise.*

LIZA:

How do you do, Professor Higgins? Are you quite well?

HIGGINS (*choking*):

Am I—(*He can say no more*).

LIZA:

But of course you are: you are never ill. So glad to see you again, Colonel Pickering. (*He rises hastily; and they shake hands*). Quite chilly this morning, isn't it? (*She sits down on his left. He sits beside her*).

HIGGINS:

Don't you dare try this game on me. I taught it to you; and it doesn't take me in. Get up and come home; and don't be a fool.

Eliza *takes a piece of needlework from her basket, and begins to stitch at it, without taking the least notice of this outburst.*

MRS HIGGINS:

Very nicely put, indeed, Henry. No woman could resist such an invitation.

HIGGINS:

You let her alone, mother. Let her speak for herself. You will jolly soon see whether she has an idea that I haven't put into her head or a word that I haven't put into her mouth. I tell you I have created this thing out of the squashed cabbage leaves of Covent Garden; and now she pretends to play the fine lady with me.

MRS HIGGINS (*placidly*):

Yes, dear; but you'll sit down, won't you?

Higgins *sits down again, savagely.*

LIZA (*to* Pickering, *taking no apparent notice of* Higgins, *and working away deftly*):

Will you drop me altogether now that the experiment is over, Colonel Pickering?

PICKERING:

Oh don't. You mustn't think of it as an experiment. It shocks me, somehow.

LIZA:

Oh, I'm only a squashed cabbage leaf—

PICKERING (*impulsively*):

No.

LIZA (*continuing quietly*):

—but I owe so much to you that I should be very unhappy if you forgot me.

PICKERING:

It's very kind of you to say so, Miss Doolittle.

LIZA:

It's not because you paid for my dresses. I know you are generous to everybody with money. But it was from you that I learnt really nice manners; and that is what makes one a lady, isn't it? You see it was so very difficult for me with the example of Professor Higgins always before me. I was brought up to be just like him, unable to control myself, and using bad language on the slightest provocation. And I should never have known that ladies and gentlemen didn't behave like that if you hadn't been there.

HIGGINS:

Well!!

PICKERING:

Oh, that's only his way, you know. He doesn't mean it.

LIZA:

Oh, *I* didn't mean it either, when I was a flower girl. It was only my way. But you see I did it; and that's what makes the difference after all.

PICKERING:

No doubt. Still, he taught you to speak; and I couldn't have done that, you know.

LIZA (*trivially*):

Of course: that is his profession.

HIGGINS:

Damnation!

LIZA (*continuing*):

It was just like learning to dance in the fashionable way: there was nothing more than that in it. But do you know what began my real education?

PICKERING:

What?

LIZA (*stopping her work for a moment*):

Your calling me Miss Doolittle that day when I first came to Wimpole Street. That was the beginning of self-respect for me. (*She resumes her stitching*). And there were a hundred little things you never noticed, because they came naturally to you. Things about standing up and taking off your hat and opening doors—

PICKERING:

Oh, that was nothing.

LIZA:

Yes: things that showed you thought and felt about me as if I were something better than a scullery-maid; though of course I know you would have been just the same to a scullery-maid if she had been let into the drawing room. You never took off your boots in the dining room when I was there.

PICKERING:

You mustn't mind that. Higgins takes off his boots all over the place.

LIZA:

I know. I am not blaming him. It is his way, isn't it? But it made such a difference to me that you didn't do it. You see, really and truly, apart from the things anyone can pick up (the dressing and the proper way of speaking, and so on), the difference between a lady and a flower girl is not how she behaves, but how she's treated. I shall always be a flower girl to Professor Higgins, because he always treats me as a flower girl, and always will; but I know I can be a lady to you, because you always treat me as a lady, and always will.

MRS HIGGINS:

Please don't grind your teeth, Henry.

PICKERING:

Well, this is really very nice of you, Miss Doolittle.

LIZA:

I should like you to call me Eliza, now, if you would.

PICKERING:

Thank you. Eliza, of course.

LIZA:

And I should like Professor Higgins to call me Miss Doolittle.

HIGGINS:

I'll see you damned first.

MRS HIGGINS:

Henry! Henry!

PICKERING (*laughing*):

Why don't you slang back at him? Don't stand it. It would do him a lot of good.

LIZA:

I can't. I could have done it once; but now I can't go back to it. Last night, when I was wandering about, a girl spoke to me; and I tried to get back into the old way with her; but it was no use. You told me, you know, that when a child is brought to a foreign country, it picks up the language in a few weeks, and forgets its own. Well, I am a child in your country. I have forgotten my own language, and can speak nothing but yours. That's the real break-off with the corner of Tottenham Court Road. Leaving Wimpole Street finishes it.

PICKERING (*much alarmed*):

Oh! but you're coming back to Wimpole Street, aren't you? You'll forgive Higgins?

HIGGINS (*rising*):

Forgive! Will she, by George! Let her go. Let her find out how she can get on without us. She will relapse into the gutter in three weeks without me at her elbow.

Doolittle *appears at the centre window. With a look of dignified reproach at* Higgins, *he comes slowly and silently to his daughter, who, with her back to the window, is unconscious of his approach.*

PICKERING:

He's incorrigible, Eliza. You won't relapse, will you?

LIZA:

No: not now. Never again. I have learnt my lesson. I don't believe I could utter one of the old sounds if I tried. (Doolittle *touches her on her left shoulder. She drops her work, losing her self-possession utterly at the spectacle of her father's splendor*) A-a-a-a-a-ah-ow-ooh!

HIGGINS (*with a crow of triumph*):

Aha! Just so. A-a-a-a-ahowooh! A-a-a-a-ahowooh! A-a-a-a-ahowooh! Victory! Victory! (*He throws himself on the divan, folding his arms, and spraddling arrogantly*).

DOOLITTLE:

Can you blame the girl? Don't look at me like that, Eliza. It ain't my fault. I've come into some money.

LIZA:

You must have touched a millionaire this time, dad.

DOOLITTLE:

I have. But I'm dressed something special today. I'm going to St George's, Hanover Square. Your stepmother is going to marry me.

LIZA (*angrily*):

You're going to let yourself down to marry that low common woman!

PICKERING (*quietly*):

He ought to, Eliza. (*To* Doolittle) Why has she changed her mind?

DOOLITTLE (*sadly*):

Intimidated, Governor. Intimidated. Middle class morality claims its victim. Won't you put on your hat, Liza, and come and see me turned off?

LIZA:

If the Colonel says I must, I—I'll (*almost sobbing*) I'll demean myself. And get insulted for my pains, like enough.

DOOLITTLE:

Don't be afraid: she never comes to words with anyone now, poor woman! respectability has broke all the spirit out of her.

PICKERING (*squeezing* Eliza's *elbow gently*):

Be kind to them, Eliza. Make the best of it.

LIZA (*forcing a little smile for him through her vexation*):

Oh well, just to show there's no ill feeling. I'll be back in a moment. (*She goes out*).

DOOLITTLE (*sitting down beside* Pickering):

I feel uncommon nervous about the ceremony, Colonel. I wish you'd come and see me through it.

PICKERING:

But you've been through it before, man. You were married to Eliza's mother.

DOOLITTLE:

Who told you that, Colonel?

PICKERING:

Well, nobody told me. But I concluded—naturally—

DOOLITTLE:

No: that ain't the natural way, Colonel: it's only the middle class way. My way was always the undeserving way. But don't say nothing to Eliza. She don't know: I always had a delicacy about telling her.

PICKERING:

Quite right. We'll leave it so, if you don't mind.

DOOLITTLE:

    And you'll come to the church, Colonel, and put me through straight?

PICKERING:

    With pleasure. As far as a bachelor can.

MRS HIGGINS:

    May I come, Mr Doolittle? I should be very sorry to miss your wedding.

DOOLITTLE:

    I should indeed be honored by your condescension, ma'am; and my poor old woman would take it as a tremenjous compliment. She's been very low, thinking of the happy days that are no more.

MRS HIGGINS (*rising*):

    I'll order the carriage and get ready. (*The men rise, except* Higgins). I shan't be more than fifteen minutes. (*As she goes to the door* Eliza *comes in, hatted and buttoning her gloves*). I'm going to the church to see your father married, Eliza. You had better come in the brougham with me. Colonel Pickering can go on with the bridegroom.

Mrs Higgins *goes out.* Eliza *comes to the middle of the room between the centre window and the ottoman.* Pickering *joins her.*

DOOLITTLE:

    Bridegroom! What a word! It makes a man realize his position, somehow. (*He takes up his hat and goes towards the door*).

PICKERING:

    Before I go, Eliza, do forgive him and come back to us.

LIZA:

    I don't think papa would allow me. Would you, dad?

DOOLITTLE (*sad but magnanimous*):

    They played you off very cunning, Eliza, them two sportsmen. If it had been only one of them, you could have nailed him. But you see, there was two; and one of them chaperoned the other, as you might say. (*To* Pickering) It was artful of you, Colonel; but I bear no malice: I should have done the same myself. I been the victim of one woman after another all my life; and I don't grudge you two getting the better of Eliza. I shan't interfere. It's time for us to go, Colonel. So long, Henry. See you in St George's, Eliza. (*He goes out*).

PICKERING (*coaxing*):

    Do stay with us, Eliza. (*He follows* Doolittle).

*Eliza goes out on the balcony to avoid being alone with* Higgins. *He rises and joins her there. She immediately comes back into the room and makes for the door; but he goes along the balcony quickly and gets his back to the door before she reaches it.*

HIGGINS:

> Well, Eliza, you've had a bit of your own back, as you call it. Have you had enough? and are you going to be reasonable? Or do you want any more?

LIZA:

> You want me back only to pick up your slippers and put up with your tempers and fetch and carry for you.

HIGGINS:

> I haven't said I wanted you back at all.

LIZA:

> Oh, indeed. Then what are we talking about?

HIGGINS:

> About you, not about me. If you come back I shall treat you just as I have always treated you. I can't change my nature; and I don't intend to change my manners. My manners are exactly the same as Colonel Pickering's.

LIZA:

> That's not true. He treats a flower girl as if she was a duchess.

HIGGINS:

> And I treat a duchess as if she was a flower girl.

LIZA:

> I see. (*She turns away composedly, and sits on the ottoman, facing the window*). The same to everybody.

HIGGINS:

> Just so.

LIZA:

> Like father.

HIGGINS (*grinning, a little taken down*):

> Without accepting the comparison at all points, Eliza, it's quite true that your father is not a snob, and that he will be quite at home in any station of life to which his eccentric destiny may call him. (*Seriously*) The great secret, Eliza, is not having bad manners or good manners or any other particular sort of manners, but having the same manner for all human souls: in short, behaving as if you were in Heaven, where there are no third-class carriages, and one soul is as good as another.

LIZA:

> Amen. You are a born preacher.

HIGGINS (*irritated*):

> The question is not whether I treat you rudely, but whether you ever heard me treat anyone else better.

LIZA (*with sudden sincerity*):

> I don't care how you treat me. I don't mind your swearing at me. I don't mind a black eye: I've had one before this. But (*standing up and facing him*) I won't be passed over.

HIGGINS:

> Then get out of my way; for I won't stop for you. You talk about me as if I were a motor bus.

LIZA:

> So you are a motor bus: all bounce and go, and no consideration for anyone. But I can do without you: don't think I can't.

HIGGINS:

> I know you can. I told you you could.

LIZA (*wounded, getting away from him to the other side of the ottoman with her face to the hearth*):

> I know you did, you brute. You wanted to get rid of me.

HIGGINS:

> Liar.

LIZA:

> Thank you. (*She sits down with dignity*).

HIGGINS:

> You never asked yourself, I suppose, whether *I* could do without you.

LIZA (*earnestly*):

> Don't you try to get round me. You'll have to do without me.

HIGGINS (*arrogant*):

> I can do without anybody. I have my own soul: my own spark of divine fire. But (*with sudden humility*) I shall miss you, Eliza. (*He sits down near her on the ottoman*). I have learnt something from your idiotic notions: I confess that humbly and gratefully. And I have grown accustomed to your voice and appearance. I like them, rather.

LIZA:

> Well, you have both of them on your gramophone and in your book of photographs. When you feel lonely without me, you can turn the machine on. It's got no feelings to hurt.

HIGGINS:

> I can't turn your soul on. Leave me those feelings; and you can take away the voice and the face. They are not you.

LIZA:

> Oh, you are a devil. You can twist the heart in a girl as easy as some could twist her arms to hurt her. Mrs Pearce warned me. Time and again she has wanted to leave you; and you always got round her at the last minute. And you don't care a bit for her. And you don't care a bit for me.

HIGGINS:

> I care for life, for humanity; and you are a part of it that has come my way and been built into my house. What more can you or anyone ask?

LIZA:

> I won't care for anybody that doesn't care for me.

HIGGINS:

> Commercial principles, Eliza. Like (*reproducing her Covent Garden pronunciation with professional exactness*) s'yollin voylets (selling violets), isn't it?

LIZA:

> Don't sneer at me. It's mean to sneer at me.

HIGGINS:

> I have never sneered in my life. Sneering doesn't become either the human face or the human soul. I am expressing my righteous contempt for Commercialism. I don't and won't trade in affection. You call me a brute because you couldn't buy a claim on me by fetching my slippers and finding my spectacles. You were a fool: I think a woman fetching a man's slippers is a disgusting sight: did I ever fetch your slippers? I think a good deal more of you for throwing them in my face. No use slaving for me and then saying you want to be cared for: who cares for a slave? If you come back, come back for the sake of good fellowship; for you'll get nothing else. You've had a thousand times as much out of me as I have out of you; and if you dare to set up your little dog's tricks of fetching and carrying slippers against my creation of a Duchess Eliza, I'll slam the door in your silly face.

LIZA:

> What did you do it for if you didn't care for me?

HIGGINS (*heartily*):

> Why, because it was my job.

LIZA:

> You never thought of the trouble it would make for me.

HIGGINS:

> Would the world ever have been made if its maker had been afraid of making trouble? Making life means making trouble.

There's only one way of escaping trouble; and that's killing things. Cowards, you notice, are always shrieking to have troublesome people killed.

LIZA:

I'm no preacher: I don't notice things like that. I notice that you don't notice me.

HIGGINS (*jumping up and walking about intolerantly*):

Eliza: you're an idiot. I waste the treasures of my Miltonic mind by spreading them before you. Once for all, understand that I go my way and do my work without caring two-pence what happens to either of us. I am not intimidated, like your father and your stepmother. So you can come back or go to the devil: which you please.

LIZA:

What am I to come back for?

HIGGINS (*bouncing up on his knees on the ottoman and leaning over it to her*):

For the fun of it. That's why I took you on.

LIZA (*with averted face*):

And you may throw me out to-morrow if I don't do everything you want me to?

HIGGINS:

Yes; and you may walk out tomorrow if I don't do everything you want me to.

LIZA:

And live with my stepmother?

HIGGINS:

Yes, or sell flowers.

LIZA:

Oh! if I only could go back to my flower basket! I should be independent of both you and father and all the world! Why did you take my independence from me? Why did I give it up? I'm a slave now, for all my fine clothes.

HIGGINS:

Not a bit. I'll adopt you as my daughter and settle money on you if you like. Or would you rather marry Pickering?

LIZA (*looking fiercely round at him*):

I wouldn't marry you if you asked me; and you're nearer my age than what he is.

HIGGINS (*gently*):

Than he is: not "than what he is."

LIZA (*losing her temper and rising*):

I'll talk as I like. You're not my teacher now.

HIGGINS (*reflectively*):

I don't suppose Pickering would, though. He's as confirmed an old bachelor as I am.

LIZA:

That's not what I want; and don't you think it. I've always had chaps enough wanting me that way. Freddy Hill writes to me twice and three times a day, sheets and sheets.

HIGGINS (*disagreeably surprised*):

Damn his impudence! (*He recoils and finds himself sitting on his heels*).

LIZA:

He has a right to if he likes, poor lad. And he does love me.

HIGGINS (*getting off the ottoman*):

You have no right to encourage him.

LIZA:

Every girl has a right to be loved.

HIGGINS:

What! By fools like that?

LIZA:

Freddy's not a fool. And if he's weak and poor and wants me, may be he'd make me happier than my betters that bully me and don't want me.

HIGGINS:

Can he make anything of you? That's the point.

LIZA:

Perhaps I could make something of him. But I never thought of us making anything of one another; and you never think of anything else. I only want to be natural.

HIGGINS:

In short, you want me to be as infatuated about you as Freddy? Is that it?

LIZA:

No I don't. That's not the sort of feeling I want from you. And don't you be too sure of yourself or of me. I could have been a bad girl if I'd liked. I've seen more of some things than you, for all your learning. Girls like me can drag gentlemen down to make love to them easy enough. And they wish each other dead the next minute.

HIGGINS:

Of course they do. Then what in thunder are we quarrelling about?

LIZA (*much troubled*):

I want a little kindness. I know I'm a common ignorant girl, and you a book-learned gentleman; but I'm not dirt under your feet. What I done (*correcting herself*) what I did was not for the dresses and the taxis: I did it because we were pleasant together and I come—came—to care for you; not to want you to make love to me, and not forgetting the difference between us, but more friendly like.

HIGGINS:

Well, of course. That's just how I feel. And how Pickering feels. Eliza: you're a fool.

LIZA:

That's not a proper answer to give me (*she sinks on the chair at the writing-table in tears*).

HIGGINS:

It's all you'll get until you stop being a common idiot. If you're going to be a lady, you'll have to give up feeling neglected if the men you know don't spend half their time snivelling over you and the other half giving you black eyes. If you can't stand the coldness of my sort of life, and the strain of it, go back to the gutter. Work till you are more a brute than a human being; and then cuddle and squabble and drink till you fall asleep. Oh, it's a fine life, the life of the gutter. It's real: it's warm: it's violent: you can feel it through the thickest skin: you can taste it and smell it without any training or any work. Not like Science and Literature and Classical Music and Philosophy and Art. You find me cold, unfeeling, selfish, don't you? Very well: be off with you to the sort of people you like. Marry some sentimental hog or other with lots of money, and a thick pair of lips to kiss you with and a thick pair of boots to kick you with. If you can't appreciate what you've got, you'd better get what you can appreciate.

LIZA (*desperate*):

Oh, you are a cruel tyrant. I can't talk to you: you turn everything against me: I'm always in the wrong. But you know very well all the time that you're nothing but a bully. You know I can't go back to the gutter, as you call it, and that I have no real friends in the world but you and the Colonel. You know well I couldn't bear to live with a low common man after you two; and it's wicked and cruel of you to insult me by pretending I could. You think I must go back to Wimpole Street because I have nowhere else to go but father's. But don't you be too sure that you have me under your feet to be trampled on and talked down. I'll marry Freddy, I will, as soon as he's able to support me.

HIGGINS (*sitting down beside her*):

Rubbish! you shall marry an ambassador. You shall marry the Governor-General of India or the Lord-Lieutenant of Ireland, or somebody who wants a deputy-queen. I'm not going to have my masterpiece thrown away on Freddy.

LIZA:

You think I like you to say that. But I haven't forgot what you said a minute ago; and I won't be coaxed round as if I was a baby or a puppy. If I can't have kindness, I'll have independence.

HIGGINS:

Independence? That's middle class blasphemy. We are all dependent on one another, every soul of us on earth.

LIZA (*rising determinedly*):

I'll let you see whether I'm dependent on you. If you can preach, I can teach. I'll go and be a teacher.

HIGGINS:

What'll you teach, in heaven's name?

LIZA:

What you taught me. I'll teach phonetics.

HIGGINS:

Ha! ha! ha!

LIZA:

I'll offer myself as an assistant to Professor Nepean.

HIGGINS (*rising in a fury*):

What! That impostor! that humbug! that toadying ignoramus! Teach him my methods! my discoveries! You take one step in his direction and I'll wring your neck. (*He lays hands on her*). Do you hear?

LIZA (*defiantly non-resistant*):

Wring away. What do I care? I knew you'd strike me some day. (*He let's her go, stamping with rage at having forgotten himself, and recoils so hastily that he stumbles back into his seat on the ottoman*). Aha! Now I know how to deal with you. What a fool I was not to think of it before! You can't take away the knowledge you gave me. You said I had a finer ear than you. And I can be civil and kind to people, which is more than you can. Aha! That's done you, Henry Higgins, it has. Now I don't care that (*snapping her fingers*) for your bullying and your big talk. I'll advertize it in the papers that your duchess is only a flower girl that you taught, and that she'll teach anybody to be a duchess just the same in six months for a thousand guineas. Oh, when I think of myself crawling under your feet and being trampled on and called names, when all the time I had only to lift up my finger to be as good as you, I could just kick myself.

HIGGINS (*wondering at her*):

You damned impudent slut, you! But it's better than snivelling; better than fetching slippers and finding spectacles, isn't it?

(*Rising*) By George, Eliza, I said I'd make a woman of you; and I have. I like you like this.

LIZA:

Yes: you turn round and make up to me now that I'm not afraid of you, and can do without you.

HIGGINS:

Of course I do, you little fool. Five minutes ago you were like a millstone round my neck. Now you're a tower of strength: a consort battleship. You and I and Pickering will be three old bachelors together instead of only two men and a silly girl.

Mrs Higgins *returns, dressed for the wedding.* Eliza *instantly becomes cool and elegant.*

MRS HIGGINS:

The carriage is waiting, Eliza. Are you ready?

LIZA:

Quite. Is the Professor coming?

MRS HIGGINS:

Certainly not. He can't behave himself in church. He makes remarks out loud all the time on the clergyman's pronunciation.

LIZA:

Then I shall not see you again, Professor. Goodbye. (*She goes to the door*).

MRS HIGGINS (*coming to* Higgins):

Goodbye, dear.

HIGGINS:

Goodbye, mother. (*He is about to kiss her, when he recollects something*). Oh, by the way, Eliza, order a ham and a Stilton cheese, will you? And buy me a pair of reindeer gloves, number eights, and a tie to match that new suit of mine, at Eale & Binman's. You can choose the color. (*His cheerful, careless, vigorous voice shows that he is incorrigible*).

LIZA (*disdainfully*):

Buy them yourself. (*She sweeps out*).

MRS HIGGINS:

I'm afraid you've spoiled that girl, Henry. But never mind, dear: I'll buy you the tie and gloves.

HIGGINS (*sunnily*):

Oh, don't bother. She'll buy 'em all right enough. Goodbye.

They kiss. Mrs Higgins *runs out.* Higgins, *left alone, rattles his cash in his pocket; chuckles; and disports himself in a highly self-satisfied manner.*

The rest of the story need not be shown in action, and indeed, would hardly need telling if our imaginations were not so enfeebled by their lazy dependence on the ready-mades and reach-me-downs of the ragshop in which Romance keeps its stock of "happy endings" to misfit all stories. Now, the history of Eliza Doolittle, though called a romance because the transfiguration it records seems exceedingly improbable, is common enough. Such transfigurations have been achieved by hundreds of resolutely ambitious young women since Nell Gwynne set them the example by playing queens and fascinating kings in the theatre in which she began by selling oranges. Nevertheless, people in all directions have assumed, for no other reason than that she became the heroine of a romance, that she must have married the hero of it. This is unbearable, not only because her little drama, if acted on such a thoughtless assumption, must be spoiled, but because the true sequel is patent to anyone with a sense of human nature in general, and of feminine instinct in particular.

Eliza, in telling Higgins she would not marry him if he asked her, was not coquetting: she was announcing a well-considered decision. When a bachelor interests, and dominates, and teaches, and becomes important to a spinster, as Higgins with Eliza, she always, if she has character enough to be capable of it, considers very seriously indeed whether she will play for becoming that bachelor's wife, especially if he is so little interested in marriage that a determined and devoted woman might capture him if she set herself resolutely to do it. Her decision will depend a good deal on whether she is really free to choose; and that, again, will depend on her age and income. If she is at the end of her youth, and has no security for her livelihood, she will marry him because she must marry anybody who will provide for her. But at Eliza's age a good-looking girl does not feel that pressure: she feels free to pick and choose. She is therefore guided by her instinct in the matter. Eliza's instinct tells her not to marry Higgins. It does not tell her to give him up. It is not in the slightest doubt as to his remaining one of the strongest personal interests in her life. It would be very sorely strained if there was another woman likely to supplant her with him. But as she feels sure of him on that last point, she has not doubt at all as to her course, and would not have any, even if the difference of twenty years in age, which seems so great to youth, did not exist between them.

As our own instincts are not appealed to by her conclusion, let us see whether we cannot discover some reason in it. When Higgins excused his indifference to young women on the ground that they had an irresistible rival in his mother, he gave the clue to his inveterate old-bachelordom. The case is uncommon only to the extent that remarkable mothers are uncommon. If an imaginative boy has a sufficiently rich mother who has intelligence, personal grace, dignity of character without harshness, and a cultivated sense of the best art of her time to enable her to make her house beautiful, she sets a standard for him against which very few women can struggle, besides effecting for him a disengagement of his affections, his sense of beauty, and his idealism from his specifically sexual impulses. This makes him a standing puzzle to the huge number of uncultivated people who have been brought up in tasteless homes by commonplace or disagreeable parents, and to whom, consequently, literature, painting, sculpture, music, and affectionate personal relations come as modes of sex if they come at all. The word passion means nothing else to them; and that Higgins could have a passion for phonetics and idealize his mother instead of Eliza, would seem to them absurd and unnatural. Nevertheless, when we look round and see that hardly anyone is too ugly or disagreeable to find a wife or a husband if he or she wants one, whilst many old maids and bachelors are above the average in quality and culture, we cannot help suspecting that the disentanglement of sex from the associations with which it is so commonly confused, a disentanglement which persons of genius achieve by sheer intellectual analysis, is sometimes produced or aided by parental fascination.

Now, though Eliza was incapable of thus explaining to herself Higgins's formidable powers of resistance to the charm that prostrated Freddy at the first glance, she was instinctively aware that she could never obtain a complete grip of him, or come between him and his mother (the first necessity of the married woman). To put it shortly, she knew that for some mysterious reason he had not the makings of a married man in him, according to her conception of a husband as one to whom she would be his nearest and fondest and warmest interest. Even had there been no mother-rival, she would still have refused to accept an interest in herself that was secondary to philosophic interests. Had Mrs Higgins died, there would still have been Milton and the Universal Alphabet. Landor's remark that to those who have the greatest power of loving, love is a secondary affair, would not have recommended Landor to Eliza. Put that along with her resentment of Higgins's domineering superiority, and her mistrust of his coaxing cleverness in getting round her and evading her wrath when he had gone too far with his impetuous bullying, and you will see that Eliza's instinct had good grounds for warning her not to marry her Pygmalion.

And now, whom did Eliza marry? For if Higgins was a predestinate old bachelor, she was most certainly not a predestinate old maid. Well, that can be told very shortly to those who have not guessed it from the indications she has herself given them.

Almost immediately after Eliza is stung into proclaiming her considered determination not to marry Higgins, she mentions the fact that young Mr Frederick Eynsford Hill is pouring out his love for her daily through the post. Now Freddy is young, practically twenty years younger than Higgins: he is a gentleman (or, as Eliza would qualify him, a toff), and speaks like one; he is nicely dressed, is treated by the Colonel as an equal, loves her unaffectedly, and is not her master, nor ever likely to dominate her in spite of his advantage of social standing. Eliza has no use for the foolish romantic tradition that all women love to be mastered, if not actually bullied and beaten. "When you go to women," says Nietzsche, "take your whip with you." Sensible despots have never confined that precaution to women: they have taken their whips with them when they have dealt with men, and been slavishly idealized by the men over whom they have flourished the whip much more than by women. No doubt there are slavish women as well as slavish men; and women, like men, admire those that are stronger than themselves. But to admire a strong person and to live under that strong person's thumb are two different things. The weak may not be admired and hero-worshipped; but they are by no means disliked or shunned; and they never seem to have the least difficulty in marrying people who are too good for them. They may fail in emergencies; but life is not one long emergency: it is mostly a string of situations for which no exceptional strength is needed, and with which even rather weak people can cope if they have a stronger partner to help them out. Accordingly, it is a truth everywhere in evidence that strong people, masculine or feminine, not only do not marry stronger people, but do not show any preference for them in selecting their friends. When a lion meets another with a louder roar "the first lion thinks the last a bore." The man or woman who feels strong enough for two, seeks for every other quality in a partner than strength.

The converse is also true. Weak people want to marry strong people who do not frighten them too much; and this often leads them to make the mistake we describe metaphorically as "biting off more than they can chew." They want too much for too little; and when the bargain is unreasonable beyond all bearing, the union becomes impossible: it ends in the weaker party being either discarded or borne as a cross, which is worse. People who are not only weak, but silly or obtuse as well, are often in these difficulties.

This being the state of human affairs, what is Eliza fairly sure to do when she is placed between Freddy and Higgins? Will she look forward to a lifetime of fetching Higgins's slippers or to a lifetime of Freddy fetching hers? There can be no doubt about the answer. Unless Freddy is biologically repulsive to her, and Higgins biologically attractive to a degree that overwhelms all her other instincts, she will, if she marries either of them, marry Freddy.

And that is just what Eliza did.

Complications ensued; but they were economic, not romantic. Freddy had no money and no occupation. His mother's jointure, a last relic of the opulence of Largelady Park, had enabled her to struggle along in Earlscourt with an air of gentility, but not to procure any serious secondary education for her children, much less give the boy a profession. A clerkship at thirty shillings a week was beneath Freddy's dignity, and extremely distasteful to him besides. His prospects consisted of a hope that if he kept up appearances somebody would do something for him. The something appeared vaguely to his imagination as a private secretaryship or a sinecure of some sort. To his mother it perhaps appeared as a marriage to some lady of means who could not resist her boy's niceness. Fancy her feelings when he married a flower girl who had become déclassée under extraordinary circumstances which were now notorious!

It is true that Eliza's situation did not seem wholly ineligible. Her father, though formerly a dustman, and now fantastically disclassed, had become extremely popular in the smartest society by a social talent which triumphed over every prejudice and every disadvantage. Rejected by the middle class, which he loathed, he had shot up at once into the highest circles by his wit, his dustmanship (which he carried like a banner), and his Nietzschean transcendence of good and evil. At intimate ducal dinners he sat on the right hand of the Duchess; and in country houses he smoked in the pantry and was made much of by the butler when he was not feeding in the dining room and being consulted by cabinet ministers. But he found it almost as hard to do all this on four thousand a year as Mrs Eynsford Hill to live in Earlscourt on an income so pitiably smaller that I have not the heart to disclose its exact figure. He absolutely refused to add the last straw to his burden by contributing to Eliza's support.

Thus Freddy and Eliza, now Mr and Mrs Eynsford Hill, would have spent a penniless honeymoon but for a wedding present of £500 from the Colonel to Eliza. It lasted a long time because Freddy did not know how to spend money, never having had any to spend, and Eliza, socially trained by a pair of old bachelors, wore her clothes as long as they held together and looked pretty, without the least regard to their being many months out of fashion. Still, £500 will not last two young people forever; and they both knew, and Eliza felt as well, that they must shift for themselves in the end. She could quarter herself on Wimpole Street because it had come to be her home; but she was quite aware that she ought not to quarter Freddy there, and that it would not be good for his character if she did.

Not that the Wimpole Street bachelors objected. When she consulted them, Higgins declined to be bothered about her housing problem when that solution was so simple. Eliza's desire to have Freddy in the house with her seemed of no more importance than if she had wanted an extra piece of bedroom furniture. Pleas as to Freddy's character, and the moral obligation on him to earn his own living, were lost on Higgins. He denied that Freddy had any character, and declared that if he tried to do any useful work some competent person would have the trouble of undoing it: a procedure involving a net loss to the community, and great unhappiness to Freddy himself, who was obviously intended by Nature for such light work as amusing Eliza, which, Higgins declared, was a much more useful and honorable occupation than working in the city. When Eliza referred again to her project of teaching phonetics, Higgins abated not a jot of his violent opposition to it. He said she was not within ten years of being qualified to meddle with his pet subject; and as it was evident that the Colonel agreed with him, she felt she could not go against them in this grave matter, and that she had no right, without Higgins's consent, to exploit the knowledge he had given her; for his knowledge seemed to her as much his private property as his watch: Eliza was no communist. Besides, she was superstitiously devoted to them both, more entirely and frankly after her marriage than before it.

It was the Colonel who finally solved the problem, which had cost him much perplexed cogitation. He one day asked Eliza, rather shyly, whether she had quite given up her notion of keeping a flower shop. She replied that she had thought of it, but had put it out of her head, because the Colonel had said, that day at Mrs Higgins's, that it would never do. The Colonel confessed that when he said that, he had not quite recovered from the dazzling impression of the day before. They broke the matter to Higgins that evening. The sole comment vouchsafed by him very nearly led to a serious quarrel with Eliza. It was to the effect that she would have in Freddy an ideal errand boy.

Freddy himself was next sounded on the subject. He said he had been thinking of a shop himself; though it had presented itself to his pennilessness as a small place in which Eliza should sell tobacco at one counter whilst he sold newspapers at the opposite one. But he agreed that it would be extraordinarily jolly to go early every morning with Eliza to Covent Garden and buy flowers on the scene of their first meeting: a sentiment which earned him many kisses from his wife. He added that he had always been afraid to propose anything of the sort, because Clara would make an awful row about a step that must damage her matrimonial chances, and his mother could not be expected to like it after clinging for so many years to that step of the social ladder on which retail trade is impossible.

This difficulty was removed by an event highly unexpected by Freddy's mother. Clara, in the course of her incursions into those artistic circles which were the highest within her reach, discovered that her conversational qualifications were expected to include a grounding in the novels of Mr H. G. Wells. She borrowed them in various directions so energetically that she swallowed them all within two months. The result was a conversion of a kind quite common today. A modern Acts of the Apostles would fill fifty whole Bibles if anyone were capable of writing it.

Poor Clara, who appeared to Higgins and his mother as a disagreeable and ridiculous person, and to her own mother as in some inexplicable way a social failure, had never seen herself in either light; for, though to some extent ridiculed and mimicked in West Kensington like everybody else there, she was accepted as a rational and normal—or shall we say inevitable?—sort of human being. At worst they called her The Pusher; but to them no more than to herself had it ever occurred that she was pushing the air, and pushing it in a wrong direction. Still, she was not happy. She was growing desperate. Her one asset, the fact that her mother was what the Epsom greengrocer called a carriage lady, had no exchange value, apparently. It had prevented her from getting educated, because the only education she could have afforded was education with the Earlscourt greengrocer's daughter. It had led her to seek the society of her mother's class; and that class simply would not have her, because she was much poorer than the greengrocer, and, far from being able to afford a maid, could not afford even a housemaid, and had to scrape along at home with an illiberally treated general servant. Under such circumstances nothing could give her an air of being a genuine product of Largelady Park. And yet its tradition made her regard a marriage with anyone within her reach as an unbearable humiliation. Commercial people and professional people in a small way were odious to her. She ran after painters and novelists; but she did not charm them; and her bold attempts to pick up and practise artistic and literary talk irritated them. She was, in short, an utter failure, an ignorant, incompetent, pretentious, unwelcome, penniless, useless little snob; and though she did not admit these disqualifications (for nobody ever faces unpleasant truths of this kind until the possibility of a way out dawns on them) she felt their effects too keenly to be satisfied with her position.

Clara had a startling eyeopener when, on being suddenly wakened to enthusiasm by a girl of her own age who dazzled her and produced in her a gushing desire to take her for a model, and gain her friendship, she discovered that this exquisite apparition had graduated from the gutter in a few months time. It shook her so violently, that when Mr H. G. Wells lifted her on the point of his puissant pen, and placed her at the angle of view from which the life she was leading and the society to which she clung appeared in its true relation to real human needs and worthy social structure, he effected a conversion and a conviction of sin comparable to the most sensational feats of General Booth or Gypsy Smith. Clara's snobbery went bang. Life suddenly began to move with her. Without knowing how or why, she began to make friends and enemies. Some of the acquaintances to whom she had been a tedious or indifferent or ridiculous affliction, dropped her: others became cordial. To her amazement she found that some "quite nice" people were saturated with Wells, and that this accessibility to ideas was the secret of their niceness. People she had thought deeply religious, and had tried to conciliate on that tack with disastrous results, suddenly took an interest in her, and revealed a hostility to conventional religion which she had never conceived possible except among the most desperate characters. They made her read Galsworthy; and Galsworthy exposed the vanity of Largelady Park and finished her. It exasperated her to think that the dungeon in which she had languished for so many unhappy years had been unlocked all the time, and that the impulses she had so carefully struggled with and stifled for the sake of keeping well with society, were precisely those by which alone she could have come into any sort of sincere human contact. In the radiance of these discoveries, and the tumult of their reaction, she made a fool of herself as freely and conspicuously as when she so rashly adopted Eliza's expletive in Mrs Higgins's drawing room; for the newborn Wellsian had to find her bearings almost as ridiculously as a baby; but nobody hates a baby for its ineptitudes, or thinks the worse of it for trying to eat the matches; and Clara lost no friends by her follies. They laughed at her to her face this time; and she had to defend herself and fight it out as best she could.

When Freddy paid a visit to Earlscourt (which he never did when he could possibly help it) to make the desolating announcement that he and his Eliza were thinking of blackening the Largelady scutcheon by opening a shop, he found the little household already convulsed by a prior announcement from Clara that she also was going to work in an old furniture shop in Dover Street, which had been started by a fellow Wellsian. This appointment Clara owed, after all, to her old social accomplishment of Push. She had made up her mind that, cost what it might, she would see Mr Wells in the flesh; and she had achieved her end at a garden party. She had better luck than so rash an enterprise deserved. Mr Wells came up to her expectations. Age had not withered him, nor could custom stale his infinite variety in half an hour. His pleasant neatness and compact-ness, his small hands and feet, his teeming ready brain, his unaffected accessibility, and a certain fine apprehensiveness which stamped him as susceptible from his topmost hair to his tipmost toe, proved irre-sistible. Clara talked of nothing else for weeks and weeks afterwards. And as she happened to talk to the lady of the furniture shop, and that lady also desired above all things to know Mr Wells and sell pretty things to him, she offered Clara a job on the chance of achiev-ing that end through her.

And so it came about that Eliza's luck held, and the expected opposition to the flower shop melted away. The shop is in the arcade of a railway station not very far from the Victoria and Albert Museum; and if you live in that neighborhood you may go there any day and buy a buttonhole from Eliza.

Now here is a last opportunity for romance. Would you not like to be assured that the shop was an immense success, thanks to Eliza's charms and her early business experience in Covent Garden? Alas! the truth is the truth: the shop did not pay for a long time, simply because Eliza and her Freddy did not know how to keep it. True, Eliza had not to begin at the very beginning: she knew the names and prices of the cheaper flowers; and her elation was unbounded when she found that Freddy, like all youths educated at cheap, pre-tentious, and thoroughly inefficient schools, knew a little Latin. It was very little, but enough to make him appear to her a Porson or Bentley, and to put him at his ease with botanical nomenclature. Unfortunately he knew nothing else; and Eliza, though she could count money up to eighteen shillings or so, and had acquired a cer-tain familiarity with the language of Milton from her struggles to qualify herself for winning Higgins's bet, could not write out a bill without utterly disgracing the establishment. Freddy's power of stat-ing in Latin that Balbus built a wall and that Gaul was divided into three parts did not carry with it the slightest knowledge of accounts or business: Colonel Pickering had to explain to him what a cheque book and a bank account meant. And the pair were by no means eas-ily teachable. Freddy backed up Eliza in her obstinate refusal to believe that they could save money by engaging a bookkeeper with some knowledge of the business. How, they argued, could you pos-sibly save money by going to extra expense when you already could not make both ends meet? But the Colonel, after making the ends meet over and over again, at last gently insisted; and Eliza, humbled to the dust by having to beg from him so often, and stung by the uproarious derision of Higgins, to whom the notion of Freddy suc-ceeding at anything was a joke that never palled, grasped the fact that business, like phonetics, has to be learned.

On the piteous spectacle of the pair spending their evenings in shorthand schools and polytechnic classes, learning bookkeeping and typewriting with incipient junior clerks, male and female, from the elementary schools, let me not dwell. There were even classes at the London School of Economics, and a humble personal appeal to the director of that institution to recommend a course bearing on the flower business. He, being a humorist, explained to them the method of the celebrated Dickensian essay on Chinese Metaphysics by the gentleman who read an article on China and an article on Metaphysics and combined the information. He suggested that they should combine the London School with Kew Gardens. Eliza, to whom the procedure of the Dickensian gentleman seemed perfectly correct (as in fact it was) and not in the least funny (which was only her ignorance) took his advice with entire gravity. But the effort that cost her the deepest humiliation was a request to Higgins, whose pet artistic fancy, next to Milton's verse, was caligraphy, and who himself wrote a most beautiful Italian hand, that he would teach her to write. He declared that she was congenitally incapable of forming a single letter worthy of the least of Milton's words; but she persisted; and again he suddenly threw himself into the task of teaching her with a combination of stormy intensity, concentrated patience, and occasional bursts of interesting disquisition on the beauty and nobility, the august mission and destiny, of human handwriting. Eliza ended by acquiring an extremely uncommercial script which was a positive extension of her personal beauty, and spending three times as much on stationery as anyone else because certain qualities and shapes of paper became indispensable to her. She could not even address an envelope in the usual way because it made the margins all wrong.

Their commercial schooldays were a period of disgrace and despair for the young couple. They seemed to be learning nothing about flower shops. At last they gave it up as hopeless, and shook the dust of the shorthand schools, and the polytechnics, and the London School of Economics from their feet forever. Besides, the business was in some mysterious way beginning to take care of itself. They had somehow forgotten their objections to employing other people. They came to the conclusion that their own way was the best, and that they had really a remarkable talent for business. The Colonel, who had been compelled for some years to keep a sufficient sum on current account at his bankers to make up their deficits, found that the provision was unnecessary: the young people were prospering. It is true that there was not quite fair play between them and their competitors in trade. Their weekends in the country cost them nothing, and saved them the price of their Sunday dinners; for the motor car was the Colonel's; and he and Higgins paid the hotel bills. Mr F. Hill, florist and greengrocer (they soon discovered that there was money in asparagus; and asparagus led to other vegetables), had an air which stamped the business as classy; and in private life he was still Frederick Eynsford Hill, Esquire. Not that there was any swank about him: nobody but Eliza knew that he had been christened Frederick Challoner. Eliza herself swanked like anything.

That is all. That is how it has turned out. It is astonishing how much Eliza still manages to meddle in the housekeeping at Wimpole Street in spite of the shop and her own family. And it is notable that though she never nags her husband, and frankly loves the Colonel as if she were his favorite daughter, she has never got out of the habit of nagging Higgins that was established on the fatal night when she won his bet for him. She snaps his head off on the faintest provocation, or on none. He no longer dares to tease her by assuming an abysmal inferiority of Freddy's mind to his own. He storms and bullies and derides; but she stands up to him so ruthlessly that the Colonel has to ask her from time to time to be kinder to Higgins; and it is the only request of his that brings a mulish expression into her face. Nothing but some emergency or calamity great enough to break down all likes and dislikes, and throw them both back on their common humanity—and may they be spared any such trial!—will ever alter this. She knows that Higgins does not need her, just as her father did not need her. The very scrupulousness with which he told her that day that he had become used to having her there, and dependent on her for all sorts of little services, and that he should miss her if she went away (it would never have occurred to Freddy or the Colonel to say anything of the sort) deepens her inner certainty that she is "no more to him than them slippers"; yet she has a sense, too, that his indifference is deeper than the infatuation of commoner souls. She is immensely interested in him. She has even secret mischievous moments in which she wishes she could get him alone, on a desert island, away from all ties and with nobody else in the world to consider, and just drag him off his pedestal and see him making love like any common man. We all have private imaginations of that sort. But when it comes to business, to the life that she really leads as distinguished from the life of dreams and fancies, she likes Freddy and she likes the Colonel; and she does not like Higgins and Mr Doolittle. Galatea never does quite like Pygmalion; his relation to her is too godlike to be altogether agreeable.

# HEARTBREAK HOUSE

## A FANTASIA IN THE RUSSIAN MANNER ON ENGLISH THEMES

# Act I

*The hilly country in the middle of the north edge of Sussex, looking very pleasant on a fine evening at the end of September, is seen through the windows of a room which has been built so as to resemble the after part of an old-fashioned high-pooped ship with a stern gallery; for the windows are ship built with heavy timbering, and run right across the room as continuously as the stability of the wall allows. A row of lockers under the windows provides an unupholstered window-seat interrupted by twin glass doors, respectively halfway between the stern post and the sides. Another door strains the illusion a little by being apparently in the ship's port side, and yet leading, not to the open sea, but to the entrance hall of the house. Between this door and the stern gallery are bookshelves. There are electric light switches beside the door leading to the hall and the glass doors in the stern gallery. Against the starboard wall is a carpenter's bench. The vice has a board in its jaws; and the floor is littered with shavings, overflowing from a waste-paper basket. A couple of planes and a centrebit are on the bench. In the same wall, between the bench and the windows, is a narrow doorway with a half door, above which a glimpse of the room beyond shews that it is a shelved pantry with bottles and kitchen crockery.*

*On the starboard side, but close to the middle, is a plain oak drawing-table with drawing-board, T-square, straightedges, set squares, mathematical instruments, saucers of water color, a tumbler of discolored water, Indian ink, pencils, and brushes on it. The drawing-board is set so that the draughtsman's chair has the window on its left hand. On the floor at the end of the table, on his right, is a ship's fire bucket. On the port side of the room, near the bookshelves, is a sofa with its back to the windows. It is a sturdy mahogany article, oddly upholstered in sailcloth, including the bolster, with a couple of blankets hanging over the back. Between the sofa and the drawing-table is a big wicker chair, with broad arms and a low sloping back, with its back to the light. A small but stout table of teak, with a round top and gate legs, stands against the port wall between the door and the bookcase. It is the only article in the room that suggests (not at all convincingly) a woman's hand in the furnishing. The uncarpeted floor of narrow boards is caulked and holystoned like a deck.*

*The garden to which the glass doors lead dips to the south before the landscape rises again to the hills. Emerging from the hollow is the cupola of an observatory. Between the observatory and the house is a flagstaff on a little esplanade, with a hammock on the east side and a long garden seat on the west.*

*A young lady, gloved and hatted, with a dust coat on, is sitting in the window-seat with her body twisted to enable her to look out at the view. One hand props her chin: the other hangs down with a volume of the Temple Shakespeare in it, and her finger stuck in the page she has been reading.*

*A clock strikes six.*

*The young lady turns and looks at her watch. She rises with an air of one who waits and is almost at the end of her patience. She is a pretty girl, slender, fair, and intelligent looking, nicely but not expensively dressed, evidently not a smart idler.*

*With a sigh of weary resignation she comes to the draughtsman's chair; sits down; and begins to read Shakespeare. Presently the book sinks to her lap; her eyes close; and she dozes into a slumber.*

*An elderly womanservant comes in from the hall with three unopened bottles of rum on a tray. She passes through and disappears in the pantry without noticing the young lady. She places the bottles on the shelf and fills her tray with empty bottles. As she returns with these, the young lady lets her book drop, awakening herself, and startling the womanservant so that she all but lets the tray fall.*

THE WOMANSERVANT:

God bless us! (*The young lady picks up the book and places it on the table*). Sorry to wake you, miss, I'm sure; but you are a stranger to me. What might you be waiting here for now?

THE YOUNG LADY:

Waiting for somebody to shew some signs of knowing that I have been invited here.

THE WOMANSERVANT:

Oh, you're invited, are you? And has nobody come? Dear! dear!

THE YOUNG LADY:

A wild-looking old gentleman came and looked in at the window; and I heard him calling out "Nurse: there is a young and attractive female waiting in the poop. Go and see what she wants." Are you the nurse?

THE WOMANSERVANT:

Yes, miss: I'm Nurse Guinness. That was old Captain Shotover, Mrs Hushabye's father. I heard him roaring; but I thought it was for something else. I suppose it was Mrs Hushabye that invited you, ducky?

THE YOUNG LADY:

> I understood her to do so. But really I think I'd better go.

NURSE GUINNESS:

> Oh, don't think of such a thing, miss. If Mrs Hushabye has forgotten all about it, it will be a pleasant surprise for her to see you, won't it?

THE YOUNG LADY:

> It has been a very unpleasant surprise to me to find that nobody expects me.

NURSE GUINNESS:

> You'll get used to it, miss: this house is full of surprises for them that don't know our ways.

CAPTAIN SHOTOVER (*looking in from the hall suddenly: an ancient but still hardy man with an immense white beard, in a reefer jacket with a whistle hanging from his neck*):

> Nurse: there is a hold-all and a handbag on the front steps for everybody to fall over. Also a tennis racquet. Who the devil left them there?

THE YOUNG LADY:

> They are mine, I'm afraid.

THE CAPTAIN (*advancing to the drawing-table*):

> Nurse: who is this misguided and unfortunate young lady?

NURSE GUINNESS:

> She says Miss Hessy invited her, sir.

THE CAPTAIN:

> And had she no friend, no parents, to warn her against my daughter's invitations? This is a pretty sort of house, by heavens! A young and attractive lady is invited here. Her luggage is left on the steps for hours; and she herself is deposited in the poop and abandoned, tired and starving. This is our hospitality. These are our manners. No room ready. No hot water. No welcoming hostess. Our visitor is to sleep in the toolshed, and to wash in the duckpond.

NURSE GUINNESS:

> Now it's all right, Captain: I'll get the lady some tea; and her room shall be ready before she has finished it. (*To the young lady*) Take off your hat, ducky; and make yourself at home (*she goes to the door leading to the hall*).

THE CAPTAIN (*as she passes him*):

> Ducky! Do you suppose, woman, that because this young lady has been insulted and neglected, you have the right to address her as you address my wretched children, whom you have brought up in ignorance of the commonest decencies of social intercourse?

NURSE GUINNESS:

> Never mind him, doty. (*Quite unconcerned, she goes out into the hall on her way to the kitchen*).

THE CAPTAIN:

> Madam: will you favor me with your name? (*He sits down in the big wicker chair*).

THE YOUNG LADY:

> My name is Ellie Dunn.

THE CAPTAIN:

> Dunn! I had a boatswain whose name was Dunn. He was originally a pirate in China. He set up as a ship's chandler with stores which I have every reason to believe he stole from me. No doubt he became rich. Are you his daughter?

ELLIE (*indignant*):

> No: certainly not. I am proud to be able to say that though my father has not been a successful man, nobody has ever had one word to say against him. I think my father is the best man I have ever known.

THE CAPTAIN:

> He must be greatly changed. Has he attained the seventh degree of concentration?

ELLIE:

> I don't understand.

THE CAPTAIN:

> But how could he, with a daughter! I, madam, have two daughters. One of them is Hesione Hushabye, who invited you here. I keep this house: she upsets it. I desire to attain the seventh degree of concentration: she invites visitors and leaves me to entertain them. (Nurse Guinness *returns with the tea-tray, which she places on the teak table*). I have a second daughter who is, thank God, in a remote part of the Empire with her numskull of a husband. As a child she thought the figure-head of my ship, the Dauntless, the most beautiful thing on earth. He resembled it. He had the same expression: wooden yet enterprising. She married him, and will never set foot in this house again.

NURSE GUINNESS (*carrying the table, with the tea-things on it, to* Ellie's *side*):

> Indeed you never were more mistaken. She is in England this very moment. You have been told three times this week that she is coming home for a year for her health. And very glad you should be to see your own daughter again after all these years.

THE CAPTAIN:

> I am not glad. The natural term of the affection of the human

animal for its offspring is six years. My daughter Ariadne was born when I was forty-six. I am now eighty-eight. If she comes, I am not at home. If she wants anything, let her take it. If she asks for me, let her be informed that I am extremely old, and have totally forgotten her.

NURSE GUINNESS:

That's no talk to offer to a young lady. Here, ducky, have some tea; and don't listen to him (*she pours out a cup of tea*).

THE CAPTAIN (*rising wrathfully*):

Now before high heaven they have given this innocent child Indian tea: the stuff they tan their own leather insides with. (*He seizes the cup and the tea-pot and empties both into the leathern bucket*).

ELLIE (*almost in tears*):

Oh, please! I am so tired. I should have been glad of anything.

NURSE GUINNESS:

Oh, what a thing to do! The poor lamb is ready to drop.

THE CAPTAIN:

You shall have some of my tea. Do not touch that fly-blown cake: nobody eats it here except the dogs. (*He disappears into the pantry*).

NURSE GUINNESS:

There's a man for you! They say he sold himself to the devil in Zanzibar before he was a captain; and the older he grows the more I believe them.

A WOMAN'S VOICE (*in the hall*):

Is anyone at home? Hesione! Nurse! Papa! Do come, somebody; and take in my luggage. *Thumping heard, as of an umbrella, on the wainscot.*

NURSE GUINNESS:

My gracious! It's Miss Addie, Lady Utterword, Mrs Hushabye's sister: the one I told the Captain about. (*Calling*) Coming, Miss, coming.

*She carries the table back to its place by the door, and is hurrying out when she is intercepted by* Lady Utterword, *who bursts in much flustered.* Lady Utterword, *a blonde, is very handsome, very well dressed, and so precipitate in speech and action that the first impression (erroneous) is one of comic silliness.*

LADY UTTERWORD:

Oh, is that you, Nurse? How are you? You don't look a day older. Is nobody at home? Where is Hesione? Doesn't she expect me? Where are the servants? Whose luggage is that on

the steps? Where's papa? Is everybody asleep? (*Seeing* Ellie)
Oh! I beg your pardon. I suppose you are one of my nieces.
(*Approaching her with outstretched arms*) Come and kiss your
aunt, darling.

ELLIE:

I'm only a visitor. It is my luggage on the steps.

NURSE GUINNESS:

I'll go get you some fresh tea, ducky. (*She takes up the tray*).

ELLIE:

But the old gentleman said he would make some himself.

NURSE GUINNESS:

Bless you! he's forgotten what he went for already. His mind
wanders from one thing to another.

LADY UTTERWORD:

Papa, I suppose?

NURSE GUINNESS:

Yes, Miss.

LADY UTTERWORD (*vehemently*):

Don't be silly, nurse. Don't call me Miss.

NURSE GUINNESS (*placidly*):

No, lovey (*she goes out with the tea-tray*).

LADY UTTERWORD (*sitting down with a flounce on the sofa*):

I know what you must feel. Oh, this house, this house! I come
back to it after twenty-three years; and it is just the same: the
luggage lying on the steps, the servants spoilt and impossible,
nobody at home to receive anybody, no regular meals, nobody
ever hungry because they are always gnawing bread and butter
or munching apples, and, what is worse, the same disorder in
ideas, in talk, in feeling. When I was a child I was used to it: I
had never known anything better, though I was unhappy, and
longed all the time—oh, how I longed!—to be respectable, to
be a lady, to live as others did, not to have to think of everything
for myself. I married at nineteen to escape from it. My husband
is Sir Hastings Utterword, who has been governor of all the
crown colonies in succession. I have always been the mistress of
Government House. I have been so happy: I had forgotten that
people could live like this. I wanted to see my father, my sister,
my nephews and nieces (one ought to, you know), and I was
looking forward to it. And now the state of the house! the way
I'm received! the casual impudence of that woman Guinness,
our old nurse! really Hesione might at least have been here:
some preparation might have been made for me. You must
excuse my going on in this way; but I am really very much hurt
and annoyed and disillusioned: and if I had realized it was to be

like this, I wouldn't have come. I have a great mind to go away without another word (*she is on the point of weeping*).

ELLIE (*also very miserable*):

Nobody has been here to receive me either. I thought I ought to go away too. But how can I, Lady Utterword? My luggage is on the steps; and the station fly has gone.

*The Captain* emerges from the pantry with a tray of Chinese lacquer and a very fine tea-set on it. He rests it provisionally on the end of the table; snatches away the drawing-board, which he stands on the floor against the table legs; and puts the tray in the space thus cleared. Ellie *pours out a cup greedily.*

THE CAPTAIN:

Your tea, young lady. What! another lady! I must fetch another cup (*he makes for the pantry*).

LADY UTTERWORD (*rising from the sofa, suffused with emotion*):

Papa! Don't you know me? I'm your daughter.

THE CAPTAIN:

Nonsense! my daughter's upstairs asleep. (*He vanishes through the half door*).

Lady Utterword *retires to the window to conceal her tears.*

ELLIE (*going to her with the cup*):

Don't be so distressed. Have this cup of tea. He is very old and very strange: he has been just like that to me. I know how dreadful it must be: my own father is all the world to me. Oh, I'm sure he didn't mean it.

The Captain *returns with another cup.*

THE CAPTAIN:

Now we are complete. (*He places it on the tray*).

LADY UTTERWORD (*hysterically*):

Papa: you can't have forgotten me. I am Ariadne. I'm little Paddy Patkins. Won't you kiss me? (*She goes to him and throws her arms round his neck*).

THE CAPTAIN (*woodenly enduring her embrace*):

How can you be Ariadne? You are a middle-aged woman: well preserved, madam, but no longer young.

LADY UTTERWORD:

But think of all the years and years I have been away, Papa. I have had to grow old, like other people.

THE CAPTAIN (*disengaging himself*):

> You should grow out of kissing strange men: they may be striving to attain the seventh degree of concentration.

LADY UTTERWORD:

> But I'm your daughter. You haven't seen me for years.

THE CAPTAIN:

> So much the worse! When our relatives are at home, we have to think of all their good points or it would be impossible to endure them. But when they are away, we console ourselves for their absence by dwelling on their vices. That is how I have come to think my absent daughter Ariadne a perfect fiend; so do not try to ingratiate yourself here by impersonating her (*he walks firmly away to the other side of the room*).

LADY UTTERWORD:

> Ingratiating myself indeed! (*With dignity*) Very well, papa. (*She sits down at the drawing-table and pours out tea for herself*).

THE CAPTAIN:

> I am neglecting my social duties. You remember Dunn? Billy Dunn?

LADY UTTERWORD:

> Do you mean that villainous sailor who robbed you?

THE CAPTAIN (*introducing* Ellie):

> His daughter. (*He sits down on the sofa*).

ELLIE (*protesting*):

> No—

Nurse Guinness *returns with fresh tea.*

THE CAPTAIN:

> Take that hogwash away. Do you hear?

NURSE GUINNESS:

> You've actually remembered about the tea! (*To* Ellie) O, miss, he didn't forget you after all! You have made an impression.

THE CAPTAIN (*gloomily*):

> Youth! beauty! novelty! They are badly wanted in this house. I am excessively old. Hesione is only moderately young. Her children are not youthful.

LADY UTTERWORD:

> How can children be expected to be youthful in this house? Almost before we could speak we were filled with notions that might have been all very well for pagan philosophers of fifty, but were certainly quite unfit for respectable people of any age.

NURSE GUINNESS:

> You were always for respectability, Miss Addy.

LADY UTTERWORD:

> Nurse: will you please remember that I am Lady Utterword, and not Miss Addy, nor lovey, nor darling, nor doty? Do you hear?

NURSE GUINNESS:

> Yes, ducky: all right. I'll tell them all they must call you my lady. (*She takes her tray out with undisturbed placidity*).

LADY UTTERWORD:

> What comfort? what sense is there in having servants with no manners?

ELLIE (*rising and coming to the table to put down her empty cup*):

> Lady Utterword: do you think Mrs Hushabye really expects me?

LADY UTTERWORD:

> Oh, don't ask me. You can see for yourself that I've just arrived; her only sister, after twenty-three years absence! and it seems that *I* am not expected.

THE CAPTAIN:

> What does it matter whether the young lady is expected or not? She is welcome. There are beds: there is food. I'll find a room for her myself (*he makes for the door*).

ELLIE (*following him to stop him*):

> Oh please—(*he goes out*). Lady Utterword: I don't know what to do. Your father persists in believing that my father is some sailor who robbed him.

LADY UTTERWORD:

> You had better pretend not to notice it. My father is a very clever man; but he always forgot things; and now that he is old, of course he is worse. And I must warn you that it is sometimes very hard to feel quite sure that he really forgets.

Mrs Hushabye *bursts into the room tempestuously, and embraces* Ellie. *She is a couple of years older than* Lady Utterword *and even better looking. She has magnificent black hair, eyes like the fishpools of Heshbon, and a nobly modelled neck, short at the back and low between her shoulders in front. Unlike her sister she is uncorseted and dressed anyhow in a rich robe of black pile that shews off her white skin and statuesque contour.*

MRS HUSHABYE:

> Ellie, my darling, my pettikins (*kissing her*): how long have you been here? I've been at home all the time: I was putting flowers and things in your room; and when I just sat down for a moment to try how comfortable the armchair was I went off to sleep. Papa woke me and told me you were here. Fancy your

finding no one, and being neglected and abandoned. (*Kissing her again*). My poor love! (*She deposits* Ellie *on the sofa. Meanwhile* Ariadne *has left the table and come over to claim her share of attention*). Oh! you've brought someone with you. Introduce me.

LADY UTTERWORD:

Hesione: is it possible that you don't know me?

MRS HUSHABYE (*conventionally*):

Of course I remember your face quite well. Where have we met?

LADY UTTERWORD:

Didn't papa tell you I was here? Oh! this is really too much. (*She throws herself sulkily into the big chair*).

MRS HUSHABYE:

Papa!

LADY UTTERWORD:

Yes: papa. Our papa, you unfeeling wretch. (*Rising angrily*) I'll go straight to a hotel.

MRS HUSHABYE (*seizing her by the shoulders*):

My goodness gracious goodness, you don't mean to say that you're Addy!

LADY UTTERWORD:

I certainly am Addy; and I don't think I can be so changed that you would not have recognized me if you had any real affection for me. And papa didn't think me even worth mentioning!

MRS HUSHABYE:

What a lark! Sit down (*she pushes her back into the chair instead of kissing her, and posts herself behind it*). You do look a swell. You're much handsomer than you used to be. You've made the acquaintance of Ellie, of course. She is going to marry a perfect hog of a millionaire for the sake of her father, who is as poor as a church mouse; and you must help me to stop her.

ELLIE:

Oh please, Hesione.

MRS HUSHABYE:

My pettikins, the man's coming here today with your father to begin persecuting you; and everybody will see the state of the case in ten minutes; so what's the use of making a secret of it?

ELLIE:

He is not a hog, Hesione. You don't know how wonderfully good he was to my father, and how deeply grateful I am to him.

MRS HUSHABYE (*to* Lady Utterword):

Her father is a very remarkable man, Addy. His name is Mazzini Dunn. Mazzini was a celebrity of some kind who knew

Ellie's grandparents. They were both poets, like the Brownings; and when her father came into the world Mazzini said "Another soldier born for freedom!" So they christened him Mazzini; and he has been fighting for freedom in his quiet way ever since. That's why he is so poor.

ELLIE:

I am proud of his poverty.

MRS HUSHABYE:

Of course you are, pettikins. Why not leave him in it, and marry someone you love?

LADY UTTERWORD (*rising suddenly and explosively*):

Hesione: are you going to kiss me or are you not?

MRS HUSHABYE:

What do you want to be kissed for?

LADY UTTERWORD:

I don't want to be kissed; but I do want you to behave properly and decently. We are sisters. We have been separated for twenty-three years. You ought to kiss me.

MRS HUSHABYE:

Tomorrow morning, dear, before you make up. I hate the smell of powder.

LADY UTTERWORD:

Oh! you unfeeling—(*she is interrupted by the return of* The Captain).

THE CAPTAIN (*to* Ellie):

Your room is ready. (Ellie *rises*). The sheets were damp; but I have changed them (*he makes for the garden door on the port side*).

LADY UTTERWORD:

Oh! What about my sheets?

THE CAPTAIN (*halting at the door*):

Take my advice: air them; or take them off and sleep in blankets. You shall sleep in Ariadne's old room.

LADY UTTERWORD:

Indeed I shall do nothing of the sort. That little hole! I am entitled to the best spare room.

THE CAPTAIN (*continuing unmoved*):

She married a numskull. She told me she would marry anyone to get away from home.

LADY UTTERWORD:

You are pretending not to know me on purpose. I will leave the house.

Mazzini Dunn *enters from the hall. He is a little elderly man with bulging credulous eyes and earnest manners. He is dressed in a blue serge jacket suit with an unbuttoned mackintosh over it, and carries a soft black hat of clerical cut.*

ELLIE:
At last! Captain Shotover: here is my father.

THE CAPTAIN:
This! Nonsense! not a bit like him (*he goes away through the garden, shutting the door sharply behind him*).

LADY UTTERWORD:
I will not be ignored and pretended to be somebody else. I will have it out with papa now, this instant. (*To Mazzini*) Excuse me. (*She follows the* Captain *out, making a hasty bow to* Mazzini, *who returns it*).

MRS HUSHABYE (*hospitably, shaking hands*):
How good of you to come, Mr Dunn! You don't mind papa, do you? He is as mad as a hatter, you know, but quite harmless, and extremely clever. You will have some delightful talks with him.

MAZZINI:
I hope so. (*To* Ellie) So here you are, Ellie, dear. (*He draws her arm affectionately through his*). I must thank you, Mrs Hushabye, for your kindness to my daughter. I'm afraid she would have had no holiday if you had not invited her.

MRS HUSHABYE:
Not at all. Very nice of her to come and attract young people to the house for us.

MAZZINI (*smiling*):
I'm afraid Ellie is not interested in young men, Mrs Hushabye. Her taste is on the graver, solider side.

MRS HUSHABYE (*with a sudden rather hard brightness in her manner*):
Won't you take off your overcoat, Mr Dunn? You will find a cupboard for coats and hats and things in the corner of the hall.

MAZZINI (*hastily releasing* Ellie):
Yes—thank you—I had better—(*he goes out*).

MRS HUSHABYE (*emphatically*):
The old brute!

ELLIE:
Who?

MRS HUSHABYE:
Who! Him. He. It (*pointing after* Mazzini). "Graver, solider tastes," indeed!

ELLIE (*aghast*):
You don't mean that you were speaking like that of my father!

MRS HUSHABYE:
I was. You know I was.

ELLIE (*with dignity*):

> I will leave your house at once. (*She turns to the door*).

MRS HUSHABYE:

> If you attempt it, I'll tell your father why.

ELLIE (*turning again*):

> Oh! How can you treat a visitor like this, Mrs Hushabye?

MRS HUSHABYE:

> I thought you were going to call me Hesione.

ELLIE:

> Certainly not now?

MRS HUSHABYE:

> Very well: I'll tell your father.

ELLIE (*distressed*):

> Oh!

MRS HUSHABYE:

> If you turn a hair—if you take his part against me and against your own heart for a moment, I'll give that born soldier of freedom a piece of my mind that will stand him on his selfish old head for a week.

ELLIE:

> Hesione! My father selfish! How little you know—

*She is interrupted by* Mazzini, *who returns, excited and perspiring*.

MAZZINI:

> Ellie: Mangan has come: I thought you'd like to know. Excuse me, Mrs Hushabye: the strange old gentleman—

MRS HUSHABYE:

> Papa. Quite so.

MAZZINI:

> Oh, I beg your pardon: of course: I was a little confused by his manner. He is making Mangan help him with something in the garden; and he wants me too—

*A powerful whistle is heard.*

THE CAPTAIN'S VOICE:

> Bosun ahoy! (*the whistle is repeated*).

MAZZINI (*flustered*):

> Oh dear! I believe he is whistling for me. (*He hurries out*).

MRS HUSHABYE:

> Now my father is a wonderful man if you like.

ELLIE:

> Hesione: listen to me. You don't understand. My father and Mr Mangan were boys together. Mr Ma——

MRS HUSHABYE:

I don't care what they were: we must sit down if you are going to begin as far back as that (*She snatches at* Ellie's *waist, and makes her sit down on the sofa beside her*). Now, pettikins: tell me all about Mr Mangan. They call him Boss Mangan, don't they? He is a Napoleon of industry and disgustingly rich, isn't he? Why isn't your father rich?

ELLIE:

My poor father should never have been in business. His parents were poets; and they gave him the noblest ideas; but they could not afford to give him a profession.

MRS HUSHABYE:

Fancy your grandparents, with their eyes in fine frenzy rolling! And so your poor father had to go into business. Hasn't he succeeded in it?

ELLIE:

He always used to say he could succeed if he only had some capital. He fought his way along, to keep a roof over our heads and bring us up well; but it was always a struggle: always the same difficulty of not having capital enough. I don't know how to describe it to you.

MRS HUSHABYE:

Poor Ellie! I know. Pulling the devil by the tail.

ELLIE (*hurt*):

Oh no. Not like that. It was at least dignified.

MRS HUSHABYE:

That made it all the harder, didn't it? *I* shouldn't have pulled the devil by the tail with dignity. I should have pulled hard— (*between her teeth*) hard. Well? Go on.

ELLIE:

At last it seemed that all our troubles were at an end. Mr Mangan did an extraordinarily noble thing out of pure friendship for my father and respect for his character. He asked him how much capital he wanted, and gave it to him. I don't mean that he lent it to him, or that he invested it in his business. He just simply made him a present of it. Wasn't that splendid of him?

MRS HUSHABYE:

On condition that you married him?

ELLIE:

Oh no, no, no. This was when I was a child. He had never even seen me: he never came to our house. It was absolutely disinterested. Pure generosity.

MRS HUSHABYE:

Oh! I beg the gentleman's pardon. Well, what became of the money?

ELLIE:

We all got new clothes and moved into another house. And I went to another school for two years.

MRS HUSHABYE:

Only two years?

ELLIE:

That was all; for at the end of two years my father was utterly ruined.

MRS HUSHABYE:

How?

ELLIE:

I don't know. I never could understand. But it was dreadful. When we were poor my father had never been in debt. But when he launched out into business on a large scale, he had to incur liabilities. When the business went into liquidation he owed more money than Mr Mangan had given him.

MRS HUSHABYE:

Bit off more than he could chew, I suppose.

ELLIE:

I think you are a little unfeeling about it.

MRS HUSHABYE:

My pettikins: you mustn't mind my way of talking. I was quite as sensitive and particular as you once; but I have picked up so much slang from the children that I am really hardly presentable. I suppose your father had no head for business, and made a mess of it.

ELLIE:

Oh, that just shews how entirely you are mistaken about him. The business turned out a great success. It now pays forty-four per cent after deducting the excess profits tax.

MRS HUSHABYE:

Then why arn't you rolling in money?

ELLIE:

I don't know. It seems very unfair to me. You see, my father was made bankrupt. It nearly broke his heart, because he had persuaded several of his friends to put money into the business. He was sure it would succeed; and events proved that he was quite right. But they all lost their money. It was dreadful. I don't know what we should have done but for Mr Mangan.

MRS HUSHABYE:

What! Did the Boss come to the rescue again, after all his money being thrown away?

ELLIE:

He did indeed, and never uttered a reproach to my father. He bought what was left of the business—the buildings and the machinery and things—from the official trustee for enough money to enable my father to pay six and eightpence in the pound and get his discharge. Everyone pitied papa so much, and saw so plainly that he was an honorable man, that they let him off at six-and-eight-pence instead of ten shillings. Then Mr Mangan started a company to take up the business, and made my father a manager in it to save us from starvation; for I wasn't earning anything then.

MRS HUSHABYE:

Quite a romance. And when did the Boss develop the tender passion?

ELLIE:

Oh, that was years after, quite lately. He took the chair one night at a sort of people's concert. I was singing there. As an amateur, you know: half a guinea for expenses and three songs with three encores. He was so pleased with my singing that he asked might he walk home with me. I never saw anyone so taken aback as he was when I took him home and introduced him to my father: his own manager. It was then that my father told me how nobly he had behaved. Of course it was considered a great chance for me, as he is so rich. And—and—we drifted into a sort of understanding—I suppose I should call it an engagement—(*she is distressed and cannot go on*).

MRS HUSHABYE (*rising and marching about*):

You may have drifted into it; but you will bounce out of it, my pettikins, if I am to have anything to do with it.

ELLIE (*hopelessly*):

No: it's no use. I am bound in honor and gratitude. I will go through with it.

MRS HUSHABYE (*behind the sofa, scolding down at her*):

You know, of course, that it's not honorable or grateful to marry a man you don't love. Do you love this Mangan man?

ELLIE:

Yes. At least—

MRS HUSHABYE:

I don't want to know about "the least": I want to know the

worst. Girls of your age fall in love with all sorts of impossible people, especially old people.

ELLIE:

I like Mr Mangan very much; and I shall always be—

MRS HUSHABYE (*impatiently completing the sentence and prancing away intolerantly to starboard*):

—grateful to him for his kindness to dear father. I know. Anybody else?

ELLIE:

What do you mean?

MRS HUSHABYE:

Anybody else? Are you in love with anybody else?

ELLIE:

Of course not.

MRS HUSHABYE:

Humph! (*The book on the drawing-table catches her eye. She picks it up, and evidently finds the title very unexpected. She looks at* Ellie, *and asks, quaintly*). Quite sure you're not in love with an actor?

ELLIE:

No, no. Why? What put such a thing into your head?

MRS HUSHABYE:

This is yours, isn't it? Why else should you be reading Othello?

ELLIE:

My father taught me to love Shakespeare.

MRS HUSHABYE (*flinging the book down on the table*):

Really! your father does seem to be about the limit.

ELLIE (*naïvely*):

Do you never read Shakespeare, Hesione? That seems to me so extraordinary. I like Othello.

MRS HUSHABYE:

Do you indeed? He was jealous, wasn't he?

ELLIE:

Oh, not that. I think all the part about jealousy is horrible. But don't you think it must have been a wonderful experience for Desdemona, brought up so quietly at home, to meet a man who had been out in the world doing all sorts of brave things and having terrible adventures, and yet finding something in her that made him love to sit and talk with her and tell her about them?

MRS HUSHABYE:

That's your idea of romance, is it?

ELLIE:

Not romance, exactly. It might really happen.

*Ellie's eyes shew that she is not arguing, but in a daydream. Mrs Hushabye, watching her inquisitively, goes deliberately back to the sofa and resumes her seat beside her.*

MRS HUSHABYE:

Ellie darling: have you noticed that some of those stories that Othello told Desdemona couldn't have happened?

ELLIE:

Oh no. Shakespeare thought they could have happened.

MRS HUSHABYE:

Hm! Desdemona thought they could have happened. But they didn't.

ELLIE:

Why do you look so enigmatic about it? You are such a sphinx: I never know what you mean.

MRS HUSHABYE:

Desdemona would have found him out if she had lived, you know. I wonder was that why he strangled her!

ELLIE:

Othello was not telling lies.

MRS HUSHABYE:

How do you know?

ELLIE:

Shakespeare would have said if he was. Hesione: there are men who have done wonderful things: men like Othello, only, of course, white, and very handsome, and—

MRS HUSHABYE:

Ah! Now we're coming to it. Tell me all about him. I knew there must be somebody, or you'd never have been so miserable about Mangan: you'd have thought it quite a lark to marry him.

ELLIE (*blushing vividly*):

Hesione: you are dreadful. But I don't want to make a secret of it, though of course I don't tell everybody. Besides, I don't know him.

MRS HUSHABYE:

Don't know him! What does that mean?

ELLIE:

Well, of course I know him to speak to.

MRS HUSHABYE:

But you want to know him ever so much more intimately, eh?

ELLIE:

No no: I know him quite—almost intimately.

MRS HUSHABYE:

You don't know him; and you know him almost intimately. How lucid!

ELLIE:

I mean that he does not call on us. I—I got into conversation with him by chance at a concert.

MRS HUSHABYE:

You seem to have rather a gay time at your concerts, Ellie.

ELLIE:

Not at all: we talk to everyone in the green-room waiting for our turns. I thought he was one of the artists: he looked so splendid. But he was only one of the committee. I happened to tell him that I was copying a picture at the National Gallery. I make a little money that way. I can't paint much; but as it's always the same picture I can do it pretty quickly and get two or three pounds for it. It happened that he came to the National Gallery one day.

MRS HUSHABYE:

One student's day. Paid sixpence to stumble about through a crowd of easels, when he might have come in next day for nothing and found the floor clear! Quite by accident?

ELLIE (*triumphantly*):

No. On purpose. He liked talking to me. He knows lots of the most splendid people. Fashionable women who are all in love with him. But he ran away from them to see me at the National Gallery and persuade me to come with him for a drive round Richmond Park in a taxi.

MRS HUSHABYE:

My pettikins, you have been going it. It's wonderful what you good girls can do without anyone saying a word.

ELLIE:

I am not in society, Hesione. If I didn't make acquaintances in that way I shouldn't have any at all.

MRS HUSHABYE:

Well, no harm if you know how to take care of yourself. May I ask his name?

ELLIE (*slowly and musically*):

Marcus Darnley.

MRS HUSHABYE (*echoing the music*):

Marcus Darnley! What a splendid name!

ELLIE:

Oh, I'm so glad you think so. I think so too; but I was afraid it was only a silly fancy of my own.

MRS HUSHABYE:

Hm! Is he one of the Aberdeen Darnleys?

ELLIE:

Nobody knows. Just fancy! He was found in an antique chest—

MRS HUSHABYE:

A what?

ELLIE:

An antique chest, one summer morning in a rose garden, after a night of the most terrible thunderstorm.

MRS HUSHABYE:

What on earth was he doing in the chest? Did he get into it because he was afraid of the lightning?

ELLIE:

Oh no, no: he was a baby. The name Marcus Darnley was embroidered on his babyclothes. And five hundred pounds in gold.

MRS HUSHABYE (*looking hard at her*):

Ellie!

ELLIE:

The garden of the Viscount—

MRS HUSHABYE:

—de Rougemont?

ELLIE (*innocently*):

No: de Larochejaquelin. A French family. A vicomte. His life has been one long romance. A tiger—

MRS HUSHABYE:

Slain by his own hand?

ELLIE:

Oh no: nothing vulgar like that. He saved the life of the tiger from a hunting party: one of King Edward's hunting parties in India. The King was furious: that was why he never had his military services properly recognized. But he doesn't care. He is a Socialist and despises rank, and has been in three revolutions fighting on the barricades.

MRS HUSHABYE:

How can you sit there telling me such lies? You, Ellie, of all people! And I thought you were a perfectly simple, straightforward, good girl.

ELLIE (*rising, dignified but very angry*):

Do you mean to say you don't believe me?

MRS HUSHABYE:

Of course I don't believe you. You're inventing every word of it. Do you take me for a fool?

Ellie *stares at her. Her candor is so obvious that* Mrs Hushabye *is puzzled.*

ELLIE:
> Goodbye, Hesione. I'm very sorry. I see now that it sounds very improbable as I tell it. But I can't stay if you think that way about me.

MRS HUSHABYE (*catching her dress*):
> You shan't go. I couldn't be so mistaken: I know too well what liars are like. Somebody has really told you all this.

ELLIE (*flushing*):
> Hesione: don't say that you don't believe him. I couldn't bear that.

MRS HUSHABYE (*soothing her*):
> Of course I believe him, dearest. But you should have broken it to me by degrees. (*Drawing her back to the seat*) Now tell me all about him. Are you in love with him?

ELLIE:
> Oh no, I'm not so foolish. I don't fall in love with people. I'm not so silly as you think.

MRS HUSHABYE:
> I see. Only something to think about—to give some interest and pleasure to life.

ELLIE:
> Just so. That's all, really.

MRS HUSHABYE:
> It makes the hours go fast, doesn't it? No tedious waiting to go to sleep at nights and wondering whether you will have a bad night. How delightful it makes waking up in the morning! How much better than the happiest dream! All life transfigured! No more wishing one had an interesting book to read, because life is so much happier than any book! No desire but to be alone and not to have to talk to anyone: to be alone and just think about it.

ELLIE (*embracing her*):
> Hesione: you are a witch. How do you know? Oh, you are the most sympathetic woman in the world.

MRS HUSHABYE (*caressing her*):
> Pettikins, my pettikins: how I envy you! and how I pity you!

ELLIE:
> Pity me! Oh, why?

*A very handsome man of fifty, with mousquetaire moustaches, wearing a rather dandified curly brimmed hat, and carrying an elaborate walking-*

*stick, comes into the room from the hall, and stops short at sight of the
women on the sofa.*

ELLIE (*seeing him and rising in glad surprise*):
> Oh! Hesione: this is Mr Marcus Darnley.

MRS HUSHABYE (*rising*):
> What a lark! He is my husband.

ELLIE:
> But how—(*she stops suddenly; then turns pale and sways*).

MRS HUSHABYE (*catching her and sitting down with her on the sofa*):
> Steady, my pettikins.

THE MAN (*with a mixture of confusion and effrontery, depositing his hat
and stick on the teak table*):
> My real name, Miss Dunn, is Hector Hushabye. I leave you to
> judge whether that is a name any sensitive man would care to
> confess to. I never use it when I can possibly help it. I have
> been away for nearly a month; and I had no idea you knew
> my wife, or that you were coming here. I am none the less
> delighted to find you in our little house.

ELLIE (*in great distress*):
> I don't know what to do. Please, may I speak to papa? Do leave
> me. I can't bear it.

MRS HUSHABYE:
> Be off, Hector.

HECTOR:
> I—

MRS HUSHABYE:
> Quick, quick. Get out.

HECTOR:
> If you think it better—(*he goes out, taking his hat with him but
> leaving the stick on the table*).

MRS HUSHABYE (*laying* Ellie *down at the end of the sofa*):
> Now, pettikins, he is gone. There's nobody but me. You can
> let yourself go. Don't try to control yourself. Have a good
> cry.

ELLIE (*raising her head*):
> Damn!

MRS HUSHABYE:
> Splendid! Oh, what a relief! I thought you were going to be
> broken-hearted. Never mind me. Damn him again.

ELLIE:
> I am not damning him: I am damning myself for being such a
> fool. (*Rising*) How could I let myself be taken in so? (*She begins*

*prowling to and fro, her bloom gone, looking curiously older and harder*).

MRS HUSHABYE (*cheerfully*):

Why not, pettikins? Very few young women can resist Hector. I couldn't when I was your age. He is really rather splendid, you know.

ELLIE (*turning on her*):

Splendid! Yes: splendid looking, of course. But how can you love a liar?

MRS HUSHABYE:

I don't know. But you can, fortunately. Otherwise there wouldn't be much love in the world.

ELLIE:

But to lie like that! To be a boaster! a coward!

MRS HUSHABYE (*rising in alarm*):

Pettikins: none of that, if you please. If you hint the slightest doubt of Hector's courage, he will go straight off and do the most horribly dangerous things to convince himself that he isn't a coward. He has a dreadful trick of getting out of one third-floor window and coming in at another, just to test his nerve. He has a whole drawerful of Albert Medals for saving people's lives.

ELLIE:

He never told me that.

MRS HUSHABYE:

He never boasts of anything he really did: he can't bear it; and it makes him shy if anyone else does. All his stories are made-up stories.

ELLIE (*coming to her*):

Do you mean that he is really brave, and really has adventures, and yet tells lies about things that he never did and that never happened?

MRS HUSHABYE:

Yes, pettikins, I do. People don't have their virtues and vices in sets: they have them anyhow: all mixed.

ELLIE (*staring at her thoughtfully*):

There's something odd about this house, Hesione, and even about you. I don't know why I'm talking to you so calmly. I have a horrible fear that my heart is broken, but that heartbreak is not like what I thought it must be.

MRS HUSHABYE (*fondling her*):

It's only life educating you, pettikins. How do you feel about Boss Mangan now?

ELLIE (*disengaging herself with an expression of distaste*):

Oh, how can you remind me of him, Hesione?

MRS HUSHABYE:

Sorry, dear. I think I hear Hector coming back. You don't mind now, do you, dear?

ELLIE:

Not in the least. I am quite cured.

Mazzini Dunn *and* Hecter *come in from the hall.*

HECTOR (*as he opens the door and allows* Mazzini *to pass in*):

One second more, and she would have been a dead woman!

MAZZINI:

Dear! dear! what an escape! Ellie, my love: Mr. Hushabye has just been telling me the most extraordinary—

ELLIE:

Yes: I've heard it (*She crosses to the other side of the room*).

HECTOR (*following her*):

Not this one: I'll tell it to you after dinner. I think you'll like it. The truth is, I made it up for you, and I was looking forward to the pleasure of telling it to you. But in a moment of impatience at being turned out of the room, I threw it away on your father.

ELLIE (*turning at bay with her back to the carpenter's bench, scornfully self-possessed*):

It was not thrown away. He believes it. I should not have believed it.

MAZZINI (*benevolently*):

Ellie is very naughty, Mr Hushabye. Of course she does not really think that. (*He goes to the bookshelves, and inspects the titles of the volumes*).

Boss Mangan *comes in from the hall, followed by the* Captain. Mangan, *carefully frock-coated as for church or for a directors' meeting, is about fifty-five, with a careworn, mistrustful expression, standing a little on an entirely imaginary dignity, with a dull complexion, straight, lustreless hair, and features so entirely commonplace that it is impossible to describe them.*

CAPTAIN SHOTOVER (*to Mrs Hushabye, introducing the newcomer*):

Says his name is Mangan. Not ablebodied.

MRS HUSHABYE (*graciously*):

How do you do, Mr Mangan?

MANGAN (*shaking hands*):

Very pleased.

CAPTAIN SHOTOVER:

Dunn's lost his muscle, but recovered his nerve. Men seldom do after three attacks of delirium tremens (*he goes into the pantry*).

MRS HUSHABYE:

I congratulate you, Mr Dunn.

MAZZINI (*dazed*):

I am a lifelong teetotaler.

MRS HUSHABYE:

You will find it far less trouble to let papa have his own way than try to explain.

MAZZINI:

But three attacks of delirium tremens, really!

MRS HUSHABYE (*to* Mangan):

Do you know my husband, Mr Mangan (*she indicates* Hector).

MANGAN (*going to* Hector, *who meets him with outstretched hand*):

Very pleased. (*Turning to* Ellie) I hope, Miss Ellie, you have not found the journey down too fatiguing. (*They shake hands*).

MRS HUSHABYE:

Hector: shew Mr Dunn his room.

HECTOR:

Certainly. Come along, Mr Dunn. (*He takes* Mazzini *out*).

ELLIE:

You haven't shewn me my room yet, Hesione.

MRS HUSHABYE:

How stupid of me! Come along. Make yourself quite at home, Mr Mangan. Papa will entertain you. (*She calls to the* Captain *in the pantry*) Papa: come and explain the house to Mr Mangan.

*She goes out with* Ellie. The Captain *comes from the pantry.*

CAPTAIN SHOTOVER:

You're going to marry Dunn's daughter. Don't. You're too old.

MANGAN (*staggered*):

Well! That's fairly blunt, Captain.

CAPTAIN SHOTOVER:

It's true.

MANGAN:

She doesn't think so.

CAPTAIN SHOTOVER:

She does.

MANGAN:

Older men than I have—

CAPTAIN SHOTOVER (*finishing the sentence for him*):

—made fools of themselves. That, also, is true.

MANGAN (*asserting himself*):

I don't see that this is any business of yours.

CAPTAIN SHOTOVER:

It is everybody's business. The stars in their courses are shaken when such things happen.

MANGAN:

I'm going to marry her all the same.

CAPTAIN SHOTOVER:

How do you know?

MANGAN (*playing the strong man*):

I intend to. I mean to. See? I never made up my mind to do a thing yet that I didn't bring it off. That's the sort of man I am; and there will be a better understanding between us when you make up your mind to that, Captain.

CAPTAIN SHOTOVER:

You frequent picture palaces.

MANGAN:

Perhaps I do. Who told you?

CAPTAIN SHOTOVER:

Talk like a man, not like a movy. You mean that you make a hundred thousand a year.

MANGAN:

I don't boast. But when I meet a man that makes a hundred thousand a year, I take off my hat to that man, and stretch out my hand to him and call him brother.

CAPTAIN SHOTOVER:

Then you also make a hundred thousand a year, hey?

MANGAN:

No. I can't say that. Fifty thousand, perhaps.

CAPTAIN SHOTOVER:

His half brother only (*he turns away from* Mangan *with his usual abruptness, and collects the empty tea-cups on the Chinese tray*).

MANGAN (*irritated*):

See here, Captain Shotover. I don't quite understand my position here. I came here on your daughter's invitation. Am I in her house or in yours?

CAPTAIN SHOTOVER:

You are beneath the dome of heaven, in the house of God. What is true within these walls is true outside them. Go out on the seas; climb the mountains; wander through the valleys. She is still too young.

MANGAN (*weakening*):

    But I'm very little over fifty.

CAPTAIN SHOTOVER:

    You are still less under sixty. Boss Mangan: you will not marry
    the pirate's child (*he carries the tray away into the pantry*).

MANGAN (*following him to the half door*):

    What pirate's child? What are you talking about?

CAPTAIN SHOTOVER (*in the pantry*):

    Ellie Dunn. You will not marry her.

MANGAN:

    Who will stop me?

CAPTAIN SHOTOVER (*emerging*):

    My daughter (*he makes for the door leading to the hall*).

MANGAN (*following him*):

    Mrs Hushabye! Do you mean to say she brought me down
    here to break it off?

CAPTAIN SHOTOVER (*stopping and turning on him*):

    I know nothing more than I have seen in her eye. She will break
    it off. Take my advice: marry a West Indian negress: they make
    excellent wives. I was married to one myself for two years.

MANGAN:

    Well, I am damned!

CAPTAIN SHOTOVER:

    I thought so. I was, too, for many years. The negress redeemed
    me.

MANGAN (*feebly*):

    This is queer. I ought to walk out of this house.

CAPTAIN SHOTOVER:

    Why?

MANGAN:

    Well, many men would be offended by your style of talking.

CAPTAIN SHOTOVER:

    Nonsense! It's the other sort of talking that makes quarrels.
    Nobody ever quarrels with me.

A gentleman, *whose firstrate tailoring and frictionless manners proclaim
the wellbred West Ender, comes in from the hall. He has an engaging air
of being young and unmarried, but on close inspection is found to be at
least over forty.*

THE GENTLEMAN:

    Excuse my intruding in this fashion; but there is no knocker on
    the door; and the bell does not seem to ring.

CAPTAIN SHOTOVER:

Why should there be a knocker? Why should the bell ring? The door is open.

THE GENTLEMAN:

Precisely. So I ventured to come in.

CAPTAIN SHOTOVER:

Quite right. I will see about a room for you (*he makes for the door*).

THE GENTLEMAN (*stopping him*):

But I'm afraid you don't know who I am.

CAPTAIN SHOTOVER:

Do you suppose that at my age I make distinctions between one fellowcreature and another? (*He goes out. Mangan and the newcomer stare at one another*).

MANGAN:

Strange character, Captain Shotover, sir.

THE GENTLEMAN:

Very.

CAPTAIN SHOTOVER (*shouting outside*):

Hesione: another person has arrived and wants a room. Man about town, well dressed, fifty.

THE GENTLEMAN:

Fancy Hesione's feelings! May I ask are you a member of the family?

MANGAN:

No.

THE GENTLEMAN:

I am. At least a connexion.

Mrs Hushabye *comes back.*

MRS HUSHABYE:

How do you do? How good of you to come!

THE GENTLEMAN:

I am very glad indeed to make your acquaintance, Hesione. (*Instead of taking her hand he kisses her. At the same moment the* Captain *appears in the doorway*). You will excuse my kissing your daughter, Captain, when I tell you that—

CAPTAIN SHOTOVER:

Stuff! Everyone kisses my daughter. Kiss her as much as you like (*he makes for the pantry*).

THE GENTLEMAN:

Thank you. One moment. Captain. (*The* Captain *halts and turns.* The gentleman *goes to him affably*). Do you happen to remember—but probably you don't, as it occurred many years ago—that your younger daughter married a numskull.

CAPTAIN SHOTOVER:

Yes. She said she'd marry anybody to get away from this house. I should not have recognized you: your head is no longer like a walnut. Your aspect is softened. You have been boiled in bread and milk for years and years, like other married men. Poor devil! (*He disappears into the pantry*).

MRS HUSHABYE (*going past* Mangan *to the gentleman and scrutinizing him*):

I don't believe you are Hastings Utterword.

THE GENTLEMAN:

I am not.

MRS HUSHABYE:

Then what business had you to kiss me?

THE GENTLEMAN:

I thought I would like to. The fact is, I am Randall Utterword, the unworthy younger brother of Hastings. I was abroad diplomatizing when he was married.

LADY UTTERWORD (*dashing in*):

Hesione: where is the key of the wardrobe in my room? My diamonds are in my dressing-bag: I must lock it up—(*recognizing the stranger with a shock*) Randall: how dare you? (*She marches at him past* Mrs Hushabye, *who retreats and joins* Mangan *near the sofa*).

RANDALL:

How dare I what? I am not doing anything.

LADY UTTERWORD:

Who told you I was here?

RANDALL:

Hastings. You had just left when I called on you at Claridge's; so I followed you down here. You are looking extremely well.

LADY UTTERWORD:

Don't presume to tell me so.

MRS HUSHABYE:

What is wrong with Mr Randall, Addy?

LADY UTTERWORD (*recollecting herself*):

Oh, nothing. But he has no right to come bothering you and papa without being invited (*she goes to the window-seat and sits down, turning away from them ill-humoredly and looking into the garden, where* Hector *and* Ellie *are now seen strolling together*).

MRS HUSHABYE:

I think you have not met Mr Mangan, Addy.

LADY UTTERWORD (*turning her head and nodding coldly to* Mangan):

I beg your pardon. Randall: you have flustered me so: I made a perfect fool of myself.

MRS HUSHABYE:

Lady Utterword. My sister. My younger sister.

MANGAN (*bowing*):

Pleased to meet you, Lady Utterword.

LADY UTTERWORD (*with marked interest*):

Who is that gentleman walking in the garden with Miss Dunn?

MRS HUSHABYE:

I don't know. She quarrelled mortally with my husband only ten minutes ago; and I didn't know anyone else had come. It must be a visitor. (*She goes to the window to look*). Oh, it is Hector. They've made it up.

LADY UTTERWORD:

Your husband! That handsome man?

MRS HUSHABYE:

Well, why shouldn't my husband be a handsome man?

RANDALL (*joining them at the window*):

One's husband never is, Ariadne (*he sits by* Lady Utterword, *on her right*).

MRS HUSHABYE:

One's sister's husband always is, Mr Randall.

LADY UTTERWORD:

Don't be vulgar, Randall. And you, Hesione, are just as bad.

Ellie *and* Hector *come in from the garden by the starboard door.* Randall *rises.* Ellie *retires into the corner near the pantry.* Hector *comes forward; and* Lady Utterword *rises looking her very best.*

MRS HUSHABYE:

Hector: this is Addy.

HECTOR (*apparently surprised*):

Not this lady.

LADY UTTERWORD (*smiling*):

Why not?

HECTOR (*looking at her with a piercing glance of deep but respectful admiration, his moustache bristling*):

I thought—(*pulling himself together*) I beg your pardon, Lady Utterword. I am extremely glad to welcome you at last under our roof (*he offers his hand with grave courtesy*).

MRS HUSHABYE:

She wants to be kissed, Hector.

LADY UTTERWORD:
> Hesione! (*but she still smiles*).

MRS HUSHABYE:
> Call her Addy; and kiss her like a good brother-in-law; and
> have done with it. (*She leaves them to themselves*).

HECTOR:
> Behave yourself, Hesione. Lady Utterword is entitled not only
> to hospitality but to civilization.

LADY UTTERWORD (*gratefully*):
> Thank you, Hector. (*They shake hands cordially*).

Mazzini Dunn *is seen crossing the garden from starboard to port.*

CAPTAIN SHOTOVER (*coming from the pantry and addressing* Ellie):
> Your father has washed himself.

ELLIE (*quite self-possessed*):
> He often does, Captain Shotover.

CAPTAIN SHOTOVER:
> A strange conversion! I saw him through the pantry window.

Mazzini Dunn *enters through the port window door, newly washed and
brushed, and stops, smiling benevolently, between* Mangan *and* Mrs
Hushabye.

MRS HUSHABYE (*introducing*):
> Mr Mazzini Dunn, Lady Ut——oh, I forgot: you've met.
> (*Indicating* Ellie) Miss Dunn.

MAZZINI (*walking across the room to take* Ellie's *hand, and beaming at
his own naughty irony*):
> I have met Miss Dunn also. She is my daughter. (*He draws her
> arm through his caressingly*).

MRS HUSHABYE:
> Of course: how stupid! Mr Utterword, my sister's—er—

RANDALL (*shaking hands agreeably*):
> Her brother-in-law, Mr Dunn. How do you do?

MRS HUSHABYE:
> This is my husband.

HECTOR:
> We have met, dear. Don't introduce us any more. (*He moves
> away to the big chair, and adds*) Won't you sit down, Lady Utter-
> word? (*She does so very graciously*).

MRS HUSHABYE:
> Sorry. I hate it: it's like making people shew their tickets.

MAZZINI (*sententiously*):

How little it tells us, after all! The great question is, not who we are, but what we are.

CAPTAIN SHOTOVER:

Ha! What are you?

MAZZINI (*taken aback*):

What am I?

CAPTAIN SHOTOVER:

A thief, a pirate, and a murderer.

MAZZINI:

I assure you you are mistaken.

CAPTAIN SHOTOVER:

An adventurous life; but what does it end in? Respectability. A ladylike daughter. The language and appearance of a city missionary. Let it be a warning to all of you (*he goes out through the garden*).

DUNN:

I hope nobody here believes that I am a thief, a pirate, or a murderer. Mrs Hushabye: will you excuse me a moment? I must really go and explain. (*He follows the* Captain).

MRS HUSHABYE (*as he goes*):

It's no use. You'd really better—(*but* Dunn *has vanished*). We had better all go out and look for some tea. We never have regular tea; but you can always get some when you want: the servants keep it stewing all day. The kitchen veranda is the best place to ask. May I shew you? (*She goes to the starboard door*).

RANDALL (*going with her*):

Thank you, I don't think I'll take any tea this afternoon. But if you will shew me the garden—?

MRS HUSHABYE:

There's nothing to see in the garden except papa's observatory, and a gravel pit with a cave where he keeps dynamite and things of that sort. However, it's pleasanter out of doors; so come along.

RANDALL:

Dynamite! Isn't that rather risky?

MRS HUSHABYE:

Well, we don't sit in the gravel pit when there's a thunderstorm.

LADY UTTERWORD:

That's something new. What is the dynamite for?

HECTOR:

To blow up the human race if it goes too far. He is trying to discover a psychic ray that will explode all the explosives at the will of a Mahatma.

ELLIE:

The Captain's tea is delicious, Mr Utterword.

MRS HUSHABYE (*stopping in the doorway*):

Do you mean to say that you've had some of my father's tea? that you got round him before you were ten minutes in the house?

ELLIE:

I did.

MRS HUSHABYE:

You little devil! (*She goes out with* Randall).

MANGAN:

Won't you come, Miss Ellie?

ELLIE:

I'm too tired. I'll take a book up to my room and rest a little. (*She goes to the bookshelf*).

MANGAN:

Right. You can't do better. But I'm disappointed. (*He follows* Randall *and* Mrs Hushabye).

Ellie, Hector, *and* Lady Utterword *are left*. Hector *is close to* Lady Utterword. *They look at* Ellie, *waiting for her to go*.

ELLIE (*looking at the title of a book*):

Do you like stories of adventure, Lady Utterword?

LADY UTTERWORD (*patronizingly*):

Of course, dear.

ELLIE:

Then I'll leave you to Mr Hushabye. (*She goes out through the hall*).

HECTOR:

That girl is mad about tales of adventure. The lies I have to tell her!

LADY UTTERWORD (*not interested in* Ellie):

When you saw me what did you mean by saying that you thought, and then stopping short? What did you think?

HECTOR (*folding his arms and looking down at her magnetically*):

May I tell you?

LADY UTTERWORD:

Of course.

HECTOR:

It will not sound very civil. I was on the point of saying "I thought you were a plain woman."

LADY UTTERWORD:

Oh for shame, Hector! What right had you to notice whether I am plain or not?

HECTOR:

> Listen to me, Ariadne. Until today I have seen only photographs of you; and no photograph can give the strange fascination of the daughters of that supernatural old man. There is some damnable quality in them that destroys men's moral sense, and carries them beyond honor and dishonor. You know that, don't you?

LADY UTTERWORD:

> Perhaps I do, Hector. But let me warn you once for all that I am a rigidly conventional woman. You may think because I'm a Shotover that I'm a Bohemian, because we are all so horribly Bohemian. But I'm not. I hate and loathe Bohemianism. No child brought up in a strict Puritan household ever suffered from Puritanism as I suffered from our Bohemianism.

HECTOR:

> Our children are like that. They spend their holidays in the houses of their respectable schoolfellows.

LADY UTTERWORD:

> I shall invite them for Christmas.

HECTOR:

> Their absence leaves us both without our natural chaperons.

LADY UTTERWORD:

> Children are certainly very inconvenient sometimes. But intelligent people can always manage, unless they are Bohemians.

HECTOR:

> You are no Bohemian; but you are no Puritan either: your attraction is alive and powerful. What sort of woman do you count yourself?

LADY UTTERWORD:

> I am a woman of the world, Hector; and I can assure you that if you will only take the trouble always to do the perfectly correct thing, and to say the perfectly correct thing, you can do just what you like. An ill-conducted, careless woman gets simply no chance. An ill-conducted, careless man is never allowed within arm's length of any woman worth knowing.

HECTOR:

> I see. You are neither a Bohemian woman nor a Puritan woman. You are a dangerous woman.

LADY UTTERWORD:

> On the contrary, I am a safe woman.

HECTOR:

> You are a most accursedly attractive woman. Mind: I am not making love to you. I do not like being attracted. But you had better know how I feel if you are going to stay here.

LADY UTTERWORD:

You are an exceedingly clever lady-killer, Hector. And terribly handsome. I am quite a good player, myself, at that game. Is it quite understood that we are only playing?

HECTOR:

Quite. I am deliberately playing the fool, out of sheer worthlessness.

LADY UTTERWORD (*rising brightly*):

Well, you are my brother-in-law. Hesione asked you to kiss me. (*He seizes her in his arms, and kisses her strenuously*). Oh! that was a little more than play, brother-in-law. (*She pushes him suddenly away*). You shall not do that again.

HECTOR:

In effect, you got your claws deeper into me than I intended.

MRS HUSHABYE (*coming in from the garden*):

Don't let me disturb you: I only want a cap to put on daddiest. The sun is setting; and he'll catch cold (*she makes for the door leading to the hall*).

LADY UTTERWORD:

Your husband is quite charming, darling. He has actually condescended to kiss me at last. I shall go into the garden: it's cooler now (*she goes out by the port door*).

MRS HUSHABYE:

Take care, dear child. I don't believe any man can kiss Addy without falling in love with her. (*She goes into the hall*).

HECTOR (*striking himself on the chest*):

Fool! Goat!

Mrs Hushabye *comes back with the* Captain's *cap.*

HECTOR:

Your sister is an extremely enterprising old girl. Where's Miss Dunn?

MRS HUSHABYE:

Mangan says she has gone up to her room for a nap. Addy won't let you talk to Ellie: she has marked you for her own.

HECTOR:

She has the diabolical family fascination. I began making love to her automatically. What am I to do? I can't fall in love; and I can't hurt a woman's feelings by telling her so when she falls in love with me. And as women are always falling in love with my moustache I get landed in all sorts of tedious and terrifying flirtations in which I'm not a bit in earnest.

MRS HUSHABYE:

Oh, neither is Addy. She has never been in love in her life, though she has always been trying to fall in head over ears. She is worse than you, because you had one real go at least, with me.

HECTOR:

That was a confounded madness. I can't believe that such an amazing experience is common. It has left its mark on me. I believe that is why I have never been able to repeat it.

MRS HUSHABYE (*laughing and caressing his arm*):

We were frightfully in love with one another, Hector. It was such an enchanting dream that I have never been able to grudge it to you or anyone else since. I have invited all sorts of pretty women to the house on the chance of giving you another turn. But it has never come off.

HECTOR:

I don't know that I want it to come off. It was damned dangerous. You fascinated me; but I loved you; so it was heaven. This sister of yours fascinates me; but I hate her; so it is hell. I shall kill her if she persists.

MRS HUSHABYE:

Nothing will kill Addy: she is as strong as a horse. (*Releasing him*) Now *I* am going off to fascinate somebody.

HECTOR:

The Foreign Office toff? Randall?

MRS HUSHABYE:

Goodness gracious, no! Why should I fascinate him?

HECTOR:

I presume you don't mean the bloated capitalist, Mangan?

MRS HUSHABYE:

Hm! I think he had better be fascinated by me than by Ellie. (*She is going into the garden when the* Captain *comes in from it with some sticks in his hand*). What have you got there, daddiest?

CAPTAIN SHOTOVER:

Dynamite.

MRS HUSHABYE:

You've been to the gravel pit. Don't drop it about the house: there's a dear. (*She goes into the garden, where the evening light is now very red*).

HECTOR:

Listen, O sage. How long dare you concentrate on a feeling without risking having it fixed in your consciousness all the rest of your life?

CAPTAIN SHOTOVER:

Ninety minutes. An hour and a half. (*He goes into the pantry*).

Hector, *left alone, contracts his brows, and falls into a daydream. He does not move for some time. Then he folds his arms. Then, throwing his hands behind him, and gripping one with the other, he strides tragically once to and fro. Suddenly he snatches his walking-stick from the teak table, and draws it; for it is a sword-stick. He fights a desperate duel with an imaginary antagonist, and after many vicissitudes runs him through the body up to the hilt. He sheathes his sword and throws it on the sofa, falling into another reverie as he does so. He looks straight into the eyes of an imaginary woman; seizes her by the arms; and says in a deep and thrilling tone* "Do you love me!" *The* Captain *comes out of the pantry at this moment; and* Hector, *caught with his arms stretched out and his fists clenched, has to account for his attitude by going through a series of gymnastic exercises.*

CAPTAIN SHOTOVER:

That sort of strength is no good. You will never be as strong as a gorilla.

HECTOR:

What is the dynamite for?

CAPTAIN SHOTOVER:

To kill fellows like Mangan.

HECTOR:

No use. They will always be able to buy more dynamite than you.

CAPTAIN SHOTOVER:

I will make a dynamite that he cannot explode.

HECTOR:

And that you can, eh?

CAPTAIN SHOTOVER:

Yes: when I have attained the seventh degree of concentration.

HECTOR:

What's the use of that? You never do attain it.

CAPTAIN SHOTOVER:

What then is to be done? Are we to be kept for ever in the mud by these hogs to whom the universe is nothing but a machine for greasing their bristles and filling their snouts?

HECTOR:

Are Mangan's bristles worse than Randall's lovelocks?

CAPTAIN SHOTOVER:

We must win powers of life and death over them both. I refuse to die until I have invented the means.

HECTOR:

Who are we that we should judge them?

CAPTAIN SHOTOVER:

What are they that they should judge us? Yet they do, unhesitatingly. There is enmity between our seed and their seed. They know it and act on it, strangling our souls. They believe in themselves. When we believe in ourselves, we shall kill them.

HECTOR:

It is the same seed. You forget that your pirate has a very nice daughter. Mangan's son may be a Plato: Randall's a Shelley. What was my father?

CAPTAIN SHOTOVER:

The damndest scoundrel I ever met. (*He replaces the drawing-board; sits down at the table; and begins to mix a wash of color*).

HECTOR:

Precisely. Well, dare you kill his innocent grandchildren?

CAPTAIN SHOTOVER:

They are mine also.

HECTOR:

Just so. We are members one of another. (*He throws himself carelessly on the sofa*). I tell you I have often thought of this killing of human vermin. Many men have thought of it. Decent men are like Daniel in the lion's den: their survival is a miracle; and they do not always survive. We live among the Mangans and Randalls and Billie Dunns as they, poor devils, live among the disease germs and the doctors and the lawyers and the parsons and the restaurant chefs and the tradesmen and the servants and all the rest of the parasites and blackmailers. What are our terrors to theirs? Give me the power to kill them; and I'll spare them in sheer—

CAPTAIN SHOTOVER (*cutting in sharply*):

Fellow feeling?

HECTOR:

No. I should kill myself if I believed that. I must believe that my spark, small as it is, is divine, and that the red light over their door is hell fire. I should spare them in simple magnanimous pity.

CAPTAIN SHOTOVER:

You can't spare them until you have the power to kill them. At present they have the power to kill you. There are millions of blacks over the water for them to train and let loose on us. They're going to do it. They're doing it already.

HECTOR:

They are too stupid to use their power.

CAPTAIN SHOTOVER (*throwing down his brush and coming to the end of the sofa*):

Do not deceive yourself: they do use it. We kill the better half of ourselves every day to propitiate them. The knowledge that these people are there to render all our aspirations barren prevents us having the aspirations. And when we are tempted to seek their destruction they bring forth demons to delude us, disguised as pretty daughters, and singers and poets and the like, for whose sake we spare them.

HECTOR (*sitting up and leaning towards him*):

May not Hesione be such a demon, brought forth by you lest I should slay you?

CAPTAIN SHOTOVER:

That is possible. She has used you up, and left you nothing but dreams, as some women do.

HECTOR:

Vampire women, demon women.

CAPTAIN SHOTOVER:

Men think the world well lost for them, and lose it accordingly. Who are the men that do things? The husbands of the shrew and of the drunkard, the men with the thorn in the flesh. (*Walking distractedly away towards the pantry*) I must think these things out. (*Turning suddenly*) But I go on with the dynamite none the less. I will discover a ray mightier than any X-ray: a mind ray that will explode the ammunition in the belt of my adversary before he can point his gun at me. And I must hurry. I am old: I have no time to waste in talk (*he is about to go into the pantry, and* Hector *is making for the hall, when* Hesione *comes back*).

MRS HUSHABYE:

Daddiest: you and Hector must come and help me to entertain all these people. What on earth were you shouting about?

HECTOR (*stopping in the act of turning the doorhandle*):

He is madder than usual.

MRS HUSHABYE:

We all are.

HECTOR:

I must change (*he resumes his door opening*).

MRS HUSHABYE:

Stop, stop. Come back, both of you. Come back. (*They return, reluctantly*). Money is running short.

HECTOR:

Money! Where are my April dividends?

MRS HUSHABYE:

Where is the snow that fell last year?

CAPTAIN SHOTOVER:

Where is all the money you had for that patent lifeboat I invented?

MRS HUSHABYE:

Five hundred pounds; and I have made it last since Easter!

CAPTAIN SHOTOVER:

Since Easter! Barely four months! Monstrous extravagance! I could live for seven years on £500.

MRS HUSHABYE:

Not keeping open house as we do here, daddiest.

CAPTAIN SHOTOVER:

Only £500 for that lifeboat! I got twelve thousand for the invention before that.

MRS HUSHABYE:

Yes, dear; but that was for the ship with the magnetic keel that sucked up submarines. Living at the rate we do, you cannot afford life-saving inventions. Can't you think of something that will murder half Europe at one bang?

CAPTAIN SHOTOVER:

No. I am ageing fast. My mind does not dwell on slaughter as it did when I was a boy. Why doesn't your husband invent something? He does nothing but tell lies to women.

HECTOR:

Well, that is a form of invention, is it not? However, you are right: I ought to support my wife.

MRS HUSHABYE:

Indeed you shall do nothing of the sort: I should never see you from breakfast to dinner. I want my husband.

HECTOR (*bitterly*):

I might as well be your lapdog.

MRS HUSHABYE:

Do you want to be my breadwinner, like the other poor husbands?

HECTOR:

No, by thunder! What a damned creature a husband is anyhow!

MRS HUSHABYE (*to the* Captain):

What about that harpoon cannon?

CAPTAIN SHOTOVER:

No use. It kills whales, not men.

MRS HUSHABYE:

Why not? You fire the harpoon out of a cannon. It sticks in the enemy's general; you wind him in; and there you are.

HECTOR:

You are your father's daughter, Hesione.

CAPTAIN SHOTOVER:

There is something in it. Not to wind in generals: they are not dangerous. But one could fire a grapnel and wind in a machine gun or even a tank. I will think it out.

MRS HUSHABYE (*squeezing the* Captain's *arm affectionately*):

Saved! You are a darling, daddiest. Now we must go back to these dreadful people and entertain them.

CAPTAIN SHOTOVER:

They have had no dinner. Don't forget that.

HECTOR:

Neither have I. And it is dark: it must be all hours.

MRS HUSHABYE:

Oh, Guinness will produce some sort of dinner for them. The servants always take jolly good care that there is food in the house.

CAPTAIN SHOTOVER (*raising a strange wail in the darkness*):

What a house! What a daughter!

MRS HUSHABYE (*raving*):

What a father!

HECTOR (*following suit*):

What a husband!

CAPTAIN SHOTOVER:

Is there no thunder in heaven?

HECTOR:

Is there no beauty, no bravery, on earth?

MRS HUSHABYE:

What do men want? They have their food, their firesides, their clothes mended, and our love at the end of the day. Why are they not satisfied? Why do they envy us the pain with which we bring them into the world, and make strange dangers and torments for themselves to be even with us?

CAPTAIN SHOTOVER (*weirdly chanting*):

I built a house for my daughters, and opened the doors
     thereof,
That men might come for their choosing, and their betters
     spring from their love;
But one of them married a numskull;

HECTOR (*taking up the rhythm*):

                              The other a liar wed;

MRS HUSHABYE (*completing the stanza*):

And now must she lie beside him, even as she made
     her bed.

LADY UTTERWORD (*calling from the garden*):

Hesione! Hesione! Where are you?

HECTOR:

The cat is on the tiles.

MRS HUSHABYE:

Coming, darling, coming (*she goes quickly into the garden*).

The Captain *goes back to his place at the table.*

HECTOR (*going into the hall*):

Shall I turn up the lights for you?

CAPTAIN SHOTOVER:

No. Give me deeper darkness. Money is not made in the light.

# Act II

*The same room, with the lights turned up and the curtains drawn.* Ellie *comes in, followed by* Mangan. *Both are dressed for dinner. She strolls to the drawing-table. He comes between the table and the wicker chair.*

MANGAN:

What a dinner! I don't call it a dinner: I call it a meal.

ELLIE:

I am accustomed to meals, Mr Mangan, and very lucky to get them. Besides, the captain cooked some macaroni for me.

MANGAN (*shuddering liverishly*):

Too rich: I can't eat such things. I suppose it's because I have to work so much with my brain. That's the worst of being a man of business: you are always thinking, thinking, thinking. By the way, now that we are alone, may I take the opportunity to come to a little understanding with you?

ELLIE (*settling into the draughtsman's seat*):

Certainly. I should like to.

MANGAN (*taken aback*):

Should you? That surprises me; for I thought I noticed this afternoon that you avoided me all you could. Not for the first time either.

ELLIE:

I was very tired and upset. I wasn't used to the ways of this extraordinary house. Please forgive me.

MANGAN:

Oh, that's all right: I don't mind. But Captain Shotover has been talking to me about you. You and me, you know.

ELLIE (*interested*):

The Captain! What did he say?

MANGAN:

Well, he noticed the difference between our ages.

ELLIE:

He notices everything.

MANGAN:

You don't mind, then?

ELLIE:

Of course I know quite well that our engagement—

MANGAN:

Oh! you call it an engagement.

ELLIE:

Well, isn't it?

MANGAN:

Oh, yes, yes: no doubt it is if you hold to it. This is the first time you've used the word; and I didn't quite know where we stood: that's all. (*He sits down in the wicker chair; and resigns himself to allow her to lead the conversation*). You were saying—?

ELLIE:

Was I? I forget. Tell me. Do you like this part of the country? I heard you ask Mr Hushabye at dinner whether there are any nice houses to let down here.

MANGAN:

I like the place. The air suits me. I shouldn't be surprised if I settled down here.

ELLIE:

Nothing would please me better. The air suits me too. And I want to be near Hesione.

MANGAN (*with growing uneasiness*):

The air may suit us; but the question is, should we suit one another? Have you thought about that?

ELLIE:

Mr Mangan: we must be sensible, mustn't we? It's no use pretending that we are Romeo and Juliet. But we can get on very well together if we choose to make the best of it. Your kindness of heart will make it easy for me.

MANGAN (*leaning forward, with the beginning of something like deliberate unpleasantness in his voice*):

Kindness of heart, eh? I ruined your father, didn't I?

ELLIE:

Oh, not intentionally.

MANGAN:

Yes I did. Ruined him on purpose.

ELLIE:

On purpose!

MANGAN:

Not out of ill-nature, you know. And you'll admit that I kept a job for him when I had finished with him. But business is business; and I ruined him as a matter of business.

ELLIE:

I don't understand how that can be. Are you trying to make me feel that I need not be grateful to you, so that I may choose freely?

MANGAN (*rising aggressively*):

No. I mean what I say.

ELLIE:

But how could it possibly do you any good to ruin my father? The money he lost was yours.

MANGAN (*with a sour laugh*):

Was mine! It is mine, Miss Ellie, and all the money the other fellows lost too. (*He shoves his hands into his pockets and shews his teeth*). I just smoked them out like a hive of bees. What do you say to that? A bit of a shock, eh?

ELLIE:

It would have been, this morning. Now! you can't think how little it matters. But it's quite interesting. Only, you must explain it to me. I don't understand it. (*Propping her elbows on the drawing-board and her chin on her hands, she composes herself to listen with a combination of conscious curiosity with unconscious contempt which provokes him to more and more unpleasantness, and an attempt at patronage of her ignorance*).

MANGAN:

Of course you don't understand: what do you know about business? You just listen and learn. Your father's business was a new business; and I don't start new businesses: I let other fellows start them. They put all their money and their friends' money into starting them. They wear out their souls and bodies trying to make a success of them. They're what you call enthusiasts. But the first dead lift of the thing is too much for them; and they havn't enough financial experience. In a year or so they have either to let the whole show go bust, or sell out to a new lot of fellows for a few deferred ordinary shares: that is, if they're lucky enough to get anything at all. As likely as not the very same thing happens to the new lot. They put in more money and a couple of years more work; and then perhaps they have to sell out to a third lot. If it's really a big thing the third lot will have to sell out too, and leave their work and their money behind them. And that's where the real business man comes in: where I come in. But I'm cleverer than some: I don't mind dropping a little money to start the process. I took your father's measure. I saw that he had a sound idea, and that he would work himself silly for it if he got the chance. I saw that he was a child in business, and was dead certain to outrun his expenses and be in too great a hurry to wait for his market. I knew that the surest way to ruin a man who doesn't know how to handle money is to give him some. I explained my idea to some friends in the city, and they found the money; for I take no risks in ideas, even when they're my own. Your father and the friends that ventured their money with him were no more to me than a heap of squeezed lemons. You've been wasting your gratitude: my kind heart is all rot. I'm sick of it. When I see your father beaming at me with his moist, grateful eyes, regularly wallowing in gratitude, I sometimes feel I must tell him the truth or burst. What stops me is that I know he wouldn't believe me. He'd think it was my modesty, as you did just now. He'd think anything rather than the truth, which is that he's a blamed fool, and I am a man that knows how to take care of himself. (*He throws himself back into the big chair with large self-approval*). Now what do you think of me, Miss Ellie?

ELLIE (*dropping her hands*):

How strange! that my mother, who knew nothing at all about business, should have been quite right about you! She always said—not before papa, of course, but to us children—that you were just that sort of man.

MANGAN (*sitting up, much hurt*):

Oh! did she? And yet she'd have let you marry me.

ELLIE:

Well, you see, Mr Mangan, my mother married a very good man—for whatever you may think of my father as a man of business, he is the soul of goodness—and she is not at all keen on my doing the same.

MANGAN:

Anyhow, you don't want to marry me now, do you?

ELLIE (*very calmly*):

Oh, I think so. Why not?

MANGAN (*rising aghast*):

Why not!

ELLIE:

I don't see why we shouldn't get on very well together.

MANGAN:

Well, but look here, you know—(*he stops, quite at a loss*).

ELLIE (*patiently*):

Well?

MANGAN:

Well, I thought you were rather particular about people's characters.

ELLIE:

If we women were particular bout men's characters, we should never get married at all, Mr Mangan.

MANGAN:

A child like you talking of "we women"! What next! You're not in earnest?

ELLIE:

Yes I am. Aren't you?

MANGAN:

You mean to hold me to it?

ELLIE:

Do you wish to back out of it?

MANGAN:

Oh no. Not exactly back out of it.

ELLIE:

Well?

*He has nothing to say. With a long whispered whistle, he drops into the wicker chair and stares before him like a beggared gambler. But a cunning look soon comes into his face. He leans over towards her on his right elbow, and speaks in a low steady voice.*

MANGAN:

Suppose I told you I was in love with another woman!

ELLIE (*echoing him*):

Suppose I told you I was in love with another man!

MANGAN (*bouncing angrily out of his chair*):

I'm not joking.

ELLIE:

Who told you *I* was?

MANGAN:

I tell you I'm serious. You're too young to be serious; but you'll have to believe me. I want to be near your friend Mrs Hushabye. I'm in love with her. Now the murder's out.

ELLIE:

I want to be near your friend Mr Hushabye. I'm in love with him. (*She rises and adds with a frank air*) Now we are in one another's confidence, we shall be real friends. Thank you for telling me.

MANGAN (*almost beside himself*):

Do you think I'll be made a convenience of like this?

ELLIE:

Come, Mr Mangan! you made a business convenience of my father. Well, a woman's business is marriage. Why shouldn't I make a domestic convenience of you?

MANGAN:

Because I don't choose, see? Because I'm not a silly gull like your father. That's why.

ELLIE (*with serene contempt*):

You are not good enough to clean my father's boots, Mr Mangan; and I am paying you a great compliment in condescending to make a convenience of you, as you call it. Of course you are free to throw over our engagement if you like; but, if you do, you'll never enter Hesione's house again: I will take care of that.

MANGAN (*gasping*):

You little devil, you've done me (*On the point of collapsing into the big chair again he recovers himself*) Wait a bit, though: you're not so cute as you think. You can't beat Boss Mangan as easy as that. Suppose I go straight to Mrs Hushabye and tell her that you're in love with her husband.

ELLIE:

She knows it.

MANGAN:

You told her!!!

ELLIE:

She told me.

MANGAN (*clutching at his bursting temples*):

Oh, this is a crazy house. Or else I'm going clean off my chump. Is she making a swop with you—she to have your husband and you to have hers?

ELLIE:

Well, you don't want us both, do you?

MANGAN (*throwing himself into the chair distractedly*):

My brain won't stand it. My head's going to split. Help! Help me to hold it. Quick: hold it: squeeze it. Save me. (Ellie *comes behind his chair; clasps his head hard for a moment; then begins to draw her hands from his forehead back to his ears*). Thank you. (*Drowsily*) That's very refreshing. (*Waking a little*) Don't you hypnotize me, though. I've seen men made fools of by hypnotism.

ELLIE (*steadily*):

Be quiet. I've seen men made fools of without hypnotism.

MANGAN (*humbly*):

You don't dislike touching me, I hope. You never touched me before, I noticed.

ELLIE:

Not since you fell in love naturally with a grown-up nice woman, who will never expect you to make love to her. And I will never expect him to make love to me.

MANGAN:

He may, though.

ELLIE (*making her passes rhythmically*):

Hush. Go to sleep. Do you hear? You are to go to sleep, go to sleep, go to sleep; be quiet, deeply deeply quiet; sleep, sleep, sleep, sleep, sleep.

*He falls asleep.* Ellie *steals away; turns the light out; and goes into the garden.*

Nurse Guinness *opens the door and is seen in the light which comes in from the hall.*

NURSE GUINNESS (*speaking to someone outside*):

Mr Mangan's not here, ducky: there's no one here. It's all dark.

MRS HUSHABYE (*without*):

Try the garden. Mr Dunn and I will be in my boudoir. Shew him the way.

NURSE GUINNESS:

Yes, ducky. (*She makes for the garden door in the dark; stumbles over the sleeping* Mangan; *and screams*) Ahoo! Oh Lord, sir! I beg your pardon, I'm sure: I didn't see you in the dark. Who is it? (*She goes back to the door and turns on the light*). Oh, Mr Mangan, sir, I hope I haven't hurt you plumping into your lap like that. (*Coming to him*) I was looking for you, sir. Mrs Hushabye says will you please—(*noticing that he remains quite insensible*) Oh, my good Lord, I hope I haven't killed him. Sir! Mr Mangan! Sir! (*She shakes him; and he is rolling inertly off the chair on the floor when she holds him up and props him against the cushion*). Miss Hessy! Miss Hessy! Quick, doty darling. Miss Hessy! (Mrs Hushabye *comes in from the hall, followed by* Mazzini Dunn). Oh, Miss Hessy, I've been and killed him.

Mazzini *runs round the back of the chair to* Mangan's *right hand, and sees that the nurse's words are apparently only too true.*

MAZZINI:

What tempted you to commit such a crime, woman?

MRS HUSHABYE (*trying not to laugh*):

Do you mean you did it on purpose?

NURSE GUINNESS:

> Now is it likely I'd kill any man on purpose? I fell over him in the dark; and I'm a pretty tidy weight. He never spoke nor moved until I shook him; and then he would have dropped dead on the floor. Isn't it tiresome?

MRS HUSHABYE (*going past* Nurse Guinness *to* Mangan's *side, and inspecting him less credulously than* Mazzini) Nonsense! he is not dead: he is only asleep. I can see him breathing.

NURSE GUINNESS:

> But why won't he wake?

MAZZINI (*speaking very politely into* Mangan's *ear*):

> Mangan! My dear Mangan! (*he blows into* Mangan's *ear*).

MRS HUSHABYE:

> That's no good (*she shakes him vigorously*). Mr Mangan: wake up. Do you hear? (*He begins to roll over*). Oh! Nurse, nurse: he's falling: help me.

Nurse Guinness *rushes to the rescue. With* Mazzini's *assistance,* Mangan *is propped safely up again.*

NURSE GUINNESS (*behind the chair; bending over to test the case with her nose*):

> Would he be drunk, do you think, pet?

MRS HUSHABYE:

> Had he any of papa's rum?

MAZZINI:

> It can't be that: he is most abstemious. I am afraid he drank too much formerly, and has to drink too little now. You know, Mrs Hushabye, I really think he has been hypnotized.

NURSE GUINNESS:

> Hip no what, sir?

MAZZINI:

> One evening at home, after we had seen a hypnotizing performance, the children began playing at it; and Ellie stroked my head. I assure you I went off dead asleep; and they had to send for a professional to wake me up after I had slept eighteen hours. They had to carry me upstairs; and as the poor children were not very strong, they let me slip; and I rolled right down the whole flight and never woke up. (Mrs Hushabye *splutters*). Oh, you may laugh, Mrs Hushabye; but I might have been killed.

MRS HUSHABYE:

> I couldn't have helped laughing even if you had been, Mr Dunn. So Ellie has hypnotized him. What fun!

MAZZINI:

Oh no, no, no. It was such a terrible lesson to her: nothing would induce her to try such a thing again.

MRS HUSHABYE:

Then who did it? *I* didn't.

MAZZINI:

I thought perhaps the Captain might have done it unintentionally. He is so fearfully magnetic: I feel vibrations whenever he comes close to me.

NURSE GUINNESS:

The Captain will get him out of it anyhow, sir: I'll back him for that. I'll go fetch him (*she makes for the pantry*).

MRS HUSHABYE:

Wait a bit. (*To* Mazzini) You say he is all right for eighteen hours?

MAZZINI:

Well, *I* was asleep for eighteen hours.

MRS HUSHABYE:

Were you any the worse for it?

MAZZINI:

I don't quite remember. They had poured brandy down my throat, you see; and—

MRS HUSHABYE:

Quite. Anyhow, you survived. Nurse, darling: go and ask Miss Dunn to come to us here. Say I want to speak to her particularly. You will find her with Mr Hushabye probably.

NURSE GUINNESS:

I think not, ducky: Miss Addy is with him. But I'll find her and send her to you. (*She goes out into the garden*).

MRS HUSHABYE (*calling* Mazzini's *attention to the figure on the chair*):

Now, Mr Dunn, look. Just look. Look hard. Do you still intend to sacrifice your daughter to that thing?

MAZZINI (*troubled*):

You have completely upset me, Mrs Hushabye, by all you have said to me. That anyone could imagine that I—*I*, a consecrated soldier of freedom, if I may say so—could sacrifice Ellie to anybody or anyone, or that I should ever have dreamed of forcing her inclinations in any way, is a most painful blow to my—well, I suppose you would say to my good opinion of myself.

MRS HUSHABYE (*rather stolidly*):

Sorry.

MAZZINI (*looking forlornly at the body*):

What is your objection to poor Mangan, Mrs Hushabye? He looks all right to me. But then I am so accustomed to him.

MRS HUSHABYE:

Have you no heart? Have you no sense? Look at the brute! Think of poor weak innocent Ellie in the clutches of this slavedriver, who spends his life making thousands of rough violent workmen bend to his will and sweat for him: a man accustomed to have great masses of iron beaten into shape for him by steam-hammers! to fight with women and girls over a halfpenny an hour ruthlessly! a captain of industry, I think you call him, don't you? Are you going to fling your delicate, sweet, helpless child into such a beast's claws just because he will keep her in an expensive house and make her wear diamonds to shew how rich he is?

MAZZINI (*staring at her in wide-eyed amazement*):

Bless you, dear Mrs Hushabye, what romantic ideas of business you have! Poor dear Mangan isn't a bit like that.

MRS HUSHABYE (*scornfully*):

Poor dear Mangan indeed!

MAZZINI:

But he doesn't know anything about machinery. He never goes near the men: he couldn't manage them: he is afraid of them. I never can get him to take the least interest in the works: he hardly knows more about them than you do. People are cruelly unjust to Mangan: they think he is all rugged strength just because his manners are bad.

MRS HUSHABYE:

Do you mean to tell me he isn't strong enough to crush poor little Ellie?

MAZZINI:

Of course it's very hard to say how any marriage will turn out; but speaking for myself, I should say that he won't have a dog's chance against Ellie. You know, Ellie has remarkable strength of character. I think it is because I taught her to like Shakespeare when she was very young.

MRS HUSHABYE (*contemptuously*):

Shakespeare! The next thing you will tell me is that you could have made a great deal more money than Mangan. (*She retires to the sofa, and sits down at the port end of it in the worst of humors*).

MAZZINI (*following her and taking the other end*):

No: I'm no good at making money. I don't care enough for it, somehow. I'm not ambitious! that must be it. Mangan is wonderful about money: he thinks of nothing else. He is so dreadfully afraid of being poor. I am always thinking of other things: even at the works I think of the things we are doing and not of what they cost. And the worst of it is, poor Mangan doesn't know what to do with his money when he gets it. He is such a baby that he doesn't know even what to eat and drink: he has ruined his liver eating and drinking the wrong things; and now he can hardly eat at all. Ellie will diet him splendidly. You will be surprised when you come to know him better: he is really the most helpless of mortals. You get quite a protective feeling towards him.

MRS HUSHABYE:

Then who manages his business, pray?

MAZZINI:

I do. And of course other people like me.

MRS HUSHABYE:

Footling people, you mean.

MAZZINI:

I suppose you'd think us so.

MRS HUSHABYE:

And pray why don't you do without him if you're all so much cleverer?

MAZZINI:

Oh, we couldn't: we should ruin the business in a year. I've tried; and I know. We should spend too much on everything. We should improve the quality of the goods and make them too dear. We should be sentimental about the hard cases among the workpeople. But Mangan keeps us in order. He is down on us about every extra halfpenny. We could never do without him. You see, he will sit up all night thinking of how to save sixpence. Won't Ellie make him jump, though, when she takes his house in hand!

MRS HUSHABYE:

Then the creature is a fraud even as a captain of industry!

MAZZINI:

I am afraid all the captains of industry are what you call frauds, Mrs Hushabye. Of course there are some manufacturers who really do understand their own works; but they don't make as high a rate of profit as Mangan does. I assure you Mangan is quite a good fellow in his way. He means well.

MRS HUSHABYE:

He doesn't look well. He is not in his first youth, is he?

MAZZINI:

After all, no husband is in his first youth for very long, Mrs Hushabye. And men can't afford to marry in their first youth nowadays.

MRS HUSHABYE:

Now if *I* said that, it would sound witty. Why can't you say it wittily? What on earth is the matter with you? Why don't you inspire everybody with confidence? with respect?

MAZZINI (*humbly*):

I think that what is the matter with me is that I am poor. You don't know what that means at home. Mind: I don't say they have ever complained. They've all been wonderful: they've been proud of my poverty. They've even joked about it quite often. But my wife has had a very poor time of it. She has been quite resigned—

MRS HUSHABYE (*shuddering involuntarily*): !!

MAZZINI:

There! You see, Mrs Hushabye. I don't want Ellie to live on resignation.

MRS HUSHABYE:

Do you want her to have to resign herself to living with a man she doesn't love?

MAZZINI (*wistfully*):

Are you sure that would be worse than living with a man she did love, if he was a footling person?

MRS HUSHABYE (*relaxing her contemptuous attitude, quite interested in* Mazzini *now*):

You know, I really think you must love Ellie very much; for you become quite clever when you talk about her.

MAZZINI:

I didn't know I was so very stupid on other subjects.

MRS HUSHABYE:

You are, sometimes.

MAZZINI (*turning his head away; for his eyes are wet*):

I have learnt a good deal about myself from you, Mrs Hushabye; and I'm afraid I shall not be the happier for your plain speaking. But if you thought I needed it to make me think of Ellie's happiness you were very much mistaken.

MRS HUSHABYE (*leaning towards him kindly*):

Have I been a beast?

MAZZINI (*pulling himself together*):

It doesn't matter about me, Mrs Hushabye. I think you like Ellie; and that is enough for me.

MRS HUSHABYE:

I'm beginning to like you a little. I perfectly loathed you at first. I thought you the most odious, self-satisfied, boresome elderly prig I ever met.

MAZZINI (*resigned, and now quite cheerful*):

I daresay I am all that. I never have been a favorite with gorgeous women like you. They always frighten me.

MRS HUSHABYE (*pleased*):

Am I a gorgeous woman, Mazzini? I shall fall in love with you presently.

MAZZINI (*with placid gallantry*):

No you won't, Hesione. But you would be quite safe. Would you believe it that quite a lot of women have flirted with me because I am quite safe? But they get tired of me for the same reason.

MRS HUSHABYE (*mischievously*):

Take care. You may not be so safe as you think.

MAZZINI:

Oh yes, quite safe. You see, I have been in love really: the sort of love that only happens once. (*Softly*) That's why Ellie is such a lovely girl.

MRS HUSHABYE:

Well, really, you are coming out. Are you quite sure you won't let me tempt you into a second grand passion?

MAZZINI:

Quite. It wouldn't be natural. The fact is, you don't strike on my box, Mrs Hushabye; and I certainly don't strike on yours.

MRS HUSHABYE:

I see. Your marriage was a safety match.

MAZZINI:

What a very witty application of the expression I used! I should never have thought of it.

Ellie *comes in from the garden, looking anything but happy.*

MRS HUSHABYE (*rising*):

Oh! here is Ellie at last. (*She goes behind the sofa*).

ELLIE (*on the threshold of the starboard door*):

Guinness said you wanted me: you and papa.

MRS HUSHABYE:

You have kept us waiting so long that it almost came to—well, never mind. Your father is a very wonderful man (*she ruffles his hair affectionately*): the only one I ever met who could resist me when I made myself really agreeable. (*She comes to the big chair, on* Mangan's *left*). Come here. I have something to shew you. (Ellie *strolls listlessly to the other side of the chair*). Look.

ELLIE (*contemplating* Mangan *without interest*):

> I know. He is only asleep. We had a talk after dinner; and he fell asleep in the middle of it.

MRS HUSHABYE:

> You did it, Ellie. You put him asleep.

MAZZINI (*rising quickly and coming to the back of the chair*):

> Oh, I hope not. Did you, Ellie?

ELLIE (*wearily*):

> He asked me to.

MAZZINI:

> But it's dangerous. You know what happened to me.

ELLIE (*utterly indifferent*):

> Oh, I daresay I can wake him. If not, somebody else can.

MRS HUSHABYE:

> It doesn't matter, anyhow, because I have at last persuaded your father that you don't want to marry him.

ELLIE (*suddenly coming out of her listlessness, much vexed*):

> But why did you do that, Hesione? I do want to marry him. I fully intend to marry him.

MAZZINI:

> Are you quite sure, Ellie? Mrs Hushabye has made me feel that I may have been thoughtless and selfish about it.

ELLIE (*very clearly and steadily*):

> Papa. When Mrs Hushabye takes it on herself to explain to you what I think or don't think, shut your ears tight; and shut your eyes too. Hesione knows nothing about me: she hasn't the least notion of the sort of person I am, and never will. I promise you I won't do anything I don't want to do and mean to do for my own sake.

MAZZINI:

> You are quite, quite sure?

ELLIE:

> Quite, quite sure. Now you must go away and leave me to talk to Mrs Hushabye.

MAZZINI:

> But I should like to hear. Shall I be in the way?

ELLIE (*inexorable*):

> I had rather talk to her alone.

MAZZINI (*affectionately*):

> Oh, well, I know what a nuisance parents are, dear. I will be good and go. (*He goes to the garden door*). By the way, do you remember the address of that professional who woke me up? Don't you think I had better telegraph to him?

MRS HUSHABYE (*moving towards the sofa*):

It's too late to telegraph tonight.

MAZZINI:

I suppose so. I do hope he'll wake up in the course of the night. (*He goes out into the garden*).

ELLIE (*turning vigorously on* Mrs Hushabye *the moment her father is out of the room*):

Hesione: what the devil do you mean by making mischief with my father about Mangan?

MRS HUSHABYE (*promptly losing her temper*):

Don't you dare speak to me like that, you little minx. Remember that you are in my house.

ELLIE:

Stuff! Why don't you mind your own business? What is it to you whether I choose to marry Mangan or not?

MRS HUSHABYE:

Do you suppose you can bully me, you miserable little matrimonial adventurer?

ELLIE:

Every woman who hasn't any money is a matrimonial adventurer. It's easy for you to talk: you have never known what it is to want money; and you can pick up men as if they were daisies. I am poor and respectable—

MRS HUSHABYE (*interrupting*):

Ho! respectable! How did you pick up Mangan? How did you pick up my husband? You have the audacity to tell me that I am a—a—a—

ELLIE:

A siren. So you are. You were born to lead men by the nose: if you weren't, Marcus would have waited for me, perhaps.

MRS HUSHABYE (*suddenly melting and half laughing*):

Oh, my poor Ellie, my pettikins, my unhappy darling! I am so sorry about Hector. But what can I do? It's not my fault: I'd give him to you if I could.

ELLIE:

I don't blame you for that.

MRS HUSHABYE:

What a brute I was to quarrel with you and call you names! Do kiss me and say you're not angry with me.

ELLIE (*fiercely*):

Oh, don't slop and gush and be sentimental. Don't you see that unless I can be hard—as hard as nails—I shall go mad. I don't care a damn about your calling me names: do you think a woman in my situation can feel a few hard words?

MRS HUSHABYE:

Poor little woman! Poor little situation!

ELLIE:

I suppose you think you're being sympathetic. You are just foolish and stupid and selfish. You see me getting a smasher right in the face that kills a whole part of my life: the best part that can never come again; and you think you can help me over it by a little coaxing and kissing. When I want all the strength I can get to lean on: something iron, something stony, I don't care how cruel it is, you go all mushy and want to slobber over me. I'm not angry; I'm not unfriendly; but for God's sake do pull yourself together; and don't think that because you're on velvet and always have been, women who are in hell can take it as easily as you.

MRS HUSHABYE (*shrugging her shoulders*):

Very well. (*She sits down on the sofa in her old place*). But I warn you that when I am neither coaxing and kissing nor laughing, I am just wondering how much longer I can stand living in this cruel, damnable world. You object to the siren: well, I drop the siren. You want to rest your wounded bosom against a grindstone. Well (*folding her arms*), here is the grindstone.

ELLIE (*sitting down beside her, appeased*):

That's better: you really have the trick of falling in with everyone's mood; but you don't understand, because you are not the sort of woman for whom there is only one man and only one chance.

MRS HUSHABYE:

I certainly don't understand how your marrying that object (*indicating* Mangan) will console you for not being able to marry Hector.

ELLIE:

Perhaps you don't understand why I was quite a nice girl this morning, and am now neither a girl nor particularly nice.

MRS HUSHABYE:

Oh yes I do. It's because you have made up your mind to do something despicable and wicked.

ELLIE:

I don't think so, Hesione. I must make the best of my ruined house.

MRS HUSHABYE:

Pooh! You'll get over it. Your house isn't ruined.

ELLIE:

Of course I shall get over it. You don't suppose I'm going to sit down and die of a broken heart, I hope, or be an old maid living on a pittance from the Sick and Indigent Roomkeepers' Association. But my heart is broken, all the same. What I mean by that is that I know that what has happened to me with Marcus will not happen to me ever again. In the world for me there is Marcus and a lot of other men of whom one is just the same as another. Well, if I can't have love, that's no reason why I should have poverty. If Mangan has nothing else, he has money.

MRS HUSHABYE:

And are there no young men with money?

ELLIE:

Not within my reach. Besides, a young man would have the right to expect love from me, and would perhaps leave me when he found I could not give it to him. Rich young men can get rid of their wives, you know, pretty cheaply. But this object, as you call him, can expect nothing more from me than I am prepared to give him.

MRS HUSHABYE:

He will be your owner, remember. If he buys you, he will make the bargain pay him and not you. Ask your father.

ELLIE (*rising and strolling to the chair to contemplate their subject*):

You need not trouble on that score, Hesione. I have more to give Boss Mangan than he has to give me: it is I who am buying him, and at a pretty good price too, I think. Women are better at that sort of bargain than men. I have taken the Boss's measure; and ten Boss Mangans shall not prevent me doing far more as I please as his wife than I have ever been able to do as a poor girl. (*Stopping to the recumbent figure*) Shall they, Boss? I think not. (*She passes on to the drawing-table, and leans against the end of it, facing the windows*). I shall not have to spend most of my time wondering how long my gloves will last, anyhow.

MRS HUSHABYE (*rising superbly*):

Ellie: you are a wicked sordid little beast. And to think that I actually condescended to fascinate that creature there to save you from him! Well, let me tell you this: if you make this disgusting match, you will never see Hector again if I can help it.

ELLIE (*unmoved*):

I nailed Mangan by telling him that if he did not marry me he should never see you again (*she lifts herself on her wrists and seats herself on the end of the table*).

MRS HUSHABYE (*recoiling*):

Oh!

ELLIE:

So you see I am not unprepared for your playing that trump

against me. Well, you just try it: that's all. I should have made a man of Marcus, not a household pet.

MRS HUSHABYE (*flaming*):

You dare!

ELLIE (*looking almost dangerous*):

Set him thinking about me if you dare.

MRS HUSHABYE:

Well, of all the impudent little fiends I ever met! Hector says there is a certain point at which the only answer you can give to a man who breaks all the rules is to knock him down. What would you say if I were to box your ears?

ELLIE (*calmly*):

I should pull your hair.

MRS HUSHABYE (*mischievously*):

That wouldn't hurt me. Perhaps it comes off at night.

ELLIE (*so taken aback that she drops off the table and runs to her*):

Oh, you don't mean to say, Hesione, that your beautiful black hair is false?

MRS HUSHABYE (*patting it*):

Don't tell Hector. He believes in it.

ELLIE (*groaning*):

Oh! Even the hair that ensnared him false! Everything false!

MRS HUSHABYE:

Pull it and try. Other women can snare men in their hair; but I can swing a baby on mine. Aha! you can't do that, Goldylocks.

ELLIE (*heartbroken*):

No. You have stolen my babies.

MRS HUSHABYE:

Pettikins: don't make me cry. You know, what you said about my making a household pet of him is a little true. Perhaps he ought to have waited for you. Would any other woman on earth forgive you?

ELLIE:

Oh, what right had you to take him all for yourself! (*Pulling herself together*) There! You couldn't help it: neither of us could help it. He couldn't help it. No: don't say anything more: I can't bear it. Let us wake the object. (*She begins stroking Mangan's head, reversing the movement with which she put him to sleep*). Wake up, do you hear? You are to wake up at once. Wake up, wake up, wake—

MANGAN (*bouncing out of the chair in a fury and turning on them*):

Wake up! So you think I've been asleep, do you? (*He kicks the chair violently out of his way, and gets between them*). You throw me into a trance so that I can't move hand or foot—I might have been buried alive! it's a mercy I wasn't—and then you think I was only asleep. If you'd let me drop the two times you rolled me about, my nose would have been flattened for life against the floor. But I've found you all out, anyhow. I know the sort of people I'm among now. I've heard every word you've said, you and your precious father, and (*to* Mrs Hushabye) you too. So I'm an object, am I? I'm a thing, am I? I'm a fool that hasn't sense enough to feed myself properly, am I? I'm afraid of the men that would starve if it weren't for the wages I give them, am I? I'm nothing but a disgusting old skinflint to be made a convenience of by designing women and fool managers of my works, am I? I'm—

MRS HUSHABYE (*with the most elegant aplomb*):
Sh-sh-sh-sh-sh! Mr Mangan: you are bound in honor to obliterate from your mind all you heard while you were pretending to be asleep. It was not meant for you to hear.

MANGAN:
Pretending to be asleep! Do you think if I was only pretending that I'd have sprawled there helpless, and listened to such unfairness, such lies, such injustice and plotting and backbiting and slandering of me, if I could have up and told you what I thought of you! I wonder I didn't burst.

MRS HUSHABYE (*sweetly*):
You dreamt it all, Mr Mangan. We were only saying how beautifully peaceful you looked in your sleep. That was all, wasn't it, Ellie? Believe me, Mr Mangan, all those unpleasant things came into your mind in the last half second before you woke. Ellie rubbed your hair the wrong way; and the disagreeable sensation suggested a disagreeable dream.

MANGAN (*doggedly*):
I believe in dreams.

MRS HUSHABYE:
So do I. But they go by contraries, don't they?

MANGAN (*depths of emotion suddenly welling up in him*):
I shan't forget, to my dying day, that when you gave me the glad eye that time in the garden, you were making a fool of me. That was a dirty low mean thing to do. You had no right to let me come near you if I disgusted you. It isn't my fault if I'm old and haven't a moustache like a bronze candlestick as your husband has. There are things no decent woman would do to a man—like a man hitting a woman in the breast.

Mrs Hushabye, *utterly shamed, sits down on the sofa and covers her face with her hands.* Mangan *sits down also on his chair and begins to cry like a child.* Ellie *stares at them.* Mrs Hushabye, *at the distressing sound he makes, takes down her hands and looks at him. She rises and runs to him.*

MRS HUSHABYE:

Don't cry: I can't bear it. Have I broken your heart? I didn't know you had one. How could I?

MANGAN:

I'm a man ain't I?

MRS HUSHABYE (*half coaxing, half rallying, altogether tenderly*):

Oh no: not what I call a man. Only a Boss: just that and nothing else. What business has a Boss with a heart?

MANGAN:

Then you're not a bit sorry for what you did, nor ashamed?

MRS HUSHABYE:

I was ashamed for the first time in my life when you said that about hitting a woman in the breast, and I found out what I'd done. My very bones blushed red. You've had your revenge, Boss. Aren't you satisfied?

MANGAN:

Serve you right! Do you hear? Serve you right! You're just cruel. Cruel.

MRS HUSHABYE:

Yes: cruelty would be delicious if one could only find some sort of cruelty that didn't really hurt. By the way (*sitting down beside him on the arm of the chair*), what's your name? It's not really Boss, is it?

MANGAN (*shortly*):

If you want to know, my name's Alfred.

MRS HUSHABYE (*springing up*):

Alfred!! Ellie: he was christened after Tennyson!!!

MANGAN (*rising*):

I was christened after my uncle, and never had a penny from him, damn him! What of it?

MRS HUSHABYE:

It comes to me suddenly that you are a real person: that you had a mother, like anyone else. (*Putting her hands on his shoulders and surveying him*) Little Alf!

MANGAN:

Well, you have a nerve.

MRS HUSHABYE:

And you have a heart, Alfy, a whimpering little heart, but a real one. (*Releasing him suddenly*) Now run and make it up with Ellie. She has had time to think what to say to you, which is more than I had (*she goes out quickly into the garden by the port door*).

MANGAN:

That woman has a pair of hands that go right through you.

ELLIE:

Still in love with her, in spite of all we said about you?

MANGAN:

Are all women like you two? Do they never think of anything about a man except what they can get out of him? You weren't even thinking that about me. You were only thinking whether your gloves would last.

ELLIE:

I shall not have to think about that when we are married.

MANGAN:

And you think I am going to marry you after what I heard there!

ELLIE:

You heard nothing from me that I did not tell you before.

MANGAN:

Perhaps you think I can't do without you.

ELLIE:

I think you would feel lonely without us all now, after coming to know us so well.

MANGAN (*with something like a yell of despair*):

Am I never to have the last word?

CAPTAIN SHOTOVER (*appearing at the starboard garden door*):

There is a soul in torment here. What is the matter?

MANGAN:

This girl doesn't want to spend her life wondering how long her gloves will last.

CAPTAIN SHOTOVER (*passing through*):

Don't wear any. I never do (*he goes into the pantry*).

LADY UTTERWORD (*appearing at the port garden door, in a handsome dinner dress*):

Is anything the matter?

ELLIE:

This gentleman wants to know is he never to have the last word?

LADY UTTERWORD (*coming forward to the sofa*):

I should let him have it, my dear. The important thing is not to have the last word, but to have your own way.

MANGAN:

She wants both.

LADY UTTERWORD:

She won't get them, Mr Mangan. Providence always has the last word.

MANGAN (*desperately*):

Now you are going to come religion over me. In this house a man's mind might as well be a football. I'm going. (*He makes for the hall, but is stopped by a hail from the* Captain, *who has just emerged from his pantry*).

CAPTAIN SHOTOVER:

Whither away, Boss Mangan?

MANGAN:

To hell out of this house: let that be enough for you and all here.

CAPTAIN SHOTOVER:

You were welcome to come: you are free to go. The wide earth, the high seas, the spacious skies are waiting for you outside.

LADY UTTERWORD:

But your things, Mr Mangan. Your bags, your comb and brushes, your pyjamas—

HECTOR (*who has just appeared in the port doorway in a handsome Arab costume*):

Why should the escaping slave take his chains with him?

MANGAN:

That's right, Hushabye. Keep the pyjamas, my lady; and much good may they do you.

HECTOR (*advancing to* Lady Utterword's *left hand*):

Let us all go out into the night and leave everything behind us.

MANGAN:

You stay where you are, the lot of you. I want no company, especially female company.

ELLIE:

Let him go. He is unhappy here. He is angry with us.

CAPTAIN SHOTOVER:

Go, Boss Mangan; and when you have found the land where there is happiness and where there are no women, send me its latitude and longitude; and I will join you there.

LADY UTTERWORD:

You will certainly not be comfortable without your luggage, Mr Mangan.

ELLIE (*impatient*):

Go, go: why don't you go? It is a heavenly night: you can sleep on the heath. Take my waterproof to lie on: it is hanging up in the hall.

HECTOR:

Breakfast at nine, unless you prefer to breakfast with the Captain at six.

ELLIE:

Good night, Alfred.

HECTOR:

Alfred! (*He runs back to the door and calls into the garden*) Randall: Mangan's Christian name is Alfred.

RANDALL (*appearing in the starboard doorway in evening dress*):

Then Hesione wins her bet.

Mrs Hushabye *appears in the port doorway. She throws her left arm round* Hector's *neck; draws him with her to the back of the sofa; and throws her right arm round* Lady Utterword's *neck.*

MRS HUSHABYE:

They wouldn't believe me, Alf.

*They contemplate him.*

MANGAN:

Is there any more of you coming in to look at me, as if I was the latest thing in a menagerie.

MRS HUSHABYE:

You are the latest thing in this menagerie.

*Before* Mangan *can retort, a fall of furniture is heard from upstairs; then a pistol shot, and a yell of pain. The staring group breaks up in consternation.*

MAZZINI'S VOICE (*from above*):

Help! A burglar! Help!

HECTOR (*his eyes blazing*):

A burglar!!!

MRS HUSHABYE:

No, Hector: you'll be shot (*but it is too late: he has dashed out past* Mangan, *who hastily moves towards the bookshelves out of his way*).

CAPTAIN SHOTOVER (*blowing his whistle*):

All hands aloft! (*He strides out after* Hector).

LADY UTTERWORD:

My diamonds! (*She follows the* Captain).

RANDALL (*rushing after her*):

No, Ariadne. Let me.

ELLIE:

Oh, is papa shot? (*she runs out*).

MRS HUSHABYE:

Are you frightened, Alf?

MANGAN:

> No. It ain't my house, thank God.

MRS HUSHABYE:

> If they catch a burglar, shall we have to go into court as witnesses, and be asked all sorts of questions about our private lives?

MANGAN:

> You won't be believed if you tell the truth.

Mazzini, *terribly upset, with a duelling pistol in his hand, comes from the hall, and makes his way to the drawing-table.*

MAZZINI:

> Oh, my dear Mrs Hushabye, I might have killed him (*He throws the pistol on the table and staggers round to the chair*). I hope you won't believe I really intended to.

Hector *comes in, marching an old and villainous looking man before him by the collar. He plants him in the middle of the room and releases him.*

> Ellie *follows, and immediately runs across to the back of her father's chair, and pats his shoulders.*

RANDALL (*entering with a poker*):

> Keep your eye on this door, Mangan. I'll look after the other (*he goes to the starboard door and stands on guard there*).

Lady Utterword *comes in after* Randall, *and goes between* Mrs Hushabye *and* Mangan.

> Nurse Guinness *brings up the rear, and waits near the door, on Mangan's left.*

MRS HUSHABYE:

> What has happened?

MAZZINI:

> Your housekeeper told me there was somebody upstairs, and gave me a pistol that Mr Hushabye had been practising with. I thought it would frighten him; but it went off at a touch.

THE BURGLAR:

> Yes, and took the skin off my ear. Precious near took the top off my head. Why don't you have a proper revolver instead of a thing like that, that goes off if you as much as blow on it?

HECTOR:

> One of my duelling pistols. Sorry.

MAZZINI:

> He put his hands up and said it was a fair cop.

THE BURGLAR:

>So it was. Send for the police.

HECTOR:

>No, by thunder! It was not a fair cop. We were four to one.

MRS HUSHABYE:

>What will they do to him?

THE BURGLAR:

>Ten years. Beginning with solitary. Ten years off my life. I shan't serve it all: I'm too old. It will see me out.

LADY UTTERWORD:

>You should have thought of that before you stole my diamonds.

THE BURGLAR:

>Well, you've got them back, lady: haven't you? Can you give me back the years of my life you are going to take from me?

MRS HUSHABYE:

>Oh, we can't bury a man alive for ten years for a few diamonds.

THE BURGLAR:

>Ten little shining diamonds! Ten long black years!

LADY UTTERWORD:

>Think of what it is for us to be dragged through the horrors of a criminal court, and have all our family affairs in the papers! If you were a native, and Hastings could order you a good beating and send you away, I shouldn't mind; but here in England there is no real protection for any respectable person.

THE BURGLAR:

>I'm too old to be giv a hiding, lady. Send for the police and have done with it. It's only just and right you should.

RANDALL (*who has relaxed his vigilance on seeing the burglar so pacifically disposed, comes forward swinging the poker between his fingers like a well-folded umbrella*):

>It is neither just nor right that we should be put to a lot of inconvenience to gratify your moral enthusiasm, my friend. You had better get out, while you have the chance.

THE BURGLAR (*inexorably*):

>No. I must work my sin off my conscience. This has come as a sort of call to me. Let me spend the rest of my life repenting in a cell. I shall have my reward above.

MANGAN (*exasperated*):

>The very burglars can't behave naturally in this house.

HECTOR:

>My good sir: you must work out your salvation at somebody else's expense. Nobody here is going to charge you.

THE BURGLAR:

Oh, you won't charge me, won't you?

HECTOR:

No. I'm sorry to be inhospitable; but will you kindly leave the house?

THE BURGLAR:

Right. I'll go to the police station and give myself up. (*He turns resolutely to the door; but* Hector *stops him*).

HECTOR: ⎱ ⎰ Oh no. You mustn't do that.

RANDALL: ⎰ ⎱ No, no. Clear out, man, can't you; and don't be a fool.

MRS HUSHABYE: ⎰ ⎱ Don't be so silly. Can't you repent at home?

LADY UTTERWORD:

You will have to do as you are told.

THE BURGLAR:

It's compounding a felony, you know.

MRS HUSHABYE:

This is utterly ridiculous. Are we to be forced to prosecute this man when we don't want to?

THE BURGLAR:

Am I to be robbed of my salvation to save you the trouble of spending a day at the sessions? Is that justice? Is it right? Is it fair to me?

MAZZINI (*rising and leaning across the table persuasively as if it were a pulpit desk or a shop counter*):

Come, come! let me shew you how you can turn your very crimes to account. Why not set up as a locksmith? You must know more about locks than most honest men?

THE BURGLAR:

That's true, sir. But I couldn't set up as a locksmith under twenty pounds.

RANDALL:

Well, you can easily steal twenty pounds. You will find it in the nearest bank.

THE BURGLAR (*horrified*):

Oh what a thing for a gentleman to put into the head of a poor criminal scrambling out of the bottomless pit as it were! Oh, shame on you, sir! Oh, God forgive you! (*He throws himself into the big chair and covers his face as if in prayer*).

LADY UTTERWORD:

Really, Randall!

HECTOR:

It seems to me that we shall have to take up a collection for this inopportunely contrite sinner.

LADY UTTERWORD:
> But twenty pounds is ridiculous.

THE BURGLAR (*looking up quickly*):
> I shall have to buy a lot of tools, lady.

LADY UTTERWORD:
> Nonsense: you have your burgling kit.

THE BURGLAR:
> What's a jemmy and a centrebit and an acetylene welding plant and a bunch of skeleton keys? I shall want a forge, and a smithy, and a shop, and fittings. I can't hardly do it for twenty.

HECTOR:
> My worthy friend, we haven't got twenty pounds.

THE BURGLAR (*now master of the situation*):
> You can raise it among you, can't you?

MRS HUSHABYE:
> Give him a sovereign, Hector; and get rid of him.

HECTOR (*giving him a pound*):
> There! Off with you.

THE BURGLAR (*rising and taking the money very ungratefully*):
> I won't promise nothing. You have more on you than a quid: all the lot of you, I mean.

LADY UTTERWORD (*vigorously*):
> Oh, let us prosecute him and have done with it. I have a conscience too, I hope; and I do not feel at all sure that we have any right to let him go, especially if he is going to be greedy and impertinent.

THE BURGLAR (*quickly*):
> All right, lady, all right. I've no wish to be anything but agreeable. Good evening, ladies and gentlemen; and thank you kindly.

*He is hurrying out when he is confronted in the doorway by* Captain Shotover.

CAPTAIN SHOTOVER (*fixing the burglar with a piercing regard*):
> What's this? Are there two of you?

THE BURGLAR (*falling on his knees before the* Captain *in abject terror*):
> Oh my good Lord, what have I done? Don't tell me it's your house I've broken into, Captain Shotover.

*The* Captain *seizes him by the collar; drags him to his feet; and leads him to the middle of the group,* Hector *falling back beside his wife to make way for them.*

CAPTAIN SHOTOVER (*turning him towards* Ellie):
> Is that your daughter? (*He releases him*).

THE BURGLAR:

Well, how do I know, Captain? You know the sort of life you and me has led. Any young lady of that age might be my daughter anywhere in the wide world, as you might say.

CAPTAIN SHOTOVER (*to* Mazzini):

You are not Billy Dunn. This is Billy Dunn. Why have you imposed on me?

THE BURGLAR (*indignantly to* Mazzini):

Have you been giving yourself out to be me? You, that nigh blew my head off! Shooting yourself, in a manner of speaking!

MAZZINI:

My dear Captain Shotover, ever since I came into this house I have done hardly anything else but assure you that I am not Mr William Dunn, but Mazzini Dunn, a very different person.

THE BURGLAR:

He don't belong to my branch, Captain. There's two sets in the family: the thinking Dunns and the drinking Dunns, each going their own ways. I'm a drinking Dunn: he's a thinking Dunn. But that didn't give him any right to shoot me.

CAPTAIN SHOTOVER:

So you've turned burglar, have you?

THE BURGLAR:

No, Captain: I wouldn't disgrace our old sea calling by such a thing. I am no burglar.

LADY UTTERWORD:

What were you doing with my diamonds?

GUINNESS:

What did you break into the house for if you're no burglar?

RANDALL:

Mistook the house for your own and came in by the wrong window, eh?

THE BURGLAR:

Well, it's no use my telling you a lie: I can take in most captains, but not Captain Shotover, because he sold himself to the devil in Zanzibar, and can divine water, spot gold, explode a cartridge in your pocket with a glance of his eye, and see the truth hidden in the heart of man. But I'm no burglar.

CAPTAIN SHOTOVER:

Are you an honest man?

THE BURGLAR:

I don't set up to be better than my fellow-creatures, and never did, as you well know, Captain. But what I do is innocent and pious. I enquire about for houses where the right sort of people live. I work it on them same as I worked it here. I break into the house; put a few spoons or diamonds in my pocket; make a noise; get caught; and take up a collection. And you wouldn't believe how hard it is to get caught when you're actually trying to. I have knocked over all the chairs in a room without a soul paying any attention to me. In the end I have had to walk out and leave the job.

RANDALL:

When that happens, do you put back the spoons and diamonds?

THE BURGLAR:

Well, I don't fly in the face of Providence, if that's what you want to know.

CAPTAIN SHOTOVER:

Guinness: you remember this man?

NURSE GUINNESS:

I should think I do, seeing I was married to him, the blackguard!

MRS HUSHABYE:    } *exclaiming* { Married to him!
LADY UTTERWORD: }  *together*   { Guinness!!

THE BURGLAR:

It wasn't legal. I've been married to no end of women. No use coming that over me.

CAPTAIN SHOTOVER:

Take him to the forecastle (*he flings him to the door with a strength beyond his years*).

NURSE GUINNESS:

I suppose you mean the kitchen. They won't have him there. Do you expect servants to keep company with thieves and all sorts?

CAPTAIN SHOTOVER:

Land-thieves and water-thieves are the same flesh and blood. I'll have no boatswain on my quarter-deck. Off with you both.

THE BURGLAR:

Yes, Captain. (*He goes out humbly*).

MAZZINI:

Will it be safe to have him in the house like that?

NURSE GUINNESS:

Why didn't you shoot him, sir? If I'd known who he was, I'd have shot him myself. (*She goes out*).

MRS HUSHABYE:

Do sit down, everybody. (*She sits down on the sofa*).

*They all move except* Ellie. Mazzini *resumes his seat*. Randall *sits down in the window seat near the starboard door, again making a pendulum of his poker, and studying it as Galileo might have done.* Hector *sits on his left, in the middle.* Mangan, *forgotten, sits in the port corner.* Lady Utterword *takes the big chair.* Captain Shotover *goes into the pantry in deep abstraction. They all look after him; and* Lady Utterword *coughs consciously.*

MRS HUSHABYE:

So Billy Dunn was poor nurse's little romance. I knew there had been somebody.

RANDALL:

They will fight their battles over again and enjoy themselves immensely.

LADY UTTERWORD (*irritably*):

You are not married; and you know nothing about it, Randall. Hold your tongue.

RANDALL:

Tyrant!

MRS HUSHABYE:

Well, we have had a very exciting evening. Everything will be an anticlimax after it. We'd better all go to bed.

RANDALL:

Another burglar may turn up.

MAZZINI:

Oh, impossible! I hope not.

RANDALL:

Why not? There is more than one burglar in England.

MRS HUSHABYE:

What do you say, Alf?

MANGAN (*huffily*):

Oh, I don't matter. I'm forgotten. The burglar has put my nose out of joint. Shove me into a corner and have done with me.

MRS HUSHABYE (*jumping up mischievously, and going to him*):

Would you like a walk on the heath, Alfred? With me?

ELLIE:

Go, Mr Mangan. It will do you good. Hesione will soothe you.

MRS HUSHABYE (*slipping her arm under his and pulling him upright*):

Come, Alfred. There is a moon: it's like the night in Tristan and Isolde. (*She caresses his arm and draws him to the port garden door*).

MANGAN (*writhing but yielding*):

How you can have the face—the heart—(*he breaks down and is heard sobbing as she takes him out.*)

LADY UTTERWORD:

What an extraordinary way to behave! What is the matter with the man?

ELLIE (*in a strangely calm voice, staring into an imaginary distance*):

His heart is breaking: that is all. (*The* Captain *appears at the pantry door, listening*). It is a curious sensation: the sort of pain that goes mercifully beyond our powers of feeling. When your heart is broken, your boats are burned: nothing matters any more. It is the end of happiness and the beginning of peace.

LADY UTTERWORD (*suddenly rising in a rage, to the astonishment of the rest*):

How dare you?

HECTOR:

Good heavens! What's the matter?

RANDALL (*in a warning whisper*):

Tch—tch—tch! Steady.

ELLIE (*surprised and haughty*):

I was not addressing you particularly, Lady Utterword. And I am not accustomed to be asked how dare I.

LADY UTTERWORD:

Of course not. Anyone can see how badly you have been brought up.

MAZZINI:

Oh, I hope not, Lady Utterword. Really!

LADY UTTERWORD:

I know very well what you meant. The impudence!

ELLIE:

What on earth do you mean?

CAPTAIN SHOTOVER (*advancing to the table*):

She means that her heart will not break. She has been longing all her life for someone to break it. At last she has become afraid she has none to break.

LADY UTTERWORD (*flinging herself on her knees and throwing her arms round him*):

Papa: don't say you think I've no heart.

CAPTAIN SHOTOVER (*raising her with grim tenderness*):

If you had no heart how could you want to have it broken, child?

HECTOR (*rising with a bound*):

Lady Utterword: you are not to be trusted. You have made a scene (*he runs out into the garden through the starboard door*).

LADY UTTERWORD:

Oh! Hector, Hector! (*she runs out after him*).

RANDALL:

Only nerves, I assure you. (*He rises and follows her, waving the poker in his agitation*):

Ariadne! Ariadne! For God's sake be careful. You will—(*he is gone*).

MAZZINI (*rising*):

How distressing! Can I do anything, I wonder?

CAPTAIN SHOTOVER (*promptly taking his chair and setting to work at the drawing-board*):

No. Go to bed. Goodnight.

MAZZINI (*bewildered*):

Oh! Perhaps you are right.

ELLIE:

Goodnight, dearest. (*She kisses him*).

MAZZINI:

Goodnight, love. (*He makes for the door, but turns aside to the bookshelves*). I'll just take a book (*he takes one*). Goodnight. (*He goes out, leaving* Ellie *alone with the* Captain).

*The* Captain *is intent on his drawing.* Ellie, *standing sentry over his chair, contemplates him for a moment.*

ELLIE:

Does nothing ever disturb you, Captain Shotover?

CAPTAIN SHOTOVER:

I've stood on the bridge for eighteen hours in a typhoon. Life here is stormier; but I can stand it.

ELLIE:

Do you think I ought to marry Mr Mangan?

CAPTAIN SHOTOVER (*never looking up*):

One rock is as good as another to be wrecked on.

ELLIE:

I am not in love with him.

CAPTAIN SHOTOVER:

Who said you were?

ELLIE:

You are not surprised?

CAPTAIN SHOTOVER:

Surprised! At my age!

ELLIE:

It seems to me quite fair. He wants me for one thing: I want him for another.

CAPTAIN SHOTOVER:

Money?

ELLIE:

Yes.

CAPTAIN SHOTOVER:
  Well, one turns the cheek: the other kisses it. One provides the cash: the other spends it.

ELLIE:
  Who will have the best of the bargain, I wonder?

CAPTAIN SHOTOVER:
  You. These fellows live in an office all day. You will have to put up with him from dinner to breakfast; but you will both be asleep most of that time. All day you will be quit of him; and you will be shopping with his money. If that is too much for you, marry a seafaring man: you will be bothered with him only three weeks in the year, perhaps.

ELLIE:
  That would be best of all, I suppose.

CAPTAIN SHOTOVER:
  It's a dangerous thing to be married right up to the hilt, like my daughter's husband. The man is at home all day, like a damned soul in hell.

ELLIE:
  I never thought of that before.

CAPTAIN SHOTOVER:
  If you're marrying for business, you can't be too businesslike.

ELLIE:
  Why do women always want other women's husbands?

CAPTAIN SHOTOVER:
  Why do horse-thieves prefer a horse that is broken-in to one that is wild?

ELLIE (*with a short laugh*):
  I suppose so. What a vile world it is!

CAPTAIN SHOTOVER:
  It doesn't concern me. I'm nearly out of it.

ELLIE:
  And I'm only just beginning.

CAPTAIN SHOTOVER:
  Yes; so look ahead.

ELLIE:
  Well, I think I am being very prudent.

CAPTAIN SHOTOVER:
  I didn't say prudent. I said look ahead.

ELLIE:
  What's the difference?

CAPTAIN SHOTOVER:
  It's prudent to gain the whole world and lose your own soul.

But don't forget that your soul sticks to you if you stick to it; but the world has a way of slipping through your fingers.

ELLIE (*wearily, leaving him and beginning to wander restlessly about the room*):

I'm sorry, Captain Shotover; but it's no use talking like that to me. Old-fashioned people are no use to me. Old-fashioned people think you can have a soul without money. They think the less money you have, the more soul you have. Young people nowadays know better. A soul is a very expensive thing to keep: much more so than a motor car.

CAPTAIN SHOTOVER:

Is it? How much does your soul eat?

ELLIE:

Oh, a lot. It eats music and pictures and books and mountains and lakes and beautiful things to wear and nice people to be with. In this country you can't have them without lots of money: that is why our souls are so horribly starved.

CAPTAIN SHOTOVER:

Mangan's soul lives on pigs' food.

ELLIE:

Yes: money is thrown away on him. I suppose his soul was starved when he was young. But it will not be thrown away on me. It is just because I want to save my soul that I am marrying for money. All the women who are not fools do.

CAPTAIN SHOTOVER:

There are other ways of getting money. Why don't you steal it?

ELLIE:

Because I don't want to go to prison.

CAPTAIN SHOTOVER:

Is that the only reason? Are you quite sure honesty has nothing to do with it?

ELLIE:

Oh, you are very very old-fashioned, Captain. Does any modern girl believe that the legal and illegal ways of getting money are the honest and dishonest ways? Mangan robbed my father and my father's friends. I should rob all the money back from Mangan if the police would let me. As they won't, I must get it back by marrying him.

CAPTAIN SHOTOVER:

I can't argue: I'm too old: my mind is made up and finished. All I can tell you is that, old-fashioned or new-fashioned, if you sell yourself, you deal your soul a blow that all the books and pictures and concerts and scenery in the world won't heal (*he gets up suddenly and makes for the pantry*).

ELLIE (*running after him and seizing him by the sleeve*):

Then why did you sell yourself to the devil in Zanzibar?

CAPTAIN SHOTOVER (*stopping, startled*):

What?

ELLIE:

You shall not run away before you answer. I have found out that trick of yours. If you sold yourself, why shouldn't I?

CAPTAIN SHOTOVER:

I had to deal with men so degraded that they wouldn't obey me unless I swore at them and kicked them and beat them with my fists. Foolish people took young thieves off the streets; flung them into a training ship where they were taught to fear the cane instead of fearing God; and thought they'd make men and sailors of them by private subscription. I tricked these thieves into believing I'd sold myself to the devil. It saved my soul from the kicking and swearing that was damning me by inches.

ELLIE (*releasing him*):

I shall pretend to sell myself to Boss Mangan to save my soul from the poverty that is damning me by inches.

CAPTAIN SHOTOVER:

Riches will damn you ten times deeper. Riches won't save even your body.

ELLIE:

Old-fashioned again. We know now that the soul is the body, and the body the soul. They tell us they are different because they want to persuade us that we can keep our souls if we let them make slaves of our bodies. I am afraid you are no use to me, Captain.

CAPTAIN SHOTOVER:

What did you expect? A Savior, eh? Are you old-fashioned enough to believe in that?

ELLIE:

No. But I thought you were very wise, and might help me. Now I have found you out. You pretend to be busy, and think of fine things to say, and run in and out to surprise people by saying them, and get away before they can answer you.

CAPTAIN SHOTOVER:

It confuses me to be answered. It discourages me. I cannot bear men and women. I have to run away. I must run away now (*he tries to*).

ELLIE (*again seizing his arm*):

You shall not run away from me. I can hypnotize you. You are the only person in the house I can say what I like to. I know you are fond of me. Sit down. (*She draws him to the sofa*).

CAPTAIN SHOTOVER (*yielding*):

Take care: I am in my dotage. Old men are dangerous: it doesn't matter to them what is going to happen to the world.

*They sit side by side on the sofa. She leans affectionately against him with her head on his shoulder and her eyes half closed.*

ELLIE (*dreamily*):

I should have thought nothing else mattered to old men. They can't be very interested in what is going to happen to themselves.

CAPTAIN SHOTOVER:

A man's interest in the world is only the overflow from his interest in himself. When you are a child your vessel is not yet full; so you care for nothing but your own affairs. When you grow up, your vessel overflows; and you are a politician, a philosopher, or an explorer and adventurer. In old age the vessel dries up: there is no overflow: you are a child again. I can give you the memories of my ancient wisdom: mere scraps and leavings; but I no longer really care for anything but my own little wants and hobbies. I sit here working out my old ideas as a means of destroying my fellow-creatures. I see my daughters and their men living foolish lives of romance and sentiment and snobbery. I see you, the younger generation, turning from their romance and sentiment and snobbery to money and comfort and hard common sense. I was ten times happier on the bridge in the typhoon, or frozen into Arctic ice for months in darkness, than you or they have ever been. You are looking for a rich husband. At your age I looked for hardship, danger, horror, and death, that I might feel the life in me more intensely. I did not let the fear of death govern my life; and my reward was, I had my life. You are going to let the fear of poverty govern your life; and your reward will be that you will eat, but you will not live.

ELLIE (*sitting up impatiently*):

But what can I do? I am not a sea captain: I can't stand on bridges in typhoons, or go slaughtering seals and whales in Greenland's icy mountains. They won't let women be captains. Do you want me to be a stewardess?

CAPTAIN SHOTOVER:

There are worse lives. The stewardesses could come ashore if they liked; but they sail and sail and sail.

ELLIE:

What could they do ashore but marry for money? I don't want to be a stewardess: I am too bad a sailor. Think of something else for me.

CAPTAIN SHOTOVER:

I can't think so long and continuously. I am too old. I must go in and out. (*He tries to rise*).

ELLIE (*pulling him back*):

You shall not. You are happy here, aren't you?

CAPTAIN SHOTOVER:

I tell you it's dangerous to keep me. I can't keep awake and alert.

ELLIE:

What do you run away for? To sleep?

CAPTAIN SHOTOVER:

No. To get a glass of rum.

ELLIE (*frightfully disillusioned*):

Is that it? How disgusting! Do you like being drunk?

CAPTAIN SHOTOVER:

No: I dread being drunk more than anything in the world. To be drunk means to have dreams; to go soft; to be easily pleased and deceived; to fall into the clutches of women. Drink does that for you when you are young. But when you are old: very very old, like me, the dreams come by themselves. You don't know how terrible that is: you are young: you sleep at night only, and sleep soundly. But later on you will sleep in the afternoon. Later still you will sleep even in the morning; and you will awake tired, tired of life. You will never be free from dozing and dreams: the dreams will steal upon your work every ten minutes unless you can awaken yourself with rum. I drink now to keep sober; but the dreams are conquering: rum is not what it was: I have had ten glasses since you came; and it might be so much water. Go get me another: Guinness knows where it is. You had better see for yourself the horror of an old man drinking.

ELLIE:

You shall not drink. Dream. I like you to dream. You must never be in the real world when we talk together.

CAPTAIN SHOTOVER:

I am too weary to resist or too weak. I am in my second childhood. I do not see you as you really are. I can't remember what I really am. I feel nothing but the accursed happiness I have dreaded all my life long: the happiness that comes as life goes, the happiness of yielding and dreaming instead of resisting and doing, the sweetness of the fruit that is going rotten.

ELLIE:

You dread it almost as much as I used to dread losing my dreams and having to fight and do things. But that is all over for me: my dreams are dashed to pieces. I should like to marry a very old, very rich man. I should like to marry you. I had much rather marry you than marry Mangan. Are you very rich?

CAPTAIN SHOTOVER:

No. Living from hand to mouth. And I have a wife somewhere in Jamaica: a black one. My first wife. Unless she's dead.

ELLIE:

What a pity! I feel so happy with you. (*She takes his hand, almost unconsciously, and pats it*). I thought I should never feel happy again.

CAPTAIN SHOTOVER:

Why?

ELLIE:

Don't you know?

CAPTAIN SHOTOVER:

No.

ELLIE:

Heartbreak. I fell in love with Hector, and didn't know he was married.

CAPTAIN SHOTOVER:

Heartbreak? Are you one of those who are so sufficient to themselves that they are only happy when they are stripped of everything, even of hope?

ELLIE (*gripping the hand*):

It seems so; for I feel now as if there was nothing I could not do, because I want nothing.

CAPTAIN SHOTOVER:

That's the only real strength. That's genius. That's better than rum.

ELLIE (*throwing away his hand*):

Rum! Why did you spoil it?

Hector *and* Randall *come in from the garden through the starboard door.*

HECTOR:

I beg your pardon. We did not know there was anyone here.

ELLIE (*rising*):

That means that you want to tell Mr Randall the story about the tiger. Come, Captain: I want to talk to my father; and you had better come with me.

CAPTAIN SHOTOVER (*rising*):

Nonsense! the man is in bed.

ELLIE:

Aha! I've caught you. My real father has gone to bed; but the father you gave me is in the kitchen. You knew quite well all along. Come. (*She draws him out into the garden with her through the port door*).

HECTOR:

That's an extraordinary girl. She has the Ancient Mariner on a string like a Pekinese dog.

RANDALL:

Now that they have gone, shall we have a friendly chat?

HECTOR:

You are in what is supposed to be my house. I am at your disposal.

Hector *sits down in the draughtsman's chair, turning it to face* Randall, *who remains standing, leaning at his ease against the carpenter's bench.*

RANDALL:

I take it that we may be quite frank. I mean about Lady Utterword.

HECTOR:

You may. I have nothing to be frank about. I never met her until this afternoon.

RANDALL (*straightening up*):

What! But you are her sister's husband.

HECTOR:

Well, if you come to that, you are her husband's brother.

RANDALL:

But you seem to be on intimate terms with her.

HECTOR:

So do you.

RANDALL:

Yes; but I am on intimate terms with her. I have known her for years.

HECTOR:

It took her years to get to the same point with you that she got to with me in five minutes, it seems.

RANDALL (*vexed*):

Really, Ariadne is the limit (*he moves away huffishly towards the windows*).

HECTOR (*coolly*):

She is, as I remarked to Hesione, a very enterprising woman.

RANDALL (*returning, much troubled*):

You see, Hushabye, you are what women consider a good-looking man.

HECTOR:

I cultivated that appearance in the days of my vanity; and Hesione insists on my keeping it up. She makes me wear these ridiculous things (*indicating his Arab costume*) because she thinks me absurd in evening dress.

RANDALL:

Still, you do keep it up, old chap. Now, I assure you I have not an atom of jealousy in my disposition—

HECTOR:

The question would seem to be rather whether your brother has any touch of that sort.

RANDALL:

What! Hastings! Oh, don't trouble about Hastings. He has the gift of being able to work sixteen hours a day at the dullest detail, and actually likes it. That gets him to the top wherever he goes. As long as Ariadne takes care that he is fed regularly, he is only too thankful to anyone who will keep her in good humour for him.

HECTOR:

And as she has all the Shotover fascination, there is plenty of competition for the job, eh?

RANDALL (*angrily*):

She encourages them. Her conduct is perfectly scandalous. I assure you, my dear fellow, I haven't an atom of jealousy in my composition; but she makes herself the talk of every place she goes to by her thoughtlessness. It's nothing more: she doesn't really care for the men she keeps hanging about her; but how is the world to know that? It's not fair to Hastings. It's not fair to me.

HECTOR:

Her theory is that her conduct is so correct—

RANDALL:

Correct! She does nothing but make scenes from morning till night. You be careful, old chap. She will get you into trouble: that is, she would if she really cared for you.

HECTOR:

Doesn't she?

RANDALL:

Not a scrap. She may want your scalp to add to her collection; but her true affection has been engaged years ago. You had really better be careful.

HECTOR:

Do you suffer much from this jealousy?

RANDALL:

Jealousy! I jealous! My dear fellow, haven't I told you that there is not an atom of—

HECTOR:

Yes. And Lady Utterword told me she never made scenes. Well, don't waste your jealousy on my moustache. Never waste jealousy on a real man: it is the imaginary hero that supplants us all in the long run. Besides, jealousy does not belong to your easy man-of-the-world pose, which you carry so well in other respects.

RANDALL:

Really, Hushabye, I think a man may be allowed to be a gentleman without being accused of posing.

HECTOR:

It is a pose like any other. In this house we know all the poses: our game is to find out the man under the pose. The man under your pose is apparently Ellie's favorite, Othello.

RANDALL:

Some of your games in this house are damned annoying, let me tell you.

HECTOR:

Yes: I have been their victim for many years. I used to writhe under them at first; but I became accustomed to them. At last I learned to play them.

RANDALL:

If it's all the same to you, I had rather you didn't play them on me. You evidently don't quite understand my character, or my notions of good form.

HECTOR:

Is it your notion of good form to give away Lady Utterword?

RANDALL (*a childishly plaintive note breaking into his huff*):

I have not said a word against Lady Utterword. This is just the conspiracy over again.

HECTOR:

What conspiracy?

RANDALL:

You know very well, sir. A conspiracy to make me out to be pettish and jealous and childish and everything I am not. Everyone knows I am just the opposite.

HECTOR (*rising*):

Something in the air of the house has upset you. It often does have that effect. (*He goes to the garden door and calls* Lady Utterword *with commanding emphasis*) Ariadne!

LADY UTTERWORD (*at some distance*):

>Yes.

RANDALL:

>What are you calling her for? I want to speak—

LADY UTTERWORD (*arriving breathless*):

>Yes. You really are a terribly commanding person. What's the matter?

HECTOR:

>I do not know how to manage your friend Randall. No doubt you do.

LADY UTTERWORD:

>Randall: have you been making yourself ridiculous, as usual? I can see it in your face. Really, you are the most pettish creature.

RANDALL:

>You know quite well, Ariadne, that I have not an ounce of pettishness in my disposition. I have made myself perfectly pleasant here. I have remained absolutely cool and imperturbable in the face of a burglar. Imperturbability is almost too strong a point of mine. But (*putting his foot down with a stamp, and walking angrily up and down the room*) I insist on being treated with a certain consideration. I will not allow Hushabye to take liberties with me. I will not stand your encouraging people as you do.

HECTOR:

>The man has a rooted delusion that he is your husband.

LADY UTTERWORD:

>I know. He is jealous. As if he had any right to be! He compromises me everywhere. He makes scenes all over the place. Randall: I will not allow it. I simply will not allow it. You had no right to discuss me with Hector. I will not be discussed by men.

HECTOR:

>Be reasonable, Ariadne. Your fatal gift of beauty forces men to discuss you.

LADY UTTERWORD:

>Oh indeed! what about your fatal gift of beauty?

HECTOR:

>How can I help it?

LADY UTTERWORD:

>You could cut off your moustache: I can't cut off my nose. I get my whole life messed up with people falling in love with me. And then Randall says I run after men.

RANDALL:

>I—

LADY UTTERWORD:

> Yes you do: you said it just now. Why can't you think of something else than women? Napoleon was quite right when he said that women are the occupation of the idle man. Well, if ever there was an idle man on earth, his name is Randall Utterword.

RANDALL:

> Ariad—

LADY UTTERWORD (*overwhelming him with a torrent of words*):

> Oh yes you are: it's no use denying it. What have you ever done? What good are you? You are as much trouble in the house as a child of three. You couldn't live without your valet.

RANDALL:

> This is—

LADY UTTERWORD:

> Laziness! You are laziness incarnate. You are selfishness itself. You are the most uninteresting man on earth. You can't even gossip about anything but yourself and your grievances and your ailments and the people who have offended you. (*Turning to* Hector) Do you know what they call him, Hector?

HECTOR: ⎱ (*speaking* ⎰ Please don't tell me.
RANDALL: ⎰ *together*) ⎱ I'll not stand it—

LADY UTTERWORD:

> Randall the Rotter: that is his name in good society.

RANDALL (*shouting*):

> I'll not bear it, I tell you. Will you listen to me, you infernal—(*he chokes*).

LADY UTTERWORD:

> Well: go on. What were you going to call me? An infernal what? Which unpleasant animal is it to be this time?

RANDALL (*foaming*):

> There is no animal in the world so hateful as a woman can be. You are a maddening devil. Hushabye: you will not believe me when I tell you that I have loved this demon all my life; but God knows I have paid for it (*he sits down in the draughtsman's chair, weeping*).

LADY UTTERWORD (*standing over him with triumphant contempt*):

> Cry-baby!

HECTOR (*gravely, coming to him*):

> My friend: the Shotover sisters have two strange powers over men. They can make them love; and they can make them cry. Thank your stars that you are not married to one of them.

LADY UTTERWORD (*haughtily*):

And pray, Hector—

HECTOR (*suddenly catching her round the shoulders; swinging her right round him and away from* Randall; *and gripping her throat with the other hand*):

Ariadne: if you attempt to start on me, I'll choke you: do you hear? The cat-and-mouse game with the other sex is a good game; but I can play your head off at it. (*He throws her, not at all gently, into the big chair, and proceeds, less fiercely but firmly*) It is true that Napoleon said that woman is the occupation of the idle man. But he added that she is the relaxation of the warrior. Well, *I* am the warrior. So take care.

LADY UTTERWORD (*not in the least put out, and rather pleased by his violence*):

My dear Hector: I have only done what you asked me to do.

HECTOR:

How do you make that out, pray?

LADY UTTERWORD:

You called me in to manage Randall, didn't you? You said you couldn't manage him yourself.

HECTOR:

Well, what if I did? I did not ask you to drive the man mad.

LADY UTTERWORD:

He isn't mad. That's the way to manage him. If you were a mother, you'd understand.

HECTOR:

Mother! What are you up to now?

LADY UTTERWORD:

It's quite simple. When the children got nerves and were naughty, I smacked them just enough to give them a good cry and a healthy nervous shock. They went to sleep and were quite good afterwards. Well, I can't smack Randall: he is too big; so when he gets nerves and is naughty, I just rag him till he cries. He will be all right now. Look: he is half asleep already (*which is quite true*).

RANDALL (*waking up indignantly*):

I'm not. You are most cruel, Ariadne. (*Sentimentally*) But I suppose I must forgive you, as usual (*he checks himself in the act of yawning*).

LADY UTTERWORD (*to* Hector):

Is the explanation satisfactory, dread warrior?

HECTOR:

Some day I shall kill you, if you go too far. I thought you were a fool.

LADY UTTERWORD (*laughing*):

Everybody does, at first. But I am not such a fool as I look. (*She rises complacently*). Now, Randall: go to bed. You will be a good boy in the morning.

RANDALL (*only very faintly rebellious*):

I'll go to bed when I like. It isn't ten yet.

LADY UTTERWORD:

It is long past ten. See that he goes to bed at once, Hector. (*She goes into the garden*).

HECTOR:

Is there any slavery on earth viler than this slavery of men to women?

RANDALL (*rising resolutely*):

I'll not speak to her tomorrow. I'll not speak to her for another week. I'll give her such a lesson. I'll go straight to bed without bidding her goodnight. (*He makes for the door leading to the hall*).

HECTOR:

You are under a spell, man. Old Shotover sold himself to the devil in Zanzibar. The devil gave him a black witch for a wife; and these two demon daughters are their mystical progeny. I am tied to Hesione's apronstring; but I'm her husband; and if I did go stark staring mad about her, at least we became man and wife. But why should you let yourself be dragged about and beaten by Ariadne as a toy donkey is dragged about and beaten by a child? What do you get by it? Are you her lover?

RANDALL:

You must not misunderstand me. In a higher sense—in a Platonic sense—

HECTOR:

Psha! Platonic sense! She makes you her servant; and when pay-day comes round, she bilks you: that is what you mean.

RANDALL (*feebly*):

Well, if I don't mind, I don't see what business it is of yours. Besides, I tell you I am going to punish her. You shall see: *I* know how to deal with women. I'm really very sleepy. Say goodnight to Mrs Hushabye for me, will you, like a good chap. Goodnight. (*He hurries out*).

HECTOR:

Poor wretch! Oh women! women! women! (*He lifts his fists in invocation to heaven*) Fall. Fall and crush. (*He goes out into the garden*).

# Act III

*In the garden,* Hector, *as he comes out through the glass door of the poop, finds* Lady Utterword *lying voluptuously in the hammock on the east side of the flagstaff, in the circle of light cast by the electric arc, which is like a moon on its opal globe. Beneath the head of the hammock, a campstool. On the other side of the flagstaff, on the long garden seat,* Captain Shotover *is asleep, with* Ellie *beside him, leaning affectionately against him on his right hand. On his left is a deck chair. Behind them in the gloom,* Hesione *is strolling about with* Mangan. *It is a fine still night, moonless.*

LADY UTTERWORD:

> What a lovely night! It seems made for us.

HECTOR:

> The night takes no interest in us. What are we to the night? (*He sits down moodily in the deck chair*).

ELLIE (*dreamily, nestling against the* Captain):

> Its beauty soaks into my nerves. In the night there is peace for the old and hope for the young.

HECTOR:

> Is that remark your own?

ELLIE:

> No. Only the last thing the Captain said before he went to sleep.

CAPTAIN SHOTOVER:

> I'm not asleep.

HECTOR:

> Randall is. Also Mr Mazzini Dunn. Mangan too, probably.

MANGAN:

> No.

HECTOR:

> Oh, you are there. I thought Hesione would have sent you to bed by this time.

MRS HUSHABYE (*coming to the back of the garden seat, into the light, with* Mangan):

> I think I shall. He keeps telling me he has a presentiment that he is going to die. I never met a man so greedy for sympathy.

MANGAN (*plaintively*):

> But I have a presentiment. I really have. And you wouldn't listen.

MRS HUSHABYE:

> I was listening for something else. There was a sort of splendid drumming in the sky. Did none of you hear it? It came from a distance and then died away.

MANGAN:

I tell you it was a train.

MRS HUSHABYE:

And *I* tell you, Alf, there is no train at this hour. The last is nine fortyfive.

MANGAN:

But a goods train.

MRS HUSHABYE:

Not on our little line. They tack a truck on to the passenger train. What can it have been, Hector?

HECTOR:

Heaven's threatening growl of disgust at us useless futile creatures. (*Fiercely*) I tell you, one of two things must happen. Either out of that darkness some new creation will come to supplant us as we have supplanted the animals, or the heavens will fall in thunder and destroy us.

LADY UTTERWORD (*in a cool instructive manner, wallowing comfortably in her hammock*):

We have not supplanted the animals, Hector. Why do you ask heaven to destroy this house, which could be made quite comfortable if Hesione had any notion of how to live? Don't you know what is wrong with it?

HECTOR:

We are wrong with it. There is no sense in us. We are useless, dangerous, and ought to be abolished.

LADY UTTERWORD:

Nonsense! Hastings told me the very first day he came here, nearly twentyfour years ago, what is wrong with the house.

CAPTAIN SHOTOVER:

What! The numskull said there was something wrong with my house!

LADY UTTERWORD:

I said Hastings said it; and he is not in the least a numskull.

CAPTAIN SHOTOVER:

What's wrong with my house?

LADY UTTERWORD:

Just what is wrong with a ship, papa. Wasn't it clever of Hastings to see that?

CAPTAIN SHOTOVER:

The man's a fool. There's nothing wrong with a ship.

LADY UTTERWORD:

Yes there is.

MRS HUSHABYE:

But what is it? Don't be aggravating, Addy.

LADY UTTERWORD:

Guess.

HECTOR:

Demons. Daughters of the witch of Zanzibar. Demons.

LADY UTTERWORD:

Not a bit. I assure you, all this house needs to make it a sensible, healthy, pleasant house, with good appetites and sound sleep in it, is horses.

MRS HUSHABYE:

Horses! What rubbish!

LADY UTTERWORD:

Yes: horses. Why have we never been able to let this house? Because there are no proper stables. Go anywhere in England where there are natural, wholesome, contented, and really nice English people; and what do you always find? That the stables are the real centre of the household; and that if any visitor wants to play the piano the whole room has to be upset before it can be opened, there are so many things piled on it. I never lived until I learned to ride; and I shall never ride really well because I didn't begin as a child. There are only two classes in good society in England: the equestrian classes and the neurotic classes. It isn't mere convention: everybody can see that the people who hunt are the right people and the people who don't are the wrong ones.

CAPTAIN SHOTOVER:

There is some truth in this. My ship made a man of me; and a ship is the horse of the sea.

LADY UTTERWORD:

Exactly how Hastings explained your being a gentleman.

CAPTAIN SHOTOVER:

Not bad for a numskull. Bring the man here with you next time: I must talk to him.

LADY UTTERWORD:

Why is Randall such an obvious rotter? He is well bred; he has been at a public school and a university; he has been in the Foreign Office; he knows the best people and has lived all his life among them. Why is he so unsatisfactory, so contemptible? Why can't he get a valet to stay with him longer than a few months? Just because he is too lazy and pleasure-loving to hunt and shoot. He strums the piano, and sketches, and runs after married women, and reads literary books and poems. He actually plays the flute; but I never let him bring it into my house. If he would only—(*she is interrupted by the melancholy strains of a flute coming from an open window above. She raises herself indig-*

*nantly in the hammock*). Randall: you have not gone to bed. Have you been listening? (*The flute replies pertly:*)

How vulgar! Go to bed instantly, Randall: how dare you? (*The window is slammed down. She subsides*). How can anyone care for such a creature!

MRS HUSHABYE:

Addy: do you think Ellie ought to marry poor Alfred merely for his money?

MANGAN (*much alarmed*):

What's that? Mrs Hushabye: are my affairs to be discussed like this before everybody?

LADY UTTERWORD:

I don't think Randall is listening now.

MANGAN:

Everybody is listening. It isn't right.

MRS HUSHABYE:

But in the dark, what does it matter? Ellie doesn't mind. Do you, Ellie?

ELLIE:

Not in the least. What is your opinion, Lady Utterword? You have so much good sense.

MANGAN:

But it isn't right. It—(Mrs Hushabye *puts her hand on his mouth*). Oh, very well.

LADY UTTERWORD:

How much money have you, Mr Mangan?

MANGAN:

Really—No: I can't stand this.

LADY UTTERWORD:

Nonsense, Mr Mangan! It all turns on your income, doesn't it?

MANGAN:

Well, if you come to that, how much money has she?

ELLIE:

None.

LADY UTTERWORD:

You are answered, Mr Mangan. And now, as you have made Miss Dunn throw her cards on the table, you cannot refuse to shew your own.

MRS HUSHABYE:

Come, Alf! out with it! How much?

MANGAN (*baited out of all prudence*):

Well, if you want to know, I have no money and never had any.

MRS HUSHABYE:

Alfred: you mustn't tell naughty stories.

MANGAN:

I'm not telling you stories. I'm telling you the raw truth.

LADY UTTERWORD:

Then what do you live on, Mr Mangan?

MANGAN:

Travelling expenses. And a trifle of commission.

CAPTAIN SHOTOVER:

What more have any of us but travelling expenses for our life's journey?

MRS HUSHABYE:

But you have factories and capital and things?

MANGAN:

People think I have. People think I'm an industrial Napoleon. That's why Miss Ellie wants to marry me. But I tell you I have nothing.

ELLIE:

Do you mean that the factories are like Marcus's tigers? That they don't exist?

MANGAN:

They exist all right enough. But they're not mine. They belong to syndicates and shareholders and all sorts of lazy good-for-nothing capitalists. I get money from such people to start the factories. I find people like Miss Dunn's father to work them, and keep a tight hand so as to make them pay. Of course I make them keep me going pretty well; but it's a dog's life; and I don't own anything.

MRS HUSHABYE:

Alfred, Alfred: you are making a poor mouth of it to get out of marrying Ellie.

MANGAN:

I'm telling the truth about my money for the first time in my life; and it's the first time my word has ever been doubted.

LADY UTTERWORD:

How sad! Why don't you go in for politics, Mr Mangan?

MANGAN:

Go in for politics! Where have you been living? I am in politics.

LADY UTTERWORD:

I'm sure I beg your pardon. I never heard of you.

MANGAN:

Let me tell you, Lady Utterword, that the Prime Minister of this country asked me to join the Government without even going through the nonsense of an election, as the dictator of a great public department.

LADY UTTERWORD:

As a Conservative or a Liberal?

MANGAN:

No such nonsense. As a practical business man. (*They all burst out laughing*). What are you all laughing at?

MRS HUSHABYE:

Oh, Alfred, Alfred!

ELLIE:

You! who have to get my father to do everything for you!

MRS HUSHABYE:

You! who are afraid of your own workmen!

HECTOR:

You! with whom three women have been playing cat and mouse all the evening!

LADY UTTERWORD:

You must have given an immense sum to the party funds, Mr Mangan.

MANGAN:

Not a penny out of my own pocket. The syndicate found the money: they knew how useful I should be to them in the Government.

LADY UTTERWORD:

This is most interesting and unexpected, Mr Mangan. And what have your administrative achievements been, so far?

MANGAN:

Achievements? Well, I don't know what you call achievements; but I've jolly well put a stop to the games of the other fellows in the other departments. Every man of them thought he was going to save the country all by himself, and do me out of the credit and out of my chance of a title. I took good care that if they wouldn't let me do it they shouldn't do it themselves either. I may not know anything about my own machinery; but I know how to stick a ramrod into the other fellow's. And now they all look the biggest fools going.

HECTOR:

And in heaven's name, what do you look like?

MANGAN:

> I look like the fellow that was too clever for all the others, don't I? If that isn't a triumph of practical business, what is?

HECTOR:

> Is this England, or is it a madhouse?

LADY UTTERWORD:

> Do you expect to save the country, Mr Mangan?

MANGAN:

> Well, who else will? Will your Mr Randall save it?

LADY UTTERWORD:

> Randall the Rotter! Certainly not.

MANGAN:

> Will your brother-in-law save it with his moustache and his fine talk.

HECTOR:

> Yes, if they will let me.

MANGAN (*sneering*):

> Ah! Will they let you?

HECTOR:

> No. They prefer you.

MANGAN:

> Very well then, as you're in a world where I'm appreciated and you're not, you'd best be civil to me, hadn't you? Who else is there but me?

LADY UTTERWORD:

> There is Hastings. Get rid of your ridiculous sham democracy; and give Hastings the necessary powers, and a good supply of bamboo to bring the British native to his senses: he will save the country with the greatest ease.

CAPTAIN SHOTOVER:

> It had better be lost. Any fool can govern with a stick in his hand. *I* could govern that way. It is not God's way: The man is a numskull.

LADY UTTERWORD:

> The man is worth all of you rolled into one. What do you say, Miss Dunn?

ELLIE:

> I think my father would do very well if people did not put upon him and cheat him and despise him because he is so good.

MANGAN (*contemptuously*):

> I think I see Mazzini Dunn getting into parliament or pushing his way into the Government. We've not come to that yet, thank God! What do you say, Mrs Hushabye?

MRS HUSHABYE:

Oh, *I* say it matters very little which of you governs the country so long as we govern you.

HECTOR:

We? Who is we, pray?

MRS HUSHABYE:

The devil's granddaughters, dear. The lovely women.

HECTOR (*raising his hands as before*):

Fall, I say; and deliver us from the lures of Satan!

ELLIE:

There seems to be nothing real in the world except my father and Shakespeare. Marcus's tigers are false; Mr Mangan's millions are false; there is nothing really strong and true about Hesione but her beautiful black hair; and Lady Utterword's is too pretty to be real. The one thing that was left to me was the Captain's seventh degree of concentration; and that turns out to be—

CAPTAIN SHOTOVER:

Rum.

LADY UTTERWORD (*placidly*):

A good deal of my hair is quite genuine. The Duchess of Dithering offered me fifty guineas for this (*touching her forehead*) under the impression that it was a transformation; but it is all natural except the color.

MANGAN (*wildly*):

Look here: I'm going to take off all my clothes (*he begins tearing off his coat.*)

| LADY UTTERWORD: | | | Mr Mangan! |
| CAPTAIN SHOTOVER: | (*in | Whats's that? |
| HECTOR: | consternation*) | Ha! ha! Do. Do. |
| ELLIE: | | | Please don't. |

MRS HUSHABYE (*catching his arm and stopping him*):

Alfred: for shame! Are you mad?

MANGAN:

Shame! What shame is there in this house? Let's all strip stark naked. We may as well do the thing thoroughly when we're about it. We've stripped ourselves morally naked: well, let us strip ourselves physically naked as well, and see how we like it. I tell you I can't bear this. I was brought up to be respectable. I don't mind the women dyeing their hair and the men drinking: it's human nature. But it's not human nature to tell everybody about it. Every time one of you opens your mouth I go like this (*he cowers as if to avoid a missile*) afraid of what will come next. How are we to have any self-respect if we don't keep it up that we're better than we really are?

LADY UTTERWORD:

> I quite sympathize with you, Mr Mangan. I have been through it all; and I know by experience that men and women are delicate plants and must be cultivated under glass. Our family habit of throwing stones in all directions and letting the air in is not only unbearably rude, but positively dangerous. Still, there is no use catching physical colds as well as moral ones; so please keep your clothes on.

MANGAN:

> I'll do as I like: not what you tell me. Am I a child or a grown man? I won't stand this mothering tyranny. I'll go back to the city, where I'm respected and made much of.

MRS HUSHABYE:

> Goodbye, Alf. Think of us sometimes in the city. Think of Ellie's youth!

ELLIE:

> Think of Hesione's eyes and hair!

CAPTAIN SHOTOVER:

> Think of this garden in which you are not a dog barking to keep the truth out!

HECTOR:

> Think of Lady Utterword's beauty! her good sense! her style!

LADY UTTERWORD:

> Flatterer. Think, Mr Mangan, whether you can really do any better for yourself elsewhere: that is the essential point, isn't it?

MANGAN (*surrendering*):

> All right: all right. I'm done. Have it your own way. Only let me alone. I don't know whether I'm on my head or my heels when you all start on me like this. I'll stay. I'll marry her. I'll do anything for a quiet life. Are you satisfied now?

ELLIE:

> No. I never really intended to make you marry me, Mr Mangan. Never in the depths of my soul. I only wanted to feel my strength: to know that you could not escape if I chose to take you.

MANGAN (*indignantly*):

> What! Do you mean to say you are going to throw me over after my acting so handsome?

LADY UTTERWORD:

> I should not be too hasty, Miss Dunn. You can throw Mr Mangan over at any time up to the last moment. Very few men in his position go bankrupt. You can live very comfortably on his reputation for immense wealth.

ELLIE:

  I cannot commit bigamy, Lady Utterword.

| MRS HUSHABYE: | | | Bigamy! Whatever on earth are you talking about, Ellie? |
|---|---|---|---|
| LADY UTTERWORD: | *(exclaiming all together)* | | Bigamy! What do you mean, Miss Dunn? |
| MANGAN: | | | Bigamy! Do you mean to say you're married already? |
| HECTOR: | | | Bigamy! This is some enigma. |

ELLIE:

  Only half an hour ago I became Captain Shotover's white wife.

MRS HUSHABYE:

  Ellie! What nonsense! Where?

ELLIE:

  In heaven, where all true marriages are made.

LADY UTTERWORD:

  Really, Miss Dunn! Really, papa!

MANGAN:

  He told me *I* was too old! And him a mummy!

HECTOR (*quoting Shelley*):

  Their altar the grassy earth outspread,
  And their priest the muttering wind.

ELLIE:

  Yes: I, Ellie Dunn, give my broken heart and my strong sound soul to its natural captain, my spiritual husband and second father.

*She draws the* Captain's *arm through hers, and pats his hand. The* Captain *remains fast asleep.*

MRS HUSHABYE:

  Oh, that's very clever of you, pettikins. Very clever. Alfred: you could never have lived up to Ellie. You must be content with a little share of me.

MANGAN (*sniffing and wiping his eyes*):

  It isn't kind—(*his emotion chokes him*).

LADY UTTERWORD:

  You are well out of it, Mr Mangan. Miss Dunn is the most conceited young woman I have met since I came back to England.

MRS HUSHABYE:

  Oh, Ellie isn't conceited. Are you, pettikins?

ELLIE:

I know my strength now, Hesione.

MANGAN:

Brazen, I call you. Brazen.

MRS HUSHABYE:

Tut tut, Alfred: don't be rude. Don't you feel how lovely this marriage night is, made in heaven? Aren't you happy, you and Hector? Open your eyes: Addy and Ellie look beautiful enough to please the most fastidious man: we live and love and have not a care in the world. We women have managed all that for you. Why in the name of common sense do you go on as if you were two miserable wretches?

CAPTAIN SHOTOVER:

I tell you happiness is no good. You can be happy when you are only half alive. I am happier now I am half dead than ever I was in my prime. But there is no blessing on my happiness.

ELLIE (*her face lighting up*):

Life with a blessing! that is what I want. Now I know the real reason why I couldn't marry Mr Mangan: there would be no blessing on our marriage. There is a blessing on my broken heart. There is a blessing on your beauty, Hesione. There is a blessing on your father's spirit. Even on the lies of Marcus there is a blessing; but on Mr Mangan's money there is none.

MANGAN:

I don't understand a word of that.

ELLIE:

Neither do I. But I know it means something.

MANGAN:

Don't say there was any difficulty about the blessing. I was ready to get a bishop to marry us.

MRS HUSHABYE:

Isn't he a fool, pettikins?

HECTOR (*fiercely*):

Do not scorn the man. We are all fools.

Mazzini, *in pyjamas and a richly colored silk dressing-gown, comes from the house, on* Lady Utterword's *side.*

MRS HUSHABYE:

Oh! here comes the only man who ever resisted me. What's the matter, Mr Dunn? Is the house on fire?

MAZZINI:

Oh no: nothing's the matter; but really it's impossible to go to sleep with such an interesting conversation going on under one's window, and on such a beautiful night too. I just had to come down and join you all. What has it all been about?

MRS HUSHABYE:

Oh, wonderful things, soldier of freedom.

HECTOR:

For example, Mangan, as a practical business man, has tried to undress himself and has failed ignominiously; whilst you, as an idealist, have succeeded brilliantly.

MAZZINI:

I hope you don't mind my being like this, Mrs Hushabye. (*He sits down on the campstool*).

MRS HUSHABYE:

On the contrary, I could wish you always like that.

LADY UTTERWORD:

Your daughter's match is off, Mr Dunn. It seems that Mr Mangan, whom we all supposed to be a man of property, owns absolutely nothing.

MAZZINI:

Well of course I knew that, Lady Utterword. But if people believe in him and are always giving him money, whereas they don't believe in me and never give me any, how can I ask poor Ellie to depend on what I can do for her?

MANGAN:

Don't you run away with this idea that I have nothing. I—

HECTOR:

Oh, don't explain. We understand. You have a couple of thousand pounds in exchequer bills, 50,000 shares worth tenpence a dozen, and half a dozen tabloids of cyanide of potassium to poison yourself with when you are found out. That's the reality of your millions.

MAZZINI:

Oh no, no, no. He is quite honest: the businesses are genuine and perfectly legal.

HECTOR (*disgusted*):

Yah! Not even a great swindler!

MANGAN:

So you think. But I've been too many for some honest men, for all that.

LADY UTTERWORD:

There is no pleasing you, Mr Mangan. You are determined to be neither rich nor poor, honest nor dishonest.

MANGAN:

There you go again. Ever since I came into this silly house I

have been made to look like a fool, though I'm as good a man
in this house as in the city.

ELLIE (*musically*):

Yes: this silly house, this strangely happy house, this agonizing
house, this house without foundations. I shall call it Heartbreak House.

MRS HUSHABYE:

Stop, Ellie; or I shall howl like an animal.

MANGAN (*breaks into a low snivelling*):

!!!

MRS HUSHABYE:

There! you have set Alfred off.

ELLIE:

I like him best when he is howling.

CAPTAIN SHOTOVER:

Silence! (Mangan *subsides into silence*). I say, let the heart break
in silence.

HECTOR:

Do you accept that name for your house?

CAPTAIN SHOTOVER:

It is not my house: it is only my kennel.

HECTOR:

We have been too long here. We do not live in this house: we
haunt it.

LADY UTTERWORD (*heart torn*):

It is dreadful to think how you have been here all these years
while I have gone round the world. I escaped young; but it has
drawn me back. It wants to break my heart too. But it shan't. I
have left you and it behind. It was silly of me to come back.
I felt sentimental about papa and Hesione and the old place. I
felt them calling to me.

MAZZINI:

But what a very natural and kindly and charming human feeling, Lady Utterword!

LADY UTTERWORD:

So I thought, Mr Dunn. But I know now that it was only the
last of my influenza. I found that I was not remembered and
not wanted.

CAPTAIN SHOTOVER:

You left because you did not want us. Was there no heartbreak
in that for your father? You tore yourself up by the roots; and
the ground healed up and brought forth fresh plants and forgot
you. What right had you to come back and probe old wounds?

MRS HUSHABYE:

You were a complete stranger to me at first, Addy; but now I feel as if you had never been away.

LADY UTTERWORD:

Thank you, Hesione; but the influenza is quite cured. The place may be Heartbreak House to you, Miss Dunn, and to this gentleman from the city who seems to have so little self-control; but to me it is only a very ill-regulated and rather untidy villa without any stables.

HECTOR:

Inhabited by—?

ELLIE:

A crazy old sea captain and a young singer who adores him.

MRS HUSHABYE:

A sluttish female, trying to stave off a double chin and an elderly spread, vainly wooing a born soldier of freedom.

MAZZINI:

Oh, really, Mrs Hushabye—

MANGAN:

A member of His Majesty's Government that everybody sets down as a nincompoop: don't forget him, Lady Utterword.

LADY UTTERWORD:

And a very fascinating gentleman whose chief occupation is to be married to my sister.

HECTOR:

All heartbroken imbeciles.

MAZZINI:

Oh no. Surely, if I may say so, rather a favorable specimen of what is best in our English culture. You are very charming people, most advanced, unprejudiced, frank, humane, unconventional, democratic, free-thinking, and everything that is delightful to thoughtful people.

MRS HUSHABYE:

You do us proud, Mazzini.

MAZZINI:

I am not flattering, really. Where else could I feel perfectly at ease in my pyjamas? I sometimes dream that I am in very distinguished society, and suddenly I have nothing on but my pyjamas! Sometimes I haven't even pyjamas. And I always feel overwhelmed with confusion. But here, I don't mind in the least: it seems quite natural.

LADY UTTERWORD:

An infallible sign that you are not now in really distinguished society, Mr Dunn. If you were in my house, you would feel embarrassed.

MAZZINI:

I shall take particular care to keep out of your house, Lady Utterword.

LADY UTTERWORD:

You will be quite wrong, Mr Dunn. I should make you very comfortable; and you would not have the trouble and anxiety of wondering whether you should wear your purple and gold or your green and crimson dressing-gown at dinner. You complicate life instead of simplifying it by doing these ridiculous things.

ELLIE:

Your house is not Heartbreak House: is it, Lady Utterword?

HECTOR:

Yet she breaks hearts, easy as her house is. That poor devil upstairs with his flute howls when she twists his heart, just as Mangan howls when my wife twists his.

LADY UTTERWORD:

That is because Randall has nothing to do but have his heart broken. It is a change from having his head shampooed. Catch anyone breaking Hastings' heart!

CAPTAIN SHOTOVER:

The numskull wins, after all.

LADY UTTERWORD:

I shall go back to my numskull with the greatest satisfaction when I am tired of you all, clever as you are.

MANGAN (*huffily*):

I never set up to be clever.

LADY UTTERWORD:

I forgot you, Mr Mangan.

MANGAN:

Well, I don't see that quite, either.

LADY UTTERWORD:

You may not be clever, Mr Mangan; but you are successful.

MANGAN:

But I don't want to be regarded merely as a successful man. I have an imagination like anyone else. I have a presentiment—

MRS HUSHABYE:

Oh, you are impossible, Alfred. Here I am devoting myself to you; and you think of nothing but your ridiculous presentiment. You bore me. Come and talk poetry to me under the stars. (*She drags him away into the darkness*).

MANGAN (*tearfully, as he disappears*):

Yes: it's all very well to make fun of me; but if you only knew—

HECTOR (*impatiently*):

How is all this going to end?

MAZZINI:

It won't end, Mr Hushabye. Life doesn't end: it goes on.

ELLIE:

Oh, it can't go on for ever. I'm always expecting something. I don't know what it is; but life must come to a point sometime.

LADY UTTERWORD:

The point for a young woman of your age is a baby.

HECTOR:

Yes, but damn it, I have the same feeling; and *I* can't have a baby.

LADY UTTERWORD:

By deputy, Hector.

HECTOR:

But I have children. All that is over and done with for me: and yet I too feel that this can't last. We sit here talking, and leave everything to Mangan and to chance and to the devil. Think of the powers of destruction that Mangan and his mutual admiration gang wield! It's madness: it's like giving a torpedo to a badly brought up child to play at earthquakes with.

MAZZINI:

I know. I used often to think about that when I was young.

HECTOR:

Think! What's the good of thinking about it? Why didn't you do something?

MAZZINI:

But I did. I joined societies and made speeches and wrote pamphlets. That was all I could do. But, you know, though the people in the societies thought they knew more than Mangan, most of them wouldn't have joined if they had known as much. You see they had never had any money to handle or any men to manage. Every year I expected a revolution, or some frightful smash-up: it seemed impossible that we could blunder and muddle on any longer. But nothing happened, except, of course, the usual poverty and crime and drink that we are used to. Nothing ever does happen. It's amazing how well we get along, all things considered.

LADY UTTERWORD:

Perhaps somebody cleverer than you and Mr Mangan was at work all the time.

MAZZINI:

> Perhaps so. Though I was brought up not to believe in anything, I often feel that there is a great deal to be said for the theory of an overruling Providence, after all.

LADY UTTERWORTH:

> Providence! I meant Hastings.

MAZZINI:

> Oh, I beg your pardon, Lady Utterword.

CAPTAIN SHOTOVER:

> Every drunken skipper trusts to Providence. But one of the ways of Providence with drunken skippers is to run them on the rocks.

MAZZINI:

> Very true, no doubt, at sea. But in politics, I assure you, they only run into jellyfish. Nothing happens.

CAPTAIN SHOTOVER:

> At sea nothing happens to the sea. Nothing happens to the sky. The sun comes up from the east and goes down to the west. The moon grows from a sickle to an arc lamp, and comes later and later until she is lost in the light as other things are lost in the darkness. After the typhoon, the flying-fish glitter in the sunshine like birds. It's amazing how they get along, all things considered. Nothing happens, except something not worth mentioning.

ELLIE:

> What is that, O Captain, my captain?

CAPTAIN SHOTOVER (*savagely*):

> Nothing but the smash of the drunken skipper's ship on the rocks, the splintering of her rotten timbers, the tearing of her rusty plates, the drowning of the crew like rats in a trap.

ELLIE:

> Moral: don't take rum.

CAPTAIN SHOTOVER (*vehemently*):

> That is a lie, child. Let a man drink ten barrels of rum a day, he is not a drunken skipper until he is a drifting skipper. Whilst he can lay his course and stand on his bridge and steer it, he is no drunkard. It is the man who lies drinking in his bunk and trusts to Providence that I call the drunken skipper, though he drank nothing but the waters of the River Jordan.

ELLIE:

> Splendid! And you haven't had a drop for an hour. You see you don't need it: your own spirit is not dead.

CAPTAIN SHOTOVER:

> Echoes: nothing but echoes. The last shot was fired years ago.

HECTOR:

And this ship we are all in? This soul's prison we call England?

CAPTAIN SHOTOVER:

The captain is in his bunk, drinking bottled ditch-water; and the crew is gambling in the forecastle. She will strike and sink and split. Do you think the laws of God will be suspended in favor of England because you were born in it?

HECTOR:

Well, I don't mean to be drowned like a rat in a trap. I still have the will to live. What am I to do?

CAPTAIN SHOTOVER:

Do? Nothing simpler. Learn your business as an Englishman.

HECTOR:

And what may my business as an Englishman be, pray?

CAPTAIN SHOTOVER:

Navigation. Learn it and live; or leave it and be damned.

ELLIE:

Quiet, quiet; you'll tire yourself.

MAZZINI:

I thought all that once, Captain; but I assure you nothing will happen.

*A dull distant explosion is heard.*

HECTOR (*starting up*):

What was that?

CAPTAIN SHOTOVER:

Something happening (*he blows his whistle*). Breakers ahead!

*The light goes out.*

HECTOR (*furiously*):

Who put that light out? Who dared put that light out?

NURSE GUINNESS (*running in from the house to the middle of the esplanade*):

I did, sir. The police have telephoned to say we'll be summoned if we don't put that light out: it can be seen for miles.

HECTOR:

It shall be seen for a hundred miles (*he dashes into the house*).

NURSE GUINNESS:

The rectory is nothing but a heap of bricks, they say. Unless we can give the rector a bed he has nowhere to lay his head this night.

CAPTAIN SHOTOVER:

The Church is on the rocks, breaking up. I told him it would unless it headed for God's open sea.

NURSE GUINNESS:

And you are all to go down to the cellars.

CAPTAIN SHOTOVER:

Go there yourself, you and all the crew. Batten down the hatches.

NURSE GUINNESS:

And hide beside the coward I married! I'll go on the roof first. (*The lamp lights up again*). There! Mr Hushabye's turned it on again.

THE BURGLAR (*hurrying in and appealing to* Nurse Guinness):

Here: where's the way to that gravel pit? The boot-boy says there's a cave in the gravel pit. Them cellars is no use. Where's the gravel pit. Them cellars is no use. Where's the gravel pit, Captain?

NURSE GUINNESS:

Go straight on past the flagstaff until you fall into it and break your dirty neck. (*She pushes him contemptuously towards the flagstaff, and herself goes to the foot of the hammock and waits there, as it were by* Ariadne's *cradle*).

*Another and louder explosion is heard. The burglar stops and stands trembling.*

ELLIE (*rising*):

That was nearer.

CAPTAIN SHOTOVER:

The next one will get us. (*He rises*). Stand by, all hands, for judgment.

THE BURGLAR:

Oh my Lordy God! (*He rushes away frantically past the flagstaff into the gloom*).

MRS HUSHABYE (*emerging panting from the darkness*):

Who was that running away? (*She comes to* Ellie). Did you hear the explosions? And the sound in the sky: it's splendid: it's like an orchestra: it's like Beethoven.

ELLIE:

By thunder, Hesione: it is Beethoven.

*She and* Mrs Hushabye *throw themselves into one another's arms in wild excitement. The light increases.*

MAZZINI (*anxiously*):

> The light is getting brighter.

NURSE GUINNESS (*looking up at the house*):

> It's Mr Hushabye turning on all the lights in the house and tearing down the curtains.

RANDALL (*rushing in in his pyjamas, distractedly waving a flute*):

> Ariadne: my soul, my precious, go down to the cellars: I beg and implore you, go down to the cellars!

LADY UTTERWORD (*quite composed in her hammock*):

> The governor's wife in the cellars with the servants! Really, Randall!

RANDALL:

> But what shall I do if you are killed?

LADY UTTERWORD:

> You will probably be killed, too, Randall. Now play your flute to shew that you are not afraid; and be good. Play us Keep the home fires burning.

NURSE GUINNESS (*grimly*):

> They'll keep the home fires burning for us: them up there.

RANDALL (*having tried to play*):

> My lips are trembling. I can't get a sound.

MAZZINI:

> I hope poor Mangan is safe.

MRS HUSHABYE:

> He is hiding in the cave in the gravel pit.

CAPTAIN SHOTOVER:

> My dynamite drew him there. It is the hand of God.

HECTOR (*returning from the house and striding across to his former place*):

> There is not half light enough. We should be blazing to the skies.

ELLIE (*tense with excitement*):

> Set fire to the house, Marcus.

MRS HUSHABYE:

> My house! No.

HECTOR:

> I thought of that; but it would not be ready in time.

CAPTAIN SHOTOVER:

> The judgment has come. Courage will not save you; but it will shew that your souls are still alive.

MRS HUSHABYE:

> Sh-sh! Listen: do you hear it now? It's magnificent.

*They all turn away from the house and look up, listening.*

HECTOR (*gravely*):

Miss Dunn: you can do no good here. We of this house are only moths flying into the candle. You had better go down to the cellar.

ELLIE (*scornfully*):

I don't think.

MAZZINI:

Ellie, dear, there is no disgrace in going to the cellar. An officer would order his soldiers to take cover. Mr Hushabye is behaving like an amateur. Mangan and the burglar are acting very sensibly; and it is they who will survive.

ELLIE:

Let them. I shall behave like an amateur. But why should you run any risk?

MAZZINI:

Think of the risk those poor fellows up there are running!

NURSE GUINNESS:

Think of them, indeed, the murdering blackguards! What next?

*A terrific explosion shakes the earth. They reel back into their seats, or clutch the nearest support. They hear the falling of the shattered glass from the windows.*

MAZZINI:

Is anyone hurt?

HECTOR:

Where did it fall?

NURSE GUINNESS (*in hideous triumph*):

Right in the gravel pit: I seen it. Serve un right! I seen it (*she runs away towards the gravel pit, laughing harshly*).

HECTOR:

One husband gone.

CAPTAIN SHOTOVER:

Thirty pounds of good dynamite wasted.

MAZZINI:

Oh, poor Mangan!

HECTOR:

`Are you immortal that you need pity him? Our turn next.

*They wait in silence and intense expectation. Mrs Hushabye and Ellie hold each other's hand tight.*

*A distant explosion is heard.*

MRS HUSHABYE (*relaxing her grip*):

Oh! they have passed us.

LADY UTTERWORD:

The danger is over, Randall. Go to bed.

CAPTAIN SHOTOVER:

Turn in, all hands. The ship is safe. (*He sits down and goes asleep*).

ELLIE (*disappointedly*):

Safe!

HECTOR (*disgustedly*):

Yes, safe. And how damnably dull the world has become again suddenly! (*He sits down*).

MAZZINI (*sitting down*):

I was quite wrong, after all. It is we who have survived; and Mangan and the burglar—

HECTOR:

—the two burglars—

LADY UTTERWORD:

—the two practical men of business—

MAZZINI:

—both gone. And the poor clergyman will have to get a new house.

MRS HUSHABYE:

But what a glorious experience! I hope they'll come again tomorrow night.

ELLIE (*radiant at the prospect*):

Oh, I hope so.


Randall *at last succeeds in keeping the home fires burning on his flute.*